Atlas of Oregon

Second Edition

Atlas of Oregon

Second Edition

Editor

William G. Loy

Authors

Stuart Allan
Aileen R. Buckley
James E. Meacham

Cartographic Editor

Stuart Allan

Contributing Editors

Lawrence J. Andreas
Gene E. Martin

Text Editor

Ross West

University of Oregon Press

The revised Atlas of Oregon was published with the assistance of grants from the University of Oregon Foundation, University of Oregon Office of the President and the University of Oregon Office of University Advancement. The book would not have been possible without the generous assistance of Allan Cartography.

First edition published by the University of Oregon Press, ©1976.

Printed in the United States of America.

Library of Congress Cataloging-in-Publication Data
Loy, William G. (editor); Allan, Stuart; Buckley, Aileen R.; Meacham, James E. (authors)
Atlas of Oregon. 2nd ed.
Revised ed. of: Atlas of Oregon, ©1976
p. cm.   Includes index and sources/bibliography

ISBN 0-87114-101-9

Summary: Revised and expanded version of Atlas of Oregon, including maps, diagrams, charts and text of Oregon geography, history, economy, demographics, politics and natural resources.

1. Atlases
2. Maps, Oregon
3. Oregon Statistics
4. Oregon Geography
5. Oregon History

Printed by Dynagraphics, Portland, Oregon.

Type set in Berkeley and Frutiger.

Table of Contents

Physical Geography

Reference Maps

Foreword

Education is one of the most important gifts that we can give. But education does not stop at graduation. It is a lifelong quest. That is why I am enthusiastic about the book you hold in your hands.

This completely revised *Atlas of Oregon* is an important addition to the literature of our state. Thanks go to the University of Oregon for funding and overseeing this outstanding project. By marrying the latest digital mapping techniques with solid information from a wide variety of state agencies and experts, the *Atlas* team has produced an astonishing tribute to our region: a solid reference book that is also beautiful to look at; a one-volume compendium of much that is special about our state; an important review of Oregon at the turn of the millennium, presented in the form of maps, charts and text that grow in value the more you study them.

I hope that this *Atlas* finds its way into the home of every Oregonian. In its pages, we can all learn a great deal about our neighbors and our state. It is my deep hope that this information is used to make a better life for all Oregonians.

Governor John A. Kitzhaber, M.D.

The University of Oregon:
125 Years of Service to the State

Why do research universities exist?

The book you hold in your hands is one answer. Put simply, leading research universities like the University of Oregon exist to do three things: to teach, to conduct original research and to provide service to their communities. The *Atlas of Oregon* accomplishes all three. It certainly represents a great teaching tool for every classroom and library in the state. It is the result of years of original research by the authors as well as hundreds of other dedicated contributors.

But perhaps most important, the *Atlas* illustrates how the University of Oregon provides service to its state and to the nation. The hundreds of maps and charts on these pages, the countless of hours of work they represent, the compelling way in which the art of mapmaking is melded with hard scientific facts in so many areas—all of these demonstrate the University of Oregon employing its intellectual and financial resources to give something important back to the people of Oregon.

The University of Oregon provides service in many other ways, of course, from the international celebration of our renowned Bach Festival to the path-breaking educational programs developed to prevent youth violence; from faculty members doing important research on our state economy to the view of the stars Oregonians and other visitors see at the University of Oregon's Pine Mountain Observatory near Bend; from our statewide classical music radio station to the treasures in our art and natural history museums.

As you peruse these pages and learn more about Oregon at the turn of the millennium, please remember how these stunning images and enlightening facts came to be put before you. This atlas is the result of teaching, research and service at the highest level. It is a gift to the state and its people. It is the University of Oregon's way of saying, "Thank you, Oregon."

Dave Frohnmayer, President of the University

Oregon's Flagship University

Oregon's flagship liberal arts and sciences university, the University of Oregon provides students a top-quality education in the liberal arts, sciences and professions. The university is the state's home for doctoral degrees in the arts and humanities and the social sciences, and it places a strong emphasis on research programs in the most advanced areas of basic science.

Five generations of outstanding leaders and citizens have studied at the University of Oregon since it opened in 1876. Today's students, like the 162,000 alumni who graduated before them, have access to the most current knowledge in courses, laboratories and seminars conducted by active researchers.

The university's academic reputation is highlighted by its stature as Oregon's only member of the prestigious Association of American Universities, one of just 34 public universities in the United States so honored. Membership in this select group signifies preeminence in graduate and professional education and basic research.

In addition to a comprehensive College of Arts and Sciences, the university is composed of the Graduate School, the Robert Donald Clark Honors College and six professional schools: the School of Architecture and Allied Arts, the Charles H. Lundquist College of Business, the College of Education, the School of Journalism and Communication, the School of Law and the School of Music. Degrees and certificates are offered in more than 110 majors and minors.

Located in the southern Willamette Valley city of Eugene, close to some of the world's most spectacular beaches, mountains, lakes and forests, the 295-acre main University of Oregon campus consists of 50 major buildings surrounded by an arboretum of more than 500 species of trees. Campus buildings date from 1876, when Deady Hall opened, to 1999, when the William W. Knight Law Center was completed. The University of Oregon Museum of Art, a member of the American Association of Museums, is noted for its collections of Oriental and Northwest art. The two-million-volume University of Oregon Library System, a member of the Association of Research Libraries, is the state's largest research library, and an important research facility for scholars throughout the Northwest.

The combination of strong academic programs, beautiful setting and moderate size draws an annual enrollment of about 17,000 students, nearly 10 percent of whom are international students from more than 80 foreign countries. Relative to its size, the University of Oregon has been ranked number one in the U.S. among major public universities in international student enrollment.

Acknowledgments

It is impossible to adequately acknowledge all of the people who helped create this atlas. Hundreds of individuals were involved as data contributors, researchers, cartographers, text writers, reviewers and proofreaders. Many people responded generously to our e-mail and telephone queries as we checked and double-checked data. Everyone was a volunteer, as all of the paid staff also worked extra hours in an effort to keep the price low and the quality high. The level of teamwork was exceptional. Many people filled multiple roles, but in this listing each name will be cited only once. Full names are given, but titles are not.

The *Atlas* was produced in two years, from mid-1999 until mid-2001. During this period many students were involved in developing materials that were later reworked by the professional staff into final graphics for the *Atlas*. Erin Aigner was a key graduate researcher and cartographer for the Economy section and Eugene A. Carpentier III filled a similar role for the Physical Geography section. Other graduate students who worked on the *Atlas* were: Michael L. Cooper, Graham K. Dalldorf, Nicolas P. Kohler, Nancy Toth, Leslie Van Allen and Mike Kulakowski. Undergraduates involved were: James P. Archer, Kevin D. Beatty, Ronni Blair, Arne Buechling, Ronald R. Funke, Craig Greene, Peter M. Griffen, Camille P. Harris, Sara V. Lasky, Sara L. Michener, Courtney Phelps, Jaime D. Schwartz, Justin Stoltzfus, Eric R. Strandhagen, Lisa A. Takashima, Laura M. Testa, David M. Theirl, Rachel R. A. Trusty, Joshua A. Warner, Ryan Walsh and Michael A. Willock.

Atlas work at the University of Oregon was centered in the Department of Geography, primarily in the InfoGraphics Laboratory. The Director of the InfoGraphics Laboratory, James E. Meacham, supervised most of the students involved and was the lead researcher for the Economy section. He was assisted by Andrea Ball, who provided GIS and computer support, and cartographers Blake E. Andrew, David W. Cutting, Mike Engelmann and Kenneth S. Kato. The Physical Geography section was largely the responsibility of Aileen Buckley, who directed several student workers. Office staff support was provided by Alla Blanca-White, Mary Milo and Vickie Stafflebach. The *Atlas* also marks the first significant book published by the University of Oregon Press in a quarter century; Tom Hager took substantial leave from his position as Director of the University of Oregon Office of Communications in order to oversee its publication. The text editor was Ross West and the Sources compiler was Jessica MacMurray. Shelly Cooper managed our financial accounts.

Allan Cartography in Medford, Oregon, was responsible for all final map production and page preparation. Stuart Allan directed the operation. Lawrence J. Andreas was Production Manager. Gene E. Martin, a former University of Oregon Geography Department member, assisted in Medford. The Allan Cartography production staff were: Neil H. Allen, Karen L. Dorey, Thaddeus A. Lenker, Bryan K. Mamaril, Curtis E. Shaffer and Frederick N. Weston. Louise A. Brandes, Joyce M. Conrad and Gale L. Hill provided office and staff support.

Making a modern atlas involves innumerable steps. After deciding what graphics will best tell the story of the geography of a particular area or theme comes the process of accessing the best data available, and finding experts who can offer advice about the data and later write appropriate explanatory texts. Other steps include checking the data for accuracy, making the necessary maps and graphs, having the graphics reviewed and text written, editing the text for style and length, involving multiple reviewers, incorporating their suggestions and then creating final page layouts that need to be proofed and prepared for the printer. To accomplish all of these steps requires the active cooperation of numerous experts. Fortunately, Oregon has the experts, and they have a real affection for the state and possess a strong sense of public service. We obtained outstanding cooperation from faculty members from the University of Oregon, Oregon State University and Portland State University. State and federal officials and many private individuals gave generously of their time and expertise.

This *Atlas* represents a very broad cooperative effort. It is impossible to acknowledge everyone fully; principal contributors are listed below alphabetically (once only, though many contributed to more than one topic), by groups of topics in Table of Contents order.

Human Geography

Historical: Edwin Bingham, Richard M. Brown, Chet Orloff, Clyde P. Patton, Elizabeth Winroth. Native Americans: C. Melvin Aikens, Stephen Dow Beckham, Jeff LaLande. Urban: Kate R. Kralik, Jessi J. Lane. Population: Barry Edmonston, Elizabeth Florez, George Hough, Gil Latz, Richard Lycan, Darrell Millner, Karen Seidel. Religion: Benton Johnson. Political: William M. Lunch. Education: Gary Andeen, Harvey O. Bennett, Bob Jones, Robert Kieran, Shannon McCarthy, Gary H. Searl, Susan Weeks. Crime: Bob O'Brien. Health: Candice Barr, John Bascom. News Media: Bill Campbell, Karl Nestvold.

The Economy

Economy: Anne Fifield, Cathleen Leué, Thomas Stave, Paul Warner, Ed Whitelaw. Employment: Art L. Ayre, Shannon Conway, Kathi R. Riddell. Business: John Mitchell. Lumber: Paul F. Ehinger.

Land: David Haney, Tonya Theiss-Skrip, Champ Vaughan. Zoning: Richard Benner, Kathleen Van Velsor. Minerals: Ron Geitgey. Fisheries: Christopher N. Carter, David B. Sampson. Timber: Jonathan Brooks, David Hulse, K. Norman Johnson. Agriculture: William G. Boggess, Ernest W. Carter, James C. Cornelius. Wine: Laura Burgess, Robin Cross, Mary Davis, Douglas Marousek, Robert E. Sogge. Energy: Bonnie B. Tatom, John G. White. Transportation: Edward P. Arabas, Steven R. Kale, David W. Ringeisen, Dennis J. Scofield. Recreation: Frank Howard, Dean Runyan.

Physical Geography

Geology: Robert Christiansen, J. Lu Clark, Dennis Fletcher, Jon Hofmeister, George W. Lienkaemper, William N. Orr, Fred Swanson, Theresa Valentine, Ray Weldon, Robert Yeats. Soils: J. Herbert Huddleston, Thor Thorson. Precipitation: George H. Taylor. Climate: Patrick Bartlein, Sarah Shafer. Hydrology: Richard M. Cooper, John A. Falk, Patricia McDowell, Benjamin F. Scales. Ecoregions: Jeff Comstock, Jim Omernik. Vegetation: Robert E. Frenkel, Cathy Whitlock. Habitat: Blair Csuti, Jimmy Kagan, Chris Kiilsgaard. Protected Areas: Darren Borgias.

Reference

Maps: Stuart Allan, Allan Cartography staff and Gene E. Martin. Geographic Names essay: Lewis L. McArthur. Sources: Jessica MacMurray. Indexing: Robin J. Allan, Gene E. Martin.

Special Mention

Special mention must be made of people who contributed greatly but who do not fit into the categories above. Robert and Joyce Beaver gave hundreds of hours to develop databases used to make maps of churches, schools and wineries. Ben Truwe proofread the *Atlas*; David Imus proofread the reference maps; Peter Eberhardt reviewed much of the *Atlas*. Although mentioned above, I would be remiss not to emphasize that Bill Orr wrote most of the text for the landforms and geology topics, Bob Frenkel for vegetation and Steve Kale for transportation. Gene Martin was responsible for most of the settlement geography topics and for the Population Centers map compilation. He also reviewed and refined nearly every other topic. He was instrumental in keeping the *Atlas* focused, not on a large collection of topics as they happen to relate to this state, but on Oregon itself.

It is difficult to express what a complicated technical production this atlas is. Twenty-five years ago when we were making the first *Atlas of Oregon*, we had folders full of sheets of plastic with lines engraved, windows opened and sheets with text and lettering waxed down. Now all the information is digital, on CD-ROMs, converted to images on printing plates, then printed on pages. Creating these digital materials is so complicated as to defy comprehension. Lawrence Andreas was involved with every individual image, every block of type and every page layout in the book. His mastery of sophisticated cartographic production in all its digital complexity is evident throughout the *Atlas*. This book would not have been possible in this form without his efforts.

Co-authors Aileen Buckley and Jim Meacham pulled together elements that became most of the Physical and Economic sections of the *Atlas* while continuing to teach courses and keeping the busy University of Oregon InfoGraphics Lab on top of all of its regular workload. The InfoGraphics Lab's success in ferreting out the significant pieces of information from ever-growing mounds of state and federal GIS data was largely due to Jim Meacham's expertise and tireless persistence. Text editor Ross West worked heroically to turn an extremely varied collection of rough drafts from more than 40 different authors into the coherent text presented here, in the face of late submissions, authorial revisions and shifting page layouts. Insofar as cats can be herded, he herded them.

In 1973 Stuart Allan arrived at the University of Oregon as a new graduate student. He quickly became my Associate Director of the original *Atlas of Oregon*, published in 1976. He went on to co-author an *Atlas of California* before starting Allan Cartography in Medford. For the past two decades Stuart has developed his cartographic expertise; Allan Cartography is well known for its Raven wall maps and Benchmark Road Atlases. For the past two years he has devoted his considerable talent and energy to creating this new atlas. Every element of the *Atlas* bears his imprint. The quality of this atlas is testimony to his dedication.

Finally, the patience and support of *Atlas* staff family members must be acknowledged. A project of this magnitude often takes precedence over family needs. Stuart and I need to express our appreciation to our wives, Karen Allan and Maude Caldwell, who have not seen much of us in the past year.

William G. Loy
Eugene
July 2001

Introduction

The quote below first appeared in the preface of *OREGON, End of the Trail*, published in 1940 by the Writers' Program of the Work Projects Administration. The book, compiled and written by an anonymous group of writers during the Great Depression, is a perceptive statement about Oregon from the viewpoint of a resident of Portland who understands the state's fundamental geographic truths.

It was easy to write about Oregon. The state has something that inspires not provincial patriotism but affection. California has climate; Iowa has corn; Massachusetts has history; Utah has religion; and New York has buildings and money and hustle and congestion; but that "lovely dappled up-and-down land called Oregon" has an ever-green beauty as seductive as the lotus of ancient myth.

It is not only the native son of pioneers who feels this affection for the land. The newcomer at first may smile at the attitude of Oregonians towards their scenery and their climate. But soon he will begin to refer to Mt. Hood as "our mountain"—significantly, not as "The Mountain," as Seattlites speak of Mt. Rainier. Soon he will try to purchase a home-site from which he can view it. And before a year of life in Oregon has passed, the sheer splendor of peaks and pines, the joy of shouting trout-filled mountain streams, the satisfying quiet of Douglas firs, the beauty of roses that bloom at Christmas, the vista of rolling wooded hills and meadows always lush and green, the scenic climax of a fiery sun sinking into earth's most majestic ocean—all will have become a part of his daily happiness, undefined and unrecognized in his consciousness, but something so vital that he can never again do without it. And he will even, as do the natives, find merit in the long winter of dismal skies and warm but chilling rains, calling himself a "webfoot" and stoutly proclaiming that he likes it—when all the while he means that he considers it poor sportsmanship to complain, since he knows that this is the annual tax he pays for eternal verdure, for trees and grass and ferns and ivy and hydrangeas and holly, and for the privilege of appreciating by contrast the short bright rainless summer cooled by the softest yet most invigorating northerly winds.

These tributes are generally inspired by only a part, not even a third part, of Oregon. Beyond the wall of the Cascades, which cuts the state into two sections sharply contrasting topographically, stretches a land whose character is that of the plateaus and deserts and mountains of the Rockies country. Yet even the climate of this eastern region has its enthusiasts, and has been thus described by Claire Warner Churchill: "It rains. It snows. It scorches. It droughts. It suspends itself in celestial moments of sheer clarity that hearten the soul. Whatever else it may do, it challenges rather than enervates. Rather than complacency it breeds philosophy."

The style and viewpoint are dated, but the geographic facts and sentiments ring perfectly true. This atlas is our attempt to illustrate and explain what lies behind them—to capture in maps the essential nature of Oregon.

A state atlas is never complete. There is hardly a subject in this book that could not have been expanded into a chapter, and there are many fascinating topics we were not able to include at all. Limitations of space, time and accessible data all shaped the table of contents. Very little information from the 2000 census was available in time to be included, and the date of "most recent" information varies greatly from subject to subject. There is therefore no single reference year for this atlas, no single authority for most topics and no single point of view. We hope the varied virtues of this collection outweigh its inconsistencies.

The first edition the *Atlas of Oregon* was constructed entirely by hand. Maps and graphs were difficult and costly to build, and were often used sparingly to illustrate text. The digital revolution has made them easier to create, and the *Second Edition* includes many more of them. That has meant less room for text, and brief discussions of subjects deserving much fuller treatment. The Sources section near the end of the *Atlas* will direct the interested reader to the detailed sources on which the maps, other graphics and text are based. The *Atlas* does not replace any of these sources. It does present in map form a great deal of information that is otherwise only available in tables and lists, and it assembles existing map information from an enormous range of sources in a single volume. The *Atlas* will certainly be a useful reference. It is also the authors' tribute to this wonderful state.

Human Geography

Settlement History and Social Development

Oregon in the World

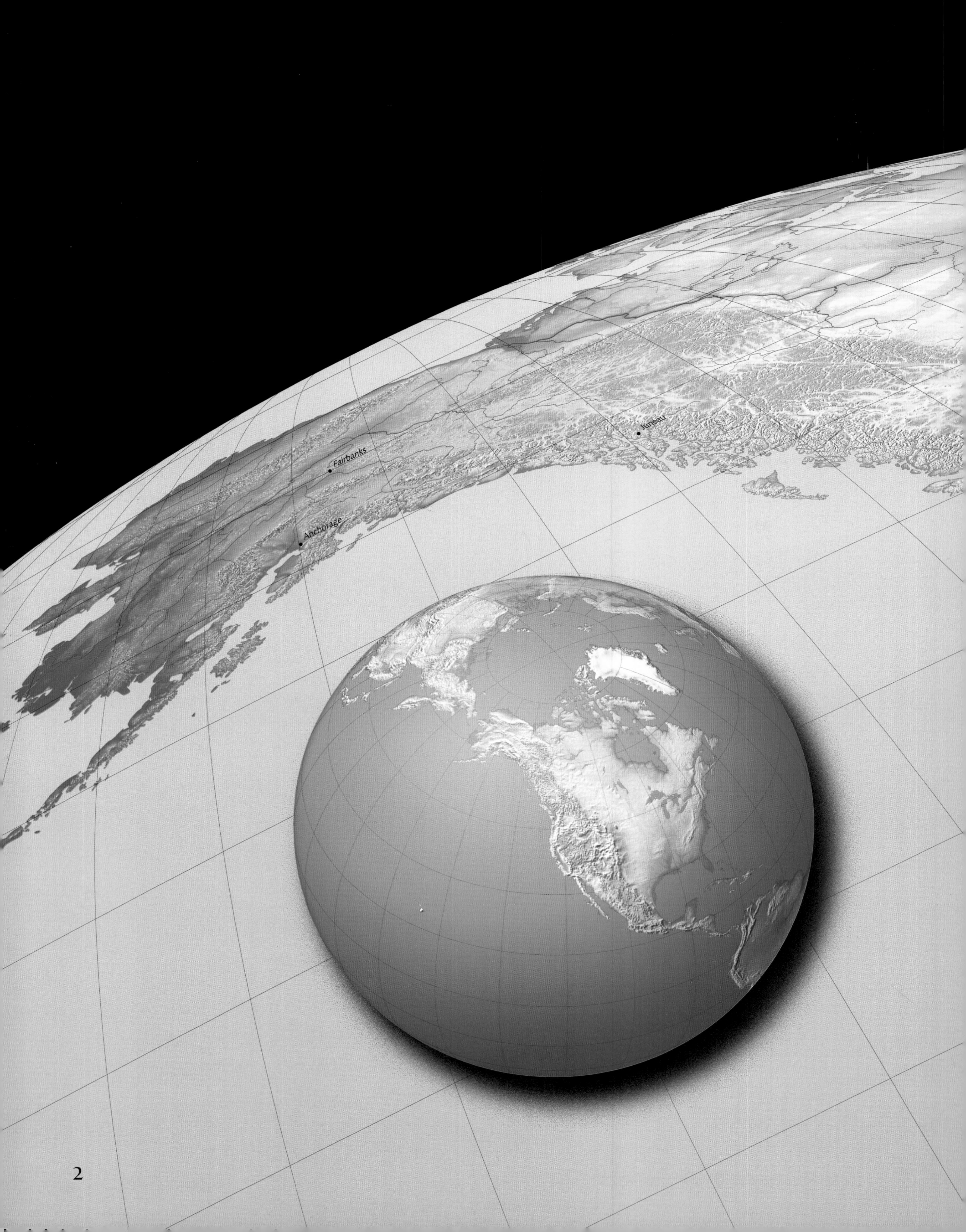
Fairbanks
Anchorage
Juneau

Thunder Bay

Winnipeg

Regina

Bismarck

Minneapolis • St Paul

Pierre

Calgary

Omaha
Lincoln

Helena

Cheyenne

Denver

Vancouver

Seattle

Olympia

Boise

Salt Lake City

Santa Fe

Portland

Salem

Eugene

Carson City

Sacramento

San Francisco

Phoenix

Los Angeles

San Diego

Oregon's location on the globe influences every aspect of the human settlement, economy and natural environment described in this atlas. Northwestern North America is effectively an extension of Northeast Asia and thus the gateway for early human settlement of the Americas. The temperate coastal route of migration leading south from Alaska passes directly through Oregon, a fact reflected in the exceptional diversity of Native American languages in the region. But the state is separated from Europe by vast ocean distances and impassable Arctic ice. Oregon was thus the last part of North America to feel the impact of European settlement and expansion. The Panama Canal and air travel have brought the Northwest closer to the Atlantic world, but Oregon remains far from the population centers of the eastern United States and Europe. The Pacific provides convenient shipping routes to and from East Asia, but even the Pacific Rim countries lie across huge expanses of the world's largest

ocean. The historical and social implications of this isolation are profound.

Oregon's physical environment is shaped by its position at the edge of the continent. The clockwise rotation of the cold Northern Pacific ocean currents and mid-latitude air circulation from west to east combine to give Western Oregon a milder "oceanic" climate than most places of similar latitude enjoy. The coastal region is part of the largest temperate rain forest on earth. The continuing tectonic collision of the North American and Pacific Plates along with the resulting volcanic activity has created the Cascades, confining the damp moderate climate to a narrow belt and giving the interior a much drier and more extreme "continental" climate. This tectonically controlled climate shift is the single dominant factor influencing nearly every natural system discussed in this book.

3

Location

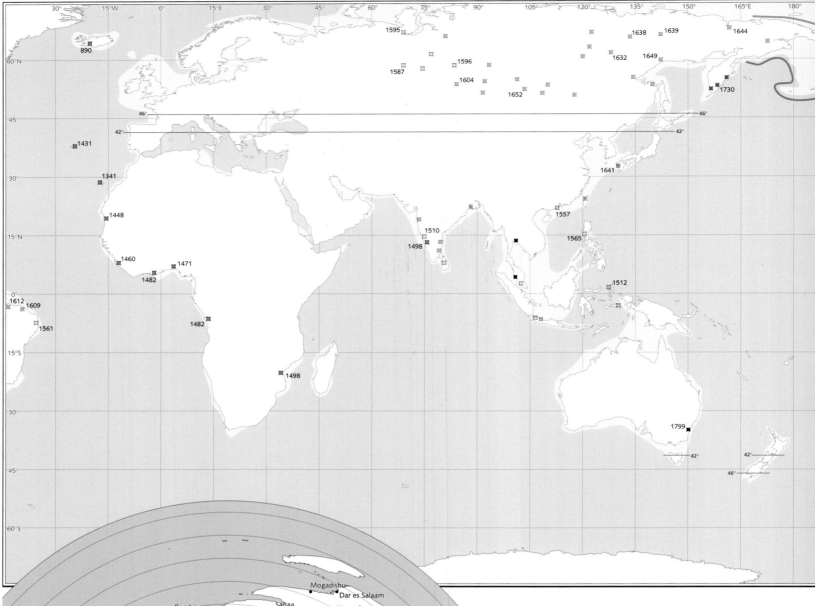

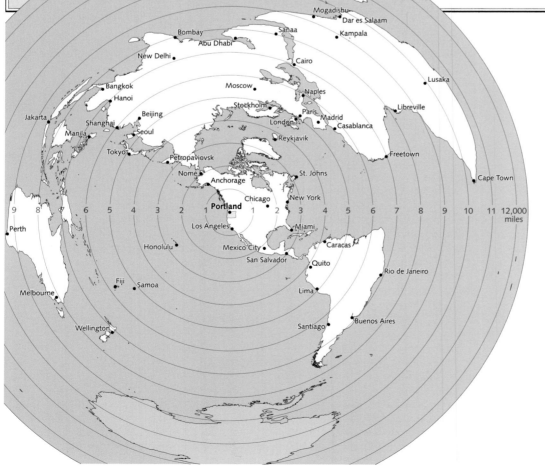

Human Settlement of Oregon

Oregon was originally settled by waves of immigrants arriving from northeastern Asia. Successive groups probably moved first into Alaska over the exposed continental shelf during periods when glacial ice accumulated a significant percentage of the earth's water. Opportunities to move southeastward into the continent depended on the varying extent of glacial ice in interior valleys and exposed shelf and marine terraces along the coast.

An archeological record of stone tools and camping sites in Alaskan and Canadian interior valleys and along the Rocky Mountain front of the Great Plains documents the existence of this route about 11,000 years ago. Archeological documentation for a possible coastal route at an equivalent or earlier date has not been found, perhaps because rising sea levels and coastal erosion have obscured the record. Nevertheless, the coast has always offered a warmer climate, abundant food supplies and water routes around impassable local barriers. Any group with effective fishing and shellfish-gathering techniques, and some means of floatation, should have been able to make its way south. Linguistic evidence supports this view. Oregon and the immediately neighboring areas of the

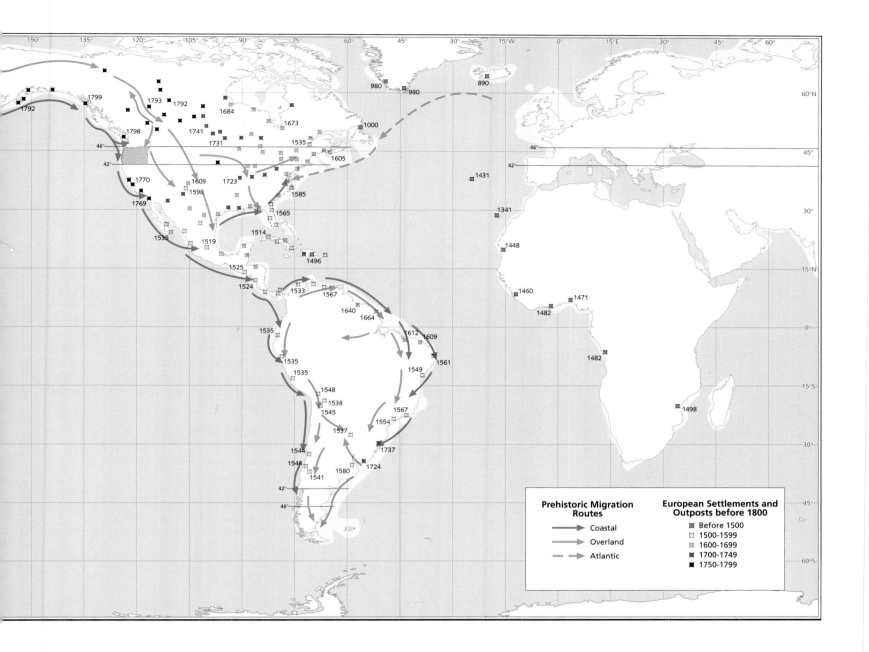

Prehistoric Migration Routes

Coastal
Overland
Atlantic

European Settlements and Outposts before 1800

- Before 1500
- 1500-1599
- 1600-1699
- 1700-1749
- 1750-1799

Northwest Coast and California include a greater number of languages than any comparable area of the continent. Nearly all the language families of North America are represented here (see pages 10 and 11). This strongly suggests the region was peopled earlier than much of the rest of the continent. The arrows on the map show the probable early routes into the Americas.

The archeological record begins in southeastern Oregon as far back as 13,500 years ago. The relationship of these earliest settlers to the peoples living in the region at the time of European contact is not known. Various groups arrived successively over a very long time. The most recent pre-European immigrants were the Athabascan language family speakers, of whom the Tututni in the Rogue River drainage were the largest Oregon group. They may have arrived in the area around 1,000 years ago.

While Oregon is on what was probably one of the main routes for early hunter-gatherer immigration into the Americas, it was extremely isolated from the later centers of seafaring populations. Some evidence exists for early transoceanic contact between the Americas and the Mediterranean classical world, the civilizations of South and East Asia

and the islanders of the South Pacific; but if such visits occurred they apparently had little impact, and certainly none in Oregon. Chinese or Japanese expeditions, or disabled vessels, may have reached the Oregon Coast —ocean currents are favorable and East Asian sailing technology was advanced. However, both countries adopted an isolationist policy in the sixteenth century, cutting off a likely source of trans-oceanic contact.

For Europeans, Oregon was one of the most remote locations on earth and their advance toward Oregon began very late. By the beginning of the sixteenth century Europeans had established trading centers along the Asian rim of the Pacific, and imperial outposts in the Caribbean. By the end of the century Northern Europeans were exploring the Atlantic Coast of North America, and Spain was sending Asian products to Spain via Mexico on the annual Manila Galleon, following a route which brought the ships close to the Oregon Coast. However, these treasure ships did no exploring. Drake reached at least as far as Northern California, and possibly Oregon, after his 1578 raid on Spanish colonial ports. He claimed the region for England as "New Albion." Vizcaino and Aguilar's 1603

expedition from Mexico reached to about 43' N, and named Cape Blanco, but the next century and a half saw no further advances. Oregon was simply too remote from maritime Western Europe.

The Russians, however, had reached the Pacific shores of Siberia by 1600. They consolidated their fur empire throughout the seventeenth century, began exploiting Alaskan waters by 1740 and were moving south. Spain responded to the challenge by building a chain of Franciscan missions in California (from 1769 onward), and actively exploring the Northwest Coast. British expeditions under Cook and Vancouver (1770s to 1790s) included systematic examination of the Northwest Coast. They found no sign of a western entrance to the fabled Northwest Passage, but in the course of their voyages they did discover an excellent market for sea otter furs in Canton. Traders promptly followed. In May, 1792, Captain Robert Gray of Massachusetts brought his ship across the Columbia River bar. Vancouver learned about the estuary from Gray, entered the Columbia, and a month later sent a small craft 100 miles up the river. Oregon's long isolation from Europe and European America had ended.

Maps: 1762–1814

Janvier 1762

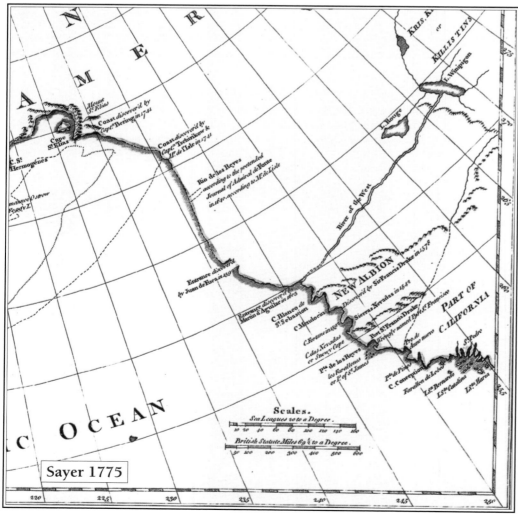

Sayer 1775

Introduction

The territory we now know as Oregon did not appear on the earliest maps of North America. Its remote location, stormy seas and prevailing ocean currents all made the region nearly inaccessible to European explorers during the first several centuries of their expansion across the globe. Sir Francis Drake wintered somewhere on the Northern California or Oregon Coast in 1579–80; Aguilar descriptively named some point north of 43 degrees "Cape Blanco" in 1603. But ships, shipboard diet and navigation technology were all inadequate for any sustained or repeated exploration. More promising conquests were available elsewhere. The Northwest Coast of North America consequently remained virtually unknown to European explorers through the middle of the eighteenth century. As late as the nineteenth century, maps still showed the interior without meaningful detail. In less than 50 years, however, mapmakers would detail the region's vast expanses and correct many existing cartographic inaccuracies. Oregon entered the charted world late, but rapidly.

Janvier's Map of 1762

The colonies of Central and South America were well known and accurately represented on maps by 1762. British and French possessions on the Atlantic Coast of North America were similarly well-mapped. In contrast, depictions of the Pacific Northwest coast and interior at this time were almost pure fantasy.

The "Sea or Bay of the West," appearing larger than Hudson Bay, derived from Verrazano's (circa 1550) observation of Pamlico Sound near Cape Hatteras on the Atlantic Coast. Verrazano hoped this bay might offer a route west to the Pacific. By 1762 mariners and cartographers alike knew that if any such opening existed, it must be in the Arctic. Nevertheless, the idea of such a passage leading to the Pacific was attractive, and no one knew for certain that it did not exist. This 1762 map by the French cartographer Janvier includes tantalizing pieces of accurate information—Cape Blanco and the Strait of Juan de Fuca, for example, are shown reasonably close to their correct latitudes. The Janvier map represents a state of ignorance that was ending even as the map was produced.

Sayer's Map of 1775

Russian power had reached the Pacific coast of Siberia by 1700. By 1741 Bering's second expedition had revealed the extent of the rich Alaskan fur territory and charted the general trend of the Northwest Coast. A map based on this work was published by the Russian Imperial Academy of Sciences in 1754. English publisher and mapmaker Robert Sayer's 1775 map was a close copy of the Russian original. The Russian explorations and resulting maps were an attempt at systematic and objective observation. The Strait of Juan de Fuca is shown as known—that is, without any speculative detail—and the mythical "Rio de los Reyes" of the fictional Da Fonte expedition

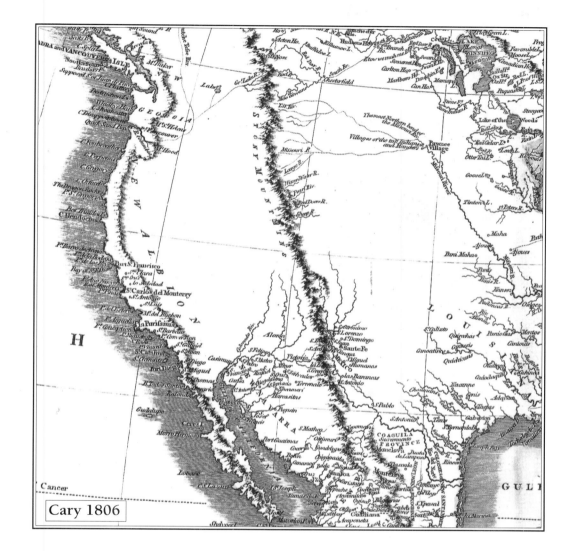

Cary 1806

is presented as such. But Sayer presents an English point of view—with Drake's "New Albion" prominently noted—and introduces a new and entirely English fantasy, the "River of the West." The idea of a river running west from the Great Lakes derived from the misunderstanding of Native American reports of an actual river, the "Ouriconsint." A copying error later transformed the name to the Ouricon—hence, eventually, Oregon. To the British of the late eighteenth century a river connecting the Great Lakes to the Pacific was too attractive to ignore—and, once again, no one knew that such a river did not exist.

Cary's Map of 1806

Cook's 1778 discovery of the Hawaiian Islands was followed immediately by his exploration of the Northwest Coast. In the ensuing decades, British, French, Russian and Spanish expeditions all systematically mapped the area. By 1800, private traders from New England were competing with the Europeans to dominate the fur trade with Native American settlements from Southeast Alaska to Northern California. Cary's map of 1806 documents this period of very rapidly growing geographic knowledge.

Spanish claims north of California were effectively ceded to Great Britain in 1790 with the Nootka Convention's principle of sovereignty by actual occupancy (by a European power, that is; no one considered the existing Native American occupants as

Continued on Page 8

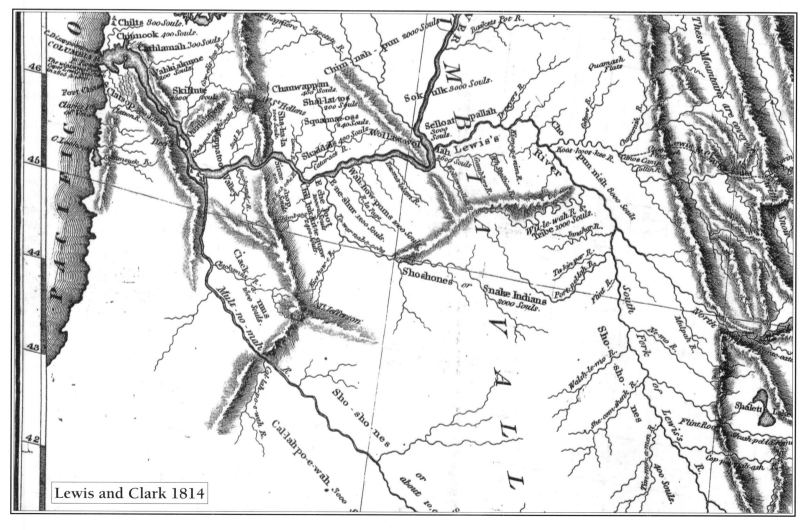

Lewis and Clark 1814

Maps: 1838–1852

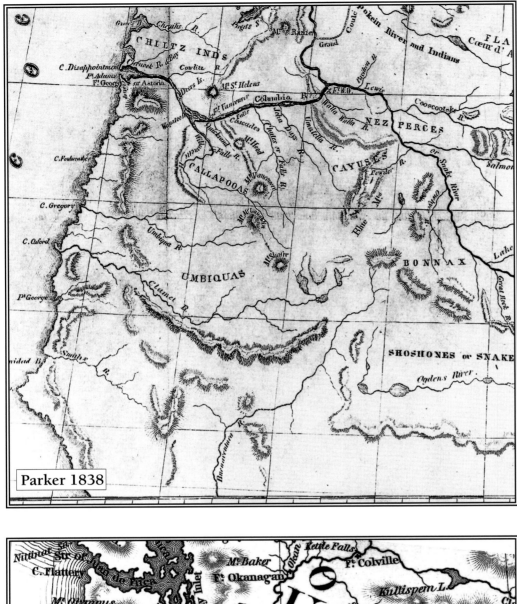

Parker 1838

Greenhow 1844

Continued from Page 7

possessing any rights of ownership). The Convention spurred competition for the region between Britain and the U.S.

While the coastline was increasingly well known around the time of Cary's map, the interior remained unmapped territory.

Lewis and Clark's Map of 1814
(Seen on Previous Page)

The discovery of the Columbia River led to McKenzie's explorations of the 1790s and to Lewis and Clark's expedition of 1804–1806. The explorers found a marked difference between the mid-continent's network of readily navigated rivers and the Northwest's more challenging waterways. Lewis and Clark did not have the advantage of the accurate chronometers used on ships, so their observations of longitude were unreliable. The resulting cumulative error displaced the Pacific Coast by about 60 miles. At the same time, Lewis and Clark necessarily relied on translations of second- and third-hand accounts of geographic features they had not actually visited. The inherent unreliability of this method led to serious errors, such as the wildly speculative course of the Willamette ("Mult-no-mah"). These obvious flaws obscure the very high quality and systematic character of Lewis and Clark's work. Their framework of careful observations brought the Northwest into the orbit of practical American ambition. They documented the upriver approaches to a region previously approached only by sea, and thus laid the foundations for overland entry from the expanding American frontier.

Parker's Map of 1838

By the time of scout and mapmaker Samuel Parker's map of 1838 the Oregon Country was well-explored, but no systematic surveys had been undertaken since Lewis and Clark. The general trend of rivers within the Columbia drainage is fairly accurate on this map, but their locations are wildly offset. The north–south orientation of the Cascades is entirely missed. Regions beyond the Columbia drainage are misrepresented significantly—the merging of the Klamath ("Clamet") and Rogue Rivers is the most notable example. Parker's emphasis on Native American tribes is typical of the fur trading period, then coming to a close.

At this time there was a growing sense that the young country's destiny was to push west across the continent. The rapid expansion of the U.S. frontier into the Mississippi Valley and its settlement by U.S. farmers established a staging area for the next wave of pioneers moving west. Oregon offered a climate well-suited to the farming and grazing economy of the frontier. It also offered abundant unclaimed lands (again, Native American possession was given no weight) with which Congress might reward those who would settle—and therefore hold—the territory for the U.S.

Greenhow's Map of 1844

By 1844 the region's economic foundation was shifting rapidly from the fur trade to pioneer farming. The land itself, not merely

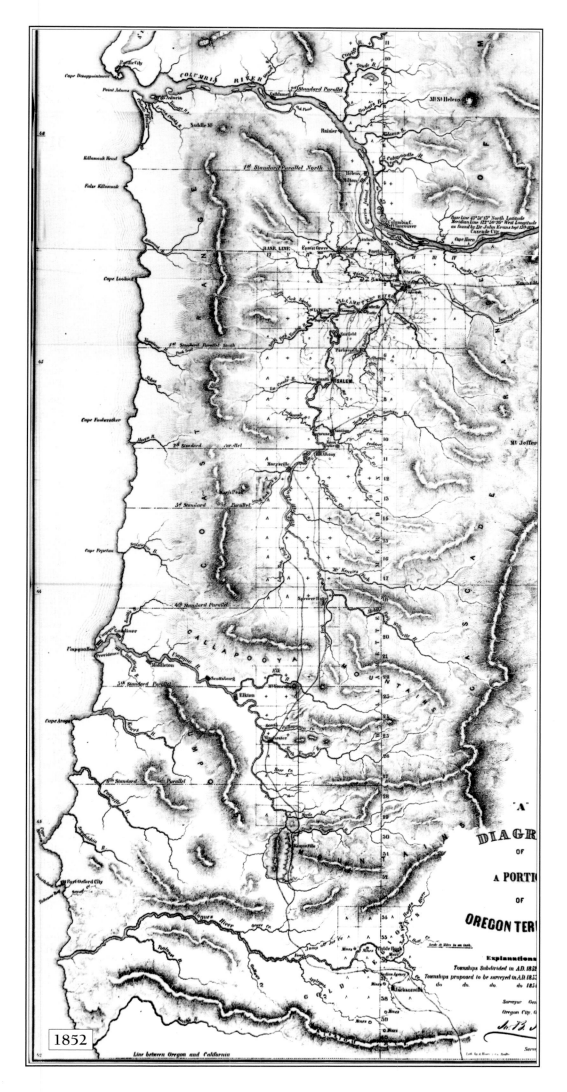

its furs, was now the object of intense interest. Robert Greenhow, a librarian at the U.S. Department of State, published a map reflecting the new conditions. Most charted river systems on the map are essentially correct, though the Malheur is wrongly shown flowing from the lakes of the Harney Basin, and the Klamath and Rogue Rivers are badly confused. The name Shasty, applied to the Rogue River and also to Mt. McLoughlin, was Hudson's Bay Company usage, not a mistake. There is a host of other errors; for example, the inaccurate southeastward trend of the Cascades is carried forward from earlier maps and Cape Blanco is greatly exaggerated. These problems are minor, however; overall, Greenhow's map is much more accurate than previous efforts. Oregon was rapidly emerging as a known region.

General Land Office Map of 1852

While this map follows Greenhow by only eight years, and Parker by 14, the growth in precise knowledge about Oregon in those few years is remarkable. Most of the good valley land had been claimed and (however thinly) settled during the previous decade. Land Office surveyors and contractors were belatedly mapping out the Public Land Survey's township and range grid of six-by-six-mile townships, the standard on which all subsequent land divisions would be based. Many of the settlements which would grow into the principal towns and cities of Oregon are shown, along with the north-south trails which remain (with some realignment) the state's most heavily traveled routes.

Early names were fluid—Cincinnati became Dallas, Marysville is now Corvallis and Kenyonville is Canyonville. Some early towns did not survive the floods and shifting channels of the Willamette—Fairfield and Parkersville are long gone. Others have been eclipsed by the growth of more successful neighbors: Linnton, Portland and Milwaukie were all hopeful contenders against the more important settlements of Vancouver and Oregon City. The California Gold Rush of 1849 abruptly created a much larger economy to the south, and set off a smaller but significant rush in Southwestern Oregon, optimistically labeled "Gold Region." The surprising concentration of settlements on the Umpqua River reflects its importance as the best regional route for moving heavy freight. Port Orford's isolation was outweighed by its value as one of the only sheltered harbors available along the busy and dangerous coastal trade route to San Francisco.

The General Land Office Map includes many inaccuracies and distortions, but these are in the details. It is an essentially modern, scientifically based map. Only 90 years—a single lifetime—had passed since Janvier's representation of the mythical "Sea or Bay of the West." In that brief period, Oregon moved from the realm of fantasy into the modern world.

Indians

The earliest Americans came through Northeast Asia and into North America along routes governed by glacial advances and retreats. Wide areas of the coastal shelf, including the well-known "land bridge" across what is now the Bering Strait, were exposed during glacial advances when water was locked in glacial ice. Conversely, glacial melting inundated coastal routes but opened previously inaccessible mountain passes; Indian legends refer to such openings in the ice. The archaeological record of human activity in the region goes back about 11,000 years, but evidence from Northeastern Asia and interior North America suggests that the earliest immigrants probably passed through the region between about 14,000 and 18,000 years ago.

Pacific Northwest and California Indians spoke an unusually large number of languages, reflecting both long-term local residence and recent in-migration. Languages of the Penutian family, spoken over much of Oregon and California, are highly diversified; Oregon includes five subfamilies with 17 separate languages and many dialects. This distribution and proliferation suggests that people speaking the ancestral Penutian mother language spread widely across the region at an early time. Oregon's Athabascan languages, in contrast, are very closely related to others spoken in Alaska and Western Canada, and probably entered Oregon within the past thousand years.

Cultural and economic patterns among Oregon Indians can be grouped into three main regional types, shown on the map of Culture Areas at right. Oregon west of the Cascades belonged to the Northwest Coast Culture Area, which includes some of the wealthiest "hunter gatherer" communities the world has ever known. The largest populations were on the resource-rich Lower Columbia and coastal estuaries. Salmon was a central economic mainstay throughout this region; settlement was in villages of plank houses; social classes were organized hierarchically; and property, inheritance and debt were regarded in terms similar to those in the European tradition. Inland and upriver interior valley groups, more dependent on less abundant game and acorns, did not sustain such large communities, but there were many local groups, and the Willamette, Rogue and other valleys were heavily populated.

Eastern Oregon was culturally part of the greater Intermountain Region. The largest sub-area was the dry, resource-poor Great Basin, which supported small, highly mobile bands that covered large areas in a seasonal circuit. Shallow lakes and marshes, the basin floor remnants of Ice Age lakes, were important sources of game and plant foods; mountains provided a very different suite of resources. This rotation through various environmental settings gave Great Basin people an austere but reliable, broadly based economy. The Northern Paiute occupants of Oregon's Great Basin were heirs to an ingenious, light weight, highly portable material culture that was developed and maintained for more than 10,000 years in the region. They are linguistic and cultural relatives of people spread over a vast area of the Intermountain West, from the Shoshone and Bannock ("Snakes") of Oregon

and Idaho southward to the Aztecs of Mexico.

The balance of Oregon's Intermountain Cultural Area, the Columbia Plateau region, was occupied by peoples of the Penutian and Salishan linguistic families. The area is typically better watered than the Great Basin, and includes the upriver reaches of important seasonal salmon streams. The Plateau accordingly supported larger and more sedentary populations than the Great Basin, based on salmon, game and root crops such as camas and biscuitroot. As in the Great Basin, the distinctive tradition and cultural history of the Plateau was developed and maintained over some 10,000 years. The Plateau also shared a long common boundary with the Northern Plains culture area, from which the horse and other cultural traits entered northeast Oregon some time in the early eighteenth century. By the time of Lewis and Clark (1804–1806) the Nez Perce and Cayuse were renowned horse breeders and handlers.

It is important to note that linguistic and cultural areas were not organized as political units. In general, each local community was politically independent, though social relationships were maintained between communities through individual marriage and trading ties. Groups of hunters and gatherers as well as trading (and raiding) parties covered great distances, and seasonal movement was common. The great salmon fishery at Celilo Falls on the Columbia brought together people from many different groups in a huge multilingual seasonal fishing settlement. The regional boundaries shown on the maps were not fixed territories, but fluid and permeable zones.

There were probably between 50,000 and 100,000 people living in what is now Oregon when the first Europeans arrived at the mouth of the Columbia. They represented most of the language groups of North America, with diverse economies and social systems. These

were well adapted to the resources available, and utilized the remarkable salmon fishery with great success. This is not to say that Oregon before European contact was idyllic. War, slave raiding, bankruptcy and starvation were all found here, as in the rest of the world. The epidemic diseases of the Old World, however, were unknown. That absence, a great advantage during the millennia before contact, meant that Indians lacked acquired immunities to these diseases. This condition proved catastrophic in the decades after contact.

Culture Areas

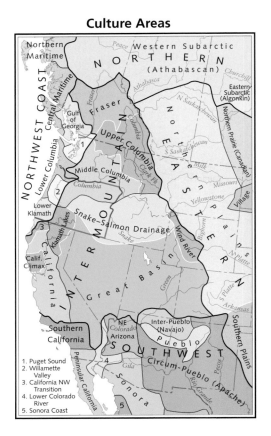

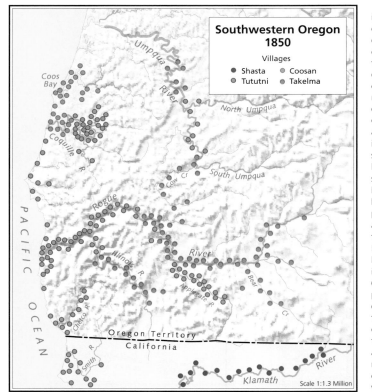

Southwestern Oregon 1850

Villages
- Shasta
- Tututni
- Coosan
- Takelma

Scale 1:1.3 Million

This map of southwestern Oregon in 1850 reflects, on the one hand, key ecological determinants of the regional culture pattern, and on the other, the comparative independence of language from other aspects of culture. Settlement distribution was to a great degree controlled by the presence of major rivers in the mountains and major estuaries or bays along the coast. The central place of salmon and other aquatic products in the diet of inhabitants is clearly indicated. People surely used the rest of this rugged landscape for such activities as hunting, seasonal berry picking and acorn harvesting, but only occasionally and briefly. When the language of the people involved is considered, the map also demonstrates how completely both the long-established speakers of Penutian (Coosan, Takelma) and Hokan languages (Shasta) and the newly immigrant speakers of Athabascan (Tututni) shared the same fundamental pattern of settlement and subsistence economics. While the language and oral traditions of the Tututni clearly demonstrate their ancestral connection to other lands far to the north, in other aspects of life they had taken on, to a remarkable degree, the practical ways of the long-established people among whom they had recently moved.

Major Native American Groups of 1850

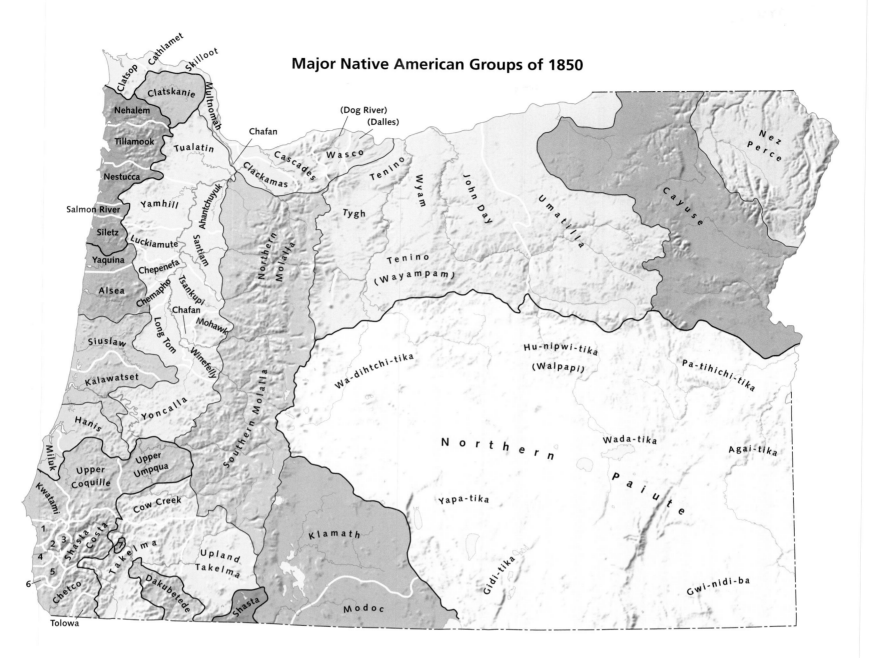

Clatsop · Cathlamet · Skilloot · Clatskanie · Multnomah · Nehalem · Chafan · (Dog River) (Dalles) · Tillamook · Tualatin · Cascades · Wasco · Nez Perce · Nestucca · Clackamas · Tenino · Wyam · John Day · Cayuse · Salmon River · Yamhill · Ahantchuyuk · Umatilla · Siletz · Luckiamute · Santiam · Tygh · Yaquina · Chepeneta · Tsankupi · Tenino (Wayampam) · Alsea · Chemapho · Chafan · Mohawk · Northern Molalla · Siuslaw · Long Tom · Winefelly · Hu-nipwi-tika (Walpapi) · Pa-tihichi-tika · Kalawatset · Yoncalla · Wa-dihtchi-tika · Hanis · Southern Molalla · Wada-tika · Agai-tika · Miluk · Upper Coquille · Upper Umpqua · Northern · Paiute · Kwatami · Cow Creek · Yapa-tika · 1 2 3 · Shasta Costa · Klamath · Gidi-tika · 4 · Takelma · 5 · Upland Takelma · 6 · Chetco · Dakubetede · Gwi-nidi-ba · Tolowa · Shasta · Modoc

---

Languages in Western North America

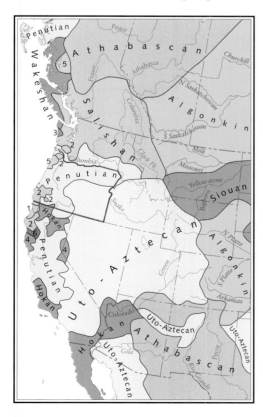

Algonkin (1)	Salishan (5)
Uto-Aztecan	Siouan
Chimakuan (3)	Wakeshan
Hokan (4)	Yuki (6)
Penutian	Athabascan (2)

The map above displays the linguistic and cultural diversity of aboriginal Oregon. East of the Cascades, less abundant resources dictated lower population density and higher group mobility; the areas covered by the speakers of a given language tended to be large. More productive areas west of the Cascades supported higher populations. The areas covered by speakers of any given language were smaller, and overall linguistic diversity was correspondingly higher. The language map illustrates graphically the effect of ecological relationships on human societies.

The 17 Oregon languages fall into five major language families shown on the map at left, along with others that did not quite reach into Oregon. Each of these large family groupings extends far beyond the state's borders and contains many languages, of which only the Oregon representatives are shown in the key at right. Each family represents a set of daughter languages descended in parallel from an original mother tongue that was spoken deep in the past. Individual languages within a major language family can be closely or only very distantly related. Some of these languages are classified on the basis of scant evidence, so any classification scheme must be tentative in some areas. The linguistic diversity of Oregon indicates a long and complex history played out among many different peoples.

Languages in Oregon

SUPERFAMILY
FAMILY
Language
Dialect

UTO-AZTECAN

☐ Northern Paiute

Wa-dihtchi-tika, Hu-nipwi-tika, Pa-tihichi-tika, Walpapi, Wada-tika, Agai-tika, Yapa-tika, Gidi-tika (Gidu-Tikadu), Gwi-nidi-ba

HOKAN

☐ Shasta

ATHABASCAN

☐ Clatskanie, Tututni

Yukichetunne (**1**), Tututni (**2**), Mikonotunne (**3**), Chemetunne (**4**), Chetleshin (**5**), Kwaishtunnetunne (**6**), Taltushtuntede (Galice) (**7**), Kwatami, Upper Coquille, Upper Umpqua, Shasta Costa, Chetco, Tolowa, Dakubetede

SALISH

☐ Tillamook

PENUTIAN
COOSAN

☐ Hanis; Miluk

CHINOOKAN

☐ Lower Chinookan

Clatsop, Cathlamet

☐ Kiksht (Upper Chinookan)

Multnomah, Clackamas, Cascades, Wasco

TAKELMAN–KALAPUYAN

☐ Tualatan, Kalapooia, Yoncalla, Takelma, Upland Takelma, Cow Creek

PLATEAU PENUTIAN

☐ Sahaptin

Tenino, Tygh, Wyam, John Day, Umatilla

☐ Nez Perce

☐ Molalla

☐ Klamath/Modoc

CAYUSE

☐ Cayuse

OTHERS

☐ Alsea

☐ Siuslaw

Exploration: 1800–1845

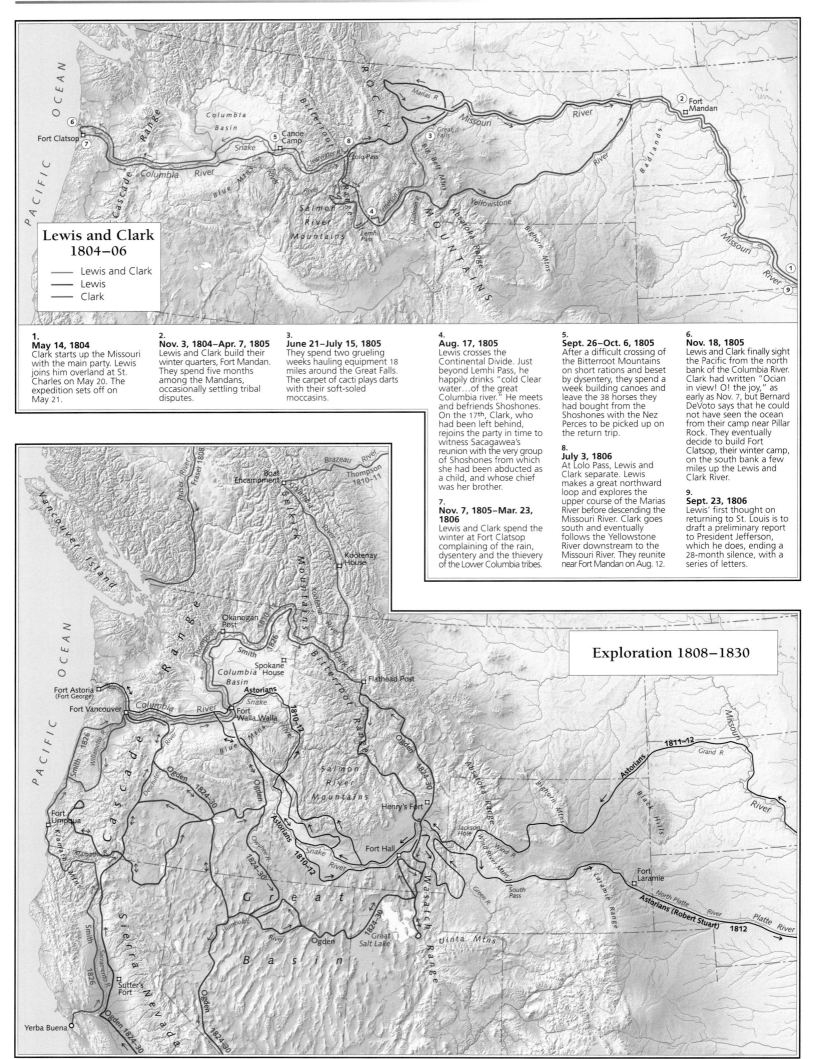

Lewis and Clark 1804–06

— Lewis and Clark
— Lewis
— Clark

1.
May 14, 1804
Clark starts up the Missouri with the main party. Lewis joins him overland at St. Charles on May 20. The expedition sets off on May 21.

2.
Nov. 3, 1804–Apr. 7, 1805
Lewis and Clark build their winter quarters, Fort Mandan. They spend five months among the Mandans, occasionally settling tribal disputes.

3.
June 21–July 15, 1805
They spend two grueling weeks hauling equipment 18 miles around the Great Falls. The carpet of cacti plays darts with their soft-soled moccasins.

4.
Aug. 17, 1805
Lewis crosses the Continental Divide. Just beyond Lemhi Pass, he happily drinks "cold Clear water…of the great Columbia river." He meets and befriends Shoshones. On the 17th, Clark, who had been left behind, rejoins the party in time to witness Sacagawea's reunion with the very group of Shoshones from which she had been abducted as a child, and whose chief was her brother.

7.
Nov. 7, 1805–Mar. 23, 1806
Lewis and Clark spend the winter at Fort Clatsop complaining of the rain, dysentery and the thievery of the Lower Columbia tribes.

5.
Sept. 26–Oct. 6, 1805
After a difficult crossing of the Bitterroot Mountains on short rations and beset by dysentery, they spend a week building canoes and leave the 38 horses they had bought from the Shoshones with the Nez Perces to be picked up on the return trip.

8.
July 3, 1806
At Lolo Pass, Lewis and Clark separate. Lewis makes a great northward loop and explores the upper course of the Marias River before descending the Missouri River. Clark goes south and eventually follows the Yellowstone River downstream to the Missouri River. They reunite near Fort Mandan on Aug. 12.

6.
Nov. 18, 1805
Lewis and Clark finally sight the Pacific from the north bank of the Columbia River. Clark had written "Ocian in view! O! the joy," as early as Nov. 7, but Bernard DeVoto says that he could not have seen the ocean from their camp near Pillar Rock. They eventually decide to build Fort Clatsop, their winter camp, on the south bank a few miles up the Lewis and Clark River.

9.
Sept. 23, 1806
Lewis' first thought on returning to St. Louis is to draft a preliminary report to President Jefferson, which he does, ending a 28-month silence, with a series of letters.

Exploration 1808–1830

Lewis and Clark, 1804–06

The first White to enter and explore the fabled "River of the West" was Robert Gray in 1792. He named it after his ship, the *Columbia*, and set the foundation for later U.S. claims to this distant enclave. Strengthening this tenuous hold, mainly with regard to control of the fur trade, was one of Thomas Jefferson's motives in sending Lewis and Clark westward. Their charge: "to explore the Missouri River, & such principal stream of it, as, by it's [sic] course & communication with the waters of the Pacific, may offer the most direct and practicable water communication across this continent, for the purpose of commerce."

Lewis and Clark did not find such a route, but they solidified the American claim in the face of the intersecting claims of Russia, Spain and Britain. Their journals are also the first written account of the physical and human geography of the enormous territory they crossed. In Bernard DeVoto's words, "If Lewis had talent for geography, Clark had genius for it." The journals also attest to the able leadership that allowed the expedition to make the astonishing traverse in 28 months with remarkably few mishaps. A rare misjudgment by Lewis near the end of the journey led to the killing of two Blackfeet bent on stealing horses. With other groups both Lewis and Clark showed firmness, but also respect and fairness—a bright strand in a dark history.

1808–1830

John Jacob Astor soon responded to the trade possibilities described by Lewis and Clark. Astoria was founded in 1811 as the Pacific headquarters of his American Fur Company. To find a practicable overland route, one of the Astorians, Robert Stuart, journeyed in 1812 from Astoria to St. Louis. His report, describing a route without serious obstacles, was widely reprinted. It was the first elaboration of the route and concept that became the "Oregon Trail."

British traders were equally active. In 1808, Simon Fraser descended to the mouth of the Fraser River. David Thompson reached Astoria in 1811 by way of Athabasca Pass and a long voyage down the Kootenay and the Columbia Rivers.

South of the Columbia River, the major exploration was carried out by Peter Skene Ogden, a British subject and employee of the Hudson's Bay Company, and by Jedediah Smith, an American working for U.S. traders. Smith's journeys (1822–1831) were among the most remarkable of all western explorations. He was the first to cross the Great Basin and the first to cross the Siskiyou Pass into Oregon, but he wrote very little. Ogden's journeys across the Basin and into Oregon are better documented. As a result of the War of 1812, U.S. presence in the region faded. The Astorians, isolated and fearful, sold out to the British. Astoria, renamed Fort George, was soon replaced by Fort Vancouver. By 1830, the British were unchallenged on the Pacific slope.

1830–1845

By 1832, Boston sea captains had displaced both the Russians and British from the sea otter trade; but on land, the Hudson's Bay Company had only begun to feel the competition of U.S. fur traders led by mountain men such as Jim Bridger, Kit Carson and Tom Fitzpatrick. Leaving few records, their names are missing from these maps even though Bridger and Fitzpatrick, for example, became proprietors of the Rocky Mountain Fur Company. While not showing the travels of the members of this company nor those of its main rival, the American Fur Company, the 1830–1845 map indicates the routes of two other competitors, Benjamin Bonneville and Nathaniel Wyeth. Bonneville, perhaps planning a takeover of the Oregon Country by the U.S., built Fort Bonneville at a strategic point on the route west. Wyeth was inspired to pit Yankee ingenuity against the British by the sight, in 1831, of the brig *Owyhee* arriving in Boston harbor with 53 barrels of smoked Columbia River salmon. Out West, he was undone by his rivals. William Sublette had built Fort Laramie in 1834 to thwart Wyeth's efforts to bolster the U.S. fur trade. Wyeth built Fort Hall to stem the penetration of the Hudson's Bay Company—the company countered with Fort Boise.

Ewing Young, a mountain man and important figure in the early history of Oregon, drove cattle from California to Oregon, then settled there in 1834. Guided by Carson and Fitzpatrick, John Fremont surveyed the Great Basin for the Army from 1843 to 1848.

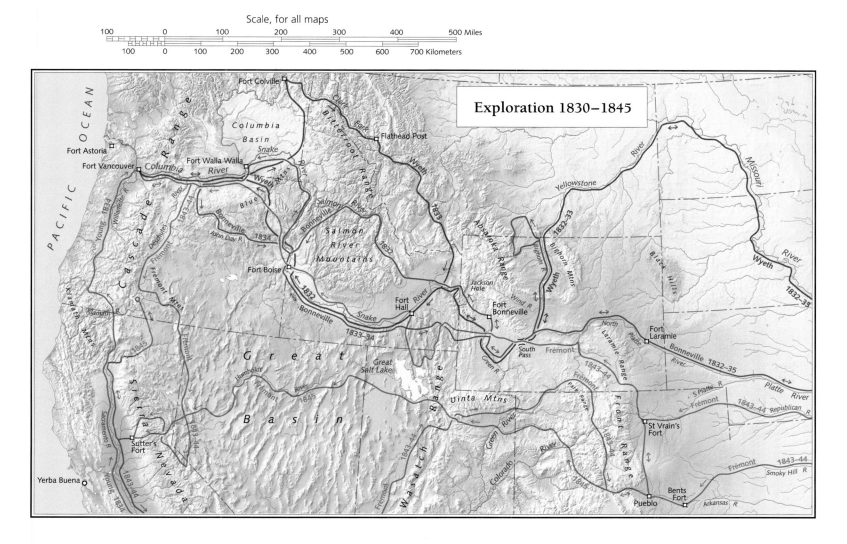

Scale, for all maps

100   0   100   200   300   400   500 Miles

100   0   100   200   300   400   500   600   700 Kilometers

Exploration 1830–1845

Oregon Trail

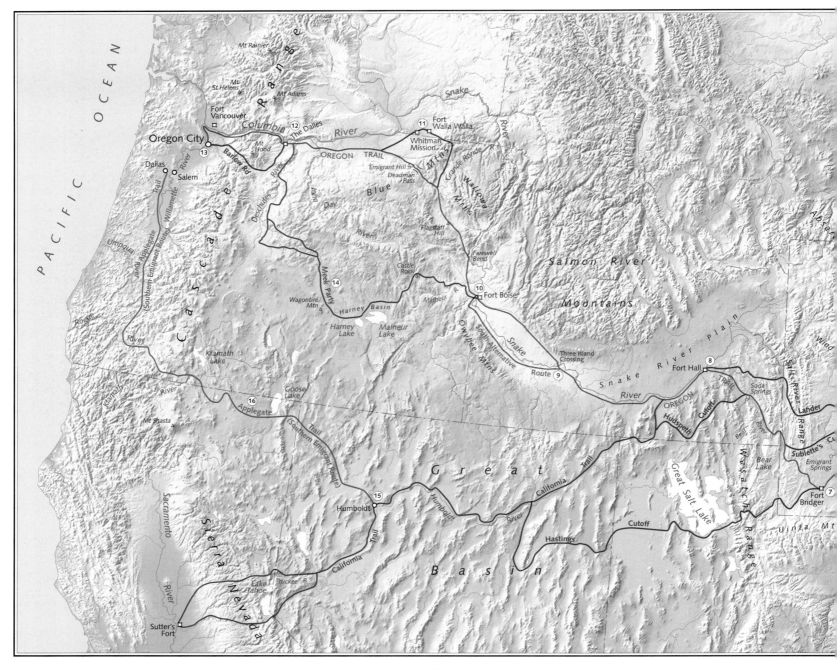

Disputed Territory

In 1819, Spain relinquished claims to all Pacific Coast lands north of 42° N latitude. The 1818 treaty between the United States and Great Britain specified "joint occupance" of the land between 42° N and 54° 40′ N. This agreement was terminated by the treaty of June 15, 1846, which defined the present boundary between the U.S. and Canada.

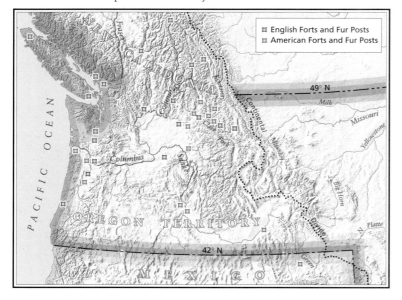

The Oregon Trail

The Oregon Trail developed out of early fur trading explorations, beginning with Robert Stuart's discovery of South Pass through the Rocky Mountains in 1812. The forts established by rival trading companies served as resting places and supply points for the westward migrations. The wagons and livestock of the pioneers, however, posed difficulties not faced by the more lightly burdened traders.

The journey west began along the gentle streams and broad valleys of the Great Plains. Beyond South Pass travel was harder. Sublette's Cutoff saved 75 miles of the long detour southward to Fort Bridger, but it ran through a bitter desert with 50 waterless miles. Most migrants chose the longer route. West of Fort Hall, travel became still more difficult. The toll of the long journey on people, animals and equipment compounded the unforeseen challenges of travel along the Snake and Columbia Rivers. The last 60 miles, from The Dalles to the mouth of the Willamette, was so arduous that most parties preferred the cost and effort of the Barlow Road.

Jesse Applegate's route, opened in 1846, avoided the perils of the Blue Mountains and the descent of the Columbia, but it was 200 miles longer and posed its own difficulties. Even so, nearly half the overland emigrants of 1853 passed this way.

The significance of the Oregon Trail was twofold. It was a "path of empire" as the nation grew, opening the Oregon Country to occupation by pioneers and acquisition by the U.S. In later years, the Trail served as an artery between the Pacific Coast and the Mississippi River, through which travel and trade flowed until the completion of the railroad through the Columbia Gorge in 1883.

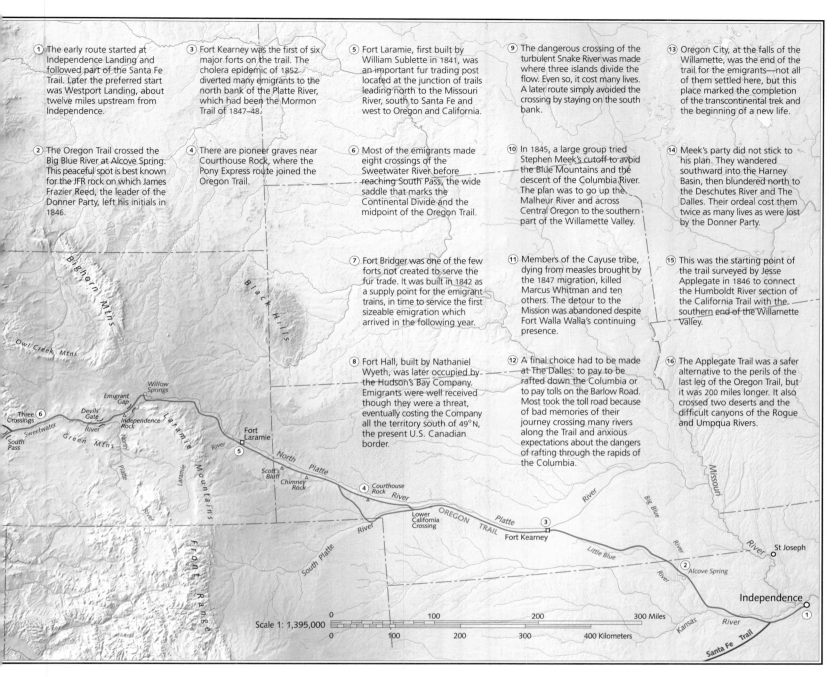

1. The early route started at Independence Landing and followed part of the Santa Fe Trail. Later the preferred start was Westport Landing, about twelve miles upstream from Independence.

2. The Oregon Trail crossed the Big Blue River at Alcove Spring. This peaceful spot is best known for the JFR rock on which James Frazier Reed, the leader of the Donner Party, left his initials in 1846.

3. Fort Kearney was the first of six major forts on the trail. The cholera epidemic of 1852 diverted many emigrants to the north bank of the Platte River, which had been the Mormon Trail of 1847–48.

4. There are pioneer graves near Courthouse Rock, where the Pony Express route joined the Oregon Trail.

5. Fort Laramie, first built by William Sublette in 1841, was an important fur trading post located at the junction of trails leading north to the Missouri River, south to Santa Fe and west to Oregon and California.

6. Most of the emigrants made eight crossings of the Sweetwater River before reaching South Pass, the wide saddle that marks the Continental Divide and the midpoint of the Oregon Trail.

7. Fort Bridger was one of the few forts not created to serve the fur trade. It was built in 1842 as a supply point for the emigrant trains, in time to service the first sizeable emigration which arrived in the following year.

8. Fort Hall, built by Nathaniel Wyeth, was later occupied by the Hudson's Bay Company. Emigrants were well received though they were a threat, eventually costing the Company all the territory south of 49°N, the present U.S. Canadian border.

9. The dangerous crossing of the turbulent Snake River was made where three islands divide the flow. Even so, it cost many lives. A later route simply avoided the crossing by staying on the south bank.

10. In 1845, a large group tried Stephen Meek's cutoff to avoid the Blue Mountains and the descent of the Columbia River. The plan was to go up the Malheur River and across Central Oregon to the southern part of the Willamette Valley.

11. Members of the Cayuse tribe, dying from measles brought by the 1847 migration, killed Marcus Whitman and ten others. The detour to the Mission was abandoned despite Fort Walla Walla's continuing presence.

12. A final choice had to be made at The Dalles: to pay to be rafted down the Columbia or to pay tolls on the Barlow Road. Most took the toll road because of bad memories of their journey crossing many rivers along the Trail and anxious expectations about the dangers of rafting through the rapids of the Columbia.

13. Oregon City, at the falls of the Willamette, was the end of the trail for the emigrants—not all of them settled here, but this place marked the completion of the transcontinental trek and the beginning of a new life.

14. Meek's party did not stick to his plan. They wandered southward into the Harney Basin, then blundered north to the Deschutes River and The Dalles. Their ordeal cost them twice as many lives as were lost by the Donner Party.

15. This was the starting point of the trail surveyed by Jesse Applegate in 1846 to connect the Humboldt River section of the California Trail with the southern end of the Willamette Valley.

16. The Applegate Trail was a safer alternative to the perils of the last leg of the Oregon Trail, but it was 200 miles longer. It also crossed two deserts and the difficult canyons of the Rogue and Umpqua Rivers.

The Emigrants

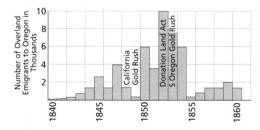

The word "emigrants" describes those pioneers who moved westward, from the eastern U.S. to the Midwest and from there to the Far West. The trickle began in 1840 and soon became a flood. In 1847 approximately 4,000 emigrants headed west along the Oregon Trail. The flow slowed briefly in 1848–49 as many migrants turned south for the California gold fields, then rose to much higher levels in the early 1850s.

The vast majority of Oregon trail emigrants, according to 1850 census data, were born in the states of Maine, Massachusetts, New York, Pennsylvania, Virginia, North Carolina, Kentucky, Tennessee and Ohio. These people migrated west first to Missouri, Illinois or Iowa and then from those states to Oregon. Missouri supplied more emigrants than any other state —40 percent of these emigrants were closely related to Kentucky-born people. Farmers, smiths, shopkeepers, doctors, teachers, leatherworkers, peddlers and salesmen left behind drought, worn-out land, malarial epidemics and economic privation. With families and supplies loaded into canvas-covered farm wagons, they headed for the Willamette Valley, a land they referred to as "Eden."

The journey was not easy. Cholera epidemics in 1849, 1850 and 1852 took heavy tolls on emigrant wagon trains. Food and water were often in short supply, especially toward the end of summer. Notwithstanding the hardships caused by ill-prepared travelers and an unforgiving landscape, most of the emigrants arrived safely with stories to boast of for the remainder of their lives.

Lawyers came in great numbers, helping to settle and litigate the numerous land claims that accompanied mass migration and land acquisition. Clergymen quickly followed their flocks. Lawyers and the clergy were perhaps the most influential new arrivals. They wrote the laws, edited newspapers and helped structure the developing frontier society.

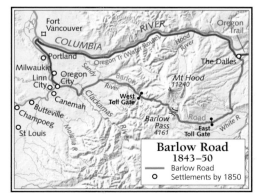

The Barlow Road

To help emigrants avoid the dangerous Columbia River passage through the Cascade Mountains and the Columbia River Gorge, pioneer road builder Samuel Barlow carved a wagon road around the south side of Mount Hood in 1845–46. In the following years, he and others improved the road, the first to traverse the mountains. While the vast majority of emigrants to the Willamette Valley traveled the Barlow Road, for many it was the most arduous stretch of their entire journey west, requiring great effort to guide wagons through nearly impenetrable forests and down precipitous hillsides.

Epidemics, Wars and Reservations

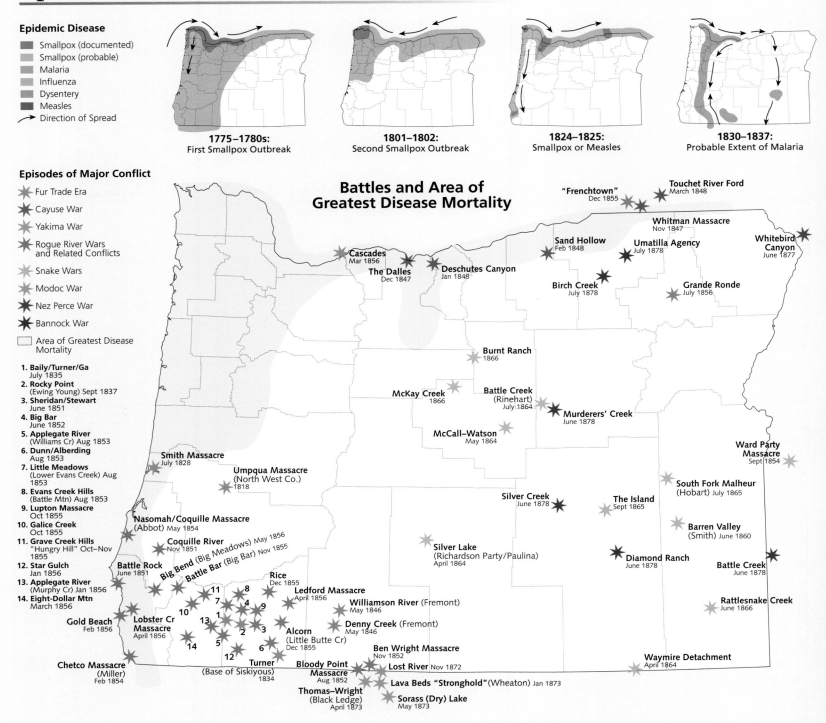

1775–1780s:
First Smallpox Outbreak

1801–1802:
Second Smallpox Outbreak

1824–1825:
Smallpox or Measles

1830–1837:
Probable Extent of Malaria

Episodes of Major Conflict

- ✶ Fur Trade Era
- ✶ Cayuse War
- ✶ Yakima War
- ✶ Rogue River Wars and Related Conflicts
- ✶ Snake Wars
- ✶ Modoc War
- ✶ Nez Perce War
- ✶ Bannock War
- ▢ Area of Greatest Disease Mortality

1. **Baily/Turner/Ga** July 1835
2. **Rocky Point** (Ewing Young) Sept 1837
3. **Sheridan/Stewart** June 1851
4. **Big Bar** June 1852
5. **Applegate River** (Williams Cr) Aug 1853
6. **Dunn/Alberding** Aug 1853
7. **Little Meadows** (Lower Evans Creek) Aug 1853
8. **Evans Creek Hills** (Battle Mtn) Aug 1853
9. **Lupton Massacre** Oct 1855
10. **Galice Creek** Oct 1855
11. **Grave Creek Hills** "Hungry Hill" Oct–Nov 1855
12. **Star Gulch** Jan 1856
13. **Applegate River** (Murphy Cr) Jan 1856
14. **Eight-Dollar Mtn** March 1856

Battles and Area of Greatest Disease Mortality

"Frenchtown" Dec 1855
Touchet River Ford March 1848
Whitman Massacre Nov 1847
Sand Hollow Feb 1848
Umatilla Agency July 1878
Whitebird Canyon June 1877
Cascades Mar 1856
The Dalles Dec 1847
Deschutes Canyon Jan 1848
Birch Creek July 1878
Grande Ronde July 1856
Burnt Ranch 1866
McKay Creek 1866
Battle Creek (Rinehart) July 1864
Murderers' Creek June 1878
McCall–Watson May 1864
Ward Party Massacre Sept 1854
Smith Massacre July 1828
Umpqua Massacre (North West Co.) 1818
Silver Creek June 1878
The Island Sept 1865
South Fork Malheur (Hobart) July 1865
Barren Valley (Smith) June 1860
Silver Lake (Richardson Party/Paulina) April 1864
Diamond Ranch June 1878
Battle Creek June 1878
Coquille River Nov 1851
Big Bend (Big Meadows) May 1856
Battle Bar (Big Bar) Nov 1855
Rice Dec 1855
Ledford Massacre April 1856
Williamson River (Fremont) May 1846
Rattlesnake Creek June 1866
Battle Rock June 1851
Nasomah/Coquille Massacre (Abbot) May 1854
Denny Creek (Fremont) May 1846
Gold Beach Feb 1856
Lobster Cr Massacre April 1856
Alcorn (Little Butte Cr) Dec 1855
Ben Wright Massacre Nov 1852
Waymire Detachment April 1864
Chetco Massacre (Miller) Feb 1854
Turner (Base of Siskiyous) 1834
Bloody Point Massacre Aug 1852
Lost River Nov 1872
Lava Beds "Stronghold" (Wheaton) Jan 1873
Thomas–Wright (Black Ledge) April 1873
Sorass (Dry) Lake May 1873

Disease

The arrival of Europeans and white Americans on the Northwest Coast in the 1790s was the beginning of a rapid and steep decline in the fortunes of Oregon Indians, who had no immunity to Old World diseases. Smallpox was already in evidence by the time of Lewis and Clark's arrival in 1805; by 1825 either two or three smallpox epidemics had swept through parts of Western and northern Oregon. The disease was probably introduced into the Lower Columbia by trading vessels, and indirectly from the northern Great Plains where it was brought by fur trappers. Mortality in each epidemic is estimated to have ranged from 15 to 40 percent. The disease was most virulent in the densely populated areas of the Columbia, the northern Willamette Valley, and the villages of the coastal bays. The same general epidemic pattern was repeated by later-arriving influenza, dysentery and measles.

Malaria arrived in 1830 via an unknown infected individual, and quickly took hold as an endemic disease carried by mosquitoes in the low-elevation valleys west of the Cascades and probably in the Klamath and Harney Basins. Malaria's ongoing debilitatation compounded the impact of recurring waves of epidemic disease. The cumulative death rate for Oregon Indians is estimated by 1850 to have ranged between 50 and 90 percent in some originally heavily populated areas. Widely dispersed bands were generally less affected by disease.

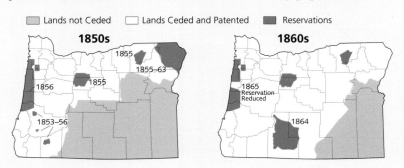

1850s
1855
1855–63
1856
1855
1853–56

1860s
1865 Reservation Reduced
1864

1870s
1875 Reservation Reduced
1872–78

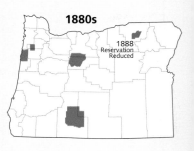

1880s
1888 Reservation Reduced

1837:
Influenza

1837–1838:
Smallpox Outbreak

1844:
Dysentery

1847–1848:
Measles

1853:
Smallpox Outbreak

Armed Conflict

What disease began, warfare completed. The exploration and fur trade era was marked by occasional and local conflicts. Episodes of slaughter occurred on both sides, but there was no general warfare. The Hudson's Bay Company maintained a semi-military administration but did not threaten Indian territorial claims or resource bases. The arrival of large numbers of Americans over the Oregon Trail after 1840 did. Settlers rapidly took the most productive lands without regard to Indian occupation, turning hogs and cattle onto the acorn-producing oak woodlands and camas and arrowroot meadows on which many Indians relied. Southwestern Oregon's gold rush in 1851 brought conflict into previously remote areas. The native population of Oregon was now directly in the path of Manifest Destiny.

White response to the Whitman Massacre (1847) was Oregon's first full-scale "Indian war," the Cayuse War. The "Yakima War" of the 1850s occurred mostly north of the Columbia in Washington Territory. During the same decade, the on-going Rogue River Indian Wars included many small skirmishes and a number of major battles. The volunteer militia, composed of gold miners and settlers (some of whom committed atrocities and called for outright extermination of the Indians), played a large role in this series of brutal conflicts. As a result, most of southwestern Oregon's surviving native people were ultimately relocated to distant reservations.

East of the Cascades, regular troops of the U.S. Army played a dominant role in the intermittent warfare of the 1860s and 1870s. The well-known Modoc and Nez Perce Wars, both fought outside Oregon, had their origins in part within the state, and resulted in the exile of the defeated Indians. In southeastern Oregon, the Army established posts during the "Snake Wars" of the 1860s. The defeated Northern Paiutes ceded most of their homeland in return for the huge Malheur Reservation. After the participation of a few Paiute bands in the 1878 Bannock War, and due to relentless political pressure from leading Oregon citizens, the reservation was dissolved and thrown open to settlement by ranchers.

Reservations

By 1880 a greatly reduced Indian population was confined to five reservations, each containing a mix of different tribal groups and languages. Further reduction in the native land base between 1885 and the 1920s followed from the federal policies of assimilation and allotment. Under the allotment scheme, collectively owned tribal lands were converted to individual ownership and, frequently, later sold to non-Indians. This trend culminated in the 1950s with the government's "Termination" policy, when the tiny remnant Siletz and Grand Ronde Reservations and the huge Klamath Reservation were abolished and then sold.

Since the 1980s a number of Oregon tribes have been restored to federal recognition; others, such as the Warm Springs and Umatilla, never lost their status as recognized tribes. Although the total acreage of land actually placed back into reservation or trust status since 1980 remains modest, several of Oregon's tribes have opened resorts, casinos and convention centers; some manage forest resources and commercial farms on tribal lands.

Unratified Treaties

Ratified Treaties

1. **April–May 1851**
Willamette Valley Treaties (6)
2. **August 1851**
Tansey Point Treaties (10)
3. **20 September 1851**
Port Orford Treaties (2)
4. **Autumn 1851**
Treaty with Clackamas Tribe
5. **25 March 1854**
Treaty with the Tualatins
6. **8 September 1855**
Coast Treaty (cedes entire Oregon Coast and overlaps cessions 2 and 3)

1. **10 September 1853**
Rogue River (Takelma and other groups)
2. **19 September 1853**
Umpqua Cow Creek Band
3. **18 November 1854**
Chasta, Scotons and Grave Creek Band
4. **29 November 1854**
Umpqua and Kalapuya
5. **22 January 1855**
Kalapuya and Confederated Bands of the Willamette Valley
6. **9 June 1855**
Walla-Wallas, Cayuses and Umatillas
7. **11 June 1855**
Nez Perces
8. **25 June 1855**
Tribes of Middle Oregon
9. **21 December 1855**
Molalla or Mollels
10. **9 June 1863**
Nez Perces
11. **14 October 1864**
Klamaths, Modocs and Yahooskin Band of Snakes
12. **12 August 1865**
Woll-Pah-Pe Snakes (also covered by 6, 8 and 11)
13. **15 November 1865**
Warm Springs

Treaties

The initial treaty program in Oregon failed. Eighteen duly negotiated, signed treaties in 1851 assured tribes of federal intentions. None was ratified. The primary argument against the treaties was that they did not remove the tribes to east of the Cascades. An unratified treaty had no legal standing. Congress set the value of all land in the territory in 1850 at $1.25 per acre. Oregon tribes were paid only a few cents per acre for their lands in annuities paid out over 20 years.

Succeeding treaties negotiated between 1852 and 1865 ceded three-fifths of the native lands to the U.S. None of the Coast nor any of southeastern Oregon was obtained by ratified treaty. Only the Warm Springs and Umatilla treaties explicitly reserved off-reservation hunting and fishing rights. The highly controversial (and ignored) ratified treaty of 1865 ceded Warm Springs off-reservation rights.

Reservations and Federally Recognized Tribes

Reservations and reservation status

Tribe-owned

See detailed land ownership on pages 82–83

⊗ Tribal Headquarters

Confederated Tribes of the Grand Ronde Community of Oregon
Grand Ronde Reservation
Tribes: Shasta, Kalapuya, Rogue (Takelma), Molalla, Umpqua, Chinook, Clackamas

Confederated Tribes of the Siletz Indian Reservation
Siletz Reservation
Tribes: Taltushtuntude, Chasta Costa, Chetco, Coquille, Tututni, Dakubetede, other Athapascan tribes, Takelma, Shasta

Confederated Tribes of the Coos, Lower Umpqua and Siuslaw Indians of Oregon
Tribe: Coos, Lower Umpqua (Kuitsh), Siuslaw

Coquille Indian Tribe
Headquarters: Coos Bay
Tribe: Coquille

Cow Creek Band of the Umpqua Tribe of Indians
Cow Creek Reservation
Tribe: Umpqua

The Klamath Tribes of Oregon
⊗ Tribes: Klamath, Modoc, Yahuskin Band of Northern Paiute

Confederated Tribes of the Umatilla Indian Reservation
Umatilla Reservation
Tribes: Umatilla, Cayuse, Walla Walla, Palouse, Nez Perce

Confederated Tribes of the Warm Springs Indian Reservation of Oregon
Warm Springs Reservation
Tribes: Tenino (Sahaptin tribes), Wasco, Northern Paiute

Burns Paiute Tribe
Burns Paiute Reservation
Tribe: Northern Paiute

Fort McDermit Paiute Indians
Fort McDermit Reservation
Tribe: Northern Paiute

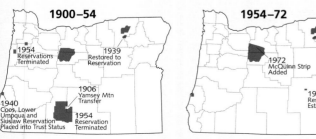

1900–54

1954
Reservations
Terminated

1939
Restored to
Reservation

1906
Yamsey Mtn
Transfer

1940
Coos, Lower
Umpqua and
Siuslaw Reservation
Placed into Trust Status

1954
Reservation
Terminated

1954–72

1972
McQuinn Strip
Added

1972
Reservation
Established

Donation Land Claims; Public Land Survey

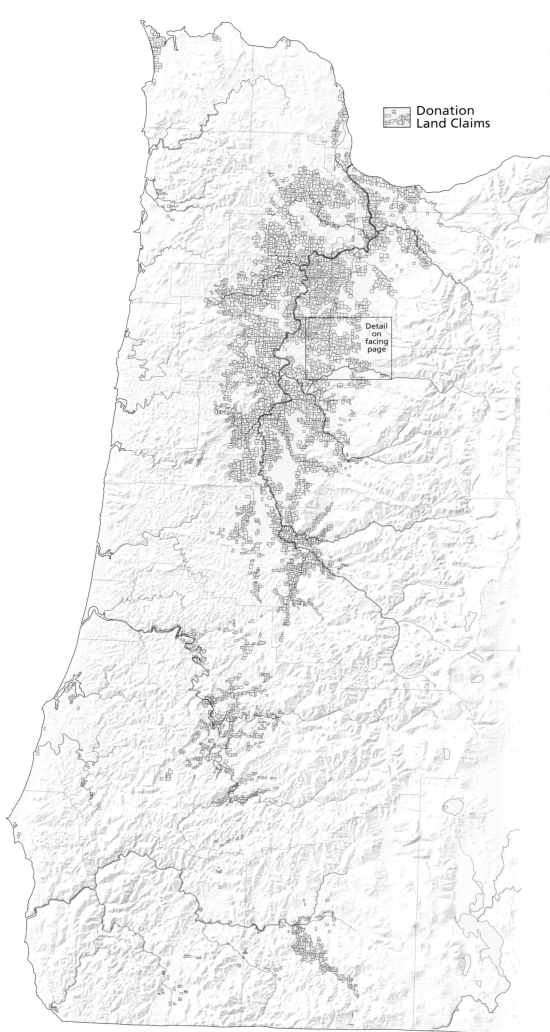

Donation
Land Claims

Detail on facing page

Public Land Survey

The U.S. Public Land Survey began in 1785 when Congress authorized a systematic scheme for surveying lands in the public domain. This scheme, known as the Township and Range System, was eventually applied to all land in the federal domain. Its basis was a series of meridians of longitude and parallels of latitude called principal

meridians and base lines. On either side of the principal meridian additional lines were drawn at six-mile intervals, thus dividing the land into north-to-south strips called ranges. Lines running east to west at six-mile intervals broke up the strips into squares, six miles on a side, called townships. These townships were further surveyed into 36 sections, each one mile per side, with 640 acres in each section. Some sections were subdivided into quarter-sections of 160 acres. Responsible for implementing the Township and Range System in Oregon, the Office of the Surveyor General was created in 1850 as part of the Donation Land Act. By 1852 this office had completed the initial survey that would serve to orient the rest of the Oregon grid. The Willamette Principal Meridian and Willamette Base Line originate at the Willamette Stone in northwest Portland.

Donation Land Claims

Viewed from an airplane, the Willamette Valley landscape appears as an irregular pattern of roads and fields. This is due in large part to the manner in which Oregon Trail immigrants settled the land after their arrival in the 1840s. They established their claims before the land was surveyed according to the regularizing provisions of the Donation Land Act of 1850. The Act, passed by Congress after Oregon had become a territory, was designed to confirm existing (often irregular) claims and define the terms of future claims. The road alignments and field boundaries established shortly after 1850 persist today.

The Act initially called for the granting of free land to end in December 1853, but that limit was later extended to 1855. Under terms of the Act married couples who arrived in Oregon before December 1850 could claim 640 acres; single men could receive 320 acres. Those who arrived after this time could claim 320 acres if married, 160 if single. Parcels claimed before townships were surveyed appear on Oregon land ownership maps as irregular shapes. They were assigned section numbers greater than 36. Parcels claimed after townships were surveyed had to conform to the regular survey pattern of square sections numbered from one to 36. These two distinct patterns are shown on the map at right depicting 12 townships in the Willamette Valley southeast of Salem.

The Progress of the Public Land Survey

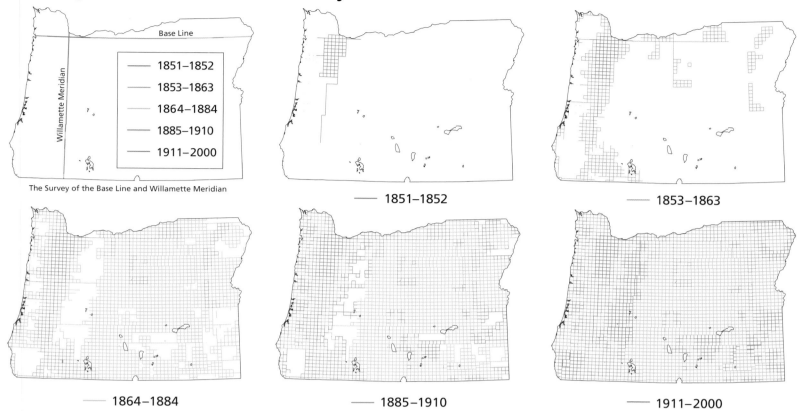

The Survey of the Base Line and Willamette Meridian

—— 1851–1852

—— 1853–1863

—— 1864–1884

—— 1885–1910

—— 1911–2000

Legend:
- 1851–1852
- 1853–1863
- 1864–1884
- 1885–1910
- 1911–2000

Detail of Donation Land Claims and the Public Land Survey

Political Boundaries

Developing Borders of Oregon

The present political borders of Oregon developed gradually, in piecemeal fashion, along lines first established by competing European powers and later by the dictates of regional economic growth. The eighteenth-century French and Spanish empires divided western North America at the 42nd parallel, far from either country's valuable colonial centers. Britain's 1767 victory over the French in Canada called that division into question. At the same time, the Russians were pushing south from their new base in Alaska. Spain hurriedly forged the chain of Franciscan missions in California to anchor its northern Mexican borders and began actively exploring the Northwest coast. English expeditions under Cook and then Vancouver systematically charted the same region, which their countryman Drake had first claimed as New Albion in 1585. Colliding interests were

1844

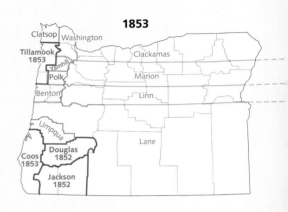

1853

Counties first organized as of the year mapped are outlined and named in bold red. Counties already in existence as of the year mapped, but whose boundaries later changed, are outlined and named in light red. Counties which had assumed their present boundaries as of the year mapped are named in gray. Present county boundaries are shown as very light gray lines.

resolved (to British advantage) in the Nootka Convention of 1792 between Britain and Spain. The Convention recognized actual occupancy as the basis for sovereignty. The effect was to extinguish Spanish claims in the Northwest, and also to encourage a (very slow-moving) race between Britain and the U.S. to occupy the region. British maps claimed New Albion (see page 14), and the Northwest Fur and Hudson's Bay Companies dominated the Lower Columbia during most of the early nineteenth century, but with no certain border.

Spanish claims below the 42nd parallel were formally recognized by the U.S. in 1819. The southern border follows the parallel, but wanders considerably due to surveyor errors, misplaced in some locations over half a mile north or south. In Western Oregon the boundary roughly corresponds to the crest of the Siskiyou Mountains, but this is pure coincidence. The southern boundary of Russian claims in the Northwest was settled at 54° 40' in 1824. Conflicting American and British claims to the whole territory between those boundaries continued for another generation, and were the subject of six negotiations between 1818 and 1846. During most of that time the effective seat of government for the region was the Hudson's Bay Company base at Fort Vancouver, on the north bank of the Columbia.

By the early 1840s American settlement on the Lower Columbia and on Puget Sound was spurred by the expansionist outlook of the period, and by a long standing movement in Congress to reward settlers with large land grants. The Hudson's Bay Company's competing effort to establish a population of long-term lease tenants north of the Columbia could not compete with the prospects of free land title. The Oregon Treaty of 1846 between Britain and the U.S. recognized the realities of this situation. The 49th parallel plus all of Vancouver Island was established as the southern boundary of British Canada. The Continental Divide marked the practical and assumed easternmost boundary of the Oregon Country.

In 1843 an assembly at Champoeg led to the establishment of a provisional government for the (as yet not formally existing) Oregon Territory. The region was divided into the four Districts of Champoeg, Clackamas, Twality (also spelled Tuality) and Yamhill, with the government seat at Oregon City. Clatsop was added from Twality District in 1844 and, a year later, Polk was added from Yamhill District and Vancouver (soon to become part of the new Washington Territory) from Clackamas District. Also in 1845, the "districts" were legally retitled "counties." Oregon was formally established as a U.S. Territory in 1848. Early settlement was concentrated in the lower Willamette Valley, which offered good farmland and river transport, but little market for crops. Settlements along the Southern Emigrant Road or Applegate Trail were even more isolated.

The California Gold Rush of 1849 suddenly created a market for Oregon crops and employment for Oregonians. Within a few years a population of experienced prospectors and miners developed; they were soon seeking and finding gold in southwestern Oregon. County development in the Territory followed rapidly, with the present boundaries (apart

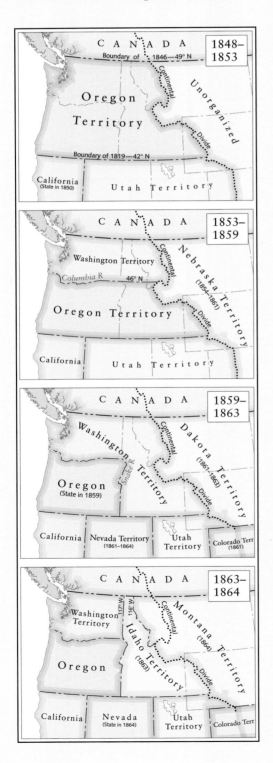

from a single minor adjustment in the Cascades, and the merger of Umpqua and Douglas Counties) established by 1856. The 1854 creation of Columbia, Multnomah and Wasco Counties reflected the growing shipping industry along the Columbia. Wasco County nominally included all territory east of the Cascades (until 1859, presumably extending to the Continental Divide), but in practice consisted of The Dalles and a few smaller river ports and their hinterlands.

Settlement around Puget Sound led to the establishment of the Washington Territory in 1853, with the boundary on the main channel of the Columbia (up to its sharp bend to the north, and from that point, east along the 46th parallel to the Continental Divide). Oregon was admitted to the Union in 1859 with its eastern boundary defined as the Snake River from the 46th parallel south to the confluence of the Owyhee River, and thence due south to the 42nd parallel. Lands east of this boundary were briefly included in the Washington Territory, but established as the Idaho Territory after the Boise gold strikes of the early 1860s.

The organization of Eastern Oregon counties followed the mining booms of the 1860s, with the eastern third of the state organized into the four counties of Umatilla, Union, Grant and Baker by 1864. The expansion of cattle ranching out of the Willamette Valley led to the organization of Lake County in 1874. Klamath, Crook, Gilliam and Morrow Counties were established by

1845

Clatsop · Tuality · Clackamas · Champoeg · Yamhill · Polk 1845 · Linn 1845

1847

Clatsop · Tuality · Clackamas · Champoeg · Yamhill · Polk · Benton 1847 · Linn

1851

Clatsop · Washington · Clackamas · Yamhill · Marion · Polk · Benton · Linn · Umpqua 1851 · Attached to Umpqua · Lane 1851

1860

Columbia 1854 · Clatsop · Multnomah 1854 · Wash. · Clackamas · Tillamook · Yamhill · Marion · Polk · Benton · Linn · Lane · Wasco 1854 · Umpqua · Coos · Douglas · Curry 1855 · Jackson · Josephine 1856

1862

Clatsop · Columbia · Tillamook · Wash. · Mult. · Clackamas · Yamhill · Marion · Umatilla 1862 · Polk · Benton · Linn · Lane · Baker 1862 · Coos · Douglas · Wasco · Curry · Jos. · Jackson

1865

Clatsop · Columbia · Tillamook · Wash. · Mult. · Clackamas · Yamhill · Marion · Umatilla · Union 1864 · Polk · Benton · Linn · Wasco · Lane · Grant 1864 · Baker · Coos · Douglas · Curry · Jos. · Jackson

1880

Clatsop · Columbia · Tillamook · Wash. · Mult. · Clackamas · Umatilla · Union · Yamhill · Marion · Wasco · Polk · Benton · Linn · Lane · Coos · Douglas · Grant · Baker · Lake 1874 · Curry · Jos. · Jackson

1885

Clatsop · Columbia · Tillamook · Wash. · Mult. · Wasco · Umatilla · Union · Yamhill · Clackamas · Gilliam 1885 · Morrow 1885 · Marion · Polk · Benton · Linn · Crook 1882 · Grant · Baker · Lane · Coos · Douglas · Lake · Curry · Jos. · Jackson · Klamath 1882

1890

Clatsop · Columbia · Tillamook · Wash. · Mult. · Wasco · Morrow · Umatilla · Wallowa 1887 · Yamhill · Clackamas · Gilliam · Sherman 1889 · Union · Marion · Polk · Benton · Linn · Crook · Grant · Baker · Lane · Coos · Douglas · Harney 1889 · Malheur 1887 · Curry · Jos. · Jackson · Lake · Klamath

1900

Clatsop · Columbia · Tillamook · Wash. · Mult. · Wasco · Sherman · Gilliam · Morrow · Umatilla · Wallowa · Yamhill · Clackamas · Union · Lincoln 1893 · Polk · Marion · Wheeler 1899 · Grant · Baker · Linn · Crook · Lane · Coos · Douglas · Harney · Malheur · Curry · Jos. · Jackson · Klamath · Lake

1910

Clatsop · Columbia · Tillamook · Wash. · Mult. · Hood River 1908 · Sherman · Gilliam · Morrow · Umatilla · Wallowa · Yamhill · Clackamas · Wasco · Union · Lincoln · Polk · Marion · Wheeler · Grant · Baker · Linn · Crook · Lane · Coos · Douglas · Harney · Malheur · Curry · Jos. · Jackson · Klamath · Lake

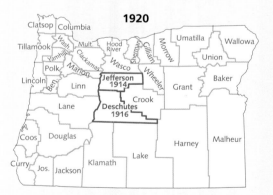

1920

Clatsop · Columbia · Tillamook · Wash. · Mult. · Hood River · Sherman · Gilliam · Morrow · Umatilla · Wallowa · Yamhill · Clackamas · Wasco · Union · Lincoln · Marion · Wheeler · Polk · Ben. · Jefferson 1914 · Grant · Baker · Linn · Crook · Lane · Deschutes 1916 · Coos · Douglas · Harney · Malheur · Curry · Jos. · Jackson · Klamath · Lake

1885, and Sherman, Wallowa, Harney and Malheur by 1889—all based on cattle ranching and wheat farming.

The 1890 U.S. census recorded the end of the American frontier—there was no longer any "edge of settlement" remaining in the West. Lincoln County was organized in 1893 from the Grand Rond Indian Reservation, and Wheeler County in 1899 from the northeast corner of Crook County. The three twentieth-century counties (Hood River, Jefferson and Deschutes) organized areas of farming, ranching and timber harvesting.

Oregon's Territorial Government moved from Oregon City to Salem in 1850. Many county seats shifted during the early years. Josephine County's seat moved from Waldo to Kerbyville in 1857, and on to Grants Pass in 1885; Curry County's from Port Orford to Ellensburg (now Gold Beach) in 1859; Baker County's from Auburn to Baker City in 1868; Umatilla County's from Umatilla City to Pendleton in 1868; Harney County's from Harney to Burns in 1890; Gilliam County's from Alkali (now Arlington) to Condon in 1890; Coos County's from Empire City to Coquille in 1896; Jackson County's from Jacksonville to Medford in 1928.

1941

Clatsop · Columbia · Tillamook · Wash. · Mult. · Hood River · Sherman · Gilliam · Morrow · Umatilla · Wallowa · Yamhill · Clackamas · Wasco · Union · Lincoln · Polk · Ben. · Marion · Jefferson · Wheeler · Grant · Baker · Linn · Crook · Lane · Deschutes · County Line Adjustment · Coos · Douglas · Harney · Malheur · Curry · Jos. · Jackson · Klamath · Lake

Land Grants

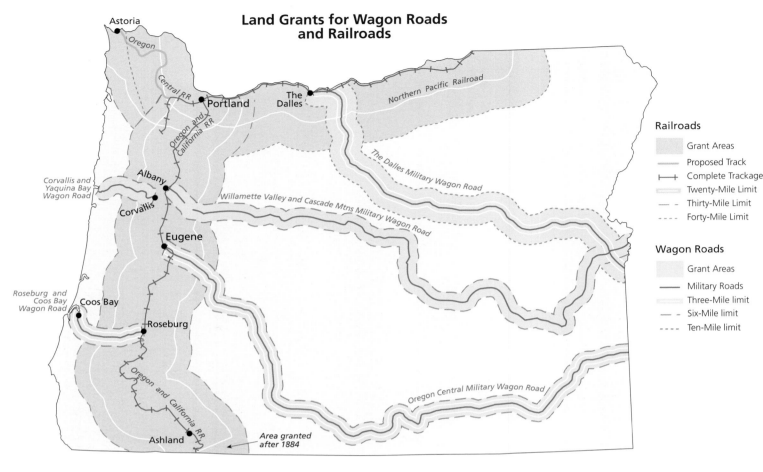

Land Grants for Wagon Roads and Railroads

Railroads

- Grant Areas
- —— Proposed Track
- ├─┤ Complete Trackage
- ▭ Twenty-Mile Limit
- – – Thirty-Mile Limit
- ···· Forty-Mile Limit

Wagon Roads

- Grant Areas
- —— Military Roads
- ▭ Three-Mile limit
- – · Six-Mile limit
- ···· Ten-Mile limit

Disposition of the Public Domain in Oregon

Category	Acres
Miscellaneous	992,921
Railroad Grants	1,588,532
Wagon-Road Grants	2,490,890
Donation Land Claims	2,614,082
Grants to State	4,329,445
Sales	6,455,551
Homesteads	11,083,779

Acres (in millions)

Homesteads
(Including commuted homesteads)

Years	Percent
1870–1879	3%
1880–1889	8%
1890–1899	16%
1900–1909	18%
1910–1919	26%
1920–1929	23%
1930–1939	5%
1940–1949	1%

Acres (in millions)

1908 Advertisement

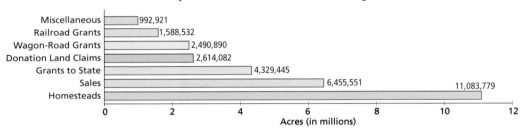

"Military" and Wagon Roads

The federal government has disposed of public domain land in various ways. In Oregon, the earliest and simplest method was to give away farm-sized parcels to settlers (see pages 18–19). Another early method was to give large grants of land to the states and transportation companies as subsidies for road and railroad building. The wagon road grants, designed to satisfy the demand for internal improvements at federal expense in the Mississippi Valley, actually had their greatest application in Oregon. Beginning in the 1860s, almost 2.5 million acres of public land were granted in Oregon for wagon roads, compared to grants of about one million acres elsewhere.

In Oregon, local speculators provided small amounts of capital to form road construction companies, in return for which they received enormous amounts of land, often fraudulently and with the connivance of state officials. New settlers were also in favor of the grants, hoping to buy inexpensive granted land and reap huge benefits. Five military roads were built in Oregon with land grant subsidies. The term "military road" was a legal fiction designed to make this use of federal lands more acceptable to congressmen from other parts of the country. These roads came with a stipulated provision of toll-free passage by military vehicles; however, only one such military use is recorded. The land grants were for the alternate, odd-numbered, square-mile sections in a band three miles wide on each side of the road. With the exception of the Corvallis and Yaquina Bay Wagon Road Company, all the road building companies are considered to have been almost total frauds that received huge amounts of land for building poor roads.

Oregon and California Lands

The checkerboard of Oregon and California lands (commonly called O & C lands) was created in 1866 when Congress authorized a grant from the public domain to subsidize the construction of a railroad from Portland to the California border. The grant consisted of 20 square-mile sections for every mile of railroad built. The land was to be selected from the odd-numbered sections within 20 miles on either side of the right-of-way, and, if necessary, from two adjacent ten-mile strips.

The Oregon Legislature designated the East Side Company to receive the grant. Because of filing delays, new federal legislation was required in 1869. This renewal stipulated that grant lands could be sold only to "actual settlers" in tracts no larger than 160 acres and at prices not to exceed $2.50 per acre. The company was reorganized in 1870 as the Oregon and California Railroad Company. By 1887 construction was completed, the O & C railroad was integrated into the Southern Pacific railroad system, and more than 3.7 million acres had become railroad property.

Most of the land granted was heavily forested and on steep slopes, and there was little demand for it by "actual settlers" interested in agriculture. Only 296,000 acres had been sold by 1890. In 1894, however, the railroad began to sell tracts for their timber value in violation of the 1869 legislation. Eighty-five percent of the 813,000 acres sold by 1903 had been disposed of illegally. Southern Pacific also decided to hold the land as a timber reserve —there would be no more sales of O & C land. Eventually Congress took action and passed the Chamberlain–Ferris Act in 1916: about 2.9 million acres of O & C land were returned to federal ownership; timber was to be sold by competitive bid; cut-over lands were to be sold at $2.50 per acre; money was appropriated to pay delinquent taxes to the counties and to pay the railroad for its lost land.

From 1916 to 1938, the 18 counties with O & C lands received only $13 million of payments in lieu of taxes. In 1937, new legislation brought the O & C Lands under sustained-yield forest management and called for a new formula for disbursing the revenue from timber sales. In 1946, the Bureau of Land Management (BLM) was created and given responsibility for managing O & C lands. Due to the BLM's strong leadership and the rapidly increasing demand for timber, the 1937 formula proved to be a bonanza for local governments, even though they were persuaded in 1952 to yield all revenues above 50 percent of receipts for road building, reforestation and other improvements of the O & C lands. Timber sales and revenue have been reduced dramatically in recent years due to environmental issues.

Oregon and California Lands Payments

	Acres	% of Total O & C Lands	2000 Receipts In $1,000s
Benton	52,496	2.81	$1,741
Clackamas	91,805	5.55	3,438
Columbia	11,079	2.06	1,276
Coos	122,001	5.90	3,655
Curry	93,506	3.65	2,261
Douglas	706,321	25.05	15,517
Jackson	437,997	15.67	9,707
Josephine	366,600	12.08	7,483
Klamath	67,305	2.34	1,450
Lane	374,215	15.27	9,459
Lincoln	9,220	0.36	233
Linn	86,166	2.64	6,635
Marion	20,712	1.46	904
Multnomah	4,247	1.09	675
Polk	42,205	2.16	1,338
Tillamook	27,570	0.56	347
Washington	11,645	0.63	390
Yamhill	41,645	0.72	446
TOTAL	**2,566,735**	**100%**	**$66,955**

Oregon and California Lands Payments
Dollars in Millions (adjusted to 1998 dollars)

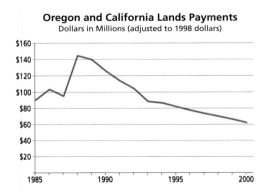

Oregon and California Lands

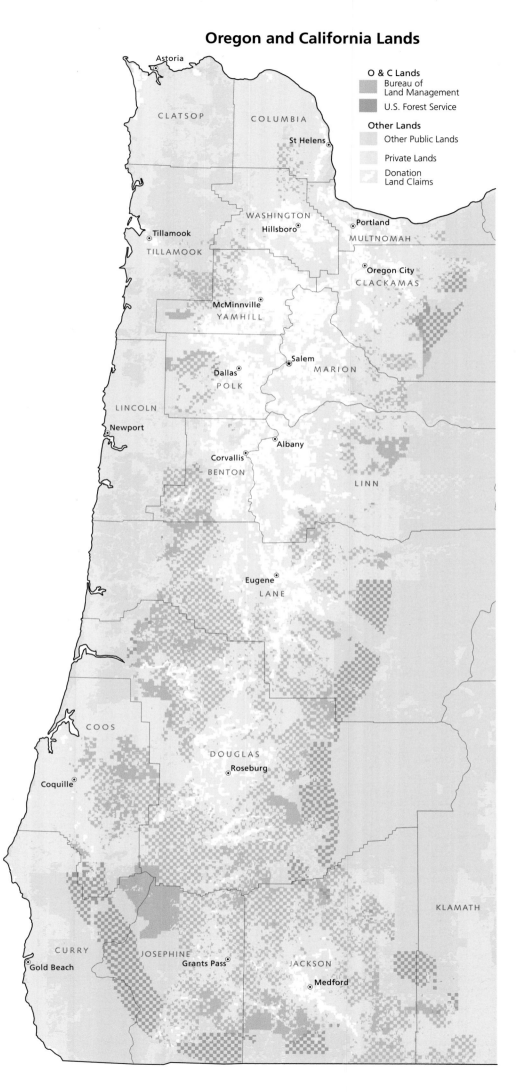

O & C Lands
- Bureau of Land Management
- U.S. Forest Service

Other Lands
- Other Public Lands
- Private Lands
- Donation Land Claims

23

Place Names

Physical Feature Names

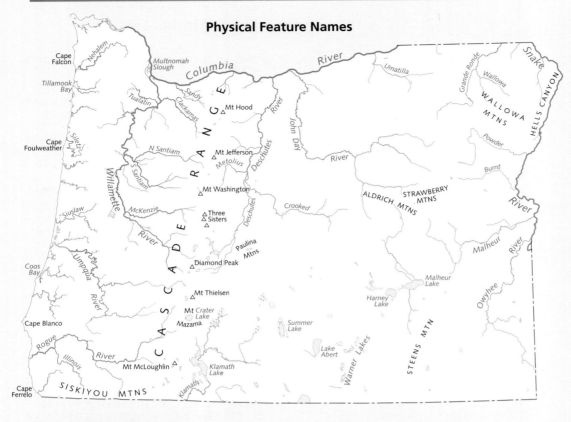

Place Name Origins

Every place name is a signpost that tells a story of settlement and of the culture of earlier generations. Place naming is discussed in detail on pages 288–291. About 1,600 place names shown on the reference maps are indexed by page and map coordinates in the Gazetteer (pages 284–288). A very brief summary is presented below of some of the state's most important physical features, and of counties and county seats. Listings give the date or period when the name was first recorded, the source of the name and, in some cases, the identity of the namer. The history of some 7,000 Oregon place names is found in McArthur's *Oregon Geographic Names* (see page 288).

Physical Feature Names

Date of the earliest written record of the name is given where known. Most names would have been in use for some years before they were recorded.

Aldrich Mtns. (c. 1880) For the Aldrich family. A son, Elmer Aldrich, was killed in a skirmish with Paiutes in 1878.

Burnt River (1825) Translation of the French *Rivière Brûlée*, probably originally a reference to an area of burned timber.

Cape Blanco (1603) It is not clear to which cape successive Spanish navigators applied the name. Vancouver called the present Cape Blanco "Cape Orford" (1792), but the name Blanco has held for the westernmost point in Oregon; by Capt. Martin de Aguilar.

Cape Falcon (1775) As with most early coastal names there is uncertainty about which cape was actually sighted; by Capt. Bruno Heceta.

Cape Ferrelo (1869) Bartolome Ferrelo commanded the northern portions of Juan Cabrillo's 1542–43 expedition which reached these latitudes; assigned commemoratively by the USC&GS.

Cape Foulweather (1778) Descriptively named for his first Oregon landfall; by Capt. James Cook.

Cascade Range (1820s) For the cascades on the Columbia River, now inundated by the reservoir behind Bonneville Dam.

Clackamas (1806) The name of a Chinookan people living along the river; mentioned by Lewis and Clark.

Columbia River (1792) For his ship, the *Columbia Rediviva* out of Boston, the first to enter the river; by Capt. Robert Gray.

Coos Bay (1805–06) For the "Cook-koo-oose" Indians living there; by Lewis and Clark.

Crater Lake (1869) Oregon's first tourist destination renamed by sightseers, displacing "Deep Blue Lake" (1853); by prospectors.

Crooked River (1820s) A practical description of the deeply incised meanders of its lower reaches; by fur trappers.

Deschutes River (1820s) "River of the Falls" for Celilo Falls on the Columbia near the Deschutes confluence; by fur trappers.

Diamond Peak (1852) For John Diamond, who surveyed an alternate route over Willamette Pass to Idaho.

Grande Ronde River (1827) Freely translated as "fine large valley surrounded by hills or mountains." Confusingly, there are two: the larger, in northeast Oregon, is indicated on the map. The smaller, west of Salem, is spelled "Grand."

Harney Lake (1859) Ogden's "Salt Lake" of the 1820s; noted by a military expedition as unfit to drink and then nevertheless (or perhaps accordingly) renamed for the major-general in charge of the Army's Department of Oregon.

Hells Canyon (1950s) Originally identifying a single deep side canyon, the name was applied for tourist promotional purposes to the whole of the Snake River Gorge.

Illinois River (1850s) By placer miners who emigrated from Peoria in 1847.

John Day River (1810s) Day fell behind Astor's overland party, was rescued by friendly Indians but later was robbed even of his clothes by hostiles near the river.

Klamath (1820s) An Indian term for the region (meaning unknown), then applied, in many early variants, to the people living there.

Lake Abert (1843) For the chief of the U.S. Army Topographical Engineers; by Fremont.

Malheur River (1820s) French "river of misfortune," from the theft of a cache of furs hidden there.

McKenzie (1834) Donald McKenzie of Astor's Pacific Fur Co. explored the Willamette Valley in 1812.

Metolius River (1855) "Light-colored salmon" in one of the languages spoken at the Warm Springs Reservation.

Mt. Hood (1792) By the Vancouver expedition for the noted British admiral under whom Vancouver had served.

Mt. Jefferson (1806) By Lewis for the President and patron of the Lewis and Clark expedition.

Mt. Mazama (1896) For the Mazama Mountaineering Club.

Mt. McLoughlin (1838) For John McLoughlin, chief factor at the Hudson's Bay Company's Oregon base at Fort Vancouver. Confusingly, originally called Shasta (like the much larger peak to the south) and, well into the twentieth century, Mt. Pitt.

Mt. Thielsen (c. 1872) For an early railroad engineer and builder—originally called "Big Cowhorn."

Mt. Washington (1867) Named for the President during a railroad survey.

Multnomah (1806) Chinook name recorded by Lewis and Clark for the Willamette River; may have identified the reach below Willamette Falls. It now applies to the side channel west of Sauvie Island.

Nehalem Salish "place where people live." The prefix "Ne-" means locale or place, and is widespread on the North Coast.

Oregon (1760s) Appears first as the "Great River of the West," the long-rumored and imaginatively mapped, but in fact nonexistent, route from the Great Lakes to the Pacific. The name was probably a corruption of "Ouriconsint"—the Wisconsin. Oregon reemerged in 1817 in Bryant's popular poem "Thanatopsis." The river was by then well-established as the Columbia, but Oregon came into general use for the region.

Owyhee River (1826) For two Hawaiian ("Owyhee") Islanders killed by Indians in 1819. The fur trade's sea routes included an important base in Hawaii, and Hawaiians were among the early trappers.

Paulina Peak The most prominent of many features named for the Paiute leader in fight against Whites 1866–68.

Powder River Probably descriptive of powdery soil along a frequented reach of the river.

Rogue (around 1820) The Tututni people of the lower Rogue often tangled with the fur trappers, who then identified them descriptively.

Sandy River (1840s) Named Barings River (for the bankers) by Vancouver in 1792; Quicksand River by Lewis and Clark in 1805; the present shorter form evolved as a handier variant.

Santiam A group of Kalapooyans, the name later applied to the river along which they lived.

Siletz River (1850s) Tututni for "black bear." The Tututni survivors of the Rogue Indian Wars were exiled to a reservation on the northern Oregon Coast. They named a local lake for its bears, and that name was adopted for the river, the reservation, and eventually the Indians (of various origins) living there.

Siskiyou Mtns. (1828) Cree (eastern Canada) "spotted horse," the name of a prize animal lost by trappers while crossing the mountains in a blizzard.

Siuslaw River (1805) An Indian word of unknown meaning, used, in various spellings, from Lewis and Clark on, applied first to a people, later to the river.

Snake River (early fur period) For the Northern Paiutes and other related Great Basin and Intermountain peoples whose common use of reptiles as food was noted by appalled Europeans and neighboring tribes as a defining characteristic.

Steens Mt. (1860s) Called the "Snow Mtns." in fur trade and pioneer times, renamed for U.S. Army Major Steens, who fought Paiutes on the mountain in 1860.

Strawberry Mtns. (1870s) For wild strawberries, first applied to a creek, then the peak, now commonly for the whole ridge.

Summer Lake (1843) For the green grass at its margins, by Fremont, several thousand feet higher and snowbound on what he accordingly named "Winter Ridge."

Three Sisters Called "Faith, Hope and Charity" by Willamette Valley missionaries of the 1830s; the simpler descriptive name seems to have grown out of that list.

Tillamook (1805) A Salish group noted by Lewis and Clark as "Killamook"; the present form was in use by the 1850s.

Tualatin River (1830s) Indian word, language unknown, probably meaning lazy or sluggish, describing the river's meandering course.

Umatilla River (1805) An Indian word of unknown meaning, spelled variously by Lewis and Clark, much later applied to tribes of the area.

Umpqua (1825) Indian name for a locale on the river, then applied to the river and to the Kalapooyan people living along it.

Wallowa River (early 1800s) Nez Perce word for a type of fish trap used in the river below Wallowa Lake.

Warner Valley (1864) "Valley of the Lakes" in the fur period, renamed much later for the U.S. Army captain killed nearby in 1849.

Willamette (1811) An Indian name that may refer to the river above the Willamette Falls.

Yamhill (1814) Likely an adaptation of a Kalapooian word for a locale on the river.

County Names

Ten Oregon counties bear Indian names. **Clackamas, Coos, Klamath, Multnomah, Tillamook, Umatilla, Wallowa** and **Yamhill** were applied first to physical features (and are discussed above). **Clatsop** and **Wasco** directly honor groups who were of central importance to the earliest White arrivals.

Columbia, Hood, Malheur and **Deschutes** refer to physical features named during the early exploration and fur trade periods. **Lake** is descriptive: its territory

originally included Crater, Klamath, Abert and Summer Lakes and the Oregon portion of Goose Lake.

Washington, Jackson, Jefferson and **Marion** honor early U.S. leaders. Marion was the "Swamp Fox" of Revolutionary War fame; Jefferson as a county name, however, refers to the mountain, and only indirectly to the man. Thirteen names honor political and military leaders of the settlement period. **Benton, Douglas** and **Linn** were prominent Senate supporters of Oregon settlement and generous land allotments; **Polk** was President when Britain ceded its claims south of the 49th parallel. **Lane** and **Curry** were territorial governors. **Gilliam** led the 1847–48 campaign against the Cayuse. **Harney** headed the Army's Department of Oregon (the county takes its name from the lake). **Crook, Sherman, Grant, Lincoln** and **Baker** honor Civil War leaders (Baker, a former U.S. Senator from Oregon and a major-general, was killed in 1862). **Union** honors the Northern cause itself.

Wheeler and **Morrow** recall early settlers in those regions. **Josephine** takes its name from a creek, in turn named for a settler's daughter.

County Seat Names

Albany (1848) For Albany, N.Y., home town of the Monteith brothers who settled locally.

Astoria (1811) Ft. Astoria was the base for Astor's NW Fur Company 1811–13; the British renamed it Ft. George until 1818. The present town name came back into use during early pioneer times.

Baker City (1866) (See county list.) The original form was modernized to Baker in 1911, then returned to Baker City in 1989 due to renewed interest in pioneer times and places.

Bend Originally Farewell Bend, a parklike resting place along a bend of the Deschutes where stock and travelers rested before heading across the Cascades. Not to be confused with the Oregon Trail's Farewell Bend at the present Baker–Malheur County line, where the trail left the Snake River.

Burns (1883) For Robert Burns, the Scottish national poet; by cofounder George McGowan.

Canyon City (1864) Describes the town's location in a steep canyon, leading from the John Day River valley to the mines which drew settlement to the area.

Condon (1884) For Harvey Condon, whose law firm handled the sale of lots in the town.

Coquille (early 1800s) For the Coquille River, in turn

commonly thought to be a French fur trapper's reference to scallops found in the river. However, Coquille appears to be derived from an Indian word or name whose original form and meaning have both been lost.

Corvallis (1853) Kitchen Latin for "Heart of the Valley"; the original "Marysville," for Mary's River, was vetoed by the U.S. Post Office to avoid confusion with Marysville, California.

Dallas For George Dallas, Polk's vice president (1845–49).

Enterprise (1887) Selected by optimistic majority vote.

Eugene (1840s) For Eugene Skinner, settler of 1846.

Fossil (1876) For fossils found by the postmaster about the time the post office was established.

Gold Beach (1850s) For beach placer mining of the 1850s.

Grants Pass (1863) Celebrates Grant's victory at Vicksburg in 1863, news of which arrived as road construction crossed a nearby divide.

Heppner (1873) For Henry Heppner, partner of Jackson Morrow in the area's first general store.

Hillsboro (1849) For David Hill of Connecticut, settler of 1842 and chairman of Executive Committee of 1843–44, "in effect, Oregon's first elected governor." Previously "Columbia" and "Columbus."

Hood River (1856) Originally "Dog River," from the diet of a party of early starving travelers; renamed by local preference.

Klamath Falls (1892) Originally Linkville (1867); renamed for the falls on the very short Link River connecting Klamath Lake with Lake Ewauna.

Lakeview (1876) Goose Lake is visible from the slopes immediately above the town.

La Grande (1862–63) For the Grande Ronde Valley.

Madras (1903) Inspired by the label on a bolt of Madras cloth.

McMinnville (1840s) For his home town in Tennessee by William Newby, settler of 1843.

Medford (1884) Railroad station name chosen for its location near the middle ford across Bear Creek.

Moro (1870s–80s) Origin uncertain, possibly for Moro, Illinois.

Newport (1868) Probably for the Rhode Island town, also a coastal resort.

Oregon City (1842) Location at Willamette Falls seemed to guarantee its early status as the metropolis of the territory.

Pendleton (1860s) George Pendleton was the Democratic vice presidential candidate in 1864.

Portland (1844) For Portland, Maine; had a coin toss gone the other way, the 16-block townsite would have been called "Boston."

Prineville (1870s) Barney Prine's bar and blacksmithery was the first business establishment.

Roseburg (1854) Tavernkeeper Aaron Rose donated three acres and $1,000 toward a courthouse.

St. Helens (1850) For the mountain; displacing Plymouth (1847). The mountain was named in 1793 for the British diplomat whose negotiation of the Nootka Treaty removed Spain from serious contention in the Northwest; by Vancouver.

Salem (1844) for Salem, Massachusetts.

The Dalles (1814) Literally "flagstones" in French; in fur trapper usage, a narrow river passage bordered by flat ledges.

Tillamook (1805) Salish tribe, noted by Lewis and Clark.

Vale (1883) Apparently for the town's situation, which fits the English, if not the American, usage of the term.

County and County Seat Names

County Populations

Population Topics, Pages 26–39

The distribution and character of Oregon settlement is presented in the following 14 pages. The growth of individual counties is treated on this page pair. The fortunes of Oregon's incorporated cities are discussed in detail on pages 28 through 31. These maps show the expansion (or contraction) of every incorporated town at each census period—a more detailed view of the general trends presented here. Pages 32 and 33 show the evolution of downtown Portland from 1879 to 1999. Population density and zoning in the Willamette Valley are discussed on pages 34 and 35, and statewide population density and overall population growth are addressed on pages 36 and 37.

County Populations

Oregon's population has grown at every census since 1850, but the growth has been unevenly distributed, and rates of growth have fluctuated sharply. Population has always been concentrated in the western third of the state, and particularly within the Willamette Valley. The census of 1860 recorded 74 percent of the state's population (of 52,465) in Willamette Valley counties. This share dropped to a low of 56 percent in 1900, a period of rapid settlement in southern and Eastern Oregon, but it has increased ever since, reaching 70 percent (of 3.4 million) in 2000.

The graphs on these pages show some striking regional differences: half the counties (three on the Coast, the other 15 east of the Cascades) contain only 8 percent of the state's population. The largest six counties (all but one in the Willamette Valley) contain 65 percent. Most counties have seen periods of absolute population decline, and nearly all exhibit sharply uneven growth over time, with boom decades followed by slow (or no) growth.

Each county's share of total population is also shown. Figures from the earliest periods are affected by the county subdivision process, which was mostly completed by 1900 (see pages 20 and 21). Eastern Oregon counties have generally declined in relative importance, with Deschutes (now seventh in size) a marked exception. The shifting role of Multnomah County is dramatic; it accounted for nearly 36 percent of the state's population in 1930, but has lost (relative) ground to its rapidly growing suburban neighbors ever since. Areas of Multnomah County growth, predominantly unincorporated between 1940 and 1980, have almost entirely been organized into incorporated cities in the past two decades.

The bottom (darker) portion of each graph shows the proportion of county population living in incorporated towns. Some "rural" agricultural counties are in fact surprisingly urban—Baker, Union and Umatilla are notable examples. Klamath County stands out at the opposite extreme.

County Populations, 1850–2000

- Total County Population
- Population of Incorporated Places
- Population as a Percentage of the State Total
- 18 Rank, of 36 Counties

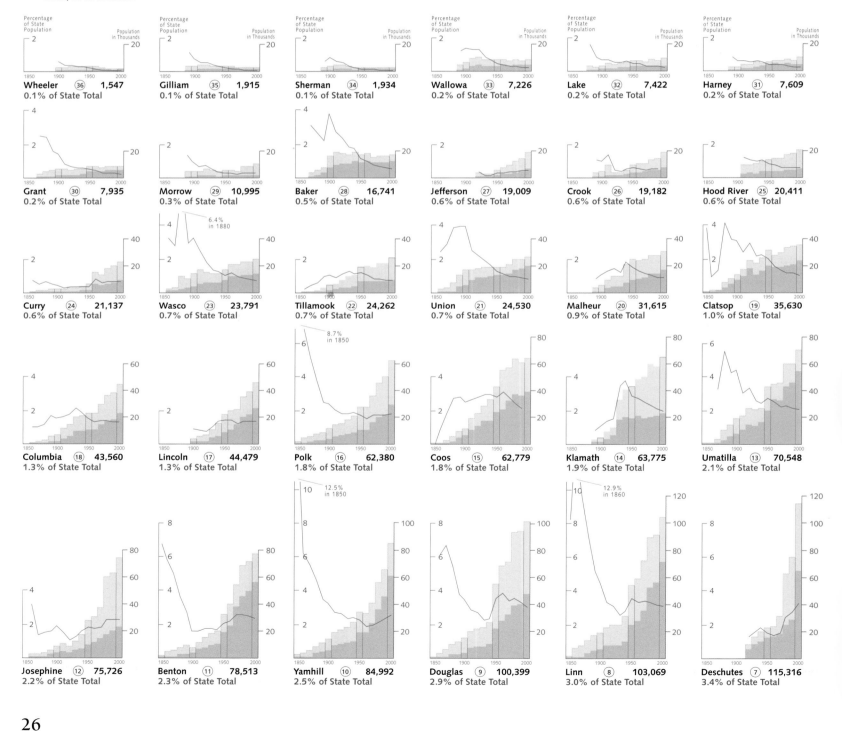

County Populations at 20-Year Interval

On each map county populations shown in thousands on sphere proportional to county population at that date.

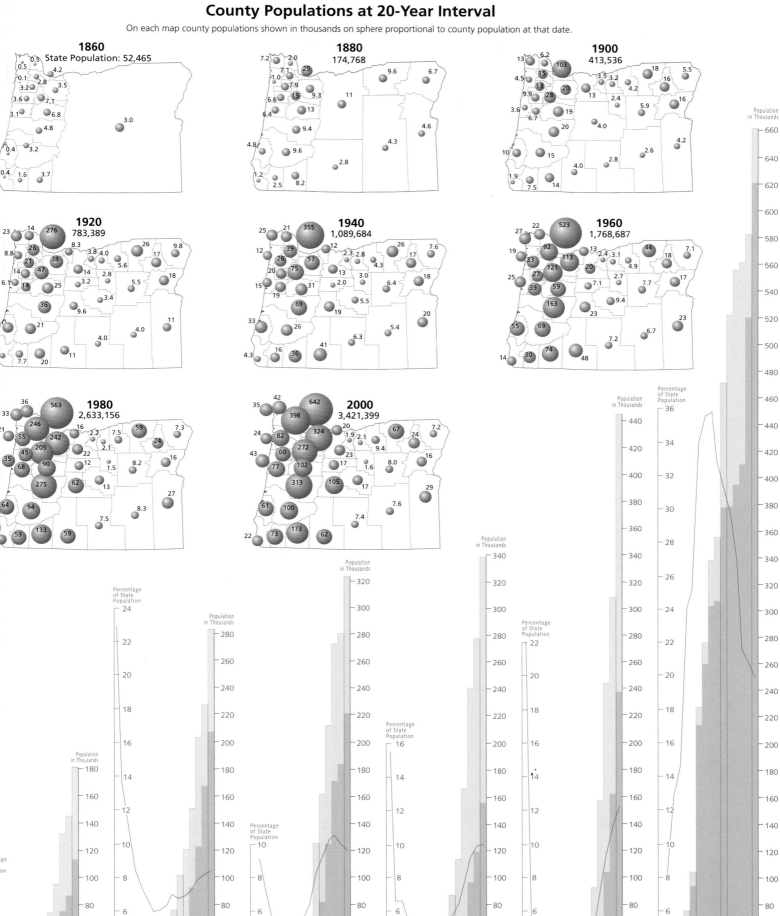

Jackson ⑥ 181,269
5.3% of State Total

Marion ⑤ 284,834
8.3% of State Total

Lane ④ 322,959
9.5% of State Total

Clackamas ③ 338,391
9.9% of State Total

Washington ② 445,342
13.0% of State Total

Multnomah ① 660,486
19.3% of State Total

Cities: 1870–1960

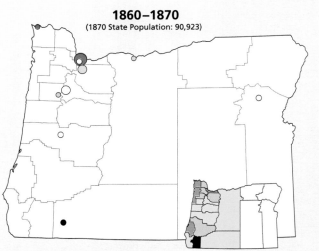

1860–1870
(1870 State Population: 90,923)

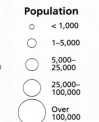

Population

○	< 1,000
○	1–5,000
○	5,000–25,000
○	25,000–100,000
○	Over 100,000

Growth Rate

Cities	Counties	
○	□	(1st Decade)
●	■	Loss
●		0–10%
○		10–25%
○		25–50%
○		50–100%
●		100–200%
●		Over 200%

1900–1910
(1910 State Population: 672,765)

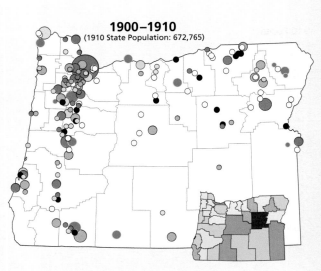

1870 Populations
All Incorporated Places

●	Portland	8,293
○	Salem	1,139
○	Oregon City	1,076
○	The Dalles	942
●	Jacksonville	865
○	Eugene	861
○	East Portland	830
●	Astoria	639
○	Independence	558
○	Baker City	312

1870–1880
(1880 State Population: 174,768)

1880 Populations
25 Largest Incorp. Places

●	Portland	17,577
●	East Portland	2,934
●	Astoria	2,803
●	Salem	2,538
●	The Dalles	2,232
○	Albany	1,867
○	Oregon City	1,263
○	Baker City	1,258
○	Corvallis	1,128
○	Eugene	1,117
○	Ashland	842
●	Jacksonville	839
○	Roseburg	822
○	Pendleton	730
○	Independence	691
○	Dallas	670
○	McMinnville	670
○	Coos Bay	642
○	Forest Grove	547
○	Weston	446
○	Junction City	428
○	Harrisburg	422
○	Union	416
○	Hillsboro	402
○	Lafayette	396

1910–1920
(1920 State Population: 783,389)

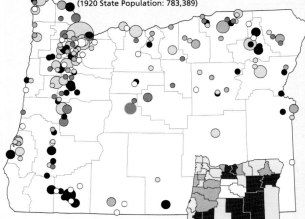

1880–1890
(1890 State Population: 317,704)

1890 Populations

●	Portland	46,385
●	East Portland	10,532
●	Astoria	6,184
●	Albina	5,129
○	Salem	3,398
○	Albany	3,079
●	Oregon City	3,062
●	The Dalles	3,029
●	Baker City	2,604
○	La Grande	2,583
●	Pendleton	2,506
○	Eugene	2,177
●	Ashland	1,784
○	Corvallis	1,527
○	Roseburg	1,472
○	Coos Bay	1,461
○	Grants Pass	1,432
●	McMinnville	1,368
○	Medford	967
○	Dallas	848
●	Lebanon	829
○	Independence	800
●	North Bend	749
●	Jacksonville	743
○	Hillsboro	691

1920–1930
(1930 State Population: 953,786)

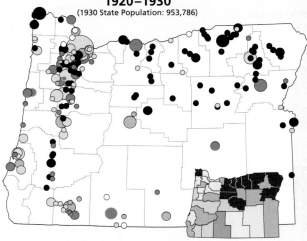

1890–1900
(1900 State Population: 413,536)

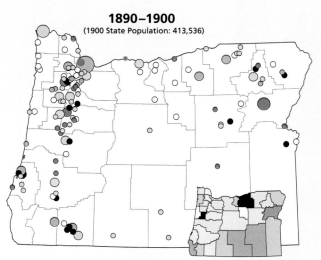

1900 Populations

●	Portland	90,426
○	Astoria	8,381
○	Baker City	6,663
○	Pendleton	4,406
○	Salem	4,258
○	The Dalles	3,542
○	Oregon City	3,494
○	Eugene	3,236
●	Albany	3,149
○	La Grande	2,991
○	Ashland	2,634
●	St. Johns	2,591
○	Grants Pass	2,290
○	Corvallis	1,819
○	Medford	1,791
○	Roseburg	1,690
●	McMinnville	1,420
○	North Bend	1,414
●	Coos Bay	1,391
○	Dallas	1,271
○	Heppner	1,146
●	Forest Grove	1,096
○	Hillsboro	980
●	Cottage Grove	974
●	Newberg	945

1930–1940
(1940 State Population: 1,089,684)

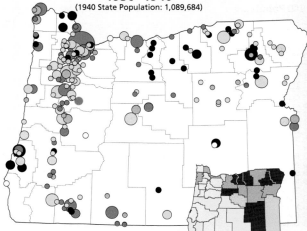

The growth rates of Oregon's cities reflect boom-and-bust economic cycles and changing attitudes about town versus country living. The Oregon Trail pioneers included many enthusiastic town builders, and the territory's resource-based market economy could not exist without urban centers. By 1870, 17 percent of the population already lived in the state's ten incorporated cities: Astoria and The Dalles (on the Columbia); Portland, East Portland, Oregon City, Independence, Salem and Eugene (on the Willamette); and in the outlying mining centers of Jacksonville and Baker City. Incorporation boomed after 1870, continuing until 1910. The percentage of state population living within incorporated towns peaked at 62 percent in 1920. The past 90 years have seen only sporadic new incorporation. City limits have expanded greatly into previously unincorporated urban fringe areas, but automobiles enabled settlement to move still farther out. Incorporated cities' share of the state's population dropped to 56 percent in 1970 and 1980. Land use controls in place since 1975 (see pages 34–35 and 86–87) have encouraged a small rise in that percentage.

Incorporation is a response to the needs of a concentrated population and also a measure of optimism about the future. As the maps on these and the following two pages show, that optimism was not always well-founded. Jacksonville lost population in every census period up to 1910 despite being a county seat. Many of Eastern Oregon's smaller mining towns have dwindled almost as steadily. Astoria grew at every census until 1930, but has lost population at every census since 1950. Towns with lumber-based economies have tended to boom as new tracts of old-growth timber open up, and then slow in growth rate or shrink as the resource is depleted. Few of Oregon's smaller farming and ranching towns have prospered in the face of mechanization and stagnant or declining farm prices.

National economic trends have an effect at the state level. The boom decade of 1900–1910 was followed by the generally dismal performance of 1910–20. Rogue Valley communities contracted sharply, with Medford losing more than one-third of its population after growing fourfold in the previous decade. The agricultural depression of the 1920s undercut prosperity in many Eastern Oregon towns, and the Depression years of the 1930s were difficult nearly everywhere. With little economic opportunity elsewhere, however, few people left.

World War II and the post-war boom brought tremendous growth to Oregon, with a tripling of population from 1940 to 2000. But regional disparities and cycles of rapid growth alternating with widespread stagnation or loss remain the rule. The rise of suburbs in the Portland metro area was a striking feature of the late twentieth century. Hillsboro, Beaverton and Gresham had a combined population of less than 11,000 in 1950. In 2000 the three cities totaled more than 235,000 inhabitants. Public concern over the loss of rural landscapes to suburban development led to the establishment of the state's land use laws in the mid-1970s. Growth patterns before and after their implementation are shown on the Population Centers maps, pages 194–249.

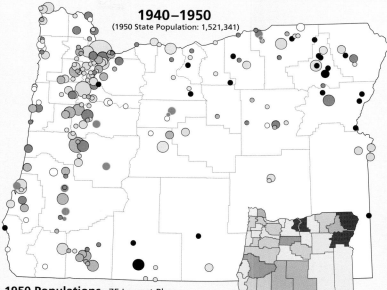

1940–1950
(1950 State Population: 1,521,341)

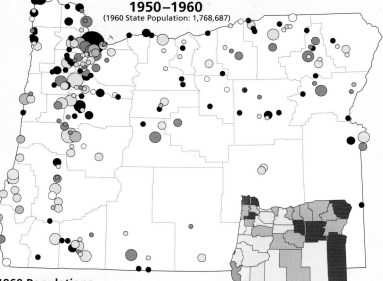

1950–1960
(1960 State Population: 1,768,687)

Cities: 1970–2000

Population

< 1,000	1–5,000	5,000–25,000	25,000–100,000	over 100,000

Growth Rate

	Cities	Counties		Cities	Counties
	○ (1st Decade)	▭		◍ 25–50%	▭
	● Loss	▨		◍ 50–100%	▭
	◍ 0–10%	▭		◍ 100–200%	▨
	○ 10–25%	▭		● over 200%	▨

1960–1970
(1970 State Population: 2,091,533)

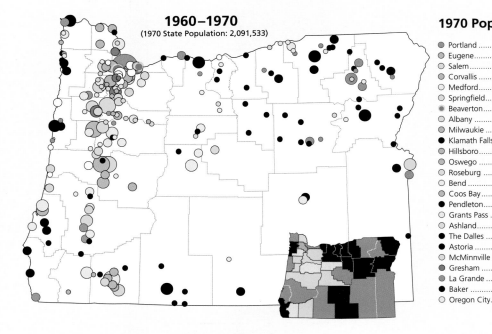

1970 Populations — 75 largest incorporated places

City	Pop.	City	Pop.	City	Pop.
Portland	379,967	North Bend	8,553	Canby	3,813
Eugene	79,028	Forest Grove	8,175	Sweet Home	3,799
Salem	68,725	Woodburn	7,495	Redmond	3,721
Corvallis	35,056	Lebanon	7,277	Oakridge	3,422
Medford	28,454	West Linn	7,091	Burns	3,293
Springfield	26,874	Ontario	6,523	Stayton	3,170
Beaverton	18,577	Newberg	6,507	Sutherlin	3,070
Albany	18,181	Tigard	6,499	Toledo	2,818
Milwaukie	16,444	Dallas	6,361	Myrtle Creek	2,733
Klamath Falls	15,775	Gladstone	6,254	Brookings	2,720
Hillsboro	14,675	St Helens	6,212	Lakeview	2,705
Oswego	14,615	Cottage Grove	6,004	Nyssa	2,620
Roseburg	14,461	Monmouth	5,237	Independence	2,594
Bend	13,710	Newport	5,188	Myrtle Point	2,511
Coos Bay	13,466	Hermiston	4,893	Winston	2,468
Pendleton	13,197	Coquille	4,437	Junction City	2,373
Grants Pass	12,455	Seaside	4,402	Florence	2,246
Ashland	12,342	Silverton	4,301	Molalla	2,005
The Dalles	10,423	Lincoln City	4,196	Mount Angel	1,973
Astoria	10,244	Milton–Freewater	4,105	Cornelius	1,903
McMinnville	10,125	Prineville	4,101	Sheridan	1,881
Gresham	10,030	Reedsport	4,039	Scappoose	1,859
La Grande	9,645	Central Point	4,004	Bandon	1,832
Baker	9,354	Hood River	3,991	Warrenton	1,825
Oregon City	9,176	Tillamook	3,968	Rainier	1,731

1970–1980
(1970 State Population: 2,633,156)

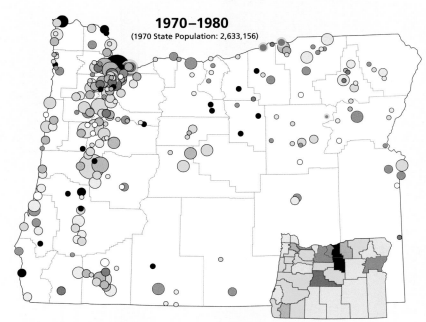

1980 Populations

City	Pop.	City	Pop.	City	Pop.
Portland	366,383	Woodburn	11,196	Milton–Freewater	5,086
Eugene	105,664	The Dalles	10,820	Reedsport	4,984
Salem	89,091	Lebanon	10,413	Sutherlin	4,560
Springfield	41,621	Newberg	10,394	Coquille	4,481
Corvallis	40,960	Astoria	9,996	Florence	4,411
Medford	39,746	North Bend	9,779	Cornelius	4,402
Gresham	33,005	Gladstone	9,500	Stayton	4,396
Beaverton	31,962	Baker	9,471	Hood River	4,329
Hillsboro	27,664	Ontario	8,814	Independence	4,024
Albany	26,511	Dallas	8,530	Tillamook	3,991
Oswego	22,527	Hermiston	8,408	Oakridge	3,680
Milwaukie	17,931	Canby	7,659	Burns	3,579
Bend	17,260	Newport	7,519	Brookings	3,384
Klamath Falls	16,661	Tualatin	7,483	Myrtle Creek	3,365
Roseburg	16,644	Cottage Grove	7,148	Winston	3,359
Grants Pass	15,032	St Helens	7,064	Junction City	3,320
Ashland	14,943	Sweet Home	6,921	Scappoose	3,213
Tigard	14,799	Redmond	6,452	Umatilla	3,199
Oregon City	14,673	Central Point	6,357	Toledo	3,151
Pendleton	14,521	Troutdale	5,908	Molalla	2,992
Coos Bay	14,424	Monmouth	5,594	Wilsonville	2,920
McMinnville	14,080	Lincoln City	5,469	Sandy	2,905
Forest Grove	11,499	Prineville	5,276	Mount Angel	2,876
West Linn	11,358	Seaside	5,193	Nyssa	2,862
La Grande	11,354	Silverton	5,168	Myrtle Point	2,859

1980–1990
(1990 State Population: 2,842,321)

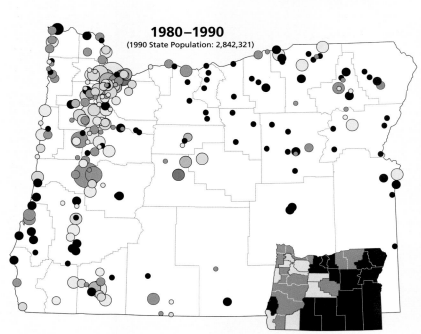

1990 Populations

City	Pop.	City	Pop.	City	Pop.
Portland	438,802	Forest Grove	13,559	Silverton	5,635
Eugene	112,733	Woodburn	13,404	Milton–Freewater	5,533
Salem	107,793	Newberg	13,086	Seaside	5,359
Gresham	68,249	La Grande	11,766	Prineville	5,355
Beaverton	53,307	The Dalles	11,021	Florence	5,171
Medford	47,021	Lebanon	10,950	Sutherlin	5,020
Corvallis	44,757	Gladstone	10,152	Stayton	5,011
Springfield	44,664	Astoria	10,069	Reedsport	4,796
Hillsboro	37,598	Hermiston	10,047	Hood River	4,632
Oswego	30,576	North Bend	9,614	Independence	4,425
Albany	29,540	Dallas	9,422	Brookings	4,400
Tigard	29,435	Ontario	9,394	Sandy	4,152
Keizer	21,884	Baker City	9,140	Coquille	4,121
Bend	20,447	Canby	8,990	Tillamook	4,001
Milwaukie	18,670	Newport	8,437	Sheridan	3,979
McMinnville	17,894	Troutdale	7,852	Winston	3,773
Klamath Falls	17,737	St Helens	7,535	Junction City	3,670
Grants Pass	17,503	Central Point	7,512	Molalla	3,651
Roseburg	17,069	Cottage Grove	7,403	Scappoose	3,529
West Linn	16,389	Redmond	7,165	Madras	3,443
Ashland	16,252	Wilsonville	7,106	Talent	3,274
Pendleton	15,142	Sweet Home	6,850	Phoenix	3,239
Coos Bay	15,076	Monmouth	6,288	Toledo	3,174
Oregon City	14,698	Cornelius	6,148	Sherwood	3,093
Tualatin	14,664	Lincoln City	5,908	Myrtle Creek	3,063

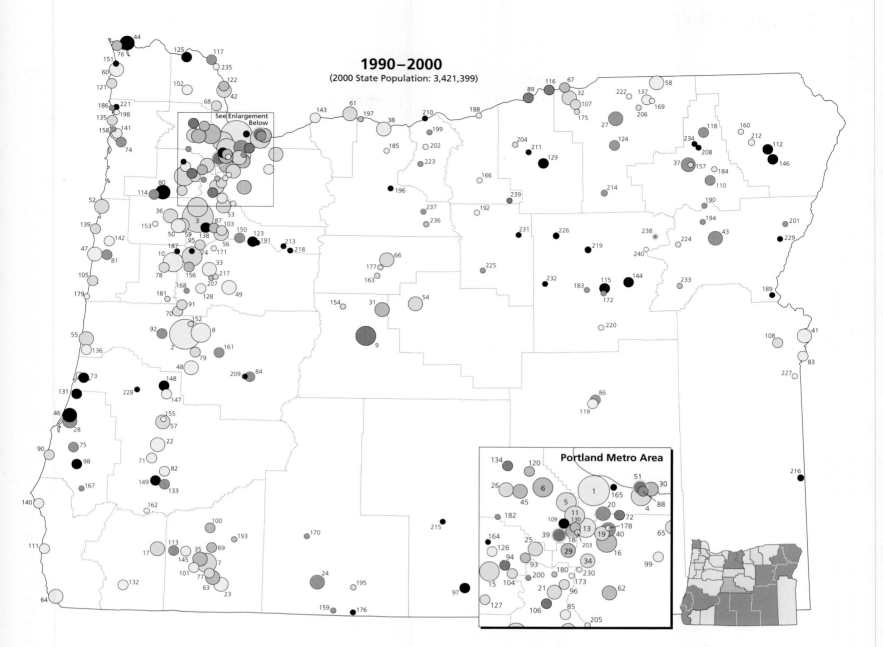

1990–2000

(2000 State Population: 3,421,399)

Portland Metro Area

2000 Populations All Incorporated Places

1 ○ Portland 529,121	41 ○ Ontario 10,985	81 ○ Toledo 3,472
2 ○ Eugene 137,893	42 ○ St. Helens...........10,019	82 ○ Myrtle Creek 3,419
3 ○ Salem................136,924	43 ● Baker City 9,860	83 ○ Nyssa 3,163
4 ○ Gresham..............90,205	44 ● Astoria 9,813	84 ● Oakridge 3,148
5 ● Beaverton 76,129	45 ○ Cornelius 9,652	85 ○ Mount Angel.........3,121
6 ● Hillsboro............70,186	46 ● North Bend 9,544	86 ● Burns 3,064
7 ● Medford.............63,154	47 ○ Newport 9,532	87 ○ Aumsville 3,003
8 ○ Springfield 52,864	48 ○ Cottage Grove........8,445	88 ● Wood Village 2,860
9 ● Bend 52,029	49 ○ Sweet Home 8,016	89 ● Boardman 2,855
10 ○ Corvallis 49,322	50 ○ Monmouth 7,741	90 ○ Bandon 2,833
11 ● Tigard 41,223	51 ● Fairview 7,561	91 ○ Harrisburg 2,795
12 ○ Albany 40,852	52 ○ Lincoln City 7,437	92 ○ Veneta 2,755
13 ● Lake Oswego 35,278	53 ○ Silverton 7,414	93 ○ Dundee 2,598
14 ○ Keizer................32,203	54 ○ Prineville 7,356	94 ● Lafayette 2,586
15 ○ McMinnville 26,499	55 ○ Florence 7,263	95 ○ Jefferson 2,487
16 ○ Oregon City 25,754	56 ○ Stayton 6,816	96 ○ Hubbard 2,483
17 ○ Grants Pass 23,003	57 ○ Sutherlin 6,669	97 ● Lakeview 2,474
18 ○ Tualatin 22,791	58 ● Milton–Freewater 6,470	98 ○ Myrtle Point 2,451
19 ○ West Linn 22,261	59 ○ Independence 6,035	99 ○ Estacada 2,371
20 ● Milwaukie 20,490	60 ● Seaside 5,900	100 ○ Shady Cove 2,307
21 ● Woodburn 20,100	61 ○ Hood River 5,831	101 ○ Jacksonville 2,235
22 ○ Roseburg 20,017	62 ● Molalla 5,647	102 ○ Vernonia 2,228
23 ● Ashland 19,522	63 ● Talent 5,589	103 ○ Sublimity 2,148
24 ● Klamath Falls.......19,462	64 ○ Brookings 5,447	104 ○ Dayton 2,119
25 ○ Newberg 18,064	65 ○ Sandy 5,385	105 ○ Waldport 2,050
26 ● Forest Grove 17,708	66 ○ Madras 5,078	106 ● Gervais 2,009
27 ● Pendleton 16,354	67 ○ Umatilla 4,978	107 ○ Stanfield..............1,979
28 ● Coos Bay 15,374	68 ○ Scappoose 4,976	108 ○ Vale 1,976
29 ● Wilsonville 13,991	69 ● Eagle Point 4,797	109 ● King City 1,949
30 ○ Troutdale 13,777	70 ○ Junction City 4,721	110 ○ Union 1,926
31 ○ Redmond 13,481	71 ○ Winston 4,613	111 ○ Gold Beach 1,897
32 ○ Hermiston 13,154	72 ● Happy Valley 4,519	112 ● Enterprise 1,895
33 ○ Lebanon 12,950	73 ● Reedsport 4,378	113 ○ Rogue River 1,847
34 ● Canby 12,790	74 ● Tillamook 4,352	114 ● Willamina.............1,844
35 ○ Central Point 12,493	75 ○ Coquille 4,184	115 ● John Day 1,821
36 ○ Dallas 12,459	76 ○ Warrenton 4,096	116 ● Irrigon 1,702
37 ● La Grande 12,327	77 ○ Phoenix 4,060	117 ○ Rainier 1,687
38 ○ The Dalles 12,156	78 ○ Philomath 3,838	118 ● Elgin 1,654
39 ● Sherwood 11,791	79 ○ Creswell 3,579	119 ○ Hines 1,623
40 ○ Gladstone 11,438	80 ● Sheridan 3,570	120 ○ North Plains.........1,605

121 ○ Cannon Beach.....1,588	161 ● Lowell 857	201 ● Halfway 337
122 ● Columbia City 1,571	162 ○ Glendale 855	202 ○ Moro 337
123 ● Mill City 1,537	163 ○ Culver 802	203 ● Rivergrove 324
124 ● Pilot Rock 1,532	164 ● Yamhill 794	204 ● Ione 321
125 ○ Clatskanie 1,528	165 ● Maywood Park 777	205 ○ Scotts Mills 312
126 ○ Carlton 1,514	166 ○ Condon 759	206 ● Adams 297
127 ○ Amity 1,478	167 ○ Powers 734	207 ● Sodaville..............290
128 ○ Brownsville 1,449	168 ○ Halsey 724	208 ● Imbler 284
129 ● Heppner 1,395	169 ○ Weston 717	209 ● Westfir 276
130 ● Durham...............1,382	170 ○ Chiloquin 716	210 ○ Rufus 268
131 ● Lakeside 1,371	171 ○ Scio 695	211 ● Lexington 263
132 ○ Cave Junction 1,363	172 ● Canyon City 669	212 ● Lostine 263
133 ● Canyonville 1,293	173 ● Aurora 655	213 ● Detroit 262
134 ● Banks 1,286	174 ● Millersburg 651	214 ● Ukiah 255
135 ● Rockaway Beach .1,267	175 ○ Echo 650	215 ● Paisley 247
136 ○ Dunes City 1,241	176 ○ Malin 638	216 ● Jordan Valley 239
137 ○ Athena 1,221	177 ● Metolius 635	217 ● Waterloo 239
138 ○ Turner 1,199	178 ● Johnson City 634	218 ● Idanha 232
139 ○ Depoe Bay 1,174	179 ○ Yachats 617	219 ● Long Creek 228
140 ○ Port Orford 1,153	180 ● Donald 608	220 ○ Seneca 223
141 ○ Bay City..............1,149	181 ○ Monroe 607	221 ● Nehalem 203
142 ○ Siletz 1,133	182 ○ Gaston 600	222 ○ Helix 183
143 ○ Cascade Locks 1,115	183 ● Mount Vernon 595	223 ● Grass Valley 171
144 ● Prairie City..........1,080	184 ● Cove 594	224 ○ Sumpter 171
145 ○ Gold Hill.............1,073	185 ● Dufur 588	225 ○ Mitchell 170
146 ● Joseph 1,054	186 ● Manzanita 564	226 ● Monument 151
147 ○ Yoncalla 1,052	187 ● Adair Village 536	227 ○ Adrian 147
148 ● Drain 1,021	188 ○ Arlington 524	228 ● Elkton 147
149 ○ Riddle 1,014	189 ● Huntington 515	229 ● Richland 147
150 ○ Lyons 1,008	190 ● North Powder........489	230 ● Barlow 140
151 ● Gearhart 995	191 ● Gates 471	231 ● Spray 140
152 ○ Coburg 969	192 ○ Fossil 469	232 ● Dayville 138
153 ○ Falls City 966	193 ● Butte Falls 439	233 ○ Unity 131
154 ○ Sisters 959	194 ● Haines 426	234 ● Summerville 117
155 ○ Oakland 954	195 ● Bonanza 415	235 ○ Prescott 72
156 ○ Tangent 933	196 ● Maupin 411	236 ● Antelope 59
157 ○ Island City 916	197 ○ Mosier 410	237 ○ Shaniko 26
158 ○ Garibaldi 899	198 ○ Wheeler 391	238 ● Granite 24
159 ○ Merrill 897	199 ○ Wasco 381	239 ● Lonerock 24
160 ○ Wallowa 869	200 ● St. Paul 354	240 ○ Greenhorn 0

31

Historic Portland

Not all the Oregon Trail pioneers had farming in mind; many settled in towns or cities and promoted their new communities with competitive zeal. Portland overtook its neighboring early rivals (Linnton and Milwaukie) and the first regional hub at Oregon City by establishing itself as the port farthest upriver that was accessible to oceangoing ships. The new town then built an all-weather plank road through the West Hills canyons to bring the Tualatin Valley's agricultural products to its riverside warehouses.

In 1879 Portland had a population of about 17,500. The city was a riverfront wharf town, with blocks of narrow commercial buildings (many of them brick and a few three and even four stories high) extending from Ash Street to Jefferson Street. Single-family residences were still plentiful above Second Avenue. Fifth Avenue boasted a newly built Federal Post Office, the Corbett mansion stood across the street to the south, and a fine brick school was just above Sixth Avenue.

By 1908 Portland was booming (though upstart Seattle had recently outstripped it in size). Four bridges now crossed the Willamette, where wharves were flanked by small manufacturing buildings. Retail structures had replaced most residences east of Broadway (formerly Seventh Avenue). The fine new Portland Hotel, showpiece of Henry Villard's railroad empire, was the largest structure in a downtown full of four-storied commercial blocks, theaters and saloons. Fashionable residences and churches were moving to the base of the West Hills, joining the Multnomah Amateur Athletic Club.

Portland in 1955 was much larger, but no longer growing. The city lost about 1,000 inhabitants between 1950 and 1960. Metro area suburbs were booming, though downtown Portland remained dominant as the retail core for the entire region. Car sales were concentrated along Burnside Street's "auto row." Parking lots and buildings converted to parking garages were widespread. The Portland Hotel was taken down in the early 1950s, its site converted to a two-storied parking lot for the Meier & Frank department store. The brick buildings of 1879's retail core—along with their elegant and decorative cast-iron fronts—were becoming rare. The wharves had disappeared in the early 1930s when a seawall was constructed along the west bank of the Willamette River. Shipping moved to wharves farther north on the river.

Downtown Portland at the turn of the twenty-first century remains Oregon's retail and administrative center, but on significantly altered terms. Suburban shopping malls and office parks have taken a large share of downtown's commercial and retail functions. The rebuilt Morrison Bridge and the I-405 freeway occupy about seven of the 80 blocks mapped. Parking lots and parking garages add another 13 blocks, for a total of nearly a quarter of non-street space devoted to cars. An alternative to the automobile, Portland's light rail system opened in 1986. Downtown is now centered on the public space of Pioneer Courthouse Square, occupying a block whose changes from 1879 to the present sum up Portland's downtown history.

Building Use:

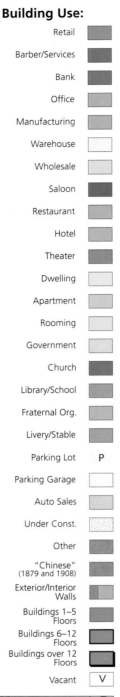

Retail
Barber/Services
Bank
Office
Manufacturing
Warehouse
Wholesale
Saloon
Restaurant
Hotel
Theater
Dwelling
Apartment
Rooming
Government
Church
Library/School
Fraternal Org.
Livery/Stable
Parking Lot — P
Parking Garage
Auto Sales
Under Const.
Other
"Chinese" (1879 and 1908)
Exterior/Interior Walls
Buildings 1–5 Floors
Buildings 6–12 Floors
Buildings over 12 Floors
Vacant — V

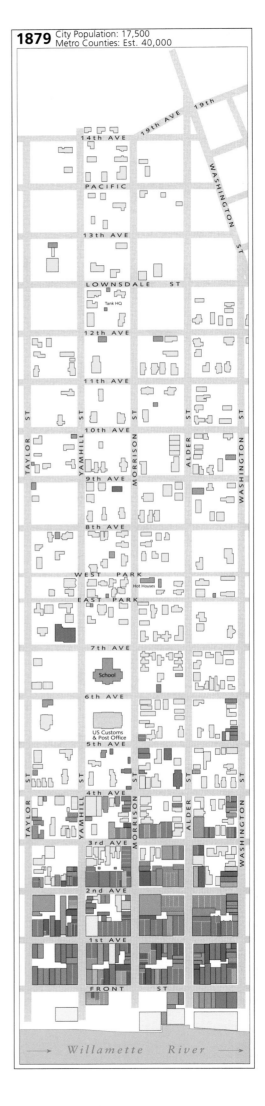

1879 City Population: 17,500 Metro Counties: Est. 40,000

32

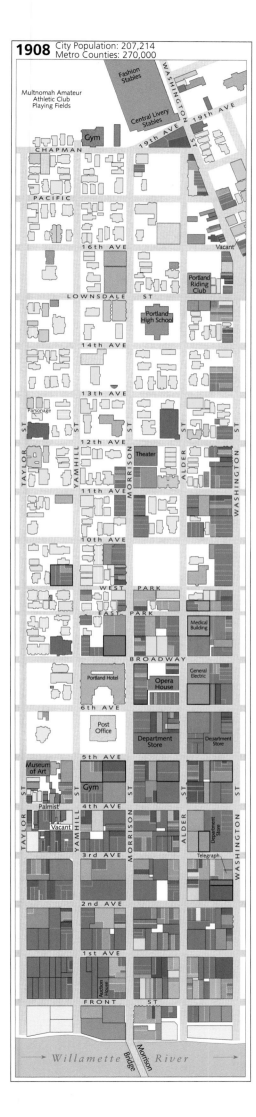

1908 City Population: 207,214
Metro Counties: 270,000

Multnomah Amateur
Athletic Club
Playing Fields

Fashion
Stables

Central Livery
Stables

WASHINGTON ST

19th AVE

Gym

CHAPMAN

PACIFIC

16th AVE

Vacant

LOWNSDALE ST

Portland
Riding
Club

Portland
High School

14th AVE

13th AVE

Parsonage

TAYLOR ST

YAMHILL ST

MORRISON ST

ALDER ST

WASHINGTON ST

12th AVE

Theater

11th AVE

10th AVE

WEST PARK

EAST PARK

Medical
Building

BROADWAY

Portland Hotel

Opera
House

General
Electric

6th AVE

Post
Office

Department
Store

Department
Store

Museum
of Art

5th AVE

Gym

Palmist

4th AVE

Vacant

Department
Store

3rd AVE

Telegraph

2nd AVE

Auction
House

1st AVE

FRONT ST

Willamette River

Morrison Bridge

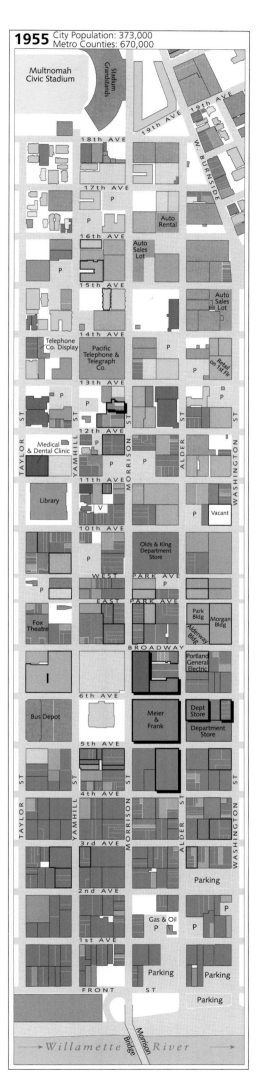

1955 City Population: 373,000
Metro Counties: 670,000

Multnomah
Civic Stadium

Stadium
Grandstands

19th AVE

19th AVE

W BURNSIDE

18th AVE

17th AVE

Auto
Rental

16th AVE

Auto
Sales
Lot

P

15th AVE

Auto
Sales
Lot

14th AVE

Telephone
Co. Display

Pacific
Telephone &
Telegraph
Co.

P

Retail
on 1st Flr

13th AVE

P

P

TAYLOR ST

YAMHILL ST

MORRISON ST

ALDER ST

WASHINGTON ST

Medical
& Dental Clinic

12th AVE

P

11th AVE

Library

V

P

Vacant

10th AVE

P

Olds & King
Department
Store

WEST PARK AVE

EAST PARK AVE

Park
Bldg

Morgan
Bldg

Fox
Theatre

Alderway
Bldg

BROADWAY

Portland
General
Electric

6th AVE

Bus Depot

Meier
&
Frank

Dept
Store

Department
Store

5th AVE

4th AVE

3rd AVE

Parking

2nd AVE

Gas & Oil
P

P

1st AVE

Parking

Parking

FRONT ST

Parking

Willamette River

Morrison Bridge

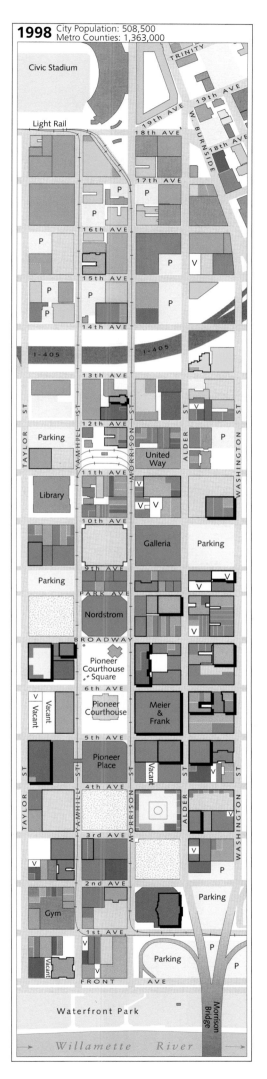

1998 City Population: 508,500
Metro Counties: 1,363,000

Civic Stadium

TRINITY

Light Rail

19th AVE

19th AVE

W BURNSIDE

18th AVE

17th AVE

P

P

16th AVE

P

P

P

V

15th AVE

P

P

14th AVE

I-405

I-405

13th AVE

V

TAYLOR ST

YAMHILL ST

MORRISON ST

ALDER ST

WASHINGTON ST

Parking

United
Way

P

11th AVE

V

Library

V V

10th AVE

Galleria

Parking

Parking

9th AVE

PARK AVE

Nordstrom

V

V

V

BROADWAY

Pioneer
Courthouse
Square

Meier
&
Frank

6th AVE

Pioneer
Courthouse

V

Vacant

Vacant

5th AVE

Pioneer
Place

Vacant

V

4th AVE

V

3rd AVE

V

P

2nd AVE

Parking

Gym

V

1st AVE

Parking

P

P

Vacant

V

FRONT AVE

Waterfront Park

Morrison
Bridge

Willamette   River

33

Willamette Valley Population

Population Density

The whole of the Willamette Valley is shown at right with a population density color scale designed to illustrate the low-density areas below the "urban threshold" value of 2,000 people per square mile. The three smaller inset maps in this column use a different density color scale to illustrate the range of densities within entirely urbanized areas. The density equivalents table on page 37 shows the characteristic settlement patterns associated with the density values shown on both legends. Values are averages for each census block. See also the Population Centers maps, pages 194–249.

Urban Population Densities

Portland

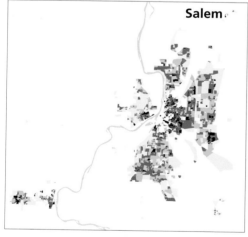

Salem

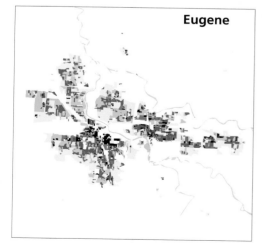

Eugene

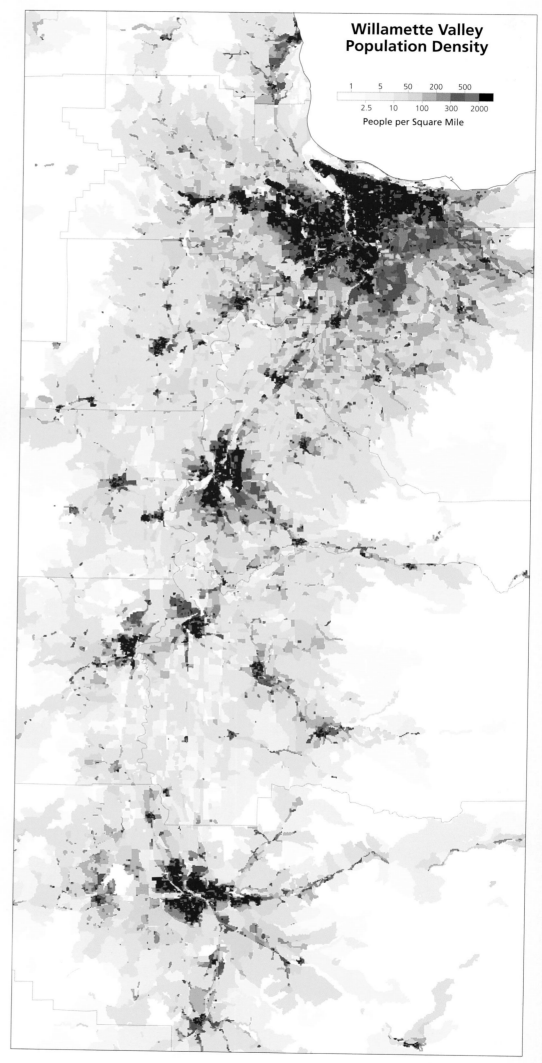

Willamette Valley Population Density

People per Square Mile

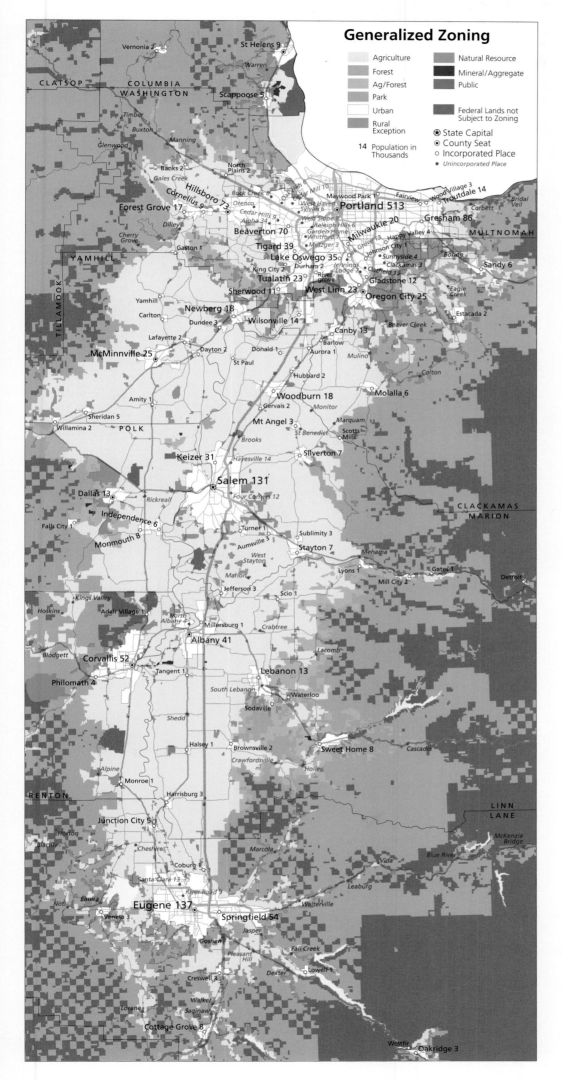

Generalized Zoning

Agriculture	Natural Resource
Forest	Mineral/Aggregate
Ag/Forest	Public
Park	
Urban	Federal Lands not Subject to Zoning
Rural Exception	

14 Population in Thousands

⊛ State Capital
⊙ County Seat
○ Incorporated Place
• Unincorporated Place

The Willamette Valley remains the core to which other parts of the state are more or less closely linked. The valley contains 70 percent of Oregon's population; three quarters of these (1.8 million people) live in the 94 incorporated cities shown here. Another 600,000 valley inhabitants live outside incorporated city boundaries—a high proportion in suburban unincorporated areas that have larger populations than all but a handful of Oregon cities outside the Willamette Valley. The historic spread of built-up areas is mapped in detail on the Population Centers maps (pages 208–221 cover the Willamette Valley).

Urban settlement remained relatively compact until the 1920s. The exception was Portland, which had sufficient population to support a streetcar system linking downtown with residential suburbs. The advent of inexpensive automobiles and increasing numbers of paved roads removed significant limitations on growth. Exploding after World War II, and particularly in the 1970s, Willamette Valley growth has been mostly outward: only very small areas in valley cities reach the densities commonly seen in larger American cities. The Oregon Land Use Plan adopted in the 1970s has attempted to curb the expansion of low-density urban sprawl with a combination of Urban Growth Boundary zoning and comprehensive plans. Large fringe areas already subdivided were recognized as rural exceptions lands, and most have remained available for rural non-farm use.

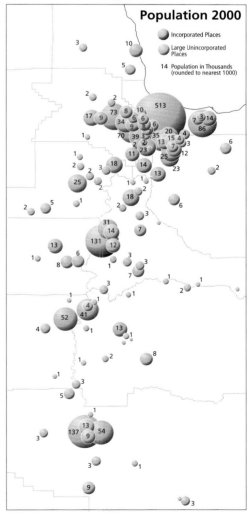

Population 2000

○ Incorporated Places
○ Large Unincorporated Places

14 Population in Thousands (rounded to nearest 1000)

Population Growth and Density

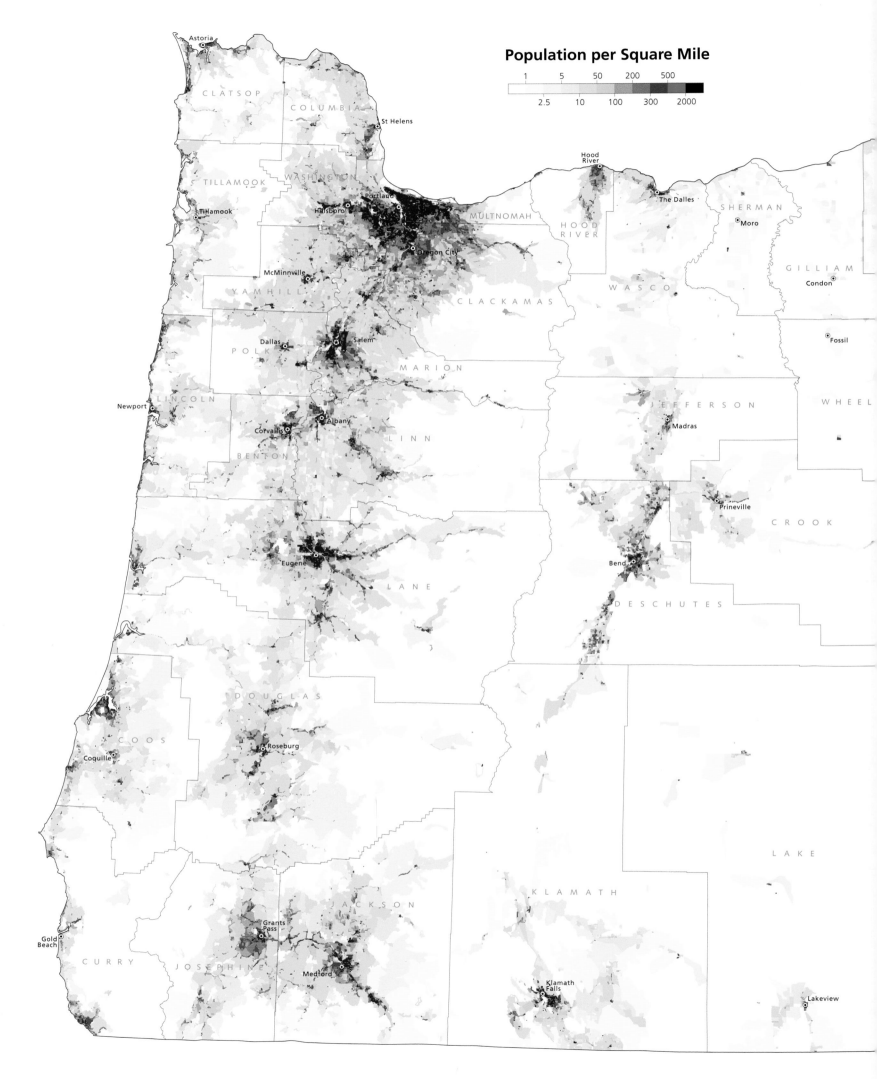

Population per Square Mile

| 1 | 5 | 50 | 200 | 500 |
| 2.5 | 10 | 100 | 300 | 2000 |

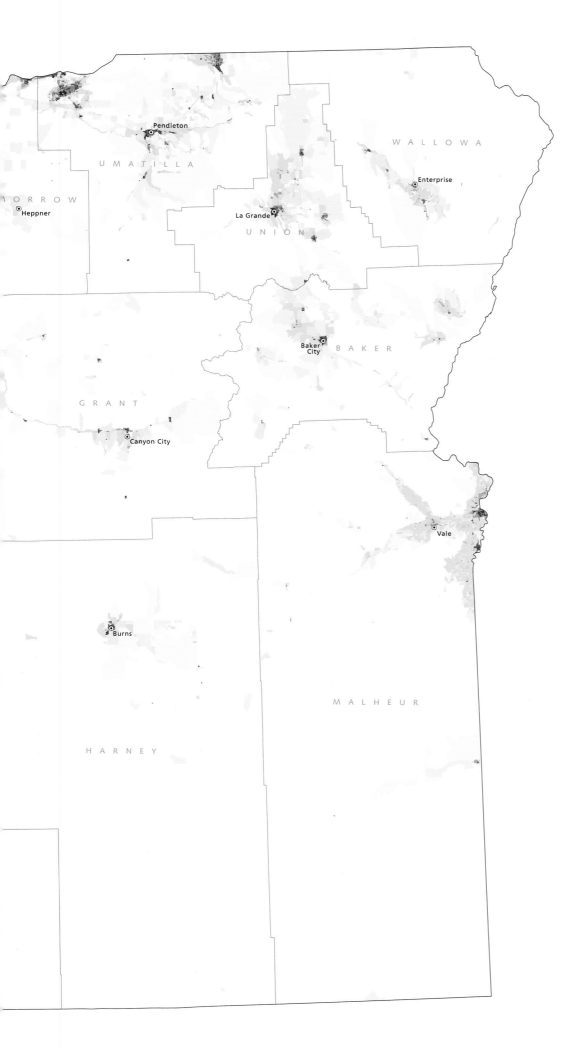

Oregon's population growth has varied greatly from year to year, but every decade has seen net growth. "Natural growth" (the surplus of births over deaths) is a function of population age structure (see pages 38–39) and prevailing attitudes toward family size. In-migration reflects both overall U.S. population growth and Oregon's prosperity relative to that of other states. The state boomed from 1900 to 1910, after World War II, during the 1970s and again in the 1990s. Oregon's "livability" draws immigrants from other areas where economic growth has led to unpalatable levels of crowding. The state as a whole had about 35 people per square mile in 2000, compared to 83 in Washington, 213 in California, 15 in Idaho and 18 in Nevada. However, the southeastern third of Oregon is almost entirely empty. Small populations are highly concentrated in towns, and thinly spread over widely separated ranching and farming valleys. The wheat country of the Deschutes–Umatilla Plateau is almost as lightly settled. A strip of denser settlement extends (with some interruptions) the length of Central Oregon, supported by irrigation water from neighboring mountains and, especially in Deschutes County, the appeal of a scenic recreation region. Western Oregon is much more heavily populated. Urban centers along the Interstate 5 corridor support scattered settlement extending into almost all low-elevation areas. The Coast is characterized by a narrow band of relatively dense settlement for much of its length.

Population per square mile
Characteristic settlement type

10,000 Urban, single-family residential neighborhoods

5,000 Low-density, urban, single-family: 2.5 houses per acre

2,000 The urban threshold: one house per acre

300 Rural, residential, 5-acre parcels

200 Rural, residential, 10-acre parcels

100 Rural, residential, 20-acre parcels; some intensive farms; vineyards; nurseries

50 Small, part-time farms of 40 acres; some intensive commercial farming; nurseries

10 Part-time farms of 200 acres; intensive commercial farming, especially orchards, vineyards, berries

5 Commercial farming of 800-acre parcels

1 Large farm operations, grazing, timber lands

Population Growth

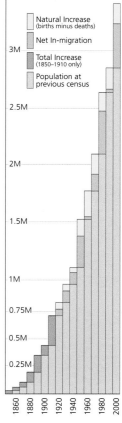

- Natural Increase (births minus deaths)
- Net In-migration
- Total Increase (1850–1910 only)
- Population at previous census

Age Structure

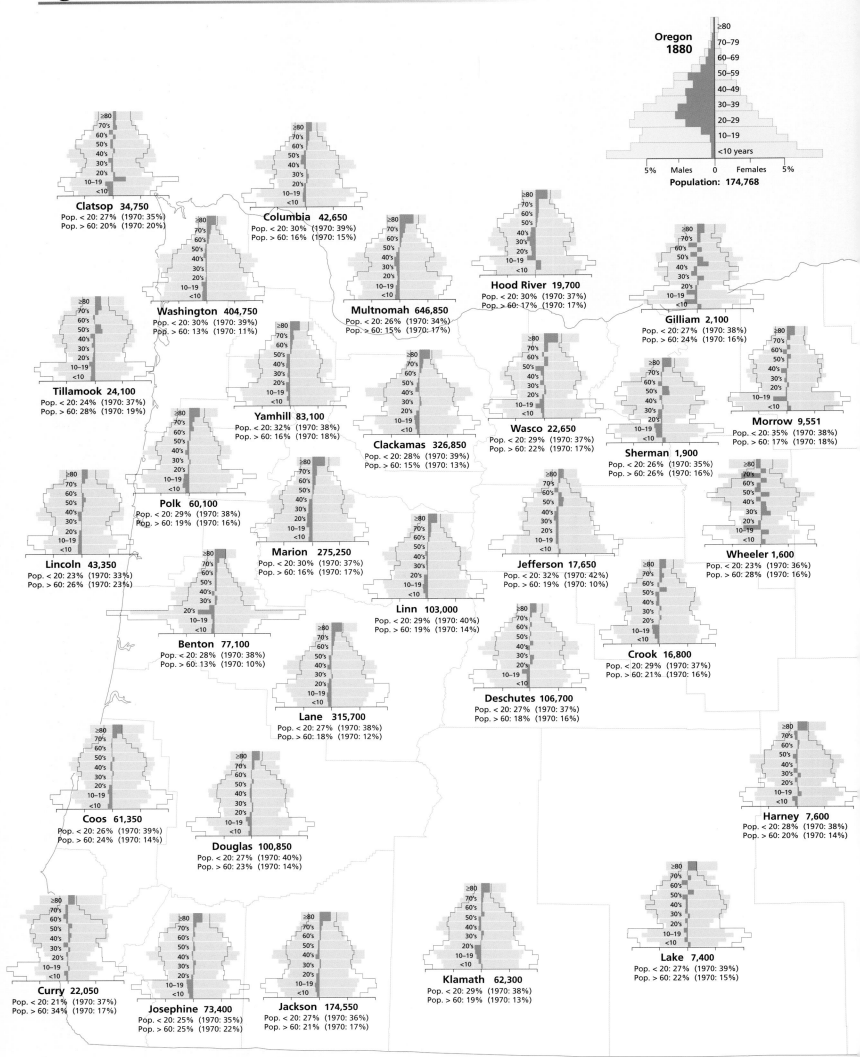

**Oregon
1880**

≥80
70–79
60–69
50–59
40–49
30–39
20–29
10–19
<10 years

5%   Males   0   Females   5%

Population: 174,768

Clatsop 34,750
Pop. < 20: 27% (1970: 35%)
Pop. > 60: 20% (1970: 20%)

Columbia 42,650
Pop. < 20: 30% (1970: 39%)
Pop. > 60: 16% (1970: 15%)

Washington 404,750
Pop. < 20: 30% (1970: 39%)
Pop. > 60: 13% (1970: 11%)

Multnomah 646,850
Pop. < 20: 26% (1970: 34%)
Pop. > 60: 15% (1970: 17%)

Hood River 19,700
Pop. < 20: 30% (1970: 37%)
Pop. > 60: 17% (1970: 17%)

Gilliam 2,100
Pop. < 20: 27% (1970: 38%)
Pop. > 60: 24% (1970: 16%)

Tillamook 24,100
Pop. < 20: 24% (1970: 37%)
Pop. > 60: 28% (1970: 19%)

Yamhill 83,100
Pop. < 20: 32% (1970: 38%)
Pop. > 60: 16% (1970: 18%)

Clackamas 326,850
Pop. < 20: 28% (1970: 39%)
Pop. > 60: 15% (1970: 13%)

Wasco 22,650
Pop. < 20: 29% (1970: 37%)
Pop. > 60: 22% (1970: 17%)

Sherman 1,900
Pop. < 20: 26% (1970: 35%)
Pop. > 60: 26% (1970: 16%)

Morrow 9,551
Pop. < 20: 35% (1970: 38%)
Pop. > 60: 17% (1970: 18%)

Polk 60,100
Pop. < 20: 29% (1970: 38%)
Pop. > 60: 19% (1970: 16%)

Marion 275,250
Pop. < 20: 30% (1970: 37%)
Pop. > 60: 16% (1970: 17%)

Jefferson 17,650
Pop. < 20: 32% (1970: 42%)
Pop. > 60: 19% (1970: 10%)

Wheeler 1,600
Pop. < 20: 23% (1970: 36%)
Pop. > 60: 28% (1970: 16%)

Lincoln 43,350
Pop. < 20: 23% (1970: 33%)
Pop. > 60: 26% (1970: 23%)

Benton 77,100
Pop. < 20: 28% (1970: 38%)
Pop. > 60: 13% (1970: 10%)

Linn 103,000
Pop. < 20: 29% (1970: 40%)
Pop. > 60: 19% (1970: 14%)

Crook 16,800
Pop. < 20: 29% (1970: 37%)
Pop. > 60: 21% (1970: 16%)

Lane 315,700
Pop. < 20: 27% (1970: 38%)
Pop. > 60: 18% (1970: 12%)

Deschutes 106,700
Pop. < 20: 27% (1970: 37%)
Pop. > 60: 18% (1970: 16%)

Coos 61,350
Pop. < 20: 26% (1970: 39%)
Pop. > 60: 24% (1970: 14%)

Douglas 100,850
Pop. < 20: 27% (1970: 40%)
Pop. > 60: 23% (1970: 14%)

Harney 7,600
Pop. < 20: 28% (1970: 38%)
Pop. > 60: 20% (1970: 14%)

Curry 22,050
Pop. < 20: 21% (1970: 37%)
Pop. > 60: 34% (1970: 17%)

Josephine 73,400
Pop. < 20: 25% (1970: 35%)
Pop. > 60: 25% (1970: 22%)

Jackson 174,550
Pop. < 20: 27% (1970: 36%)
Pop. > 60: 21% (1970: 17%)

Klamath 62,300
Pop. < 20: 29% (1970: 38%)
Pop. > 60: 19% (1970: 13%)

Lake 7,400
Pop. < 20: 27% (1970: 39%)
Pop. > 60: 22% (1970: 15%)

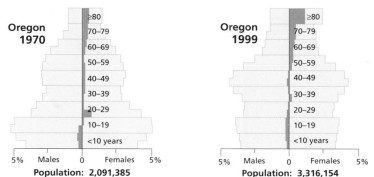

Oregon 1910
≥80 / 70–79 / 60–69 / 50–59 / 40–49 / 30–39 / 20–29 / 10–19 / <10 years
5% Males 0 Females 5%
Population: 672,765

Oregon 1940
data n/a
≥70 / 60–69 / 50–59 / 40–49 / 30–39 / 20–29 / 10–19 / <10 years
5% Males 0 Females 5%
Population: 1,089,684

Oregon 1970
≥80 / 70–79 / 60–69 / 50–59 / 40–49 / 30–39 / 20–29 / 10–19 / <10 years
5% Males 0 Females 5%
Population: 2,091,385

Oregon 1999
≥80 / 70–79 / 60–69 / 50–59 / 40–49 / 30–39 / 20–29 / 10–19 / <10 years
5% Males 0 Females 5%
Population: 3,316,154

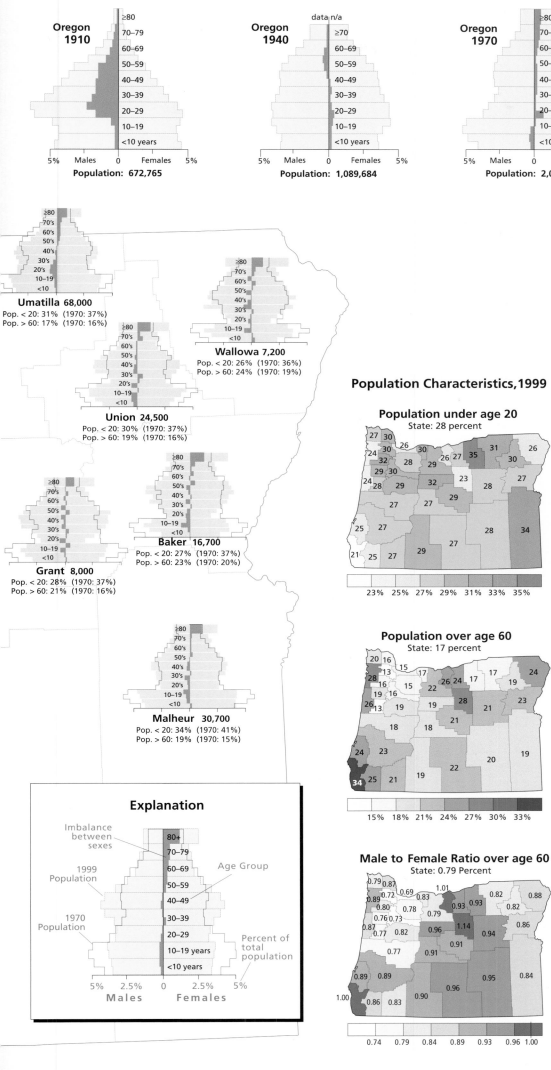

Umatilla 68,000
Pop. < 20: 31% (1970: 37%)
Pop. > 60: 17% (1970: 16%)

Wallowa 7,200
Pop. < 20: 26% (1970: 36%)
Pop. > 60: 24% (1970: 19%)

Union 24,500
Pop. < 20: 30% (1970: 37%)
Pop. > 60: 19% (1970: 16%)

Baker 16,700
Pop. < 20: 27% (1970: 37%)
Pop. > 60: 23% (1970: 20%)

Grant 8,000
Pop. < 20: 28% (1970: 37%)
Pop. > 60: 21% (1970: 16%)

Malheur 30,700
Pop. < 20: 34% (1970: 41%)
Pop. > 60: 19% (1970: 15%)

Explanation
Imbalance between sexes
1999 Population
1970 Population
80+ / 70–79 / 60–69 / 50–59 / 40–49 / 30–39 / 20–29 / 10–19 years / <10 years
Age Group
Percent of total population
5% 2.5% 0 2.5% 5%
Males Females

Population Characteristics, 1999

Population under age 20
State: 28 percent
23% 25% 27% 29% 31% 33% 35%

Population over age 60
State: 17 percent
15% 18% 21% 24% 27% 30% 33%

Male to Female Ratio over age 60
State: 0.79 Percent
0.74 0.79 0.84 0.89 0.93 0.96 1.00

Age and Sex

A combination of constantly shifting factors determines the age and sex characteristics of a population: birth rates, survival rates, patterns of in-migration and out-migration and the demographic profile of the migrants.

In 1850 the territory was a frontier and, despite the many family groups arriving over the Oregon Trail, it had a mostly young male population. The U.S. census counted 13,294 residents in the Oregon Territory (excluding Native Americans): 62 percent male with 28 percent of all males in the 20- to 40-year-old group. By 1880 (the first figures graphed here) the economy was based on agriculture, timber harvesting and mining, thus explaining the continuing dominant share of males. Families, however, were producing large numbers of children; one generation later, in 1910, the imbalance between males and females had declined, though it was still pronounced in segments of the population older than 20. Statistics for 1940 reflect an aging population, small families and only a modest residual of the earlier, predominantly male population. The 1970 graph reveals the low birthrates of the Depression era (seen here in the 30- to 40-year-old group) and the strikingly high birthrates of the post-World War II "baby boom." Numerical imbalance between the sexes was minor, reflecting the natural slight surplus of male births, and, beyond the age of 20, higher male death rates and absence in the armed forces. In its early stages in 1970, the post-baby boom decline in births is clearly evident by 1999. The growth in the population more than 80 is marked, as is the increasing number of older women.

The geographic distribution of these trends is shown by the small state maps and the 36 county graphs shown here. Conspicuous in most counties are the differences between the figures for 1999 and 1970. The sharp reduction in children as a percentage of total population is seen throughout the state along with an increasing percentage of people in the top age bracket. Another trend is the "pinched waist" graphs for rural counties due to post-high school out-migration; conversely, due to in-migration, Multnomah County has more 20- to 29-year-olds than 10- to 19-year-olds. Local anomalies from state norms include the disproportionate significance of Oregon State University students in mostly rural Benton County, the slight increase in the percentage of children under five in Multnomah and Washington Counties and the "top heavy" pattern of Curry County with its unusually high percentage of retirees.

Immigration

The initial settlement of the Willamette Valley in the mid-nineteenth century included many immigrants from Germany and the United Kingdom. In Eastern Oregon, the largest single immigrant group was Chinese, who worked almost exclusively in mining. As the numbers of immigrant laborers coming into the U.S. increased in the period from 1860 to 1880, so did some native-born residents' opposition to the influx. Congress passed the Chinese Exclusion Act of 1882 to limit cheap immigrant labor. Originally specific only to the Chinese, concern about Asian immigration expanded to include the Japanese, who were restricted from immigrating in 1907.

The major immigrant groups arriving in Oregon between 1880 and 1910 were from Canada, Germany and Italy. Fewer in number, Scandinavians settled mostly on the Coast, where they played an important part in the development of fishing and maritime-related industries.

Early in the twentieth century various groups in the U.S. feared that immigrants might take jobs from native-born Americans and lobbied for tight immigration enforcement laws. In 1924, Congress limited immigration severely, putting into place a set of national-origin quotas that capped immigration from Europe and barred immigration from Asia.

Immigration into the U.S. and Oregon increased steadily in the prosperous decades following World War II. Deaths among the foreign-born living in Oregon outnumbered new arrivals in the period from 1945 to 1960, however, resulting in an overall population decrease for immigrants.

Immigration laws were substantially changed in 1965, when major amendments to the Immigration and Nationality Act became law. The act removed quotas and placed all countries on an equal footing with similar numerical quotas. The quotas were largely filled (about 80 percent) by foreign-born relatives of U.S. citizens; the remaining openings went primarily to those with desirable job skills and their dependents. The main countries of origin for U.S. immigrants became Mexico, the Philippines, Vietnam, the Dominican Republic and China.

Immigration from Europe and Canada decreased steadily both in absolute and relative terms since 1960, accounting for only 14 percent of legal immigrants by 1990. In relative terms, the biggest gain has been by Asia, which accounted for 6 percent of legal immigrants in the 1950s and 44 percent in the 1980s. About 2.6 million Asians entered the U.S. legally in the 1980s, more than all immigrants in the 1950s.

Latin American immigration grew from 26 percent of legal immigration in the 1950s to 40 percent in the 1960s, where it has remained. In the 1980s, Latin America accounted for 2.4 million legal immigrants. Mexico is the single largest source of legal immigrants—12 to 14 percent of the flow during each of the past four decades. When illegal immigration is included, Latin America surpasses Asia as the main source for immigrants to the U.S., and Mexico becomes the predominant single source.

Origin of the Foreign-Born, 1870–1990

Counties are colored to show the country of origin of the largest foreign-born groups at each census. Countries with no legend color are those whose immigrants were never the largest group in any county. Foreign-born groups amounting to one percent or more of total county population are identified by letter code, as follows:

(**H**) 5% or more of total population
(H) 2–4.9%
(h) 1–1.9%

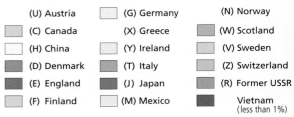

(U) Austria
(C) Canada
(H) China
(D) Denmark
(E) England
(F) Finland
(G) Germany
(X) Greece
(Y) Ireland
(T) Italy
(J) Japan
(M) Mexico
(N) Norway
(W) Scotland
(V) Sweden
(Z) Switzerland
(R) Former USSR
Vietnam (less than 1%)

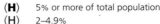

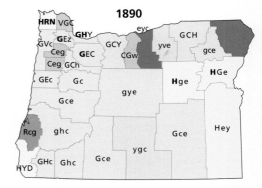

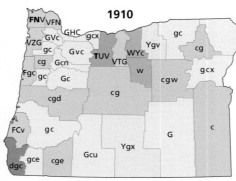

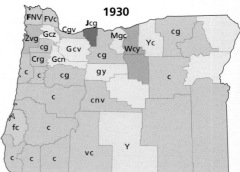

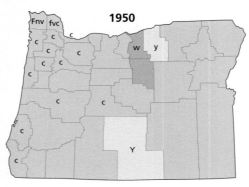

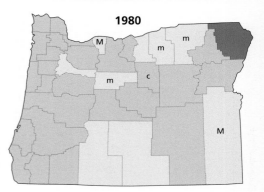

The maps above show the distribution of the foreign-born in Oregon changing over time. In 1870, the immigrant population in the Willamette Valley and Coast were almost entirely from the United Kingdom, Canada and Germany. In Eastern Oregon, the predominant immigrant population was Chinese, with more than 40 percent of immigrants in Grant County originating in China. Between 1870 and 1910, European immigrants settled throughout the state, with sizable Scandinavian settlement along the Coast; in this period many Japanese immigrants located in Hood River. No single group predominated among immigrants from 1930 to 1980, but by 1990 immigrants from Mexico emerged as the major immigrant group in almost half of Oregon's counties.

Percentage Foreign-Born 1990

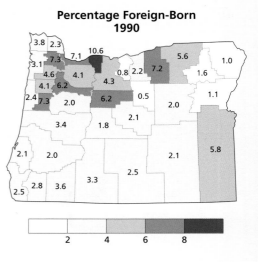

2   4   6   8

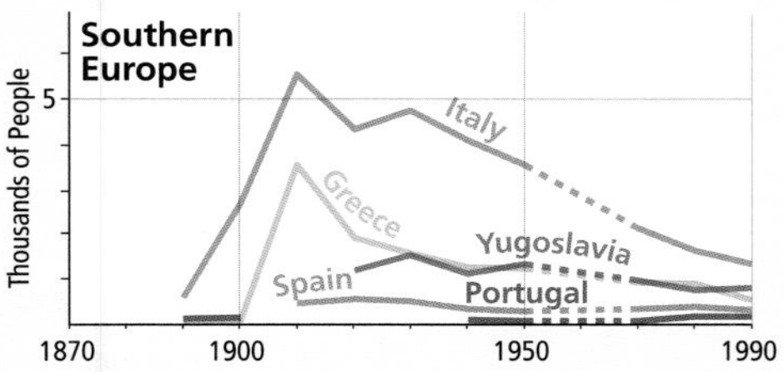

Regions of Origin

Total number of immigrants is shown by region and country, in seven graphs at a common scale. The graph at right shows foreign-born as a percentage of total population.

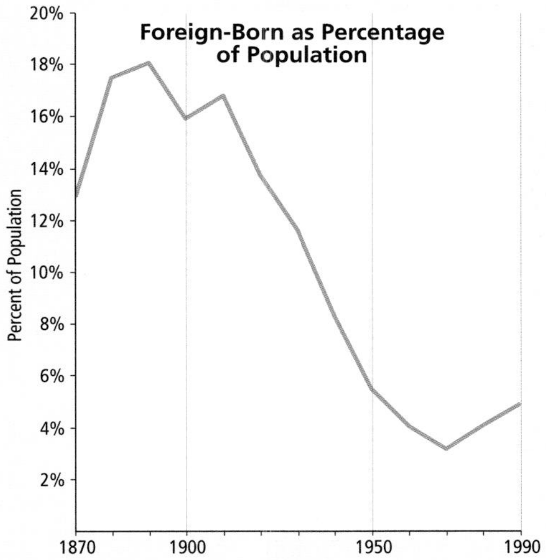

Southern Europe

Thousands of People

Italy
Greece
Yugoslavia
Spain
Portugal

1870　1900　1950　1990

Eastern Europe

Thousands of People

Former
USSR
Austria
Poland
Czecho-slovakia
Hungary

1870　1900　1950　1990

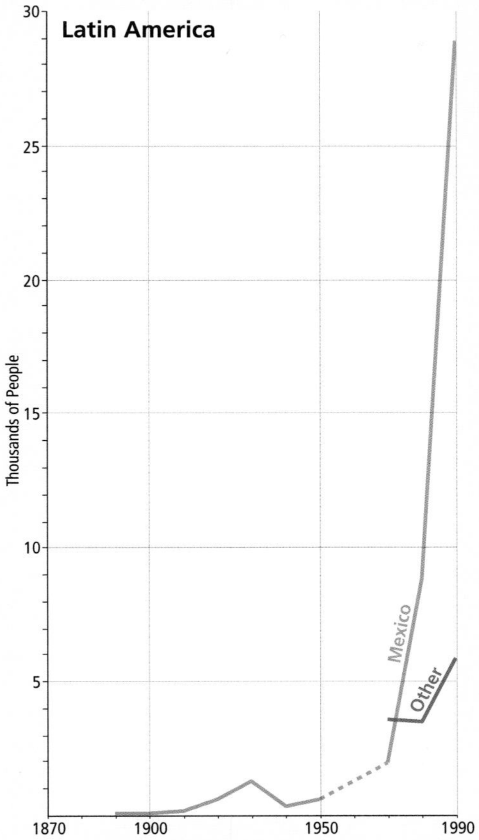

Scandinavia

Thousands of People

Sweden
Norway
Finland
Denmark

1870　1900　1950　1990

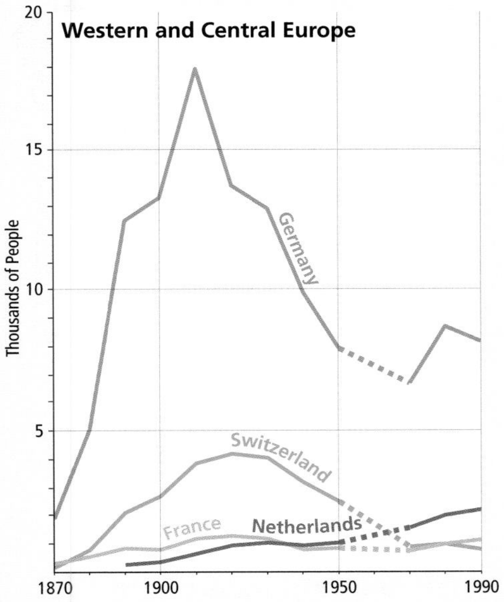

Western and Central Europe

Thousands of People

Germany
Switzerland
France
Netherlands

1870　1900　1950　1990

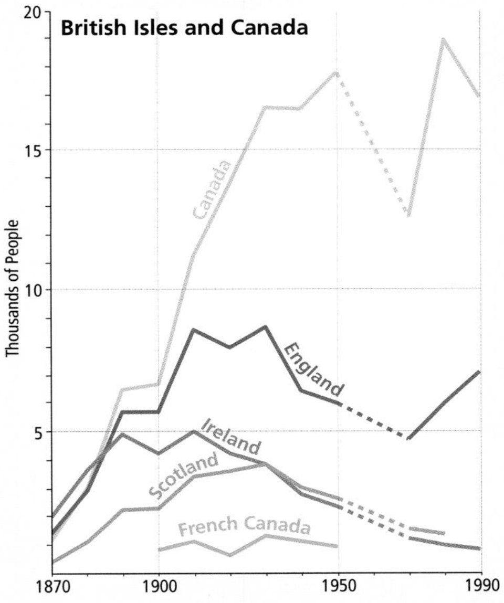

Latin America

Thousands of People

Mexico
Other

1870　1900　1950　1990

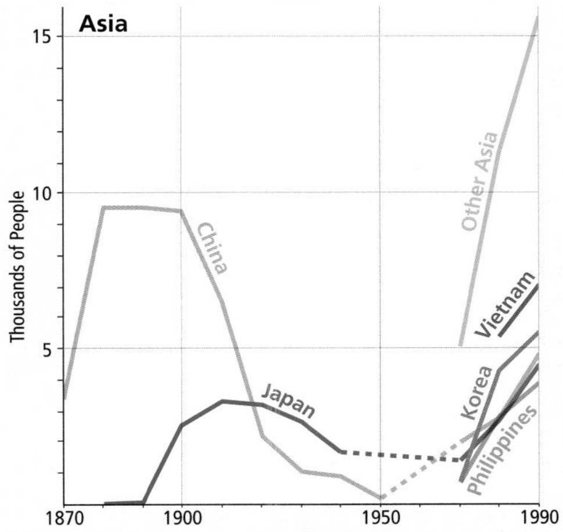

British Isles and Canada

Thousands of People

Canada
England
Ireland
Scotland
French Canada

1870　1900　1950　1990

Foreign-Born as Percentage of Population

Percent of Population

20%
18%
16%
14%
12%
10%
8%
6%
4%
2%

1870　1900　1950　1990

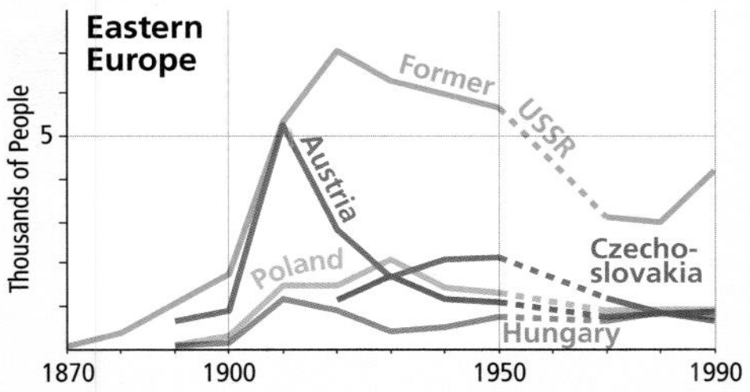

Asia

Thousands of People

China
Other Asia
Japan
Vietnam
Korea
Philippines

1870　1900　1950　1990

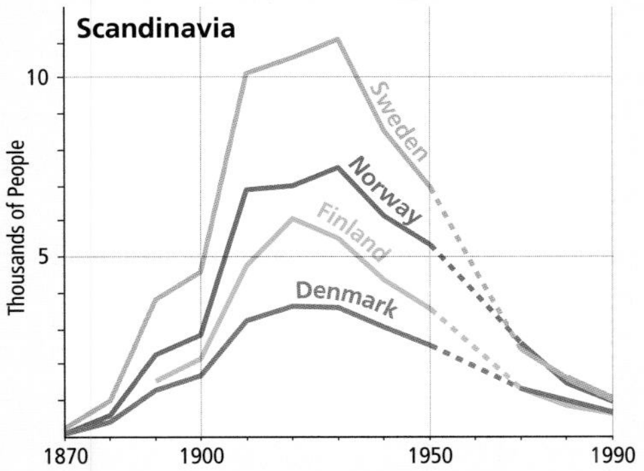

Moving to Oregon from Other States

Migration to Oregon from within the U.S. is reflected in numbers of out-of-state drivers licenses turned in during the process of obtaining an Oregon license. The maps below show 1995–2000 annual average values. The graph shows the 5-year trend.

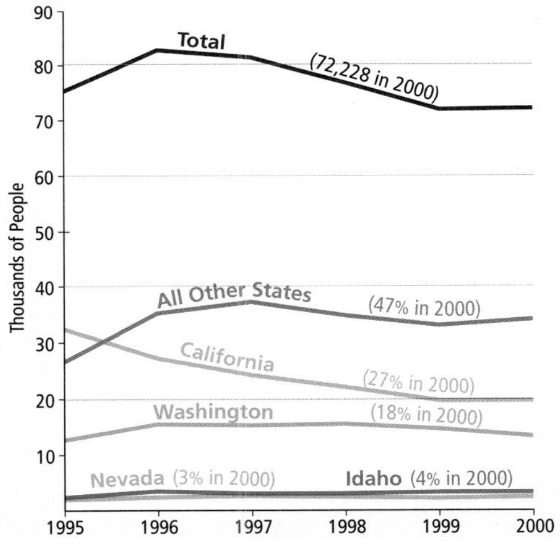

Thousands of People

90
80
70
60
50
40
30
20
10

Total (72,228 in 2000)
All Other States (47% in 2000)
California (27% in 2000)
Washington (18% in 2000)
Nevada (3% in 2000)　Idaho (4% in 2000)

1995　1996　1997　1998　1999　2000

Drivers Licenses Turned In By State of Issue

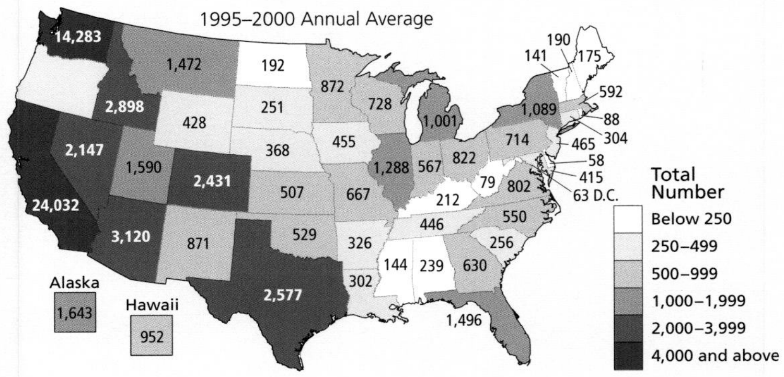

1995–2000 Annual Average

14,283
1,472
192
190
175
141
2,898
428
251
872
728
592
88
2,147
1,590
368
455
1,001
1,089
304
714
465
24,032
2,431
507
1,288
567
822
79
802
415
667
212
550
63 D.C.
3,120
871
529
326
446
256
144
239
630
302
2,577
1,496

Alaska 1,643
Hawaii 952

Total Number
Below 250
250–499
500–999
1,000–1,999
2,000–3,999
4,000 and above

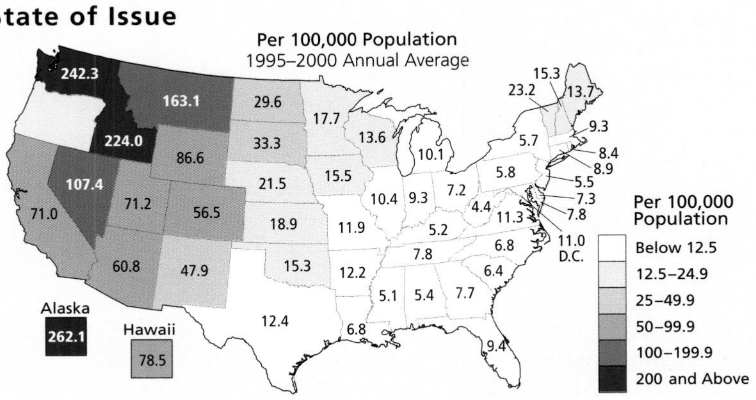

Per 100,000 Population
1995–2000 Annual Average

242.3
163.1
29.6
15.3
13.7
23.2
224.0
86.6
17.7
13.6
5.7
9.3
107.4
71.2
33.3
15.5
10.1
5.8
8.4
71.0
56.5
21.5
10.4　9.3
7.2
4.4
5.5
8.9
7.3
11.3
7.8
60.8
47.9
18.9
11.9
5.2
6.8
11.0 D.C.
15.3
12.2
7.8
6.4
5.1　5.4　7.7
12.4
6.8
9.4

Alaska 262.1
Hawaii 78.5

Per 100,000 Population
Below 12.5
12.5–24.9
25–49.9
50–99.9
100–199.9
200 and Above

Race and Ethnicity

Non-White Population in 1990

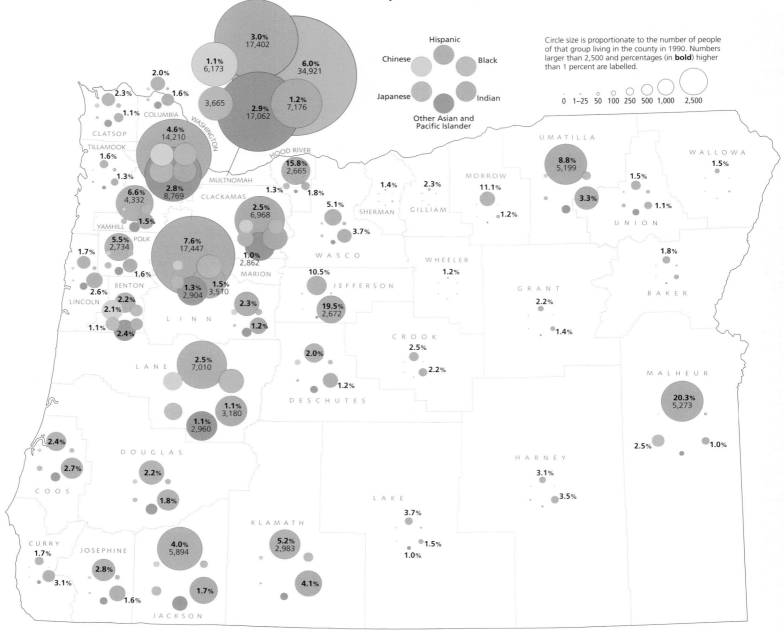

Circle size is proportionate to the number of people of that group living in the county in 1990. Numbers larger than 2,500 and percentages (in **bold**) higher than 1 percent are labelled.

0 1–25 50 100 250 500 1,000 2,500

Hispanic
Chinese — Black
Japanese — Indian
Other Asian and Pacific Islander

Between 50,000 and 100,000 Indians were living in present-day Oregon at the time of contact with explorers and settlers, according to current estimates. Drastically reduced in number by disease and war (see pages 16–17), Oregon Indians were forced by the 1870s onto a handful of reservations. Indians did not begin to grow as a percentage of the state population until the 1950s, and are still mostly concentrated in a few areas.

Compared to other states, Oregon's African American population is small, only 1.6 percent of the state's 2000 population. The 1857 Constitution of Oregon barred any "free negro, or mulatto" from owning land or even residing in Oregon—the census of 1860 identified only 124 "blacks and mulattoes." The first significant numbers of African Americans came to Oregon during the late 1800s as a result of railroad employment and resided mostly in areas near Portland's Union Station. As their numbers grew they expanded northward across the Willamette into the Albina neighborhood. Oregon's African American population grew slowly until World War II. At that time, jobs at the Kaiser Corporation shipyards in Portland drew thousands of African Americans, mainly

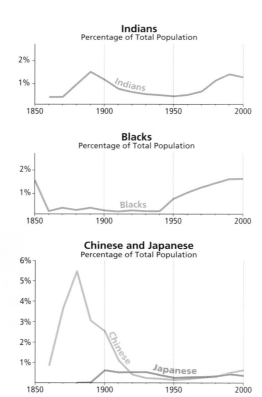

Indians
Percentage of Total Population

Blacks
Percentage of Total Population

Chinese and Japanese
Percentage of Total Population

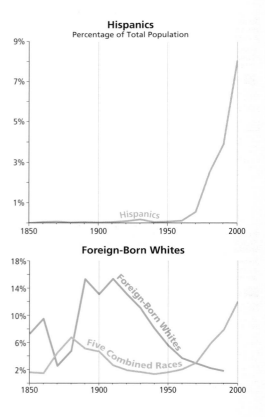

Hispanics
Percentage of Total Population

Foreign-Born Whites

White High School Students

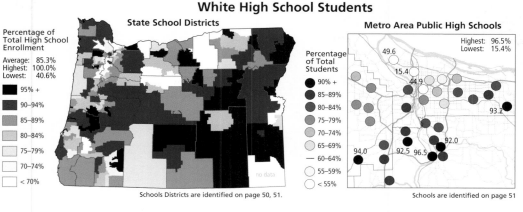

State School Districts

Percentage of Total High School Enrollment

Average: 85.3%
Highest: 100.0%
Lowest: 40.6%

- ■ 95% +
- 90–94%
- 85–89%
- 80–84%
- 75–79%
- 70–74%
- □ < 70%

Schools Districts are identified on page 50, 51.

Metro Area Public High Schools

Percentage of Total Students

Highest: 96.5%
Lowest: 15.4%

- ● 90% +
- 85–89%
- 80–84%
- 75–79%
- 70–74%
- 65–69%
- — 60–64%
- 55–59%
- ○ < 55%

49.6 15.4 44.9 93.2 94.0 92.5 96.5 92.0

Schools are identified on page 51

Schools Districts are identified on page 50, 51. / Schools are identified on page 51

Race and Ethnicity in the Schools

The maps on this page show the ethnic composition of Oregon high schools in the 2000–2001 school year. Values are shown for all districts, and for individual high schools in the Portland area. Districts and schools are identified on page 51.

Non-Hispanic Whites total over 85 percent of all students. The state and Portland area maps show Whites as a percentage of all students.

Hispanics total 8.7 percent of students statewide. Blacks total 0.8 percent, Indians 2.5 percent and Asians 1.9 percent. The state maps show the levels of these groups as a percentage of their state average figures. For example, a district or school in which Indians total 5 percent of the student body had 200 percent of the state average.

The maps of Portland area schools, in contrast, show the percent of the student body each group represents. The highest and lowest values for each group are labeled.

Hispanic High School Students

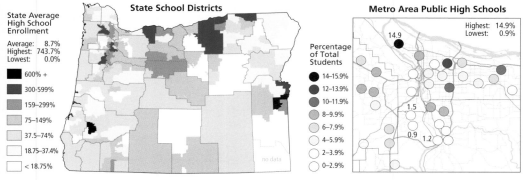

State School Districts

State Average High School Enrollment

Average: 8.7%
Highest: 743.7%
Lowest: 0.0%

- ■ 600% +
- 300–599%
- 159–299%
- 75–149%
- 37.5–74%
- 18.75–37.4%
- □ < 18.75%

Metro Area Public High Schools

Percentage of Total Students

Highest: 14.9%
Lowest: 0.9%

- ● 14–15.9%
- 12–13.9%
- 10–11.9%
- 8–9.9%
- 6–7.9%
- 4–5.9%
- 2–3.9%
- ○ 0–2.9%

14.9 1.5 0.9 1.2

Black High School Students

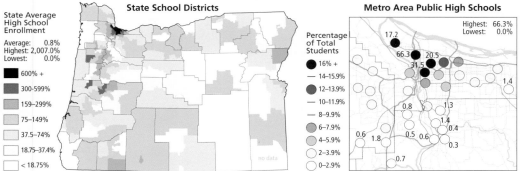

State School Districts

State Average High School Enrollment

Average: 0.8%
Highest: 2,007.0%
Lowest: 0.0%

- ■ 600% +
- 300–599%
- 159–299%
- 75–149%
- 37.5–74%
- 18.75–37.4%
- □ < 18.75%

Metro Area Public High Schools

Percentage of Total Students

Highest: 66.3%
Lowest: 0.0%

- ● 16% +
- — 14–15.9%
- 12–13.9%
- 10–11.9%
- 8–9.9%
- ● 6–7.9%
- 4–5.9%
- 2–3.9%
- ○ 0–2.9%

17.2 66.3 20.5 31.5 1.4 0.8 1.3 1.4 0.6 1.8 0.5 0.6 0.4 0.3 0.7

Indian High School Students

State School Districts

State Average High School Enrollment

Average: 2.5%
Highest: 1,399.9%
Lowest: 0.0%

- ■ 600% +
- 300–599%
- 159–299%
- 75–149%
- 37.5–74%
- 18.75–37.4%
- □ < 18.75%

Metro Area Public High Schools

Percentage of Total Students

Highest: 4.07%
Lowest: 0.0%

- ● 4% +
- — 3.5–3.9%
- 3–3.4%
- 2.5–2.9%
- 2–2.4%
- 1.5–1.9%
- 1–1.4%
- 0.5–0.9%
- ○ 0–0.4%

4.07 0.4 0.2 0.3 0.3 0.1 0.1

Asian High School Students

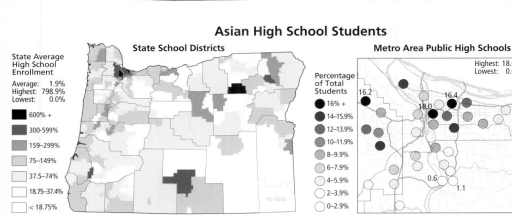

State School Districts

State Average High School Enrollment

Average: 1.9%
Highest: 798.9%
Lowest: 0.0%

- ■ 600% +
- 300–599%
- 159–299%
- 75–149%
- 37.5–74%
- 18.75–37.4%
- □ < 18.75%

Metro Area Public High Schools

Percentage of Total Students

Highest: 18.0%
Lowest: 0.6%

- ● 16% +
- 14–15.9%
- 12–13.9%
- 10–11.9%
- 8–9.9%
- 6–7.9%
- 4–5.9%
- 2–3.9%
- ○ 0–2.9%

16.2 16.4 18.0 0.6 1.1

---

from the South: from 1940 to 1950 the Black population quadrupled. Due in part to discriminatory real estate practices, African Americans remained concentrated in the northeast core of Portland. During the 1980s and 1990s, this once predominantly African American area became more racially and ethnically diverse.

Chinese immigrants played an important role in Oregon's history. Mostly contract laborers, they worked in railroad construction, mining and the Columbia River canning industry. In the 1870s and 1880s Chinese populations up and down the West Coast tended to cluster in "Chinatowns," due in part to anti-Chinese bigotry (see Historic Portland, page 32). Oregon's Japanese population grew rapidly early in the twentieth century, largely in the Columbia River canning industry, but a 1924 federal immigration law reduced Japanese immigration to a trickle. The Japanese population of all three Pacific Coast states was interned at inland camps during World War II—the small concentration of Japanese in Malheur County is a legacy of this episode. Following the Vietnam War, many Vietnamese, as well as members of other Southeast Asian ethnic groups, immigrated to the U.S. During the 1990s, the growth of the high technology industry in Oregon, especially in Portland, spurred additional Asian immigration. In the 2000 census, the number of Vietnamese was nearly as large as the number of Chinese.

Early in the twentieth century, a substantial number of Mexicans resided in Oregon, mainly in rural areas, working mostly as seasonal agriculture workers. The northward flow of Mexicans greatly increased during World War II when the "bracero" program recruited contract workers to alleviate serious agricultural labor shortages in the U.S. The present racial makeup of Oregon reflects the sharp rise in immigration that followed the federal immigration reforms of 1965 (see Immigration, pages 40–41). Hispanics are now the state's most numerous minority group and have been since they were first separately identified in the 1970 census. From 1990 to 2000, the numbers of Oregon Hispanics, the state's fastest growing minority group, more than doubled, increasing from 112,707 to 275,314. The group is largely of Mexican origin, although Portland has a substantial number of Central American immigrants. During the 1990s more Mexican immigrants were employed outside of the agricultural sector, and more were living in urban areas.

Income

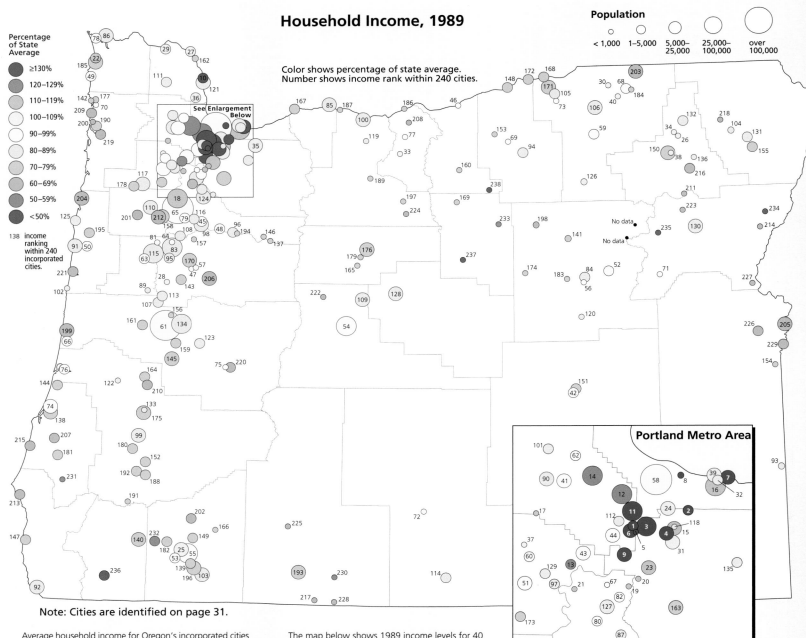

Household Income, 1989

Percentage of State Average

- ≥130%
- 120–129%
- 110–119%
- 100–109%
- 90–99%
- 80–89%
- 70–79%
- 60–69%
- 50–59%
- <50%

138 income ranking within 240 incorporated cities.

Color shows percentage of state average. Number shows income rank within 240 cities.

Population

- < 1,000
- 1–5,000
- 5,000–25,000
- 25,000–100,000
- over 100,000

Portland Metro Area

Note: Cities are identified on page 31.

Average household income for Oregon's incorporated cities is mapped above. Income figures (the most recent available for cities) are for 1989. Colors show income as a percentage of state average; numbers show the income-level rank of each city. See page 31 for the names and populations of cities.

The map below shows 1989 income levels for 40 incorporated cities and unincorporated places in the Portland Metro Area. Color shows income as a percentage of the Metro Area (not state) average; numbers show income-level rank within the Metro Area.

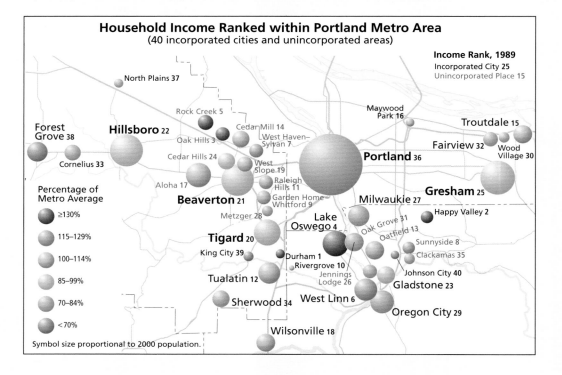

Household Income Ranked within Portland Metro Area
(40 incorporated cities and unincorporated areas)

Income Rank, 1989
Incorporated City 25
Unincorporated Place 15

North Plains 37
Rock Creek 5
Maywood Park 16
Forest Grove 38
Hillsboro 22
Cedar Mill 14
West Haven–Sylvan 7
Troutdale 15
Oak Hills 3
Cornelius 33
Cedar Hills 24
Fairview 32
Wood Village 30
West Slope 19
Portland 36
Aloha 17
Raleigh Hills 11
Beaverton 21
Garden Home–Whitford 9
Gresham 25
Metzger 28
Milwaukie 27
Happy Valley 2
Lake Oswego 4
Oak Grove 31
Oatfield 13
Tigard 20
Sunnyside 8
King City 39
Clackamas 35
Durham 1
Rivergrove 10
Johnson City 40
Tualatin 12
Jennings Lodge 26
Gladstone 23
Sherwood 34
West Linn 6
Oregon City 29
Wilsonville 18

Percentage of Metro Average

- ≥130%
- 115–129%
- 100–114%
- 85–99%
- 70–84%
- <70%

Symbol size proportional to 2000 population.

Personal income for Oregon residents totaled $85 billion in 1998. This accounted for 1.16 percent of total U.S. personal income generated in that year. Personal income consists of wages and salaries, other labor income such as employer-provided health insurance, transfers such as Social Security payments, dividends, interest and rent and proprietor's income. State personal income is adjusted for payroll taxes and commuters who live in one state and work in another.

Oregon's per capita personal income (total personal income in the state divided by total population) stood at $25,912 in 1998. This compares with $16,062 in 1988 and $8,476 in 1978. Oregon per capita personal income was 95 percent of the U.S. average ($27,203) in 1998, ranking 24th among the states.

Per capita personal income varies widely across Oregon's 36 counties and is consistently higher in urbanized areas. The Portland Metropolitan Area (Multnomah, Clackamas and Washington Counties) showed the state's highest per capita income in 1998. Relatively high income can be found in the Willamette

1999 Income per Capita by Type

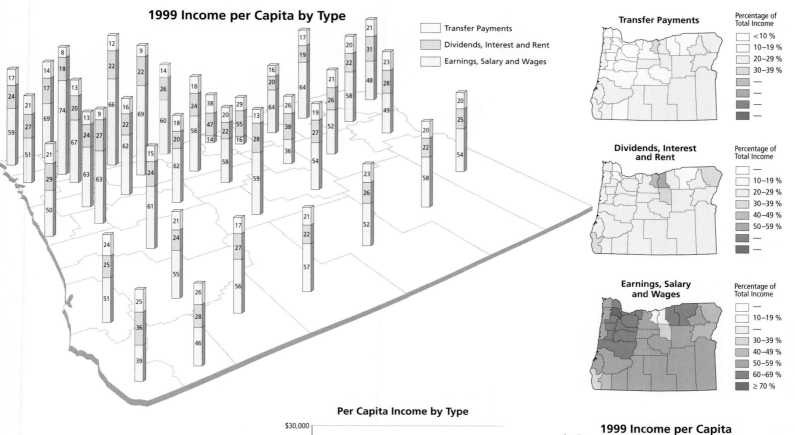

Legend:
- Transfer Payments
- Dividends, Interest and Rent
- Earnings, Salary and Wages

Transfer Payments

Percentage of Total Income
- <10 %
- 10–19 %
- 20–29 %
- 30–39 %

Dividends, Interest and Rent

Percentage of Total Income
- 10–19 %
- 20–29 %
- 30–39 %
- 40–49 %
- 50–59 %

Earnings, Salary and Wages

Percentage of Total Income
- 10–19 %
- 30–39 %
- 40–49 %
- 50–59 %
- 60–69 %
- ≥ 70 %

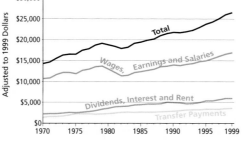

Per Capita Income by Type

Adjusted to 1999 Dollars

Total

Wages, Earnings and Salaries

Dividends, Interest and Rent

Transfer Payments

$30,000 / $25,000 / $20,000 / $15,000 / $10,000 / $5,000 / $0

1970 1975 1980 1985 1990 1995 1999

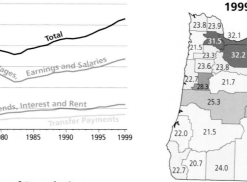

1999 Income per Capita

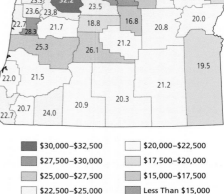

- $30,000–$32,500
- $27,500–$30,000
- $25,000–$27,500
- $22,500–$25,000
- $20,000–$22,500
- $17,500–$20,000
- $15,000–$17,500
- Less Than $15,000

Valley (Marion, Benton and Lane Counties), southern Oregon (Jackson County) and Central Oregon (Deschutes County). In 1998, all counties east of the Cascade Mountains (except Deschutes) had per capita income at least $3,000 below the statewide average.

Earnings consist of wages and salaries, other labor income and proprietor's income. Net earnings are calculated by adjusting for social insurance contributions and interstate commuters. Net earnings made up 64.2 percent of total personal income for Oregonians in 1998. Transfer payments (the largest component of this category is Social Security income) accounted for 13.1 percent, while dividends, interest and rent constituted 22.7 percent. Net earnings tend to be a more important source of income in metropolitan areas. Dividends, interest and rent and transfer payments are closely tied to age. Curry County, for example, with its high proportion of retirees, is relatively dependent on transfer payments as well as dividends, interest and rent income.

Inflation-adjusted net earnings fell sharply in the early 1980s as employment declined and wage increases lagged behind inflation. Since that time net earnings have grown steadily, with the exception of the mild 1990–91 recession. Boosted by in-migration of retirees and the aging of long-term residents, transfer payments have also grown steadily. Dividends, interest and rent income declined through much of the 1990s—interest income slipped because interest rates declined in the early 1990s and remained generally low throughout the decade. At the same time, rapid stock price appreciation triggered strong growth in capital gains income—from $1.2 billion to $4.7 billion between 1990 and 1998.

Percentage of Population in Poverty, 1997

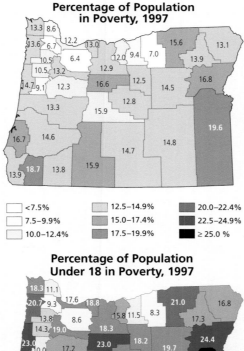

- <7.5 %
- 7.5–9.9 %
- 10.0–12.4 %
- 12.5–14.9 %
- 15.0–17.4 %
- 17.5–19.9 %
- 20.0–22.4 %
- 22.5–24.9 %
- ≥ 25.0 %

Percentage of Population Under 18 in Poverty, 1997

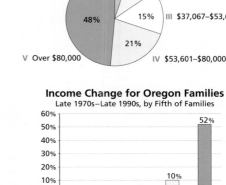

Income Inequality

Shares of total income enjoyed by poorest to wealthiest families. Each group contains 20 percent of Oregon families. In the late 1990s, the poorest 20 percent received 5 percent of the total income; the wealthiest 20 percent received 48 percent.

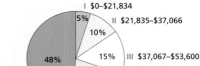

- I $0–$21,834 — 5%
- II $21,835–$37,066 — 10%
- III $37,067–$53,600 — 15%
- IV $53,601–$80,000 — 21%
- V Over $80,000 — 48%

Income Change for Oregon Families

Late 1970s–Late 1990s, by Fifth of Families

60% / 50% / 40% / 30% / 20% / 10% / 0% / -10% / -20%

Poorest I: -13%
Second II: -8%
Middle III: 0%
Fourth IV: 10%
Richest V: 52%

Religion

A nationwide survey of religious preferences conducted in 1991 showed that Oregonians differ from other Americans in three notable ways. First, no other state has such a high proportion of adults who say they have no religion at all. Second, Oregon is the only state in which the number of people claiming no religion exceeds the number who identify themselves with the state's largest religion. And finally, Oregonians are much less likely than other Americans to be Catholics, Baptists or Methodists—in the nation at large, over half the population identifies with one of these faiths compared with only 29 percent of Oregonian residents.

Other differences are less striking. Oregon has relatively more Mormons, Lutherans, Presbyterians, Buddhists, Jehovah's Witnesses and Seventh-day Adventists than other states; and relatively fewer Jews.

Church membership totals for Oregon's 12 largest denominations reveal that the Catholic Church has more members than any other religious body. That is in line with its leading place in the religious preferences study, results of which are shown in the table at the right. The Church of Jesus Christ of Latter-day Saints, sometimes known as the Mormon Church or LDS, is the state's second-largest denomination—not surprising in view of Oregon's proximity to Utah and Southern Idaho, where the Mormon Church is dominant. Based on Oregonians' individual preferences, one would expect both the United Methodist and the Presbyterian Church (USA) to have far more members than the LDS Church. In fact, the Mormon Church is almost three times larger than either of these two bodies. Similarly, based on individual preferences the Assemblies of God should have far fewer members than the Methodists or Presbyterians, but it nevertheless ranks as the third largest denomination in the state.

Religious preference statistics are somewhat unreliable indicators of the relative strength of various religious denominations for several reasons. Not everyone who has a religious preference belongs to a religious congregation. Furthermore, members of some denominations do not always use the same term to identify their faith. Congregations affiliated with the Christian Churches and Churches of Christ almost never use this name to identify themselves. The names they do use —either Christian Church or Church of Christ—are also used by congregations of other denominations. Likewise, many congregations of the Church of the Foursquare Gospel do not advertise their denominational affiliation, preferring names such as Faith Center or Living Faith Church.

More than a quarter of Oregonians use the general terms "Christian" or "Protestant" to identify themselves. But even a more exact term such as "Baptist" is somewhat ambiguous since it does not signify a specific church among the many Baptist denominations. Denominational membership statistics are only rough indicators of the number of people who participate actively in church life. Some denominations, for example, the Catholics, include baptized infants as members as well as baptized adults who seldom if ever go to church. Other denominations, for example, the Conservative Baptists, do not count young children or inactive adults as members.

Over the years the growth of the Assemblies of God, the Foursquare Church and the Southern Baptists has been truly remarkable. In 1926, Oregon had no Southern Baptist congregations, the Foursquare Church had not been founded and in the entire state there were only 613 members of the Assemblies of God. Mormon growth, though less spectacular, has been strong and steady. An active recruiting program elevated this denomination from ninth place in 1926 to second place by 1980.

As these vigorous denominations have grown, others have stagnated or declined in member numbers. Most of the old-line Protestant bodies, both in Oregon and elsewhere in the U.S., have lost a substantial number of members since the mid-1960s. Between 1971 and 2000 the Presbyterian Church (USA) lost 31 percent of its Oregon members, the United Methodist Church lost 41 percent and the Episcopal Church lost 45 percent. After 1980, Presbyterian and Episcopal membership losses became less severe, and by 2000 Episcopal Church membership had stabilized at the level of 1990. United Methodist losses, on the other hand, accelerated in each decade since 1971. By 2000, the number of Methodists in Oregon had fallen to approximately the number the Census Bureau reported in 1926.

Stated Religious Preference, 1991

	Oregon (%)	U.S. (%)		Oregon (%)	U.S. (%)
None	17.2	7.5	Buddhist	0.5	0.2
Roman Catholic	15.3	26.2	Jewish	0.4	1.8
Protestant	14.7	9.8	Born Again/		
Christian	11.7	4.6	Evangelical	0.4	0.3
Baptist	8.7	19.4	Church of Christ	0.4	1.0
Lutheran	6.7	5.2	Unitarian	0.4	0.3
Methodist	4.9	8.0	Assemblies of God	0.3	0.4
Presbyterian	4.2	2.8	Nazarene	0.3	0.3
Refused to answer	2.4	2.3	Mennonite	0.2	0.2
LDS/Mormon	2.4	1.4	Orthodox Christian	0.2	0.3
Episcopal	2.2	1.7	Congregationalist	0.1	0.2
Other religion	1.7	1.4	Muslim	0.1	0.3
Pentecostal	1.2	1.8	Holiness/Holy	0	0.3
Agnostic	1.2	0.7	Church of God	0	0.3
Jehovah's Witness	1.1	0.8	Hindu	0	0.1
Seventh-day Adventist	1.1	0.4			

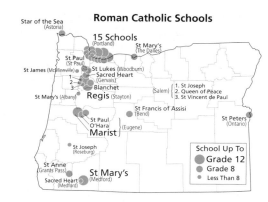

Roman Catholic Schools

Star of the Sea (Astoria) · 15 Schools (Portland) · St Mary's (The Dalles) · St Paul (St Paul) · St James (McMinnville) · St Lukes (Woodburn) · Sacred Heart (Gervais) · Blanchet · 1. St Joseph · 2. Queen of Peace · 3. St Vincent de Paul (Salem) · Regis (Stayton) · St Mary's (Albany) · St Francis of Assisi (Bend) · St Peters (Ontario) · St Paul O'Hara (Eugene) · Marist · St Joseph (Roseburg) · St Anne (Grants Pass) · Sacred Heart (Medford) · St Mary's (Medford)

School Up To: Grade 12 / Grade 8 / Less Than 8

Lutheran Schools

Trinity Grace Portland (Portland) · Forest Hills (Cornelius) · Pilgrim (Beaverton) · Concordia (Salem) · Zion (Corvallis) · Life (Eugene) · Trinity (Bend) · St Paul (Roseburg) · Grace (Ashland)

School Up To: Grade 12 / Grade 8 / Grade 6 / Grade 4

Non-Christian Congregations

● Muslim ○ Buddhist ○ Jewish · Portland · Beaverton · Gresham · Tualatin · Salem · Corvallis · Eugene · Pendleton · Ontario · Ashland

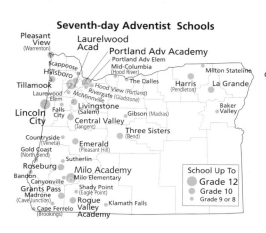

Seventh-day Adventist Schools

Pleasant View (Warrenton) · Laurelwood Acad · Portland Adv Academy · Scappoose · Portland Adv Elem · Mid-Columbia (Hood River) · Hillsboro · Hood View (Portland) · The Dalles · Harris (Pendleton) · Milton Stateline · La Grande · Tillamook · Laurelwood Elem · McMinnville · Rivergate (Gladstone) · Livingstone (Salem) · Gibson (Madras) · Baker Valley · Lincoln City · Falls City · Central Valley (Tangent) · Three Sisters (Bend) · Countryside (Veneta) · Emerald (Pleasant Hill) · Gold Coast (North Bend) · Sutherlin · Roseburg · Milo Academy · Milo Elementary · Bandon · Canyonville · Shady Cove (Eagle Point) · Grants Pass · Madrone (Cave Junction) · Rogue Valley · Klamath Falls · Cape Ferrelo (Brookings) · Academy

School Up To: Grade 12 / Grade 10 / Grade 9 or 8

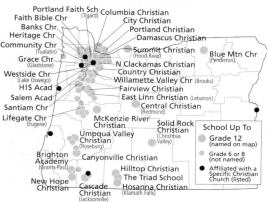

Christian Schools

Portland Faith Sch (Tigard) · Columbia Christian · Faith Bible Chr · City Christian · Banks Chr · Portland Christian · Heritage Chr · Damascus Christian · Community Chr (Tualatin) · Summit Christian (Hood River) · Blue Mtn Chr (Pendleton) · Grace Chr (Gladstone) · N Clackamas Christian · Westside Chr (Lake Oswego) · Country Christian · HIS Acad · Willamette Valley Chr (Brooks) · Fairview Christian · Salem Acad · East Linn Christian (Lebanon) · Santiam Chr · Central Christian (Redmond) · Lifegate Chr (Eugene) · McKenzie River Christian · Solid Rock Christian (Christmas Valley) · Umpqua Valley Christian (Roseburg) · Brighton Academy (Grants Pass) · Canyonville Christian · New Hope Christian · Cascade Christian (Jacksonville) · Hilltop Christian · The Triad School · Hosanna Christian (Klamath Falls)

School Up To: Grade 12 (named on map) / Grade 6 or 8 (not named) / ● Affiliated with a Specific Christian Church (listed)

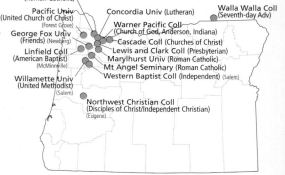

Accredited Colleges with Religious Affiliation

Univ of Portland (Roman Catholic) · Pacific Univ (United Church of Christ) · Concordia Univ (Lutheran) · Walla Walla Coll (Seventh-day Adv) · Warner Pacific Coll (Church of God, Anderson, Indiana) · George Fox Univ (Friends) (Newberg) · Cascade Coll (Churches of Christ) · Linfield Coll (American Baptist) (McMinnville) · Lewis and Clark Coll (Presbyterian) · Marylhurst Univ (Roman Catholic) · Mt Angel Seminary (Roman Catholic) · Willamette Univ (United Methodist) (Salem) · Western Baptist Coll (Independent) (Salem) · Northwest Christian Coll (Disciples of Christ/Independent Christian) (Eugene)

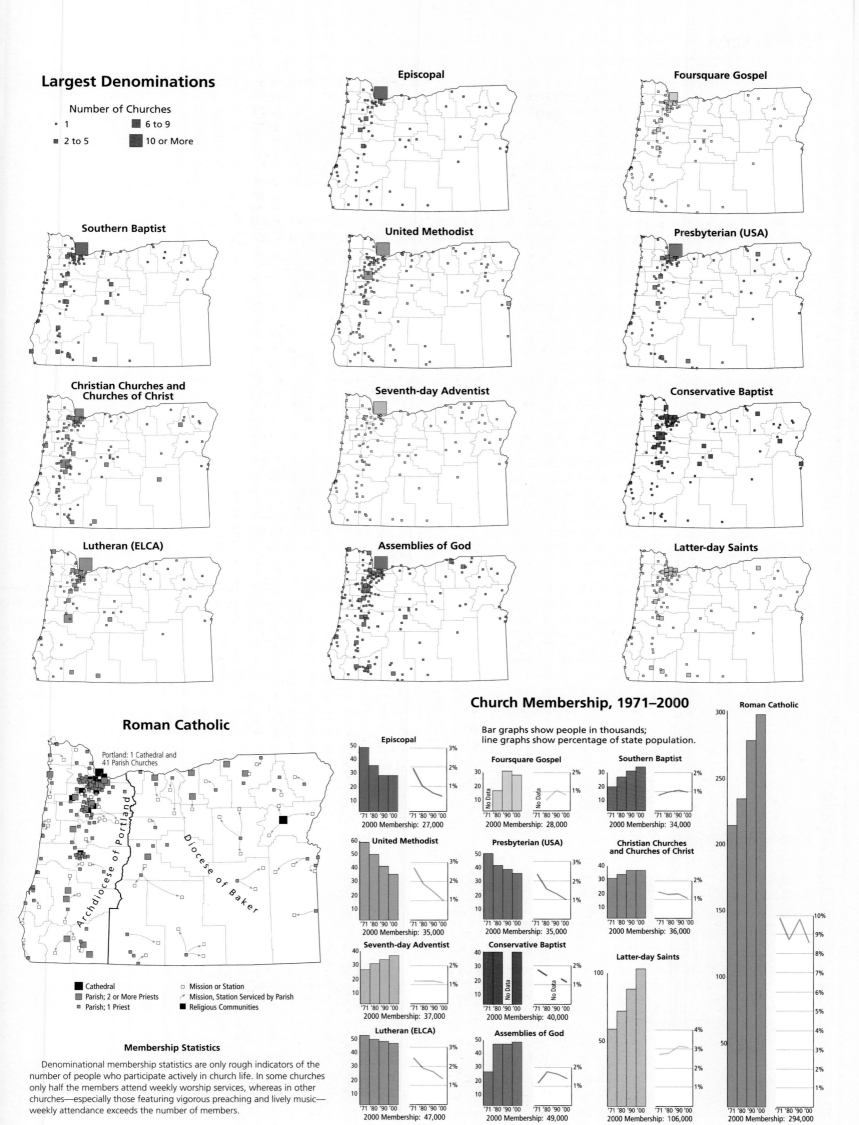

Largest Denominations

Number of Churches
- 1
- 2 to 5
- 6 to 9
- 10 or More

Episcopal

Foursquare Gospel

Southern Baptist

United Methodist

Presbyterian (USA)

Christian Churches and Churches of Christ

Seventh-day Adventist

Conservative Baptist

Lutheran (ELCA)

Assemblies of God

Latter-day Saints

Roman Catholic

Portland: 1 Cathedral and 41 Parish Churches

Archdiocese of Portland

Diocese of Baker

- ■ Cathedral
- ■ Parish; 2 or More Priests
- ■ Parish; 1 Priest
- □ Mission or Station
- ⤳ Mission, Station Serviced by Parish
- ■ Religious Communities

Membership Statistics

Denominational membership statistics are only rough indicators of the number of people who participate actively in church life. In some churches only half the members attend weekly worship services, whereas in other churches—especially those featuring vigorous preaching and lively music—weekly attendance exceeds the number of members.

Church Membership, 1971–2000

Bar graphs show people in thousands; line graphs show percentage of state population.

Episcopal
2000 Membership: 27,000

Foursquare Gospel
2000 Membership: 28,000

Southern Baptist
2000 Membership: 34,000

United Methodist
2000 Membership: 35,000

Presbyterian (USA)
2000 Membership: 35,000

Christian Churches and Churches of Christ
2000 Membership: 36,000

Seventh-day Adventist
2000 Membership: 37,000

Conservative Baptist
2000 Membership: 40,000

Latter-day Saints
2000 Membership: 106,000

Lutheran (ELCA)
2000 Membership: 47,000

Assemblies of God
2000 Membership: 49,000

Roman Catholic
2000 Membership: 294,000

Politics

During the nineteenth century Oregon politics were fairly stable: Republicans were the majority party, but the Democrats were active and modestly successful. During this time of strong regional influence in American politics, Oregon resembled most other northern (or Union) states. Through the first third of the twentieth century Oregon became solidly Republican. From 1900 to 1928, Oregon voted for the Republican candidate for President in six of seven elections; in U.S. Senate elections, Grand Old Party (GOP) candidates prevailed eight of 11 times.

Economic reverses during the Great Depression of the 1930s made class rather than region the focus of political divisions. In Oregon and the nation, the New Deal made the Democrats much more competitive. This revival is reflected in the voter registration figures below, showing a rapid increase among the Democrats from 1930 to 1936. The 1932 and 1936 maps show the broad pattern of Franklin Roosevelt's first two victories—again reflecting national trends. But by the post-war years, Oregon trended back toward the Republican side, with state victories by Republican presidential candidates in 1948, 1952 and 1956. During this period, the Oregon congressional delegation also largely reverted to its GOP roots.

But by the mid-1950s, increasing urbanization and effective organizing by liberal political activists helped the Democrats. From that period to the late 1970s, Democrats expanded their urban and labor core (with significant support among registered voters in rural Oregon) to become the majority party in the state.

But the political wheel turned again starting roughly in 1980, as Ronald Reagan easily carried Oregon and the nation. The GOP captured control of the state House of Representatives in 1990 and the state Senate in 1994. But through the 1990s, with rare exceptions, the Republicans were unable to win most statewide contests. For example, since 1986 three Democratic governors have been elected to four successive terms.

There is now strong urban–rural political regionalism in Oregon, clearly seen in the maps for presidential elections since 1988. Both Portland and Multnomah County are heavily Democratic, as are the university-influenced cities of Eugene and Corvallis and a number of coastal counties which are home to intense ongoing labor–management conflicts. Rural counties in Eastern and southern Oregon—including some in northeast Oregon that were once solidly Democratic—have shifted decisively to the GOP. Thus the urban Democratic preference is almost balanced by the rural tilt toward to the Republicans.

Since about 1980, many more voters have either declined to affiliate with a major party or registered with a minor party. Two important sources for these voters are (1) rural blue collar workers, formerly Democrats, who have been alienated by the influence of urban environmentalists on the party, and (2) moderate suburbanites, particularly women, alienated from the Republican party by the influence of religious conservatives.

Presidental Elections 1928–2000

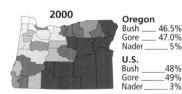

1928

Oregon
Hoover _____ 64%
Smith _____ 34%
U.S.
Hoover _____ 59%
Smith _____ 41%

1932

Oregon
Roosevelt ___ 58%
Hoover _____ 37%
Thomas _____ 4%
U.S.
Roosevelt ___ 58%
Hoover _____ 40%
Thomas _____ 2%

1952

Oregon
Eisenhower ___ 60%
Stevenson ___ 38%
U.S.
Eisenhower ___ 55%
Stevenson ___ 45%

1956

Oregon
Eisenhower ___ 54%
Stevenson ___ 44%
U.S.
Eisenhower ___ 58%
Stevenson ___ 42%

1976

Oregon
Carter _____ 47.6%
Ford _____ 47.8%
McCarthy _____ 4%
U.S.
Carter _____ 51%
Ford _____ 49%

1980

Oregon
Reagan _____ 48%
Carter _____ 39%
Anderson ___ 10%
U.S.
Reagan _____ 52%
Carter _____ 42%
Anderson _____ 7%

2000

Oregon
Bush _____ 46.5%
Gore _____ 47.0%
Nader _____ 5%
U.S.
Bush _____ 48%
Gore _____ 49%
Nader _____ 3%

Bush is listed first despite placing second in the popular vote, since he prevailed in the Electoral College.

2000 election shown with proportional symbols (see note at right)

Maps in this series show counties colored according to the division of the two-party vote in each. The 2000 presidential election is also presented in a second map, colored in the same way, but showing counties as circles proportional in size to the number of votes cast. This second presentation corrects for disparities in geographic size—a useful adjustment since it is votes, not square miles, that count in elections. Proportional circles make individual counties and their color classes more difficult to identify, but gives a more accurate representation of the statewide vote. Space constraints limit this "double map" presentation to this single example, but all the maps on these pages (and elsewhere in this atlas) should be interpreted with county populations in mind. See pages 26–27.

Republican   50%   55%   60%   65%   70%

Democratic   70%   65%   60%   55%   50%

Percentage of Two-Party Votes

Colors indicate percentages of the two-party vote. Listed percentages reflect the total vote, and include third-party candidates receiving over 1 percent of votes cast.

Voter Registration 2000

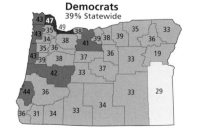

Democrats
39% Statewide

Percentage of Registered Voters

15–20%	35–40%
20–25%	40–45%
25–30%	45–50%
30–35%	>50%

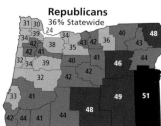

Republicans
36% Statewide

Non-Affiliated, Independents
22% Statewide

Percentage of Two-Party Registration

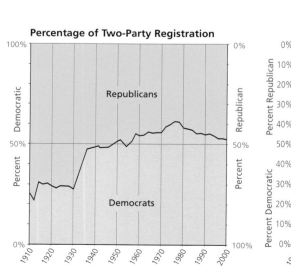

Republicans

Democratic

Republican

Democrats

Percent

Registration of All Voters

☐ Other Parties
☐ Non-Affiliated Voters

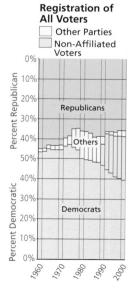

Republicans

Others

Democrats

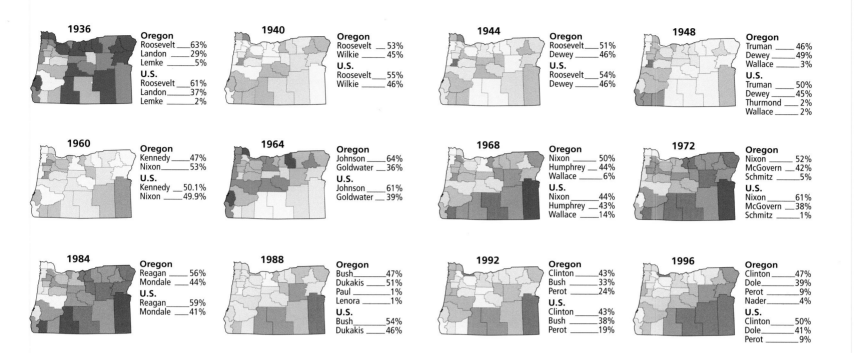

1936 — Oregon: Roosevelt 63%, Landon 29%, Lemke 5%; U.S.: Roosevelt 61%, Landon 37%, Lemke 2%

1940 — Oregon: Roosevelt 53%, Wilkie 45%; U.S.: Roosevelt 55%, Wilkie 46%

1944 — Oregon: Roosevelt 51%, Dewey 46%; U.S.: Roosevelt 54%, Dewey 46%

1948 — Oregon: Truman 46%, Dewey 49%, Wallace 3%; U.S.: Truman 50%, Dewey 45%, Thurmond 2%, Wallace 2%

1960 — Oregon: Kennedy 47%, Nixon 53%; U.S.: Kennedy 50.1%, Nixon 49.9%

1964 — Oregon: Johnson 64%, Goldwater 36%; U.S.: Johnson 61%, Goldwater 39%

1968 — Oregon: Nixon 50%, Humphrey 44%, Wallace 6%; U.S.: Nixon 44%, Humphrey 43%, Wallace 14%

1972 — Oregon: Nixon 52%, McGovern 42%, Schmitz 5%; U.S.: Nixon 61%, McGovern 38%, Schmitz 1%

1984 — Oregon: Reagan 56%, Mondale 44%; U.S.: Reagan 59%, Mondale 41%

1988 — Oregon: Bush 47%, Dukakis 51%, Paul 1%, Lenora 1%; U.S.: Bush 54%, Dukakis 46%

1992 — Oregon: Clinton 43%, Bush 33%, Perot 24%; U.S.: Clinton 43%, Bush 38%, Perot 19%

1996 — Oregon: Clinton 47%, Dole 39%, Perot 9%, Nader 4%; U.S.: Clinton 50%, Dole 41%, Perot 9%

Progressive Party candidate Henry Wallace ran to Truman's political left, drawing less than 2 percent nationally but more than 3 percent in Oregon. George Wallace's 1968 state's rights and segregationist campaign generally won less than 10 percent of the vote outside the South, but surpassed that in four southern Oregon counties. Oregon gave Ross Perot one of his best showings, particularly in Eastern Oregon. Dissatisfaction with the major parties was again a factor in Nader's strong performance in Oregon, but Nader's principal appeal was to environmentalists.

Minor Presidental Candidates

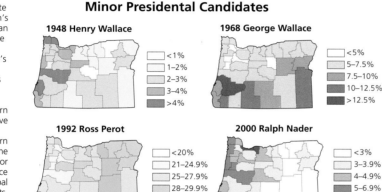

1948 Henry Wallace — <1%, 1–2%, 2–3%, 3–4%, >4%

1968 George Wallace — <5%, 5–7.5%, 7.5–10%, 10–12.5%, >12.5%

1992 Ross Perot — <20%, 21–24.9%, 25–27.9%, 28–29.9%, ≥30%

2000 Ralph Nader — <3%, 3–3.9%, 4–4.9%, 5–6.9%, ≥7%

State Ballot Measures

One of the first states to adopt a ballot measure initiative process (1902), Oregon initiatives can qualify with fewer signatures than initiatives in most other states permitting the process. In the late 1980s, courts ruled that paid petition circulators could not be prohibited, and the use of initiatives expanded greatly. Measure 5 in 1990 reflected a widespread Western tax revolt which began in 1978 with California's Proposition 13. Measure 5's passage cut property taxes nearly in half, requiring greater state reliance on income taxes for funding. A decade later, the passage of Measure 7 required compensation to property owners for land use planning and zoning restrictions (later struck down by the courts). Measure 18 in 1994 restricting hunting clearly reflected the state's urban–rural split. The same divide is apparent in the approval of Measure 67 (1998), authorizing the use of marijuana for medical purposes, and the defeat of Measure 9 (2000), which proposed to deny legal protection to homosexuals.

Percentage of All Votes

Yes — 50% 55% 60% 65% 70%

No — 70% 65% 60% 55% 50%

Ballot measure maps show majority "yes" vote percentages in green, and majority "no" vote percentages in brown.

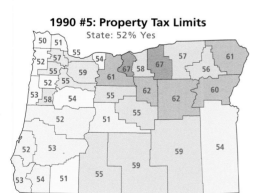

1990 #5: Property Tax Limits — State: 52% Yes

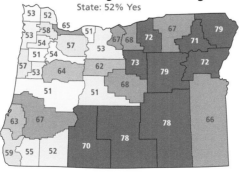

1994 #18: Hunting Bears and Cougars — State: 52% Yes

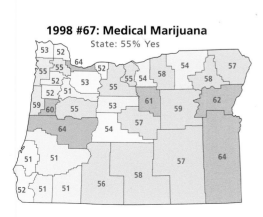

1998 #67: Medical Marijuana — State: 55% Yes

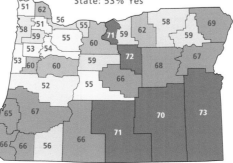

2000 #7: Regulatory Takings — State: 53% Yes

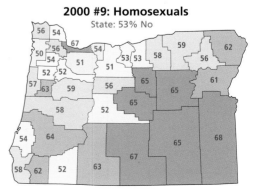

2000 #9: Homosexuals — State: 53% No

School Districts

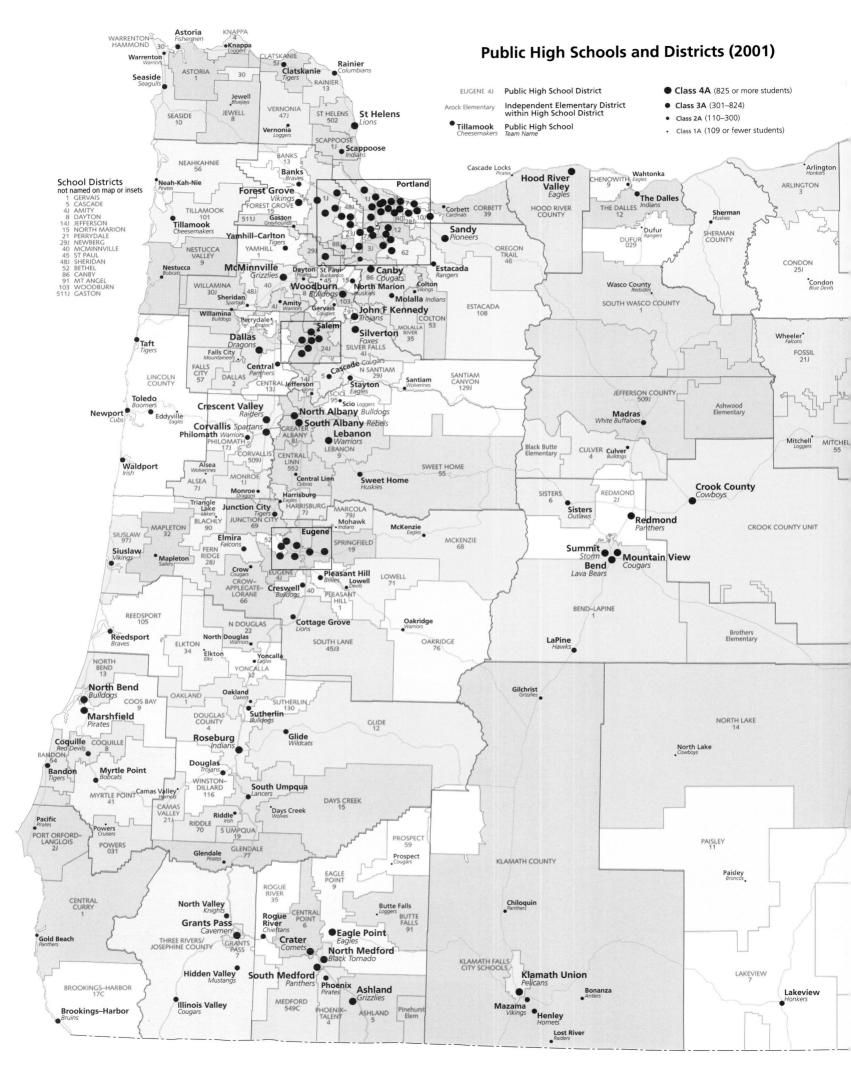

Public High Schools and Districts (2001)

EUGENE 4J	Public High School District	
Arock Elementary	Independent Elementary District within High School District	
Tillamook Cheesemakers	Public High School Team Name	

● Class 4A (825 or more students)
● Class 3A (301–824)
• Class 2A (110–300)
· Class 1A (109 or fewer students)

School Districts
not named on map or insets
1   GERVAIS
5   CASCADE
4J   AMITY
8   DAYTON
14J   JEFFERSON
15   NORTH MARION
21   PERRYDALE
29J   NEWBERG
40   MCMINNVILLE
45   ST PAUL
48J   SHERIDAN
52   BETHEL
86   CANBY
91   MT ANGEL
103   WOODBURN
511J   GASTON

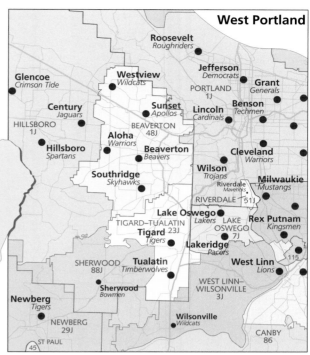

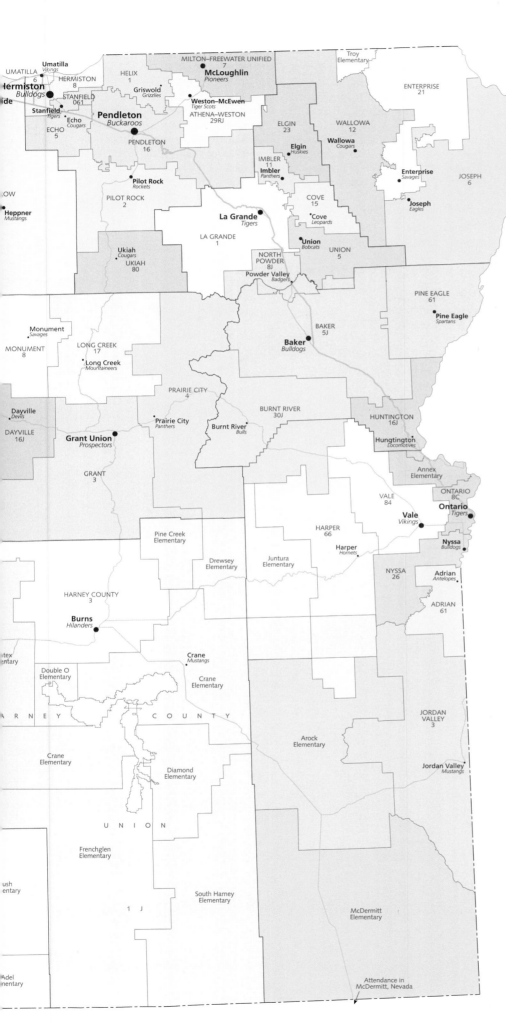

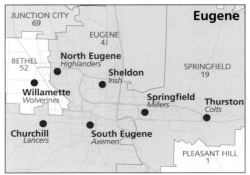

Education

Oregon was slow to develop its system of public education beyond the elementary level. Competition from private denominational schools and other schools associated with private religious colleges discouraged the development of public high schools. Taxpayers were not eager to support education beyond the elementary level, an attitude fanned by 20 years of editorial opposition by editor Harvey W. Scott of *The Oregonian*, who attacked the public high school as the creator of an over-educated class of "drones" and a "powerful promoter of communism." Oregon's first four-year high school opened in Portland in 1869, but the second, in Astoria, did not appear until 1895 (there were, however, three-year high schools in Ashland, Baker City, Grants Pass, Medford and Roseburg by that date). The competition from preparatory departments of universities delayed the arrival of public four-year high schools in Eugene and Salem until 1900 and 1902 respectively. Enthusiasm and support for high school education increased rapidly after the turn of the twentieth century.

Education was a decidedly local affair during most of Oregon's history. The number of (mostly elementary) districts increased as settlement widened, reaching a peak of 2,556 in 1917–1918, but a steady trend toward consolidations and mergers has reduced this number. By 1998–1999 there were 198 school districts, 179 of them unified school districts

offering all grade levels. The disparity in size among school districts is extreme: Portland 1J had more than 53,000 students in 2000–01, while Double 0 28 in Harney County had four. Declining enrollments in some areas of the state (see Age Structure, pages 38–39) make further consolidations likely.

Public school funding mechanisms, too, have changed over time. In 1980 about 70 percent of K–12 funding came from local property taxes. After voters approved Ballot Measure 5 in 1990 (see Politics, page 49) local funding declined, with state revenue now providing about tw--thirds of K–12 funding. In fall 2000, Oregon public schools and school districts employed 56,195 people, one for every nine students. Almost exactly half were teachers. Another 4.4 percent were administrators, 2.2 percent counselors, 1

percent librarians and 42 percent support staff.

Religious-based schools have a long history in Oregon. Protestant denominations historically focused their efforts on colleges, but the Roman Catholic Church has operated a very substantial parallel school system in Oregon's larger towns. The Seventh-day Adventist Church has also operated a large school network for many years. The wider growth of Protestant "Christian" schools, most of them non-denominational, is a comparatively recent development (see Religion, page 46). Non-religious private ("independent") schools are few and small. Altogether, religious and independent schools account for just over 6 percent of enrollment. Most of these schools participate with public schools in athletic conferences, where religious schools play a significant role in Class IA and IIA leagues.

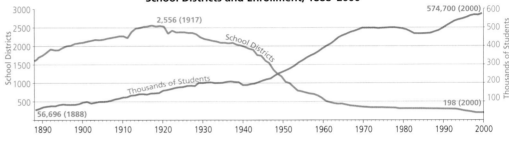

School Districts and Enrollment, 1888–2000

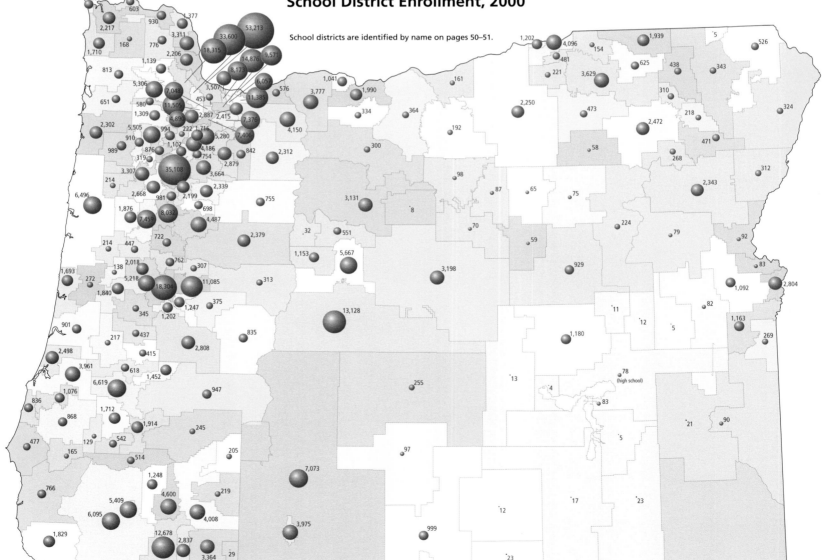

School District Enrollment, 2000

School districts are identified by name on pages 50–51.

Religious and Independent High Schools

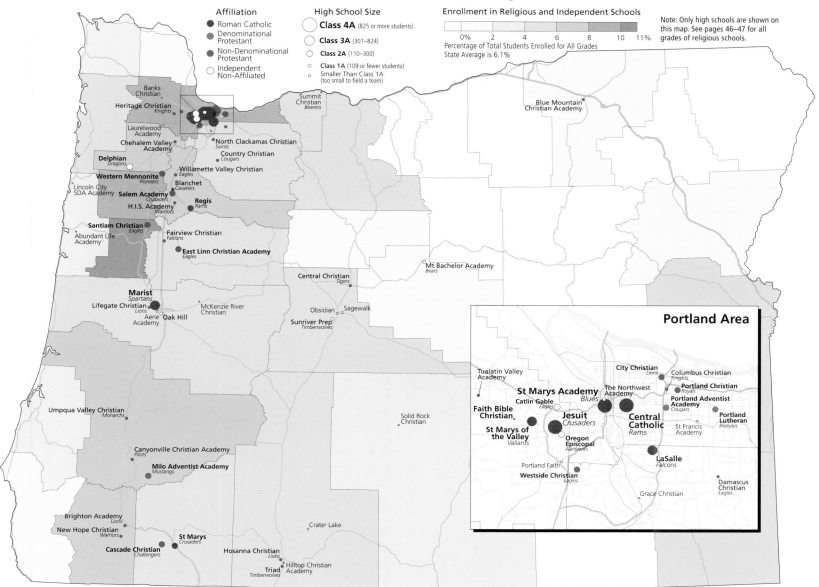

Affiliation
- Roman Catholic
- Denominational Protestant
- Non-Denominational Protestant
- Independent Non-Affiliated

High School Size
- Class 4A (825 or more students)
- Class 3A (301–824)
- Class 2A (110–300)
- Class 1A (109 or fewer students)
- Smaller Than Class 1A (too small to field a team)

Enrollment in Religious and Independent Schools

0% 2 4 6 8 10 11%

Percentage of Total Students Enrolled for All Grades
State Average is 6.1%

Note: Only high schools are shown on this map. See pages 46–47 for all grades of religious schools.

Portland Area

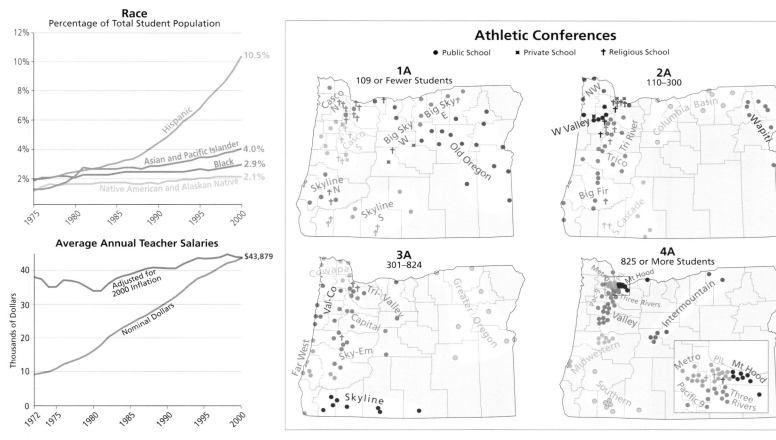

Race
Percentage of Total Student Population

- Hispanic 10.5%
- Asian and Pacific Islander 4.0%
- Black 2.9%
- Native American and Alaskan Native 2.1%

Average Annual Teacher Salaries

- Adjusted for 2000 Inflation
- Nominal Dollars
- $43,879

Athletic Conferences

- ● Public School
- ✖ Private School
- † Religious School

1A 109 or Fewer Students

2A 110–300

3A 301–824

4A 825 or More Students

53

Colleges and Universities

Higher education in Oregon began early in the state's history. The forerunner of Willamette University was established at the Methodist mission in Salem in 1842, before any cities were incorporated and before the arrival of the Oregon Trail's "Great Migration" of 1843. Pacific (Church of Christ) and Linfield (Baptist) followed in 1849. The first public institution, the Oregon Normal School (now Western Oregon State University), was established at Monmouth in 1856, three years before statehood. Oregon Agricultural College

(now Oregon State University) was founded in 1868 after the Morrill Act provided its Land Grant funding source. The University of Oregon followed in 1876. With the exception of Reed College (founded in 1909), all private colleges had religious denominational roots, and nearly all schools, both public and private, were located in small towns.

Sixteen regionally accredited nonprofit private colleges are now in Oregon, accounting for 12 percent of post-secondary enrollment. Most serve a predominantly in-state student

base, though Willamette, Lewis and Clark and Reed attract more than half their students from out of state.

About 89,600 students (full-time equivalent), or 53 percent of 2000–2001 post-secondary enrollment, attend Oregon's 17 community colleges. This network was created after World War II to provide both vocational training and affordable lower division college courses. In 2000–2001, 38 percent of community college students were in lower division collegiate programs. Another 32

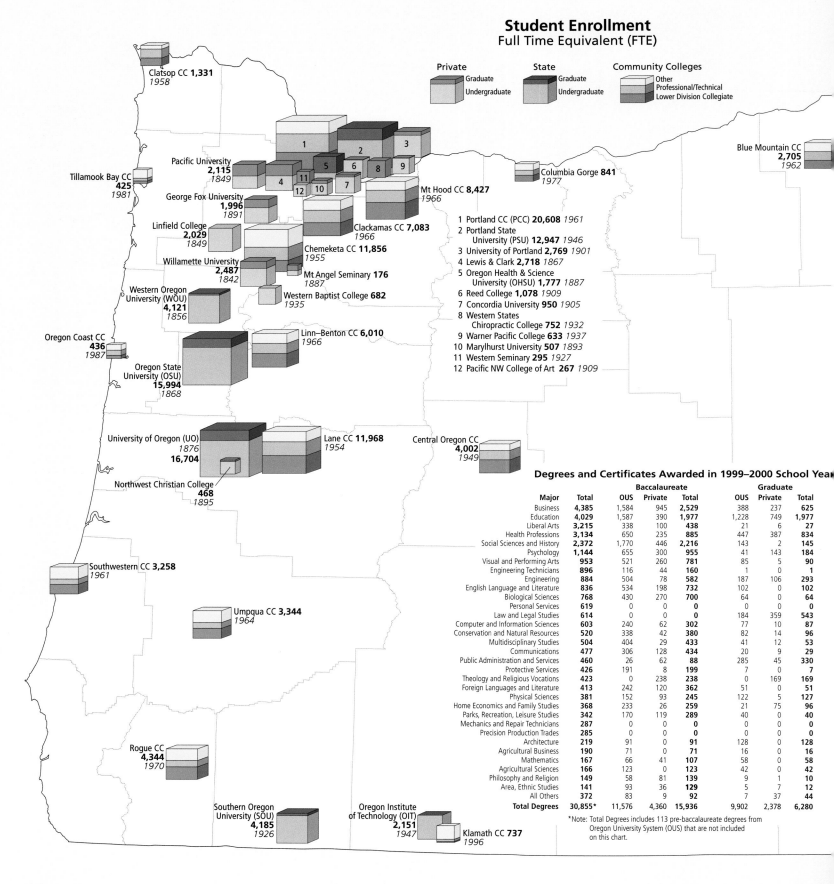

Student Enrollment
Full Time Equivalent (FTE)

1 Portland CC (PCC) **20,608** *1961*
2 Portland State University (PSU) **12,947** *1946*
3 University of Portland **2,769** *1901*
4 Lewis & Clark **2,718** *1867*
5 Oregon Health & Science University (OHSU) **1,777** *1887*
6 Reed College **1,078** *1909*
7 Concordia University **950** *1905*
8 Western States Chiropractic College **752** *1932*
9 Warner Pacific College **633** *1937*
10 Marylhurst University **507** *1893*
11 Western Seminary **295** *1927*
12 Pacific NW College of Art **267** *1909*

Clatsop CC **1,331** *1958*
Tillamook Bay CC **425** *1981*
Pacific University **2,115** *1849*
George Fox University **1,996** *1891*
Linfield College **2,029** *1849*
Willamette University **2,487** *1842*
Western Oregon University (WOU) **4,121** *1856*
Oregon Coast CC **436** *1987*
Oregon State University (OSU) **15,994** *1868*
University of Oregon (UO) *1876* **16,704**
Northwest Christian College **468** *1895*
Clackamas CC **7,083** *1966*
Chemeketa CC **11,856** *1955*
Mt Angel Seminary **176** *1887*
Western Baptist College **682** *1935*
Linn–Benton CC **6,010** *1966*
Mt Hood CC **8,427** *1966*
Columbia Gorge **841** *1977*
Blue Mountain CC **2,705** *1962*
Lane CC **11,968** *1954*
Central Oregon CC **4,002** *1949*
Southwestern CC **3,258** *1961*
Umpqua CC **3,344** *1964*
Rogue CC **4,344** *1970*
Southern Oregon University (SOU) **4,185** *1926*
Oregon Institute of Technology (OIT) **2,151** *1947*
Klamath CC **737** *1996*

Degrees and Certificates Awarded in 1999–2000 School Year

Major	Total	Baccalaureate OUS	Baccalaureate Private	Baccalaureate Total	Graduate OUS	Graduate Private	Graduate Total
Business	**4,385**	1,584	945	**2,529**	388	237	**625**
Education	**4,029**	1,587	390	**1,977**	1,228	749	**1,977**
Liberal Arts	**3,215**	338	100	**438**	21	6	**27**
Health Professions	**3,134**	650	235	**885**	447	387	**834**
Social Sciences and History	**2,372**	1,770	446	**2,216**	143	2	**145**
Psychology	**1,144**	655	300	**955**	41	143	**184**
Visual and Performing Arts	**953**	521	260	**781**	85	5	**90**
Engineering Technicians	**896**	116	44	**160**	1	0	**1**
Engineering	**884**	504	78	**582**	187	106	**293**
English Language and Literature	**836**	534	198	**732**	102	0	**102**
Biological Sciences	**768**	430	270	**700**	64	0	**64**
Personal Services	**619**	0	0	**0**	0	0	**0**
Law and Legal Studies	**614**	0	0	**0**	184	359	**543**
Computer and Information Sciences	**603**	240	62	**302**	77	10	**87**
Conservation and Natural Resources	**520**	338	42	**380**	82	14	**96**
Multidisciplinary Studies	**504**	404	29	**433**	41	12	**53**
Communications	**477**	306	128	**434**	20	9	**29**
Public Administration and Services	**460**	26	62	**88**	285	45	**330**
Protective Services	**426**	191	8	**199**	7	0	**7**
Theology and Religious Vocations	**423**	0	238	**238**	0	169	**169**
Foreign Languages and Literature	**413**	242	120	**362**	51	0	**51**
Physical Sciences	**381**	152	93	**245**	122	5	**127**
Home Economics and Family Studies	**368**	233	26	**259**	21	75	**96**
Parks, Recreation, Leisure Studies	**342**	170	119	**289**	40	0	**40**
Mechanics and Repair Technicians	**287**	0	0	**0**	0	0	**0**
Precision Production Trades	**285**	0	0	**0**	0	0	**0**
Architecture	**219**	91	0	**91**	128	0	**128**
Agricultural Business	**190**	71	0	**71**	16	0	**16**
Mathematics	**167**	66	41	**107**	58	0	**58**
Agricultural Sciences	**166**	123	0	**123**	42	0	**42**
Philosophy and Religion	**149**	58	81	**139**	9	1	**10**
Area, Ethnic Studies	**141**	93	36	**129**	5	7	**12**
All Others	**372**	83	9	**92**	7	37	**44**
Total Degrees	**30,855***	11,576	4,360	**15,936**	9,902	2,378	**6,280**

*Note: Total Degrees includes 113 pre-baccalaureate degrees from Oregon University System (OUS) that are not included on this chart.

percent were in professional and technical programs. A very large percentage of community college students attend part time, making these schools much larger than any of the state's four-year schools in terms of "head count" enrollment.

Oregon's seven public universities and one affiliate, the Oregon Health & Science University, are organized within the Oregon University System. This unified system was intended in part to prevent duplication of programs. The smaller public universities retain much of their original character as teachers colleges. Oregon Institute of Technology concentrates on applied engineering. Portland State University has a generally older student body and many working part-time students (and thus the highest head count enrollment). Oregon State University and the University of Oregon, with their traditionally divergent emphases on applied sciences and theoretical sciences respectively, have the state's highest full-time enrollments, reflecting large numbers of residential students.

Community College Districts, 1999

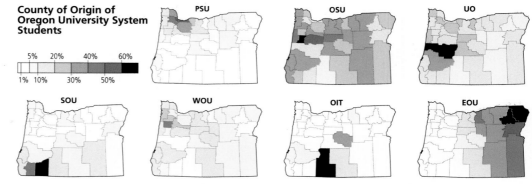

County of Origin of Oregon University System Students

5% 20% 40% 60%
1% 10% 30% 50%

PSU OSU UO
SOU WOU OIT EOU

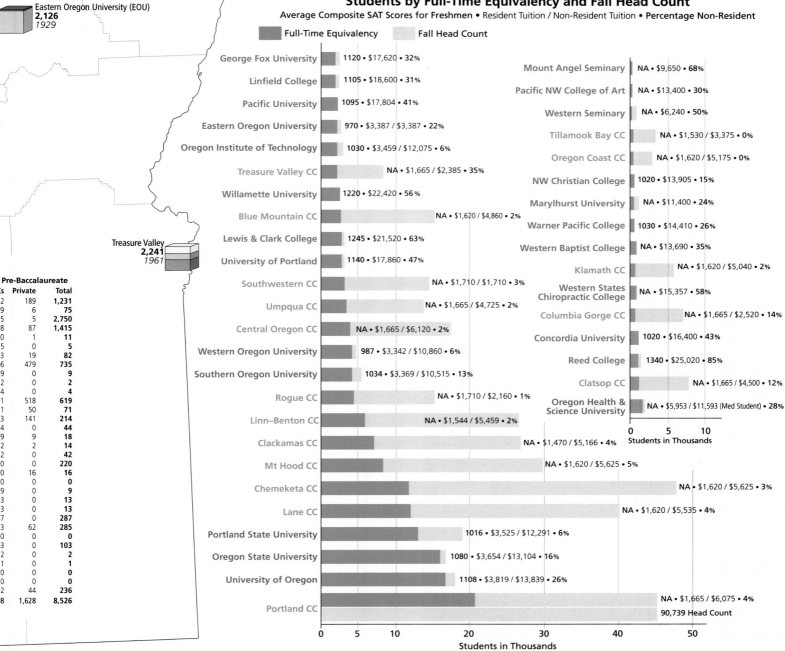

Eastern Oregon University (EOU)
2,126
1929

Treasure Valley
2,241
1961

Pre-Baccalaureate

	CCs	Private	Total
	1,042	189	1,231
	69	6	75
	2,745	5	2,750
	1,328	87	1,415
	10	1	11
	5	0	5
	63	19	82
	256	479	735
	9	0	9
	2	0	2
	4	0	4
	101	518	619
	21	50	71
	73	141	214
	44	0	44
	9	9	18
	12	2	14
	42	0	42
	220	0	220
	0	16	16
	0	0	0
	9	0	9
	13	0	13
	13	0	13
	287	0	287
	223	62	285
	0	0	0
	103	0	103
	2	0	2
	1	0	1
	0	0	0
	0	0	0
	192	44	236
	6,898	1,628	8,526

Students by Full-Time Equivalency and Fall Head Count

Average Composite SAT Scores for Freshmen • Resident Tuition / Non-Resident Tuition • Percentage Non-Resident

■ Full-Time Equivalency   ▢ Fall Head Count

George Fox University — 1120 • $17,620 • 32%
Linfield College — 1105 • $18,600 • 31%
Pacific University — 1095 • $17,804 • 41%
Eastern Oregon University — 970 • $3,387 / $3,387 • 22%
Oregon Institute of Technology — 1030 • $3,459 / $12,075 • 6%
Treasure Valley CC — NA • $1,665 / $2,385 • 35%
Willamette University — 1220 • $22,420 • 56%
Blue Mountain CC — NA • $1,620 / $4,860 • 2%
Lewis & Clark College — 1245 • $21,520 • 63%
University of Portland — 1140 • $17,860 • 47%
Southwestern CC — NA • $1,710 / $1,710 • 3%
Umpqua CC — NA • $1,665 / $4,725 • 2%
Central Oregon CC — NA • $1,665 / $6,120 • 2%
Western Oregon University — 987 • $3,342 / $10,860 • 6%
Southern Oregon University — 1034 • $3,369 / $10,515 • 13%
Rogue CC — NA • $1,710 / $2,160 • 1%
Linn–Benton CC — NA • $1,544 / $5,459 • 2%
Clackamas CC — NA • $1,470 / $5,166 • 4%
Mt Hood CC — NA • $1,620 / $5,625 • 5%
Chemeketa CC — NA • $1,620 / $5,625 • 3%
Lane CC — NA • $1,620 / $5,535 • 4%
Portland State University — 1016 • $3,525 / $12,291 • 6%
Oregon State University — 1080 • $3,654 / $13,104 • 16%
University of Oregon — 1108 • $3,819 / $13,839 • 26%
Portland CC — NA • $1,665 / $6,075 • 4%   90,739 Head Count

Mount Angel Seminary — NA • $9,650 • 68%
Pacific NW College of Art — NA • $13,400 • 30%
Western Seminary — NA • $6,240 • 50%
Tillamook Bay CC — NA • $1,530 / $3,375 • 0%
Oregon Coast CC — NA • $1,620 / $5,175 • 0%
NW Christian College — 1020 • $13,905 • 15%
Marylhurst University — NA • $11,400 • 24%
Warner Pacific College — 1030 • $14,410 • 26%
Western Baptist College — NA • $13,690 • 35%
Klamath CC — NA • $1,620 / $5,040 • 2%
Western States Chiropractic College — NA • $15,357 • 58%
Columbia Gorge CC — NA • $1,665 / $2,520 • 14%
Concordia University — 1020 • $16,400 • 43%
Reed College — 1340 • $25,020 • 85%
Clatsop CC — NA • $1,665 / $4,500 • 12%
Oregon Health & Science University — NA • $5,953 / $11,593 (Med Student) • 28%

Students in Thousands
0   5   10

Students in Thousands
0   5   10   20   30   40   50

Crime and Prisons

Urban Multnomah County has the state's highest rates of violent crime (120 per 10,000 people), property crime (743 per 10,000) and drug offenses (115 per 10,000). This pattern of high crime in urban areas holds for the U.S. as a whole, where, in 1999, the rate of crimes against persons and property was more than twice as great in metropolitan areas as it was in rural counties. High property crime rates in Oregon generally occur in more highly populated counties; but outside Multnomah County, the correlation one might expect between population density and crimes against people appears only weakly, or not at all. Drug offense rates show no apparent statewide pattern. While most of the rates for crimes against persons and property declined in Oregon (and in the country as a whole) during the 1990s, drug offense rates increased. This may reflect a real increase in illicit drug use or an increase in enforcement activity. Most drug convictions lead to probation or community control, not to prison terms. Increasing prison populations in Oregon over the past two decades result from tougher sentencing guidelines and mandatory minimum sentencing rules. The rising inmate population is mirrored by the spread of new prisons beyond the Department of Corrections' traditional base in Salem. Prison admission rates, shown on the facing page by county of jurisdiction (normally the county in which the crime occurred) were higher—barely—in Malheur County than in Multnomah County during the two years graphed; Josephine County was third. These areas differ in many respects, but Josephine and Malheur Counties led the state in 1997 in percentage of population living in poverty (see Income, pages 44–45).

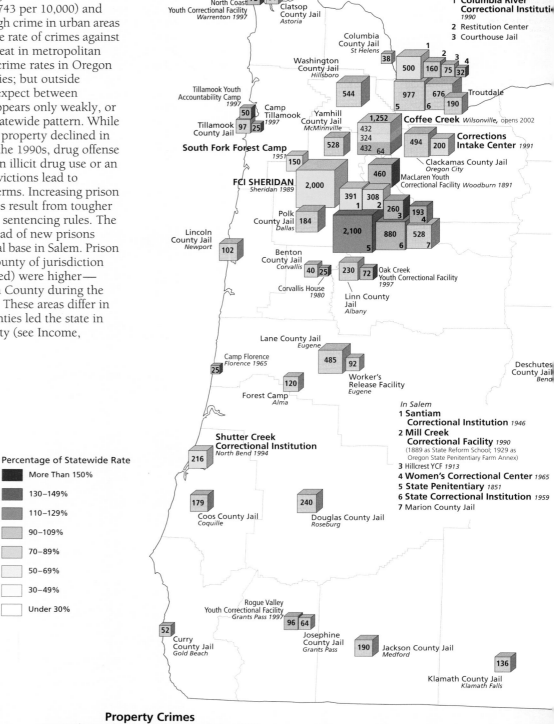

In Portland
1 **Columbia River Correctional Institution** 1990
2 Restitution Center
3 Courthouse Jail

In Salem
1 **Santiam Correctional Institution** 1946
2 **Mill Creek Correctional Facility** 1990
(1889 as State Reform School; 1929 as Oregon State Penitentiary Farm Annex)
3 **Hillcrest YCF** 1913
4 **Women's Correctional Center** 1965
5 **State Penitentiary** 1851
6 **State Correctional Institution** 1959
7 Marion County Jail

North Coast Youth Correctional Facility *Warrenton 1997*
Clatsop County Jail *Astoria*
Columbia County Jail *St Helens*
Washington County Jail *Hillsboro*
Tillamook Youth Accountability Camp
Camp Tillamook *1997*
Tillamook County Jail
Yamhill County Jail *McMinnville*
Coffee Creek *Wilsonville, opens 2002*
Corrections Intake Center 1991
South Fork Forest Camp *1951*
FCI SHERIDAN *Sheridan 1989*
Clackamas County Jail *Oregon City*
MacLaren Youth Correctional Facility *Woodburn 1891*
Polk County Jail *Dallas*
Lincoln County Jail *Newport*
Benton County Jail *Corvallis*
Corvallis House *1980*
Oak Creek Youth Correctional Facility
Linn County Jail *Albany*
Lane County Jail *Eugene*
Camp Florence *Florence 1965*
Worker's Release Facility *Eugene*
Forest Camp *Alma*
Deschutes County Jail *Bend*
Shutter Creek Correctional Institution *North Bend 1994*
Coos County Jail *Coquille*
Douglas County Jail *Roseburg*
Rogue Valley Youth Correctional Facility *Grants Pass 1997*
Curry County Jail *Gold Beach*
Josephine County Jail *Grants Pass*
Jackson County Jail *Medford*
Klamath County Jail *Klamath Falls*
Troutdale

Murder, Rape, Assault and Robbery
State Rate: 42.8 / 10,000 People
1996–1999

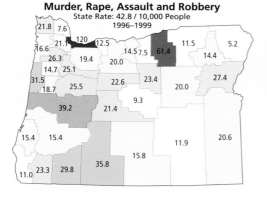

Percentage of Statewide Rate
- More Than 150%
- 130–149%
- 110–129%
- 90–109%
- 70–89%
- 50–69%
- 30–49%
- Under 30%

Burglary, Larceny and Motor Vehicle Theft
State Rate: 535 / 10,000 People
1996–1999

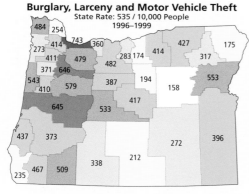

Drug Offenses
State Rate: 63.0 / 10,000 People
1996–1999

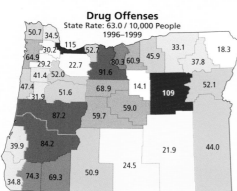

Property Crimes
Reported Crime Rates per 10,000 Population, 1999

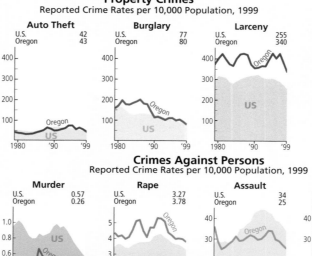

Auto Theft
U.S. 42
Oregon 43

Burglary
U.S. 77
Oregon 80

Larceny
U.S. 255
Oregon 340

Crimes Against Persons
Reported Crime Rates per 10,000 Population, 1999

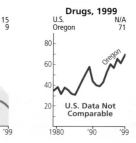

Murder
U.S. 0.57
Oregon 0.26

Rape
U.S. 3.27
Oregon 3.78

Assault
U.S. 34
Oregon 25

Robbery
U.S. 15
Oregon 9

Drugs, 1999
U.S. N/A
Oregon 71

U.S. Data Not Comparable

Crime Rate Trends
Comparing crime rate trends can be difficult. Trend data are only meaningful in context, and due to the nature of the criminal justice system that context can change over time. For example, some officially recorded crime rates, such as those for rape and drug crimes, are subject to changing definitions, reporting and enforcement.

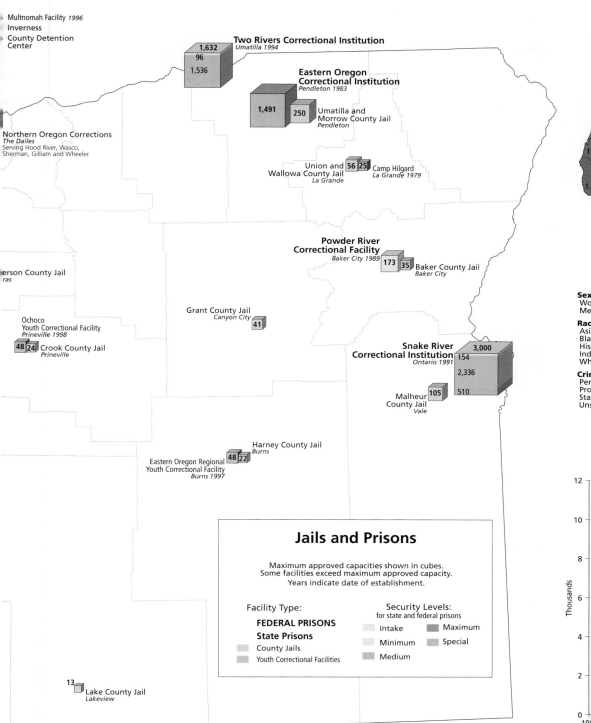

Multnomah Facility *1996*
Inverness
County Detention
Center

Two Rivers Correctional Institution
Umatilla 1994
1,632
96
1,536

Eastern Oregon Correctional Institution
Pendleton 1983
1,491 250 Umatilla and Morrow County Jail
Pendleton

Northern Oregon Corrections
The Dalles
Serving Hood River, Wasco, Sherman, Gilliam and Wheeler

Union and Wallowa County Jail 56 25 Camp Hilgard
La Grande *La Grande 1979*

Powder River Correctional Facility
Baker City 1989 173 35 Baker County Jail
Baker City

erson County Jail
ras

Grant County Jail
Canyon City 41

Ochoco Youth Correctional Facility
Prineville 1998 48 24 Crook County Jail
Prineville

Snake River Correctional Institution
Ontario 1991 3,000
154
2,336
Malheur 105 510
County Jail
Vale

Harney County Jail
Burns 48 22
Eastern Oregon Regional Youth Correctional Facility
Burns 1997

13 Lake County Jail
Lakeview

Jails and Prisons

Maximum approved capacities shown in cubes.
Some facilities exceed maximum approved capacity.
Years indicate date of establishment.

Facility Type:

FEDERAL PRISONS
State Prisons
County Jails
Youth Correctional Facilities

Security Levels:
for state and federal prisons

Intake   Maximum
Minimum Special
Medium

Prison Admissions by County of Origin
1998–2000 Annual Average
Rate per 1,000 Population

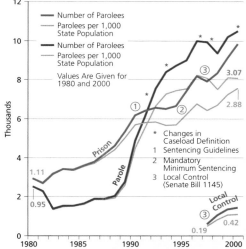

1.27 0.9
0.79 1.99 0.66 1.59 0.28
0.91 1.32 0.48 0.37
0.76 0.52 0.84 1.29
0.53 0.63 1.23
1.07 1.5 0.93 0.38
0.47 1.6 0.98
1.18 1.07 2.0
1.62 1.25 0.72
1.52 1.76 0.90 1.18 1.01

▢ 0.25–0.49	▢ 0.75–0.99	▣ 1.25–1.49	▣ 1.75–1.99
▢ 0.50–0.74	▢ 1–1.24	▣ 1.50–1.74	■ 2.0 and Above

Offender Characteristics
as of 1/1/00

	Probation	Local Control	Prison	Parole	Total	Percentage of Total
Sex						
Women	4,778	220	536	1,376	6,910	17%
Men	13,868	1,123	8,891	10,097	33,979	83%
Race						
Asian	175	14	103	87	379	1%
Black	1,165	123	1,087	1,370	3,745	9%
Hispanic	751	72	962	698	2,483	6%
Indian	247	20	225	202	694	2%
White	16,308	1,114	7,050	9,116	33,588	82%
Crime Type						
Person	3,691	220	7,003	4,238	15,152	37%
Property	5,420	417	1,286	2,991	10,114	25%
Statute	9,535	655	1,094	4,029	15,313	38%
Unspecified	—	51	44	215	310	<1%
	18,646	1,343	9,427	11,473	40,889	

Prison and Community Corrections Populations

Number of Parolees
Parolees per 1,000 State Population
Number of Parolees
Parolees per 1,000 State Population
Values Are Given for 1980 and 2000

* Changes in Caseload Definition
1 Sentencing Guidelines
2 Mandatory Minimum Sentencing
3 Local Control (Senate Bill 1145)

Thousands

1.11
0.95
3.07
2.88
0.19 0.42

Prison
Parole
Local Control

1980 1985 1990 1995 2000

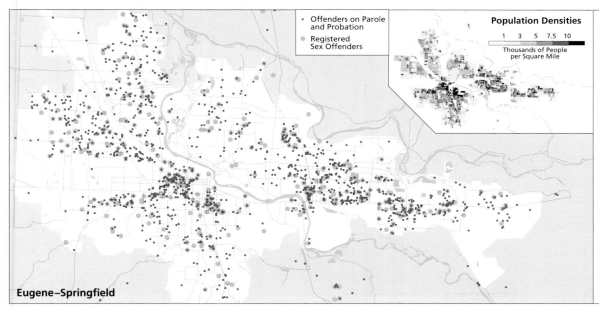

Offenders on Parole and Probation
Registered Sex Offenders

Population Densities
1 3 5 7.5 10
Thousands of People per Square Mile

Eugene–Springfield

Community Supervision

Roughly 31,000 supervised criminal offenders (parolees and offenders on probation) were living in Oregon communities in 2000. This is nearly 1 percent of overall population in the state and more than three times the number of people incarcerated. The map at left shows the distribution of this population in Eugene–Springfield, the second largest urban area in the state. (The largest, Portland, is too big to show at a useful scale in the space available.) Eugene–Springfield had a total population of about 190,000 in 2000, including about 2,900 supervised criminal offenders. They lived in virtually every residential neighborhood. There are a few exceptions: not many offenders live in the high-density dormitory area and faculty housing districts around the University of Oregon (see page 218–219 for a detailed map of Eugene–Springfield), and some newer high-density subdivisions have similarly low rates. In general, however, concentrations of offenders closely parallel the overall population densities shown in the small inset map.

Health Care

The past century has seen dramatic improvements in health and longevity, in Oregon as elsewhere. Maternal and infant death rates have dropped sharply; more people are living longer. In 1920, people under 65 years old accounted for about 67 percent of all Oregon deaths; by 1998 they represented only 23 percent. In this period the median age at death rose from 53 to 78 years. Causes of death reflect differences in population characteristics between Oregon and the U.S.; environmental influences may also be a factor. Tobacco-related deaths are low in strongly Mormon Malheur County, for example, while deaths of all kinds are low in university-dominated Benton County.

About 11,000 people were living in Oregon nursing homes in 2000, filling to roughly 80 percent of capacity the state's 13,600 available nursing home beds. Acute care hospitals had a total licensed capacity of about 8,500 beds, but only about 5,200 of these were "staffed beds," or beds in regular use. The average census of hospital inpatients was lower still, at about 3,500, or one per thousand Oregon residents. Oregon's hospitals are heavily concentrated in Portland, which is also the site of the state's only medical school. Only four counties lack hospitals, but small outlying hospitals tend to have very low utilization. The trend is toward consolidation of hospital organizations; the largest are the Providence, Adventist, Legacy, Samaritan and Sacred Heart systems. Psychiatric hospitals are fewer and smaller than a generation ago, a result of outpatient treatment with drugs. There were about 35,000 physicians, dentists and registered nurses in Oregon in 1999—about 1 percent of the state's total population.

Licensed Hospital Beds

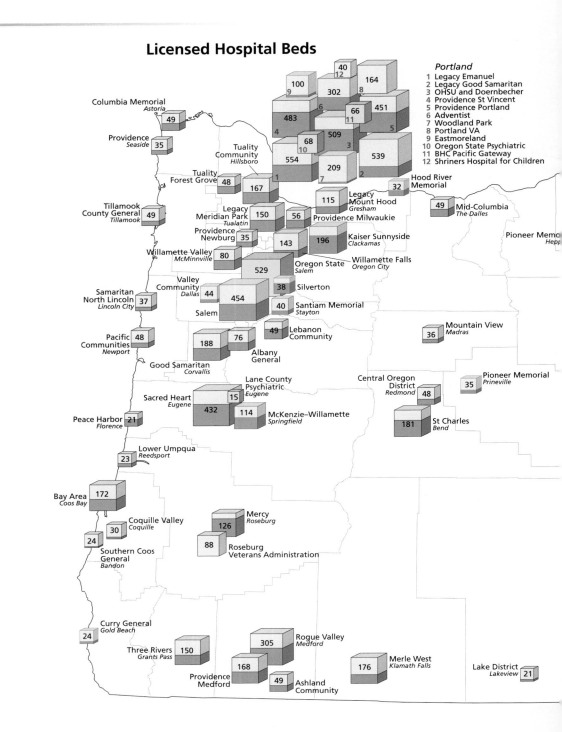

Portland
1 Legacy Emanuel
2 Legacy Good Samaritan
3 OHSU and Doernbecher
4 Providence St Vincent
5 Providence Portland
6 Adventist
7 Woodland Park
8 Portland VA
9 Eastmoreland
10 Oregon State Psychiatric
11 BHC Pacific Gateway
12 Shriners Hospital for Children

Percentage of Population Without Health Care Coverage

- Below 10%
- 10–12.4%
- 12.5–14.9%
- 15–17.4%
- 17.5–19.9%
- 20% and above

Alaska
Hawaii

Percentage of Uninsured Children by Region

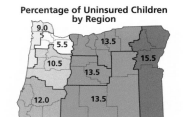

Immunization of Two-Year-Olds

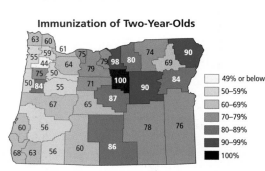

- 49% or below
- 50–59%
- 60–69%
- 70–79%
- 80–89%
- 90–99%
- 100%

Maternal Deaths

Rate per 100,000 Live Births

— Oregon Rate
— U.S. Rate

Infant and Fetal Deaths

Rate per 1,000 Live Births

Infant Deaths
— Oregon Rate
— U.S. Rate
Fetal Deaths
— Oregon Rate
— U.S. Rate

Infant Deaths

Fetal Deaths

* No Data

Twenty Leading Causes of Death, 1994, 1995, 1997, Averaged
Listed in Order by Number of Deaths to Oregon Residents

Cause of Death	Age-Adjusted Rates Oregon	Age-Adjusted Rates U.S.	Percent Difference	State Rank
1. Diseases of the Heart	105.9	136.2	-22.2	45
2. Malignant Neoplasms	124.2	129.0	-3.6	33
3. Cerebrovascular Disease	27.4	24.7	10.9	12
4. Chronic Obstructive Pulmonary Disease	23.3	20.9	12.0	18
5. Unintended Injuries	42.1	37.9	12.3	20
6. Pneumonia and Influenza	10.1	12.9	-21.9	46
7. Diabetes Mellitus	12.0	13.3	-9.6	32
8. Alzheimer's Disease	6.1	4.0	53.2	5
9. Suicide	14.9	11.0	35.5	10
10. Other Diseases of the Arteries	5.4	5.3	1.9	24
11. Alcoholism and Allied Conditions	7.6	5.8	29.7	11
12. AIDS	6.7	12.2	-48.3	29
13. Arteriosclerosis	2.9	2.2	27.9	11
14. Hypertension, with or without Renal Disease	2.3	2.2	4.3	16
15. Parkinsonism	2.4	1.6	47.9	5
16. Homicide and Legal Intervention	5.2	9.3	-44.2	35
17. Congenital Anomalies	4.3	4.3	0.4	27
18. Nephritis and Nephrosis	2.5	4.4	-41.9	46
19. Septicemia	2.1	4.0	-47.3	46
20. Hernia and Intestinal Obstruction	0.9	0.9	0	34

Rates are adjusted to the U.S. standard million population and are per 100,000.

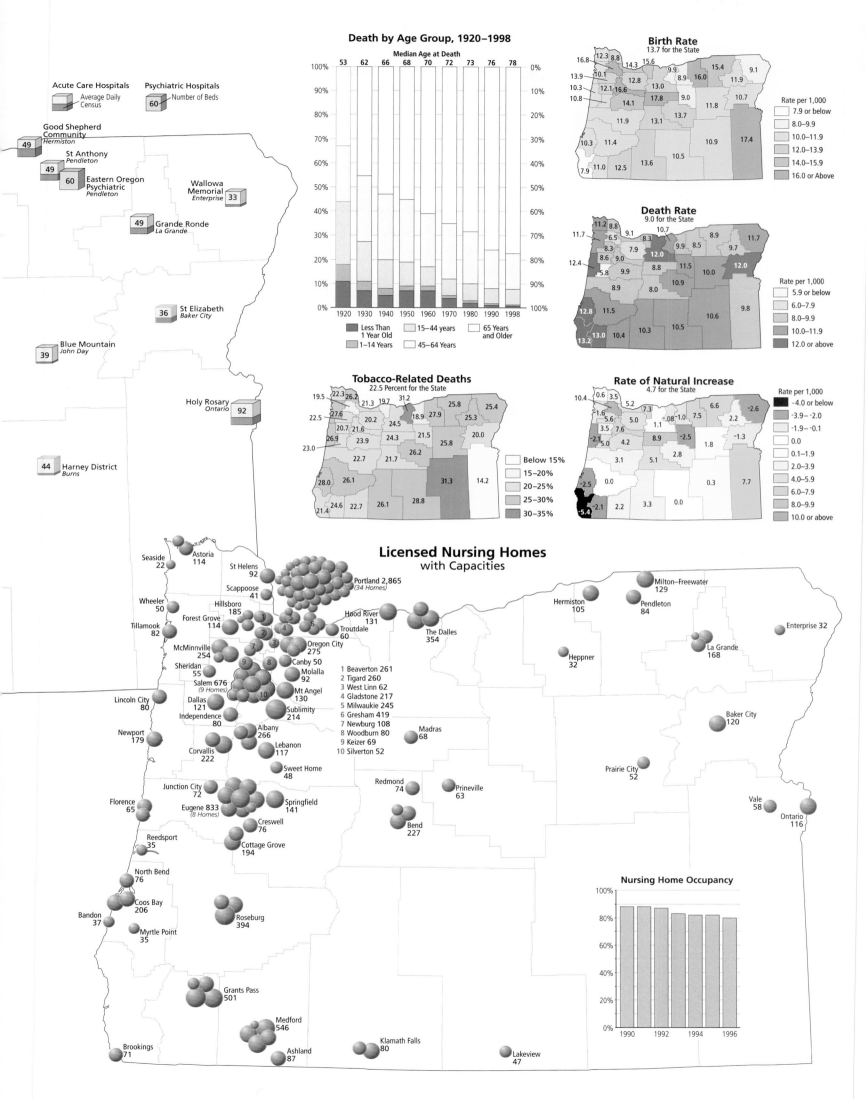

Death by Age Group, 1920–1998

Median Age at Death: 53 62 66 68 70 72 73 76 78

Legend:
- Less Than 1 Year Old
- 1–14 Years
- 15–44 years
- 45–64 Years
- 65 Years and Older

Years: 1920 1930 1940 1950 1960 1970 1980 1990 1998

Birth Rate
13.7 for the State

Rate per 1,000
- 7.9 or below
- 8.0–9.9
- 10.0–11.9
- 12.0–13.9
- 14.0–15.9
- 16.0 or Above

Death Rate
9.0 for the State

Rate per 1,000
- 5.9 or below
- 6.0–7.9
- 8.0–9.9
- 10.0–11.9
- 12.0 or above

Tobacco-Related Deaths
22.5 Percent for the State

- Below 15%
- 15–20%
- 20–25%
- 25–30%
- 30–35%

Rate of Natural Increase
4.7 for the State

Rate per 1,000
- -4.0 or below
- -3.9 – -2.0
- -1.9 – -0.1
- 0.0
- 0.1–1.9
- 2.0–3.9
- 4.0–5.9
- 6.0–7.9
- 8.0–9.9
- 10.0 or above

Acute Care Hospitals
Average Daily Census

Psychiatric Hospitals
Number of Beds — 60

- Good Shepherd Community, *Hermiston* — 49
- St Anthony, *Pendleton* — 49
- Eastern Oregon Psychiatric, *Pendleton* — 60
- Wallowa Memorial, *Enterprise* — 33
- Grande Ronde, *La Grande* — 49
- St Elizabeth, *Baker City* — 36
- Blue Mountain, *John Day* — 39
- Holy Rosary, *Ontario* — 92
- Harney District, *Burns* — 44

Licensed Nursing Homes
with Capacities

- Seaside 22
- Astoria 114
- St Helens 92
- Scappoose 41
- Wheeler 50
- Hillsboro 185
- Forest Grove 114
- Tillamook 82
- McMinnville 254
- Sheridan 55
- Lincoln City 80
- Dallas 121
- Independence 80
- Newport 179
- Corvallis 222
- Junction City 72
- Florence 65
- Eugene 833 (8 Homes)
- Reedsport 35
- North Bend 76
- Coos Bay 206
- Bandon 37
- Myrtle Point 35
- Salem 676 (9 Homes)
- Canby 50
- Molalla 92
- Mt Angel 130
- Sublimity 214
- Albany 266
- Lebanon 117
- Sweet Home 48
- Creswell 76
- Springfield 141
- Cottage Grove 194
- Roseburg 394
- Grants Pass 501
- Medford 546
- Ashland 87
- Brookings 71
- Klamath Falls 80
- Lakeview 47
- Portland 2,865 (34 Homes)
- Hood River 131
- Troutdale 60
- The Dalles 354
- Oregon City 275
- Hermiston 105
- Heppner 32
- Milton–Freewater 129
- Pendleton 84
- La Grande 168
- Enterprise 32
- Baker City 120
- Prairie City 52
- Madras 68
- Redmond 74
- Prineville 63
- Bend 227
- Vale 58
- Ontario 116

1 Beaverton 261
2 Tigard 260
3 West Linn 62
4 Gladstone 217
5 Milwaukie 245
6 Gresham 419
7 Newburg 108
8 Woodburn 80
9 Keizer 69
10 Silverton 52

Nursing Home Occupancy
1990 1992 1994 1996

Newspapers and Broadcasting

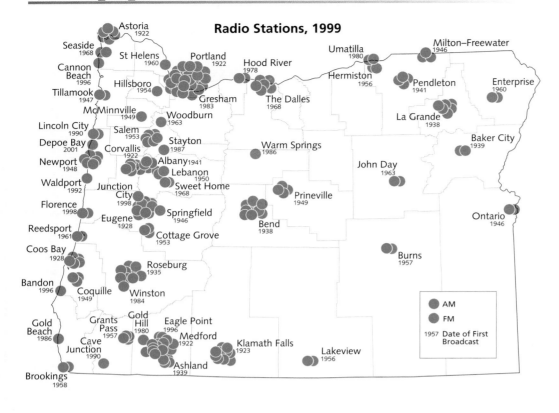

Radio Stations, 1999

Astoria 1922
Seaside 1968
St Helens 1960
Cannon Beach 1996
Tillamook 1947
Hillsboro 1954
Portland 1922
Hood River 1978
Umatilla 1980
Hermiston 1956
Milton–Freewater 1946
Pendleton 1941
Enterprise 1960
McMinnville 1949
Gresham 1983
The Dalles 1968
La Grande 1938
Lincoln City 1990
Woodburn 1963
Salem 1953
Stayton 1987
Baker City 1939
Depoe Bay 2001
Corvallis 1922
Warm Springs 1986
Newport 1948
Albany 1941
Lebanon 1950
John Day 1963
Waldport 1992
Junction City 1998
Sweet Home 1968
Florence 1998
Prineville 1949
Springfield 1946
Eugene 1928
Bend 1938
Ontario 1946
Reedsport 1961
Cottage Grove 1953
Coos Bay 1928
Roseburg 1935
Burns 1957
Bandon 1996
Coquille 1949
Winston 1984
Gold Beach 1986
Grants Pass 1957
Gold Hill 1980
Eagle Point 1996
Medford 1922
Klamath Falls 1923
Lakeview 1956
Cave Junction 1990
Ashland 1939
Brookings 1958

AM
FM
1957 Date of First Broadcast

Radio Station Formats, 1999

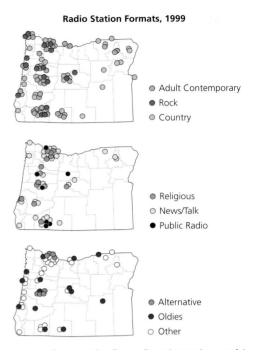

- Adult Contemporary
- Rock
- Country

- Religious
- News/Talk
- Public Radio

- Alternative
- Oldies
- Other

Formats change continually as radio stations seek successful marketing strategies. These maps show the distribution of formats at a single point in 1999.

Oregon has mirrored the national development and progression of media information and entertainment—from newspapers, to radio and television broadcast stations, to cable TV, to satellite reception and Internet news sources. While this growth in Oregon covers a shorter period than in many states, it still dates back to 1846, beginning with the *Oregon Spectator* newspaper in Oregon City. The *Oregonian* was started in Portland in 1850 and remains today the state's longest-lived media operation. Newspapers, either dailies or weeklies, began publishing in many other cities and towns in Oregon before 1900. Oregon now has 19 daily newspapers and 72 weekly or multi-weekly paid circulation newspapers—nearly every community has a newspaper of some type. The Willamette Valley's population supports the heaviest newspaper circulation in the state, led by the *Oregonian's* weekday readership of nearly 350,000. Most of the daily newspapers in the state are owned by national companies; this includes the *Oregonian* (Newhouse), the Salem *Statesman Journal* (Gannett), the Medford *Mail Tribune* (Ottaway) and the Coos Bay *World* (Pulitzer). A majority of the weekly or multi-weekly papers in the state are under in-state ownership. Although generally growing in step with the state's steadily advancing population, major daily newspapers in Oregon are being challenged by increasingly diverse media options. These options—now including cable TV, the World Wide Web and satellite-connected communications services—are cutting into large daily newspaper circulation figures, especially in less densely populated areas of Eastern Oregon. In addition to paid circulation newspapers, there are many free distribution papers in Oregon. Two of the largest and most significant are *Willamette Week* in Portland and *Eugene Weekly* in Eugene.

As it did elsewhere in the U.S., the broadcasting era in Oregon began in the 1920s with the start-up of a small number of standard AM radio stations. The most vigorous period of expansion in Oregon broadcasting occurred in the decades after World War II, first with more AM radio stations, then with the advent of television and later with the growth of FM radio.

Today Oregon has 194 AM and FM radio stations. The total number of small market radio stations greatly exceeds the number of small market newspapers, because nearly all small market radio station operations include both AM and FM outlets. The great expansion of FM stations in the U.S. took place in the 1960s and 1970s, when FM radio began broadcasting in stereo.

Oregon's first television station, KPTV in Portland, started broadcasting in 1952—initially as the nation's first UHF (ultra high frequency) station, then as channel 12, its current location, on the VHF (very high frequency) broadcast spectrum. Predating KPTV by four years, the nation's first two CATV (community antenna television) or cable systems began operating in Oregon and in Pennsylvania in 1948. Oregon's was in Astoria, where a receiving antenna was erected at an elevated location to pull in television signals from Seattle and later from Portland. The original purpose of such cable systems was to bring television programming from distant stations into small communities, especially those where hills or mountains would obstruct

Television Stations and Market Areas, 1999

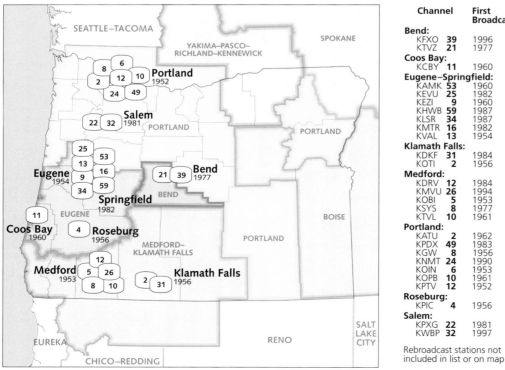

SEATTLE–TACOMA
YAKIMA–PASCO–RICHLAND–KENNEWICK
SPOKANE
Portland 1952
8 6
2 12 10
24 49
Salem 1981
22 32
PORTLAND
PORTLAND
Eugene 1954
25 53
13 16
9 59
34
Bend 1977
21 39
Springfield 1982
BEND
BOISE
Coos Bay 1960
11
EUGENE
Roseburg 1956
4
MEDFORD–KLAMATH FALLS
PORTLAND
Medford 1953
12
5 26
8 10
Klamath Falls 1956
2 31
EUREKA
SALT LAKE CITY
RENO
CHICO–REDDING

	Channel	First Broadcast
Bend:		
KFXO	39	1996
KTVZ	21	1977
Coos Bay:		
KCBY	11	1960
Eugene–Springfield:		
KAMK	53	1960
KEVU	25	1982
KEZI	9	1960
KHWB	59	1987
KLSR	34	1987
KMTR	16	1982
KVAL	13	1954
Klamath Falls:		
KDKF	31	1984
KOTI	2	1956
Medford:		
KDRV	12	1984
KMVU	26	1994
KOBI	5	1953
KSYS	8	1977
KTVL	10	1961
Portland:		
KATU	2	1962
KPDX	49	1983
KGW	8	1956
KNMT	24	1990
KOIN	6	1953
KOPB	10	1961
KPTV	12	1952
Roseburg:		
KPIC	4	1956
Salem:		
KPXG	22	1981
KWBP	32	1997

Rebroadcast stations not included in list or on map.

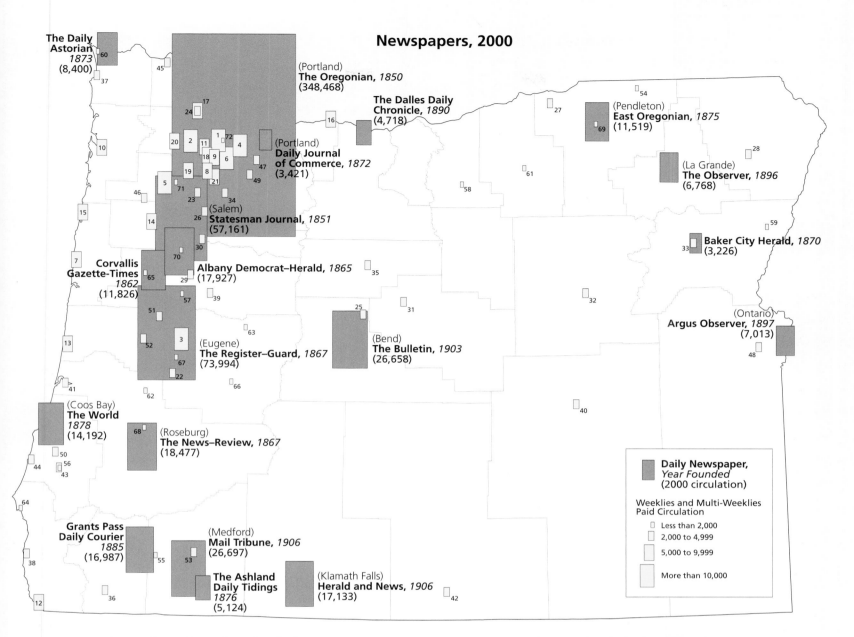

Newspapers, 2000

The Daily Astorian *1873* (8,400)

(Portland) **The Oregonian**, *1850* (348,468)

The Dalles Daily Chronicle, *1890* (4,718)

(Portland) **Daily Journal of Commerce**, *1872* (3,421)

(Salem) **Statesman Journal**, *1851* (57,161)

(Pendleton) **East Oregonian**, *1875* (11,519)

(La Grande) **The Observer**, *1896* (6,768)

Baker City Herald, *1870* (3,226)

Corvallis Gazette-Times *1862* (11,826)

Albany Democrat–Herald, *1865* (17,927)

(Eugene) **The Register–Guard**, *1867* (73,994)

(Bend) **The Bulletin**, *1903* (26,658)

(Ontario) **Argus Observer**, *1897* (7,013)

(Coos Bay) **The World** *1878* (14,192)

(Roseburg) **The News–Review**, *1867* (18,477)

Grants Pass Daily Courier *1885* (16,987)

(Medford) **Mail Tribune**, *1906* (26,697)

The Ashland Daily Tidings *1876* (5,124)

(Klamath Falls) **Herald and News**, *1906* (17,133)

Daily Newspaper, *Year Founded* (2000 circulation)

Weeklies and Multi-Weeklies Paid Circulation
- Less than 2,000
- 2,000 to 4,999
- 5,000 to 9,999
- More than 10,000

Oregonian Daily and Sunday Circulation, 1981–2000

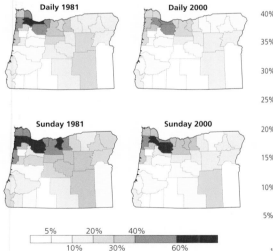

Daily 1981 — Daily 2000

Sunday 1981 — Sunday 2000

Sunday / Daily

Percent of Households Receiving Daily and Sunday Oregonian, 1981–2000

1981 1985 1990 1995 2000

40% 35% 30% 25% 20% 15% 10% 5%

5% 20% 40% / 10% 30% 60%

Weeklies and Multi-Weeklies, 1999

1 Portland Observer
2 Hillsboro Argus
3 Springfield News
4 Gresham Outlook
5 (McMinnville) News–Register
6 Clackamas Review
7 (Newport) News–Times
8 Wilsonville Spokesman
9 Lake Oswego Review
10 (Tillamook) Headlight–Herald
11 Beaverton Valley Times
12 (Brookings) Curry Coastal Pilot
13 (Florence) The Siuslaw News
14 (Monmouth) The Polk County Itemizer–Observer
15 (Lincoln City) The News Guard
16 Hood River News
17 (St. Helens) The Chronicle and Sentinel Mist
18 Tigard Tualatin Times
19 (Newberg) The Graphic
20 Forest Grove News Times
21 The Canby Herald/ Wilsonville Spokesman
22 Cottage Grove Sentinel
23 Woodburn Independent
24 (St. Helens) The South County Spotlight

25 The Redmond Spokesman
26 Silverton Appeal Tribune/ Mt. Angel News
27 The Hermiston Herald
28 (Enterprise) Wallowa County Chieftain
29 Lebanon Express
30 Stayton Mail
31 (Prineville) Central Oregonian
32 (John Day) The Blue Mountain Eagle
33 (Baker City) Record–Courier
34 Molalla Pioneer
35 The Madras Pioneer
36 (Cave Junction) Illinois Valley News
37 Seaside Signal
38 (Gold Beach) Curry County Reporter
39 (Sweet Home) The New Era
40 Burns Times–Herald
41 Reedsport Courier
42 (Lakeview) Lake County Examiner
43 (Myrtle Point) Umpqua Free Press
44 Bandon Western World
45 Clatskanie Chief
46 (Sheridan) The Sun
47 Sandy Post
48 (Vale) Malheur Enterprise

49 (Estacada) Clackamas County News
50 Coquille Valley Sentinel
51 (Junction City) Tri-County News
52 (Veneta) West Lane News
53 (Eagle Point) Upper Rogue Independent
54 (Milton–Freewater) Valley Times
55 Rogue River Press
56 Myrtle Point Herald
57 (Brownsville) The Times
58 (Condon) The Times-Journal
59 (Halfway) Hells Canyon Journal
60 (Astoria) The Columbia Press
61 The Heppner Gazette Times
62 Drain Enterprise
63 (Blue River) McKenzie River Reflections
64 Port Orford News
65 Benton Bulletin
66 (Oakridge) Dead Mountain Echo
67 Creswell Chronicle
68 (Sutherlin) The Sun Tribune
69 The Pendleton Record
70 Jefferson Review
71 Dayton Tribune
72 (Portland) Multnomah Village Post

reception. Now cable systems also function in major markets and provide customers not only with clear local TV signals but also with a variety of national cable networks, distant stations and other communication services. Oregon has 27 VHF and UHF television stations that originate programming. While the map of Oregon television stations identifies no stations in Eastern Oregon, local cable systems

and dozens of signal translators provide widespread coverage of Eastern Oregon with television signals from cities such as Portland, Boise, Spokane and the Tri-Cities, as well as national TV programming on local cable systems. The Oregon Public Broadcasting network (OPB) is a prime example of using television signal translators and rebroadcast stations. OPB programming originates in

Portland, where the home station is KOPB-TV. OPB airs its program schedule on four rebroadcast stations (in Corvallis, Eugene, Bend and La Grande), on nearly 40 signal translators scattered across the entire state and now also on high-definition digital TV stations in Portland and Corvallis.

The Economy

Resource Organization, Transformation and Use

Employment and Labor Force

Taxation and Revenue

Manufacturing

Land Use and Ownership

Agriculture

Energy

Transportation

Recreation

Economic Sectors

Employment by Sector, 1997

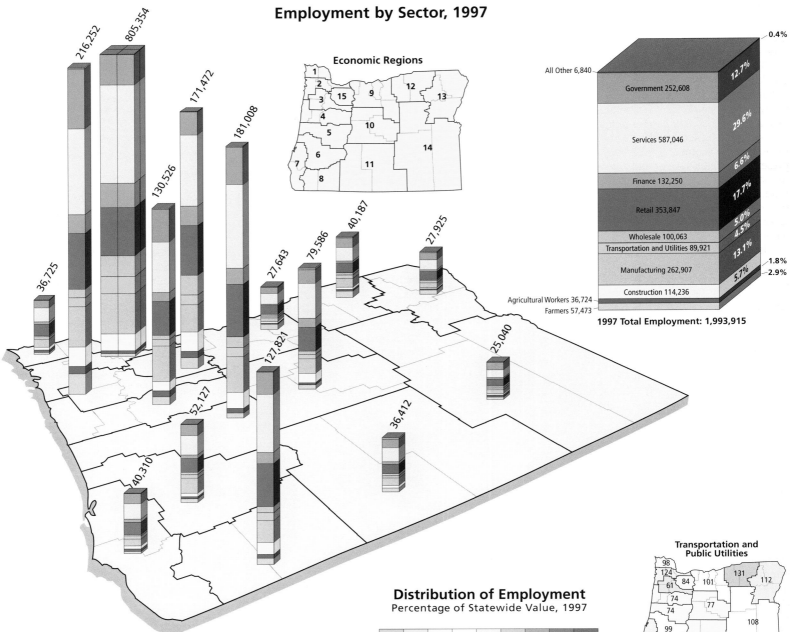

Economic Regions

All Other 6,840

Government 252,608	12.7%
Services 587,046	29.6%
Finance 132,250	6.6%
Retail 353,847	17.7%
Wholesale 100,063	5.0%
Transportation and Utilities 89,921	4.5%
Manufacturing 262,907	13.1%
Construction 114,236	5.7%

0.4%

1.8%
2.9%

Agricultural Workers 36,724
Farmers 57,473

1997 Total Employment: 1,993,915

Distribution of Employment
Percentage of Statewide Value, 1997

50 70 90 110 130 150 170 190

Transportation and Public Utilities

Services

Finance, Insurance and Real Estate

Construction

Retail Trade

Wholesale Trade

Agriculture Services, Forestry and Fishing

Manufacturing

Government

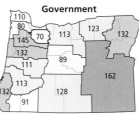

Farm Employment

Oregon's bounty of natural resources helped lure early settlers to the territory, as rich agricultural lands, vast forests and abundant fish and wildlife promised prosperity to anyone who would take advantage of them. More recently, the Great Depression and World War II spurred large-scale development of the region's resources. Large hydropower projects on the Columbia River created jobs, and the energy they produced underwrote the development of the aluminum, pulp-and-paper and other heavy industries. Shipping facilities expanded to transport timber, grain and other products derived from Oregon's natural resources to the rest of the world. Through the first half of the twentieth century, natural resources drove most of Oregon's economic activity.

During the post-war years, further development of the state's natural resources contributed to America's booming economy. The hydropower, timber and irrigated-agriculture industries expanded rapidly, as did Oregon's cities. In the early 1980s, however, Oregon's reliance on natural resources cost it dearly. A nationwide recession reduced demand for housing, and orders for lumber dropped. The state lost population as Oregonians moved elsewhere to find jobs. Oregon needed to move beyond the extractive industries and toward diversifying its economic base.

Oregon's economy did diversify, and quickly. Its economic reaction to drastic cuts in harvests from federally owned timberlands in the 1990s was a complete turnaround from its reaction to reduced timber demand in the 1980s. In response to public demand for increased environmental protection, such as preserving habitat for endangered species, timber harvests on federal lands declined dramatically between 1988 and 1998—by 91 percent on federal lands and 59 percent on all lands. But instead of slowing as logging harvests were reduced, the state's economy accelerated, easily outpacing the nation's economy. Total employment increased by 33 percent; per capita income, in real dollars (inflation-adjusted), grew by 24 percent, and real gross state product added 68 percent. Oregon's economy no longer depended on converting forests into commodities.

Employment grew in many industries during the 1990s. In manufacturing, the bulk of the growth came from industrial machinery and equipment. Wholesale and retail trade added about 100,000 jobs, roughly one-fifth of all new jobs during the 1990s. Services grew even more, with most growth in the business- and health-services industries. Employment in finance, insurance and real estate also grew, as did employment in government, but only at the local level—state and federal employment declined.

While much of Oregon's economy no longer depends on extracting wealth from its lands, the economy remains tied to the landscape. Oregon's quality of life is an important component of the state's economic development. More than 40 percent of incoming residents, for example, cite the state's quality of life as a major reason for moving to Oregon. Easy access to clean rivers, mountaintop trails and bucolic landscapes are all part of Oregon's lure. The natural landscape has been shaped by the efforts of state policy makers; Oregon's land use planning system has limited urban development in agricultural and forest lands and provides protective measures for waterways. Income in Oregon is lower than the nationwide average, in part because state residents have traded higher income elsewhere for a higher quality of life in Oregon. By one estimate, Oregonians, on average, would need a 14 percent increase in annual pay to leave the state.

Growth has been strong for the state as a whole, but prosperity has not spread itself evenly across geographic regions, industries or income groups. Prosperity and growth have focused on Oregon's metropolitan areas, especially in the Willamette Valley, while many rural areas have grown only slowly. Unemployment in rural counties is higher, and average incomes are lower. Many rural counties rely on the timber industry, which continues to decline, and agriculture, which faces oversupply and reduced prices for commodities worldwide.

At the start of the new century, Oregon's economy is diverse. The state is home to jobs in those industries traditionally associated with Oregon, such as timber and agriculture, and also supports jobs in growing industries, such as computer parts manufacturing, tourism and health-related industries. Analysts expect Oregon's economy to continue the current expansion, but no one expects the expansion to benefit evenly all the state's geographic regions.

Employment

Slightly fewer than two million people were employed in Oregon in 1997. Almost half of these employees worked in the greater Portland area. More than 800,000 worked in Multnomah, Washington or Tillamook Counties. An additional 171,000 worked in neighboring Clackamas County. The next highest concentration of employment was in the region immediately to the south of the greater Portland area. More than 216,000 people worked in Marion, Polk and Yamhill Counties. Other large concentrations of employment include Benton, Linn and Lincoln Counties, with more than 130,000 employees; Lane County, with more than 181,000 employees; and Jackson and Josephine Counties, with almost 128,000 employees. Employment beyond those areas is much sparser, as the map on the facing page shows.

Of all industries, the services industry employs the most people in Oregon. According to 1997 U.S. Bureau of Economic Analysis data, 29.4 percent of all Oregon jobs were in the services industry. Retail trade provided almost 18 percent of all jobs. Manufacturing was the third-largest employer, with slightly more than 13 percent, followed closely by government, with less than 13 percent. These four industry groups accounted for almost three-quarters of Oregon's total full- and part-time employment in 1997.

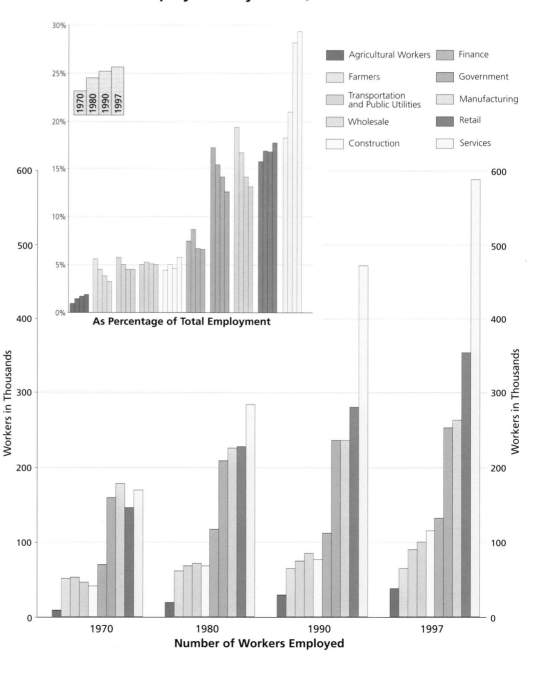

Employment by Sector, 1970–1997

As Percentage of Total Employment

Workers in Thousands

Number of Workers Employed

Labor

Oregon's labor force tripled between 1940 and 1990, a pace of growth much faster than that of most other states in the nation. This growth was due to a combination of factors, including strength in the lumber and wood products industry during the housing boom of the 1960s and 1970s. A key element of the state's recent growth was expansion of the high technology industry during the 1990s. Oregon's labor force is now about 1.8 million, or slightly more than half of the state's 3.4 million residents. Most of those who are not in the labor force are younger than 16 years old, 65 years old or older or voluntarily absent from the labor force.

Oregon's labor force has grown somewhat faster than its population, due mostly to the trend of women participating more fully in the paid labor force. The portion of the paid labor force composed of women grew from 22 percent in 1940 to nearly half (45 percent) in 1990. This trend is evident at the national as well as the state level, and is associated with an increase in the purchase of restaurant meals, prepared groceries and child care services.

The state's annual average unemployment rate reached 11.5 percent in 1982 as the national recession hit Oregon's manufacturing industries. Since then, unemployment has been more moderate. The national recession in the early 1990s caused the state's unemployment rate to rise to 7.5 percent in 1992. The rate fell from 5.7 percent in 1999 to 4.9 percent in 2000.

Oregon's monthly unemployment rates are usually at their highest during the first few months of the year. The state's largest seasonal industries and activities—agriculture, lumber and wood products and much of tourism—contract to their lowest levels of employment during these months. The retail industry hires many seasonal holiday workers in the fall.

Workers laid off in late December or early January add to the seasonally unemployed.

Unemployment rates vary considerably by county. All counties' unemployment rates were higher during the national recession of the early 1980s than afterwards. A few rural counties had unemployment rates higher than 15 percent during this period. Harney County's unemployment rate surpassed 20 percent in 1980 and 1981. Benton County, along with Multnomah County and its neighboring counties, have had some of the state's lowest unemployment rates.

Some state regions have a relatively high concentration of certain occupations. The accompanying maps indicate the concentration of eight major occupational categories by region. The Multnomah, Washington and Tillamook Counties region in northwestern Oregon, which accounts for the bulk of employment in Portland, has a relatively high

Average Annual Unemployment Rate, 1980–2000

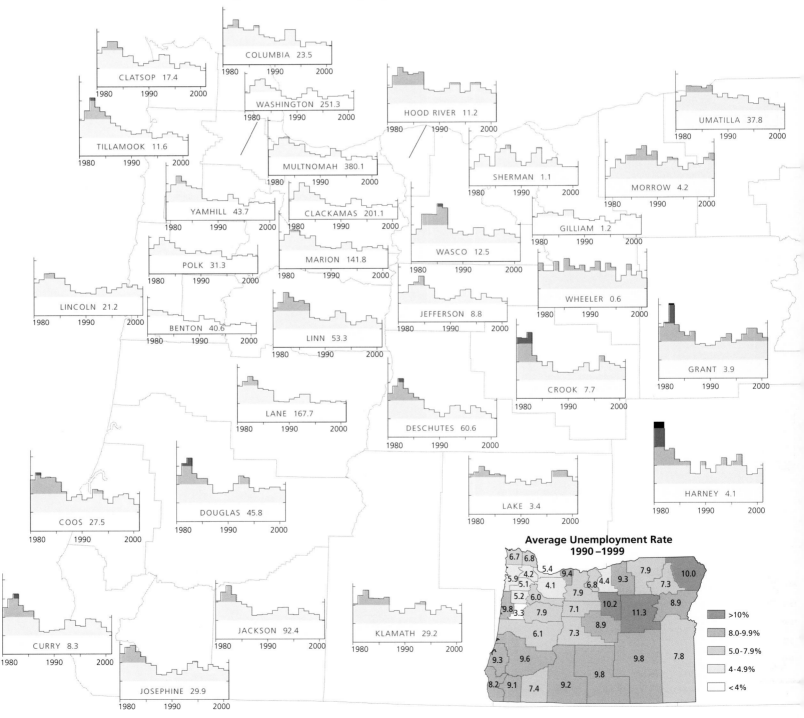

Average Unemployment Rate 1990–1999

>10%
8.0-9.9%
5.0-7.9%
4-4.9%
<4%

66

concentration of managers and administrators, professional and technical workers and clerical and administrative support workers. Benton, Linn and Lincoln Counties in west–central Oregon have, as a region, a relatively high concentration of student and leased workers and of professional and technical workers. Professional and technical workers form a large portion of the work force in many regions: northeastern Oregon, home of Eastern Oregon University; Lane County in Western Oregon, home of the University of Oregon; Benton County, home of Oregon State University; and Marion, Polk and Yamhill Counties in northwestern Oregon, near the state capital. Two regions with a high concentration of workers in the agriculture, forestry and fishing occupational group (but principally agriculture and forestry workers) are Grant, Harney and Malheur Counties in southeastern Oregon and Hood River, Wasco, Sherman, Gilliam and Wheeler Counties in north–central Oregon.

Composition of the Labor Force, 1998

Production, Construction, Operators and Maintenance
State 25.6%

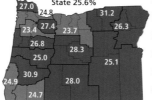

State Total: 406,085

Motor Vehicle Operators — 49,493
Hand Workers and Assemblers — 40,504
Machine Mechanics and Repairers — 19,159
Mobile Equip. Mech. and Repairers — 18,695
Material Moving Equip. Operators — 15,659
Carpentry and Related Workers — 14,456

Professional and Technical
State 20.5%

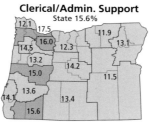

State Total: 325,217

Primary and Secondary Teachers — 57,544
Health Care Specialists — 31,104
Computer Specialists — 20,703
Social Workers and Counselors — 20,324
Engineers — 19,358
Financial Specialists — 17,480

Clerical/Admin. Support
State 15.6%

State Total: 247,366

Gen. Office Clerks — 42,811
Bookkeeping and Acctg. Clerks — 27,707
Secretaries — 26,716
Receptionists/Info. Clerks — 16,896
Banking, Finance and Credit Wkrs. — 16,745
Mail and Message Distribution Workers — 7,194

Service Occupations
State 15.2%

State Total: 242,088

Food Prep and Service Wkrs. — 118,115
Building Service and Cleaning Wkrs. — 34,714
Health Service Occupations — 27,373
Fire and Police Protection Wkrs. — 13,586
Child Care Wkrs. — 5,581
Personal and Home Care Aides — 4,709

Sales Related Occupations
State 11.7%

State Total: 185,211

Retail Sales — 55,014
Cashiers — 29,873
Sales Supervisors — 23,668
Non-technical Sales Reps — 14,723
Sales Floor Stock Clerks — 11,027
Real Estate Agents — 7,608

Agriculture, Forestry, Fishing Workers
State 3.5%

State Total: 55,834

Farmworkers — 16,132
Gardeners and Groundskeepers — 10,180
Nursery Workers — 6,620
Forest and Conservation Workers — 5,294
Agricultural Graders and Sorters — 3,289
Farm Equipment Operators — 1,520

Managers and Administrators
State 5.4%

State Total: 86,354

General Managers/ Top Executives — 26,950
Financial Mgrs. — 7,413
Property and Estate Managers — 6,398
Marketing/Public Relations Mgrs. — 6,070
Education Administrators — 4,389
Food Service and Lodging Mgrs. — 4,234

Student and Leased Workers
State 2.5%

State Total: 40,162

Leased Workers — 24,412
Student Workers — 15,221
Sheltered Workshop Workers — 529

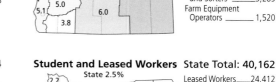

0   2   4   6   8   10   15   20   25   30

Percent of Total Labor Force

WALLOWA 3.5
1980   1990   2000

UNION 12.6
1980   1990   2000

BAKER 7.3
1980   1990   2000

MALHEUR 14.9
1980   1990   2000

Oregon and U.S. Unemployment Rates

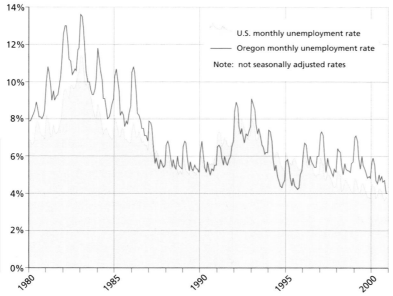

U.S. monthly unemployment rate
Oregon monthly unemployment rate
Note: not seasonally adjusted rates

Labor Force by Sex, 1940–1990

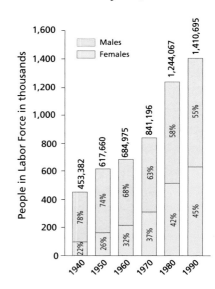

67

Public Employment

Public sector employment includes jobs in the federal government—both civilian and military branches—and in state and local governments. Nationwide, 13.7 percent of all jobs were in the public sector in 1998. Oregon, at 12.6 percent, ranked 38th among all states for its share of total employment in the public sector. Government employment in Oregon grew from about 165,000 in 1970 to about 260,000 in 1998. Despite this gain, government employment fell as a share of total employment from almost 18 percent in 1970 to 12.6 percent in 1998.

The nation's employment in the public sector, particularly in federal government, grew substantially as a share of all employment in the decades following the Great Depression. With the social programs put into place by the New Deal and the military expansion caused by World War II, federal government employment grew from about 3 percent of total non-farm payroll employment in 1939 to about 7 percent in the mid-1940s. Soon after the war, federal jobs declined to between 4 and 5 percent of total employment, then drifted downward to about 3 percent in the 1980s and 2 percent by 2000. In addition to U.S. Postal Service jobs, much of Oregon's federal civilian employment is related to the management of federal lands through the U.S. Forest Service and the Bureau of Land Management. The share of total employment in federal civilian government jobs fell in Oregon from about 2.75 percent in 1970 to 1.5 percent in 1998, well below the nation's level of 1.8 percent. Oregon ranked 29th among all states in federal civilian employment in 1998.

Combined state and local government employment almost doubled its share of total employment between the late 1940s and the mid-1970s. More recently, the share of employment in state and local governments

Federal Civilian Employment

U.S. Rate 1.8%
High: Maryland 5.2%
Low: Wisconsin 0.9%
Oregon Ranked 29th

Percentage of Total Employment
- <1.25%
- 1.25%–1.49%
- 1.50%–1.99%
- 2.00%–2.99%
- ≥3.00%

Alaska 4.4%
Hawaii 4.0%

Oregon Rate 1.5%
High: Grant Co. 8.2%
Low: Washington Co. 0.3%

Percentage of Total Employment
- <1.0%
- 1.0%–2.4%
- 2.5%–4.9%
- 5.0%–7.4%
- ≥7.5%

Federal Civilian Employment In Oregon

Military Employment

U.S. Rate 1.3%
High: Hawaii 7.4%
Low: Michigan 0.4%
Oregon Ranked 42nd

Percentage of Total Employment
- <1.00%
- 1.00%–1.49%
- 1.50%–1.99%
- 2.00%–2.99%
- ≥3.00%

Alaska 5.9%
Hawaii 7.4%

Oregon Rate 0.6%
High: Clatsop Co. 2.2%
Low: Multnomah Co. 0.5%

Percentage of Total Employment
- <0.6%
- 0.6%–0.79%
- 0.8%–0.99%
- 1.0%–1.19%
- ≥1.2%

Military Employment in Oregon

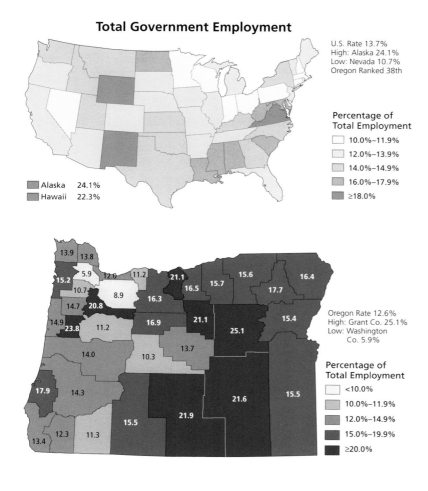

Total Government Employment

U.S. Rate 13.7%
High: Alaska 24.1%
Low: Nevada 10.7%
Oregon Ranked 38th

Percentage of Total Employment
- 10.0%–11.9%
- 12.0%–13.9%
- 14.0%–14.9%
- 16.0%–17.9%
- ≥18.0%

Alaska 24.1%
Hawaii 22.3%

Oregon Rate 12.6%
High: Grant Co. 25.1%
Low: Washington Co. 5.9%

Percentage of Total Employment
- <10.0%
- 10.0%–11.9%
- 12.0%–14.9%
- 15.0%–19.9%
- ≥20.0%

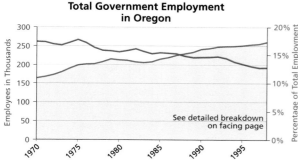

Total Government Employment in Oregon

Government employment rose from about 160,000 in 1970 to about 260,000 in 1998, but declined as a percentage of all employment from 17% to 13%. The graph on the facing page breaks these totals down by government level.

See detailed breakdown on facing page

has remained below its mid-1970s peak but well above its late-1940s level. The baby boom generation added substantially to local and state government employment in the area of education during this period. Since the late 1960s, education employment has accounted for about 40 percent of state government employment and about 55 percent of local government employment.

Oregon ranked 39th among all states in its concentration of employment in state government jobs (2.9 percent versus the national average of 3.0 percent). State government employment in Oregon grew from about 50,000 in 1980 to almost 65,000 in 1995, then declined to about 58,000 jobs—due in part to the transfer of Oregon Health Sciences University from a state government to local government employment classification. Benton County, home of Oregon State University, had Oregon's highest concentration (16.3 percent) of total employment in state government jobs in 1998. Marion County, with the state's capital, had the second highest concentration (11.1 percent). Washington County, where many of Oregon's large high-technology businesses are located, had only 0.3 percent of its total employment in state government jobs.

Local government employment includes those working in elementary and secondary schools and community colleges, fire and police departments, county health facilities, community recreation programs, city and county transportation departments and various other programs.

Local Government Employment

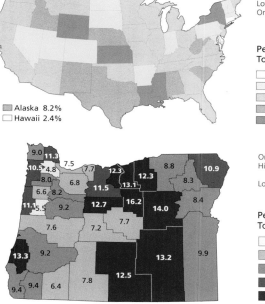

U.S. Rate 7.7%
High: Wyoming 11.2%
Low: Hawaii 2.4%
Oregon Ranked 20th

■ Alaska 8.2%
□ Hawaii 2.4%

Percentage of
Total Employment
□ <6.00%
□ 6.00%–6.99%
▨ 7.00%–7.99%
▨ 8.00%–8.99%
■ ≥9.00%

Oregon Rate 7.6%
High: Wheeler
Co. 16.2%
Low: Washington
Co. 4.8%

Percentage of
Total Employment
□ <6.0%
▨ 6.0%–7.9%
▨ 8.0%–9.9%
▨ 10.0%–11.9%
■ ≥12.0%

Local Government Employment in Oregon

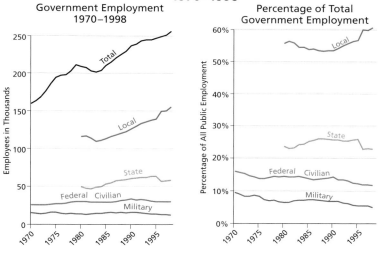

Top Ten Public Employers, 2000

Federal Employers	Employees
U.S. Postal Service	9,345
U.S. Forest Service	4,482
Civilian Department of Defense	2,814
Veterans Administration	2,135
Bureau of Land Management	1,838
Bonneville Power Administration	1,358
Intermittent Census Workers	1.303
Department of Veterans Affairs Medical	744
Internal Revenue Service	715
U.S. Dept. of Health and Human Services	640

State Employers	Employees
Oregon Department of Transportation	4,846
Oregon State University	4,516
University of Oregon	4,207
Department of Corrections	3,294
Portland State University	2,361
Adult and Family Services	1,954
Services to Children and Families	1,815
Judicial Department	1,617
Employment Department	1,400
State Police Department	1,391

Public Employment by Level of Government 1970–1998

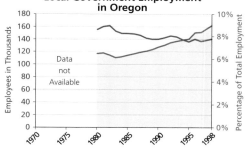

State Government Employment

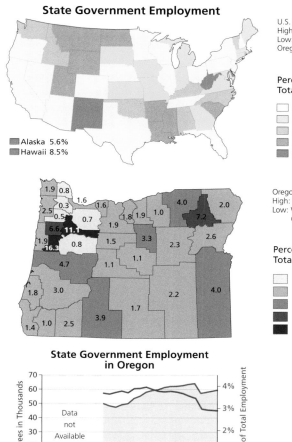

U.S. Rate 3.0%
High: Hawaii 8.5%
Low: Illinois 2.2%
Oregon Ranked 39th

Percentage of
Total Employment
□ <3.00%
□ 3.00%–3.49%
▨ 3.50%–3.99%
▨ 4.00%–4.99%
■ ≥5.00%

■ Alaska 5.6%
■ Hawaii 8.5%

Oregon Rate 2.9%
High: Benton Co.16.3%
Low: Washington
Co. 0.3%

Percentage of
Total Employment
□ <1.0%
□ 1.0%–2.9%
▨ 3.0%–4.9%
▨ 5.0%–9.9%
■ ≥10.0%

State Government Employment in Oregon

Occupational Categories, 1998
Top 12 Occupational Categories

Federal Government		State Government		Local Government	
Total Employment: 30,148		Total Employment: 58,010		Total Employment: 160,228	
Communications/Mail	4,900	Teachers and Educators	7,622	Teachers and Educators	64,797
Scientists and Related	3,100	Secretarial	6,231	Secretarial	14,687
Schedule/Dispatch	2,719	Student Workers	5,907	Fire and Police	9,725
Management Support	2,133	Management Support	5,427	Social/Recreation	6,180
Secretarial	1,721	Social/Recreation	3,411	Transportation	5,054
Health Specialists	1,687	Fire and Police	2,409	Health Specialists	4,646
Engineers and Related	1,567	Clerical/Administrative	1,900	Student Workers	4,619
Mechanics	1,136	Scientists and Related	1,582	Building Service/Cleaning	4,444
Computer Operators	646	Computer/Mathematics	1,472	Management Support	4,121
Computer/Mathematics	612	Health Service	1,422	Clerical/Administrative	3,558
Legal and Related	570	Construction	1,271	Food Service	3,426
Transportation	482	Engineers and Related	1,183	Mechanics	3,100

Taxation and Revenue

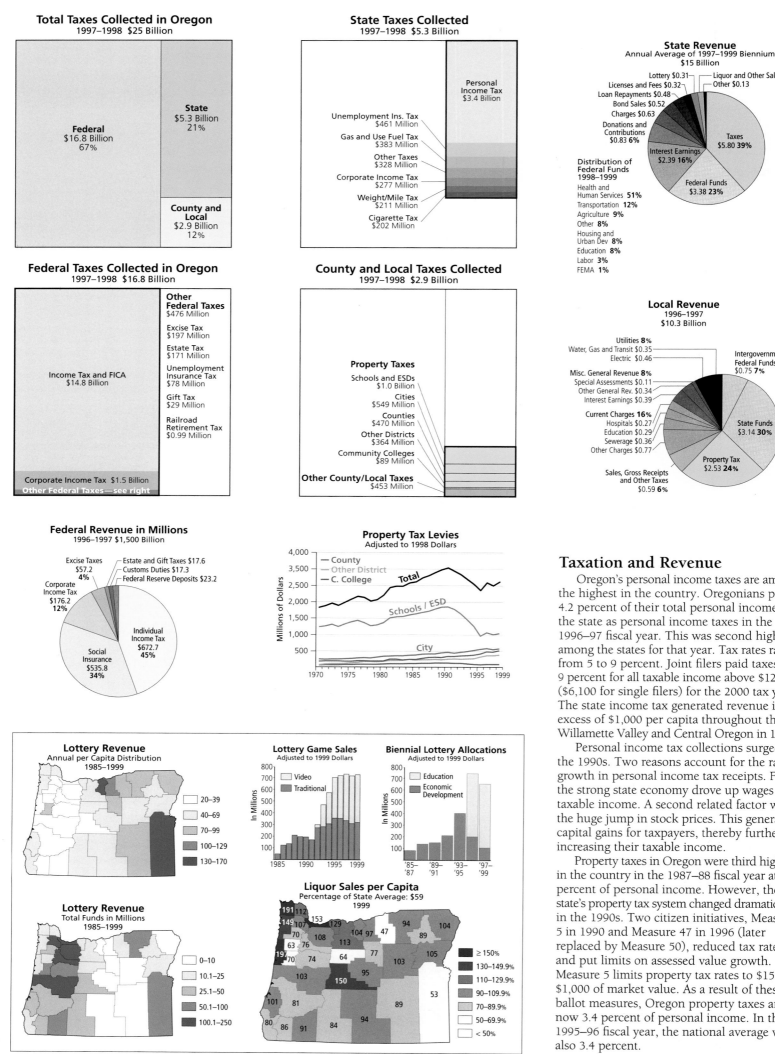

Total Taxes Collected in Oregon
1997–1998 $25 Billion

- **Federal** $16.8 Billion 67%
- **State** $5.3 Billion 21%
- **County and Local** $2.9 Billion 12%

State Taxes Collected
1997–1998 $5.3 Billion

- **Personal Income Tax** $3.4 Billion
- Unemployment Ins. Tax $461 Million
- Gas and Use Fuel Tax $383 Million
- Other Taxes $328 Million
- Corporate Income Tax $277 Million
- Weight/Mile Tax $211 Million
- Cigarette Tax $202 Million

State Revenue
Annual Average of 1997–1999 Biennium $15 Billion

- Lottery $0.31
- Licenses and Fees $0.32
- Loan Repayments $0.48
- Bond Sales $0.52
- Charges $0.63
- Donations and Contributions $0.83 6%
- Interest Earnings $2.39 16%
- Liquor and Other Sales $0.23
- Other $0.13
- Taxes $5.80 39%
- Federal Funds $3.38 23%

Distribution of Federal Funds 1998–1999
- Health and Human Services 51%
- Transportation 12%
- Agriculture 9%
- Other 8%
- Housing and Urban Dev 8%
- Education 8%
- Labor 3%
- FEMA 1%

Federal Taxes Collected in Oregon
1997–1998 $16.8 Billion

- Income Tax and FICA $14.8 Billion
- Corporate Income Tax $1.5 Billion
- Other Federal Taxes—see right
- **Other Federal Taxes** $476 Million
- Excise Tax $197 Million
- Estate Tax $171 Million
- Unemployment Insurance Tax $78 Million
- Gift Tax $29 Million
- Railroad Retirement Tax $0.99 Million

County and Local Taxes Collected
1997–1998 $2.9 Billion

- **Property Taxes**
  - Schools and ESDs $1.0 Billion
  - Cities $549 Million
  - Counties $470 Million
  - Other Districts $364 Million
  - Community Colleges $89 Million
- **Other County/Local Taxes** $453 Million

Local Revenue
1996–1997 $10.3 Billion

- Utilities 8%
  - Water, Gas and Transit $0.35
  - Electric $0.46
- Misc. General Revenue 8%
  - Special Assessments $0.11
  - Other General Rev. $0.34
  - Interest Earnings $0.39
- Current Charges 16%
  - Hospitals $0.27
  - Education $0.29
  - Sewerage $0.36
  - Other Charges $0.77
- Sales, Gross Receipts and Other Taxes $0.59 6%
- Intergovernmental Federal Funds $0.75 7%
- State Funds $3.14 30%
- Property Tax $2.53 24%

Federal Revenue in Millions
1996–1997 $1,500 Billion

- Excise Taxes $57.2 4%
- Estate and Gift Taxes $17.6
- Customs Duties $17.3
- Federal Reserve Deposits $23.2
- Corporate Income Tax $176.2 12%
- Individual Income Tax $672.7 45%
- Social Insurance $535.8 34%

Property Tax Levies
Adjusted to 1998 Dollars

- County
- Other District
- C. College

(Total, Schools / ESD, City) — graph from 1970 to 1999, Millions of Dollars axis 0–4,000

Lottery Revenue
Annual per Capita Distribution 1985–1999

- 20–39
- 40–69
- 70–99
- 100–129
- 130–170

Lottery Revenue
Total Funds in Millions 1985–1999

- 0–10
- 10.1–25
- 25.1–50
- 50.1–100
- 100.1–250

Lottery Game Sales
Adjusted to 1999 Dollars

- Video
- Traditional

(graph 1985–1999, In Millions 0–800)

Biennial Lottery Allocations
Adjusted to 1999 Dollars

- Education
- Economic Development

(graph '85–'87 to '97–'99, In Millions 0–800)

Liquor Sales per Capita
Percentage of State Average: $59 1999

- ≥ 150%
- 130–149.9%
- 110–129.9%
- 90–109.9%
- 70–89.9%
- 50–69.9%
- < 50%

Taxation and Revenue

Oregon's personal income taxes are among the highest in the country. Oregonians paid 4.2 percent of their total personal income to the state as personal income taxes in the 1996–97 fiscal year. This was second highest among the states for that year. Tax rates range from 5 to 9 percent. Joint filers paid taxes at 9 percent for all taxable income above $12,200 ($6,100 for single filers) for the 2000 tax year. The state income tax generated revenue in excess of $1,000 per capita throughout the Willamette Valley and Central Oregon in 1997.

Personal income tax collections surged in the 1990s. Two reasons account for the rapid growth in personal income tax receipts. First, the strong state economy drove up wages and taxable income. A second related factor was the huge jump in stock prices. This generated capital gains for taxpayers, thereby further increasing their taxable income.

Property taxes in Oregon were third highest in the country in the 1987–88 fiscal year at 5.5 percent of personal income. However, the state's property tax system changed dramatically in the 1990s. Two citizen initiatives, Measure 5 in 1990 and Measure 47 in 1996 (later replaced by Measure 50), reduced tax rates and put limits on assessed value growth. Measure 5 limits property tax rates to $15 per $1,000 of market value. As a result of these ballot measures, Oregon property taxes are now 3.4 percent of personal income. In the 1995–96 fiscal year, the national average was also 3.4 percent.

Despite the effects of voter-approved initiatives, property taxes remain the largest source of revenue for local governments, other than schools. Oregon governments levied $2.8 billion in property taxes in 1999–2000. The levies are distributed as follows: schools and education service districts 41 percent, cities 22 percent, counties 19 percent, community colleges 4 percent and special districts 14 percent. In 1989–90, before the passage of Measure 5, schools and education service districts received 62 percent of property tax levies. Schools now receive about 70 percent of their operating revenue from the state and 30 percent from property tax collections. These proportions were reversed in 1989. Property tax revenue varies widely across the state on a per capita basis. The primary reason is differences in property value. Another reason is the ratio of assessed value to market value— the direct result of Measure 50, which limited assessed value increases to 3 percent per year. Differing county tax rates also contribute to the uneven levels of per capita tax revenues collected in Oregon.

Lottery

In the wake of a serious economic downturn between 1979 and 1982, Oregon voters approved an initiative in 1984 that created a state lottery. The Oregon constitution limits administrative expense to 16 percent of lottery revenue and requires that at least 50 percent of gross revenue be returned to the players as prizes. Initially, lottery funds—generated from scratch-off tickets and lotto games—were to be used for economic development. The introduction of keno in 1991 and video poker in 1992 dramatically increased revenues. Video games accounted for 79 percent of anticipated lottery revenues in the 1999–2001 budget period ($621.7 million). Lottery earnings are used for education, parks, gambling addiction treatment and other uses selected by the Legislature. The existence of the state lottery opened the way for Indian casinos in Oregon under the 1988 Indian Gaming Act. In 1989, the Legislature initiated Sports Action as a separate lottery game. Proceeds from this game are distributed to intercollegiate athletic programs around the state.

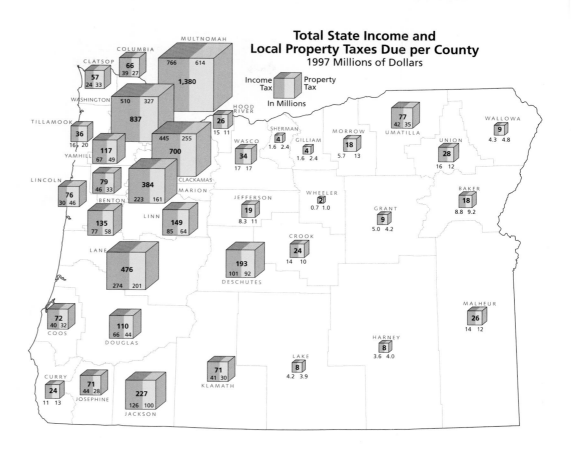

Total State Income and Local Property Taxes Due per County
1997 Millions of Dollars

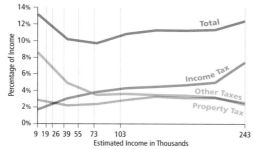

Effective Tax Rate by Income Level
State and Local

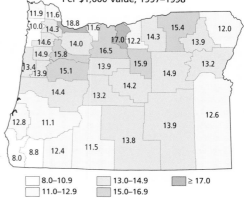

State Income and Local Property Tax Collections
Adjusted to 1998 Dollars

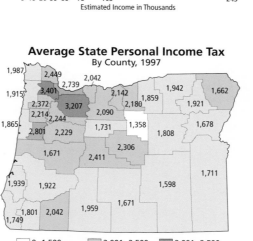

Average State Personal Income Tax
By County, 1997

☐ 0–1,500	☐ 2,001–2,500	■ 3,001–3,500
☐ 1,501–2,000	☐ 2,501–3,000	

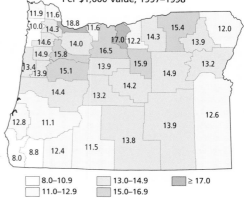

Average Local Property Tax Rate
Per $1,000 Value, 1997–1998

☐ 8.0–10.9	☐ 13.0–14.9	■ ≥ 17.0
☐ 11.0–12.9	☐ 15.0–16.9	

All State and Local Taxes
As Percentage of Personal Income
U.S. Average 11.30%

☐ 8.01–10.00	☐ 12.01–13.00	☐ 11.01–12.00
☐ 10.01–11.00	■ 13.01–15.00	

State Personal Income Tax
As Percentage of Personal Income
U.S. Average 2.41%

☐ 0	☐ 2.01–3.00%	■ 4.01–5.00%
☐ 0.01–2.00%	☐ 3.01–4.00%	

Local Property Tax
As Percentage of Personal Income
U.S. Average 3.43%

☐ 0.00–2.00	☐ 3.01–4.00	■ 5.01–6.00
☐ 2.01–3.00	☐ 4.01–5.00	

Manufacturing

In the U.S., manufacturing as a share of output slowly trended down in the 1990s with a combination of rising real output, increasing productivity and slowly declining employment. The Oregon experience was very different, with manufacturing output as a share of the state product increasing from 19.5 percent in 1987 to 28 percent in 1998. Oregon's exceptional performance can be traced to three key economic sectors— electronic equipment and instruments, transportation equipment and machinery— along with rapidly increasing employment and productivity gains.

Oregon's manufacturing sector has undergone major changes in recent decades; the most dramatic shift being the decline in forest products employment, coupled with rapid growth in the electronic equipment component. In 1998, the forest products sector (including paper) was the major component of manufacturing employment from Salem south and in much of the eastern part of the state (except Morrow, Umatilla and Malheur Counties, where food processing dominates). The electronic equipment and instruments sector is represented mostly in the urban counties in Western Oregon and in

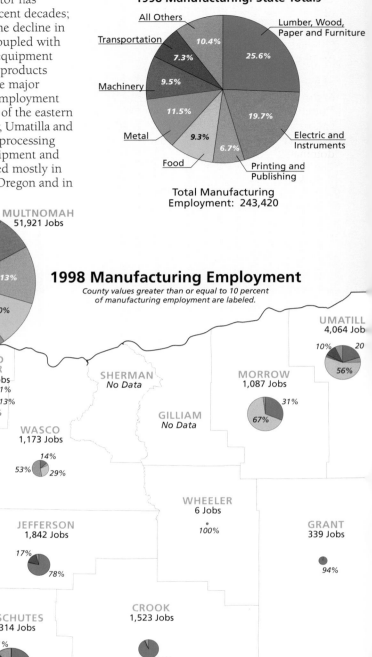

1998 Manufacturing: State Totals

All Others 10.4%
Transportation 7.3%
Machinery 9.5%
Metal 11.5%
Food 9.3%
Printing and Publishing 6.7%
Electric and Instruments 19.7%
Lumber, Wood, Paper and Furniture 25.6%

Total Manufacturing Employment: 243,420

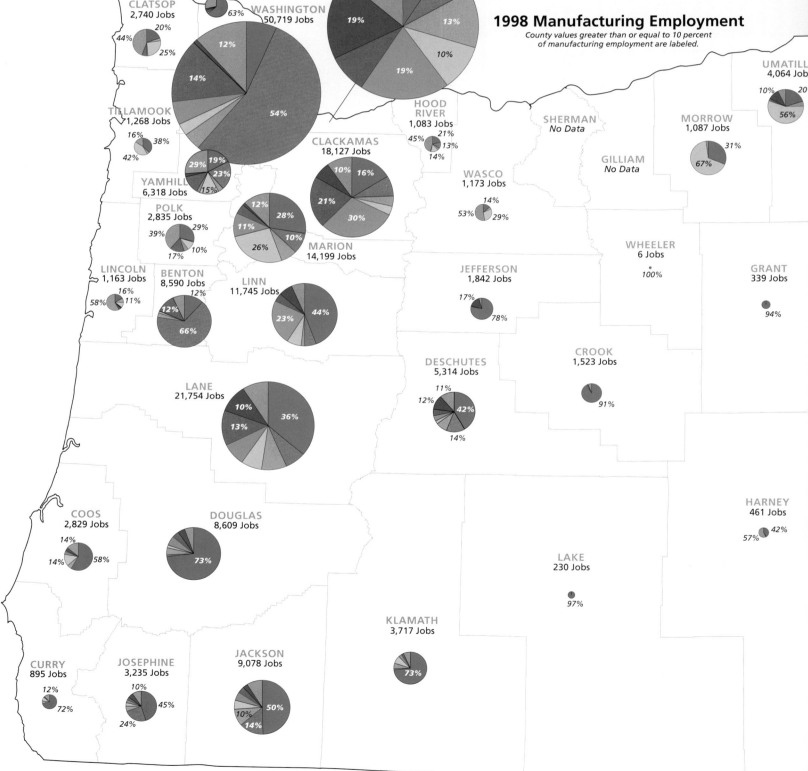

1998 Manufacturing Employment
County values greater than or equal to 10 percent of manufacturing employment are labeled.

Deschutes County. In Benton County much of the employment is accounted for by Hewlett–Packard operations; Intel employment in Oregon is concentrated in Washington County.

The transportation equipment component of manufacturing, based mostly in Multnomah, Clackamas, Linn and Lane Counties, includes heavy trucks, aircraft, rail cars, trailers and recreational vehicles. Potato and other vegetable processing operations dominate the food processing industry in Eastern Oregon. In southern Oregon there are large fruit processors, while dairy and seafood plants predominate on the Coast. The metals industry in the state includes steel mills and casting firms in the Portland area, titanium operations in Linn County and aluminum smelters in The Dalles and Troutdale.

The manufacturing component of the Oregon economy in the late 1990s has been a microcosm of the patterns seen nationally: these have been difficult times in the commodity businesses, such as metals and forest products, with strong competition and declining prices. Technology grew in a long national upturn characterized by high levels of business investment. The state has made efforts to encourage expansion in the manufacturing sector with the Strategic Investment Program of property tax caps for investments in excess of $100 million (at the option of the county), as well as infrastructure assistance and enterprise zones.

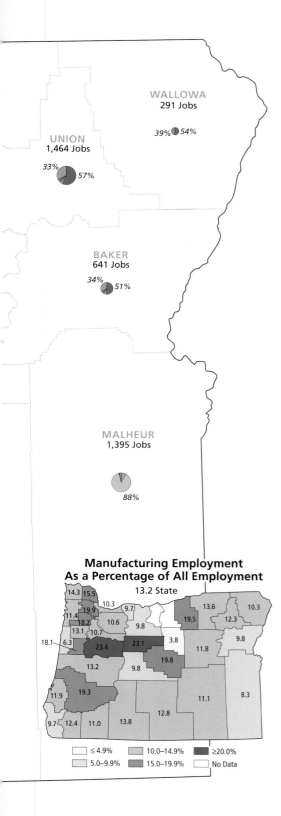

Manufacturing Employment As a Percentage of All Employment
13.2 State

≤ 4.9%   10.0–14.9%   ≥20.0%
5.0–9.9%   15.0–19.9%   No Data

1998 Manufacturing Employment
Top Subcategories in Each Manufacturing Sector

Wood, Paper and Furniture	**62,423**
Sawmills and Planing Mills	13,496
Softwood Veneer and Plywood	8,633
Electric and Instruments	**47,971**
Semiconductors and Related Devices	24,118
Instruments to Measure Electricity	5,094
Primary and Fabricated Metal	**27,939**
Steel Investment Foundries	2,284
Plating and Polishing	1,742
Industrial Machinery and Equipment	**23,244**
Computer Peripheral Equipment	4,100
Electronic Computers	2,166
Food and Kindred Products	**22,674**
Frozen Fruits and Vegetables	6,271
Baked Goods	2,154
Transportation Equipment	**17,662**
Motor Vehicles and Car Bodies	5,013
Aircraft Parts and Equipment	2,425
Printing and Publishing	**16,321**
Lithographic Commercial Printing	5,112
Newspapers	4,820
All Others	**25,186**
Rubber and Miscellaneous Plastics	7,616
Stone, Clay and Glass Products	5,119

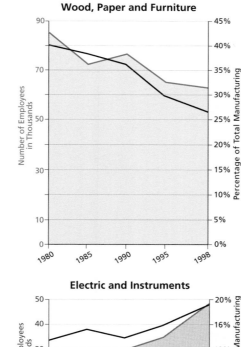

Wood, Paper and Furniture

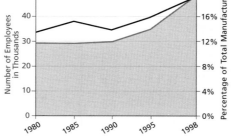

Electric and Instruments

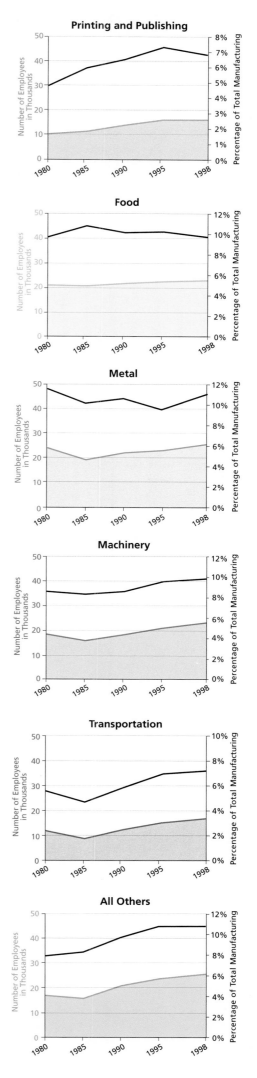

Printing and Publishing

Food

Metal

Machinery

Transportation

All Others

Lumber and Wood Products

Located in the "Persian Gulf of timber," Oregon is the leading producer of forest products in the nation. In the decade of the 1990s the industry went through a period of wrenching change. A multi-agency Forest Planning Process, the 1990 placement of the northern spotted owl and other species on the Endangered Species List, and the continuation of contentious environmental disputes have limited timber harvests, primarily on federal lands. In addition, fundamental changes in some federal forest practices led to fewer jobs. Cutting some private forests for short-term

gains, reduction in the harvest of federally owned old-growth forests and an increase of industry investment to the southeastern U.S., Canada and overseas all added pressure to the volatile situation. In 1993 the Clinton Administration held a "Timber Summit" in Portland to resolve the complex issues related to the management of federal forests in the region, but at the end of the century courtroom battles over these issues were still ongoing. The net effect in Oregon was to reduce the total timber harvest by more than half, with 85 percent of this reduction attributable to the

change in the management direction for federal forests. In 1988 the Oregon timber harvest was 8.6 billion board feet, with 3.49 billion board feet harvested from national forests and 1.44 billion board feet from Bureau of Land Management (BLM) acreage. By 1998 the harvest was 3.53 billion board feet, with 333 million board feet from national forests and 122 million board feet from BLM forests. Public lands have essentially been removed from the timber base. Between 1990 and 1995, 99 sawmill and panel operations closed in Oregon—nearly one-half of the mill closures over the period from 1980 to 1995. Reflecting the location of public timber, the mill closures were concentrated in the southern Willamette Valley and in the Coast Range in Lane, Coos, Linn, Josephine, Jackson and Klamath Counties.

The closures were accompanied by declines in forest products employment. In 1988,

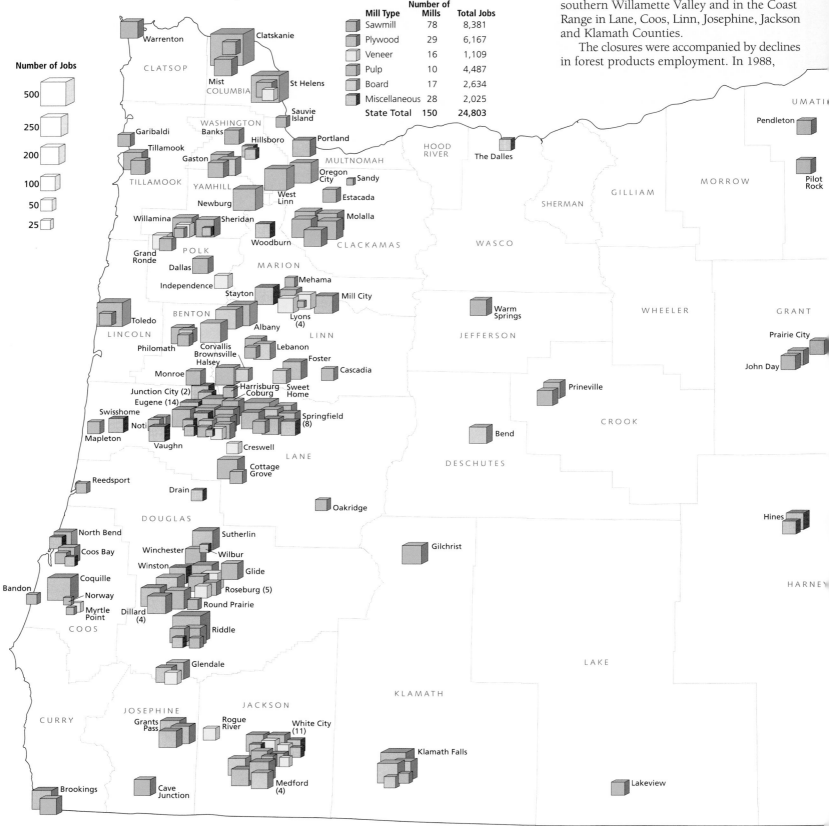

Employment in Mills

Mill Type	Number of Mills	Total Jobs
Sawmill	78	8,381
Plywood	29	6,167
Veneer	16	1,109
Pulp	10	4,487
Board	17	2,634
Miscellaneous	28	2,025
State Total	150	24,803

Number of Jobs
500
250
200
100
50
25

Oregon's annual average wage and salary jobs in forest products totaled 68,800 and the industry dominated the manufacturing sector in many non-metropolitan areas. By 1999, annual average employment in forest products was 49,000. Between 1988 and 1999 employment in the related paper industry fell from 8,600 to 8,300. The contraction of the forest products industry resulted in periods of employment decline or weakness in many parts of the state. Efforts to retrain forest workers and attract other economic activity in small, rural timber communities were initiated or accelerated. In some counties a significant share of revenues for schools and roads had come from federal timber receipts, which declined with falling sales; in 2000, federal legislation provided funds to make up for these losses.

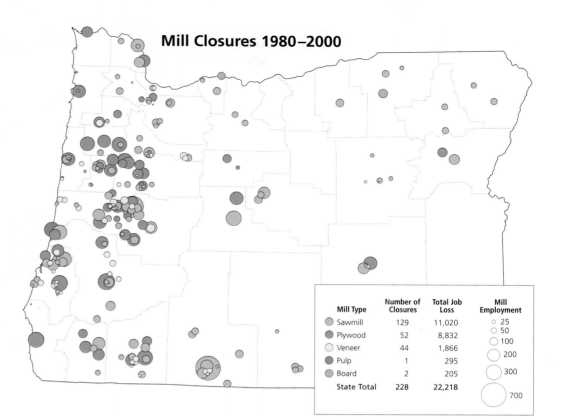

Mill Closures 1980–2000

Mill Type	Number of Closures	Total Job Loss	Mill Employment
Sawmill	129	11,020	○ 25
Plywood	52	8,832	○ 50
Veneer	44	1,866	○ 100
Pulp	1	295	○ 200
Board	2	205	○ 300
State Total	228	22,218	○ 700

Oregon's Largest Wood Products Mills By Employment

Company	Mill Type	Location	Employees
Georgia Pacific/Fort James	Pulp	Clatskanie	1,100
Boise Cascade	Pulp	St. Helens	675
Roseburg Forest Products #4	Plywood	Riddle	650
Weyerhaeuser	Pulp	Springfield	570
Georgia–Pacific	Pulp	Toledo	500
Columbia Forest Products	Plywood	Klamath Falls	450
States Industries	Plywood	Eugene	375
Roseburg Forest Products #6	Plywood	Coquille	375
S.P. Newsprint Co.	Pulp	Newburg	350
Willamette Industries	Pulp	Albany	342
West Linn Paper Co.	Pulp	West Linn	310
Roseburg Forest Products	Board	Dillard	300
Blue Heron Paper Co.	Pulp	Oregon City	275
Weyerhaeuser	Sawmill	Cottage Grove	265
Willamette Industries	Board	Albany	250
Boise Cascade	Plywood	Elgin	250
The Murphy Co.	Plywood	Sutherlin	250
Evanite Corp.	Board	Corvallis	250
Collins Pine Co.	Board	Klamath Falls	240
McKenzie Forest Products	Plywood	Springfield	240

Timber Harvest and Wood Products Production, 1945–1999

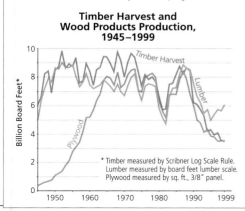

* Timber measured by Scribner Log Scale Rule.
Lumber measured by board feet lumber scale.
Plywood measured by sq. ft., 3/8" panel.

Wood Products Manufacturing Employment, 1977–1997

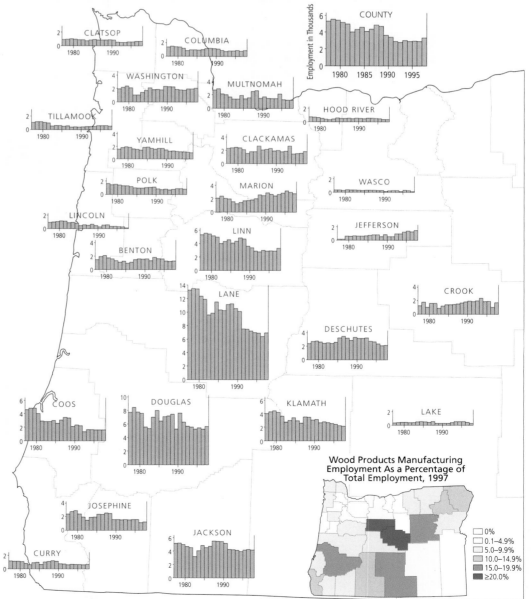

Wood Products Manufacturing Employment As a Percentage of Total Employment, 1997

□	0%
□	0.1–4.9%
□	5.0–9.9%
□	10.0–14.9%
□	15.0–19.9%
■	≥20.0%

High Technology

High-Tech Companies, 2000

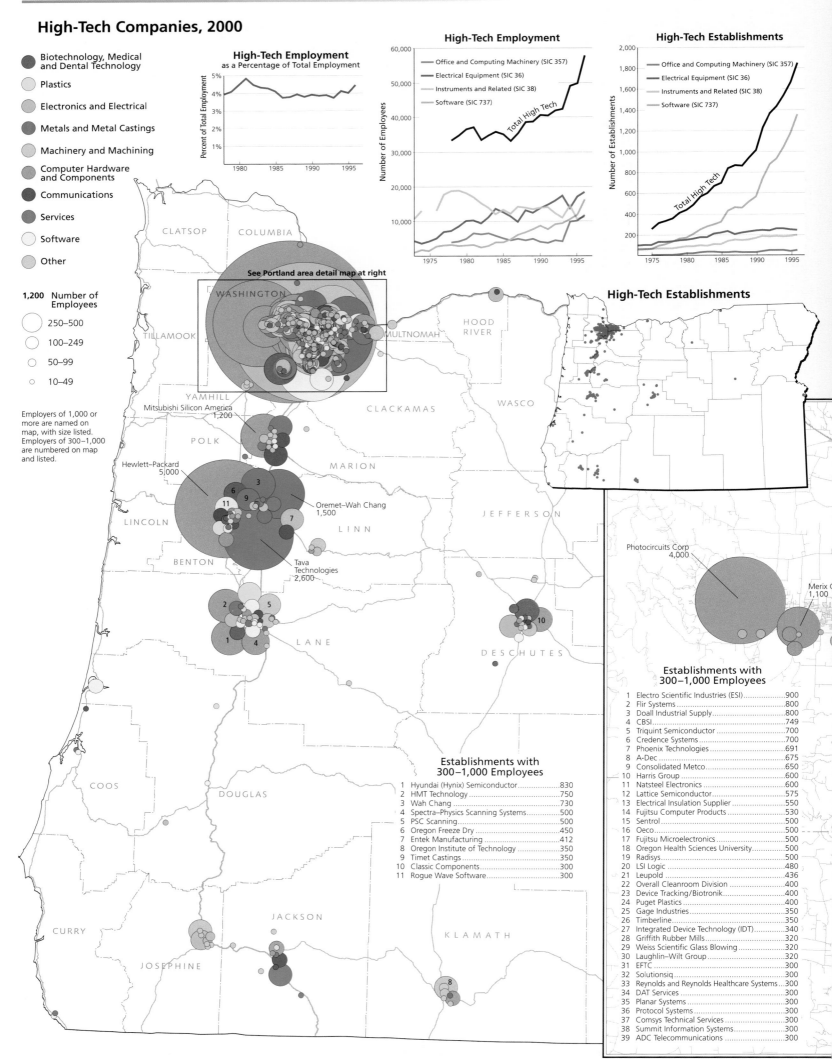

Biotechnology, Medical and Dental Technology

Plastics

Electronics and Electrical

Metals and Metal Castings

Machinery and Machining

Computer Hardware and Components

Communications

Services

Software

Other

1,200 Number of Employees

250–500
100–249
50–99
10–49

Employers of 1,000 or more are named on map, with size listed. Employers of 300–1,000 are numbered on map and listed.

High-Tech Employment
as a Percentage of Total Employment

High-Tech Employment

- Office and Computing Machinery (SIC 357)
- Electrical Equipment (SIC 36)
- Instruments and Related (SIC 38)
- Software (SIC 737)

Total High Tech

High-Tech Establishments

- Office and Computing Machinery (SIC 357)
- Electrical Equipment (SIC 36)
- Instruments and Related (SIC 38)
- Software (SIC 737)

Total High Tech

High-Tech Establishments

See Portland area detail map at right

Mitsubishi Silicon America
1,200

Hewlett–Packard
5,000

Oremet–Wah Chang
1,500

Tava Technologies
2,600

Photocircuits Corp
4,000

Merix C
1,100

Establishments with 300–1,000 Employees

1	Hyundai (Hynix) Semiconductor	830
2	HMT Technology	750
3	Wah Chang	730
4	Spectra–Physics Scanning Systems	500
5	PSC Scanning	500
6	Oregon Freeze Dry	450
7	Entek Manufacturing	412
8	Oregon Institute of Technology	350
9	Timet Castings	350
10	Classic Components	300
11	Rogue Wave Software	300

Establishments with 300–1,000 Employees

1	Electro Scientific Industries (ESI)	900
2	Flir Systems	800
3	Doall Industrial Supply	800
4	CBSI	749
5	Triquint Semiconductor	700
6	Credence Systems	700
7	Phoenix Technologies	691
8	A-Dec	675
9	Consolidated Metco	650
10	Harris Group	600
11	Natsteel Electronics	600
12	Lattice Semiconductor	575
13	Electrical Insulation Supplier	550
14	Fujitsu Computer Products	530
15	Sentrol	500
16	Oeco	500
17	Fujitsu Microelectronics	500
18	Oregon Health Sciences University	500
19	Radisys	500
20	LSI Logic	480
21	Leupold	436
22	Overall Cleanroom Division	400
23	Device Tracking/Biotronik	400
24	Puget Plastics	400
25	Gage Industries	350
26	Timberline	350
27	Integrated Device Technology (IDT)	340
28	Griffith Rubber Mills	320
29	Weiss Scientific Glass Blowing	320
30	Laughlin–Wilt Group	320
31	EFTC	300
32	Solutionsiq	300
33	Reynolds and Reynolds Healthcare Systems	300
34	DAT Services	300
35	Planar Systems	300
36	Protocol Systems	300
37	Comsys Technical Services	300
38	Summit Information Systems	300
39	ADC Telecommunications	300

The number of high-tech firms and employees in Oregon increased rapidly in the late 1980s and throughout the 1990s. By the late 1990s, employment in high technology industries surpassed employment in the lumber and wood products industry (see pages 74–75). The rapid expansion in the high-tech sector in the mid-1990s drove Oregon's gross state product at a rate of growth well ahead of the national average.

Oregon's high technology sector is divided into four classifications, including three in manufacturing and one in services. About half (50.2 percent) of Oregon's estimated 72,200 high-tech employees in 1998 worked in the electrical equipment sector, 24.7 percent in software services, 15.9 percent in scientific instruments and 9.2 percent in computer machinery. Oregon's "Silicon Forest" is rooted principally in the Portland metropolitan area and along the Interstate 5 corridor, with a few firms scattered in other parts of the state.

High technology in Oregon has its beginnings in the 1940s with the founding of instrument manufacturers Brown Engineering

Company (now Electro Scientific Industries) and Tektronix. The expansion of these firms and the large number of talented workers they employed gave rise to start-ups and spin-offs including firms such as Floating Point Systems, Planar and TriQuint Semiconductor. Several high-tech industry giants located branch plants in Oregon: the Hewlett–Packard calculator plant in Corvallis (1975) and Intel's integrated circuit plant in Aloha (1976). Both Tektronix and Intel would spend time as the state's largest private employer.

Oregon has emerged as a center of semiconductor production, with many producers and suppliers to the industry locating in the state. In 2000 the list of high-tech firms with large operations in the Portland metropolitan area includes Intel, Fujitsu Microelectronics, Integrated Device Technology, LSI Logic and wafer producers Wacker Siltronic Corp and Komatsu Silicon America. Hyundai (now Hynix) Semiconductor America is located in Eugene, and Mitsubishi Silicon is in Salem.

Agglomeration economies (reductions in

costs realized by locating near other firms in an industry) help explain the concentration of firms in the Portland area. In 1999, Oregon's high-tech industry produced the lion's share of the state's commodity exports (68 percent of value), with electronic equipment including semiconductors accounting for roughly half of the high-tech exports. Public policy has played a role in the expansion of the semiconductor industry with the Strategic Investment Program, which, at the option of the county government, caps the assessed value of large new facilities such as semiconductor plants at $100 million for purposes of property taxation. The law has been used to offset the burden of property taxes on the capital intensive semiconductor industry. The high-tech industry is cyclical and sensitive to international economic fluctuations. Economic weakness in Asia between 1997 and 1999, for example, had repercussions for Oregon, resulting in project delays and cancellations as well as reductions in employment after years of rapid growth.

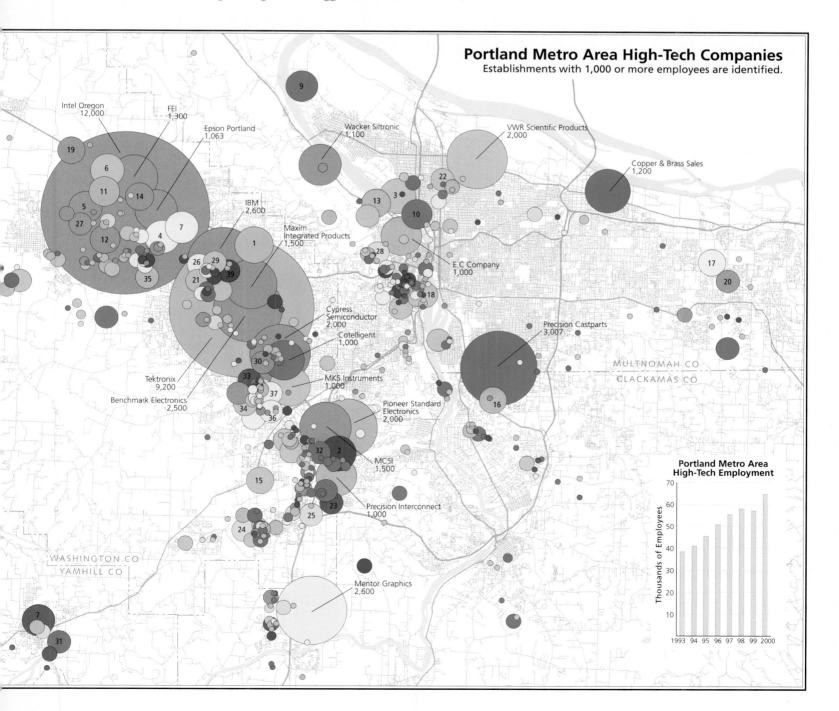

Portland Metro Area High-Tech Companies
Establishments with 1,000 or more employees are identified.

Intel Oregon 12,000
FEI 1,300
Epson Portland 1,063
Wacker Siltronic 1,100
VWR Scientific Products 2,000
Copper & Brass Sales 1,200
IBM 2,600
Maxim Integrated Products 1,500
E.C Company 1,000
Cypress Semiconductor 2,000
Cotelligent 1,000
Precision Castparts 3,007
MKS Instruments 1,000
Tektronix 9,200
Benchmark Electronics 2,500
Pioneer Standard Electronics 2,000
MCSI 1,500
Precision Interconnect 1,000
Mentor Graphics 2,600

MULTNOMAH CO
CLACKAMAS CO
WASHINGTON CO
YAMHILL CO

Portland Metro Area High-Tech Employment
Thousands of Employees
1993 94 95 96 97 98 99 2000

Business Activity

Between 1979 and 1982 Oregon endured an economic downturn that was among the worst experienced by any state since the Great Depression. This traumatic period included a 12 percent drop in employment along with an absolute decline in population. Between 1987 and 1997 the economy slowly recovered, entering a period of growth in population, income and employment above national rates. The U.S. Department of Commerce estimated that Oregon's gross state product, which is a measure of the output of goods and services produced within the state, rose at an annual average rate of 7.2 percent between 1992 and 1998, far above the national rate of 3.9 percent. Growth was particularly strong in manufacturing, construction and retail and wholesale trade. Oregon's performance is partially reflected in the changing list of the state's largest private employers. The steady increase in Intel's ranking in the top ten private sector employers is evident, and the addition of Freightliner to the 2000 list represents the surge in transportation equipment production that took place during the 1990s. Nike, Inc. joined the 2000 list of largest employers, demonstrating both the success of an Oregon start-up and growing activity in the wholesale distribution sector. Structural changes that have swept through some sectors of the U.S. economy are also seen in the list. Fred Meyer, Inc. and U.S. Bank were both founded in Oregon and have consistently been on the list of large employers. They were both purchased by out-of-state firms in the late 1990s; their headquarters then shifted to Cincinnati, Ohio, and Minneapolis, Minnesota, respectively.

Legend for Top 25 Employers List

SIC* Description	SIC Codes	SIC Description	SIC Codes
Manufacturing	2000–3900	Banking and Insurance	6000, 6300
Trucking and Warehousing	4200	Business Services	7300
Communications and Utility Services	4800, 4900	Health Services	8000
Retail and Wholesale Trade	5100–5400	All Others	

*Standard Industrial Classification

Top 100 Multi-Million-Dollar Businesses Based in Oregon

Circles represent the number of the top 100 Oregon business in each of 15 counties. The largest business in each of these counties is named and its 1999 sales listed. (The largest businesses in Washington and Clackamas Counties, Nike and Tektronix, are listed below among the top ten in the state, along with eight Multnomah County businesses.)

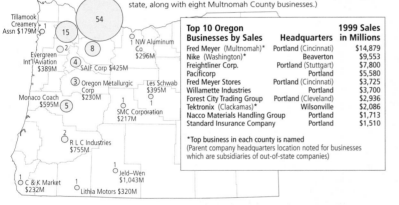

Top 10 Oregon Businesses by Sales	Headquarters	1999 Sales in Millions
Fred Meyer (Multnomah)*	Portland (Cincinnati)*	$14,879
Nike (Washington)*	Beaverton	$9,553
Freightliner Corp.	Portland (Stuttgart)	$7,800
Pacificorp	Portland	$5,580
Fred Meyer Stores	Portland (Cincinnati)	$3,725
Willamette Industries	Portland	$3,700
Forest City Trading Group	Portland (Cleveland)	$2,936
Tektronix (Clackamas)*	Wilsonville	$2,086
Nacco Materials Handling Group	Portland	$1,713
Standard Insurance Company	Portland	$1,510

*Top business in each county is named
(Parent company headquarters location noted for businesses which are subsidiaries of out-of-state companies)

Total Number of Businesses in 1999

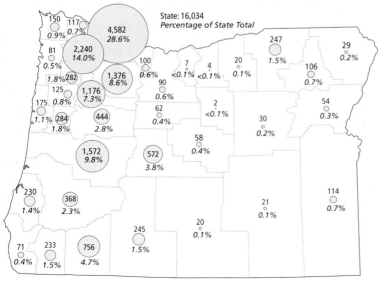

State: 16,034
Percentage of State Total

Top 25 Private-Sector Employers in Oregon

2000

	Company Name	Average Oregon Employment		SIC Description	Headquarters
1.	Intel Corporation	14,000		Semiconductors and related devices	Santa Clara, Calif.
2.	Fred Meyer	13,785		Department store	Cincinnati, Ohio
3.	Providence Health System	12,422		Integrated health system	Portland, Ore.
4.	Barrett Business Services	10,000		Temporary employment service	Portland, Ore.
5.	Safeway Stores	9,000		Grocery store	Pleasanton, Calif.
6.	Legacy Emanuel Hospital	6,935		Hospital, general medical and surgical	Portland, Ore.
7.	Wal Mart Stores	6,700		Department store	Bentonville, Ark.
8.	Kaiser Permanente	6,500		Doctors of medicine, offices and clinics	Oakland, Calif.
9.	Nike	5,900		Footwear, wholesale	Beaverton, Ore.
10.	Freightliner Corporation	5,200		Motor vehicles and car bodies	Stuttgart, Germany
11.	Albertsons	5,017		Grocery store	Boise, Idaho
12.	Hewlett–Packard	5,000		Semiconductors and related devices	Palo Alto, Calif.
13.	US Bank	4,902		Bank, national commercial	Minneapolis, Minn.
14.	Jeld-Wen	3,769		Millwork	Klamath Falls, Ore.
15.	Nordstrom	3,600		Retail department store	Seattle, Wash.
16.	PeaceHealth	3,575		Hospital, general medical and surgical	Bellevue, Wash.
17.	Roseburg Forest Products	3,500		Plywood and veneer, softwood	Roseburg, Ore.
18.	Qwest	3,440		Telephone communications	Denver, Colo.
19.	Asante Health Center	3,300		M.D., offices and clinics	Medford, Ore.
20.	Regal Cinemas	3,292		Movie theatre and concessions	Knoxville, Tenn.
21.	Willamette Industries	3,000		Plywood and veneer, softwood	Portland, Ore.
22.	Salem Hospital	2,900		Hospital, general medical and surgical	Salem, Ore.
23.	Portland General Electric	2,827		Electric power services	Portland, Ore.
24.	Wells Fargo	2,588		Bank, national commercial	San Francisco, Calif.
25.	Tektronix	2,500		Electrical measurement and test equip.	Beaverton, Ore.
25.	Regence Blue Cross and Blue Shield of Oregon	2,500		Health insurance provider	Chicago, Ill.

1998

	Company Name	Employment		SIC Description	Headquarters
1.	Fred Meyer	12,842		Department store	Cincinnati, Ohio
2.	Intel Corporation	11,000		Semiconductors and related devices	Santa Clara, Calif.
3.	Providence Health System	10,889		Integrated health system	Portland, Ore.
4.	Safeway Stores	9,568		Grocery store	Pleasanton, Calif.
5.	Barrett Business Services	7,050		Temporary employment service	Portland, Ore.
6.	US Bank	6,989		Bank, national commercial	Minneapolis, Minn.
7.	Kaiser Permanente	5,764		Doctors of medicine, offices and clinics	Oakland, Calif.
8.	Hewlett–Packard	5,708		Semiconductors and related devices	Palo Alto, Calif.
9.	Wal Mart Stores	5,140		Department store	Bentonville, Ark.
10.	Tektronix	5,000		Electrical measurement and test equip.	Beaverton, Ore.
11.	Nike	5,000		Footwear, wholesale	Beaverton, Ore.
12.	Albertsons	4,570		Grocery store	Boise, Idaho
13.	Wells Fargo	3,979		Bank, national commercial	San Francisco, Calif.
14.	Freightliner Corporation	3,900		Motor vehicles and car bodies	Stuttgart, Germany
15.	United Parcel Service	3,751		Courier services	Atlanta, Ga.
16.	US West	3,700		Telephone communications	Denver, Colo.
17.	Willamette Industries	3,650		Plywood and veneer, softwood	Portland, Ore.
18.	PeaceHealth	3,622		Hospital, general medical and surgical	Bellevue, Wash.
19.	Roseburg Forest Products	3,445		Plywood and veneer, softwood	Dillard, Ore.
20.	Boise Cascade Corporation	3,309		Boxes, corrugated and solid fiber	Boise, Idaho
21.	RiteAid Corporation	3,050		Variety stores	Camp Hill, Pa.
22.	Salem Hospital	2,776		Hospital, general medical and surgical	Salem, Ore.
23.	Portland General Electric	2,736		Electric power services	Portland, Ore.
24.	Legacy Emanuel Hospital	2,720		Hospital, general medical and surgical	Portland, Ore.
25.	Jeld-Wen	2,658		Millwork	Klamath Falls, Ore.

1995

	Company Name	Employment		SIC Description	Headquarters
1.	Fred Meyer	11,500		Department store	Portland, Ore.
2.	Safeway Stores	9,286		Grocery store	Oakland, Calif.
3.	Providence Health System	7,676		Integrated health system	Portland, Ore.
4.	US National Bank of Oregon	7,466		Bank, national commercial	Portland, Ore.
5.	Intel Corporation	6,723		Semiconductors and related devices	Santa Clara, Calif.
6.	Barrett Business Services	4,862		Temporary employment service	Portland, Ore.
7.	Kaiser Permanente	4,553		Doctors of medicine, offices and clinics	Oakland, Calif.
8.	Tektronix	4,520		Electrical measurement and test equip.	Beaverton, Ore.
9.	Albertsons	4,363		Grocery store	Boise, Idaho
10.	First Interstate Bank	4,305		Bank, national commercial	Los Angeles, Calif.
11.	US West	4,102		Telephone communications	Denver, Colo.
12.	Hewlett–Packard	4,000		Semiconductors and related devices	Palo Alto, Calif.
13.	Freightliner Corporation	3,961		Motor vehicles and car bodies	Stuttgart, Germany
14.	PeaceHealth	3,697		Hospital, general medical and surgical	Bellevue, Wash.
15.	Wal Mart Stores	3,696		Department store	Bentonville, Ark.
16.	Willamette Industries	3,650		Plywood and veneer, softwood	Portland, Ore.
17.	Meier & Frank	3,448		Retail department stores	St. Louis, Mo.
18.	Roseburg Forest Products	3,445		Plywood and veneer, softwood	Roseburg, Ore.
19.	Payless Drug Stores NW	3,361		Retail department stores	Wilsonville, Ore.
20.	Boise Cascade Corporation	3,300		Boxes, corrugated and solid fiber	Boise, Idaho
21.	Legacy Emanuel Hospital	3,282		Hospital, general medical and surgical	Portland, Ore.
22.	United Parcel Service	3,248		Courier services	Atlanta, Ga.
23.	Weyerhaeuser	3,135		Lumber	Federal Way, Wash.
24.	Nordstrom–Best	2,826		Retail department stores	Seattle, Wash.
25.	Nike	2,778		Footwear, wholesale	Beaverton, Ore.

1989

	Company Name	Employment		SIC Description	Headquarters
1.	Fred Meyer	9,700		Department store	Portland, Ore.
2.	Tektronix	9,000		Electrical measurement and test equip.	Beaverton, Ore.
3.	Safeway Stores	7,800		Grocery store	Oakland, Calif.
4.	US National Bank of Oregon	6,525		Bank, national commercial	Portland, Ore.
5.	Kaiser Permanente	5,300		Doctors of medicine, offices and clinics	Oakland, Calif.
6.	US West	4,600		Telephone communications	Denver, Colo.
7.	First Interstate Bank	4,546		Bank, national commercial	Los Angeles, Calif.
8.	Kelly Services	4,187		Temporary employment services	Detroit, Mich.
9.	McDonald's	4,100		Fast food restaurants	Oakbrook, Ill.
10.	Weyerhaeuser	4,000		Lumber	Federal Way, Wash.
11.	Payless Drug Stores NW	3,980		Retail department stores	Wilsonville, Ore.
12.	James River Corporation	3,500		Paper	Richmond, Va.
13.	Roseburg Forest Products	3,500		Plywood and veneer, softwood	Roseburg, Ore.
14.	Intel Corporation	3,200		Semiconductors and related devices	Santa Clara, Calif.
15.	Boise Cascade Corporation	3,200		Boxes, corrugated and solid fiber	Boise, Idaho
16.	Freightliner Corporation	3,150		Motor vehicles and car bodies	Stuttgart, Germany
17.	Consolidated Freightways	3,100		Long distance trucking	Portland, Ore.
18.	Willamette Industries	3,078		Plywood and veneer, softwood	Portland, Ore.
19.	Albertsons	3,036		Grocery store	Boise, Idaho
20.	Portland General Electric	3,000		Electric power services	Portland, Ore.
21.	Precision Castparts Corp.	3,000		Steel investment castings	Portland, Ore.
22.	Manpower Inc. of Portland	2,900		Temporary employment services	Portland, Ore.
23.	Meier & Frank	2,858		Retail department stores	St. Louis, Mo.
24.	Norpac Foods	2,600		Frozen fruits and vegetables	Stayton, Ore.
25.	Hewlett–Packard	2,600		Semiconductors and related devices	Palo Alto, Calif.

Much of the state's business activity is concentrated along the Interstate 5 corridor. There are now contiguous metropolitan areas from the Eugene–Springfield area in Lane County to the counties comprising the Portland metropolitan area. Business centers are also growing in Deschutes County in Central Oregon and Umatilla County in northeastern Oregon. Deschutes County is consistently among the most rapidly growing counties in the state in terms of population and employment and will likely become a metropolitan area in the near future. Umatilla County transportation, distribution, software support and incarceration activities grew rapidly in the late 1990s.

Oregon is one of five states without a general retail sales tax; the others are Alaska, Montana, New Hampshire and Delaware. This fiscal characteristic, coupled with Oregon's location—a state bordered by states that do use general sales taxes—diverts some retail activity to Oregon that would normally take place in surrounding states. Such cross-border economic activity is particularly evident in the Portland, Medford and Ontario areas. The lack of a sales tax is also a factor in the establishment of factory outlet centers in Lincoln City, Seaside, Troutdale, Bend and Woodburn. Wholesale activity is concentrated along the major transportation and population corridor. Some national and regional distributors have established facilities in Oregon to serve as bases for distribution to Washington and California.

The pattern of commercial bank deposits and savings deposits in Oregon reflects both a changing mix of institutions and alterations in the kinds of assets that consumers and businesses hold. Many of the nation's savings institutions went out of business during the wave of thrift failures in the late 1980s and early 1990s. The relatively large deposits in rural areas of Oregon reflect the use of locally based institutions such as the Columbia River Bank and Klamath First Bancorp and regional firms including Washington Federal Savings and Washington Mutual, the nation's largest thrift. The financial asset portfolios of consumers have changed, with diminishing shares held in savings accounts and increases in stocks, mutual funds and various retirement accounts. The structure of banks and savings institutions in Oregon has shifted in step with the national regulatory framework. First Interstate is now part of San Francisco-based Wells Fargo. U.S. Bancorp was purchased by First Bank Systems, which in turn was acquired by Firstar. Oregon-based Benjamin Franklin Savings and Loan was taken over by the Resolution Trust Corporation and in turn sold to Bank of America. Community banks have grown rapidly in the wake of these large bank consolidations.

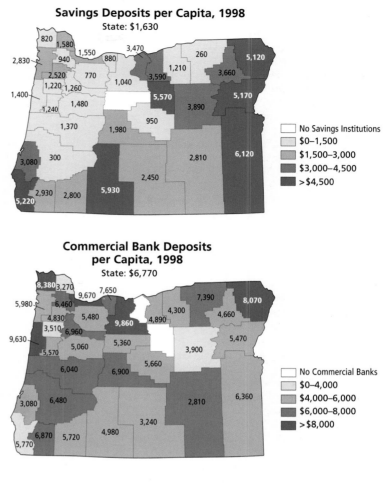

Savings Deposits per Capita, 1998
State: $1,630

- No Savings Institutions
- $0–1,500
- $1,500–3,000
- $3,000–4,500
- >$4,500

Commercial Bank Deposits per Capita, 1998
State: $6,770

- No Commercial Banks
- $0–4,000
- $4,000–6,000
- $6,000–8,000
- >$8,000

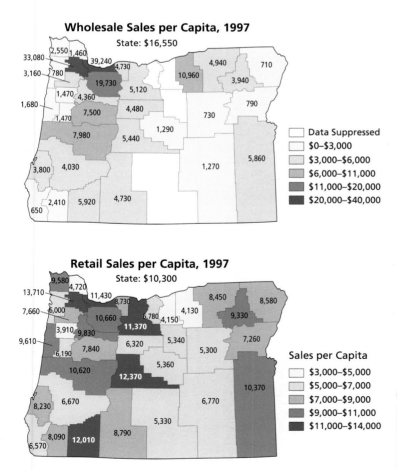

Wholesale Sales per Capita, 1997
State: $16,550

- Data Suppressed
- $0–$3,000
- $3,000–$6,000
- $6,000–$11,000
- $11,000–$20,000
- $20,000–$40,000

Retail Sales per Capita, 1997
State: $10,300

Sales per Capita
- $3,000–$5,000
- $5,000–$7,000
- $7,000–$9,000
- $9,000–$11,000
- $11,000–$14,000

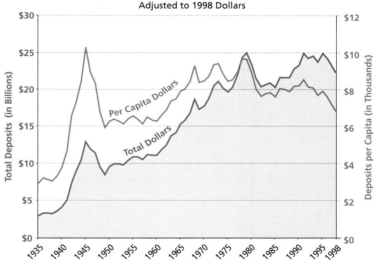

Deposits to Insured Commercial Banks
Adjusted to 1998 Dollars

Per Capita Dollars
Total Dollars

Wholesale Sales per Capita
Adjusted to 1997 Dollars

$14,015 (1972)
$17,304 (1977)
$16,091 (1982)
$14,839 (1987)
$15,855 (1992)
$16,551 (1997)

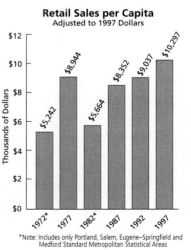

Retail Sales per Capita
Adjusted to 1997 Dollars

$5,242 (1972*)
$8,944 (1977)
$5,664 (1982*)
$8,352 (1987)
$9,037 (1992)
$10,297 (1997)

*Note: Includes only Portland, Salem, Eugene–Springfield and Medford Standard Metropolitan Statistical Areas

79

International Investments

In recent decades Oregonians in both the public and private sectors have worked to attract foreign investment as a means of encouraging economic growth. Direct foreign investment in Oregon rose sharply from the 1980s to the mid-1990s. In August 1984, a time when Oregon was still emerging from the sharp economic downturn of 1979 to 1982, the Oregon Legislature under the leadership of Governor Victor Atiyeh held a one-day session and repealed the worldwide unitary method of taxation. This technique of taxation imposed taxes on foreign firms based on their worldwide earnings; following the repeal, taxes were based on the firm's earnings in the U.S. This act was followed by a wave of investment, particularly from Japan, including Fujitsu, Epson and NEC. Trade offices were established in Tokyo and Taipei to foster trade and investment. Oregon governors and trade delegations made and continue to make overseas visits, mostly to Asia, to build relationships.

Direct foreign investments in plants, equipment and regional offices generate employment and income in the state. Foreign investment in Oregon is heavily concentrated, both in terms of location and jobs generated by foreign-owned companies, in the northern Willamette Valley. Foreign investments are

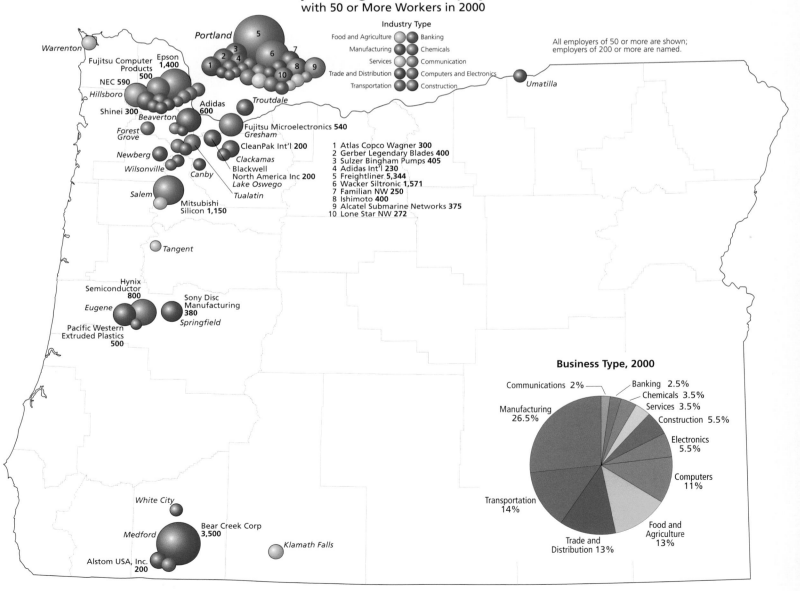

Jobs in Foreign-Owned Companies, 2000

Warrenton 120
Hillsboro 3,684
Portland 12,300
Boardman 38
Umatilla 85
Salem 1,314
Silverton 32
Stayton 40
Albany 11
Tangent 70
Eugene 1,363
Springfield 410
Creswell 35
North Bend 7
White City 115
Medford 3,814
Grants Pass 13
Klamath Falls 130

1	Forest Grove	115
2	Newberg	130
3	Wilsonville	134
4	Aurora	25
5	Canby	72
6	Tigard	31
7	Tualatin	447
8	Beaverton	831
9	Lake Oswego	217
10	Clackamas	324
11	Gresham	540
12	Troutdale	180

Major Foreign-Owned Employers
with 50 or More Workers in 2000

Industry Type

Food and Agriculture — Banking
Manufacturing — Chemicals
Services — Communication
Trade and Distribution — Computers and Electronics
Transportation — Construction

All employers of 50 or more are shown; employers of 200 or more are named.

Warrenton
Portland
Fujitsu Computer Products 500
Epson 1,400
NEC 590
Hillsboro
Shinei 300
Beaverton
Adidas 600
Troutdale
Forest Grove
Fujitsu Microelectronics 540
Gresham
Newberg
CleanPak Int'l 200
Clackamas
Wilsonville
Blackwell North America Inc 200
Canby
Lake Oswego
Salem
Tualatin
Mitsubishi Silicon 1,150
Umatilla

1 Atlas Copco Wagner **300**
2 Gerber Legendary Blades **400**
3 Sulzer Bingham Pumps **405**
4 Adidas Int'l **230**
5 Freightliner **5,344**
6 Wacker Siltronic **1,571**
7 Familian NW **250**
8 Ishimoto **400**
9 Alcatel Submarine Networks **375**
10 Lone Star NW **272**

Tangent
Hynix Semiconductor 800
Sony Disc Manufacturing 380
Eugene
Springfield
Pacific Western Extruded Plastics 500

White City
Bear Creek Corp 3,500
Medford
Klamath Falls
Alstom USA, Inc. 200

Business Type, 2000

Communications 2%
Banking 2.5%
Chemicals 3.5%
Services 3.5%
Construction 5.5%
Manufacturing 26.5%
Electronics 5.5%
Computers 11%
Food and Agriculture 13%
Transportation 14%
Trade and Distribution 13%

Major Foreign-Owned Companies
and Number of Employees

Company	Employees
Freightliner Corp. *Heavy and Medium Duty Trucks*	5,344 Germany
Bear Creek Corp. *Gift Products*	3,500 Japan
Wacker Siltronic Corp. *Monocrystalline Silicon Wafers*	1,571 Germany
Epson Portland, Inc. *Inkjet Printers and Dot Matrix Printheads*	1,400 Japan
Mitsubishi Silicon America *Silicon and Epitaxial Wafers*	1,150 Korea
Hynix Semiconductor *Semiconductors*	800 Korea
Adidas America *Apparel*	600 Germany
NEC America, Inc. *Fiberoptic Equipment*	590 Japan
Fujitsu Microelectronics, Inc. *Integrated Circuits, DRAM and ASIC Chips*	540 Japan
Fujitsu Computer Products of America, Inc. *Information Processing Equipment*	500 Japan
Pacific Western Extruded Plastics *Plastic Pipes*	500 Japan
Sulzer Bingham Pumps, Inc. *Heavy Pump Manufacturer*	405 Switzerland
Gerber Legendary Blades *Sports Knives*	400 Finland
Ishimoto America, Inc. *Facility Design, Construction Management*	400 Japan
Sony Disc Manufacturing *Optical Discs*	380 Japan
Alcatel Submarine Networks, Inc. *Underwater Fiberoptic Cable and System Assembly*	375 France
Atlas Copco Wagner, Inc. *Design and Mfr. of Underground Mining Vehicles*	300 Sweden
Shinei USA, Inc. *Precision Sheet Metal Parts and Sub-Assemblies*	300 Singapore
Lone Star Northwest *Cement*	272 Japan
Familian Northwest, Inc. *Distribution of Plumbing Materials*	250 United Kingdom
Adidas International *Footwear and Athletic Wear*	230 Germany
Alstom USA, Inc. *Instrument and Distribution Transformers*	200 France
Blackwell North America, Inc. *Booksellers*	200 United Kingdom
Cleanpak International, Inc. *Mfr. of Heating, Ventilation and A/C Equipment*	200 Japan
JAE Oregon, Inc. *Electronic Connectors*	182 Japan
TKS Industrial Company *Design, Fabrication and Installation of Cleanrooms*	180 Japan
Toyo Tanso USA *Graphite Crucibles and Other Products*	180 Japan
Weiss Scientific Glass Blowing Co., Inc. *Quartz Products for Semiconductor Industry*	180 Japan
Riverplace Associates *Property Management and Development*	152 Japan
BT Office Products International *Distribution of Office Products*	150 Netherlands
Elf Atochem *Chemicals: Chlorine and Chlorate*	150 France
Rodgers Instrument *Organs and Pianos*	150 Japan
Rexam Graphics *Coding of Paper*	135 United Kingdom
Masami Foods *Beef and Pork Processing*	130 Japan
Ushio Oregon, Inc. *Specialty Lighting*	130 Japan
Pacific Surimi Joint Venture, LLC *Frozen Ground Fish*	120 Japan
Scala Electronics *Electronics and Broadcast Antennas*	114 Germany
AGPR (Asahi Glass/Pacific Rundum) *Industrial Ceramics, Semiconductor Industry*	100 Japan
Air Liquide America Corporation *Industrial Medical Gases*	100 France
GranPac Foods *Processed Frozen Foods*	100 Japan
Komatsu Silicon America *Silicon Wafers*	100 Japan
Kyotaru Oregon, Inc. *Food Processing (Imitation Crab Meat)*	100 Japan
Matsushita Electronic Materials, Inc. *Printed Circuit Board Material*	100 Japan
Nissho Iwai American Corporation *International Trading Company*	100 Japan
Tokyo Electron Oregon, Inc. *Diffusion Furnaces, Semiconductor Industry*	100 Japan
Truck Project Corp. (Freightliner) *Lightweight Commercial Truck Design*	100 Germany
Union Bank of California *Banking Services*	100 Japan

Jobs Provided by Foreign-Owned Companies by Country, 2000

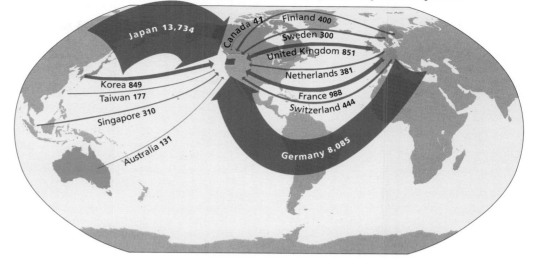

most evident in manufacturing, especially in the technology sector, with firms such as Fujitsu, Epson, Alcatel Submarine Networks, Sumitomo, Mitsubishi and Hyundai, but there are also financial institutions such as Union Bank and the Bank of Nova Scotia, as well as food processors such as Bear Creek Corporation. Oregon's role as a transshipping point results in foreign transportation and freight companies maintaining offices in the state—Danzas, a Swiss freight forwarder, for example, and Pan Pacific Shipping Company, a Taiwanese firm. The Portland area, already a leader in athletic shoe design and distribution, attracted Adidas America. Many of the foreign firms with a presence in the state are not widely recognized as such; their names do not obviously imply foreign ownership: Kershaw Knives, plumbing distributor Familian Northwest and advertising agency Cole and Weber. Germany and Japan dominate foreign investment in Oregon; combined, they account for over 80 percent of employment at foreign-owned businesses.

Jobs in Foreign-Owned Companies

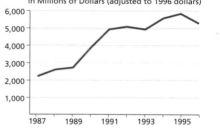

Assets of Foreign-Owned Companies
in Millions of Dollars (adjusted to 1996 dollars)

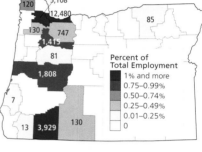

Country of Ownership
of Foreign-Owned Companies with 50 or More Workers in 2000

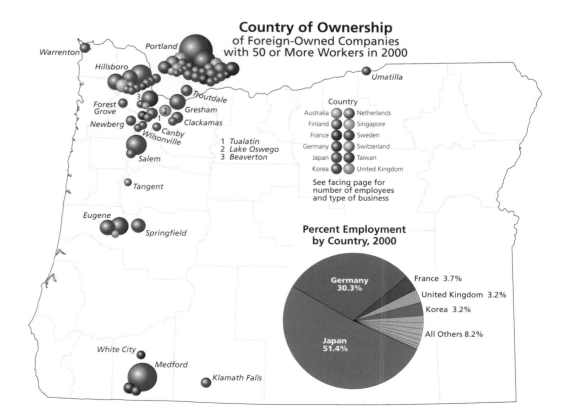

Public Lands

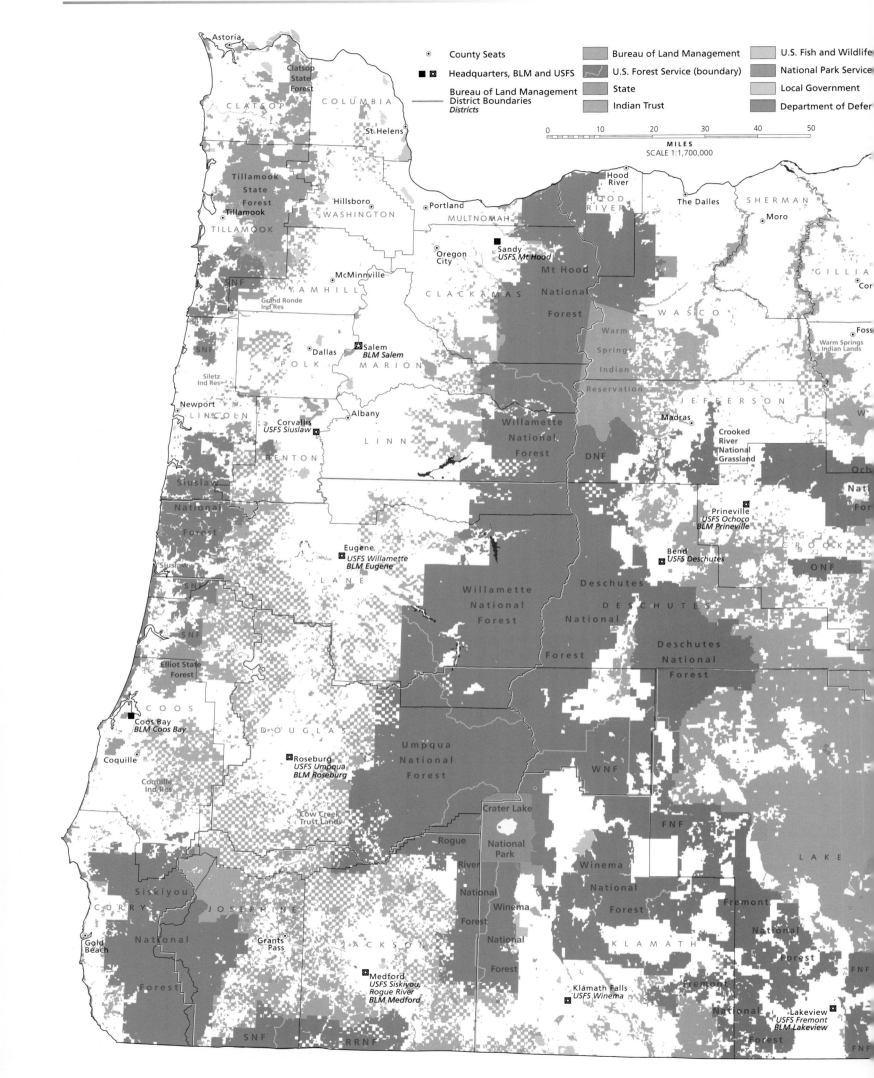

Legend:
- County Seats
- Headquarters, BLM and USFS
- Bureau of Land Management District Boundaries *Districts*
- Bureau of Land Management
- U.S. Forest Service (boundary)
- State
- Indian Trust
- U.S. Fish and Wildlife
- National Park Service
- Local Government
- Department of Defense

MILES
SCALE 1:1,700,000
0 10 20 30 40 50

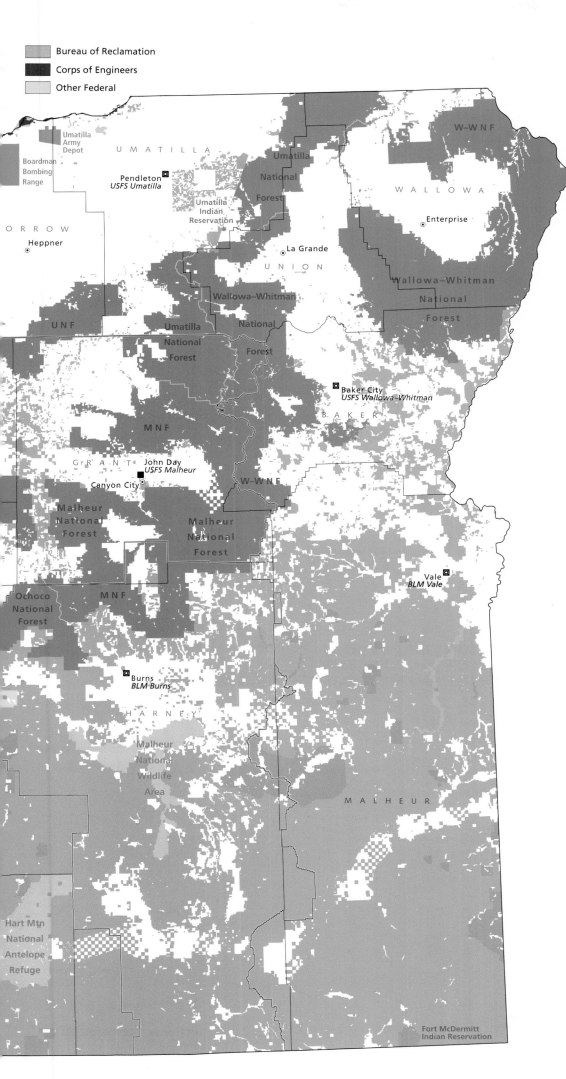

Bureau of Reclamation

Like most Western states, Oregon is owned in large part by the federal government, with the vast majority of federal lands administered by the Bureau of Land Management (BLM) and the Forest Service. State and local government land ownership is relatively minor, though locally significant. All of Oregon became part of the public domain in 1846 when the U.S. secured jurisdiction by treaty with Great Britain. The process of preemption settlement and private land claims actually began several years before 1846 and was reinforced under terms of the provisional government established in 1843. This was the year the Great Migration to Oregon began, spurred by the attraction of free land.

The Oregon Territorial Act of 1848 had no provisions for recognizing the early land claims. Congress filled this gap with the Donation Land Claim Act of 1850, which indirectly confirmed the early claims and provided authorization for new donation land claims until 1855. The Act also provided for the rectangular land survey of Oregon (see Public Land Survey, page 19).

Because of its agricultural potential and suitable climate, the Willamette Valley was the primary destination of early immigrants until all the best lands were taken. Attention then turned to Eastern Oregon and other parts of the state. Generally, lands that remain in public ownership today have little or no agricultural value, or are areas set aside for national forests, parks and other public purposes.

In the 1850s, provisions were made for the recognition of Indian tribal lands, in greatly reduced form, by the establishment of reservations primarily made up of Indian Trust lands.

The disposition of the public domain continued through additional land transfer mechanisms, including the homestead laws, land sales and land grants. Oregon statehood in 1859 resulted in various land grants to the state, including school land grants which were comprised of sections 16 and 36 in each surveyed township. Where these sections were not available, the state selected other lands in lieu thereof. The Tillamook and Elliot State Forests shown near the Coast on the map to the left are examples of the state concentrating many of its in-lieu sections. Over time, large areas of tax-delinquent, burned-over lands received by the counties were transferred to the state forests for reforestation and timber resource management.

Land grants were also made to transportation companies to aid in the construction of railroads and wagon roads. These land grants consisted of a checkerboard pattern of odd-numbered sections within the boundaries of wide swaths of land centered on the proposed transportation routes. Construction of the railroads and wagon roads was financed by the sale of these lands to settlers and other parties. As a prime example, the Oregon and California Railroad received 3.7 million acres of public domain lands in Western Oregon for the construction of a railroad from Portland to the California border. A majority of these highly productive timberlands were eventually returned to the U.S. (see Land Grants, pages 22–23). These tracts, known as the O & C lands, are today administered primarily by the BLM.

Land Ownership

Private Ownership
27,181,000 Acres

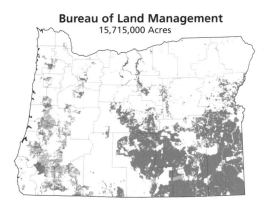

Bureau of Land Management
15,715,000 Acres

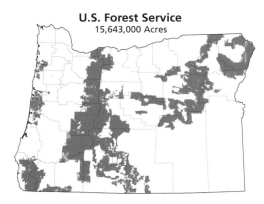

U.S. Forest Service
15,643,000 Acres

State of Oregon
1,557,000 Acres

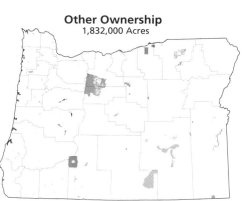

Other Ownership
1,832,000 Acres

Ownership in Thousands of Acres

COUNTIES	Private	% of Total	BLM	% of Total	USFS	% of Total	State	% of Total	Other	% of total	Total
NORTHWEST											
Benton	332	76%	59	14%	17	4%	20	5%	7	2%	436
Clatsop	364	68%	—	0%	—	0%	158	30%	10	2%	533
Columbia	410	92%	12	3%	—	0%	10	2%	15	3%	446
Lincoln	407	65%	22	3%	173	28%	19	3%	5	1%	626
Polk	420	88%	41	9%	1	0%	13	3%	3	1%	478
Tillamook	237	34%	50	7%	103	15%	306	44%	4	1%	700
Washington	398	86%	11	2%	—	0%	49	11%	4	1%	462
Yamhill	385	84%	31	7%	22	5%	1	0%	17	4%	455
SOUTHWEST											
Coos	675	67%	151	15%	79	8%	80	8%	23	2%	1,008
Curry	347	33%	68	7%	616	59%	14	1%	—	0%	1,046
Josephine	300	29%	297	28%	407	39%	42	4%	1	0%	1,047
WEST CASCADES											
Clackamas	558	46%	74	6%	545	45%	12	1%	18	1%	1,207
Douglas	1,503	47%	593	18%	1,054	33%	65	2%	13	0%	3,228
Hood River	122	36%	—	0%	216	64%	—	0%	—	0%	338
Jackson	866	48%	452	25%	443	25%	12	1%	17	1%	1,790
Lane	1,198	41%	297	10%	1,403	48%	41	1%	13	0%	2,953
Linn	896	60%	90	6%	468	32%	21	1%	7	0%	1,482
Marion	505	66%	20	3%	199	26%	30	4%	6	1%	760
Multnomah	215	70%	4	1%	78	25%	4	1%	6	2%	308
EAST CASCADES											
Deschutes	462	24%	487	25%	1,004	51%	1	0%	—	0%	1,954
Jefferson	583	51%	40	3%	276	24%	—	0%	246	21%	1,146
Klamath	1,677	43%	249	6%	1,728	44%	31	1%	212	5%	3,896
Wasco	881	57%	84	5%	160	10%	16	1%	398	26%	1,539
COLUMBIA											
Gilliam	741	93%	54	7%	—	0%	—	0%	2	0%	797
Morrow	1,077	83%	2	0%	151	12%	—	0%	66	5%	1,296
Sherman	475	90%	50	9%	—	0%	—	0%	—	0%	525
Umatilla	1,576	75%	15	1%	422	20%	1	0%	88	4%	2,101
BLUE MOUNTAINS											
Baker	955	49%	359	18%	640	33%	1	0%	6	0%	1,961
Crook	967	51%	511	27%	422	22%	4	0%	8	0%	1,913
Grant	1,141	40%	186	6%	1,546	54%	5	0%	6	0%	2,883
Union	684	52%	7	1%	612	47%	1	0%	—	0%	1,305
Wallowa	860	43%	13	1%	1,142	56%	—	0%	8	0%	2,023
Wheeler	738	67%	144	13%	179	16%	1	0%	33	3%	1,094
SOUTHEAST											
Harney	1,547	24%	4,085	62%	508	8%	192	3%	223	3%	6,555
Lake	1,329	25%	2,594	49%	1,025	19%	122	2%	266	5%	5,336
Malheur	1,350	21%	4,565	72%	3	0%	284	5%	100	2%	6,302
STATE TOTAL	**27,181**	**44%**	**15,715**	**25%**	**15,643**	**25%**	**1,557**	**3%**	**1,832**	**3%**	**61,928**

Note: Approximate figures derived from Geographic Information System (GIS) database. Ownership figures of less than 1,000 acres are indicated by a dash (—). Percentages have been rounded to the nearest whole number.

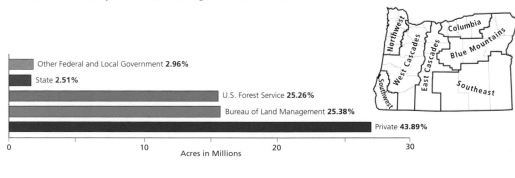

- Other Federal and Local Government **2.96%**
- State **2.51%**
- U.S. Forest Service **25.26%**
- Bureau of Land Management **25.38%**
- Private **43.89%**

Acres in Millions

Land Trades and Exchanges

Land ownership patterns change due to various forms of transfer, primarily land trades or exchanges. Land exchanges between private parties and federal and state agencies are common for the primary purpose of consolidating land holdings into more manageable tracts. While exchanged lands ordinarily have equal fair market value, the acreage can vary greatly depending on the appraised value. Annually, land exchanges are generally insignificant statewide, but over time can accumulate into substantial changes in land ownership patterns.

Federal Lands Payments to Oregon

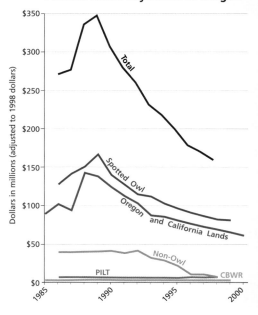

Private ownership accounts for less than 44 percent of the land area of Oregon but covers the most productive agricultural lands and a sizable share of productive timberlands. Once early immigrants claimed the choice agricultural lands in the valleys of Western Oregon, the next wave of settlers pursued ownership of federal lands in other parts of the state through the homestead laws and other land disposal authorities. The public lands survey of Oregon could never keep up with the influx of settlers. Consequently, many homesteads were settled by "squatter sovereignty" or preemption rights, with settlers waiting years for surveys to be completed before they could receive clear title to their land. Although Oregon was not considered a major mineral producer, there were significant deposits of gold and other minerals; these lured many prospectors to locate and settle mining claims on federal lands.

By 1900, the donation land claims in the Willamette Valley had largely passed from the hands of the original owners or their descendants. Stock-raising homesteads were available in parts of Eastern Oregon and attracted many inhabitants from the western part of the state. Settlers also took advantage of the opportunity to purchase grant lands from railroad and wagon road companies. Large timber companies often bought up parcels of timber land from settlers and other parties with the intention of consolidating their holdings into larger blocks of land. The map to the right demonstrates the concentration of private timber company holdings in Western Oregon. A similar consolidation has taken place on range lands in Eastern Oregon, where larger livestock ranches prove to be more economical to operate.

During the twentieth century, the federal government's policy of vigorous land disposal began to shift to land retention. Large areas were set aside for national forests, parks and other public purposes to benefit future generations. The federal government has also acquired private lands to protect critical environmental areas, sites needed for vital public purposes and large areas of submarginal farm lands in Central Oregon to rescue farmers in economic distress.

Federal Land Payments

More than half of Oregon remains in federal ownership, a situation common in Western states. Federal lands are not subject to state and local government taxation, so tax payments to many Oregon counties are greatly restricted. Congress has provided for fiscal relief through a series of revenue sharing and payment arrangements. These include Payment In Lieu of Taxes (PILT) applying to original public domain lands still in federal ownership, and receipt sharing from the sale or lease of natural resources such as timber and minerals. Receipt sharing covers four categories of land: (1) lands subject to spotted owl protection, (2) lands not subject to owl protection, (3) revested O & C Railroad Grant Lands (see pages 22 and 23), and (4) reconveyed Coos Bay Wagon Road Lands (CBWR). A downward trend in payments is clearly evident on the graph to the left, and is primarily due to environmental issues which have reduced federal timber sales.

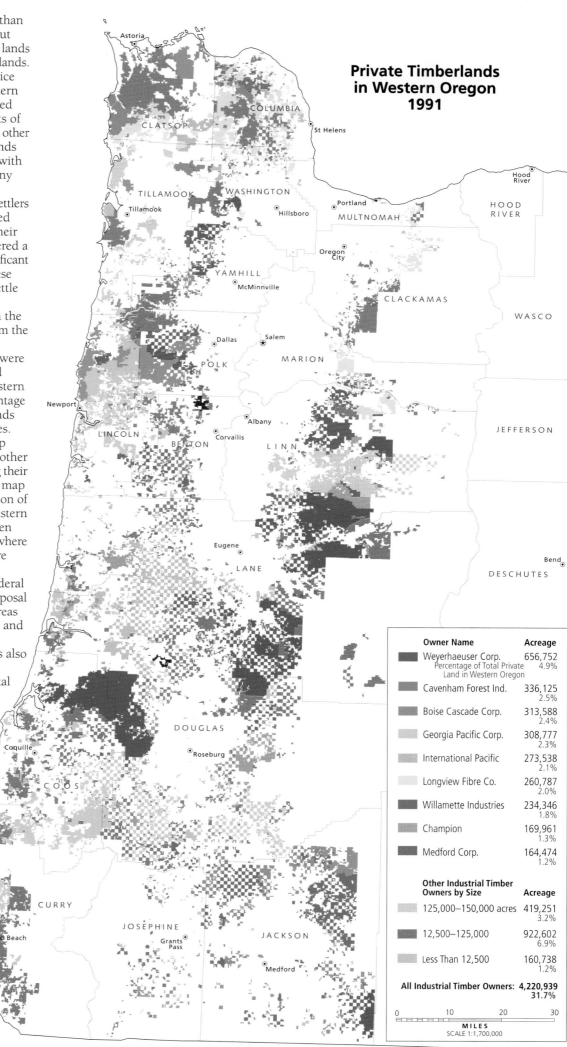

Private Timberlands in Western Oregon 1991

Owner Name	Acreage
Weyerhaeuser Corp.	656,752
Percentage of Total Private Land in Western Oregon	4.9%
Cavenham Forest Ind.	336,125
	2.5%
Boise Cascade Corp.	313,588
	2.4%
Georgia Pacific Corp.	308,777
	2.3%
International Pacific	273,538
	2.1%
Longview Fibre Co.	260,787
	2.0%
Willamette Industries	234,346
	1.8%
Champion	169,961
	1.3%
Medford Corp.	164,474
	1.2%

Other Industrial Timber Owners by Size	Acreage
125,000–150,000 acres	419,251
	3.2%
12,500–125,000	922,602
	6.9%
Less Than 12,500	160,738
	1.2%
All Industrial Timber Owners:	**4,220,939**
	31.7%

0   10   20   30
MILES
SCALE 1:1,700,000

Zoning

Generalized Zoning

- Agriculture/Forest Mix
- Agriculture
- Forest
- Urban Growth Boundary
- Rural Exception
- Ag/Rural Residential Mix
- Mineral/Aggregate Resource
- Natural Resource
- Park Designation
- Public/Airports
- Rangeland

All non-federal lands concealed by inset map are rangelands.

Non-Designated Uses

- Special Geological Area
- Wildlife Refuge

Areas without color are federal and Indian lands not subject to zoning.

Federal and Indian Lands
Shown in white

Oregon adopted a comprehensive land use planning system in 1973 under the leadership of Governor Tom McCall. The foundation of this program is a set of 19 statewide planning goals that serve as standards for local jurisdictions. They encompass economic development, natural and commodity resources, transportation, housing and urban land use efficiency. Two key points of these goals are to direct counties and cities to protect their productive agricultural lands and forestlands and to contain urban growth. Statewide goals are achieved on the local and regional levels through comprehensive plans and zoning.

State law allows counties to take varied approaches when zoning, so long as the resulting plans are consistent with statewide planning goals. This map is a generalized mosaic of each county's zoning maps. Federally owned lands (see inset map) are not normally subject to state or local land use plans or zoning and have been left uncolored on these maps. Federal agencies have control over land uses within their respective jurisdictions.

Agriculture and forestry are vital to Oregon's economic health (see pages 74–75 and 92–99). Protecting the state's productive agricultural and forest resource lands is one major aim of the land use planning system. In total, almost 25 million acres of Oregon's rural lands are zoned for these two uses (approximately 16 million acres are zoned for agriculture including rangeland uses and another 9 million acres are zoned for forest uses). The state's most productive farmlands are concentrated in the Willamette Valley. Premier forestlands are located primarily in Western Oregon. East of the Cascades, drier, less productive soils and harsher growing conditions dictate rangeland uses of a large portion of the lands zoned for agriculture.

The main tool provided by the statewide land use planning system to prevent urban development from encroaching on productive agricultural lands and forestlands is the creation of urban growth boundaries (UGBs). UGBs are intended to accommodate continued growth while encouraging efficient uses of land. One effect of this zoning policy is to establish an orderly transition between urban to rural land uses. All incorporated cities adopted UGBs by the mid-1980s. These boundaries can be amended, but boundary adjustments are neither frequent nor extensive. (Population Centers maps show UGBs and actual settlement patterns in great detail, see pages 194–195 for index map and legend.) Rural areas which were heavily committed to industrial, commercial or residential uses before the adoption of the statewide land use planning system and deemed no longer suited for exclusive farm or forest use are indicated on this map (in red) as Rural Exception lands.

Zoning for mineral and aggregate resources supports resource extraction necessary for industrial and construction activities (see pages 88 and 89). Coastal areas and estuaries have special zoning restrictions to protect these important resources. Across the state communities inventory and plan for use of natural resources, including scenic and historic areas and open spaces.

87

Minerals and Mining

Gold

Gold was discovered in southwest Oregon in 1850 and in northeast Oregon in 1861. Additional deposits were discovered in the Cascade Range and in Central and Eastern Oregon—more than 2,000 deposits are now known. The first production was from placer deposits, flakes and nuggets of gold in stream gravels and beach sands. These deposits could often be mined profitably with simple equipment and only a few workers. Oregon gold production—never exceeding a small fraction of U.S. production—peaked between 1850 and 1900. Underground mining of hard rock, or lode, deposits began in the 1890s—copper, lead and zinc as well as gold were often recovered. Mining was critical to the early economy of the state, triggering development of housing, transportation, logging, cattle and agricultural industries.

The gold mining industry collapsed in 1942 when the U.S. War Production Board issued Order L-208, which diverted experienced miners to the production of metals more important to the war effort. Oregon's postwar production never recovered. In the 1980s high gold prices set off a gold rush throughout the Western U.S., and several new deposits were discovered in Oregon. Gold prices have since dropped, however, and none of these deposits has been mined. Currently, gold production is almost entirely from small placer operations and amounts to only a few thousand ounces per year.

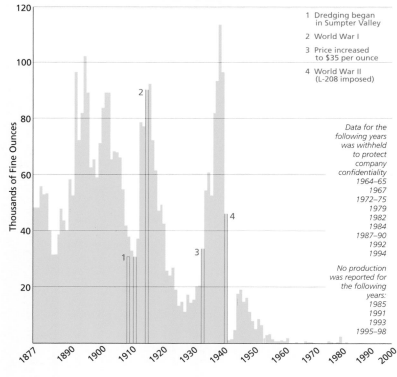

Gold Mining

- ○ Small Production Mining Districts
- Principal Gold Mining Areas
- Areas of Known or Probable Potential
- Beach Placers

North Santiam · Ashwood · Spanish Gulch · Blue Mountains · Quartzville · Howard · Blue River · Fall Creek · Bohemia · Harney · Zinc Creek · Al Serena · Lost Cabin · Klamath Mountains · Barron · High Grade · Pueblo Mountains · Beach Placers

Gold Production

Thousands of Fine Ounces

1 Dredging began in Sumpter Valley
2 World War I
3 Price increased to $35 per ounce
4 World War II (L-208 imposed)

Data for the following years was withheld to protect company confidentiality
1964–65
1967
1972–75
1979
1982
1984
1987–90
1992
1994

No production was reported for the following years:
1985
1991
1993
1995–98

Other Metals

Nickel

Nickel is an essential element in many types of stainless steel alloys, making them harder and more corrosion-resistant. Nickel is not widespread throughout the world, occurring only in certain rock types or soils derived from those rocks. More than 70 nickel deposits are known in Oregon. The only nickel mine in the U.S. was at Nickel Mountain at Riddle in Douglas County, where the metal was mined, smelted and processed starting in 1954. The plant closed in 1998. Significant nickel deposits remain in Oregon, but the U.S. now imports all of its nickel from foreign sources.

Chrome

Chrome, or chromium, is used in stainless steel and to make heat-resistant materials. It occurs in similar rock types as nickel, and in stream and beach placers resulting from erosion of those rocks. More than 500 chrome deposits—typically small and scattered—are known in Oregon. Production has been limited and occurred only in times of national emergency and government subsidies, such as during World War II, when need was critical and foreign sources were inaccessible. No chrome is currently mined in Oregon, since none of the deposits is large enough or rich enough to compete with foreign sources.

Copper, Lead and Zinc

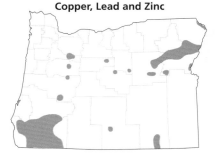

Copper, lead and zinc are three of the most important metals; their primary uses, respectively, are in electrical transmission, storage batteries and rust-proofing steel. More than 600 occurrences are known in Oregon, but total production has been extremely small compared to total U.S. production. Only two Oregon mines were primarily copper producers, the Iron Dyke in Baker County and the Queen of Bronze in Lane County. All other production was from ores—often the by-products of gold mining—containing a mixture of the metals. Oregon now produces none of these metals, as other domestic sources are larger and much easier to mine.

Mercury

Mercury is used in the production of certain chemicals, in batteries and in electric lamps. The U.S. imports all of its primary (non-recycled) mercury, since there are no longer any operating domestic mines. More than 300 occurrences have been identified scattered widely around the state. Nearly all of Oregon's mercury production has been from three areas: around Black Butte in southwest Lane County and adjacent Douglas County, the Horse Heaven area in eastern Jefferson County and the McDermitt area in southwestern Malheur County. Significant amounts were produced between 1927 and 1957—in some years these mines accounted for as much as 10 percent of U.S. production.

Uranium

Uranium is used primarily for electric power generation and military purposes. Western states were prospected intensely during the 1950s, when the federal government was purchasing large quantities of uranium. More than 80 occurrences were identified in Oregon, most of them associated with young volcanic rocks. Only two deposits produced significant amounts of uranium ore: the White King and Lucky Lass mines, both near Lakeview in Lake County. Both mines had ceased operation by 1965. Total production was quite small compared with production in other states.

Minerals and Aggregate

Construction aggregate (sand, gravel and quarry rock) is the largest mining industry in Oregon in terms of tonnage, dollar value and workers employed. Aggregate is essential for all types of concrete and asphalt construction, including highways, bridges, buildings, houses, driveways and sidewalks. More than 2,500 sites have been mined since 1972, and more than 1,000 sites are being mined currently. Aggregate consumption increases as population increases, and costs are lower if aggregate pits and quarries are located near population centers. Land use conflicts are inevitable. Only certain types of deposits are suitable for aggregate; as these sites become regarded as undesirable by residents or are engulfed by new construction, more distant sources must be found and used. This generates additional conflicts and increases hauling costs. Increasing amounts of aggregate are being transported longer distances to urban markets by rail and barge.

Oregon also produces an array of industrial minerals for local and regional markets. Portland cement is manufactured in Baker County from local shale and limestone deposits. Cement is an essential component in concrete, and this plant is one of the few in the Pacific Northwest. Diatomite, a rock composed of countless microscopic plant fossils, is mined in Eastern Oregon and processed into filter material used to purify edible oils, beverages and the water in swimming pools. Diatomite is also mined in northern Lake County for use in cat litter and other absorbent products. Oregon continues to be the nation's leading producer of pumice, a frothy volcanic glass that is used in potting soils and in lightweight concrete blocks. Perlite, a type of volcanic glass that expands when heated, much like popcorn, is used in ceiling tile, fireproof doors and potting soils. Bentonite, a clay that expands more than 10 times when wet, is used as a waterproof sealant in water wells, ponds, building foundations and waste disposal sites. Zeolite is mined in two locations and used to absorb odors, purify water and to carry and slowly release plant fertilizers. Clay is mined in Multnomah County and used to manufacture bricks. Small amounts of dune sand are used to produce green and brown glass bottles. Emery is a rock composed of very hard minerals. The only emery mine in the U.S., in Linn County, produces granules for making long-wearing, non-skid coatings for concrete and steel surfaces such as bridges. Soapstone, a very soft rock composed primarily of talc, is quarried in Jackson County for art sculpture. Gem and lapidary material, including agate, opal, jasper, sunstone and thunder eggs are mined in many counties, especially in the eastern part of the state.

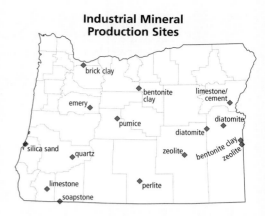

Industrial Mineral Production Sites

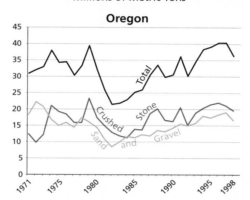

Aggregate Production, 1971–1998
Millions of Metric Tons

Oregon

United States

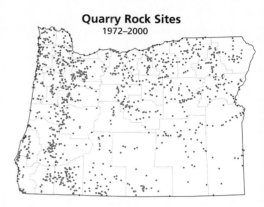

Quarry Rock Sites
1972–2000

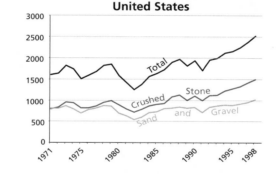

Sand and Gravel Sites
1972–2000

Fossil Fuel

Oregon has never had extensive production of fossil fuels, in part because much of the state is underlain by volcanic rocks, which typically do not contain organic material. Natural gas is produced from one area near Mist in Columbia County. This field, which supplies only a fraction of the state's need, is also used to store natural gas brought in by pipeline for use in Oregon during periods of peak demand. Several other areas, including offshore, have been explored to a limited extent; while occurrences of gas have been found, no commercial fields have been discovered. Current geologic information suggests the possibility of more natural gas, but further exploration will be increasingly expensive and will take place only when demand drives prices significantly higher.

Coal occurs in at least 16 Oregon counties. Many small deposits were mined for local use starting in the 1800s, but only the Coos Bay area has produced coal commercially. Large amounts of Coos Bay coal were mined between 1890 and 1910 and shipped to California. Smaller amounts were used to drive steam locomotives. Production decreased steadily after oil was discovered in California, and no mines have been in operation since about 1950. Coal beds with possible commercial value have been identified in southeastern Coos County and northern Wallowa County, but neither area can be mined profitably under current market conditions.

■ Known Coal Fields
☐ Potential Hydrocarbon Production Areas

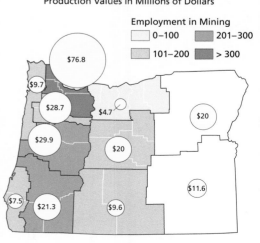

Mining Employment and Production by Region, 1993
Production Values in Millions of Dollars

Employment in Mining
☐ 0–100   ▨ 201–300
▨ 101–200 ■ > 300

Fisheries

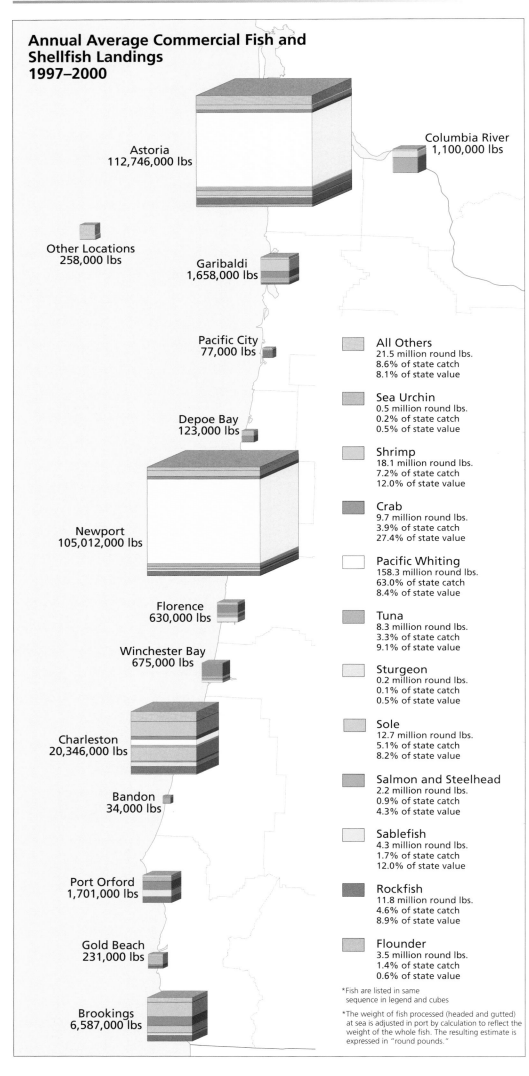

Annual Average Commercial Fish and Shellfish Landings 1997–2000

Columbia River 1,100,000 lbs

Astoria 112,746,000 lbs

Other Locations 258,000 lbs

Garibaldi 1,658,000 lbs

Pacific City 77,000 lbs

Depoe Bay 123,000 lbs

Newport 105,012,000 lbs

Florence 630,000 lbs

Winchester Bay 675,000 lbs

Charleston 20,346,000 lbs

Bandon 34,000 lbs

Port Orford 1,701,000 lbs

Gold Beach 231,000 lbs

Brookings 6,587,000 lbs

All Others
21.5 million round lbs.
8.6% of state catch
8.1% of state value

Sea Urchin
0.5 million round lbs.
0.2% of state catch
0.5% of state value

Shrimp
18.1 million round lbs.
7.2% of state catch
12.0% of state value

Crab
9.7 million round lbs.
3.9% of state catch
27.4% of state value

Pacific Whiting
158.3 million round lbs.
63.0% of state catch
8.4% of state value

Tuna
8.3 million round lbs.
3.3% of state catch
9.1% of state value

Sturgeon
0.2 million round lbs.
0.1% of state catch
0.5% of state value

Sole
12.7 million round lbs.
5.1% of state catch
8.2% of state value

Salmon and Steelhead
2.2 million round lbs.
0.9% of state catch
4.3% of state value

Sablefish
4.3 million round lbs.
1.7% of state catch
12.0% of state value

Rockfish
11.8 million round lbs.
4.6% of state catch
8.9% of state value

Flounder
3.5 million round lbs.
1.4% of state catch
0.6% of state value

*Fish are listed in same sequence in legend and cubes

*The weight of fish processed (headed and gutted) at sea is adjusted in port by calculation to reflect the weight of the whole fish. The resulting estimate is expressed in "round pounds."

Oregon's coastal waters support commercial and recreational fisheries that yield a variety of fish and crustaceans. The fisheries are highly dynamic, with large seasonal and annual changes in the availability of some of the most important species.

During the early 1970s the commercial fishery in Oregon largely relied on harvests of salmon and albacore tuna for support, followed in terms of landed value by harvests of crab, shrimp and groundfish—bottom-dwelling fish such as flatfish and rockfish. By the early 1980s, however, catches of groundfish surpassed those of salmon, tuna and shellfish in terms of pounds and were comparable to them in value. Salmon landings during the 1980s averaged about 9.4 million pounds annually (58 percent chinook, 38 percent coho) and accounted for about a quarter of the landed value of Oregon's commercial fish and shellfish catch. During the 1990s groundfish catches (including Pacific whiting) continued to grow, accounting for 79 percent of the pounds and 47 percent of the value of the commercial fishery. The 1990s also saw the salmon fishery severely limited because of the endangered species status of several stocks that spawn in the Columbia River and coastal rivers.

Oregon's commercial fish harvests are landed mostly at Astoria, Newport and Charleston (Coos Bay). Compared to Oregon's smaller ports, Astoria, Newport and Charleston have well-developed infrastructure, and their entrances are dredged regularly to maintain safe shipping channels. Even so, during high winds and rough seas it can be perilous to "cross the bar" at these harbors. In 1997 Astoria ranked 12th in seafood landings among all U.S. ports and Newport ranked 14th; in 1998 Newport ranked 11th and Astoria ranked 15th.

Salmon and albacore tuna landed in Oregon are caught primarily by trollers towing lures or baited hooks. Salmon are also harvested commercially from the Columbia River using gillnets and setnets. With the restricted salmon harvests of the 1990s, many of the salmon fishers who operate relatively small boats switched to fishing for albacore tuna during summer and Dungeness crab during the winter. Shrimp, mostly the small cocktail variety, are caught spring through fall using trawl nets towed just above the ocean floor. Bottom trawls, dragged along the ocean floor by relatively large trawlers, take the harvests of most groundfish species, although longlines

Annual Average Personal Income from Fisheries, 1995–1998

$3,380
$6,216
$3,873
$2,483
$1,076
$649
$75
$766
$742
$647
$549
$17,665
$1,797
$64
$766
$4,228
$21
$29
$4,658
$342
$142
$6,055
$2,873
$63
$18
$24
$3,288
$374
$367
$151

Thousands of Dollars

- >$15,000
- $5,000–$10,000
- $1,000–$4,999
- $100–$999
- $15–$99
- 0 or no data

Value and Pounds by Type, 1970–1999

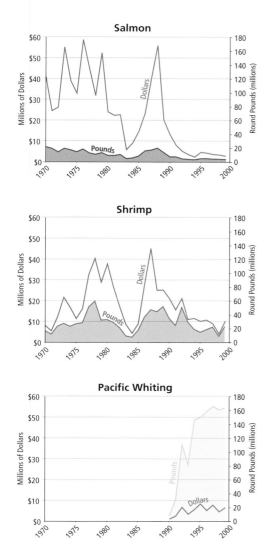

Salmon

Shrimp

Pacific Whiting

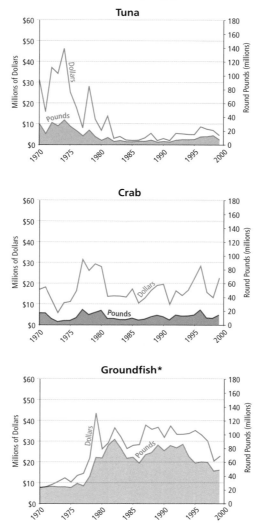

Tuna

Crab

Groundfish*

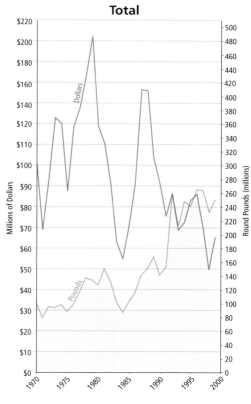

Total

*Note: Groundfish includes flounder, halibut, rockfish, sablefish, sole and other deep-habitat or non-schooling fish, but does not include Pacific Whiting.

Dollar amounts on all graphs have been adjusted to 1999 dollars.

and fish pots, operated from smaller vessels, are important gear for certain species. Pacific whiting, which form dense schools off the ocean floor, are caught mostly by large trawlers.

Usually it is necessary to constrain fishing so that harvests do not outstrip a species' ability to maintain its population. The Pacific Fishery Management Council, in conjunction with the federal government and U.S. West Coast states, manages Oregon's marine fisheries for salmon and groundfish. Species that reside primarily within the three-mile limit of Oregon's territorial waters, such as most shellfish species,

do not fall under federal jurisdiction and are managed by the Oregon Department of Fish and Wildlife. Management agencies use a variety of techniques to regulate fishing operations including: restrictions on the types or sizes of fishing gear, minimum size limits for fish that may be retained, closed seasons and areas, trip limits restricting how much each boat can land during a fixed time span, and annual quotas on the landings by the entire fleet. Almost all of Oregon's commercial fisheries have regulations to limit the number of fishers and fishing vessels. Limited entry

programs were implemented in 1979 and 1980 for the shrimp and salmon fisheries, and in 1995 for the groundfish and Dungeness crab fisheries.

Although most of Oregon's harvests of fish and shellfish are captured from naturally reproducing populations, salmon hatcheries on the Columbia River and the Oregon Coast are an important source of salmon production. Oysters are raised by private aquaculture operations at leased sites in the estuaries of Tillamook, Netarts, the Yaquina River (Newport) and Coos Bay.

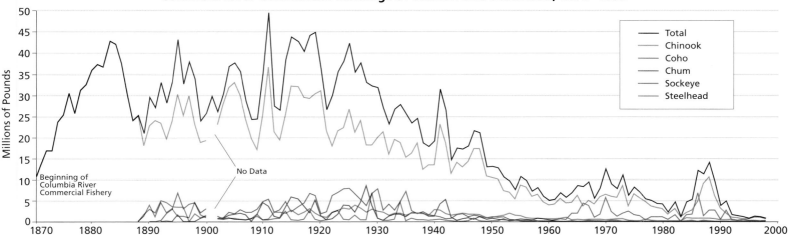

Columbia River Commercial Landings of Salmon and Steelhead, 1870–1998

Timber

Forests cover almost half of Oregon's total land area. These forests can be divided into the "wetter" ecoregions—generally Western Oregon—which have relatively high levels of precipitation; and the "drier" ecoregions—generally Eastern Oregon—which have relatively low levels of precipitation. In the west, the Douglas-fir is the most commercially important tree species, and clearcutting has been the primary form of timber harvest. In the east, harvesters have focused on the ponderosa pine and used partial cutting methods of harvest.

Oregon's commercial timber harvests began in the 1850s. Timber came exclusively from private lands, especially along the north Coast. Harvest remained at relatively low levels for decades, then, after the turn of the century, large-scale harvesting operations spread to Lane County and the eastern Cascades. Until World War II, the harvest still came largely from private lands, but the beginning of the war opened a new era in Oregon's timber production. Logging operations worked ever farther up the slopes, moving from private to public holdings.

The post-war economic boom resulted in record harvests from Oregon's forests, with only occasional dips keyed to recessions. In the 1960s through 1980s, Oregon consistently harvested more timber than any other state, with that harvest almost equally divided between private and federal lands. Lane and Douglas Counties alone accounted for more harvested timber than most states.

In the early 1990s, management of Oregon's federal forests became a national issue when the northern spotted owl joined the American political lexicon. In the policy changes that resulted, the state experienced a major reduction in timber harvest from federal lands; management of these lands refocused on protection of biodiversity as a primary goal (see pages 74–75). These changes created hardship for people and communities economically connected with the harvest of timber from federal lands. Still, these changes appear permanent. In the future most of Oregon's greatly reduced timber harvest, estimated at approximately 4 billion board feet per year, will come primarily from private land in Western Oregon.

A long-term historical pattern of high-intensity fires resulted in mostly even-aged stands in Western Oregon, with Douglas-fir the major species at low and middle elevations. The infrequent nature of these fires allowed for the development of the old-growth stands for which Western Oregon is famous. Most of the "merchantable timber" shown in Western Oregon on the 1914 Forest Cover map was such old growth.

The Landsat satellite image of the central Cascades illustrates forest conditions in much of Western Oregon. About 70 percent of the area is national forest, and most of the rest belongs to the forest industry. Industry lands are concentrated toward the western edge of the image and in the light-colored area in the northwest corner. The light-colored patches indicate recent harvests. The relatively small light-colored patches with uncut darker areas between them are in the national forests and reflect the policy of staggering small clearcuts

across the landscape. Past plans called for the uncut buffers also to be harvested as the clearcut patches grew back. The larger areas of continuous young forest on industry land reflects a past policy of harvesting bigger units. Almost all of the harvested area has been successfully restocked with conifers, although these stands often are densely stocked and lack structural and species diversity. As a result of long-term harvesting practices, today's old growth forests (much of the dark green in the image) are far smaller than those seen in the past, but have the potential to increase significantly under the Northwest Forest Plan for federal forests. Under this plan, about half of the forest in the image will be devoted to growing old forest.

A Landsat image of the forests of Eastern Oregon, such as those in the Blue Mountains where federal ownership predominates, would show less clearcutting, more continuous cover and more large, recently burned areas. Before the nineteenth century a pattern of frequent, low to moderate intensity fires at low and middle elevations resulted in multi-aged stands of ponderosa pine, along with mixed conifer stands dominated by Douglas-fir on moister sites. During the twentieth century these forests were significantly altered by timber harvest,

Average Annual Harvest
Volume Removed in Board Feet

1925–1929

Average Annual Total Harvest: 4,999,500*

Clatsop..........538,207
Columbia......505,610
Klamath........418,910
Lane.............331,654
Coos.............312,668

*In board feet; top five counties listed

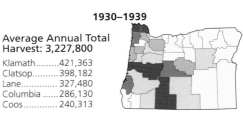

1930–1939

Average Annual Total Harvest: 3,227,800

Klamath.........421,363
Clatsop..........398,182
Lane..............327,480
Columbia......286,130
Coos.............240,313

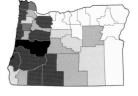

1940–1949

Average Annual Total Harvest: 6,952,100

Lane..............852,643
Douglas........570,443
Linn..............546,019
Klamath........412,402
Coos.............405,087

1950–1959

Average Annual Total Harvest: 8,713,300

Douglas.....1,524,973
Lane............1,233,749
Coos.............629,742
Jackson..........540,583
Linn..............518,058

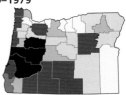

1960–1969

Average Annual Total Harvest: 8,780,500

Lane...........1,224,635
Douglas.....1,190,291
Coos.............527,028
Linn..............504,112
Jackson..........367,795

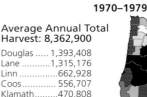

1970–1979

Average Annual Total Harvest: 8,362,900

Douglas.....1,393,408
Lane...........1,315,176
Linn..............662,928
Coos.............556,707
Klamath.........470,808

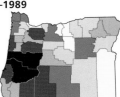

1980–1989

Average Annual Total Harvest: 7,522,600

Douglas.....1,272,150
Lane...........1,235,542
Linn..............574,572
Klamath........473,044
Coos.............444,203

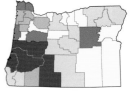

1990–1998

Average Annual Total Harvest: 4,815,666

Lane..............629,124
Douglas.........583,625
Klamath........330,338
Coos.............329,760
Linn..............243,097

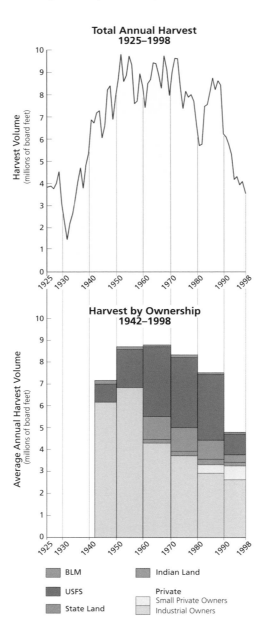

Total Annual Harvest 1925–1998

Harvest Volume (millions of board feet)

Harvest by Ownership 1942–1998

Average Annual Harvest Volume (millions of board feet)

BLM
USFS
State Land
Indian Land
Private
Small Private Owners
Industrial Owners

Volume data for BLM and State Land begins in 1962.

fire suppression and cattle grazing. Timber harvesters first focused on removing large, old, decadent trees to reduce insect hazard and, later, on removing the most valuable trees and creating a fast growing, more uniform forest. As a result, relatively few large ponderosa pine trees remain, trees that once were the symbol of the area. The combined effect of timber harvest and fire suppression produced significant increases in stand densities, fuel loadings and proportions of shade-tolerant species, especially on federal land.

This satellite image from 1995 covers about 1,050 square miles of Linn, Jefferson and Deschutes Counties. The view straddles the Cascade crest on either side of Santiam Pass, in the right central part of the image. The peaks of Mount Washington and Three Fingered Jack stand out clearly. Geologically recent lava flows from Belknap Crater and west of Santiam Pass appear as smooth gray unforested areas. The large light-colored area extending east-to-west just south of Santiam Pass and north of Big Lake is a burn from the 1960s. Other light-colored areas are in various stages of growth after logging or fire. Square-mile (640-acre) clearcuts can be seen on private land along both sides of the crest, but are especially obvious on the drier east side. A huge industrial block on the Middle Santiam River above Green Peter Lake, recognizable on page 95 (Timber Ownership), abuts the uncut Middle Santiam Wilderness just upstream. The Mount Jefferson, Mount Washington and Three Sisters Wilderness Areas similarly stand out from the distinctive pattern of small clearcuts on the Willamette and Deschutes National Forests (see pages 82–83 and 190–191). Much of this national forest land has been designated as Late Successional Reserve (see page 191).

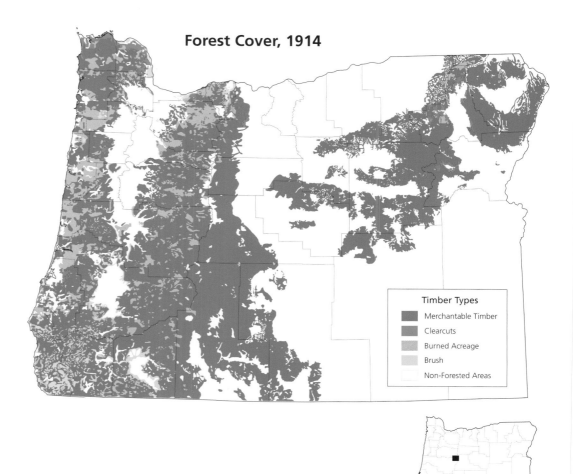

Forest Cover, 1914

Timber Types

- Merchantable Timber
- Clearcuts
- Burned Acreage
- Brush
- Non-Forested Areas

Forest Cover in the Central Cascades, 1995

This image area is shown in its wider geographic setting on page 188.

| 0 | 5 | 10 | 15 | 20 Miles |

Quartzville Creek

North Santiam

Middle Santiam River

Green Peter Lake

Three Fingered Jack

Santiam Junction

Santiam Pass

Suttle Lake

South Santiam River

Tombstone Pass

Clear Lake

Big Lake

Smith Res

Mt Washington

Belknap Crater

Lava Field

McKenzie Pass

McKenzie River

Blue River

H.J. Andrews Experimental Forest

Farmlands

Agriculture is an important part of Oregon's economy and landscape. Farms and ranches occupy a little more than a quarter of the state's total land area (nearly 17.5 million acres in 1997) and nearly 60 percent of privately owned land. About one-third of agricultural land is cropland; the remainder is largely woodlands, pasture and rangeland. Roughly half of Oregon —mostly mountains, range and desert—is publicly owned, the majority of which is unsuitable for cultivation. More than half of the public range and forest land (some 20 million acres) is leased for grazing.

The geographical distribution of farmlands and rangelands reflects the spatial distribution of soil quality, topography and water availability. The most productive soils are concentrated in the alluvial flood plains of river valleys and in the loess hills of the Columbia Plateau. Water availability tends to decrease from west to east across Oregon and to a lesser extent from north to south. Topography also plays a role, as farming is generally infeasible in areas with high elevations or steep slopes. Cropland is concentrated in the Willamette Valley and along the Columbia River, with smaller pockets of mainly irrigated croplands, scattered across the state. Rangelands predominate in the drier central and southeast regions and in the more rugged areas along the Coast and in southwestern Oregon.

The average Oregon farm size of 513 acres is misleading. West of the Cascades, relatively small farms (typically 50–200 acres) are most common. These farms produce a variety of high-value crops, reflected in the high proportions of harvested cropland, proportion of sales arising from crops and high land values. Tillamook County, which derives the majority of sales from dairy production, is the only county west of the Cascades where sales of animal products exceed sales from crops. On the drier east side, cattle ranching is the main use of rangelands. Ranches here are typically large (1,000–5,000 acres) and of lower per-acre valued land. Income results

Farm and Range Lands

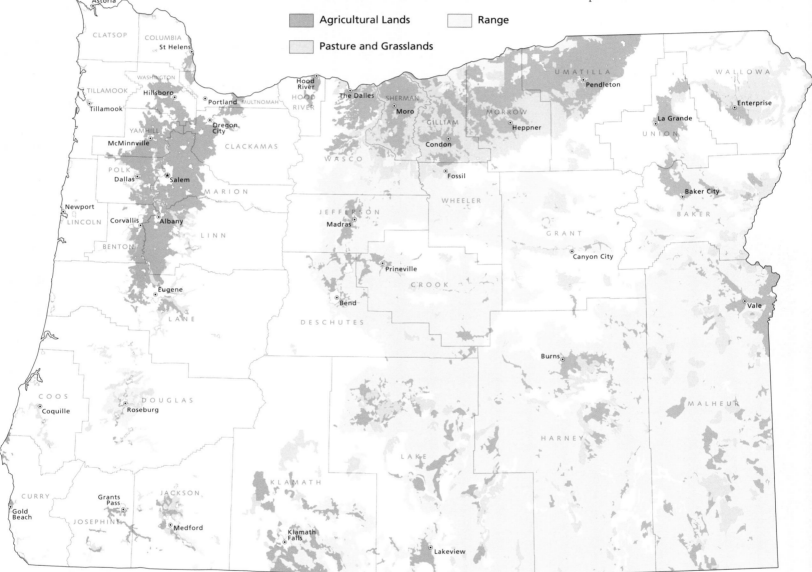

Legend:
- Agricultural Lands
- Pasture and Grasslands
- Range

1997 Agricultural Land Use

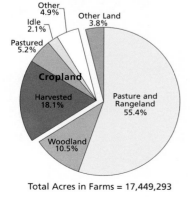

Other 4.9%
Idle 2.1%
Pastured 5.2%
Cropland — Harvested 18.1%
Woodland 10.5%
Other Land 3.8%
Pasture and Rangeland 55.4%

Total Acres in Farms = 17,449,293

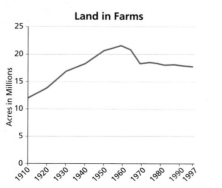

Land in Farms

Acres in Millions

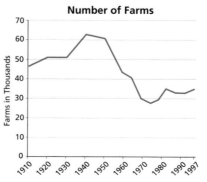

Number of Farms

Farms in Thousands

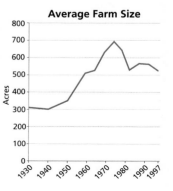

Average Farm Size

Acres

mostly from sales of cattle. Many ranches rely on small tracts of irrigated hay and pasture for supplemental forage. Farms east of the Cascades are generally of two major types: dryland wheat farms of the Columbia Plateau and irrigated crop farms in the Hermiston, La Grande, Vale, Klamath Falls and Madras areas.

More than half of the harvested cropland in Oregon was irrigated in 1997. With the exception of dryland wheat grown on the Columbia Plateau, crop farming is not possible in the high desert east of the Cascades without irrigation. Even in wet Western Oregon, much of the specialized agriculture requires irrigation during the dry summer months.

Agricultural land values have fluctuated widely in the past three decades. Heavily influenced by development pressures, the highest land values are found along Interstate 5 (I-5), the Coast and around Bend. Land values tend to steadily increase south to north up the I-5 corridor.

Land In Farms As a Percentage of Total Land
State: 28%

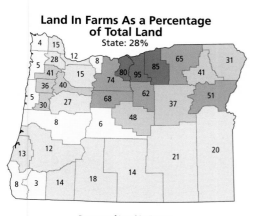

Percent of Land in Farms
<10%　10–29%　30–49%　50–79%　>80%

Harvested Cropland As a Percentage of all Farmland
State: 18%

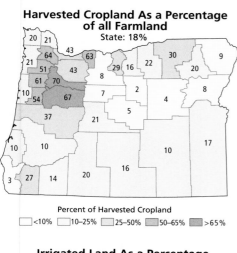

Percent of Harvested Cropland
<10%　10–25%　25–50%　50–65%　>65%

Irrigated Land As a Percentage of Total Farmland
State: 11%

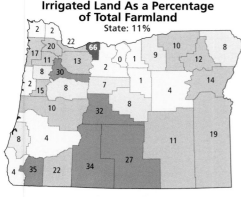

Percent of Irrigated Farmland
<5%　5–10%　10–25%　25–60%　>60%

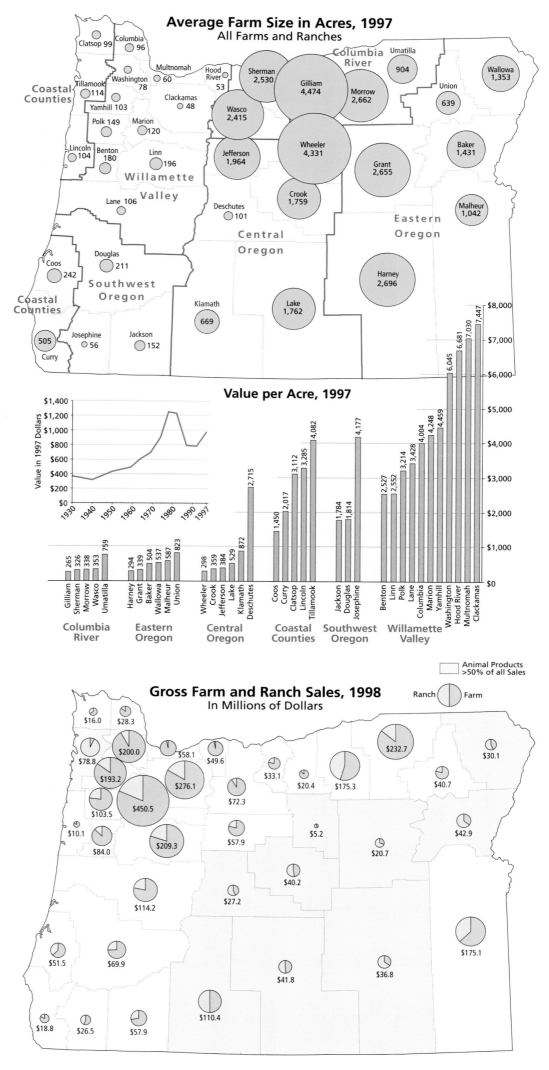

Average Farm Size in Acres, 1997
All Farms and Ranches

Value per Acre, 1997

Gross Farm and Ranch Sales, 1998
In Millions of Dollars

Cattle and Crops

There are more than 125 different farm commodities grown in Oregon. Factors such as rainfall, temperature, growing season, soils, proximity to population centers and access to economic infrastructure influence the production of individual commodities. These production variables combine to create several different agricultural regions within the state. Oregon's agricultural commodities can be classified most broadly as livestock or crops. In recent years, crops have accounted for roughly 75 percent of the total dollar value of farm output, and livestock the remaining 25 percent. By area, crops comprise only about 30 percent of total farmland.

Beef cattle are the most important commodity in Oregon's livestock industry. The majority of beef cattle are produced on the grazing lands east of the Cascade Mountains. Separate from the beef sector, dairy production is centered in the upper Willamette Valley and the north Coast.

Field crops including grains, hay and grass seed account for the largest proportion of crop acreage in the state. Wheat is the most important grain, grown primarily as a dry land (non-irrigated) crop in the Columbia Plateau counties. Hay and alfalfa are grown throughout the state, often in conjunction with livestock enterprises. Grass seed crops account for more than half of the cropland in the Willamette Valley. Oregon is the largest producer of grass seed in the U.S., offering varieties specialized for lawns, playing fields, livestock forage and soil conservation.

Although field crops account for the majority of Oregon's crop acreage, the single highest valued commodity group in terms of

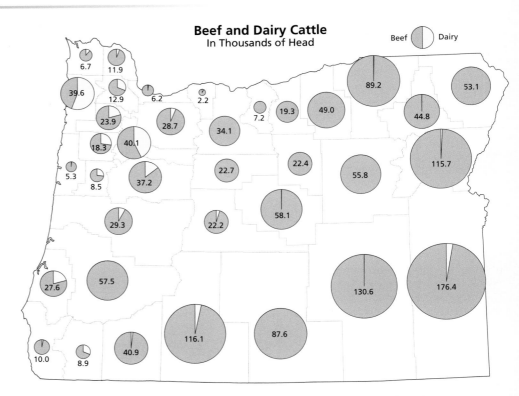

Beef and Dairy Cattle
In Thousands of Head

Beef | Dairy

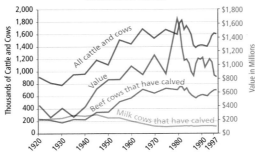

Cattle and Cows

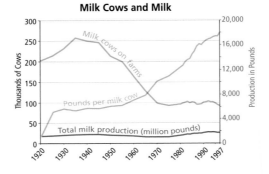

Milk Cows and Milk

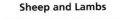

Sheep and Lambs

Livestock, Dairy and Poultry Value of Production

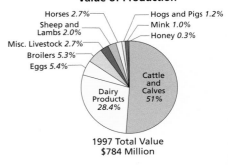

Horses 2.7%
Sheep and Lambs 2.0%
Misc. Livestock 2.7%
Broilers 5.3%
Eggs 5.4%
Hogs and Pigs 1.2%
Mink 1.0%
Honey 0.3%
Cattle and Calves 51%
Dairy Products 28.4%

1997 Total Value
$784 Million

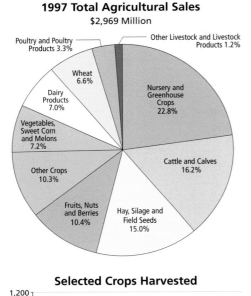

1997 Total Agricultural Sales
$2,969 Million

Poultry and Poultry Products 3.3%
Other Livestock and Livestock Products 1.2%
Wheat 6.6%
Dairy Products 7.0%
Vegetables, Sweet Corn and Melons 7.2%
Nursery and Greenhouse Crops 22.8%
Other Crops 10.3%
Cattle and Calves 16.2%
Fruits, Nuts and Berries 10.4%
Hay, Silage and Field Seeds 15.0%

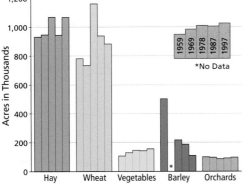

Selected Crops Harvested

1959 1969 1978 1987 1997
*No Data

Hay | Wheat | Vegetables | Barley | Orchards

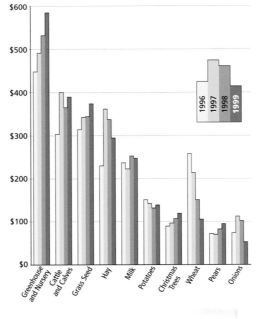

Top 10 Crops by Value of Production
In Millions of Dollars

1996 1997 1998 1999

Greenhouse and Nursery | Cattle and Calves | Grass Seed | Hay | Milk | Potatoes | Christmas Trees | Wheat | Pears | Onions

farm sales receipts is greenhouse and nursery crops. This category includes flowers and flowering plants and container and bedding plants, as well as field-grown plants. Production is centered in the upper Willamette Valley, taking advantage of the mild climate, productive soils and proximity to the state's urban population centers. Orchard crops are concentrated primarily in the Willamette and Rogue River Valleys and the Hood River region. Smaller, specialized tree fruit operations are located throughout the state. Vegetable production is concentrated in the irrigated acreage of the Willamette Valley, the Umatilla Basin near Hermiston, the Klamath Basin and the Ontario district in Malheur County. Within these general crop categories, individual commodities often grow within an even more limited range. Hazelnuts, for example, are grown almost exclusively in the Willamette Valley, pears in the Hood River and Medford regions and green peas in Umatilla County.

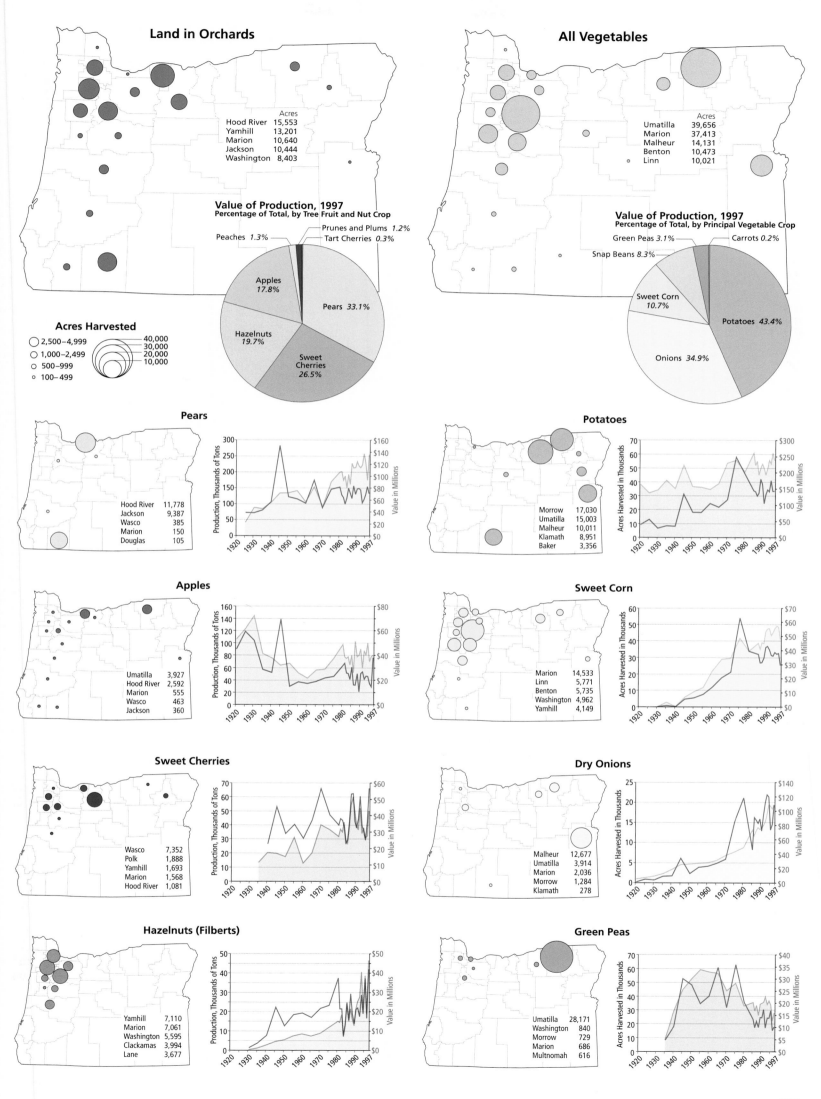

Land in Orchards

	Acres
Hood River	15,553
Yamhill	13,201
Marion	10,640
Jackson	10,444
Washington	8,403

Value of Production, 1997
Percentage of Total, by Tree Fruit and Nut Crop

- Prunes and Plums 1.2%
- Tart Cherries 0.3%
- Peaches 1.3%
- Apples 17.8%
- Pears 33.1%
- Hazelnuts 19.7%
- Sweet Cherries 26.5%

Acres Harvested

- 2,500–4,999
- 1,000–2,499
- 500–999
- 100–499
- 40,000
- 30,000
- 20,000
- 10,000

All Vegetables

	Acres
Umatilla	39,656
Marion	37,413
Malheur	14,131
Benton	10,473
Linn	10,021

Value of Production, 1997
Percentage of Total, by Principal Vegetable Crop

- Green Peas 3.1%
- Carrots 0.2%
- Snap Beans 8.3%
- Sweet Corn 10.7%
- Potatoes 43.4%
- Onions 34.9%

Pears

Hood River	11,778
Jackson	9,387
Wasco	385
Marion	150
Douglas	105

Potatoes

Morrow	17,030
Umatilla	15,003
Malheur	10,011
Klamath	8,951
Baker	3,356

Apples

Umatilla	3,927
Hood River	2,592
Marion	555
Wasco	463
Jackson	360

Sweet Corn

Marion	14,533
Linn	5,771
Benton	5,735
Washington	4,962
Yamhill	4,149

Sweet Cherries

Wasco	7,352
Polk	1,888
Yamhill	1,693
Marion	1,568
Hood River	1,081

Dry Onions

Malheur	12,677
Umatilla	3,914
Marion	2,036
Morrow	1,284
Klamath	278

Hazelnuts (Filberts)

Yamhill	7,110
Marion	7,061
Washington	5,595
Clackamas	3,994
Lane	3,677

Green Peas

Umatilla	28,171
Washington	840
Morrow	729
Marion	686
Multnomah	616

Crops and Wine

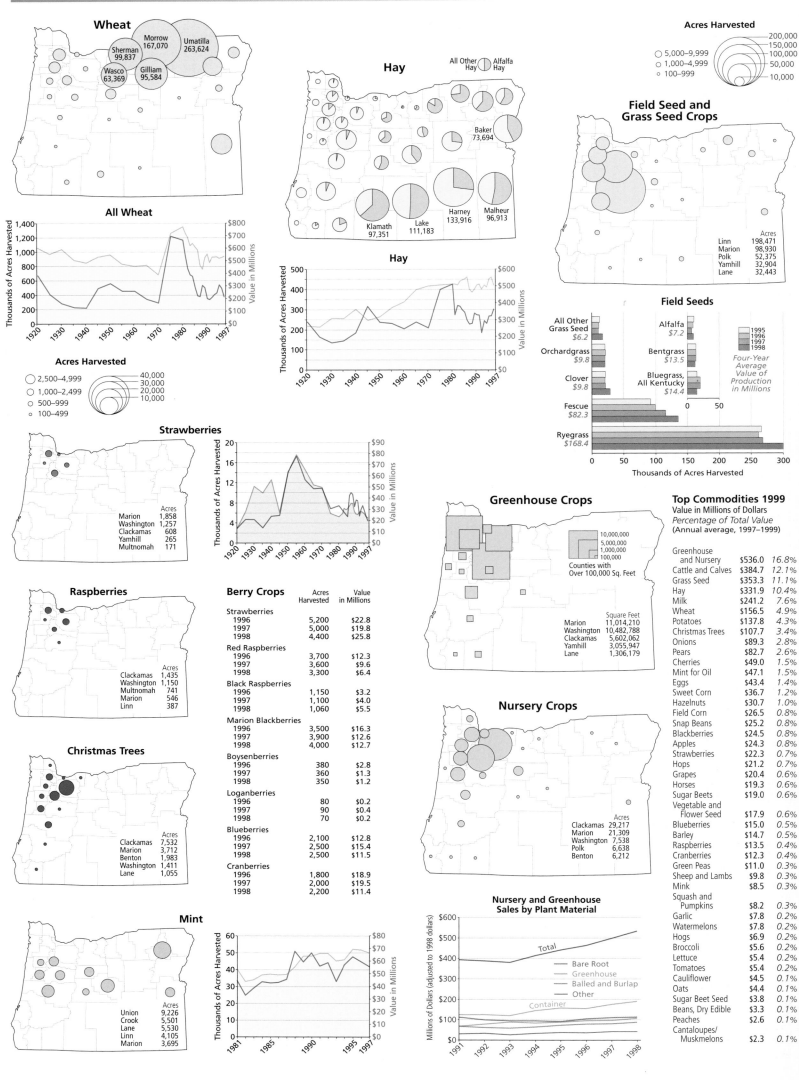

Wheat

Sherman 99,837
Morrow 167,070
Umatilla 263,624
Wasco 63,369
Gilliam 95,584

Acres Harvested
5,000–9,999
1,000–4,999
100–999
200,000
150,000
100,000
50,000
10,000

All Wheat

Thousands of Acres Harvested / Value in Millions

Hay

All Other Hay / Alfalfa Hay

Baker 73,694
Klamath 97,351
Lake 111,183
Harney 133,916
Malheur 96,913

Hay

Thousands of Acres Harvested / Value in Millions

Field Seed and Grass Seed Crops

	Acres
Linn	198,471
Marion	98,930
Polk	52,375
Yamhill	32,904
Lane	32,443

Field Seeds

All Other Grass Seed *$6.2*
Orchardgrass *$9.8*
Clover *$9.8*
Fescue *$82.3*
Ryegrass *$168.4*
Alfalfa *$7.2*
Bentgrass *$13.5*
Bluegrass, All Kentucky *$14.4*

1995 1996 1997 1998

Four-Year Average Value of Production in Millions

Thousands of Acres Harvested

Acres Harvested
2,500–4,999
1,000–2,499
500–999
100–499
40,000
30,000
20,000
10,000

Strawberries

	Acres
Marion	1,858
Washington	1,257
Clackamas	608
Yamhill	265
Multnomah	171

Thousands of Acres Harvested / Value in Millions

Greenhouse Crops

10,000,000
5,000,000
1,000,000
100,000
Counties with Over 100,000 Sq. Feet

	Square Feet
Marion	11,014,210
Washington	10,482,788
Clackamas	5,602,062
Yamhill	3,055,947
Lane	1,306,179

Top Commodities 1999
Value in Millions of Dollars
Percentage of Total Value
(Annual average, 1997–1999)

Greenhouse and Nursery	$536.0	*16.8%*
Cattle and Calves	$384.7	*12.1%*
Grass Seed	$353.3	*11.1%*
Hay	$331.9	*10.4%*
Milk	$241.2	*7.6%*
Wheat	$156.5	*4.9%*
Potatoes	$137.8	*4.3%*
Christmas Trees	$107.7	*3.4%*
Onions	$89.3	*2.8%*
Pears	$82.7	*2.6%*
Cherries	$49.0	*1.5%*
Mint for Oil	$47.1	*1.5%*
Eggs	$43.4	*1.4%*
Sweet Corn	$36.7	*1.2%*
Hazelnuts	$30.7	*1.0%*
Field Corn	$26.5	*0.8%*
Snap Beans	$25.2	*0.8%*
Blackberries	$24.5	*0.8%*
Apples	$24.3	*0.8%*
Strawberries	$22.3	*0.7%*
Hops	$21.2	*0.7%*
Grapes	$20.4	*0.6%*
Horses	$19.3	*0.6%*
Sugar Beets	$19.0	*0.6%*
Vegetable and Flower Seed	$17.9	*0.6%*
Blueberries	$15.0	*0.5%*
Barley	$14.7	*0.5%*
Raspberries	$13.5	*0.4%*
Cranberries	$12.3	*0.4%*
Green Peas	$11.0	*0.3%*
Sheep and Lambs	$9.8	*0.3%*
Mink	$8.5	*0.3%*
Squash and Pumpkins	$8.2	*0.3%*
Garlic	$7.8	*0.2%*
Watermelons	$7.8	*0.2%*
Hogs	$6.9	*0.2%*
Broccoli	$5.6	*0.2%*
Lettuce	$5.4	*0.2%*
Tomatoes	$5.4	*0.2%*
Cauliflower	$4.5	*0.1%*
Oats	$4.4	*0.1%*
Sugar Beet Seed	$3.8	*0.1%*
Beans, Dry Edible	$3.3	*0.1%*
Peaches	$2.6	*0.1%*
Cantaloupes/ Muskmelons	$2.3	*0.1%*

Raspberries

	Acres
Clackamas	1,435
Washington	1,150
Multnomah	741
Marion	546
Linn	387

Berry Crops

	Acres Harvested	Value in Millions
Strawberries		
1996	5,200	$22.8
1997	5,000	$19.8
1998	4,400	$25.8
Red Raspberries		
1996	3,700	$12.3
1997	3,600	$9.6
1998	3,300	$6.4
Black Raspberries		
1996	1,150	$3.2
1997	1,100	$4.0
1998	1,060	$5.5
Marion Blackberries		
1996	3,500	$16.3
1997	3,900	$12.6
1998	4,000	$12.7
Boysenberries		
1996	380	$2.8
1997	360	$1.3
1998	350	$1.2
Loganberries		
1996	80	$0.2
1997	90	$0.4
1998	70	$0.2
Blueberries		
1996	2,100	$12.8
1997	2,500	$15.4
1998	2,500	$11.5
Cranberries		
1996	1,800	$18.9
1997	2,000	$19.5
1998	2,200	$11.4

Christmas Trees

	Acres
Clackamas	7,532
Marion	3,712
Benton	1,983
Washington	1,411
Lane	1,055

Nursery Crops

	Acres
Clackamas	29,217
Marion	21,309
Washington	7,538
Polk	6,638
Benton	6,212

Nursery and Greenhouse Sales by Plant Material

Millions of Dollars (adjusted to 1998 dollars)

Total
Bare Root
Greenhouse
Balled and Burlap
Other
Container

Mint

	Acres
Union	9,226
Crook	5,501
Lane	5,530
Linn	4,105
Marion	3,695

Thousands of Acres Harvested / Value in Millions

Crops

In the latter part of the twentieth century Oregon agriculture gradually shifted away from bulk, homogeneous farm products such as wheat, toward higher valued, specialized products including nursery crops and grass seed. Oregon ranks as one of the top-producing states for peppermint, snap beans, hops, cane berries, winter peas, prunes, hazelnuts (filberts), Christmas trees, onions, flower seeds, pears and wine grapes. About half of the total value of agricultural production in the state is from the Willamette Valley. Led by farm output in Marion and Clackamas Counties, Willamette Valley agriculture yields a diverse, high-value mix of commodities. Umatilla, Malheur and Klamath Counties account for the largest agricultural sales output from counties east of the Cascades. Agriculture in these counties is a blend of high-value irrigated crops, traditional grains and forage, as well as extensive beef cattle production. Tillamook County is associated with dairy production, Hood River with tree fruits, Sherman and Gilliam Counties with dry land grains, and Coos and Curry Counties with cranberries.

Technological improvements in production practices and crop varieties have permitted Oregon farmers to significantly boost yield over time, even though the acreage base or livestock herd has remained relatively constant. Total potato production, for example, has tripled since 1945 although acreage devoted to the crop has not changed significantly. Nearly all of Oregon's agricultural products exhibit significant year-to-year variation in output and sales value due to a combination of growing conditions and economic factors.

Wine

Oregon shares the temperate 45th parallel with many of the world's finest wine-growing regions. Early vines came to Oregon from a vineyard planted at Fort Vancouver in 1825. Pioneer Jesse Applegate established the first southern Oregon vineyard in 1876. In 1883, German immigrant Ernest Rueter planted a vineyard in Forest Grove; his "Klevner" wine won a gold medal at the 1904 St. Louis Exposition. Inspiring the pioneers of Oregon's post-Prohibition wine industry, Richard Somer planted Hillcrest Vineyard at the southern end of the Umpqua Valley in 1961. The Eyrie Vinyard brought international attention to Oregon at the 1979 "Olympiads of the Wines of the World" held in Paris, where its 1975 vintage Pinot noir bested the renowned wines of Burgundy, France. Pinot Noir remains Oregon's flagship variety.

The wines from each of the six wine appellations (regions of origin) shown on the map reflect the unique "characteristic of place" imparted by the local climate, soil and geography. Currently about 480 vineyards produce 18,600 tons of fruit annually valued at roughly $26 million. Oregon's price per ton ($1,400) is the highest in the nation, compared to $899 in Washington and $497 in California. In the past 13 years, vineyard acreage has grown from 3,019 acres to 10,500 acres. The share of Oregon wine sold outside Oregon and Washington more than doubled in this period from 18 to 40 percent, as Oregon's reputation as a premium wine producer has grown.

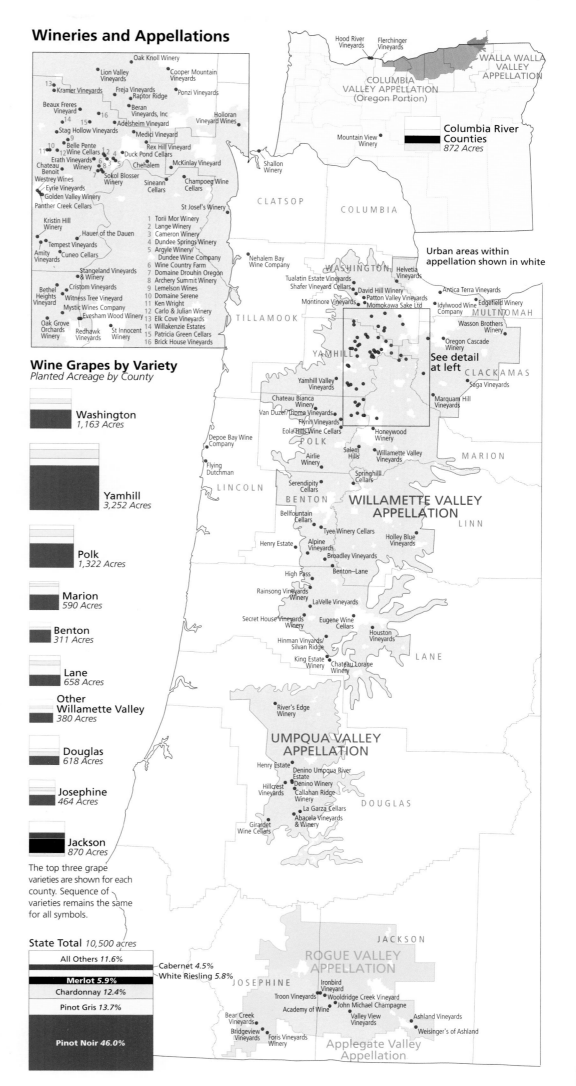

Wineries and Appellations

Oak Knoll Winery
Lion Valley Vineyards
Cooper Mountain Vineyards
13
Kramer Vineyards
Freja Vineyards
Ponzi Vineyards
Beaux Freres Vineyard
Raptor Ridge
Beran Vineyards, Inc
14
16
15
Holloran Vineyard Wines
Stag Hollow Vineyards
Adelsheim Vineyard
Medici Vineyard
9
Belle Pente
Wine Cellars
12 4
Rex Hill Vineyard
10
11
Erath Vineyards
6 8 3
Duck Pond Cellars
McKinlay Vineyard
Chateau Benoit
5
Chehalem
Westrey Wines
Sokol Blosser Winery
Champoeg Wine Cellars
Eyrie Vineyards
Sineann Cellars
Golden Valley Winery
Panther Creek Cellars
St Josef's Winery
Kristin Hill Winery
Hauer of the Dauen
Tempest Vineyards
Amity Vineyards
Cuneo Cellars
Stangeland Vineyards & Winery
Bethel Heights Vineyard
Cristom Vineyards
Witness Tree Vineyard
Mystic Wines Company
Evesham Wood Winery
Oak Grove Orchards Winery
Redhawk Vineyards
St Innocent Winery

1 Torii Mor Winery
2 Lange Winery
3 Cameron Winery
4 Dundee Springs Winery
5 Argyle Winery/ Dundee Wine Company
6 Wine Country Farm
7 Domaine Drouhin Oregon
8 Archery Summit Winery
9 Lemelson Wines
10 Domaine Serene
11 Ken Wright
12 Carlo & Julian Winery
13 Elk Cove Vineyards
14 Willakenzie Estates
15 Patricia Green Cellars
16 Brick House Vineyards

Wine Grapes by Variety
Planted Acreage by County

Washington
1,163 Acres

Yamhill
3,252 Acres

Polk
1,322 Acres

Marion
590 Acres

Benton
311 Acres

Lane
658 Acres

Other Willamette Valley
380 Acres

Douglas
618 Acres

Josephine
464 Acres

Jackson
870 Acres

The top three grape varieties are shown for each county. Sequence of varieties remains the same for all symbols.

State Total *10,500 acres*

All Others 11.6%	Cabernet 4.5%
	White Riesling 5.8%
Merlot 5.9%	
Chardonnay 12.4%	
Pinot Gris 13.7%	
Pinot Noir 46.0%	

Hood River Vineyards
Flerchinger Vineyards
WALLA WALLA VALLEY APPELLATION
COLUMBIA VALLEY APPELLATION (Oregon Portion)

Columbia River Counties
872 Acres

Mountain View Winery

Shallon Winery

CLATSOP
COLUMBIA

Urban areas within appellation shown in white

Nehalem Bay Wine Company
WASHINGTON
Helvetia Vineyards
Tualatin Estate Vineyards
Shafer Vineyard Cellars
David Hill Winery
Patton Valley Vineyards
Antica Terra Vineyards
Montinore Vineyards
Momokawa Sake Ltd
Idylwood Wine Company
Edgefield Winery
MULTNOMAH
Wasson Brothers Winery
Oregon Cascade Winery
TILLAMOOK
YAMHILL
See detail at left
CLACKAMAS
Yamhill Valley Vineyards
Saga Vineyards
Chateau Bianca Winery
Van Duzer/Thoma Vineyards
Marquam Hill Vineyards
Flynn Vineyards
Eola Hills Wine Cellars
Honeywood Winery
Depoe Bay Wine Company
POLK
Salem Hills
Airlie Winery
Willamette Valley Vineyards
MARION
Flying Dutchman
LINCOLN
Serendipity Cellars
Springhill Cellars
BENTON
WILLAMETTE VALLEY APPELLATION
Bellfountain Cellars
LINN
Tyee Winery Cellars
Holley Blue Vineyards
Henry Estate
Alpine Vineyards
Broadley Vineyards
Benton–Lane
High Pass
Rainsong Vineyards Winery
LaVelle Vineyards
Secret House Vineyards Winery
Eugene Wine Cellars
Houston Vineyards
Hinman Vinyards/ Silvan Ridge
LANE
King Estate Winery
Chateau Lorane Winery
River's Edge Winery
UMPQUA VALLEY APPELLATION
Henry Estate
Denino Umpqua River Estate
Denino Winery
Hillcrest Vineyards
Callahan Ridge Winery
DOUGLAS
La Garza Cellars
Abacela Vineyards & Winery
Girardet Wine Cellars
JACKSON
ROGUE VALLEY APPELLATION
Ironbird Vineyard
Troon Vineyards
Wooldridge Creek Vineyard
JOSEPHINE
John Michael Champagne
Academy of Wine
Valley View Vineyards
Ashland Vineyards
Bear Creek Vineyards
Weisinger's of Ashland
Bridgeview Vineyards
Foris Vineyards Winery
Applegate Valley Appellation

Energy Sources

Energy Sources

Most of Oregon's petroleum products, including gasoline, come from Northern Alaska. Natural gas burned in Oregon comes mostly from Alberta, Canada. Hydroelectric generators on the Columbia River system provide most of the state's electricity. While these intermediate sources are geographically distinct, the vast majority of the energy used in Oregon comes from a single ultimate source: the sun. Millions of years of sunlight was needed to grow the marine organisms whose accumulation and decay resulted in the oil and gas deposits now being tapped. The sun's energy also grew the ancient, mostlt aquatic vegetation that formed the coal now being mined. Biomass energy comes from the decay or burning of relatively new vegetation, which grew using sunlight. Differences in air pressure caused by the sun unevenly heating the earth's surface result in wind, the source of wind power. Electrical energy may be generated directly from the sun using photovoltaic cells. Electrical energy from hydroelectric generators is derived from a complicated chain of events that begins with the sun's rays coming 93 million miles to the earth. These rays heat and evaporate water, some of it in the tropical western Pacific Ocean. Next, the water vapor in this tropical air is transported clockwise around the northern Pacific Ocean by atmospheric circulation past Japan and Alaska to the West Coast. The prevailing westerly winds move the moist air inland into the drainage of the Columbia River, the largest river that flows into the Pacific Ocean. Rain and snow fall in the mountains, and the resulting runoff is trapped behind dams in the region's many reservoirs. As the water is released through hydroelectric turbines electricity is generated. Only two common sources of energy do not rely on the sun: geothermal energy, which is based on radioactive decay within the earth, and nuclear energy.

Hydropower Facilities

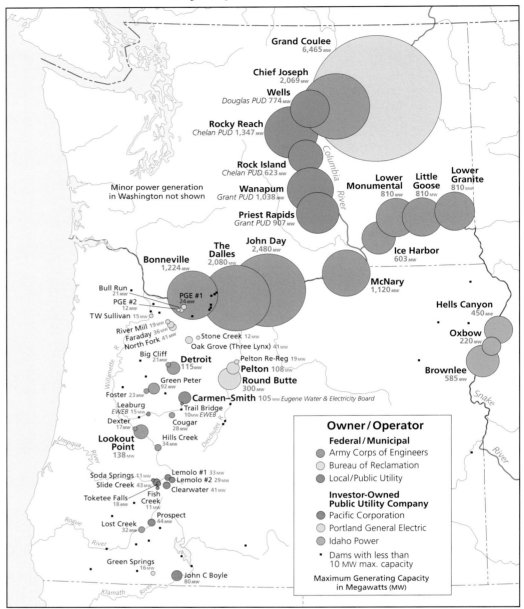

Electrical Power

Electricity was first produced commercially in Oregon by a hydropower facility installed at Willamette Falls in 1889. A transmission line carried the power 14 miles from Oregon City to Portland. Large-scale production of hydropower began in the 1930s when the federal government built dams and power plants on the Columbia River and its tributaries. Dams and power plants also were built on the main stem and tributaries of the Umpqua, Rogue and Klamath Rivers in southwestern Oregon. Hydropower plants account for most of Oregon's electricity generation. The largest hydropower plants are at four dams on the Columbia River: Bonneville, The Dalles, John Day and McNary. Generating capacity at these dams ranges from 1,120 to 2,480 megawatts (MW). The John Day Dam is the largest and newest of the Columbia River dams. Three dams on the Snake River along the Oregon–Idaho border are the next largest dams in generating capacity.

Coal and natural gas each account for 5 to 10 percent of Oregon's electricity generation. Portland General Electric produces electricity at a 530-MW coal-fired facility near Boardman.

The generation of electricity from natural gas increased substantially in the 1990s; in the early twenty-first century natural gas appears to have become the fuel of choice for new energy producers. The state's only atomic energy generating facility, the Trojan Nuclear Plant, near Rainier, stopped producing electricity in 1992.

Facilities with Greater Than 10 MW Capacity	Owner/ Operator	Date in Service	Current Capacity (MW)
Columbia			
Bonneville Dam	USACE	1938	1,224
Chief Joseph Dam	USACE	1961	2,069
Grand Coulee Dam	BuRec	1942	6,465
John Day Dam	USACE	1968	2,480
McNary Dam	USACE	1953	1,120
Priest Rapids Dam	Grant PUD	1961	907
Rock Island	Chelan PUD	1933	623
Rocky Reach	Chelan PUD	1961	1,347
The Dalles Dam	USACE	1957	2,080
Wanapum Dam	Grant PUD	1964	1,038
Wells Dam	Douglas PUD	1967	774
Lower Snake			
Brownlee Dam	ID Power	1959	585
Hells Canyon Dam	ID Power	1967	450
Ice Harbor Dam	USACE	1962	603
Little Goose Dam	USACE	1970	810
Lower Monumental Dam	USACE	1975	810
Lower Granite Dam	USACE	1969	810
Oxbow Dam	ID Power	1961	220

Willamette			
Big Cliff Dam	USACE	1954	21
Carmen–Smith Project	EWEB	1963	105
Cougar Dam	USACE	1964	28
Detroit Dam	USACE	1953	115
Dexter Dam	USACE	1955	17
Faraday Dam	PGE	1965	36
Foster Dam	USACE	1968	23
Green Peter Dam	USACE	1967	92
Hills Creek Dam	USACE	1962	34
Leaburg Dam	EWEB	1930	15
Lookout Point Dam	USACE	1954	138
North Fork Dam	PGE	1958	41
Oak Grove (Three Lynx)	PGE	1923	41
River Mill Dam	PGE	1911	19
Stone Creek	PGE	1956	12
T.W. Sullivan	PGE	1923	15
Trail Bridge Dam	EWEB	1963	10
Sandy/Deschutes			
Bull Run Dam	PGE	1894	21
PGE (Bull Run) No.1	PGE	1929	24
PGE (Bull Run) No.2	PGE	1962	12
Pelton Dam	PGE	1957	108
Pelton Re-Regulating Dam	PGE	1958	19
Round Butte Dam	PGE	1961	300
Umpqua/Rogue/Klamath			
Clearwater Dam	PacCorp	1953	41
Fish Creek Dam	PacCorp	1952	11
Green Springs/Keene Cr. Dam	BuRec	1959	16
John C. Boyle Dam	PacCorp	1958	80
Lemolo Dam/Plant No.2	PacCorp	1956	29
Lemolo Plant No.1	PacCorp	1955	33
Lost Creek/William L. Jess Dam	USACE	1976	32
Prospect Dam	PacCorp	1911	44
Slide Creek Dam	PacCorp	1951	43
Soda Springs Dam	PacCorp	1952	11
Toketee Falls Dam	PacCorp	1949	18

Petroleum Pipelines

No petroleum is produced in Oregon. Oil comes by pipeline primarily from Washington, Rocky Mountain states and Canada. Pipelines are located in Eastern Oregon and the Willamette Valley. The eight-inch pipeline in Eastern Oregon was built in 1950 and is operated by the Chevron Pipe Line Company. A second eight-inch petroleum pipeline was constructed in 1962 between Portland and Eugene, with terminals at both ends as well as in Albany. In 1965, a 14-inch Olympic Pipeline Company line was put into service between Renton, Washington and Portland. Much of Oregon's petroleum is delivered via this pipeline.

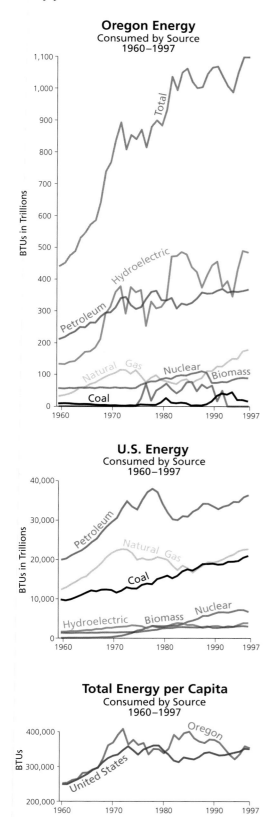

Oregon Energy
Consumed by Source
1960–1997

U.S. Energy
Consumed by Source
1960–1997

Total Energy per Capita
Consumed by Source
1960–1997

Petroleum and Natural Gas Distribution

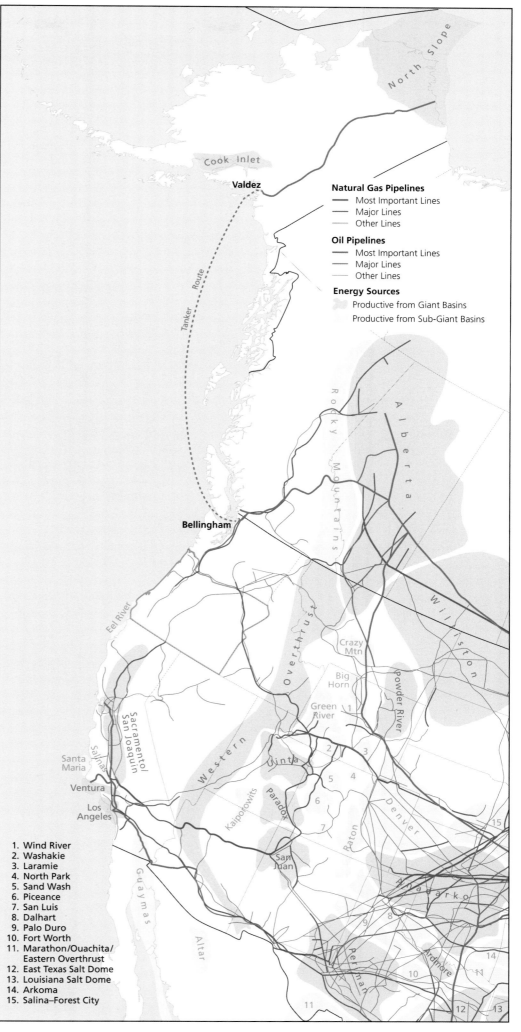

Natural Gas Pipelines
— Most Important Lines
— Major Lines
— Other Lines

Oil Pipelines
— Most Important Lines
— Major Lines
— Other Lines

Energy Sources
Productive from Giant Basins
Productive from Sub-Giant Basins

1. Wind River
2. Washakie
3. Laramie
4. North Park
5. Sand Wash
6. Piceance
7. San Luis
8. Dalhart
9. Palo Duro
10. Fort Worth
11. Marathon/Ouachita/ Eastern Overthrust
12. East Texas Salt Dome
13. Louisiana Salt Dome
14. Arkoma
15. Salina–Forest City

101

Energy Distribution

West Coast Power Grid

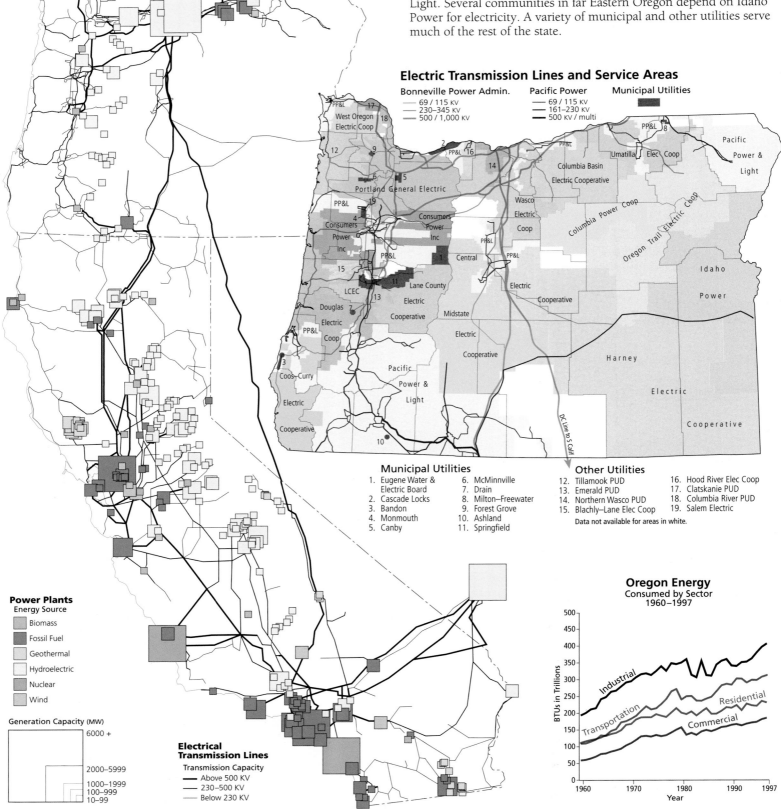

Electrical Distribution

The West Coast power grid consists of numerous electricity generating facilities and connecting transmission lines. Hydroelectric facilities comprise the vast majority of generating plants, and account for more utility-generated electricity than any other source in Oregon, Washington and California. The Bonneville Power Administration operates transmission lines associated with major generating facilities. Pacific Power & Light is another important operator of transmission lines, especially in southwestern and Eastern Oregon. Utilities in Oregon exchange electricity with other states and Canada. California, for example, typically imports electricity from Oregon during the summer and exports electricity northward during the winter. State-level deregulation of the electric utility industry and other supply and demand considerations influence the timing and geographical pattern of electricity exchanges. Portland General Electric generates about half of retail sales revenue for Oregon's electrical utilities; another 35 percent is attributable to Pacific Power & Light. Several communities in far Eastern Oregon depend on Idaho Power for electricity. A variety of municipal and other utilities serve much of the rest of the state.

Electric Transmission Lines and Service Areas

Bonneville Power Admin.
— 69 / 115 KV
— 230–345 KV
— 500 / 1,000 KV

Pacific Power
— 69 / 115 KV
— 161–230 KV
— 500 KV / multi

Municipal Utilities

Municipal Utilities
1. Eugene Water & Electric Board
2. Cascade Locks
3. Bandon
4. Monmouth
5. Canby
6. McMinnville
7. Drain
8. Milton–Freewater
9. Forest Grove
10. Ashland
11. Springfield

Other Utilities
12. Tillamook PUD
13. Emerald PUD
14. Northern Wasco PUD
15. Blachly–Lane Elec Coop
16. Hood River Elec Coop
17. Clatskanie PUD
18. Columbia River PUD
19. Salem Electric

Data not available for areas in white.

Power Plants
Energy Source
- Biomass
- Fossil Fuel
- Geothermal
- Hydroelectric
- Nuclear
- Wind

Generation Capacity (MW)
- 6000 +
- 2000–5999
- 1000–1999
- 100–999
- 10–99

Electrical Transmission Lines
Transmission Capacity
— Above 500 KV
— 230–500 KV
— Below 230 KV

Oregon Energy
Consumed by Sector 1960–1997

Industrial
Transportation
Residential
Commercial

BTUs in Trillions

Natural Gas

Before natural gas became widely available via pipelines, gas was produced from coal or petroleum at several locations in Oregon. Coal mined in Coos County was a source for some of the state's early gas production. Propane continues to be used as a source of gas in a number of locations where natural gas is not available. Biogas from waste is produced at several landfills and wastewater treatment plants. Although a small amount of natural gas is produced near Mist in Columbia County, most comes by pipeline from Canada and several Rocky Mountain states. Williams Gas Pipeline provides long-distance gas transmission service between Portland and the Rogue Valley. In Eastern Oregon, PG&E Gas Transmission provides long-distance service roughly between Umatilla and Klamath Falls. Some utilities and industrial users of natural gas have lower-cost "interruptible contracts" (see graph below) with suppliers. When natural gas demand reaches its peak these users have their supply cut—heating oil is often used as a replacement fuel.

Natural Gas Deliveries in Oregon By Sector, 1985–1999

Legend:
- Large Industrial—Open Market
- Interruptible
- Commercial/Industrial
- Residential

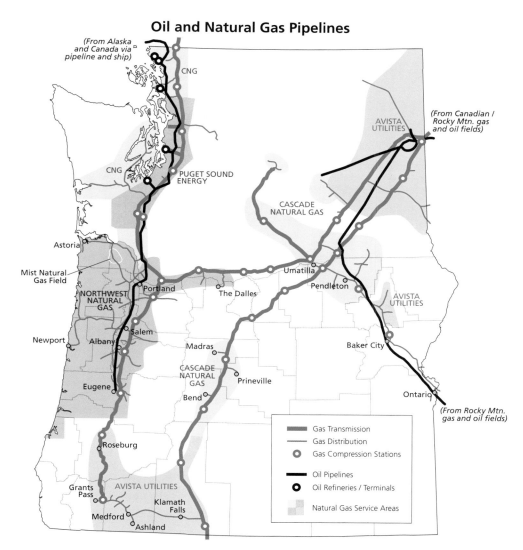

Oil and Natural Gas Pipelines

(From Alaska and Canada via pipeline and ship)

CNG

CNG

PUGET SOUND ENERGY

AVISTA UTILITIES

(From Canadian / Rocky Mtn. gas and oil fields)

CASCADE NATURAL GAS

Astoria

Mist Natural Gas Field

NORTHWEST NATURAL GAS

Portland

Umatilla

Pendleton

AVISTA UTILITIES

The Dalles

Newport

Albany

Salem

Madras

Baker City

CASCADE NATURAL GAS

Eugene

Bend

Prineville

Ontario

(From Rocky Mtn. gas and oil fields)

Roseburg

Legend:
- Gas Transmission
- Gas Distribution
- ◯ Gas Compression Stations
- Oil Pipelines
- ◉ Oil Refineries / Terminals
- Natural Gas Service Areas

Grants Pass

AVISTA UTILITIES

Klamath Falls

Medford

Ashland

Renewable Energy

More than half of Oregon's electricity comes from hydropower. About 1 percent comes from other renewable sources, primarily biomass and wind. Solar photovoltaic panels supply a small amount of electricity, mostly in remote locations. Further development of electric generation from various kinds of renewable sources hinges on reducing capital costs and increasing generating efficiency.

Biomass, solar and geothermal sources provide direct-use alternatives to reliance on electricity produced from natural gas and coal. Wood, mill residues and pulping liquor are sizable biomass sources of energy for steam, heat and power generation at pulp and lumber mills. Many Oregon households use wood for heating their homes.

Transportation accounts for about 39 percent of energy use in the state, nearly all supplied from petroleum sources. Ethanol, a renewable fuel made from biomass, is used as an additive to make gasoline burn cleaner and to add octane to premium gasoline. Oregon motorists use an estimated 30 million gallons of ethanol annually.

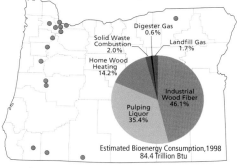

Biomass Projects

- Digester Gas 0.6%
- Solid Waste Combustion 2.0%
- Landfill Gas 1.7%
- Home Wood Heating 14.2%
- Industrial Wood Fiber 46.1%
- Pulping Liquor 35.4%

Estimated Bioenergy Consumption, 1998
84.4 Trillion Btu

● Biogas Facility   ● Biomass Combustion Facility

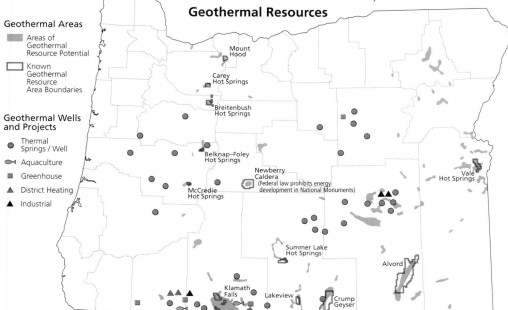

Geothermal Resources

Geothermal Areas
- Areas of Geothermal Resource Potential
- Known Geothermal Resource Area Boundaries

Geothermal Wells and Projects
- ● Thermal Springs / Well
- ⋈ Aquaculture
- ▪ Greenhouse
- ▲ District Heating
- ▲ Industrial

Mount Hood

Carey Hot Springs

Breitenbush Hot Springs

Belknap–Foley Hot Springs

Newberry Caldera (Federal law prohibits energy development in National Monuments)

McCredie Hot Springs

Vale Hot Springs

Summer Lake Hot Springs

Alvord

Klamath Falls

Lakeview

Crump Geyser

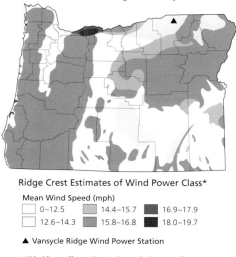

Annual Average Wind Speed

Ridge Crest Estimates of Wind Power Class*

Mean Wind Speed (mph)
- 0–12.5
- 14.4–15.7
- 16.9–17.9
- 12.6–14.3
- 15.8–16.8
- 18.0–19.7

▲ Vansycle Ridge Wind Power Station

* Wind Power Class estimates do not depict anomalies or variability caused by local terrain features.

103

Development of the Road Network

The network of stage roads crossing Oregon in 1889 was the precursor of today's highway system. Then as now, most of the main routes in the system connected the more populated areas, as well as other areas of special economic or strategic importance. Exceptions included the Oregon Coast, where no stage route preceded US 101; the Coast Range, where few stage routes crossed the mountains; and Oregon east of the Cascade Mountains, where most stage routes ran east-to-west and few ran north-to-south. In some locations, especially in Eastern Oregon, portions of stage routes were bypassed when the state highway system was built.

The Historic Columbia River Highway was the first modern highway in the Pacific Northwest and the first scenic highway constructed in the U.S. Built from 1913 to 1922, the highway extended 74 miles through the Columbia Gorge from Troutdale to The Dalles. Parts of the highway were closed or removed during construction of Interstate Highway 84 (I-84) in the 1950s and 1960s. In May 2000 the federal government designated about 51 of the remaining 55 miles of roadway as a National Historic Landmark.

Other paved highways in 1920 consisted primarily of unconnected segments of Oregon Highway 99 (OR 99) from Portland to the California border, a few roads in the Willamette Valley and a road along the Columbia River from Astoria to the Portland area. By 1930, the network had expanded to include paved roads from Astoria to the Idaho border except for a short stretch in the Blue Mountains (US 30), and from Washington to California (OR 99 and US 97). Two paved roads traversed the Coast Range, and two had been constructed over the Oregon Cascades by way of Crater Lake and Mount Hood.

During the 1930s, US 101 was paved along the entire Oregon Coast, and communities such as Burns, John Day and Lakeview got their first all-weather roads. By 1940, paving had been completed on US 30, which became the only continuous west-east paved road reaching across the state.

Between 1919 and 1932, Conde B. McCullough, head of the Oregon Highway Department's Bridge Division, supervised the design and construction of 162 bridges. These included most of the bridges on the Oregon Coast Highway, the final three of which were completed over Coos Bay, Alsea Bay and Yaquina Bay in 1936.

The last major link in Oregon's primary highway system was completed in 1941 with the construction of the Willamette Pass Highway (OR 58). This highway system was supplemented by the construction of federally designated interstate highways from the latter half of the 1950s into the 1980s. I-405 in Portland and most of I-5 and I-84 (previously known as I-80N) were built during the 1960s. Two major milestones were celebrated in 1966: the opening of the Astoria Bridge spanning the mouth of the Columbia River, and completion of I-5 through California, Oregon and Washington. I-205 in Portland and I-105 in Eugene were built mostly in the 1970s. The I-205 Glen Jackson Bridge was completed in 1982, linking Oregon and Washington near the Portland International Airport. Oregon's newest segment of interstate highway, I-82, was finished in September 1988 between I-84 and the Washington border near Umatilla.

Oregon's rapid population and economic growth between 1985 and 2000 led to proposals for new freeways to meet traffic demands and reduce congestion. Proposed projects included the Mount Hood Parkway, the Sunrise Corridor and the Western Bypass in the Portland area and the West Eugene Parkway in Eugene. For a variety of reasons including funding constraints, environmental concerns and citizen opposition, none of the projects was constructed. The Bend Parkway in Bend is one of the few major highway projects to be constructed in recent years. Completion of the project, which has a projected cost of more than $100 million, is still several years away.

Portland Freeways 1965–1985

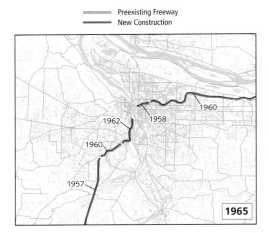

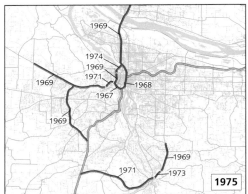

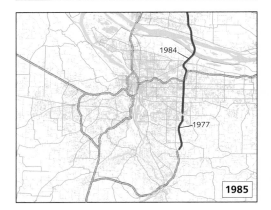

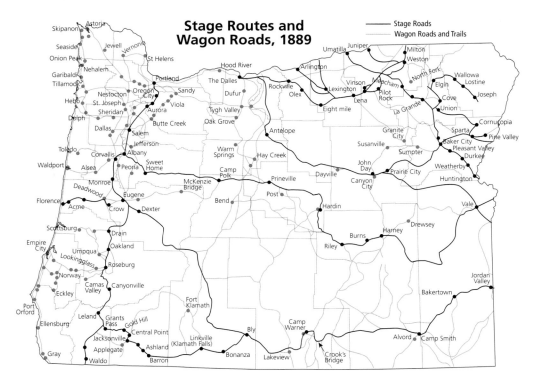

Stage Routes and Wagon Roads, 1889

Road System, 19

Paved Roads 1920–1990

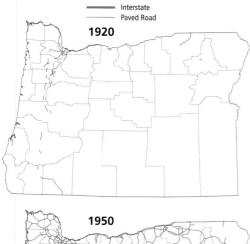

1920

1930

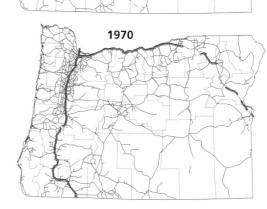

1940

1950

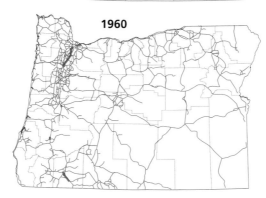

1960

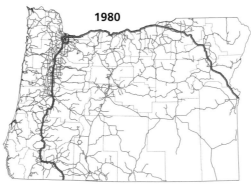

1970

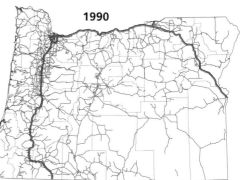

1980

1990

In 1999, Oregon had more than 83,000 miles of roads—a decrease of 24 percent from 1979 and 38 percent from the 20-year high in 1984. U.S. Forest Service closures accounted for most of the drop during the 1980s. The decrease in the 1990s was due to reductions in mileage reported by the U.S. Bureau of Land Management. Ownership by public sector agencies in 1999 was: county, 40 percent; federal, 35 percent; state, 14 percent; and city, 11 percent.

Road System, 2000

Interstate
Divided Highway
Highway
Major Through Roads
Other Through Roads
Gravel

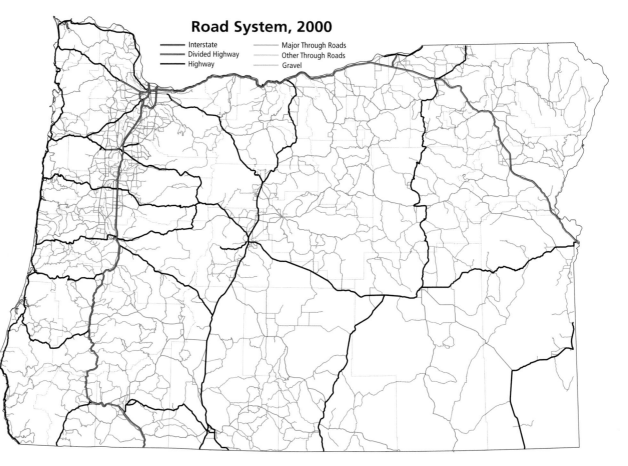

Highway Traffic

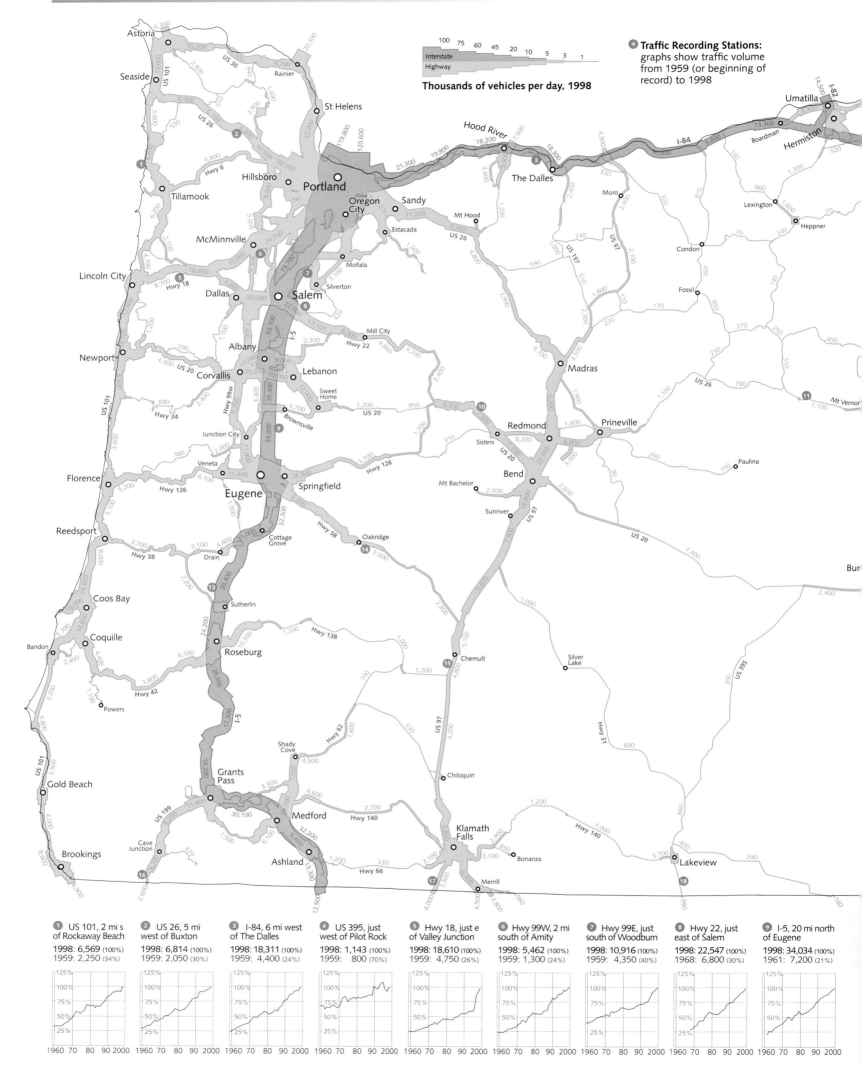

Traffic Recording Stations: graphs show traffic volume from 1959 (or beginning of record) to 1998

Thousands of vehicles per day, 1998

1 US 101, 2 mi s of Rockaway Beach
1998: 6,569 (100%)
1959: 2,250 (34%)

2 US 26, 5 mi west of Buxton
1998: 6,814 (100%)
1959: 2,050 (30%)

3 I-84, 6 mi west of The Dalles
1998: 18,311 (100%)
1959: 4,400 (24%)

4 US 395, just west of Pilot Rock
1998: 1,143 (100%)
1959: 800 (70%)

5 Hwy 18, just e of Valley Junction
1998: 18,610 (100%)
1959: 4,750 (26%)

6 Hwy 99W, 2 mi south of Amity
1998: 5,462 (100%)
1959: 1,300 (24%)

7 Hwy 99E, just south of Woodburn
1998: 10,916 (100%)
1959: 4,350 (40%)

8 Hwy 22, just east of Salem
1998: 22,547 (100%)
1968: 6,800 (30%)

9 I-5, 20 mi north of Eugene
1998: 34,034 (100%)
1961: 7,200 (21%)

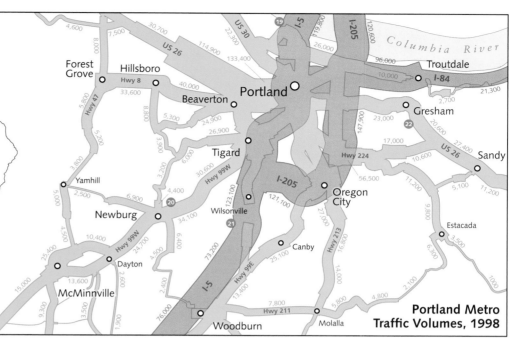

**Portland Metro
Traffic Volumes, 1998**

Daily traffic volumes at selected locations across the state are about two to three times greater than they were 40 years ago. Percentage increases were particularly high on US 20 northwest of Sisters, I-5 north of Eugene, and I-5 near Oakland. On Hwy 18 near Valley Junction, a notable spike in growth occurred in the mid-1990s. This change is likely associated with the opening of nearby casinos and other visitor attractions.

⑲ I-5, on bridge north of Portland
1998: 119,745 (100%)
1959: 38,500 (32%)

⑳ Hwy 99W, just east of Newberg
1998: 32,174 (100%)
1959: 6,250 (19%)

㉑ I-5, just south of Wilsonville
1998: 75,359 (100%)
1974: 26,200 (35%)

㉒ US 26, just east of Gresham
1998: 36,275 (100%)
1959: 8,300 (23%)

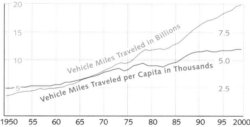

The number of vehicle miles traveled (vmt) has increased substantially in the past 50 years. The rate of vmt growth is expected to moderate as employment growth slows, as growth in the number of vehicles per licensed driver decreases and as congestion becomes more severe.

Highway Traffic

Highway traffic volumes are greatest in Oregon's five metropolitan areas (Corvallis, Eugene–Springfield, Medford–Ashland, Salem and Portland) and in major urban areas such as Albany, Bend, Coos Bay–North Bend, Klamath Falls and Roseburg. In 1998, the highest volumes statewide were on I-84 (Banfield Freeway) about three miles east of its interchange with I-5 in Portland, where approximately 164,000 vehicles traveled daily. Nearly the same number of vehicles used I-205 near its interchange with US 26 in Portland.

Highest volumes (156,000 daily) on I-5 are near its interchange with Hwy 217 in the Tigard–Lake Oswego area south of Portland. Volumes on portions of I-405 also exceed 100,000 vehicles daily.

Representative daily volumes at other locations on I-5 were approximately 40,000 in Medford and Roseburg, 55,000 in Eugene, 40,000 in Albany and 70,000 in Salem. For I-84, volumes range from 10,000 to 20,000 vehicles daily between Portland and Pendleton, and from 5,000 to 10,000 daily between Pendleton and the Idaho border. On non-interstate highways outside metropolitan areas, traffic volumes are highest on major federal and state highways, including US 97, US 101 and several routes over the Cascade Mountains and between the Oregon Coast and I-5.

Since 1950 the number of Oregon's licensed drivers has increased at about the same rate as population growth while the number of registered vehicles has increased more rapidly. Licensed drivers outnumbered registered vehicles at mid-century, but by 2000, there were about 1.6 vehicles per licensed driver.

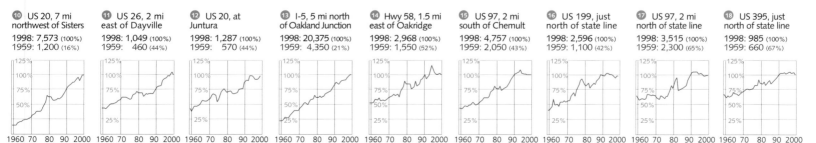

⑩ US 20, 7 mi northwest of Sisters
1998: 7,573 (100%)
1959: 1,200 (16%)

⑪ US 26, 2 mi east of Dayville
1998: 1,049 (100%)
1959: 460 (44%)

⑫ US 20, at Juntura
1998: 1,287 (100%)
1959: 570 (44%)

⑬ I-5, 5 mi north of Oakland Junction
1998: 20,375 (100%)
1959: 4,350 (21%)

⑭ Hwy 58, 1.5 mi east of Oakridge
1998: 2,968 (100%)
1959: 1,550 (52%)

⑮ US 97, 2 mi south of Chemult
1998: 4,757 (100%)
1959: 2,050 (43%)

⑯ US 199, just north of state line
1998: 2,596 (100%)
1959: 1,100 (42%)

⑰ US 97, 2 mi north of state line
1998: 3,515 (100%)
1959: 2,300 (65%)

⑱ US 395, just north of state line
1998: 985 (100%)
1959: 660 (67%)

Railroads

Oregon's first railroad was a wooden tramway, built in 1846, to connect Abernethy Island in the Willamette River to Oregon City. Construction and operation of wooden tramways started in the early 1850s on both sides of the Columbia River near present-day Cascade Locks, and by 1862, the first steam locomotive on the West Coast was operating along the south side of the river. Steamboats carried freight to the tramways were it was portaged by primitive rail cars around rapids in the river.

Oregon's first north-south railroad was built in the late 1860s and early 1870s, and by 1872 extended from Portland to Roseburg. The line reached Ashland by 1884 and over the Siskiyou Mountains three years later. A number of other lines were built in the Willamette Valley in the 1870s and 1880s, as well as a line from Corvallis to Yaquina City near present-day Newport. The latter line had been extended eastward to Idanha in the Cascade Mountains by 1889.

Oregon's first transcontinental connection was completed in 1883 from Portland through The Dalles to connect with the Northern Pacific Railroad in Washington state. A connection from Portland to Tacoma also was completed in 1883, and a second transcontinental link was established through northeastern Oregon to Idaho in 1884. By 1898, a line extended from Seaside to Portland along the Oregon Coast and the Columbia River corridor.

Between 1900 and 1930 railroad trackage more than doubled in length from 1,850 miles to nearly 4,350 miles. Major new segments were added during this period: several lines to the Oregon Coast (including one that extended from Eugene to Coos Bay and back inland to Powers), a north-south line through Central Oregon, a line over the Cascade Mountains between Eugene and Central Oregon and numerous branch lines in Eastern Oregon. In addition to the construction of main line and branch line railroads, logging railroads were built to move timber to other railroads or lumber mills. After nearby timber was harvested, logging railroads often were removed then rebuilt in other forested areas.

Since peaking in the 1930s, rail track mileage in Oregon has decreased substantially. Many of the losses occurred after timber mills closed along or at the end of branch lines. Federal rail deregulation in 1980 resulted in less stringent requirements for railroads seeking to

1874

1881

1884

1900

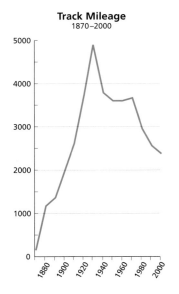

Track Mileage
1870–2000

1911

1930

Rail Freight Tonnage by Commodity

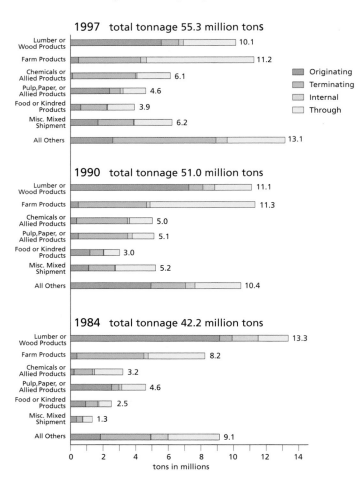

1997 total tonnage 55.3 million tons

Lumber or Wood Products	10.1
Farm Products	11.2
Chemicals or Allied Products	6.1
Pulp, Paper, or Allied Products	4.6
Food or Kindred Products	3.9
Misc. Mixed Shipment	6.2
All Others	13.1

Originating / Terminating / Internal / Through

1990 total tonnage 51.0 million tons

Lumber or Wood Products	11.1
Farm Products	11.3
Chemicals or Allied Products	5.0
Pulp, Paper, or Allied Products	5.1
Food or Kindred Products	3.0
Misc. Mixed Shipment	5.2
All Others	10.4

1984 total tonnage 42.2 million tons

Lumber or Wood Products	13.3
Farm Products	8.2
Chemicals or Allied Products	3.2
Pulp, Paper, or Allied Products	4.6
Food or Kindred Products	2.5
Misc. Mixed Shipment	1.3
All Others	9.1

tons in millions

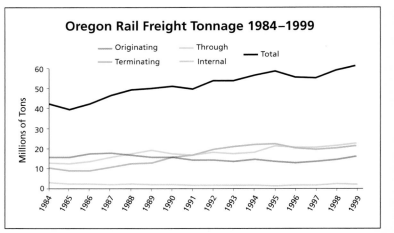

Oregon Rail Freight Tonnage 1984–1999

Originating — Through — Total — Terminating — Internal

abandon rail lines. Rail deregulation legislation also provided for the establishment and expansion of short-line railroads, many of which operate on branch lines that might otherwise have been abandoned or converted to trails.

Oregon now has two major railroads (the Union Pacific Railroad and the Burlington Northern and Santa Fe Railway), 16 short-line railroads, and three terminal railroads providing services for shippers and carriers in northwest Portland and the Medford area. In 1999 these railroads moved 63.5 million tons over about 2,400 miles of rail line.

The Union Pacific operates the most trackage in Oregon—just over 900 miles. This includes the former main line of the Southern Pacific Railroad connecting Portland, Eugene, Klamath Falls and California. Gennesee and Wyoming, Inc. operates the most short-line railroad trackage in Oregon; this consists of about 390 miles of the Portland and Western Railroad, including trackage operated formerly by the

Burlington Northern Santa Fe and Southern Pacific railroads. The Central Oregon and Pacific, which operates over former Southern Pacific lines between Eugene and the Coos Bay area and between Eugene and California via Roseburg and Medford, has the second most trackage among Oregon's short-line railroads—378 miles. Altogether, nearly as much of Oregon's rail mileage is operated by the short-line railroads as by the UP and BNSF.

Lumber and wood products and pulp and paper are the leading commodities originating within Oregon, accounting for nearly 60 percent of the total moved by rail. Of commodities terminating in Oregon, farm products and chemicals and allied products account for about 40 percent of the total.

From 1984 to 1999 tonnage moved on Oregon's rail lines grew from 42 to 63.5 million tons, an increase of more than 50 percent. In 1984 more rail tonnage originated in Oregon than terminated or passed through the state. By 1991, through traffic and terminating traffic had both surpassed the amount of rail traffic originating in Oregon. Between 1984 and 1999, tonnage of food and kindred products originating in Oregon declined by 40 percent, and tonnage of lumber and wood products fell by 24 percent.

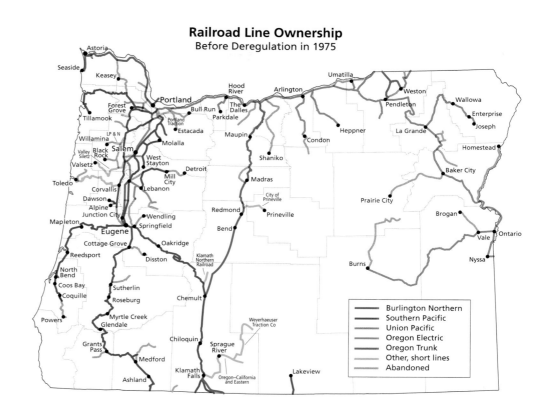

Railroad Line Ownership
Before Deregulation in 1975

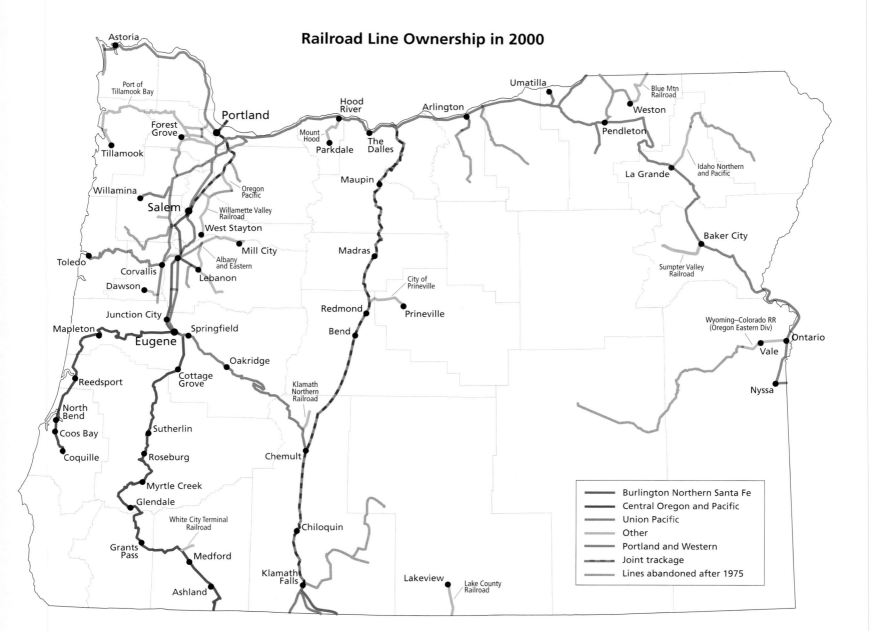

Railroad Line Ownership in 2000

Public Transportation and Airports

Railroad Passenger Service
in 1926 and 2000

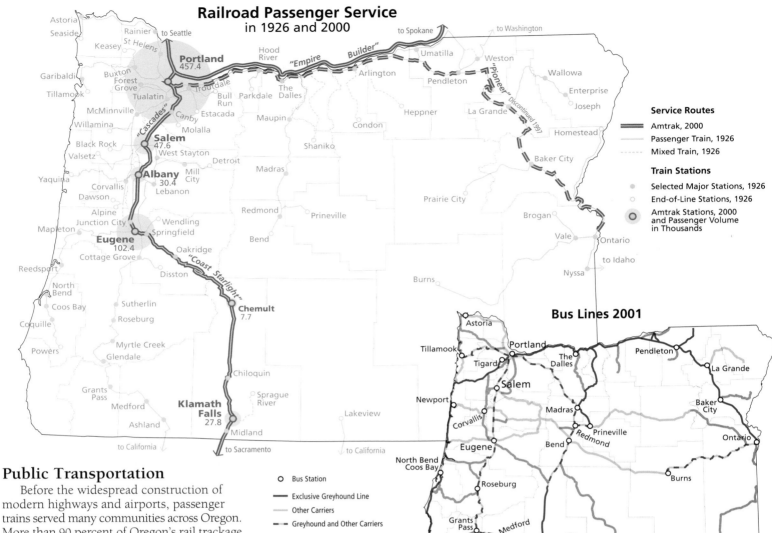

Service Routes
- Amtrak, 2000
- Passenger Train, 1926
- Mixed Train, 1926

Train Stations
- Selected Major Stations, 1926
- End-of-Line Stations, 1926
- Amtrak Stations, 2000 and Passenger Volume in Thousands

Bus Lines 2001

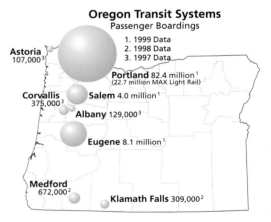

- Bus Station
- Exclusive Greyhound Line
- Other Carriers
- Greyhound and Other Carriers
- Discontinued Since 1972

Public Transportation

Before the widespread construction of modern highways and airports, passenger trains served many communities across Oregon. More than 90 percent of Oregon's rail trackage offered passenger service in 1926, a time when the state's passenger train system was near its peak. At that time, a traveler could choose from 11 daily trains in each direction between Eugene and Portland. In 2000, about 675,000 passengers rode Amtrak trains to or from six stations in Oregon: Klamath Falls, Chemult, Eugene, Albany, Salem and Portland. Union Station in Portland accounts for about two-thirds of the state's rail passenger trips. The passenger line from Eugene to Portland is part of the federally designated Northwest High Speed Rail Corridor, which extends to

Vancouver, British Columbia. Federal and state governments are funding service and infrastructure improvements to increase train speeds and reduce travel times. Improvements since the mid-1990s are thought to have contributed to ridership increases of more than 60 percent since 1994. Oregon was served daily in 2001 by Amtrak's Coast Starlight train between Los Angeles and Seattle, two Amtrak Cascade trains between Eugene and Seattle and one Amtrak Cascade train between Portland and Seattle. In addition, Amtrak's Empire Builder train between Chicago and Seattle runs daily through Portland via Spokane and the Washington side of the Columbia River Gorge—until May 1997, Amtrak operated the Pioneer Train between Seattle and Chicago via Portland and the I-84 corridor.

In addition to passengers, Amtrak trains carry a small but increasing amount of freight. Amtrak Thruway buses provide twice-daily service between Eugene and Portland as well as daily service between Amtrak stations in the Willamette Valley and Ashland, Astoria, Canyonville, Grants Pass, Medford, Newport and Roseburg. Since deregulation of the inter-city bus industry in the early 1980s the number of communities with service has decreased substantially. Service is concentrated along the state's interstate and U.S. highway corridors between large population centers. Greyhound operates the majority of inter-city

routes, with smaller carriers providing connecting service.

More than 240 mass transit districts, transportation districts, county service districts, city and county governments, private operators and private non-profit organizations provide fixed-route and demand-response public transportation services in Oregon. The Tri-County Metropolitan Transportation District of Oregon (Tri-Met), which serves portions of Clackamas, Multnomah and Washington Counties, accounted for 82 million transit trips in 1999—more than 80 percent of all transit trips in Oregon. The MAX light rail line accounted for about 23 million trips in 1999, 28 percent of transit trips in the Tri-Met service area.

Amtrak Passengers
Boardings and Deboardings in Thousands

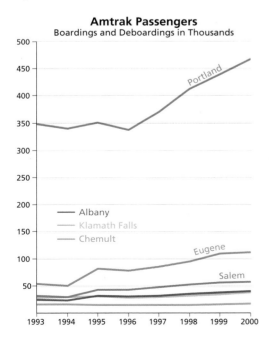

Oregon Transit Systems
Passenger Boardings

1. 1999 Data
2. 1998 Data
3. 1997 Data

- Astoria 107,000[3]
- Portland 82.4 million[1] (22.7 million MAX Light Rail)
- Corvallis 375,000[3]
- Salem 4.0 million[1]
- Albany 129,000[3]
- Eugene 8.1 million[1]
- Medford 672,000[2]
- Klamath Falls 309,000[2]

Airport Annual Operations, 1994

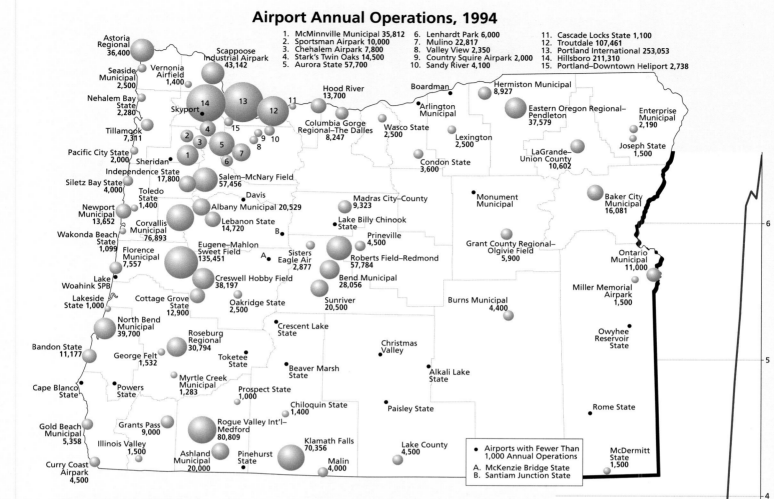

1. McMinnville Municipal 35,812
2. Sportsman Airpark 10,000
3. Chehalem Airpark 7,800
4. Stark's Twin Oaks 14,500
5. Aurora State 57,700
6. Lenhardt Park 6,000
7. Mulino 22,817
8. Valley View 2,350
9. Country Squire Airpark 2,000
10. Sandy River 4,100
11. Cascade Locks State 1,100
12. Troutdale 107,461
13. Portland International 253,053
14. Hillsboro 211,310
15. Portland–Downtown Heliport 2,738

Astoria Regional 36,400
Seaside Municipal 2,500
Vernonia Airfield 1,400
Scappoose Industrial Airpark 43,142
Nehalem Bay State 2,280
Skyport
Tillamook 7,311
Hood River 13,700
Boardman
Hermiston Municipal 8,927
Arlington Municipal
Eastern Oregon Regional–Pendleton 37,579
Enterprise Municipal 2,190
Pacific City State 2,000
Sheridan
Columbia Gorge Regional–The Dalles 8,247
Wasco State 2,500
Lexington 2,500
Joseph State 1,500
Independence State 17,800
Salem–McNary Field 57,456
Condon State 3,600
LaGrande–Union County 10,602
Siletz Bay State 4,000
Toledo State 1,400
Davis
Albany Municipal 20,529
Madras City–County 9,323
Monument Municipal
Baker City Municipal 16,081
Newport Municipal 13,652
Corvallis Municipal 76,893
Lebanon State 14,720
Lake Billy Chinook State
Prineville 4,500
Grant County Regional–Olgivie Field 5,900
Wakonda Beach State 1,099
Florence Municipal 7,557
Eugene–Mahlon Sweet Field 135,451
Sisters Eagle Air 2,877
Roberts Field–Redmond 57,784
Ontario Municipal 11,000
Lake Woahink SPB
Creswell Hobby Field 38,197
Bend Municipal 28,056
Miller Memorial Airpark 1,500
Lakeside State 1,000
Cottage Grove State 12,900
Oakridge State 2,500
Sunriver 20,500
Burns Municipal 4,400
North Bend Municipal 39,700
Crescent Lake State
Owyhee Reservoir State
Bandon State 11,177
Roseburg Regional 30,794
Christmas Valley
George Felt 1,532
Toketee State
Beaver Marsh State
Alkali Lake State
Cape Blanco State
Myrtle Creek Municipal 1,283
Prospect State 1,000
Rome State
Powers State
Chiloquin State 1,400
Paisley State
Gold Beach Municipal 5,358
Grants Pass 9,000
Rogue Valley Int'l–Medford 80,809
Klamath Falls 70,356
Lake County 4,500
Illinois Valley 1,500
Ashland Municipal 20,000
Pinehurst State
Malin 4,000
McDermitt State 1,500
Curry Coast Airpark 4,500

● Airports with Fewer Than 1,000 Annual Operations
A. McKenzie Bridge State
B. Santiam Junction State

Airports

Oregon has more than 100 public-use airports—86 are publicly owned—and more than 300 privately owned, private-use airports. Airports in seven Oregon communities—Eugene, Klamath Falls, Medford, North Bend, Pendleton, Portland and Redmond—provide regularly scheduled passenger and freight service. When market and other conditions are supportive, commercial carriers have provided service in other Oregon communities, including Astoria, Corvallis, Newport and Salem. Commercial service airports in Boise and Lewiston, Idaho, and Pasco and Walla Walla, Washington also serve northeastern and Eastern Oregon.

Of the seven Oregon airports with regularly scheduled service, Portland International Airport (PIA, but also commonly referred to as PDX) accounts for 90 percent of passengers. During the 1990s, the number of passengers more than doubled at PIA. The number of passengers also doubled at the Redmond airport in response to rapid growth and tourism in Central Oregon. Passenger growth has been more modest at Oregon's other airports, with one (Eastern Oregon Regional at Pendleton) serving fewer passengers in the 1990s than in the 1960s. The number of passengers at Oregon's airports decreased following industry deregulation in the late 1970s, though passenger numbers at most sites recovered by the 1990s.

Portland International Airport also accounts for more than 90 percent of the state's air cargo, and ranks in the top 25 nationally in air cargo tonnage. In recent years, air cargo tonnage at PIA has increased about three times as fast as passenger travel. Oregon's fast-growing high technology industry depends on timely and reliable air cargo shipments. Forecasts for the Portland area predict that over the next 30 years shipments will grow at a faster rate for cargo moving by air than for cargo moving by other modes of transport.

Airport Passenger Volume
Enplaned Passengers, 1999

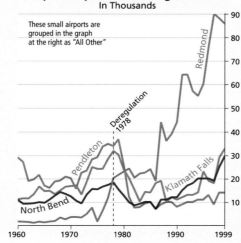

Total Enplanements 1998: 7,182,800

Portland International 6,510,300
Eastern Oregon Regional–Pendleton 14,000
Eugene Airport–Mahlon Sweet Field 302,600
Redmond Municipal–Roberts Field 86,000
North Bend Municipal 29,800
Rogue Valley Int'l–Medford 186,400
Klamath Falls Int'l 33,700

Airport Enplaned Passenger Volume
In Thousands

These small airports are grouped in the graph at the right as "All Other"

Deregulation 1978

Redmond

Pendleton

Klamath Falls

North Bend

Airport Enplaned Passenger Volume
In Millions

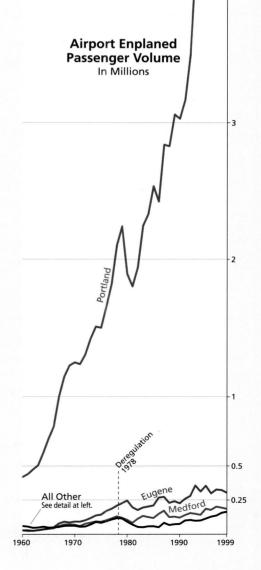

Portland

Deregulation 1978

All Other
See detail at left.

Eugene

Medford

Ports and Trade

Oregon's economy benefits from the state's location on the Pacific Rim. Oregon's 1999 exports, worth more than $11 billion, ranked 17th in value among all states, and 4th among Western states. High technology products are the leading exports to eight of Oregon's 10 leading trading partners. Other important exports include transportation equipment, which is the leading export to Canada, and agricultural products, which is the leading export to Japan. Exports to Mexico and Canada have increased substantially since the 1993 ratification of the North American Free Trade Agreement (NAFTA). In 1999, exports to Mexico were more than $900 million, up from slightly more than $100 million before passage of NAFTA. Exports to Canada have nearly

doubled since NAFTA was enacted. Overall, however, Oregon imports more from Canada and Mexico than it exports to them. By surface modes (truck and rail), imports represented about 62 percent of Oregon's trade with Canada and Mexico in 1999, while exports were about 38 percent.

Of the 23 port districts operating on the Pacific Coast and along the Columbia River, Portland ranks third after Los Angeles and Long Beach in terms of tonnage shipped. In 1999, 51 million tons of cargo were shipped through various deep-water ports from Portland to the mouth of the Columbia River; terminals in the Portland area accounted for about 30 million tons or 60 percent of the total shipped on the Lower Columbia River. Exports

Oregon Exports, 1999
Values in Millions of Dollars

High Tech	$6,588
Electronic Equip.	$3,386
Industrial and Commerical Computer Equip.	$2,581
Measuring Instruments	$621
Agriculture	$1,559
Crops	$1,228
Food and Kindred Products	$329
Livestock and Animal Specialties	$2
Transportation Equipment	$1,176
Wood Products	$712
Lumber and Wood Products	$500
Paper and Allied Products	$187
Furniture and Fixtures	$22

Other Manufacturing	$672
Chemicals	$325
Leather Products	$152
Stone, Clay, Glass, Concrete	$93
Metals	$370
Primary Metal Industries	$196
Fabricated Metal Products	$174
Non-Manufacturing	$232
Scrap and Waste	$86
Military	$63
Charity	$40
Rubber and Plastics	$84
Other	$52
Fishing and Hunting	$26
Printing and Publishing	$26

Oregon's Exports to Top 10 Countries, 1999
By Major Commodity Type

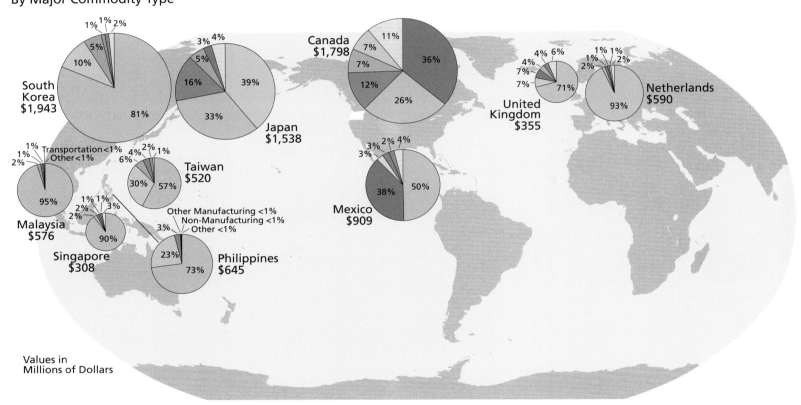

Values in Millions of Dollars

Oregon Exports by Region, 1999

Top 5 Countries in Each Region are shown

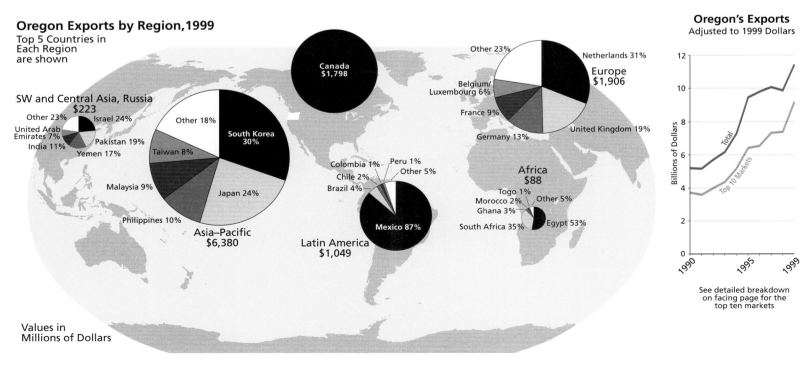

Values in Millions of Dollars

Oregon's Exports
Adjusted to 1999 Dollars

See detailed breakdown on facing page for the top ten markets

Oregon's Exports to Top 10 Markets
Adjusted to 1999 Dollars

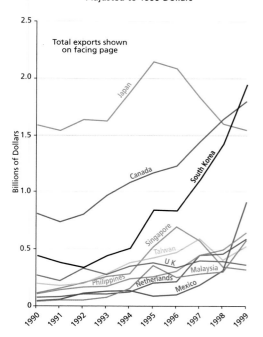

Total exports shown on facing page

Major Freight Corridors

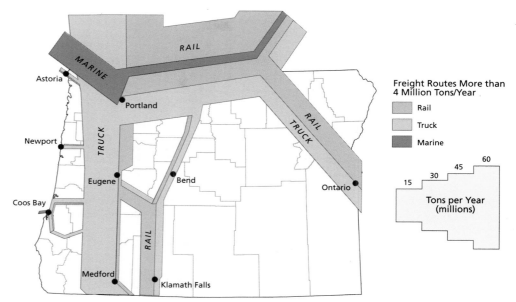

Freight Routes More than 4 Million Tons/Year
- Rail
- Truck
- Marine

Tons per Year (millions)

Major Freight Corridors

Much of Oregon's freight is moved on highways, rail lines and waterways in the Interstate Highway 5 (I-5) and Interstate Highway 84 (I-84) corridors. The I-84 corridor accounts for the most total freight moved, with rail lines on the Oregon and Washington sides of the Columbia River carrying a majority of the freight.

I-5 is one of the most heavily traveled truck freight corridors in the western United States. Seattle-to-Portland truck tonnages rank first among major metropolitan origin-destination pairs. Eugene-to-Portland tonnages rank second, followed by Los Angeles-to-San Francisco in third place and Portland-to-Eugene in fourth. The U.S. 97 corridor is Oregon's most important north-south corridor east of the Cascade Mountains: the OR 58 corridor and the southern part of the U.S. 97 corridor serve as important alternatives for freight moving by truck and rail between the Willamette Valley and northern California.

accounted for less than half of shipments below Portland; coastal and internal movements accounted for another third. Imports and "through movements" (where cargo passes through a port that is not its final destination) represented 20 percent of marine cargo shipments below Portland. The Port of Portland and other ports in Oregon and Washington along the Lower Columbia are seeking approval to deepen the river channel from 40 to 43 feet to accommodate ships that require more draft.

Marine terminals in the Coos Bay area rank second among Oregon's ports with about 2.6 million tons shipped in 1999. Forest products are the leading commodities shipped through Coos Bay as well as through other smaller deep-draft ports on the Oregon Coast and Columbia River. Other leading products shipped through Oregon's ports include grains and petroleum products. Wheat is the predominant grain shipped—Portland is the largest wheat exporting port in the U.S. Petroleum products are the leading commodities shipped upriver and the second leading commodity grouping overall, accounting for 24 percent of the tonnage moved through Portland in 1999. Manufactured products account for only a small portion of the tonnage shipped but are higher in overall value than bulk commodities. Motor vehicle imports and exports are among the manufactured products moving through marine terminals in Portland, which ranks fifth nationally, and second on the West Coast, in automobile handling.

Commercial traffic uses the 465-mile Columbia-Snake River system as far inland as Lewiston, Idaho. Wheat is the main product barged downstream; petroleum products dominate upstream movements. An increasing amount of cargo movement occurs by containers on barges. More containers move through the Port of Morrow at Boardman than through any other inland port in the U.S.

Marine Freight Ports
1998 and 1999 Averages

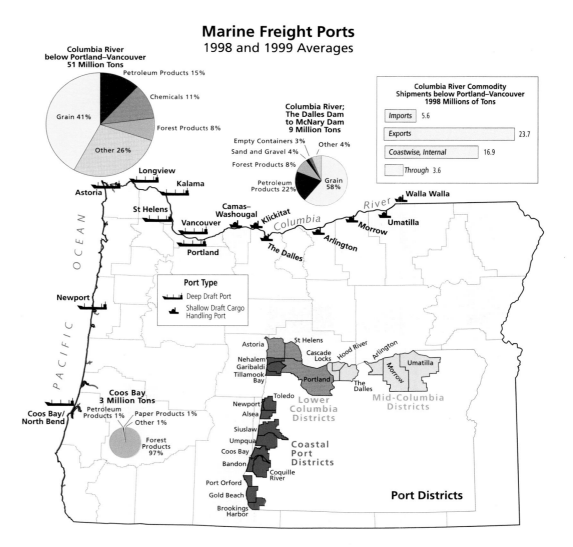

Columbia River below Portland–Vancouver 51 Million Tons
- Petroleum Products 15%
- Chemicals 11%
- Forest Products 8%
- Other 26%
- Grain 41%

Columbia River; The Dalles Dam to McNary Dam 9 Million Tons
- Empty Containers 3%
- Sand and Gravel 4%
- Other 4%
- Forest Products 8%
- Petroleum Products 22%
- Grain 58%

Columbia River Commodity Shipments below Portland–Vancouver 1998 Millions of Tons

Imports	5.6
Exports	23.7
Coastwise, Internal	16.9
Through	3.6

Coos Bay 3 Million Tons
- Petroleum Products 1%
- Paper Products 1%
- Other 1%
- Forest Products 97%

Port Type
- Deep Draft Port
- Shallow Draft Cargo Handling Port

Port Districts

Tourism and Recreation

Money spent in Oregon for tourism or travel has risen steadily in the past decade and now accounts for well over $5 billion annually. Many businesses benefit from sales to travelers, in particular businesses offering accommodations, transportation, food and beverage, retail and recreation services. For some of these businesses (for example, accommodations) travelers account for a majority of the clientele, while for others (most restaurants and retail establishments), travelers represent a much smaller percentage of clients. The bulk of Oregon's out-of-state visitors are from nearby states, in particular Washington and California. Population growth in these states has helped generate an increasing demand for Oregon's recreational resources.

A strong statewide planning process and environmental controls have helped maintain resource quality and manage growth in the state's agricultural and forest areas. Oregon has been particularly successful at retaining open space necessary for a variety of recreation activities. Many of the state's best coastal areas are in public ownership. Similarly, a high proportion of the state's forest resources is publicly owned. Agencies such as the Forest Service and the Bureau of Land Management are increasingly managing these lands for recreation purposes.

The travel industry is largest in Oregon's urban areas, Portland in particular, but it is also important in many rural locations. Oregon's Coast, forests and deserts are appealing tourist destination areas. For decades, many of these rural areas were oriented to the management and extraction of natural resources such as timber and fish—resources now less available than they were in the past. Businesses in these areas are responding to changing economic realities by expanding offerings to meet recreational demand. Along with bringing economic benefit, these changes have increased the need for roads and other transportation infrastructure, recreation access

and public facilities. In some locations these needs have not been adequately addressed, resulting in traffic congestion and other problems for residents and visitors alike. Parts of the state that have undergone substantial transformation toward recreation-oriented businesses include Central Oregon, the Columbia River Gorge and the Oregon Coast.

Recreation centered on built facilities and attractions is also gaining popularity in Oregon. The most attractive destination regions feature substantial recreation facilities along with accessible, high-quality natural areas. Central Oregon draws visitors with skiing, golf and the amenities of destination resorts such as Sunriver, Black Butte Ranch and Eagle Crest. Recreational areas east of Portland include the natural and built attractions of Mount Hood and the Columbia River Gorge. The Gorge has grown rapidly over the past decade as a recreation destination, combining water-related recreation opportunities for sailboarding and sailing with cultural attractions as well as sightseeing in the Columbia River Gorge National Scenic Area. The Coast has long supported a number of small- and moderate-sized motels and resorts, as well as marinas, retail areas and recreation businesses. The Oregon Coast Aquarium in Newport is an example of a large and relatively new public

Major Resorts

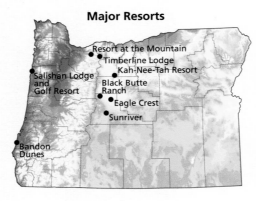

Tourism / Travel Dollars, 1998
per Capita

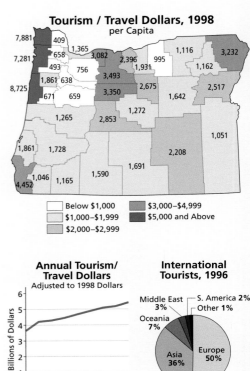

Below $1,000
$1,000–$1,999
$2,000–$2,999
$3,000–$4,999
$5,000 and Above

Annual Tourism/ Travel Dollars
Adjusted to 1998 Dollars

International Tourists, 1996

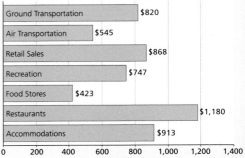

Tourism/Travel Dollars by Business 1999

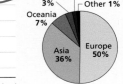

Business	Spending
Ground Transportation	$820
Air Transportation	$545
Retail Sales	$868
Recreation	$747
Food Stores	$423
Restaurants	$1,180
Accommodations	$913

Million Dollars in Spending

Tourist Accommodation Choice 1999

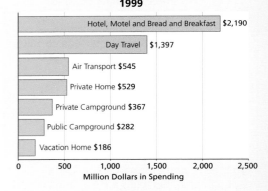

Accommodation	Spending
Hotel, Motel and Bread and Breakfast	$2,190
Day Travel	$1,397
Air Transport	$545
Private Home	$529
Private Campground	$367
Public Campground	$282
Vacation Home	$186

Million Dollars in Spending

Annual State Park Attendance 1999

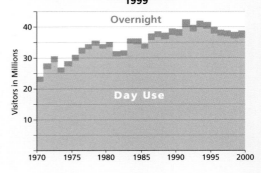

Overnight

Day Use

State Park Annual Visitors 1999

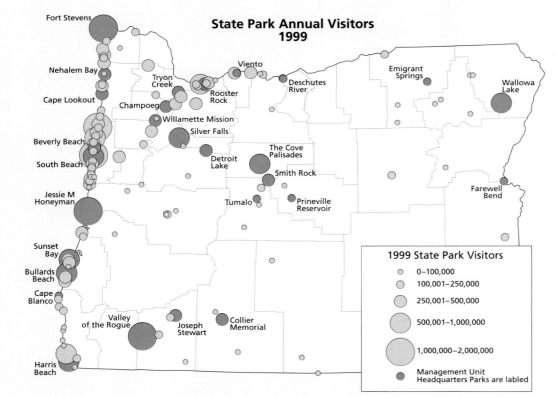

1999 State Park Visitors

- 0–100,000
- 100,001–250,000
- 250,001–500,000
- 500,001–1,000,000
- 1,000,000–2,000,000

Management Unit Headquarters Parks are labled

Golf Courses

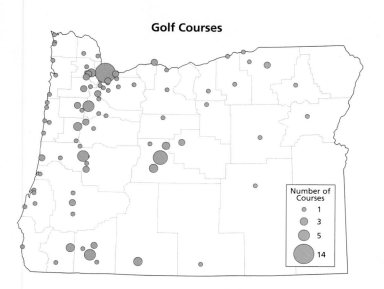

Number of Courses
- 1
- 3
- 5
- 14

Skiing, 1999–2000
Day Visits

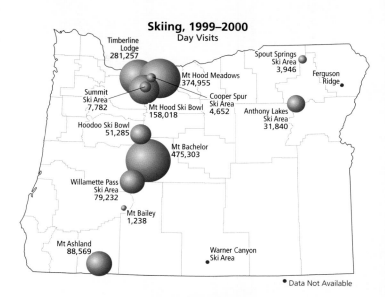

Timberline Lodge 281,257
Mt Hood Meadows 374,955
Summit Ski Area 7,782
Cooper Spur Ski Area 4,652
Mt Hood Ski Bowl 158,018
Spout Springs Ski Area 3,946
Ferguson Ridge
Anthony Lakes Ski Area 31,840
Hoodoo Ski Bowl 51,285
Mt Bachelor 475,303
Willamette Pass Ski Area 79,232
Mt Bailey 1,238
Mt Ashland 88,569
Warner Canyon Ski Area

• Data Not Available

Annual Ski Visitation
Day Visits

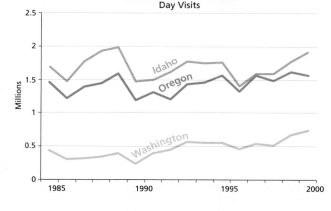

Millions — Idaho, Oregon, Washington
1985 / 1990 / 1995 / 2000

attraction in this area. Many of Oregon's golf courses are concentrated in destination regions—the Coast, Central Oregon and southern Oregon—where they are part of the recreation package that is marketed both in-state and to domestic and international visitors. Other easily accessible golf facilities in the Portland metro area and Willamette Valley cater to the region's growing resident population.

Casinos represent another rapidly growing recreation activity in Oregon, with nearly all facilities operated by Indian tribes. The state's larger casinos are typically located in small communities that are easily accessible to metro areas by high-volume highways.

Cultural events provide recreation for Oregonians and out-of-state visitors. The Oregon Shakespeare Festival in Ashland, the Oregon Bach Festival in Eugene, numerous Portland events and concerts and music festivals at venues across the state draw hundreds of thousands of culture enthusiasts each year.

Oregon has long supported an excellent inventory of state parks, dating back to 1921 when the Legislature authorized the State Highway Department to acquire park properties to protect roadside forests and scenery. Most parks today are located either on the Coast or on an inland body of water. Coastal state parks in particular are very much in demand, often filling during summer periods. The state operates a campsite reservation system to handle visitors at its most popular facilities.

A wide variety of water-related recreational activities takes place at Oregon's world-famous white water rivers, pristine lakes and Pacific coastline. There are 200,000 registered motorboats and sailboats in Oregon and an estimated 500,000 canoes, rafts, kayaks and drift boats. Many boaters use their craft while fishing for wild fish or those raised in one of the Oregon Department of Fish & Wildlife's (ODFW) 34 fish hatcheries. ODFW also manages the state's hunting and fishing license system. In 1999 this system oversaw the purchase of approximately 287,000 fishing licenses for adults and 33,000 for juveniles, 146,000 hunting licenses and 150,000 combination licenses good for both hunting and fishing.

Yearly Licenses Sold

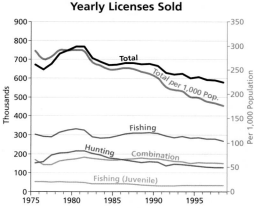

Thousands — Per 1,000 Population
Total
Total per 1,000 Pop.
Fishing
Hunting
Combination
Fishing (Juvenile)
1975 / 1980 / 1985 / 1990 / 1995

Combination Licenses
By County of Residence, 1999
Sold per 1,000 Population

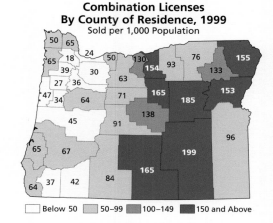

Below 50 | 50–99 | 100–149 | 150 and Above

Registered Boats in Oregon

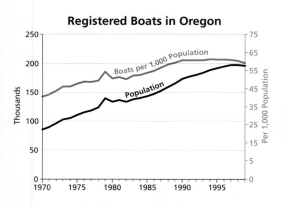

Thousands — Per 1,000 Population
Boats per 1,000 Population
Population
1970 / 1975 / 1980 / 1985 / 1990 / 1995

Fishing Licenses
By County of Residence, 1999
Sold per 1,000 Population

Below 75 | 75–99 | 100–124 | 125 and Above

Hunting Licenses
By County of Residence, 1999
Sold per 1,000 Population

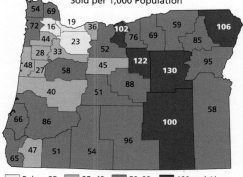

Below 25 | 25–49 | 50–99 | 100 and Above

115

Physical Geography

The Natural Setting and Its Processes

Landforms

Oregon in the Ice Age

Volcanoes and Earthquakes

Geology and Soils

Climate

Rivers and Lakes

Drainage Basins

Ecoregions and Habitats

Vegetation

Landforms: Elevation

SCALE 1:1,700,000

MILES

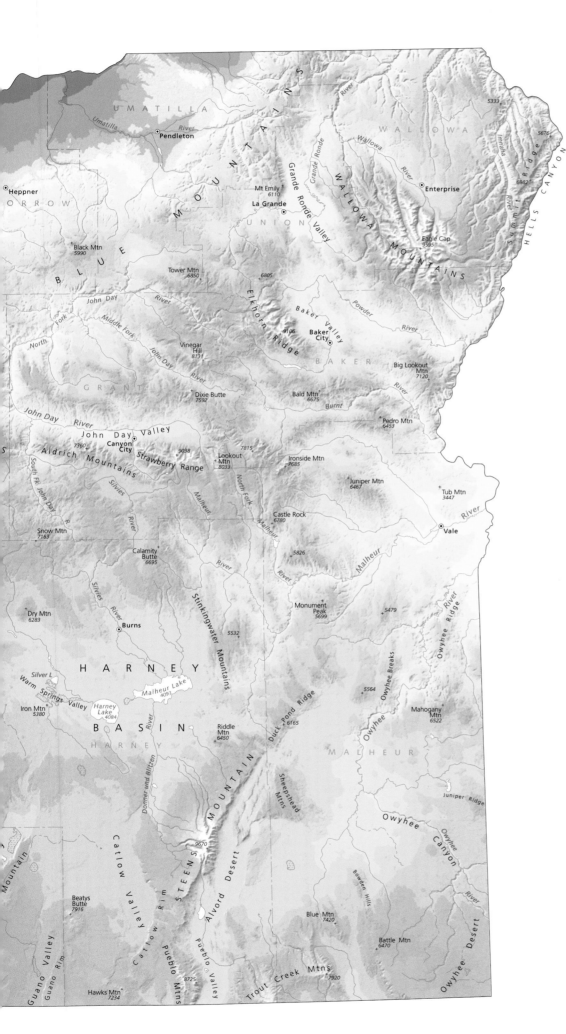

The state's most profound topographic feature, the Cascade Mountain Range, rises nearly two miles above sea level. These towering volcanic peaks set apart the eastern two-thirds of the state as a mile-high desert. To the west, Oregon's Coast Range is being elevated slowly while the Willamette Valley, already near sea level, is sinking. This movement is apparent today at raised beaches and headlands; it will be unmistakably apparent in the Willamette Valley far in the future when sea water begins to invade the valley. Barring intervention, the area will become Willamette Sound, like its northern counterpart, Puget Sound. Heavily eroded drainage systems and long, meandering estuaries give the western edge of the continent a ragged appearance.

The political boundaries of Oregon position the state at the crossroads of many massive landform regions called physiographic provinces. Only 40 percent of the Klamath Mountains project into southwest Oregon from California, while in the northeast the Blue Mountains are almost fully within the state's boundaries. The Cascade Range, extending from Northern California across Oregon and Washington into British Columbia, has about 35 percent of its length in Oregon; the Coast Range is shared almost evenly with Washington. The Columbia Plateau has roughly 20 percent of its exposure in north–central Oregon, but less than 5 percent of the vast Basin and Range province lies in south–central Oregon. Representing about 12 percent of the whole, the Owyhee Plateau, part of the Payette section that reaches into the southeastern corner of Oregon, is the southwestern end of a linear track of volcanic activity that stretches through Idaho and Wyoming.

Physiographic Provinces and Sections

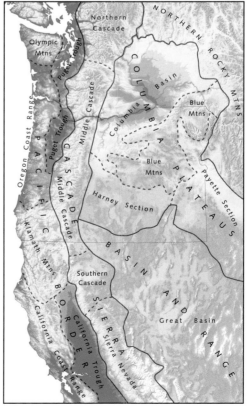

Landforms: Shaded Relief

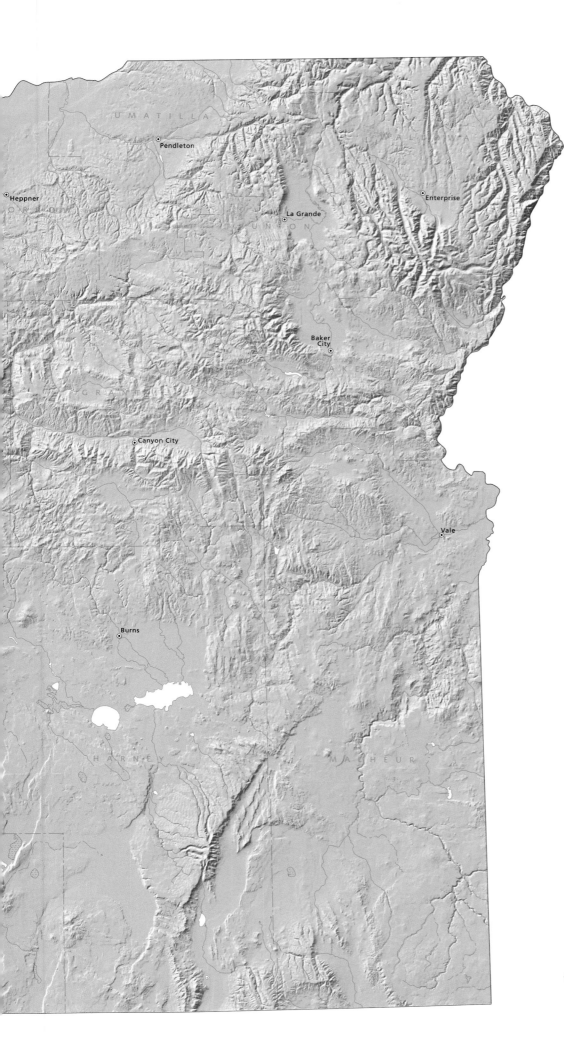

On the leading edge of the westward-moving North American continental plate, Oregon has for millions of years been variously stretched, compressed and elevated. These processes continue today, with North America moving at a velocity of approximately 1.5 inches per year. In the northeast and southwest corners of the state, the Blue and Klamath Mountains suffered extreme compression as they were being annexed to North America. The ancient rocks were elevated to high altitudes and extensively shaped by glaciers. Streams following fractures and fault patterns give the topography a distinctive rectangular grain (for detail, see page 127). Between Coquille and Newport in the central Coast area a series of lakes is trapped behind vast high dunes of clean white quartz sand delivered by streams and piled up by strong ocean winds (for detail, see page 126). The distinctive cones of the Cascades and High Lava Plains to the southeast tell a recent—geologically speaking—and tumultuous chapter in Oregon's volcanic history. Appearing on this map as smooth bumps, the volcanic peaks dotting the High Cascades are generally less than five million years old. These newly formed peaks have not yet been subject to the extensive erosion that has carved and "wrinkled" the much older Western Cascades. Remnants of what were once vast Ice Age pluvial lakes are today shallow bodies of water in the south–central portion of the state. Extensive erosion due to high rainfall has given both the Coast Range and the Western Cascades a thoroughly dissected "mature" physiography with steep valleys and deep canyons. East of the Cascades many of the streams are incised deeply into the flat volcanic plateaus.

The earth's crust beneath Oregon is anything but uniform. In the south–central part of the state intense stretching has pulled the area to more than twice its original width and left the crust only a few miles thick. In the northeast and southwest corners of the state great blocks of exotic rock project several tens of miles into the subsurface. Seventy miles beneath the eastern edge of the Cascade Range, the eastbound Juan de Fuca oceanic crustal plate is melting as it slips under the North American Plate. Along the axis of the Cascades volcanic conduits make their way to the surface from a depth in excess of 60 miles, inter-mittently pouring out lava and ash. A tangible reminder of ancient volcanic activity is seen clearly in the flat plateaus across the northern and central sections of the state. These regions are floored by near-continuous sheets of what was once an extremely hot fluid lava.

Detailed views of six areas are shown on the following pages, 126–129

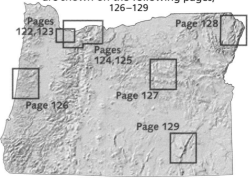

121

Landforms: Portland

Portland's turbulent geologic past and potentially troubled future can be read in its landforms. The city sits at the confluence not only of two great rivers, but of distinct geologic provinces. The Willamette River drains the southernmost portion of the great Puget Willamette Trough, a structural valley formed by the uplift of the Coast Range and simultaneous depression of the lowland to its east. The northern end of the lowland is submerged under Puget Sound. The structural grain of the Coast Range in the Portland area runs northwest by southeast. Ridges west of the Willamette generally follow that trend, as do many stream channels following old faults and fractures. The parallel alignment of the lower Tualatin and Willamette Rivers between Oregon City and Lake Oswego, as well as the former channels of the Clackamas River between the towns of Clackamas and Milwaukie, reflects this regional trend.

The most impressive northwest–southeast feature on the map is also the most ominous. Portland's West Hills follow the very straight line marking the Portland Hills Fault. The steep slopes with their fine views of the Cascades are also evidence of the young age of the uplift which raised the hills above the water-deposited lowland fill on the bank of the Willamette. The East Valley Fault runs parallel to the Portland Hills Fault just east of the river. Both line up with faults in the Cascades and across southeastern Oregon, making them part of one of the most extensive geological structures in the state. The destructive effects of a major earthquake along this system or nearby would be increased by the looseness of the Columbia River-deposited Troutdale Formation sands, gravels and clays underlying the city. (Earthquakes are discussed on pages 138–139).

The numerous buttes and small cone- or dome-shaped hills in the center of the map are the Boring volcanoes, a swarm of vents which were active between 1.2 and 3.9 million years ago. Similar small volcanoes occur in great numbers over much of Oregon. In the western parts of the state heavy tree cover contributes to their relative anonymity.

A long series of devastating Missoula Floods inundated the Portland area repeatedly between 18,000 and 12,000 years ago (see pages 134–135). These floods surged through the Columbia Gorge, roaring across east Portland and covering what is today the downtown area with 400 feet of muddy water. The floodwaters left behind a pattern of scoured channels and depositional bars where they flowed around the resistant rocks of Mount Tabor, Rocky Butte, Kelly Butte and the northwest edge of the Boring volcanoes. These features, easily overlooked on the ground, are startlingly obvious on this landforms map. Much of Portland resembles a beach at low tide, but on a gigantic scale.

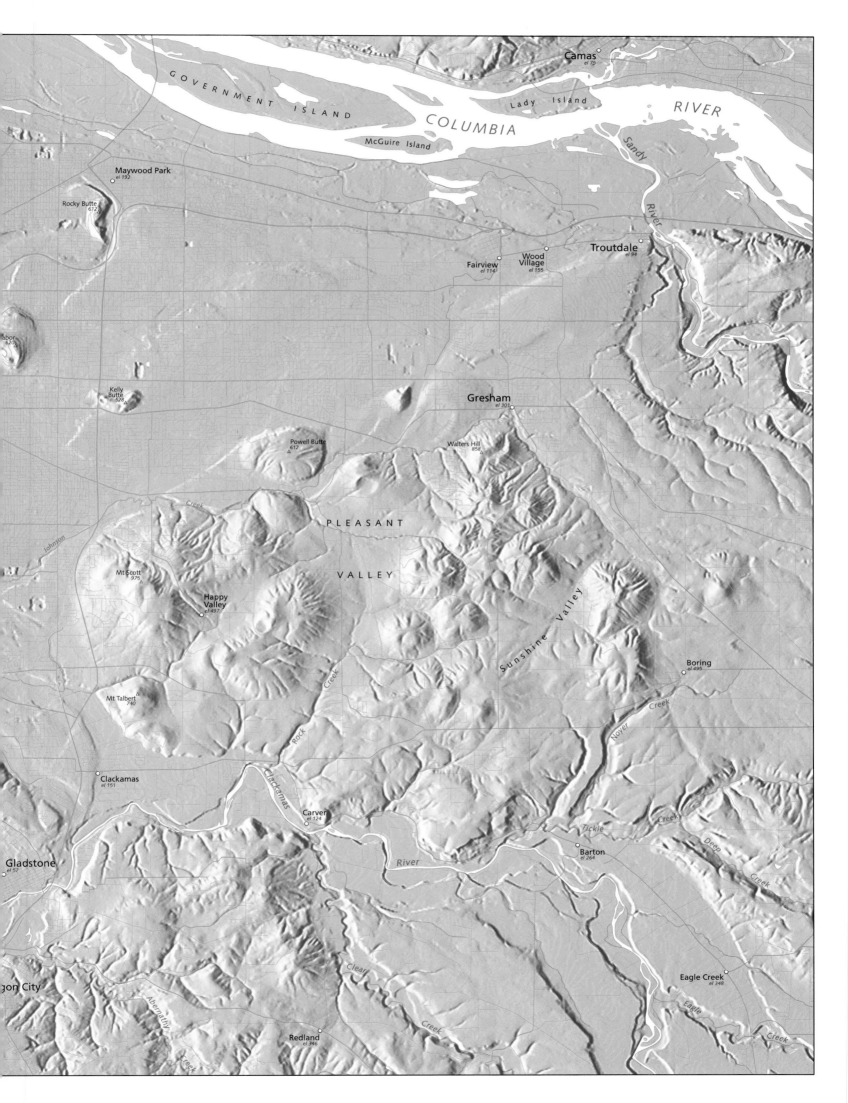

Camas
el 75

GOVERNMENT ISLAND

Lady Island

COLUMBIA

RIVER

McGuire Island

Sandy

River

Maywood Park
el 192

Rocky Butte
612

Troutdale
el 94

Fairview
el 114

Wood
Village
el 155

abor
620

Kelly
Butte
528

Gresham
el 301

Powell Butte
612

Walters Hill
858

Creek

PLEASANT

Johnson

VALLEY

Mt Scott
975

Happy
Valley
el 497

Sunshine Valley

Boring
el 495

Mt Talbert
740

Creek

Rock

Creek

Noyer

Creek

Clackamas
el 151

Clackamas

Carver
el 124

Tickle

Creek

Barton
el 264

Deep

Gladstone
el 57

River

Creek

on City

Clear

Eagle Creek
el 348

Abernathy

Eagle

Redland
el 346

Creek

Creek

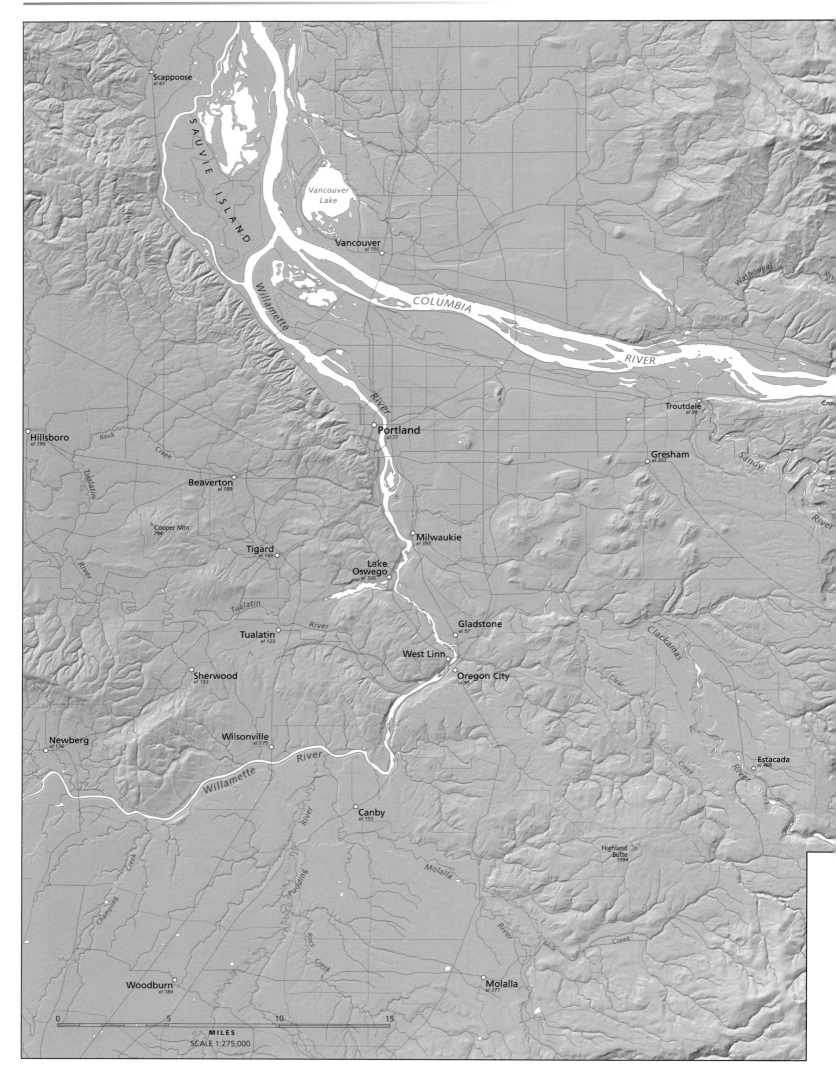

Scappoose
el 67

SAUVIE ISLAND

Vancouver
Lake

Vancouver
el 150

COLUMBIA

Willamette

RIVER

Washougal River

River

Hillsboro
el 196

Rock

Creek

Portland
el 77

Troutdale
el 94

Crow

Tualatin

Beaverton
el 189

Gresham
el 301

Sandy

River

△ Cooper Mtn
794

Tigard
el 169

Milwaukie
el 397

River

Lake
Oswego
el 100

Tualatin

River

Gladstone
el 57

Clackamas

Tualatin
el 123

West Linn

Sherwood
el 193

Oregon City
el 55

Clear

Newberg
el 176

Wilsonville
el 175

Willamette   River

Creek

River

Estacada
el 465

Champoeg   Creek

Pudding

River

Canby
el 153

Molalla

Highland
Butte
1594

Rock

Creek

River

Milk

Creek

Woodburn
el 184

Molalla
el 371

0   5   10   15
MILES
SCALE 1:275,000

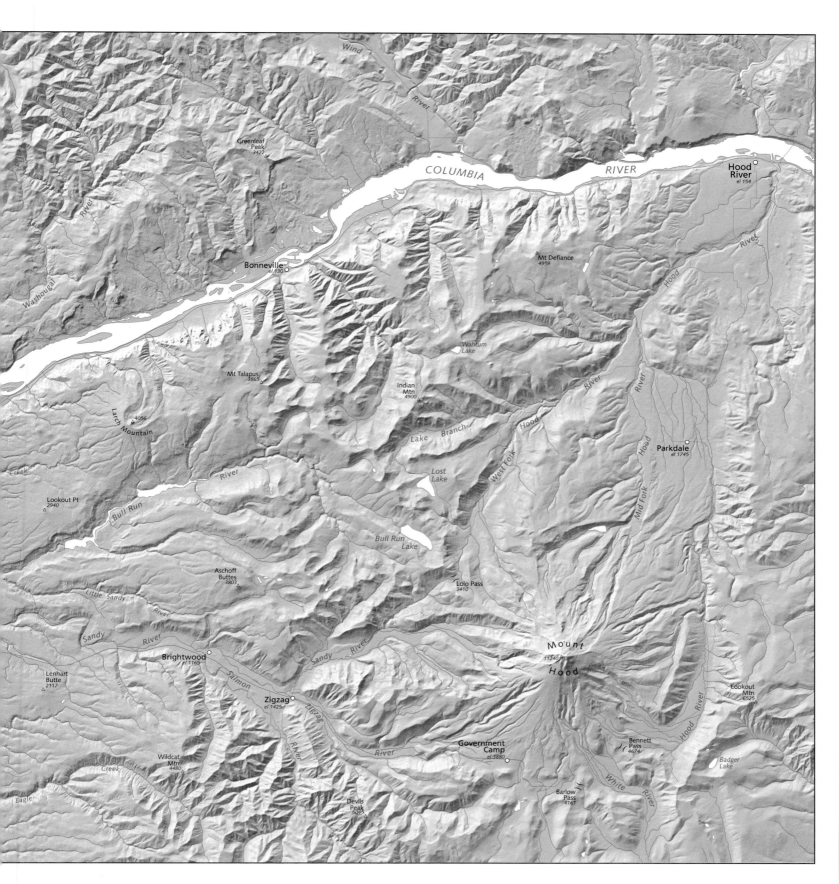

The Columbia River Gorge

The Columbia River cuts through the Cascades to emerge just north of Portland into the Puget Willamette Trough. The Willamette Valley (the northern end of which appears at left) was not cut by the river which drains it but was formed by the depression of the Willamette Lowland and simultaneous uplift of the Coast Range. Its remarkably flat surface is in part the result of the repeated deposition of Missoula Flood sediments (see pages 134–135). East of the Willamette Valley, the Cascade Range includes the Old Cascades,

formed about 40 million years ago, and the spectacular and geologically young stratocone volcanoes of the High Cascades, including Mount Hood. The Old Cascades are deeply eroded, displaying many fractures and fault lines which water and glacial erosion followed. Dormant but not extinct, Mount Hood rises to 11,240 feet, interrupting wet marine winds and precipitating the heavy snows that perpetuates its remaining active glaciers. Glacial canyons fan out from the peak in a radial pattern, probable routes for the mudflows which would follow a major eruption and

threaten neighboring communities such as Gresham, Troutdale, Hood River and Parkdale. Major eruptions 15,000 years ago built up layers of volcanic rock up to 500 feet thick on the south and southwest flanks of Mount Hood. The Columbia Gorge follows a boundary between newer volcanic rocks south of the river and older volcanics to the north. The south walls of the Gorge rise as nearly vertical cliffs, while the north slopes have repeatedly failed in large landslides. A major landslide (see page 141) occurred 300 years ago near Bonneville.

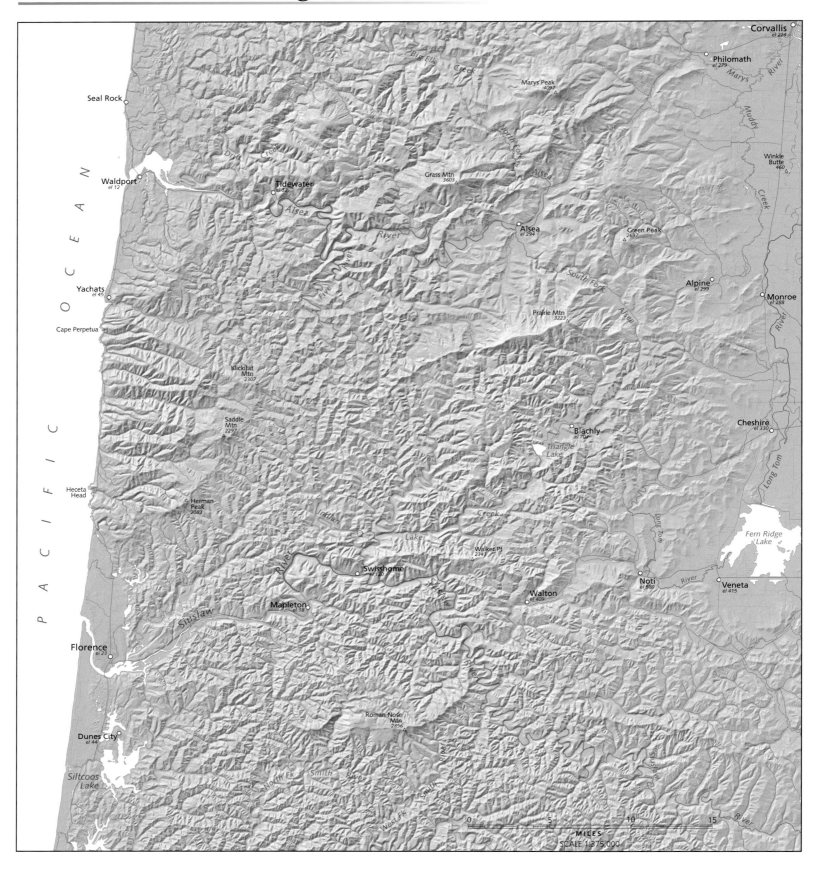

Coast Range

The collision of the Juan de Fuca Microplate with the North American Plate elevated the Coast Range in a number of stages beginning in the Miocene epoch (for geologic time scale, see Geologic Ages, pages 144–145). The regional grain of this area appears as northwest by southeast–oriented valleys which follow faults imposed by the uplift and arching of the Coast Range. Much of this region is underlain by silt as well as delta and deep sea fan sands dating back 50 million years. Higher elevations in the range—such as Roman Nose Mountain, Prairie Mountain and Marys Peak—are supported by intrusive crystalline rocks that date from the Oligocene epoch. The Oregon Coast today is a series of rocky volcanic headlands interspersed with long sandy beaches and pocket coves. The headlands of Heceta Head and Yachats are armored by the locally derived volcanic Yachats Eocene Basalt rocks which date back 40 to 42 million years. At Seal Rock, however, the lavas that form rugged sea cliffs originated at vents several hundred miles away in Eastern Oregon and Western Idaho. Termed "invasive basalts," these much younger lavas of Miocene epoch—only 16 to 17 million years old—are part of the famed Columbia River Basalt Group that spread over much of southeastern Washington and northeastern Oregon before pouring through the Columbia River Gorge to eventually reach the Pacific. Today the Coast Range is steadily tilting toward the east and being elevated as much as an inch in ten years, even as the Willamette Valley is slowly sinking.

Heart of the Blue Mountains

The John Day River is the longest river in Oregon. Shown here in Grant County, the central portion of the river cuts through some of Oregon's oldest rocks. These "terranes" originated far out in the Pacific Ocean before colliding with and being annexed to North America. Most of the map is underlain by Baker Terrane rocks, which result from deep, muddy ocean floor environments that existed 250 million years ago. The Izee Terrane to the south in the Aldrich Mountains is a much shallower and younger formation, roughly 180 million years old. Both of these terranes were deposited well to the west of the present-day North American landmass. They were attached or "accreted" to this continent approximately 140 million years ago. Within the rocks of these terranes even the fossil remains of plants and animals are decidedly exotic to North America. Atop all of these terranes, layer upon layer of Miocene epoch Columbia River Basalt Group lavas create the high plateaus of northeast Oregon (for geologic time scale, see Geologic Ages, pages 144–145). Sandwiched between these lavas and the older terranes, fossil-rich rocks of the Clarno, John Day, Mascal and Rattlesnake Formations provide a superb near-continuous 50-million-year record of life in Oregon from the Eocene through Miocene epochs. The soft crumbly volcanic ash of these fossil-bearing rock formations combined with low rainfall characteristic of areas east of the Cascade Mountains creates a "badlands" topography over much of the area shown on this map. Faults, folds and intrusive rocks across the area trend northwest by southeast as shown by the pathways of many of the streams and valleys.

Landforms: Hells Canyon; Steens Mountain

Hells Canyon

Along the state's eastern margin the sheer walls of Hells Canyon rise even higher than those of Arizona's Grand Canyon. West of the Snake River a level platform of 17-million-year-old Miocene lavas marks some of the earliest flows from the volcanic episode geologists call the Columbia River Basalt Group (for geologic time scale, see Geologic Ages, pages 144–145). In the southwestern corner of the region shown, granites of the Wallowa Mountains protrude like islands

above the basalt flows. The Wallowas were heavily eroded by ice during the Pleistocene epoch. One of the most striking glacial features of the area is Wallowa Lake just south of Joseph. This three-mile-long lake is trapped between steep mounds of glacial debris, called lateral moraines, left by northward-moving lobes of ice flowing down the valley from what is now the Eagle Cap Wilderness. (see Wallowa map on page 135).

Within Hells Canyon a rock "package" called the Wallowa Terrane is represented by

volcanic rocks of the Seven Devils Group that are up to 250 million years old. This peculiar and distinctive suite of rocks, which was annexed or "accreted" to North America some 140 million years ago, has been recognized on Vancouver Island, the Queen Charlotte Islands and well up into Southeast Alaska. These rocks represent some of the best evidence for the exotic nature of much of the Blue Mountains.

Steens Mountain

In this area of Oregon's Basin and Range province, tensional faults criss-cross the land, trending both northwest and northeast. Bounded by faults, Steens Mountain represents a "horst" or block of the earth's surface raised in relation to the surrounding land, while the Alvord Desert is a "graben," a depression or down-thrown block. Crustal stretching of this province has thinned as well as broken (by faults) the crust enough to create many hot springs where shallow ground water comes in contact with warm lower crustal rocks. Steens Mountain is a remnant of a broad volcanic plateau of black, dense granular basalt rock that cooled about 16 million years ago.

Nearly every tilted fault block mountain in Oregon has its steep face toward the west —these mountains did not have glaciers. But Steens Mountain has its steep face to the east and a long gentle slope that rises up from Frenchglen (elevation 4,184 feet) more than a vertical mile to the crest at 9,670 feet. During the ice ages the prevailing moisture-bearing winds from the west blew up this long slope and deposited quantities of snow that became the huge Pleistocene glaciers that eroded the U-shaped canyons of Kiger Gorge, Little Blitzen Gorge and Big Indian Gorge. Most of the basins oriented north–to–south, such as Catlow Valley and the Alvord Desert, were the sites of immense pluvial lakes that resulted from heavy rain during the cool, moist interval of the ice ages as recently as 12,000 years ago. These now-dry lakebeds are littered with the fossilized bones of prehistoric mammals, fish, water birds and mollusks.

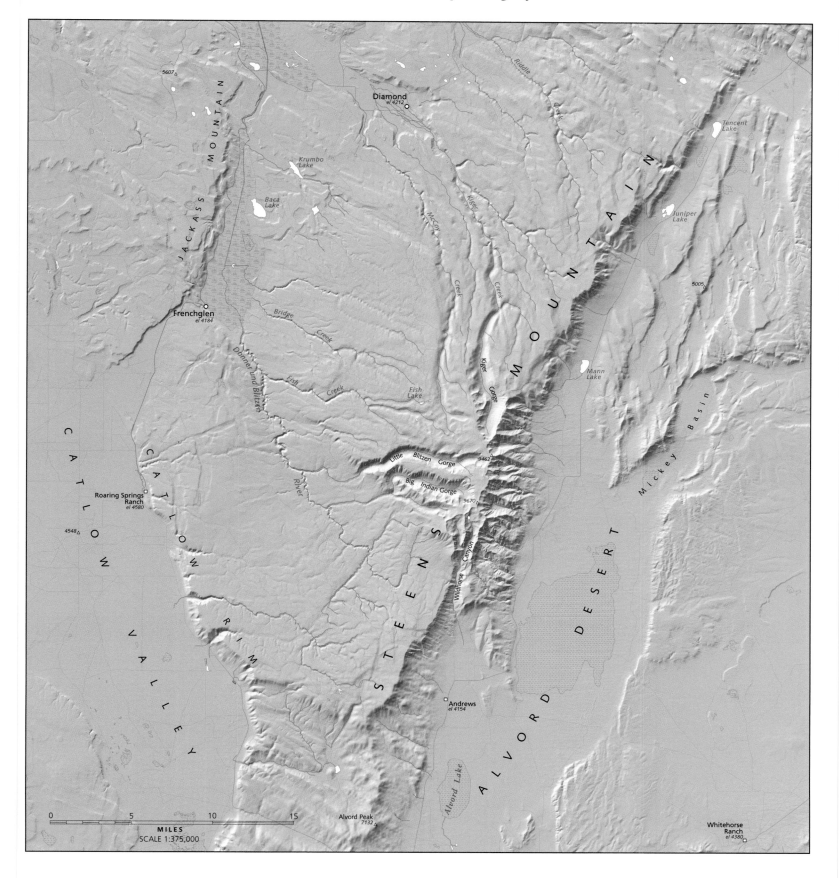

MILES
SCALE 1:375,000

129

Cross Sections

These cross sections highlight the remarkable diversity of topography across the state. The land surface is shown with an extreme vertical exaggeration, required at this small scale to make the state's relief visible —if the vertical and horizontal scales were the same, Mount Hood would appear less than one-tenth of an inch high.

The three north-to-south transects illustrate markedly different landscapes. The Coast Range is generally low and very steep, cut by the innumerable streams of this notably wet region. In the south, the Klamath Mountains are geologically distinct and much higher than the mountains in the north, but also deeply dissected. In contrast, the Cascade crest is a comparatively level ridge, punctuated by a series of volcanoes too recent to have been heavily eroded. The third cross section shows the dramatic uplift of the Strawberry Mountains and the impressive fault block of Steens Mountain. Both of these features rise far above the nearly level plateaus and basins of Central Oregon and are deeply cut by glacial erosion (see pages 132-133).

The three west-to-east transects show the regional differences within the Coast Range along with the contrasting character of the western and eastern slopes of the Cascades. The western side is much wetter, drops to a lower elevation and is consequently much more deeply eroded. The Cascade volcanoes are generally symmetrical—even in collapse, as Crater Lake shows. The tilted fault block mountains of Central and Eastern Oregon are distinctly asymmetrical. They typically rise steadily from a "hinged" baseline to an abrupt edge at the fault plane. When the blocks are composed of erosion-resistant basalts, as in Winter Ridge and Steens Mountain, the exposed uplifted face forms a spectacular near-vertical wall.

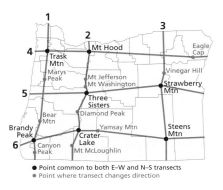

● Point common to both E–W and N–S transects
● Point where transect changes direction

1 Coast Range from North to South

2 Crest of the Cascades from North to South

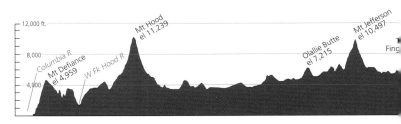

3 Eastern Oregon from North to South

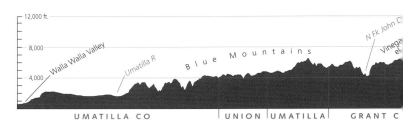

4 Pacific Ocean at Cape Lookout to the Snake River at Hells Canyon

5 Pacific Ocean at Florence to the Snake River at Ontario

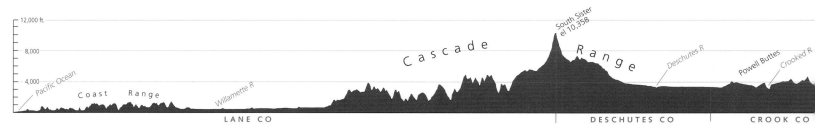

6 Pacific Ocean at Gold Beach to the Idaho Border South of Jordan Valley

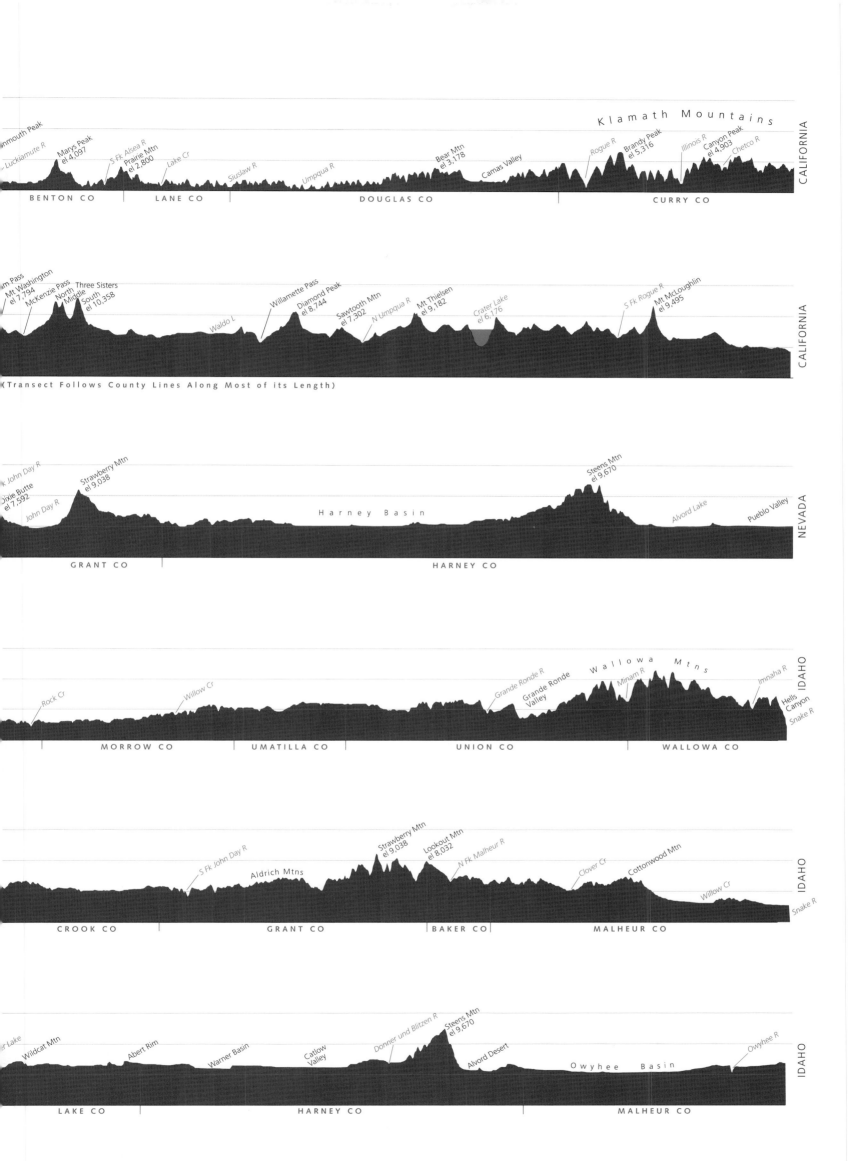

Ice Age Lakes and Floods

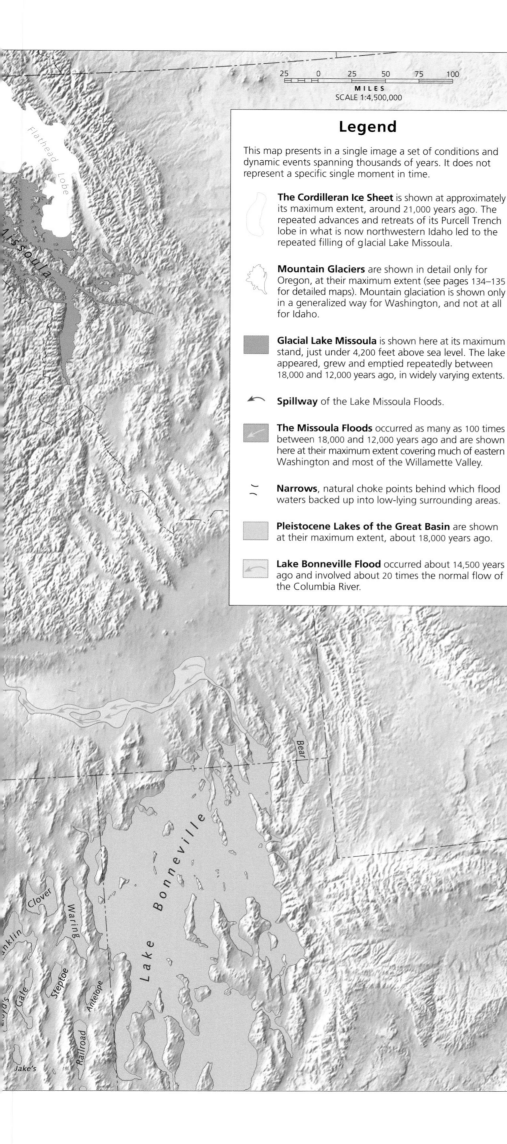

MILES
SCALE 1:4,500,000

Legend

This map presents in a single image a set of conditions and dynamic events spanning thousands of years. It does not represent a specific single moment in time.

The Cordilleran Ice Sheet is shown at approximately its maximum extent, around 21,000 years ago. The repeated advances and retreats of its Purcell Trench lobe in what is now northwestern Idaho led to the repeated filling of glacial Lake Missoula.

Mountain Glaciers are shown in detail only for Oregon, at their maximum extent (see pages 134–135 for detailed maps). Mountain glaciation is shown only in a generalized way for Washington, and not at all for Idaho.

Glacial Lake Missoula is shown here at its maximum stand, just under 4,200 feet above sea level. The lake appeared, grew and emptied repeatedly between 18,000 and 12,000 years ago, in widely varying extents.

Spillway of the Lake Missoula Floods.

The Missoula Floods occurred as many as 100 times between 18,000 and 12,000 years ago and are shown here at their maximum extent covering much of eastern Washington and most of the Willamette Valley.

Narrows, natural choke points behind which flood waters backed up into low-lying surrounding areas.

Pleistocene Lakes of the Great Basin are shown at their maximum extent, about 18,000 years ago.

Lake Bonneville Flood occurred about 14,500 years ago and involved about 20 times the normal flow of the Columbia River.

The Missoula Floods

The most far-reaching and catastrophic events of the Pleistocene Ice Age in the Pacific Northwest were the Missoula Floods. These cataclysmic deluges occurred repeatedly when a lobe of the Canadian Cordilleran Ice Sheet advanced across the Clark Fork River in what is today northwestern Montana and northern Idaho. As the river valley filled with ice and glacial debris, the Clark Fork backed up, filling neighboring valleys to a distance of up to 200 miles to the southeast. Glacial Lake Missoula at its greatest extent held over 360 cubic miles of water, roughly the volume of today's Lake Ontario in the Great Lakes system. When the ice dam failed, the entire lake emptied in a matter of days, sending a wall of water across the Idaho Panhandle into Washington's Columbia Basin, and then through the Columbia Gorge and out to the Pacific. The cycle of damming, lake filling and catastrophic flooding may have occurred as many as 50 or even 100 times at the end of the Pleistocene epoch, between 18,000 and 12,000 years ago. In volume, each of these floods contained several times the combined flow of all the rivers on the globe. The Missoula Floods may have been the largest discharges of water in the history of the earth.

As the floodwaters roared southwestward across eastern Washington, they scoured the surface topography down to bedrock to create the rugged landscape today called the Channeled Scablands. At several choke points or narrows, the floodwaters briefly backed up to create large ephemeral lakes, one of which (Lake Allison) flooded nearly all of the Willamette Valley.

Floodwaters transported slabs of floating glacial ice, which carried embedded sedimentary debris, including boulders, from the mountains of Montana. As flood lakes receded, ice rafts stranded and melted, leaving behind transported sediments and large "erratic" boulders. In the Willamette Valley these erratics number in the hundreds and bear witness to the presence of standing water at least as far south as Harrisburg, just north of Eugene. The Willamette Formation represents fine sediments that settled out of the turbid waters onto the lakebed before the valley drained out to the north.

Ice Age Lakes

During a period of substantially increased rain and snowfall approximately 50,000 years ago, natural depressions in the Basin and Range region began to fill, creating large "pluvial lakes." The largest, Lake Bonneville, filled to the point of overtopping a divide nearly 800 feet above the present level of the Great Salt Lake, sending floodwaters north into the Snake River and down Hells Canyon into the Columbia. Outflow from Lake Modoc on the California–Oregon border deepened the Klamath Gorge. The rest of these lakes expanded and shrank within closed basins. Lush wetland vegetation brought sizable populations of fish, birds and mammals, including Pleistocene elephants, horses, bison and sheep. Reduced precipitation after about 11,000 years ago has shrunk these pluvial lakes to the much smaller but still fluctuating lakes of the present.

Ice Age Glaciers

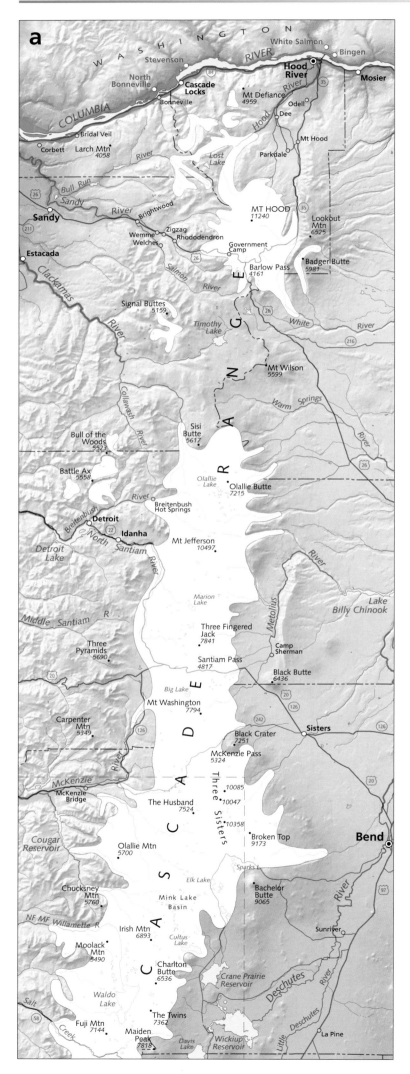

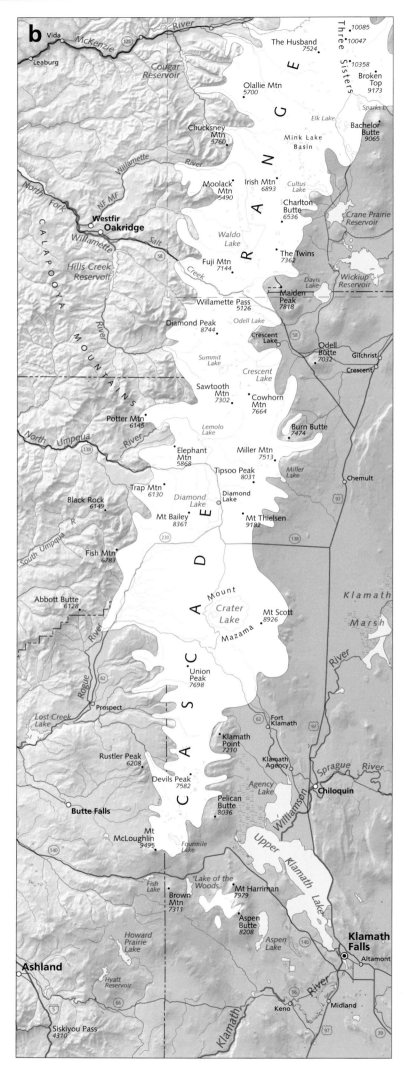

Oregon lies just south of the most southerly advance of the continental ice sheet which covered much of northern North America during the two-million-year Ice Age, or Pleistocene epoch. In Canada as well as in Northern Europe and Siberia, ice sheets accumulated to depths of many thousands of feet. The exact causes of the multiple ice advances that mark this period remain unclear. There were at least four major periods of advancing and retreating ice and innumerable local variations, presumably initiated by changes in the earth's delicate climatic balance. Repeated advances and retreats of a Cordilleran Ice Sheet lobe in northern Washington and Idaho triggered the Missoula Floods which helped shape both the Columbia River Gorge and the Willamette Valley (see pages 132–133).

Within Oregon, Ice Age glaciers developed in virtually all mountain areas with elevations more than about 5,800 feet. Glaciers reshaped the landscape of the High Cascades and Steens Mountain, as well as the

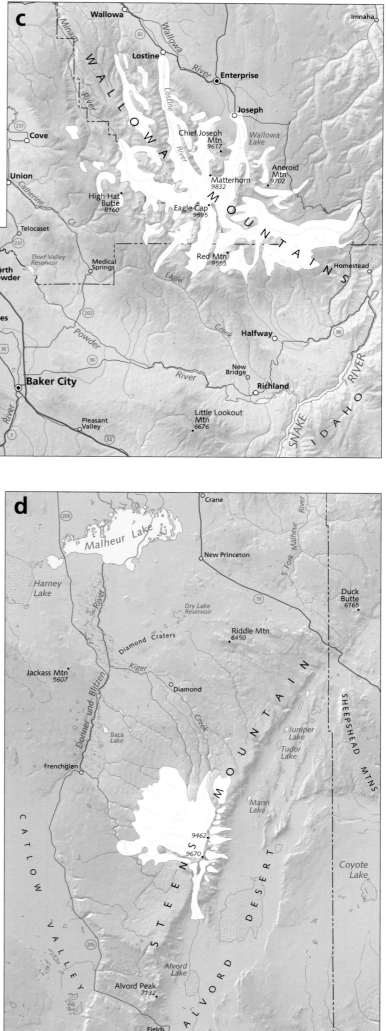

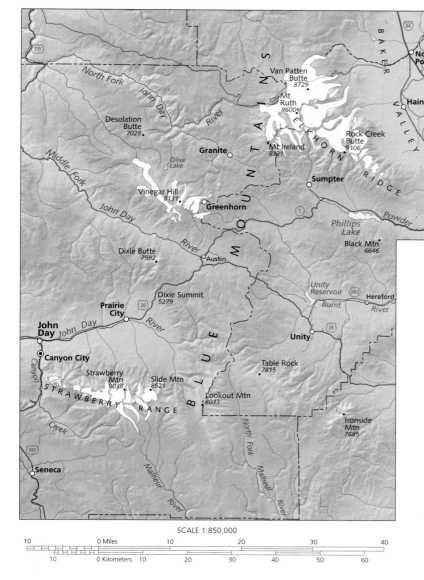

SCALE 1:850,000

Wallowa, Elkhorn, Strawberry and Greenhorn Mountains. The many deep valleys descending from the Cascade crest (see pages 120–121) are evidence of the land-shaping power of moving ice. Distinctive U-shaped glacial valleys are illustrated on page 129 (Steens Mountain) and 124–125 (Mount Hood and the Columbia Gorge). Wallowa Lake, a classic moraine feature, is shown on page 247. In the Northern Willamette Valley, fan-shaped deposits of glacial debris radiate into the valley from the western edge of the Cascades, displacing the Willamette River to its current westerly path. In the past 12,000 years glaciers have disappeared from all but the highest elevations in Oregon; remnants persist on Mount Hood and the Three Sisters.

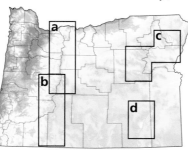

Volcanoes

Oregon's volcanoes reflect the state's location on the "Ring of Fire." This belt of volcanoes and earthquakes circles the Pacific Ocean, tracing the active boundaries of the Pacific and other neighboring crustal plates. Off the Pacific Northwest, a spreading ridge divides the Pacific Plate, moving to the northwest, from the Farallon Plate, moving to the southeast. The oceanic Farallon Plate meets the North American Plate in the Cascadia Subduction Zone, where it is overriden by the lighter continental material. The once immense Farallon Plate is now almost completely gone, subducted or recycled under the North American Plate. Three trailing remnants—the Gorda, Juan de Fuca, and Explorer Microplates—remain geologically important. At a depth of some 60 miles the subducted plate slab melts, sending plumes of molten rock, or magma, rising toward the surface, where some emerge as volcanoes. The Oregon Cascades are part of the archipelago of volcanoes that extends from Mount Lassen in Northern California into the Mount Garibaldi area in British Columbia.

As the rate of plate collision has changed over time, the geometry of the plates being subducted beneath the Cascades has correspondingly altered. The result has been the steady movement of the volcanic crest eastward during the past 40 million years.

The active volcanic peaks are at present confined to the narrow belt known as the High Cascade Range and the adjacent western part of the High Lava Plains. The belt of active peaks was much broader during the Miocene epoch about 18 million years ago (see pages 146–147).

Typical volcanic forms include steep-sided stratovolcanoes like Mount Hood (see page 125); lower, more rounded domelike shield volcanoes like Newberry Crater; smaller swarms of volcanoes like those of the Boring Volcanic Field shown on page 123; cinder cones; and eroded remnants of all of these.

Cascade stratovolcanoes tend to erupt only very intermittently (as measured on a human time scale—on a geologic time scale they are extremely active). Unlike earthquakes, they almost always warn well in advance of an impending eruption, with elevated heat flow, micro-earthquakes and harmonic tremors, surface bulging and gas venting. The actual eruption can be a cataclysmic event of great force causing widespread destruction. The Mount St. Helens eruption in 1980 was a classic example, blasting 1,300 feet off the top of the mountain and leaving a crater floor nearly 3,500 feet below the former summit. Mount St. Helens is a small and young volcano, with its oldest deposits no more than 50,000 years old, and its now partially destroyed cone only about 2,200 years old. It is also the most active. Mount Mazama is about half a million years old and many times larger, with a peak estimated at 12,000 feet when it erupted repeatedly 6,600 years ago. The mountain then fell in on itself in a "collapse caldera" now occupied by Crater Lake. The high points remaining on the rim of its shattered cone are about 4,000 feet lower than the former summit, and the bottom of Crater Lake is another 4,000 feet below the rim. Newberry Crater, a low-profile shield volcano, formed a similar collapse caldera after eruptions about 7,000 years ago. The present appearance of all three features is strikingly similar. The digital oblique views on the facing page, showing landform details which are obscured in photographs by tree cover or haze, reveal many common characteristics. The smooth slopes of Mount St. Helens reflect its young age. Early stages of rebuilding are evident in the crater's central lava dome. Newberry Crater and Mount Mazama were also modified by subsequent lava flows and cinder cone development. Glacial valleys on the slopes of Mount Mazama testify to the size of the mountain that no longer exists. Cascade-type volcanoes typically experience episodes of growth punctuated by long periods of inactivity, so it is premature to consider any of the High Cascades volcanoes extinct.

Tectonic Plates

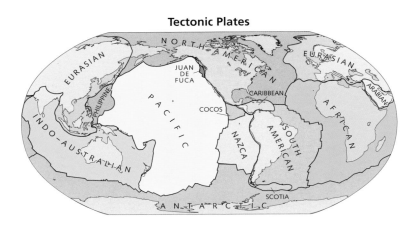

Ring of Fire: Volcanoes Around the Pacific

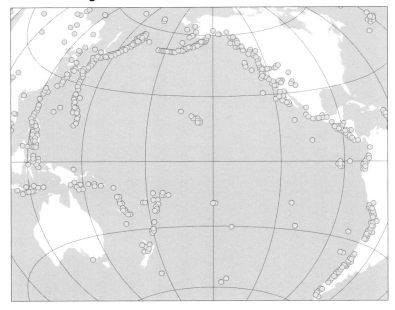

Subduction and Volcanism

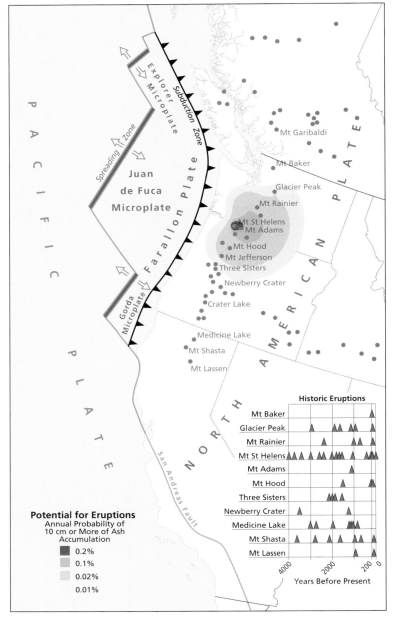

Volcanoes and Vents

Major volcanoes are named.
Smaller vents are shown as red dots.

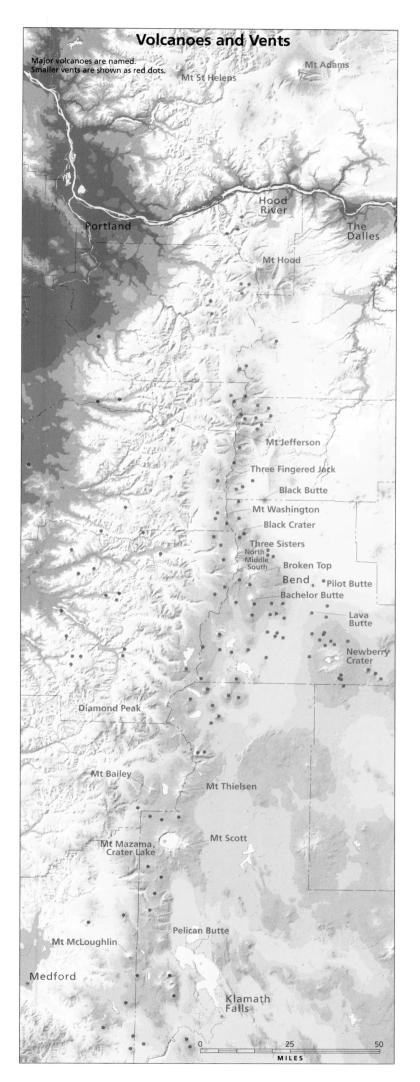

Mt Adams

Mt St Helens

Hood
River

The
Dalles

Portland

Mt Hood

Mt Jefferson

Three Fingered Jack

Black Butte

Mt Washington

Black Crater

Three Sisters
North
Middle
South

Broken Top

Bend

Pilot Butte

Bachelor Butte

Lava
Butte

Newberry
Crater

Diamond Peak

Mt Bailey

Mt Thielsen

Mt Mazama,
Crater Lake

Mt Scott

Pelican Butte

Mt McLoughlin

Medford

Klamath
Falls

0   25   50
MILES

Mount St. Helens

View from the Northwest.

Newberry Crater

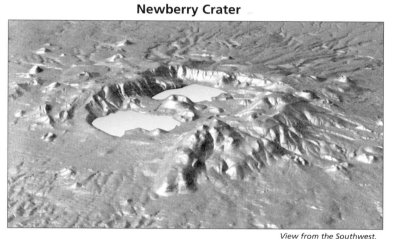

View from the Southwest.

Mount Mazama, Crater Lake

View from the Southwest.

Mount Mazama and Mount St. Helens Ash Fall

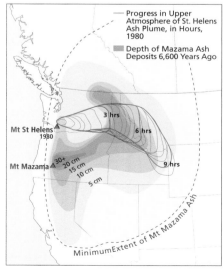

Progress in Upper
Atmosphere of St. Helens
Ash Plume, in Hours,
1980

Depth of Mazama Ash
Deposits 6,600 Years Ago

Mt St Helens
1980

3 hrs

6 hrs

9 hrs

Mt Mazama
30+
20 cm
15 cm
10 cm
5 cm

Minimum Extent of Mt Mazama Ash

Mount St. Helens in Washington is one of the smaller Cascade volcanoes, but in recent millennia the most active one. Its violent eruption in 1980 sent an enormous cloud of fine-grained, choking, abrasive ash into the upper atmosphere, where it circled the globe in only a few days. The red lines on the map record the movement of the ash plume within the first nine hours after the eruption. The much larger Mount Mazama eruption of 6,600 years ago left measurable ash deposits across virtually all of the Northwest and most of the Great Basin. This unmistakable layer is an important chronological marker for Northwest archeology and oceanography. Ash deposition is an accident of the wind currents at the time of an eruption. Mud and ash flows down glacial and river valleys are confined to narrow areas, but are potentially much more destructive (see page 125).

137

Earthquakes

Earthquakes are caused by the bending and breaking of rocks along faults, which are most abundant in boundary zones between tectonic plates (see page 136). Two of the world's largest plates, the North American and Pacific Plates, are involved in a slow, glancing collision along the western margin of the U.S. This process accounts for the numerous earthquakes shown here on both the West Coast and Oregon maps. While most of the movement between these plates is localized to California and the Gulf of California, where the earthquakes are most frequent, deformation and earthquakes due to these plate movements extend as far east as Colorado and north into Canada and Alaska. Trapped between these two large plates are smaller plates, including the Juan de Fuca Plate that lies between the coast of the Pacific Northwest (see page 136) and the offshore zone of earthquakes that form the boundary of the Pacific Plate. The Juan de Fuca Plate is being forced under the North American Plate, rather than sliding past it. This "subduction" results in volcanic activity; it also causes earthquakes, which are not numerous but can be extremely violent.

Earthquakes are located and measured by seismometers which record ground movement. The size and location of past earthquakes can be a powerful tool for predicting where future earthquakes will occur. However, because very large earthquakes occur infrequently, the short instrumental record of seismometer readings now available can be misleading. The largest known earthquake in the Western U.S. occurred in 1700 AD just off the Oregon Coast, but there have been no major earthquakes (and very few of any size) in that area since seismometers have been installed. Historical records and geologic evidence are relied on to create longer records of earthquakes for hazard maps like those shown on the next page.

In addition to the plate boundary zones offshore, Oregon has many faults that produce earthquakes during infrequent bursts of activity

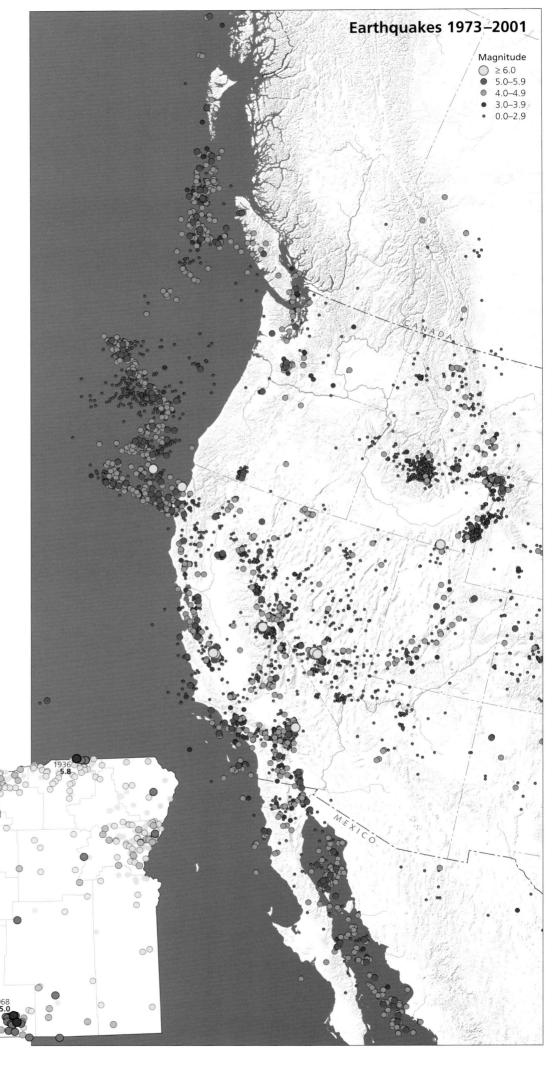

Earthquakes 1973–2001

Magnitude
≥ 6.0
5.0–5.9
4.0–4.9
3.0–3.9
0.0–2.9

Earthquakes in Oregon 1840–1998

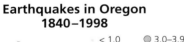

< 1.0   3.0–3.9
1.0–1.9   4.0–4.9
2.0–2.9   ≥ 5.0

Universal Building Code Soils
Susceptibility to Damage from Earthquakes

Hard Rock
Rock
Urban Growth Boundary

Very Dense Soil and Soft Rock
Stiff Soil Profile
Soft Soil Profile

Special Studies: Soil Requiring Site-Specific Evaluation

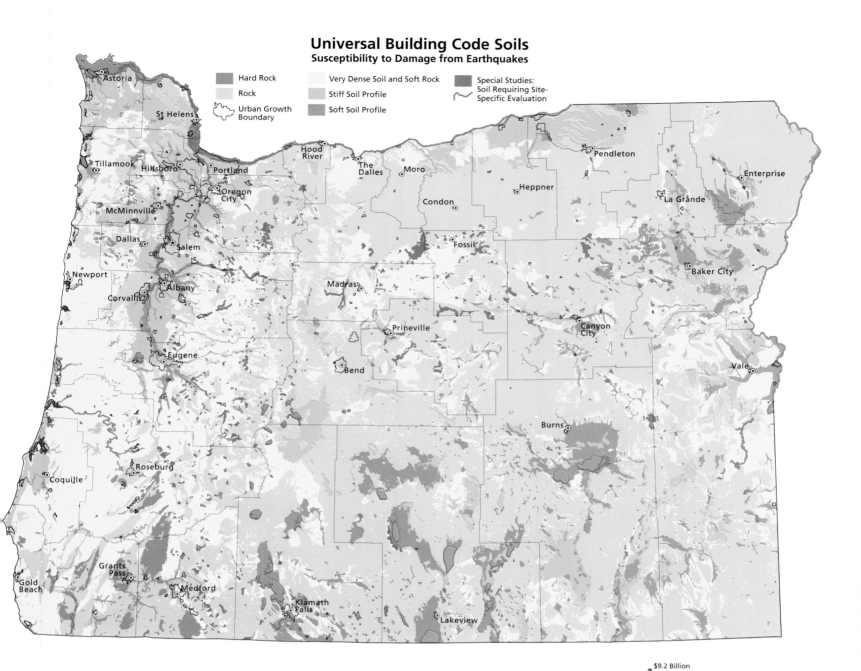

called swarms or clusters, shown on the Historic Earthquakes map. In the short interval of time represented by the instrumented record, only a few of these faults have produced such clusters. Recent activity has been concentrated in zones near Klamath Falls and in the Warner Valley. Adding the historic earthquakes to the instrumented record fills in the picture to some degree. Over a much longer, geologic period of time, all the active faults can be expected to experience earthquakes.

Earthquakes cause shaking, ground rupture, liquefaction, landslides and other forms of ground failure that can lead to loss of life and property. The large map above locates various types of soils which respond differently during earthquakes. Soft, porous, unconsolidated soils amplify shaking and are more susceptible to ground failure during earthquakes. The particularly unstable "Special Study" soils indicated on the map are mostly wetlands or old landslides. The Seismic Hazard map shows the maximum level of shaking likely to occur during a fixed interval of time (here, 1,000 years) from all possible earthquakes. Damage becomes significant at shaking levels of about 20 percent of the pull of gravity and becomes almost total above 60 percent. The third map

shows the projected economic value of damage expected from all possible earthquakes during a 500 year period. The loss ratio is the expected loss divided by the economic base. Settlement in Oregon is heavily concentrated along rivers, where there are abundant unconsolidated soils and wetlands (often covered with loose fill for development purposes), and projected losses are accordingly very high.

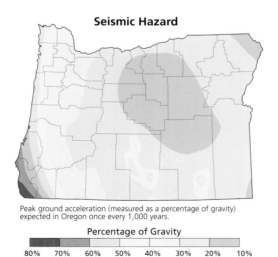

Seismic Hazard

Peak ground acceleration (measured as a percentage of gravity) expected in Oregon once every 1,000 years.

Percentage of Gravity

80% 70% 60% 50% 40% 30% 20% 10%

Earthquake Total Loss (in $Billions)

$1.5
$1.0
$0.5
$0.1
$.05

Earthquake Loss Ratio (Percentage)*

0–2.68
2.69–8.11
8.12–12.9
13.0–17.07
17.08–25.89

*Amount of economic losses divided by the economic base of the community; includes expected losses, such as transportation facilities, utilities and lost wages over 500 years from earthquakes.

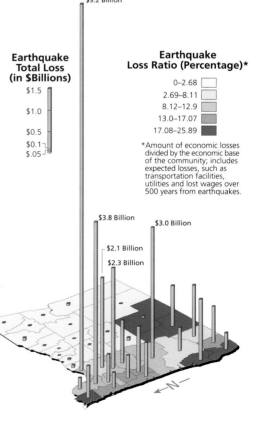

$9.2 Billion

$3.8 Billion

$3.0 Billion

$2.1 Billion

$2.3 Billion

139

Landslides

1996–1997 Landslides in Western Oregon

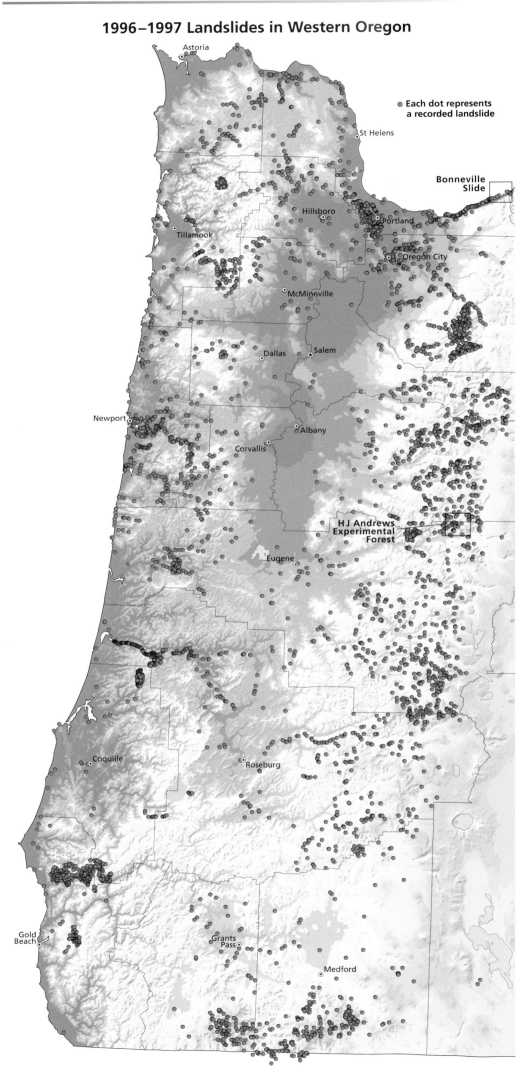

Each dot represents a recorded landslide

Landslides are common in Western Oregon as a result of favorable conditions—steep slopes and high rainfall. Water increases the weight of porous materials, and lubricates both soil and rock particles and fracture planes, increasing the potential for movement. Slides are generally seasonal; rare during the dry summer and fall months, common in winter and spring. Slide conditions may develop over long periods of time, but there is a variety of typical triggering events. These include undercutting of steep slopes by stream erosion or by road building. The combination of clearcut logging and logging road construction on steep slopes has been a major source of slope failures, some lethal. Clearcut logging appears to increase landslide frequency for a decade or more; roads have an even longer-lasting effect.

1996–1997 Landslides in Oregon

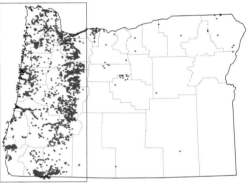

Area Shown at Left

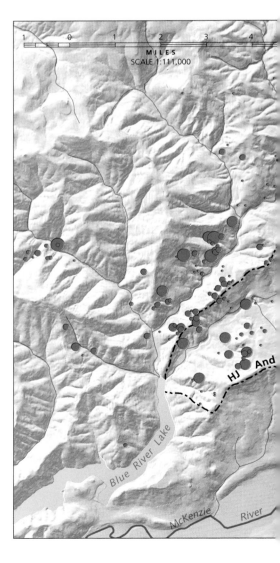

MILES
SCALE 1:111,000

The role of earthquakes as a triggering mechanism is not well understood but is certainly important. Continuous shaking during an earthquake may cause liquefaction of clay soils, a condition in which even very slight slopes can flow, and steep slopes fail spectacularly. Slides commonly involve more horizontal movement than vertical drop, a characteristic illustrated by the enormous Bonneville Slide, discussed at lower right. A slide on this scale is a rare event on the historical time scale, if not on the geological time scale, but smaller slides are frequent.

A 50-year record of small rapid landslides (as distinguished from gradual earth movement) in the U.S. Forest Service's H. J. Andrews Experimental Forest reveals high frequency in areas of steep slopes, clay-rich soils and rapid snowmelt. Upper elevations at this site have more stable soils and more persistent snowpacks, so landslides are less common despite locally steep slopes. Most inventoried landslides occurred during only three storms. Landslides have varied ecological effects, disturbing riparian ecosystems but also creating complex stream habitats.

Bonneville Slide, Overhead View

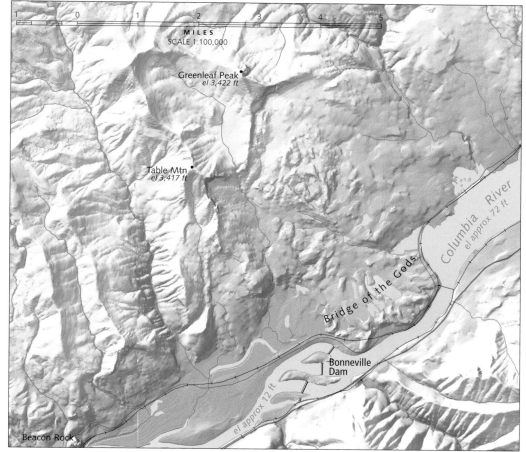

Recorded Landslides in the H.J. Andrews Experimental Forest and Adjacent Area

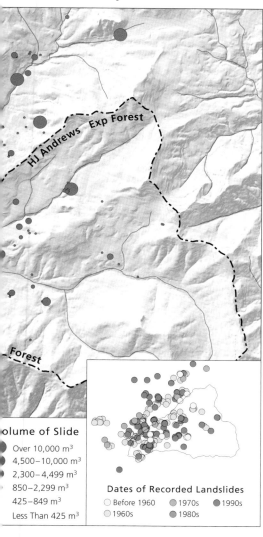

Volume of Slide
- Over 10,000 m³
- 4,500–10,000 m³
- 2,300–4,499 m³
- 850–2,299 m³
- 425–849 m³
- Less Than 425 m³

Dates of Recorded Landslides
- Before 1960
- 1960s
- 1970s
- 1980s
- 1990s

Bonneville Slide, Oblique View

Bonneville Slide

The massive Bonneville Slide collapsed into the Columbia River around 1700, at the time of the last big subduction earthquake (see pages 138–139). The 14-square-mile slide pushed the river southward and temporarily blocked it with a 200-foot-high land bridge, described in regional Indian legend as the Bridge of the Gods. Ancient ash and mudflow layers lying beneath the Columbia River basalts erode easily, and glacial flooding has removed the supporting "toes" from the base of steep slopes, so landslides are common in the area. Most are on the older, less stable north side of the gorge. The Bonneville Slide illustrates on a vast scale the landforms of many smaller slides: a sheer exposed upper face, surprising horizontal extent, and hummocky surface of low rounded mounds and shallow depressions.

Geology

Bedrock Type

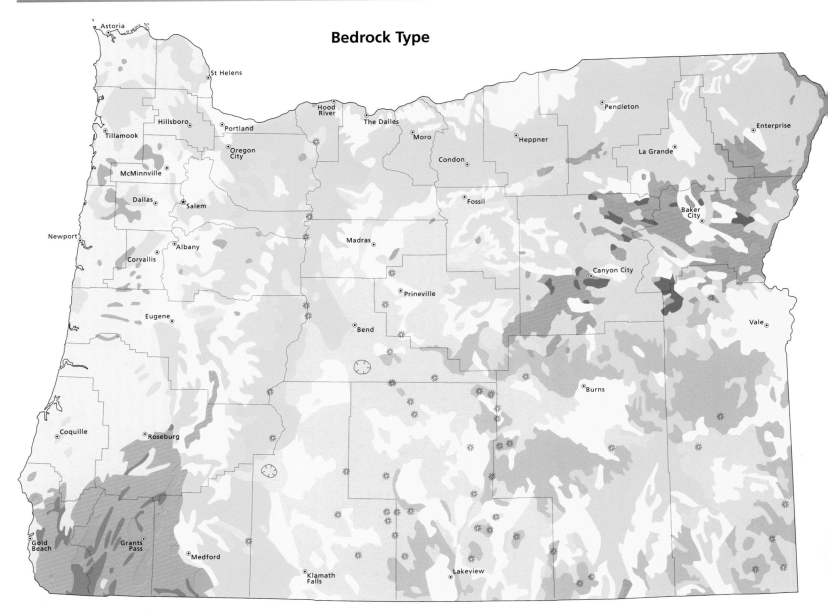

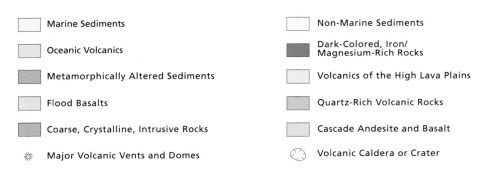

Marine Sediments

Oceanic Volcanics

Metamorphically Altered Sediments

Flood Basalts

Coarse, Crystalline, Intrusive Rocks

✳ Major Volcanic Vents and Domes

Non-Marine Sediments

Dark-Colored, Iron/ Magnesium-Rich Rocks

Volcanics of the High Lava Plains

Quartz-Rich Volcanic Rocks

Cascade Andesite and Basalt

⊘ Volcanic Caldera or Crater

Oregon's rich and turbulent geological past is reflected in this map of bedrock types. Splashed across the center of the map, the Cascade volcanics in yellow mark the axis of Oregon. To the northeast in the Blue Mountains and the southwest in the Klamath Mountains, blue and green colors represent the metamorphic rocks of the exotic terranes that anchor the state. While much of the Coast Range and Willamette Valley is composed of older sedimentary rocks, a veneer of lava flows in the northern part, and volcanic headlands along the Coast, stand out as erosion-resistant knobs and sheets above the softer sediments.

Eastern Oregon is predominantly volcanic in origin, consisting of both lava flows and ash layers interspersed with shallow fossil-bearing basins. The dry high desert environment of Eastern Oregon preserves these features remarkably well. In contrast, volcanic structures in Western Oregon are subdued by the aggressive effects of heavy rainfall and weathering.

▢ Marine Sediments

Exposed in the Coast Range and along the margins of the Willamette Valley, oceanic sediments, shown on the map as light tan,

date back as much as 50 million years. These sediments, deposited underwater, blanket older volcanic rocks. Originating in both the Cascade and Klamath Mountains and carried to an ancient ocean in the process of erosion, these sediments represent a variety of marine environments from shoreline and deltas to continental slope depths. Fossils in the sediments attest to the tropical nature of the local climate at the time of deposition.

▢ Oceanic Volcanics

Peeking from beneath the marine sediments, a series of oceanic volcanic rocks, composed predominantly of basaltic lavas, floors the Coast Range. These rocks represent an ancient oceanic submarine platform formed 50 to 60 million years ago some distance offshore from Oregon before being accreted (annexed) to the state. The most distinctive of these oceanic volcanics is a type of rock called "pillow basalt." Represented by bulbous blobs of rock, pillow basalt is the result of lava erupting underneath the water.

Metamorphically Altered Sediments

Green patches in the Klamath and Blue Mountains on this map represent sedimentary rocks that date back hundreds of millions of years. These ancient rocks were transported to North America by the conveyor belt mechanism of plate tectonics, then attached or accreted to this continent. In the process of accretion, the rocks were heated and compressed to such a degree that new mineral crystals began to form within them. Fossils entombed and still visible in these metamorphic rocks clearly show their exotic nature.

Flood Basalts

Salmon-colored patches on this map in the north-central part of the state and into the northern Willamette Valley represent lava flows dating back 10 to 17 million years. These lavas, or flood basalts, called the Columbia River Basalt Group, are a flat black finely crystalline rock that flowed easily, owing to its high-temperature source deep within the earth at the margin of the lower crust and upper mantle regions. Flowing from fissures and cracks in the crust of Idaho and Eastern Oregon, the lavas made their way to the Oregon Coast several hundred miles away, invading as far south as Salem. Today these rocks make up most of the scenic headlands along the northern Coast.

Coarse, Crystalline, Intrusive Rocks

The bright pink areas of the map in the northern Coast Range, Klamath and Blue Mountains are coarsely crystalline plutonic rocks such as granites and dolerites. These rocks, which cooled very slowly far below the earth's surface, were later exposed by erosion. They represent the "glue" which joins the exotic terrane rocks to North America. Economically, these granites are important for their gold content. Similar rocks underlie much of the state beneath the Cascade Mountains, but it will be millions of years before erosion exposes them.

Non-Marine Sediments

The buff-colored patterns scattered across most of Eastern Oregon on this map represent non-marine (freshwater) lake and stream sediments dating back as much as 40 million years. These small basins were created typically when volcanic activity disrupted and blocked stream systems, causing water to pond up behind the dams of lava and ash. The rich fossil record of plants and animals preserved in the soft sediments yields a superb account of life in Oregon's distant past.

Dark-Colored Iron/Magnesium-Rich Rocks

Dark blue smaller exposures in the Klamath and Blue Mountains on this map represent volcanic and sedimentary rocks that were severely compressed and heated during the annexation to North America of these two great provinces. The alteration process of metamorphism in these rocks is so thorough that very little remains of the original parent rock, and any fossil remains have been obliterated.

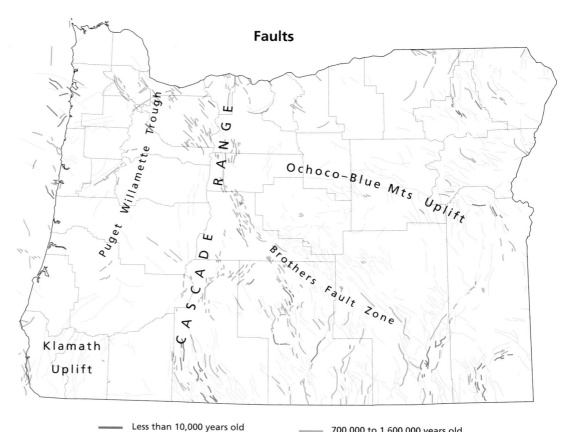

Faults

Less than 10,000 years old

10,000 to 700,000 years old

700,000 to 1,600,000 years old

Assumed inactive

Volcanics of the High Lava Plains

Shown in a light purple color on this map, volcanics in the high lava plains cover a vast tract across southeast Oregon, representing eruptions dating back 15 million years. These basaltic lavas escaped as runny fluids from the crust as the Great Basin was stretched and greatly thinned. The dry climate of Eastern Oregon preserves much of this volcanic complexion as low cones and domes.

Quartz-Rich Volcanic Rocks

Shown in light pink on the map, these quartz-rich volcanics represent both rhyolite (gray to pink fine-grained volcanics) and its glassy equivalent, obsidian. Derived from much shallower reservoirs of magma higher in the crust than the basalts, the quartz-rich volcanics tend to erupt very violently and form small domes and cinder cones. Their high quartz content makes them stand up well—much better than the basalts—against processes of erosion and decomposition.

Cascade Andesite and Basalt

Shown in bright yellow on the map in a north–south line across the western part of the state, the Cascade volcanics are still a work in progress, as many of the volcanoes in this region are still active. The Cascade Range sits astride a broad platform of shield volcanoes of dark black fine-grained basalt. The High Cascade peaks are predominantly andesite (first named in the Andes of South America). In contrast to the black, dense basalt, andesite is a less dense gray rock that forms the splendid stratovolcanoes which characterize the Cascade Mountains.

Faults

Under great pressure, rock will eventually fail, creating faults, or slip planes; these fractures impart a grain or pattern to the geology of an area. The pattern reflects differing intervals of pressure and tension over time. Individual faults have a limited life span, active for thousands to millions of years, before being bypassed by younger faults. The different colors on this map show how recently a fault has been active; the more recent the activity, the greater likelihood of an earthquake in the future (see Earthquakes, pages 138–139). Oregon contains numerous faults that generally fall into discrete zones, often forming the boundaries between more stable blocks in between. The faults along the Coast separate the soft accretionary wedge of oceanic sediments from the harder crystalline continental crust. The faults in the Cascades separate the advancing edge of the North American Plate from the more stable interior. The faults in Eastern Oregon surround stable, generally uplifted, blocks of continental crust. A well developed northwest–southeast fault trend can be found over much of the state, but it is perhaps best shown along the Brothers Fault Zone. Very ancient faults trending primarily north–south in the Blue and Klamath Mountains marks the telescoping, emplacement and annexation of these massive crustal blocks to North America more than 100 million years ago. Parallel to the Cascade crest a series of north–south faults mark the stretching of the crust that has accompanied volcanic activity here dating back 40 million years.

Geologic Ages

Some of Oregon's surface rocks are hundreds of millions of years old, others are only a few thousand years old. Some rocks came to Oregon from distant parts of the globe, others arrived in liquid form as massive lava flows welling up from within the earth. The oldest rocks in Oregon are from the Paleozoic era and the Triassic and Jurassic periods, but, like so many things in Oregon, these rocks are not natives. Pieces of exotic terranes dating from these periods and originating at distant parts of the globe were annexed to North America during the Cretaceous period. Geologists made strides toward understanding the movement of such crustal plates in the early twentieth century, but plate tectonics, as the field is known, has become a mature science only in the past 20 years. As the field has developed, scientists have come to understand how a series of separate crustal plates, moving at extremely slow speeds over millions of years, collided with, were forced under and, to varying degrees, fused onto the huge North American Plate. After this process was complete, these early terranes were largely covered by later rock formations, much as a rising tide inundates progressively more beach rocks. Only small areas of Oregon's most ancient rocks remain visible today. These areas are almost exclusively in the Klamath and Blue Mountains. Scientists have discovered the age and exotic origin of the rocks by examining the fossils embedded in sediments. In the central portion of the state, fossil-bearing marine sediments from the Cretaceous period bear witness to the last time ocean waters covered the areas east of the Cascades. In the Klamath and Blue Mountains,

Cretaceous rocks are primarily crystalline (granite-related), and mark the joining of older terranes firmly to the North American continent.

Rocks from the Paleocene, Eocene and Oligocene epochs in Western Oregon are marine volcanic platforms draped with fossil-bearing sediments. Lava flows in the Western Cascades mark the earliest instances of volcanism there. Until late Oligocene time Oregon had a broad coastal plain that extended all the way to what is now the eastern margin of the Willamette Valley. During the Miocene, that coastal plain was elevated as the Coast Range—Oregon began to assume much of its modern complexion. Volcanic rocks of Miocene age in the Cascades, as well as across the southeast part of Oregon, represent the greatest outpourings of lava the state has ever seen. Intermixed with these flows are sedimentary basins bearing fossils that nicely chronicle the local environments and climate of that period. At the extreme western margin of the state, Miocene marine (oceanic) rocks and volcanics formed very near the present-day shorelines. Pleistocene (Ice Age) deposits of volcanic origin appear mostly in the central part of the state along its axis at the High Cascades. In the Willamette Valley as well as in southeast Oregon, rocks laid down during a time of vast inland waterways and wetlands preserve a splendid record of Oregon's Ice Age plants and animals. Holocene volcanic deposits are densely concentrated in the High Cascades—other parts of the state feature evenly distributed stream and lake deposits from this period.

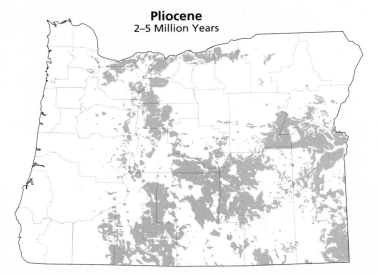

Pliocene
2–5 Million Years

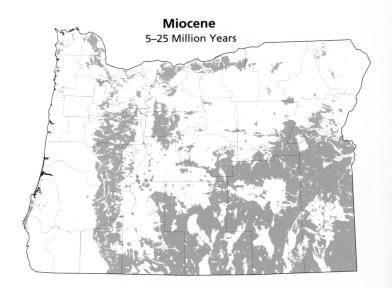

Miocene
5–25 Million Years

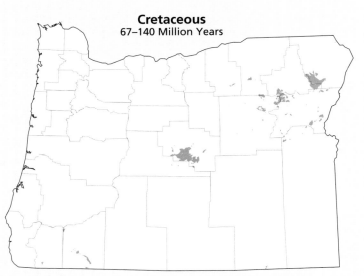

Cretaceous
67–140 Million Years

Jurassic
140–200 Million Years

Holocene
Pleistocene
Pliocene
Present
Miocene Oligocene Eocene–Paleocene Cretaceous Jurassic Triassic Pe

Quat. | Tertiary | Mesozoic
Cenozoic

2M 5M   25M   38M   67M   140M   200M   (Millions of Years)   250M

Holocene
Present–10,000 Years

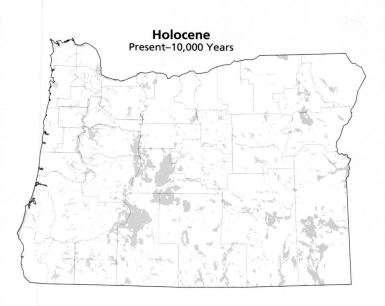

Pleistocene
10,000 Years–2 Million Years

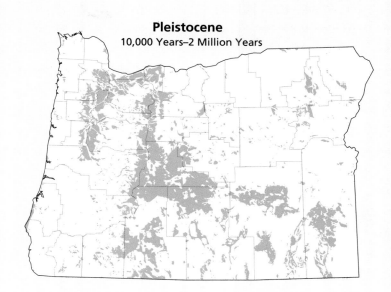

Oligocene
25–38 Million Years

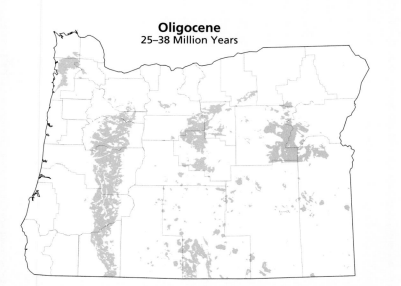

Eocene–Paleocene
38–67 Million Years

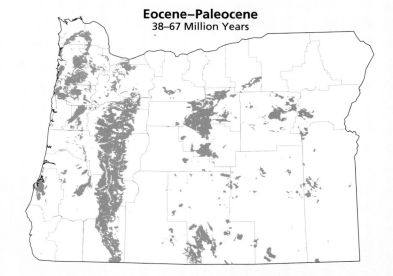

Triassic
200–250 Million Years

Paleozoic
250–544 Million Years

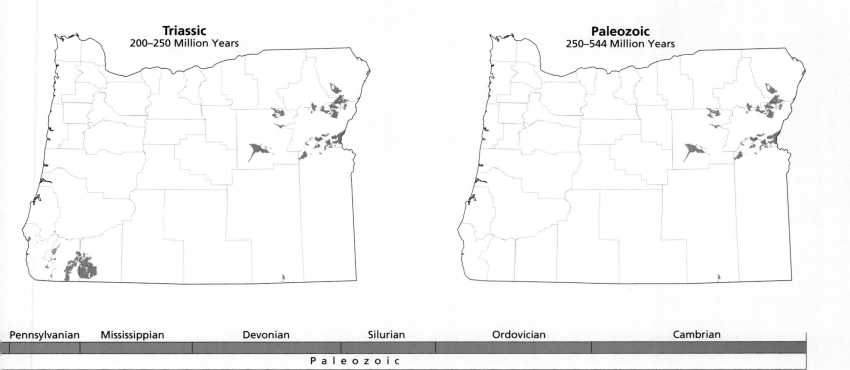

| Pennsylvanian | Mississippian | Devonian | Silurian | Ordovician | Cambrian |

Paleozoic

544M

145

Geologic Evolution

Oregon is the only state other than Hawaii that was not part of any continent one billion years ago. Fragments of island arcs similar to the modern Japanese islands collided with the ancestral North American continent, especially during the Mesozoic era (see Geologic Ages, p. 144). During the early part of the Cenozoic era, the last oceanic crustal block, called Siletzia, attached itself to the continent, forming the basaltic basement of what would become the Oregon and Washington Coast Range. As a result, Oregon is a volcanic state, with a greater variety of volcanic rocks than Hawaii.

Evolution Legend

Offshore

▪ Oceanic plates

Sedimentary Deposits

▪ Continental slope and shelf deposits

▫ Continental alluvial basin filling

Magmatic Units

▪ Magmatic Arc: associated with off-shore subduction Mafic to intermediate volcanic rocks

▪ Magmatic Belts: associated with interior extension Andesite to rhyolite plutons and volcanic fields

▪ Alkalic Magmatic Centers: basalt to intermediate in composition

▪ Rhyolite to trachyandesite centers

▨ Dikes

Tectonic Zones

▨ Areas of extension

▪ Area of folding and thrusting associated with Basin and Range extension

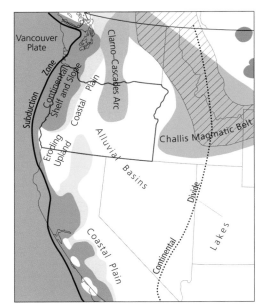

55–43 Million Years Ago

Subduction drove oceanic crust beneath Western North America. As it did, magma rose to the surface to form volcanoes, but at different locations than the present Cascade Range. The earliest of these volcanic ranges was called the Clarno–Cascades Arc. It produced abundant volcanic rocks in Central and Eastern Oregon and as far west as the southern Willamette Valley, where volcanic rocks from this period are found today in oil-exploratory wells. West of these volcanoes, rivers deposited sediment at what was then the Oregon Coast, one segment of which extended from Eugene to Portland. Light-colored shallow-marine to non-marine sandstone of Eocene epoch forms the reservoir for the Mist Gas Field in Columbia County. Farther west, near the present-day northern Oregon Coast, sediments of that age were deposited in deep ocean water. Near Coos Bay, these coastal and non-marine deposits resulted in commercial deposits of coal.

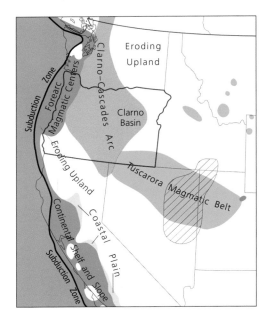

43–37 Million Years Ago

From 43 to 37 million years ago, during the late Eocene epoch, basaltic lava welled up through the older basaltic Siletzia crust, forming younger volcanic rocks in the Tillamook Highlands, Cascade Head and Yachats areas. The Clarno–Cascades Arc expanded to cover a large part of Eastern Oregon with volcanic rock.

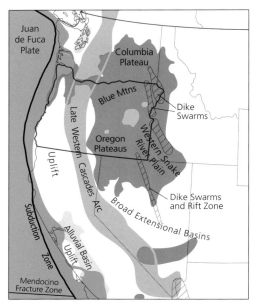

17–14 Million Years Ago

Starting about 17 million years ago, during the Miocene epoch, huge eruptions of basaltic lava called the Columbia River Basalt Group (shown in red) gushed up through fissures in northeastern Oregon and adjacent Idaho and southeastern Washington. These lavas flowed across the Columbia Plateau and between the Cascade volcanoes into the Willamette Valley as far south as Salem and across the not-yet-uplifted Coast Range into the sea near Astoria. The solidified flows are found today in the walls of the Columbia Gorge as well as areas in Portland and many parts of northeastern Oregon. Basalts at Cape Lookout, Cape Foulweather, Yaquina Head and Seal Rock were also part of the Columbia River Basalt Group. The greatest volume of lava came out between 17 and 14 million years ago, but smaller amounts continued to flow down the ancestral Columbia River as recently as six million years ago.

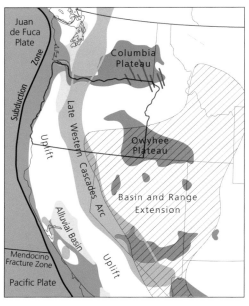

14–10 Million Years Ago

Starting about 14 million years ago, the Basin and Range of Nevada and adjacent southeastern Oregon began to spread apart, forming fault block mountains extending from Steens Mountain in southeastern Oregon westward as far as Klamath Lake. Modoc Point north of Klamath Falls is made up of one of the fault scarps of the Basin and Range. Some of these faults are still active and can produce earthquakes, such as the 1993 earthquakes near Klamath Falls. The western rim of the northern Basin and Range is the Western Cascades Arc; expansion of the crust westward is causing the Cascades and all areas west of them to move slowly westward and to rotate clockwise. The Columbia River Basalt Group continued to flow westward toward Portland but in reduced amounts, while lava flows in southeastern Oregon expanded.

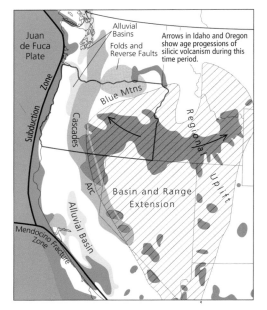

10–5 Million Years Ago

Volcanic activity continued in the High Lava Plains of southeastern Oregon, where the center of volcanic activity shifted northwestward from southeasternmost Oregon toward Newberry Crater southeast of Bend. The Cascades Arc continued to be active east of the older arc, though at a reduced level. Sediments from the Cascades Arc were deposited in the Willamette Lowland, which was isolated from the sea by the rising Coast Range. Deep marine sediments accumulated offshore, with the coastline similar to that of the present day. Sediments of the offshore Juan de Fuca Plate began to accrete to the North America Plate because of continued subduction.

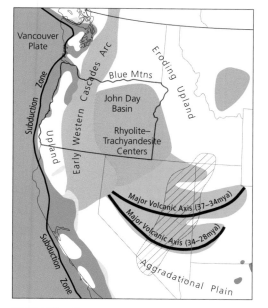

37–28 Million Years Ago

During the Oligocene epoch—starting 37 million years ago—the Clarno volcanics in Central and Eastern Oregon were succeeded by the lighter-colored John Day volcanic rocks and associated non-marine, brightly colored sediments now found at John Day Fossil Beds National Monument. Some of the John Day lava flows in the Deschutes Basin came from volcanoes now buried by the younger volcanoes of the High Cascades Arc.

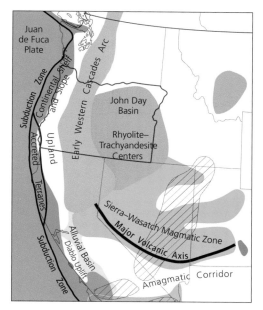

28–21 Million Years Ago

Both the John Day volcanics and the Early Western Cascades Arc continued to accumulate in Eastern Oregon. This arc was bordered on the west by a coastal plain. Shoreline deposits accumulated close to the present Oregon Coast; farther west, sedimentary rocks of this age were deposited in deep water. The subduction zone may have been closer to shore during this period than it is today.

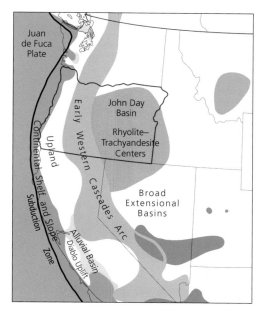

21–17 Million Years Ago

Geologic activity during this time period was similar to that of the preceding period, with volcanics and non-marine deposits in Eastern Oregon, volcanics of the Cascades Arc, a coastal plain and a subduction zone probably east of the present one.

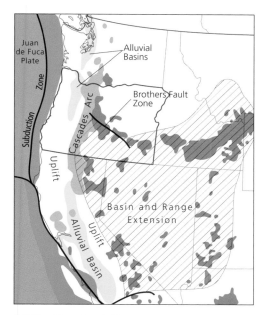

5 Million Years Ago to Present

The present situation is marked by subduction of the oceanic Juan de Fuca Plate beneath Western Oregon, accompanied by eruption of lavas to form the modern volcanoes of the High Cascades Arc. Oregon is at great risk from earthquakes on this subduction zone with potential magnitudes as large as 9 on the Moment Magnitude Scale. The most recent great earthquake (estimated magnitude 9) struck January 26, 1700. Earthquakes also occur in the crust of Western Oregon as well as deep down in the Juan de Fuca Plate. The most recent earthquake in the downgoing slab was the Nisqually Earthquake of February 28, 2001, causing major damage to Olympia and Seattle. Volcanoes also pose a hazard—recently demonstrated by Mount St. Helens. Basin and Range extension continues across southeastern Oregon from Klamath Falls and Summer Lake to Steens Mountain, raised on a great active fault at the edge of the Alvord Desert.

Structural/Physiographic Provinces

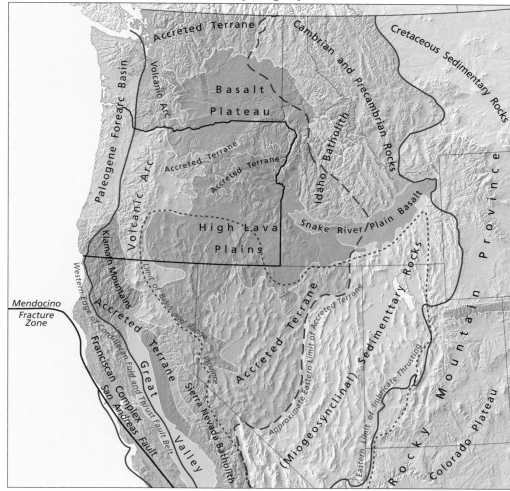

Soil Orders

Oregon's unique characteristics give rise to its bounty of soils—more than 1,500 in all. Individual soils result from a combination of local factors: climate, vegetation types, rock (or other parent material) type and landscape position. Each distinct soil is known as a soil series, and each soil series is named for a locale or feature: a Woodburn series in the Willamette Valley, a Bandon series on the south Coast, and so on. Soil classification in the U.S. uses a six-category system: order, suborder, great group, subgroup, family and series. Twelve soil orders categorize all the soils in the U.S.

Of these, Oregon lacks only Gelisols, found in permafrost soils in Alaska, and Oxisols, highly weathered tropical soils found mainly in Hawaii. This map shows the general distribution of the 10 orders that occur in Oregon. Each area on the map is colored for the single soil order dominant there, though all areas include soils in one or more other orders as well.

Soil Descriptions

Inceptisols
Soils that are beginning to form and have weakly developed soil profiles. Inceptisols are most common in the Coast Range, where they have dark surface horizons (or layers, as when viewed in cross-section) enriched with organic matter and subsoils in which only brighter colors and better structures differentiate the soil from the parent material. Inceptisols in the Klamath Mountains are similar, but have thinner surface horizons that are lower in organic matter.

Ultisols
Red soils with strongly developed subsoil horizons of clay accumulation. Oregon Ultisols are mostly paleosols (old soils) that formed long ago when the climate was warmer and wetter. Ultisols are prominent in the foothills on both sides of the Willamette Valley and also occur on foothills in Douglas, Josephine and Jackson Counties. They are widely used to produce grapes, Christmas trees, grass seed and timber.

Alfisols
Soils that have thin surface horizons enriched with organic matter and subsoil horizons of clay accumulation. Alfisols occur mainly in Western and southern Oregon. Typical examples include the reddish brown Willakenzie soils in the foothills of the Willamette Valley and the reddish brown Abegg and Ruch soils on old terraces in Jackson County.

Andisols
Soils developed in materials of volcanic origin. Coast Range Andisols are black, light-weight soils developed from basalt under cool, humid conditions. Cascade Range Andisols develop from mixed ash and weathered andesite. Andisols from Crater Lake northeastward to Newberry Crater are developed mainly from pumice. Andisols in northeastern Oregon are formed in a blanket of white ash mainly from the eruption of Mount Mazama.

Spodosols
Soils with white near-surface horizons over iron-rich subsoils formed in sandy materials under pine or spruce in cool, humid areas. Spodosols are the dominant soil at high elevations along the crest of the Cascades, but they are also prominent components of the landscape along the Coast from Newport to Brookings. Many coastal Spodosols in Coos and Curry Counties are intensively used for cranberry production.

Histosols
Highly organic soils, composed almost entirely of the decayed remains of plants that grew in marshy environments. Histosols are dominant only in the vicinity of Upper Klamath Lake, but they are perhaps better known in the small, finger-like areas of Lake Labish just north of Salem, where the Semiahmoo series is used intensively to produce Spanish onions.

Aridisols
Soils found in the driest parts of southeastern Oregon, mainly in old playas and lake basins and on surrounding uplands in Lake, Harney and Malheur Counties. Surface horizons for these soils are light in color and low in organic matter. Many Aridisols have subsoil horizons enriched with clay. Some have accumulations of free lime in the subsoil. A few, where the seasonal water table is close to the surface, are salty. Many Aridisols are underlain at shallow depth by either volcanic bedrock or by a soil-formed hardpan.

Mollisols
Soils formed mainly in association with grassland vegetation. Mollisols have relatively thick, dark surface horizons rich in organic matter under which are subsoils that are either weakly developed or enriched in clay or carbonates. More than 650 Oregon soil series are Mollisols—this order occupies the largest area of any soil order in the state. On the main floor of the Willamette Valley they are deep, dark, fertile soils. In Eastern Oregon they have lower amounts of organic matter and are more likely to be associated with carbonate accumulations, hardpans, or shallow bedrock.

Vertisols
Clay soils that shrink and swell appreciably upon wetting and drying. Vertisols are dominant soils only in small areas of south-central Oregon, but they form important components of the soil landscape on low foothills and in tributary valleys of the Willamette Valley (Bashaw series), Douglas County (Curtin series) and Jackson County (Carney and Coker series).

Entisols
Soils found mainly in recently deposited parent materials that are too young to have developed soil horizons. The largest area dominated by Entisols is the Columbia Basin in Morrow and Umatilla Counties. Irrigation with Columbia River water has made these sandy soils agriculturally productive. Other Entisols occur in small areas on floodplains of rivers and streams, where frequent flooding continually adds new sediments to the land surface.

Rock   Water

Note: Gray lines within soil orders are boundaries of suborders shown on the following two pages.

Soil Suborders

Suborders are groups of soils within each soil order. They indicate a major feature or environmental condition influencing the character and behavior of the soil. Suborder names have two components, each of which tells something about the suborder. Each name consists of a syllable identifying its order (for example, "oll" from the Mollisol order) and a prefix signaling a particular suborder attribute (for example, "Aquoll," a wet Mollisol).

Many suborders are based on the degree of soil wetness or the amount and action of the precipitation it receives. Others are based on the characteristics of the parent material, or the degree of soil development expressed by the kinds of soil horizons present. Very cold soils are broken out at the suborder level, as are some soils with excessive accumulations of soluble salts. Relationships among these suborder criteria are illustrated in the diagram on the right, and each of the suborder prefixes is defined on the next page.

Colors (excluding gray) on the suborder maps show areas dominated by a particular suborder. The sum of all brightly colored areas equals the area dominated by a given soil order, as shown on the Soil Orders map. All of the suborder-dominated areas shown here contain at least some soils in other suborders—the scale of these maps does not allow all of the natural variability that exists in the soil landscape to be shown.

Gray areas on these maps illustrate areas where soil of a given order exists but is not dominant. On the Vertisol map, for example, the few

areas in south-central Oregon that are dominated by Vertisols are in fact dominated by wet Vertisols, the Aquerts. Vertisols, however, are much more widely distributed in Oregon, but only as minor components of the soil landscape assemblage. This map shows clearly that Vertisols are present throughout the Willamette Valley, in a large part of Jackson County and throughout large areas of Lake and Harney Counties.

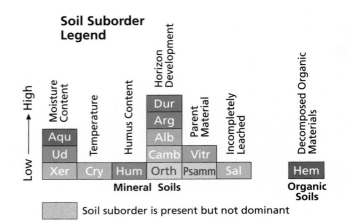

Soil Suborder Legend

Alfisols

Aqu Aqualfs   Xer Xeralfs

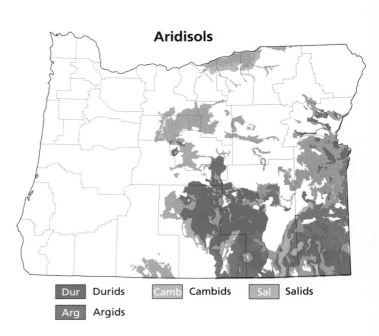

Aridisols

Dur Durids   Camb Cambids   Sal Salids
Arg Argids

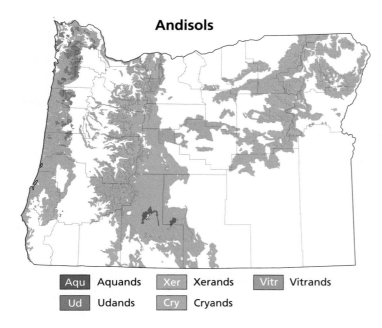

Andisols

Aqu Aquands   Xer Xerands   Vitr Vitrands
Ud Udands   Cry Cryands

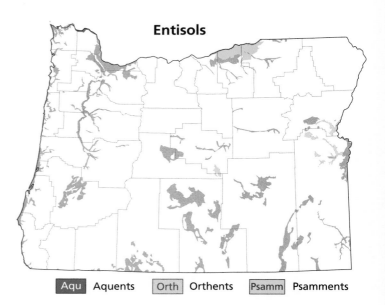

Entisols

Aqu Aquents   Orth Orthents   Psamm Psamments

Soil Suborder Prefixes

Alb	Soils with a light-colored (albino), strongly leached horizon at or below the soil surface
Aqu	Wet soils with water tables at or near the surface for long periods of time
Arg	Soils that have a subsoil horizon of clay accumulation (argillic horizon)
Camb	Soils with weakly developed subsoils (cambic horizons) that lack distinct accumulations of clay, carbonate, organic matter or iron
Cry	Soils in very cold climates at high elevations
Dur	Soils that have a duripan, or silica-cemented hardpan, in the subsoil
Hem	Organic soils formed by accumulation of partially decomposed plant remains
Hum	Soils characterized by an unusually high amount of organic matter, or humus
Orth	Young soils lacking development on active, recently eroded hillslopes
Psamm	Young soils lacking development in sandy parent materials
Sal	Soils in arid regions that have accumulations of soluble salts at or near the surface
Ud	Soils in areas where rain falls mainly throughout the growing season and is sufficient to support rain-fed agriculture
Vitr	Soils dominated by volcanic glass (vitreous)
Xer	Soils in Mediterranean climates where summers are warm and dry and winters are cool and wet

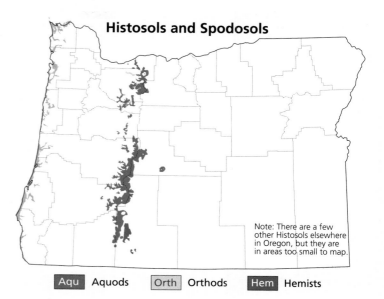

Histosols and Spodosols

Note: There are a few other Histosols elsewhere in Oregon, but they are in areas too small to map.

Aqu Aquods   **Orth** Orthods   **Hem** Hemists

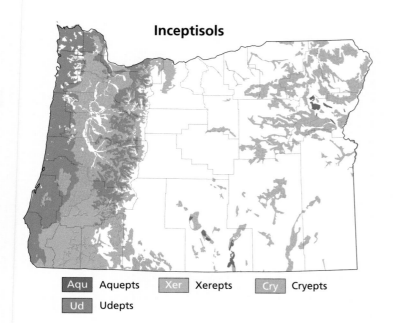

Inceptisols

Aqu Aquepts   **Xer** Xerepts   **Cry** Cryepts
Ud Udepts

Ultisols

Hum Humults

Mollisols

Aqu Aquolls   **Cry** Cryolls   **Alb** Albolls
Xer Xerolls

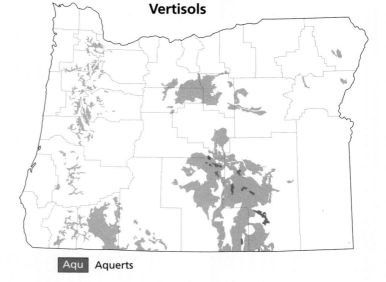

Vertisols

Aqu Aquerts

151

Soil Interpretations

Soil Interpretations

Basic soil properties are important to practitioners of many human endeavors, for example agriculture, forestry, land use planning and urban development. These properties can be interpreted—and mapped—for specific use by various industries or professions. Three such interpretive maps are shown on these pages.

Land Capability

Land Capability Classes are broad groupings of soils differing from one another according to two criteria: their limitations for sustained production of cultivated crops, permanent pasture and rangeland vegetation; and the risks of soil damage if mismanaged. Examples of soil limitations are excessive wetness, erosion potential, steep slope, shallow depth and stone content; any and all of these limitations make it more difficult to manage soil for crop production. Soil damage refers mainly to loss of the most important part of the soil resource, the topsoil, by erosion; a secondary meaning is the damage to soils and water bodies

elsewhere by sediment deposition. Class I soils have essentially no limitations and pose the least risk of damage under intensive agricultural management. Both the number of limitations and the severity of their impact increase in successive classes. Soils in Classes I–IV can be used safely for crop production, but Class IV soils require major investments in conservation practices such as erosion control terraces, grassed waterways, minimum tillage and residue management. Risks of damage are too high for sustained crop production on Class VI and VII soils, but they can be used for hay, pasture and rangeland grazing enterprises.

Potential Prime Farmland

The U.S. Department of Agriculture Prime Farmland Classification system creates four very broad categories of agriculturally suitable soils: Prime Farmland, Unique Farmland, Farmland of Statewide Importance and Farmland of Local Importance. Prime Farmland soils are the very best and must meet several specific criteria—soil depth, pH, water holding capacity, erosion characteristics and moisture supply. Some soils meet all the requisite physical properties but occur in areas of

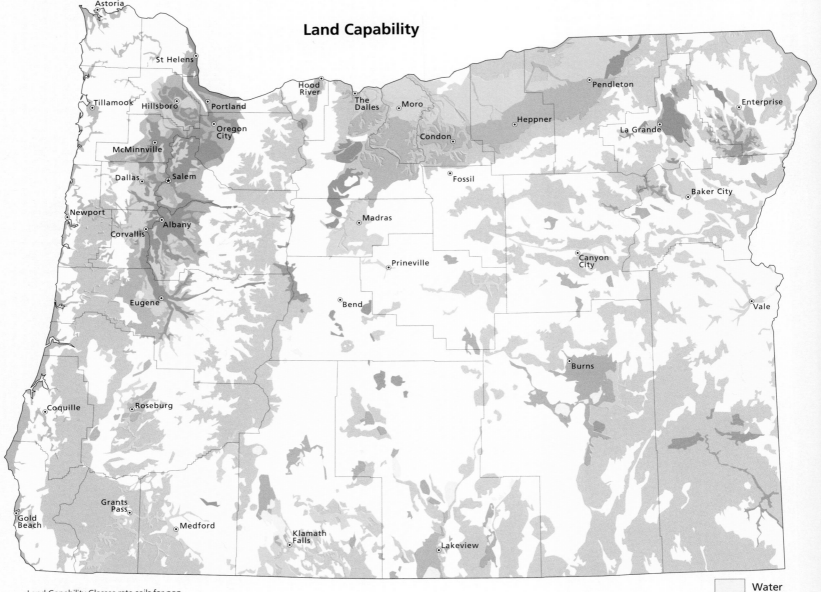

Land Capability

Land Capability Classes rate soils for non-irrigated agricultural uses. Increasing class numbers indicate progressively greater limitations and narrower options for use. Some classe designations may change if water becomes available.

Oregon has a few Class I soils, but they occur in areas too small to be visible on a map at this scale.

 Class II

Soils in Class II have some limitations that reduce the choice of plants or require moderate conservation practices.

 Class III

Soils in Class III have severe limitations that reduce the choice of plants, require moderate conservation practices or both.

 Class IV

Soils in Class IV have very severe limitations that reduce the choice of plants, require moderate conservation practices or both.

Water

Class V

Soils in Class V have little or no erosion hazard but have other limitations, primarily cold temperatures and short growing seasons, that limit their use.

Class VI

Soils in Class VI have severe limitations that make them generally unsuited to cultivation and that limit their use to pasture and similar low-intensity uses.

Class VII

Soils in Class VII have very severe limitations that make them generally unsuited to cultivation and that restrict their use to grazing and similar low-intensity uses.

 Class VIII

Class VIII soils are essentially rock outcrops or very steep, shallow, rocky soils that have no value for agriculture.

Potential Prime Farmland

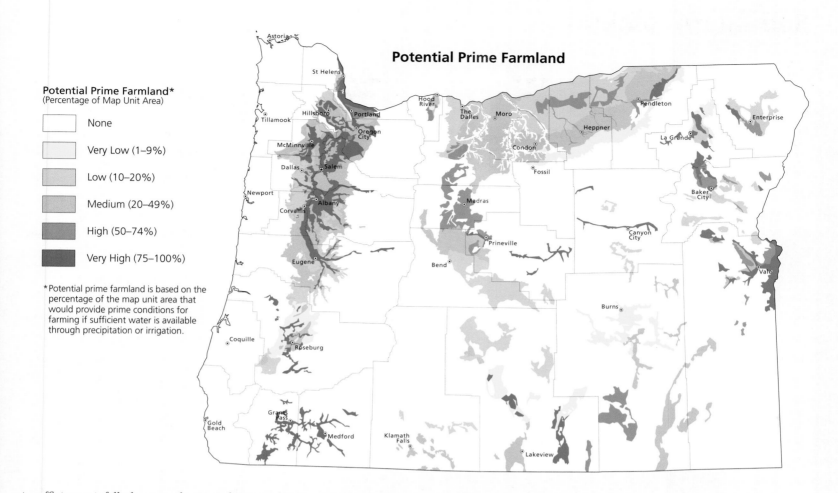

Potential Prime Farmland*
(Percentage of Map Unit Area)

- None
- Very Low (1–9%)
- Low (10–20%)
- Medium (20–49%)
- High (50–74%)
- Very High (75–100%)

*Potential prime farmland is based on the percentage of the map unit area that would provide prime conditions for farming if sufficient water is available through precipitation or irrigation.

insufficient rainfall; these are designated Potential Prime Farmland soils because they can be made prime with irrigation. Most Prime Farmland is concentrated in valleys of Western and southern Oregon. Smaller tracts are found in some valleys of Eastern Oregon and in the more humid areas of the Columbia Plateau. Mountainous areas and dry areas of Eastern Oregon have little or no Prime Farmland.

Hydric Soils

The hydric soils interpretation is useful in identifying and delineating wetlands. Wetlands are important landscape resources because they serve as resting, feeding and breeding sites for migratory waterfowl;

they help absorb the energy of floodwaters; and they help purify water that passes through them to surface streams or groundwater. Hydric soils are flooded or saturated at or near the surface for long periods of time. They support plants such as sedges, rushes and ash trees that are particularly adapted to live with their roots in the water for a long time. The large blocks of pale-colored areas in south-central Oregon on the map of hydric soils are somewhat deceptive. Hydric soils are present in these landscapes, but only in very small amounts. Hydric soils occupy much greater proportions of the landscape in areas mapped in blue and black colors, mainly along the Coast, in the Willamette Valley and in some of the large, dry lakebeds in Harney, Lake and Klamath Counties.

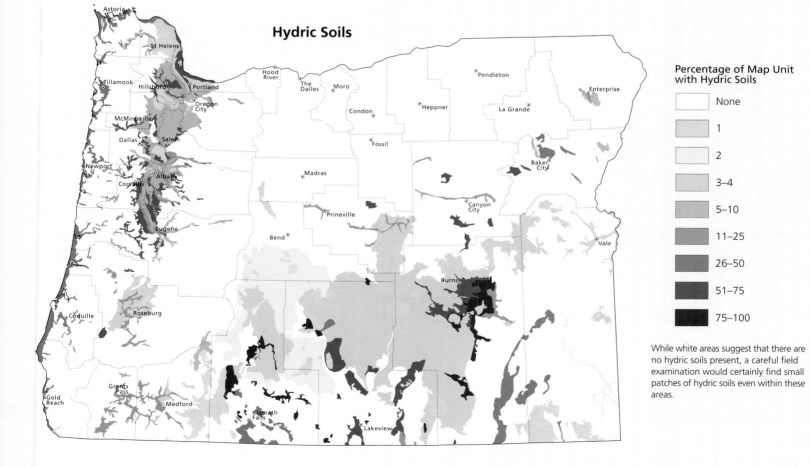

Hydric Soils

Percentage of Map Unit with Hydric Soils

- None
- 1
- 2
- 3–4
- 5–10
- 11–25
- 26–50
- 51–75
- 75–100

While white areas suggest that there are no hydric soils present, a careful field examination would certainly find small patches of hydric soils even within these areas.

153

Annual Precipitation

Oregon precipitation originates in the Pacific Ocean, where water evaporates from the surface, becoming water vapor. This vapor is transported by the prevailing winds, which blow from west to east during most of the year. Active Pacific storms with strong winds, clouds and rain blow ashore in Oregon with the greatest frequency and intensity between October and March.

If it were possible to station a rain gauge 50 miles off the Oregon Coast, the instrument would likely receive about 30 inches of rainfall per year. Much more rain falls onshore due to the effects of terrain. Not far inland, the eastward-moving storms meet the slopes of the Coast Range, which force the storms to ascend. As air rises, it cools; as it cools, its capacity to retain water (in the form of water vapor) diminishes. Some of the water vapor in the cooling air turns to liquid in a process known as "condensation." When water condenses, clouds form, and when the condensation reaches a critical point, precipitation begins to fall. Because the air

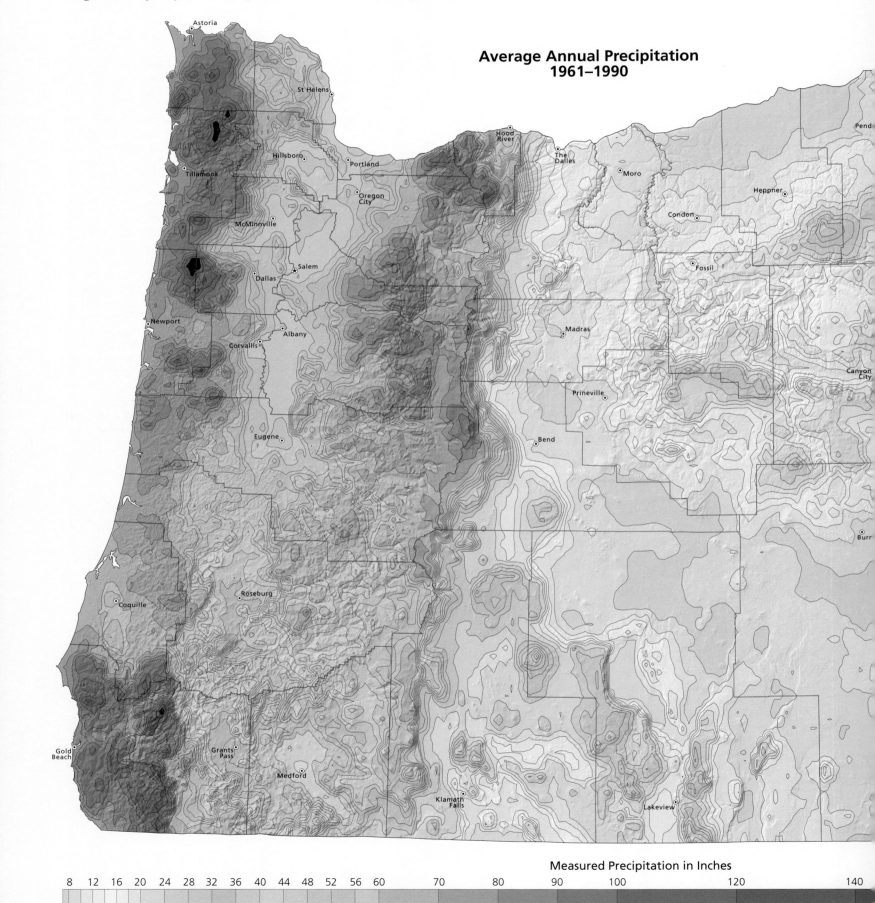

**Average Annual Precipitation
1961–1990**

Measured Precipitation in Inches

| 8 | 12 | 16 | 20 | 24 | 28 | 32 | 36 | 40 | 44 | 48 | 52 | 56 | 60 | 70 | 80 | 90 | 100 | 120 | 140 |

7 10 14 18

moving into Western Oregon is very humid (contains a great deal of water vapor), and because the slope of the Coast Range is steep, the air rises, cools and condenses quite violently, resulting in heavy precipitation.

While coastal areas typically receive 60 to 80 inches of rain annually, even greater amounts fall at higher elevations in the Coast Range, where the full effect of terrain-induced rain (also known as "orographic precipitation") pours from the sky. In an average year 180 to 200 inches of rain deluge some portions of the Coast Range, typically at elevations of 2,000 to 4,000 feet. Though there are no rain gauges in the wettest areas, the volume of water flowing down streams provides a reliable estimate of rainfall in a drainage basin. These estimates are reflected in the Average Annual Precipitation map shown here.

Even after dropping huge volumes of water (or snow, if temperatures are low enough) while passing over the mountains, the storms entering the Willamette Valley remain so moist that a significant amount of precipitation still falls. The lowest elevations in the valley (where most Oregonians live) average 35 to 45 inches of precipitation per year—only 20 percent of what falls in some parts of the Coast Range.

Continuing eastward, the storms approach the Cascade Range and are forced once again to ascend. Because much of the water vapor has condensed and fallen already, the drier air must get much higher to cool enough to reach "saturation," the point at which condensation begins to occur. In the Cascades this often will not occur until an elevation of 3,000 to 4,000 feet. However, since the Cascades are very high, air passing over the range gets very cool, causing nearly all the water vapor to condense.

As storms cross the Cascades and descend into the plains and valleys to the east, little moisture remains in the air mass. Even if a significant mountain barrier were encountered (and there are many in Eastern Oregon), little precipitation would occur because of this moisture deficit. This effect, known as a "rain shadow," explains the relative dryness of lower elevation sites downwind of large terrain obstacles. Much of the state east of the Cascades is classified as "high desert," with relatively high elevations, but generally dry conditions. The driest part of the state, the Alvord Desert in southeast Oregon, gets only about five inches of rain in an average year. Widespread areas get less than 12 inches. A few mountainous areas in Eastern Oregon are wetter because of orographic precipitation, but their totals of 50 to 80 inches per year are well below their Western Oregon counterparts.

Interestingly, despite Oregon's reputation as a place where it "rains all the time," most of the state is classified as "semi-arid." The western third of Oregon is quite wet, the eastern two-thirds mostly dry. In terms of precipitation distribution, Oregon is two very distinct regions inside one political boundary.

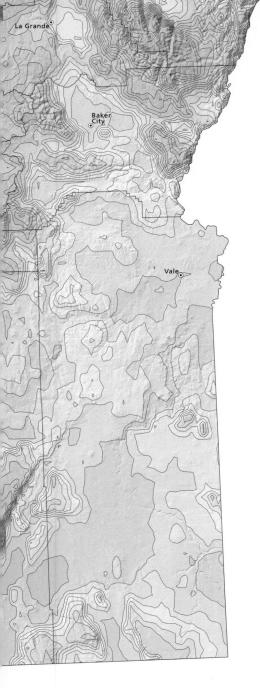

Water Equivalent of Snowfall

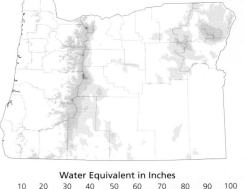

Water Equivalent in Inches

0   10   20   30   40   50   60   70   80   90   100

Average Annual Snowfall
1961–1990

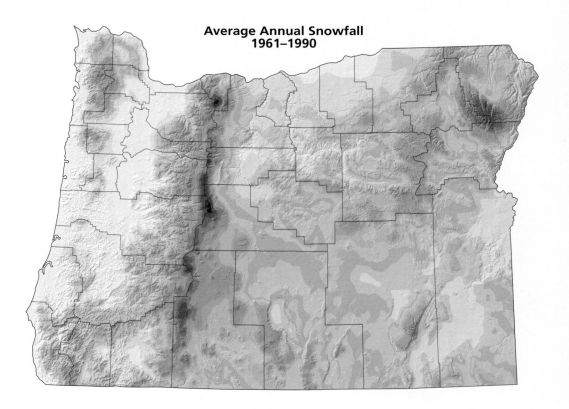

Measured Snowfall in Inches

20 40 60 80 100   200   300   400   500+

10   30

160   180+

155

Precipitation and Seasonality

Annual Totals, 1910–2000

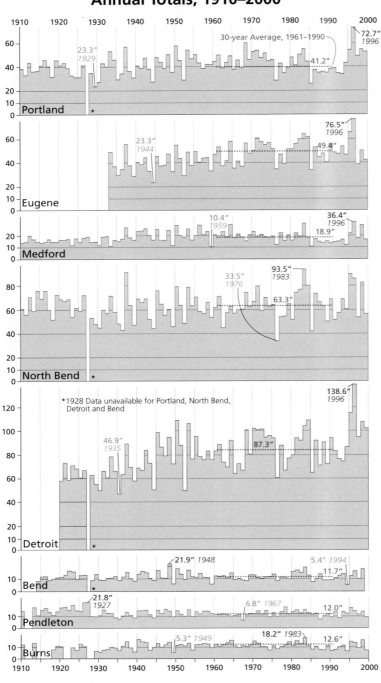

The climate of Oregon is a study in contrasts. Western Oregon is hot and dry in the summer and mild and moist in the winter; Eastern Oregon is drier year-round with hot summers and cold winters. Across the state, upland regions are cooler and moister than the adjacent lowlands. These contrasts are imparted by the state's landforms or physiography: the High Cascades act as a barrier to Pacific moisture that flows into the state from the west, and to cold polar air masses that are for the most part confined to the east. Seasonal variations in solar radiation, storminess and moisture availability also contribute to climatic variation throughout the state.

In the Northern Hemisphere the wintertime jet stream is stronger than in summer. November through March is the wet season in Oregon. Pacific storm systems frequently form or intensify in the Gulf of Alaska. As these systems move onshore, precipitation is often heavy along "rainbands" that mark the boundaries between the cool moist air from the North Pacific and warmer drier air to the south and east.

The precipitation pattern in Western Oregon reflects topography. Rainfall is heaviest along the Coast and in the Coast Range (with snow at higher elevations). In the Cascades, abundant rain falls at low elevations, with snow at high elevations. In Eastern Oregon, precipitation is higher in the upland regions, though not as high as in Western Oregon. A weaker jet stream than in winter and fewer, less intense storm systems result in less precipitation in the transitional months—April, May and June in the spring and September and October in the fall. July and August are the dry months across the state; what little precipitation occurs is generally related to afternoon thunderstorms in the Cascades, Blue Mountains and Wallowas, and to storm systems that brush the far northwest of the state.

Precipitation varies from one year to the next (left). It does not follow regular cycles, although there is a tendency for wet years to cluster together somewhat, particularly after 1970, and for annual precipitation to generally increase. Both features have been noted throughout the Western U.S. and Canada, and are consistent with the precipitation changes expected with global warming (see Future Climates, page 161). Year-to-year variations in precipitation are larger in the wetter western part of the state than in the east, but the smaller variations east of the Cascades are nevertheless significant for agriculture and water resources.

Statewide Precipitation Patterns by Month

The precipitation patterns shown below were constructed using data collected at individual weather stations around the state (those shown on the next page plus others). There is considerable variation in precipitation in Oregon, both across the state and throughout the year. The overall range of precipitation across the state each month is shown by the rectangular box on the individual scales. While there are regional differences in precipitation during every month, the range is low during the summer months. Differences in annual precipitation across Oregon are mostly the result of the differences in winter precipitation.

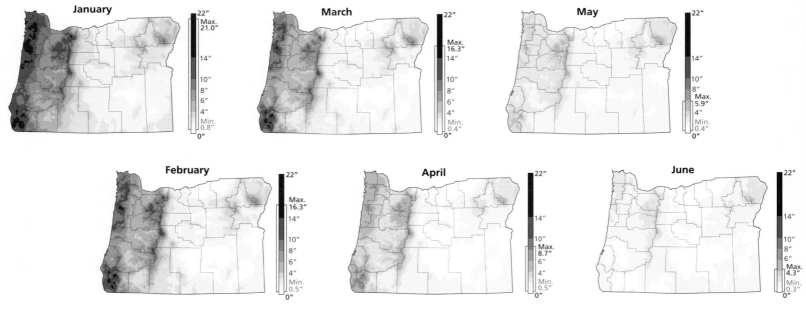

Precipitation Regimes

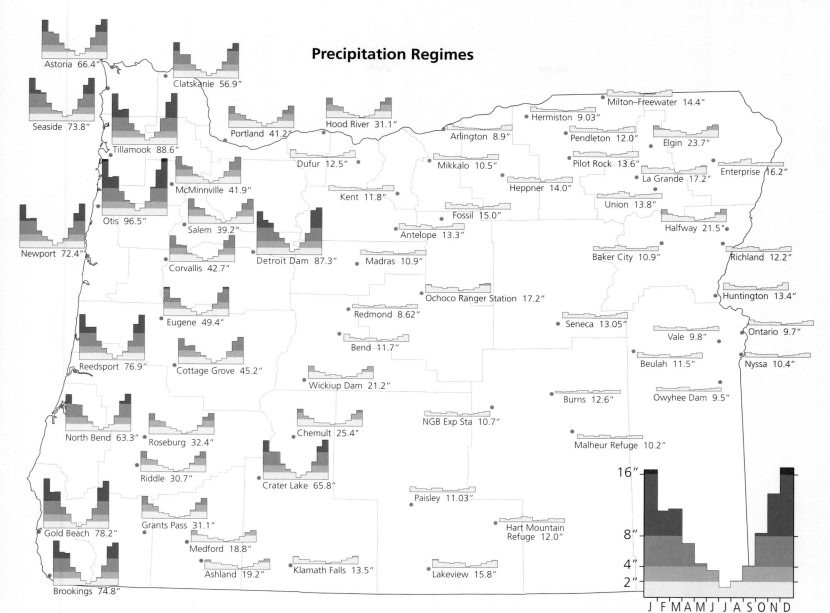

Regional and Seasonal Variation

The strong seasonal and regional variations of precipitation in Oregon are shown by the bar graphs above. Along the Oregon Coast and in the Coast and Cascade Ranges precipitation is highest overall, and greatest in the winter months. Weather stations in the Willamette Valley and in the valleys of southwestern Oregon show a similar winter-wet pattern, but of smaller amplitude than in the mountains. East of the Cascades the same basic pattern holds, but the total amounts are much lower. Stations in the northern Great Basin record a slight May–June maximum as moist subtropical air pushes into the region, triggering more frequent thunderstorms. Across the state, precipitation decreases gradually from its wintertime maximum, but increases more abruptly following the summertime dry season.

Weather Station Data

Precipitation bar graphs are plotted above for a set of weather stations across Oregon. There is one bar for each month, and the height of each bar is proportional to the total average precipitation during that month. The shading of the bars reflects the precipitation totals. The individual bar graphs can be read for the details of precipitation at individual stations, while the overall shape and color of the graphs illustrate the main precipitation gradients across the state.

Temperature and Seasonality

Temperature Regimes

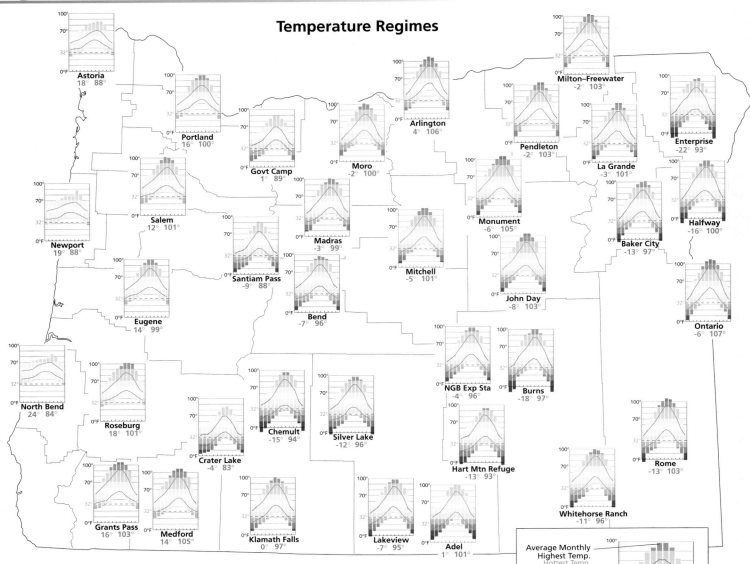

Temperature Graphs

The temperature graphs above show the average monthly highest temperature (top of bar) and lowest temperature (bottom of bar) recorded at each temperature measuring station for the 1951–1980 period. The graphs illustrate the strong gradient in "continentality" across the state: stations along the Coast show less variability of temperature during the year and are generally warmer, while stations in the northeastern part of the state show the very cold winters and hot summers that occur there, produced by strong radiational (solar) heating in summer and the intrusion of cold polar air masses in the winter. Despite its elevation, the highest station on the map, Crater Lake, does not experience the coldest winters, because of the moderating influence of the Pacific Ocean. Like the precipitation regimes shown on previous page, temperature regimes are slightly asymmetrical, featuring long springs, but brief autumns.

Monthly Temperature Patterns

Average Annual Temperature

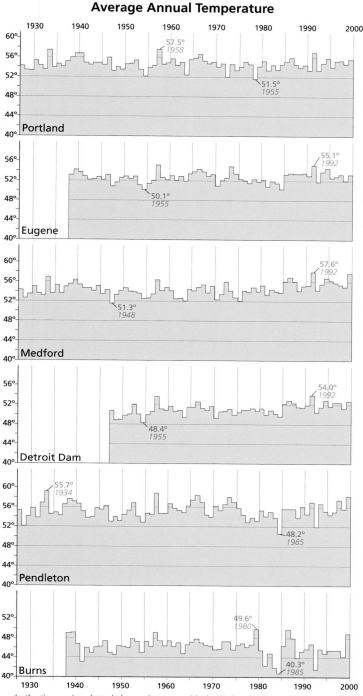

Portland

Eugene

Medford

Detroit Dam

Pendleton

Burns

In the time series plotted above, the years with the highest and lowest annual totals are identified. Below, the spatial pattern of temperatures is shown. The overall range of temperature across the state each month is indicated by the open box on each scale.

Monthly Temperatures

The year-round pattern of temperature across Oregon (small maps below) reflects the influence of four major factors: (1) the seasonal cycle of solar radiation, (2) the Cascade Range, which forms a barrier that generally confines mild Pacific air masses west of the crest and cold continental polar air masses to the east, (3) the moderating influence of the Pacific Ocean and (4) elevation in general, with upland areas being colder than lowland areas.

During the winter, days are short, the sun never rises very high in the sky, and the total amount of solar radiation received is low. In the summer, days are longer, the sun is higher in the sky, and the total amount of energy received is at its maximum. Because summer is the dry season, the amount of water that can be evaporated is low; more of the energy from solar radiation heats the land surface. Consequently, summers are hotter than they would be if Oregon had a wet summer climate. This same mechanism helps to explain why late July and August are the warmest months despite the occurrence of the solar radiation maximum in June, and why late afternoons and early evenings are often the warmest time of the day, despite the sun being highest in the sky around noon.

Throughout the year, the Cascade Range forms a barrier to the flow of air. This effect is particularly important in winter, when comparatively mild and moist Pacific air seldom reaches Eastern Oregon, and cold continental air masses are generally confined to the east. Only occasionally does cold polar air move into Western Oregon. When atmospheric circulation patterns permit, cold polar air, which is denser than warm air, flows through the Columbia River Gorge, cooling the Willamette Valley from its northern end southward toward Eugene.

The Pacific Ocean, like oceans in general, heats up and cools down more slowly than the land surface. As a result, the Pacific does not reach its coolest and warmest points until February and August. West of the Cascades this is a mediating influence, helping to keep winters warmer and summers cooler than they would be otherwise. Comparison of the January and July maps shows that the moderation is more important in winter than in summer.

Because the earth's atmosphere is heated from its base, temperatures generally decrease with increasing elevation (about 4° Fahrenheit per 1,000 feet). This effect, present at all times of the year, is why mountains and valleys are so strongly expressed in the patterns on the temperature maps shown here.

The cold season in Oregon runs from November through March, with the coldest time of the year in January. The hottest months are July and August. Comparison of the spring (April through June) and autumn (September and October) maps show why springtime seems to go on for months while winter rolls in so quickly. As is the case for precipitation, there has been a slight increase in annual-average temperatures over Oregon and the Western U.S. in the past century, a trend consistent with global warming.

Climate Indicators and Change

Growing Degree-Days (5°C Base)
Cumulative Degree-Days (dd)

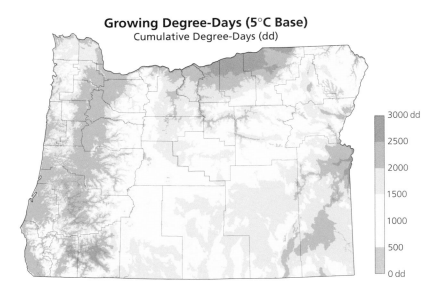

3000 dd
2500
2000
1500
1000
500
0 dd

Moisture Index

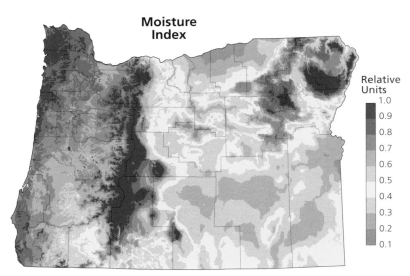

Relative Units
1.0
0.9
0.8
0.7
0.6
0.5
0.4
0.3
0.2
0.1

Climate strongly influences the plants that populate the natural, agricultural and urban landscapes of Oregon. This control is evident in the general pattern of vegetation across the state. Trees dominate in moist Western Oregon and in the mountains of Eastern Oregon, while grasslands and steppe dominate drier regions such as the Willamette and Rogue Valleys as well as the high desert of Eastern Oregon. Tundra plants prevail at the highest and coldest elevations of the Cascade Range and mountains of Eastern Oregon.

Climate determines which plants can survive in a particular area and which plants thrive. Warmth and moisture are the key controls. Three specific indicators highlight the relationship between vegetation and climate: (1) "growing degree-days," an overall measure of the length and warmth of the growing season, and of the energy potentially available to plants for photosynthesis and the production of new biomass, (2) winter temperature, which may exclude some plant species from a region and (3) moisture availability for photosynthesis.

Growing degree-days are the total number of degrees Celsius that average daily temperature exceeds some threshold (5°C in this case), accumulated over the year. Growing degree-days are highest along the central and southern Coast and in the Willamette and Rogue Valleys, where winters are mild and the growing season is long; and in the Columbia and Snake Valleys and in southeastern Oregon, where the growing season is shorter but hotter. Growing degree-days are lowest at high elevations along the crest of the Cascades and in mountains of Eastern Oregon, where summers are cool and the growing season short.

Low winter temperatures may exclude frost-intolerant plants from a region, and are also important because some plants require a particular low temperature before leafing out (in order to avoid premature bud burst and subsequent frost damage). A common index of winter cold is the average temperature of the coldest month of the year. This index is above freezing over much of Western Oregon at elevations below 3,000–3,330 feet, and along the Columbia River east of the Cascades.

For gardeners and farmers, however, a more significant index may be an area's number of frost-free days. While the ability of crops or ornamentals to survive or reproduce over the long run is not an issue (because they are planted, sometimes each year), the occurrence of freezing temperatures in spring or autumn is of primary importance.

Moisture availability involves a trade-off between precipitation or snowmelt, which recharge soil moisture, and evapotranspiration which depletes it. Evapotranspiration is the conversion of water to water vapor, from the soil by evaporation and from plants by transpiration. Moisture availability can be represented by the moisture index, defined as the ratio of actual evapotranspiration to potential evapotranspiration (how much would occur if water were not limited). Potential evapotranspiration depends on energy availability; its map pattern resembles that of July temperature. Actual evapotranspiration is higher in the wetter parts of the state, or where the soil water-holding capacity is high, enabling the soils to carry over moisture from the wet season to the dry season. A moisture-index value of 0.65 provides a point above which an area is potentially wet enough for trees to dominate and below which it is not.

Actual Evapotranspiration

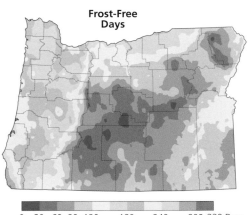

Potential Evapotranspiration

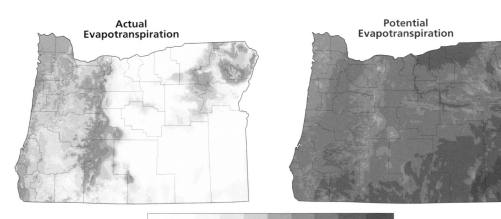

12 15 18 21 24 27 30 33 36 39 Inches

Frost-Free Days

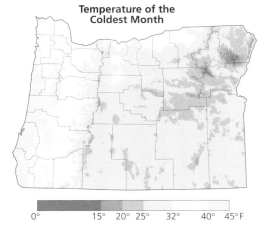

0 30 60 90 120 180 240 300 330 Days

Temperature of the Coldest Month

0° 15° 20° 25° 32° 40° 45°F

Soil Water-Holding Capacity

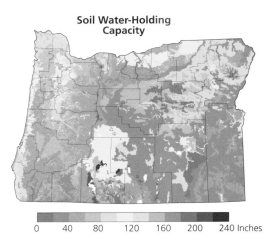

0 40 80 120 160 200 240 Inches

Future Temperature Scenarios (HADCM2 Model)

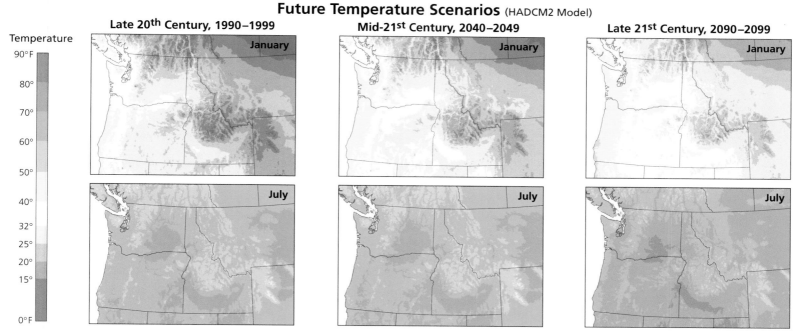

Temperature
90°F
80°
70°
60°
50°
40°
32°
25°
20°
15°
0°F

Late 20th Century, 1990–1999 — January, July
Mid-21st Century, 2040–2049 — January, July
Late 21st Century, 2090–2099 — January, July

Future Climates

At the beginning of the twenty-first century there is abundant evidence that global climate is changing as a result of human action. Projections of future climate changes have been made by the Intergovernmental Panel on Climate Change (IPCC), an organization of hundreds of scientists and technical reviewers from more than 100 countries. The projections are made in three steps: (1) estimates of future population, the global economy and energy consumption are used to create various "scenarios" of carbon dioxide emissions, (2) models of the global carbon cycle are used to estimate what proportion of those emissions will remain in the atmosphere and (3) global climate models are used to estimate future climates. The projections shown at right were made using the scenarios in the middle of the range of those produced by the IPCC. The maps show the actual climate for the late twentieth century (1990–1999), and the simulated climate for the mid- and late twenty-first century (2040–2049 and 2090–2099, respectively). January temperature in the projections increases dramatically—by the end of the century nearly all of Oregon experiences above-freezing average temperatures. July temperature also increases, with temperatures now typical of the hottest parts of the Snake River Plain and Columbia Basin covering much of the region. January precipitation increases in the projections, particularly in the western part of the state: warmer air can hold more moisture than colder air, and so Pacific storms may deliver even more precipitation than they do at present, with more falling as rain, less as snow. Projected July precipitation changes the least in these projections, but in other projections summers become even drier across the region.

Climate Projection Modeling

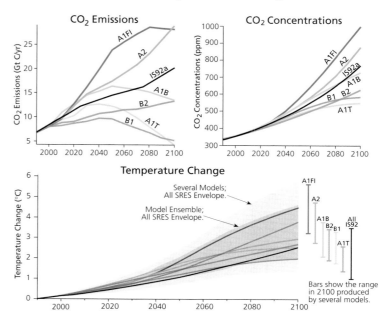

Future Precipitation Scenarios (HADCM2 Model)

Precipitation
32 Inches
16
8
4
2
0.5
0 Inches

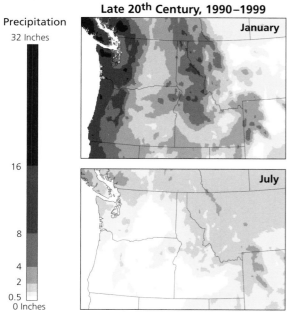

Late 20th Century, 1990–1999 — January, July

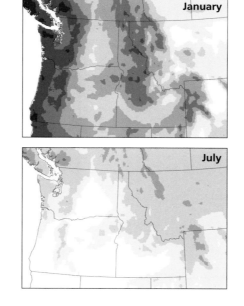

Mid-21st Century, 2040–2049 — January

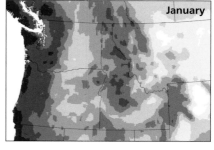

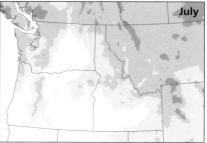

Late 21st Century, 2090–2099 — January, July

161

Rivers

Rivers and streams are perhaps Oregon's greatest environmental assets. The state is known around the U.S. and the world as a place of beautiful, rushing rivers flowing through forested valleys and teeming with wild fish. This image, however, is only partly true. Oregon does have many large, beautiful rivers, but in some parts of the state rivers are widely separated and small or even dry during much of the year.

The pattern of rivers flowing west, north, east and south from the center of the state reflects Oregon's major drainage divides: the Cascades, Coast Range, Klamath–Siskiyous and Blue Mountains. The state can be divided into four major hydrographic regions (see Drainage Basins, pages 168–169). The Umpqua and Rogue river systems, as well as a number of smaller rivers along the Coast, flow directly to the Pacific Ocean and form the Oregon Coastal hydrologic region. The Klamath River flows through northwestern California to reach the Pacific Ocean about 40 miles south of the Oregon boundary. These coastal rivers drain agricultural valleys and forested mountain canyons. The Willamette, Deschutes, John Day and Umatilla River systems are all tributaries of the Columbia River, the great river of the Western U.S. The Columbia's extensive headwaters drains parts of British Columbia, Montana, Idaho, Wyoming and Nevada. Spreading across nearly 260,000 square miles, the Columbia River system has the fifth largest drainage basin in North America. The Columbia River has been the major regional transportation network for canoes, steamboats and barges throughout Oregon's history. The Columbia River has also been a major supplier of fish and other foods, drinking and irrigation water and, for the past seventy years, hydroelectric power. Oregon's Columbia River tributaries rise in the Cascades and Blue Mountains, and flow northward through valleys largely used for agriculture and ranching. Along the eastern edge of Oregon, the Grande Ronde, Imnaha, Powder, Malheur and Owyhee river systems flow into the Snake River, the major southern branch of the Columbia River system. The Snake River tributaries have steep mountain headwaters and flow through some of Oregon's most spectacular canyons. An unusual drainage system, the Oregon Closed Basins hydrologic region is found in the arid south–central part of the state. Here, small rivers and dry streams feed closed basins and marshes, including Malheur Lake, Harney Lake, the Warner Lakes, Summer Lake, Lake Abert and Paulina Marsh. In these closed basins, the runoff collects and evaporates.

The following pages show how these river systems influence, and are used by, inhabitants of the state of Oregon. Water quantity in flowing rivers is illustrated on the Streamflow pages, while other water features are shown on the Lakes pages. The Drainage Basins pages shows how the river systems form natural land units for management of water resources and for planning. Water quality and the extensive human modifications of Oregon's rivers are shown on the Water Quality and Dams pages.

Streamflow

Western Oregon is blessed with an abundance of notable rivers, while Eastern Oregon's rivers are smaller and more widely spaced. Average flows are 6,000 cubic feet per second (cfs) or more in the three big rivers of Western Oregon; the Willamette, the Umpqua and the Rogue. In contrast, flows are only 3,000 to as little as a few hundred cfs in the largest rivers of Eastern Oregon: the Klamath, John Day, Umatilla, Grande Ronde, Malheur and Owyhee. Only the Deschutes River, which drains the eastern flank of the Cascades, rivals the large Western Oregon rivers in flow, though all are dwarfed by the Columbia.

Seasonal variation in streamflow influences water availability for human use, as well as ecological conditions in the rivers. Many large rivers have relatively low flow during the summer and fall. The greatest monthly flow is five to 10 times larger than the flow in the driest months. In many rivers a portion of river flow is stored in reservoirs during the winter and spring months to supply needs such as irrigated agriculture and drinking water during the dry months. The Deschutes River, fed by a number of large springs rather than exclusively by surface runoff, has the most even monthly flow of any large Oregon river.

Some rivers have peak flows closely tied to rainfall, while others are controlled by snowmelt. In the Willamette and Rogue Rivers, the highest flows occur in the heavy rain months of December and January. In higher elevation river basins where colder temperatures prevail, winter precipitation is stored as snow, and the peak flows are shifted to spring (April on the Owyhee River, June on the Columbia River at The Dalles).

Oregon's largest recorded flood occurred in December 1964 on many rivers in Western and north-central Oregon (although the 1894 flood was larger on the Columbia River). The February 1996 flood in Western Oregon was potentially as big as the 1964 flood, but more flood control dams were in place in 1996. The historic peak flow records for the Willamette River (bottom of page) show the effectiveness of flood control dams after 1965.

During droughts, flow may drop to 3 percent or less of average. Rivers such as the Illinois, Chetco and Nehalem are drought-prone in that they have less ground water and surface storage capacity to buffer the effects of dry years. Historic low flows have been less severe, only 10 to 20 percent of average flows, in the McKenzie, Rogue, Grande Ronde, Willamette and Columbia Rivers.

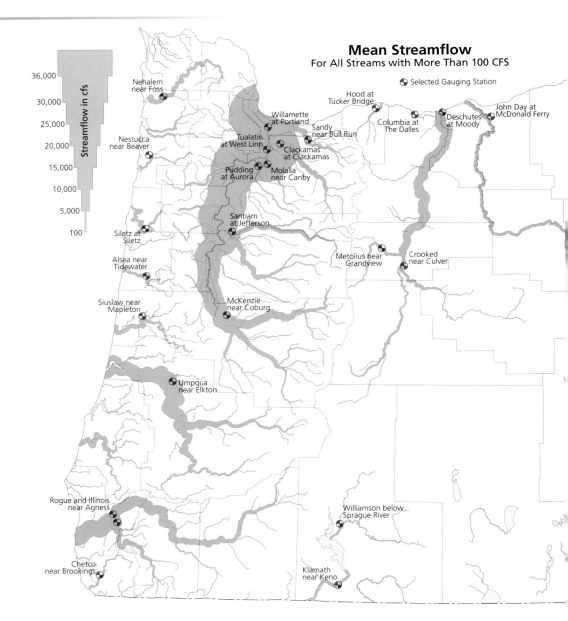

Mean Streamflow
For All Streams with More Than 100 CFS

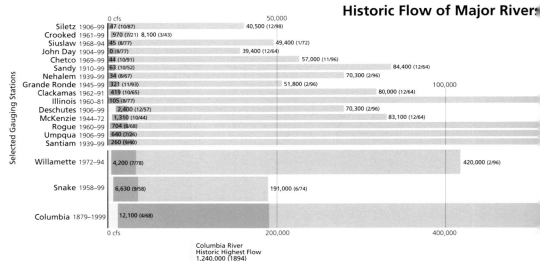

Historic Flow of Major Rivers

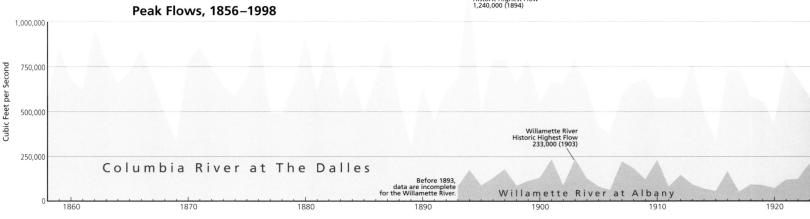

Peak Flows, 1856–1998

164

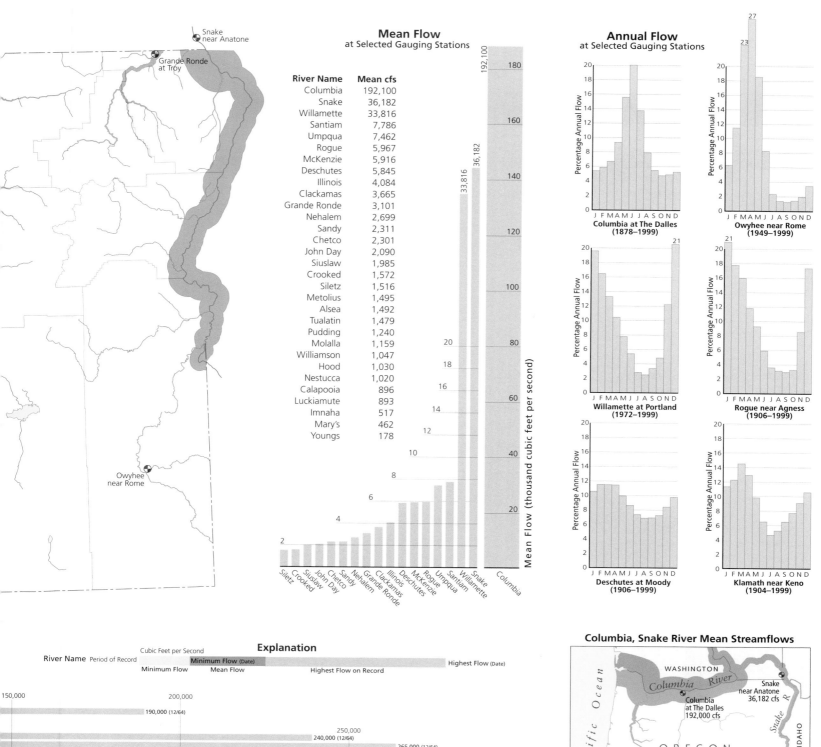

Mean Flow at Selected Gauging Stations

River Name	Mean cfs
Columbia	192,100
Snake	36,182
Willamette	33,816
Santiam	7,786
Umpqua	7,462
Rogue	5,967
McKenzie	5,916
Deschutes	5,845
Illinois	4,084
Clackamas	3,665
Grande Ronde	3,101
Nehalem	2,699
Sandy	2,311
Chetco	2,301
John Day	2,090
Siuslaw	1,985
Crooked	1,572
Siletz	1,516
Metolius	1,495
Alsea	1,492
Tualatin	1,479
Pudding	1,240
Molalla	1,159
Williamson	1,047
Hood	1,030
Nestucca	1,020
Calapooia	896
Luckiamute	893
Imnaha	517
Mary's	462
Youngs	178

Annual Flow at Selected Gauging Stations

Columbia at The Dalles (1878–1999)
Owyhee near Rome (1949–1999)
Willamette at Portland (1972–1999)
Rogue near Agness (1906–1999)
Deschutes at Moody (1906–1999)
Klamath near Keno (1904–1999)

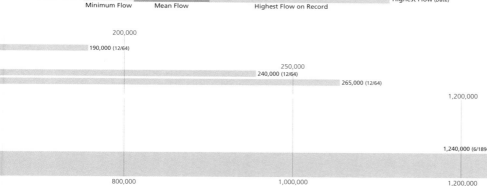

Explanation

Columbia, Snake River Mean Streamflows

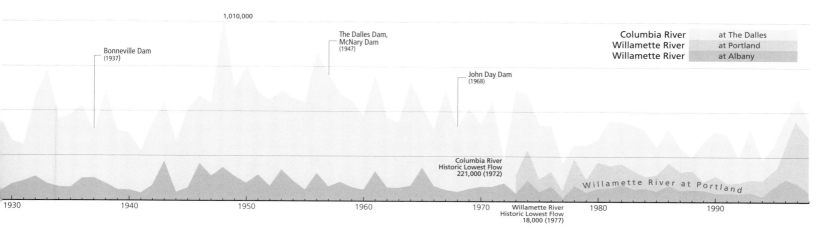

Lakes

Natural lakes can be classified as perennial (with water all year long), intermittent (with episodes of drying out entirely) or ephemeral, sometimes also called dry (with water only during brief periods after heavy rains or snowmelt). The distinction between intermittent and dry lakes is a matter of degree or frequency. On the map below, most of the smaller lakes of southeastern Oregon are shown as dry. All the lakes of this area are small successors of the much larger lakes of 10,000 to 20,000 years ago (see pages 132–133).

Oregon's coastal lakes are the product of sand dunes blocking small streams; water moving to the ocean is filtered through the sand. The many very small inland lakes of the Willamette Valley and the surviving large lakes on the Lower Columbia are remnants of old river channels. These lakes were much more numerous before nineteenth-century settlement and drainage.

High Cascade lakes are created and sustained by a combination of snowmelt, natural volcanic dams and porous or fractured rock. Occupying the caldera of Mount Mazama, Crater Lake, with a depth of 1,932 feet, is the deepest lake in North America. Paulina and East Lakes are less spectacular examples of caldera lakes. Crater Lake contains by far the largest volume of water of any Oregon lake, but the largest surface areas belong to the shallow lakes in the southeast. Klamath Lake is unique among these in being perennial and in being fed by Cascade snowmelt and drained by a large river. The other large lakes southeast of the Cascades occupy sumps (lowest part of

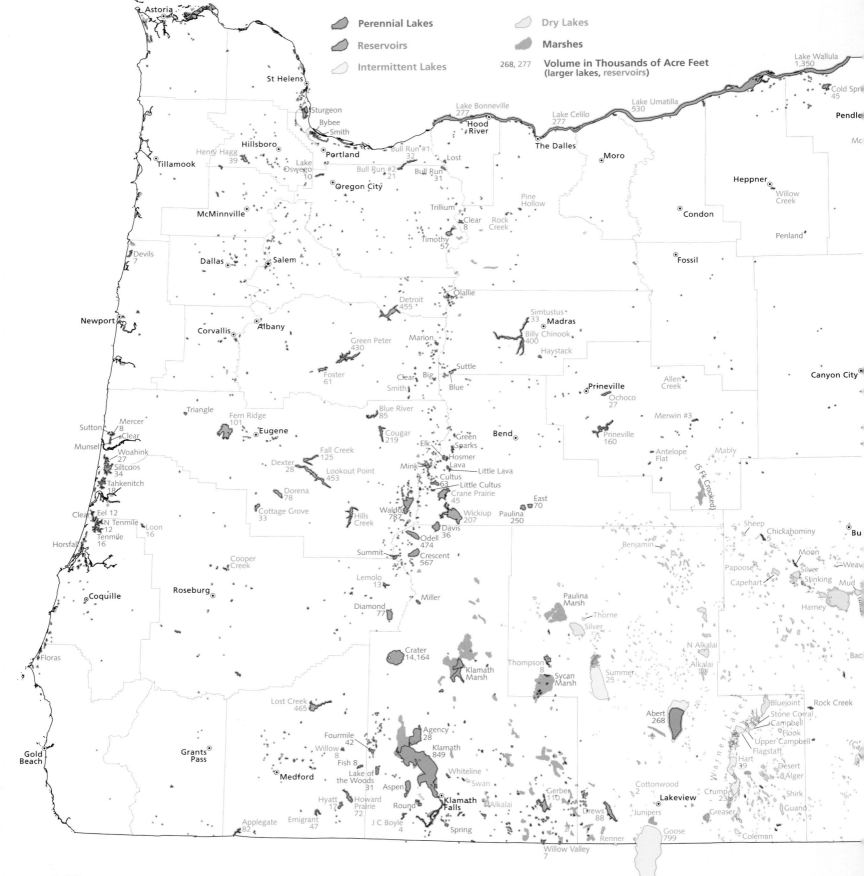

a larger basin), expanding during periods of very high rainfall, and sometimes remaining entirely dry for years at a time. Of these, only Lake Abert has never dried up completely during historic times. Surface areas of these very shallow lakes (Abert has a maximum depth of 11 feet; Malheur of five feet) fluctuate greatly, and during wet periods they sometimes extend beyond the limits mapped here.

Reservoirs are commonly managed for a combination of purposes including flood control, irrigation, hydroelectric power generation, fish passage, recreation and (on the Columbia) barge traffic. Oregon's prevailing dry summer conditions cause most reservoirs to be at very low levels by early fall.

Oregon's 50 Largest Lakes and Reservoirs

Name	Area sq mi (rank)		Volume thousands of acre ft (rank)		Depth (ft) max	Depth (ft) avg	Name	Area sq mi (rank)		Volume thousands of acre ft (rank)		Depth (ft) max	Depth (ft) avg
Abert L	57.1	6	268	19	11	7	Hells Canyon Res	3.8	39	183	23	—	—
Agency L	14.5	16	28	41	7	3	Hills Creek R	4.3	38	356	16	299	130
Antelope R	5.1	33	26	42	28	11	Howard Prairie R	3.2	40	72	32	80	35
Beulah R	3.2	41	69	33	85	33	Lake Bonneville	32.2	9	277	45	—	—
Billy Chinook R	6.1	27	400	15	415	102	Lake Celilo	17.5	13	277	18	—	—
Brownlee Res	23.4	10	1,427	2	—	—	Lake Umatilla	85.9	3	530	9	—	—
Cold Springs R	2.4	48	45	36	71	32	Lake Wallula	60.6	5	1,350	3	—	—
Cottonwood R	4.6	37	2	49	46	16	Lookout Point R	6.8	23	453	13	234	104
Crane Prairie R	6.5	25	45	35	20	11	Lost Creek R	5.4	32	465	11	322	136
Crater L	20.5	12	14,164	1	1,932	1,078	Malheur L	77.7	4	85	29	5	2
Crescent L	7.1	22	567	8	265	124	Odell L	5.6	30	474	10	282	132
Crump L	12	18	23	44	6	3	Owyhee R	21.7	11	1,122	4	117	81
Davis L	6.1	28	36	39	20	9	Paulina L	2.4	47	250	20	250	163
Detroit R	5.6	31	455	12	440	121	Phillips R	2.3	50	61	34	125	41
Diamond L	5	34	77	31	52	24	Prineville R	4.9	36	160	24	130	51
Dorena R	2.9	43	78	30	97	42	Siltcoos L	4.9	35	34	40	22	11
Drews R	8.7	21	88	28	50	16	Summer L	39.1	8	25	43	2	1
Fall Creek R	2.9	42	125	25	161	67	Tahkenitch L	2.6	45	18	46	23	11
Fern Ridge R	14.6	15	101	27	33	11	Tenmile L	2.5	46	16	47	22	10
Fourmile L	12.1	17	42	37	175	55	Thompson R	2.8	44	8	48	22	4
Gerber R	6.3	26	110	26	65	27	Upper Klamath L	96.2	2	849	5	50	14
Goose L	152.2	1	799	6	12	8	Waldo L	9.8	20	787	7	420	128
Green Peter R	5.8	29	430	14	315	114	Wallowa L	2.4	49	244	21	299	161
Harney L	41.3	7	—	50	—	—	Warm Springs R	6.6	24	285	17	140	68
Hart L	11.3	19	39	38	11	5	Wickiup R	16.1	14	207	22	70	20

Water Volume

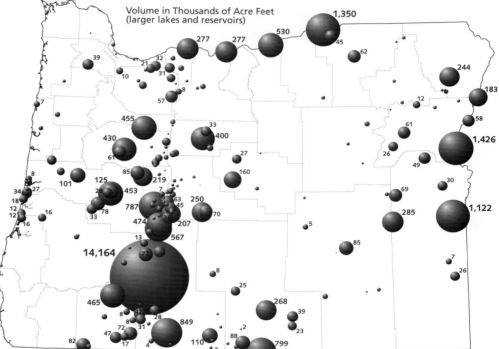

Volume in Thousands of Acre Feet (larger lakes and reservoirs)

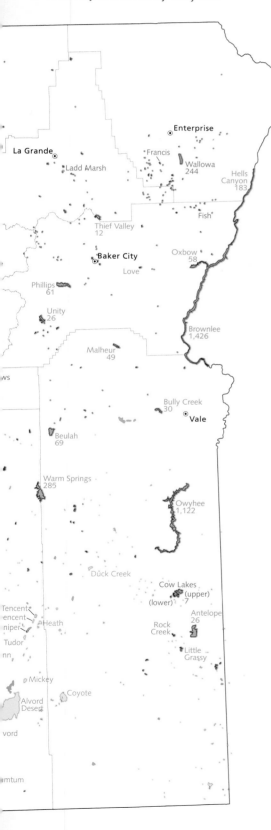

Nutrient Status of Lakes

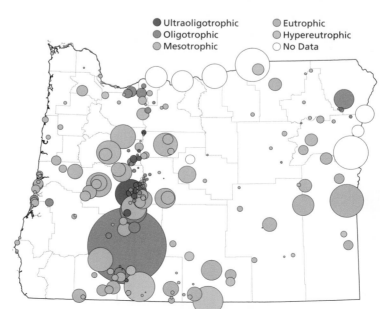

- Ultraoligotrophic
- Oligotrophic
- Mesotrophic
- Eutrophic
- Hypereutrophic
- No Data

This map shows the nutrient status of the fifty largest Oregon lakes and reservoirs. The lowest primary productivity and the lowest concentrations of nutrients used by aquatic plants and animals are found in ultraoligotrophic lakes. Hypereutrophic lakes are the highest in primary productivity and nutrients, often supporting large algae blooms and other aquatic plants. Lakes in the drier parts of Oregon tend to be naturally eutrophic, because dissolved nutrients are concentrated by evaporation. The hypereutrophic lakes are located in southeastern Oregon, and also in areas affected by urban and agricultural runoff (for example, Lake Oswego, Upper Klamath Lake and Cold Spring Reservoir). Lakes in the Cascades are naturally oligotrophic due to high precipitation and acidic vegetation and soils. Crater Lake is the largest oligotrophic lake in southern Oregon.

Drainage Basins

168

REGION

SubRegion

Basin

Sub-Basin

Sub-Basin

Sub-Basin boundaries which define major river drainages are shown in black.

A river's watershed, or drainage basin, is the area above a specified point that contributes surface runoff to the river. Watersheds are defined by drainage divides, the ridges that determine which way surface runoff will flow. All of Oregon lies in one of four regional watersheds. Most rivers of northern and Eastern Oregon flow into the Columbia

River or its major tributary, the Snake River. The western edge of the state contains a group of smaller watersheds that each flow directly into the Pacific Ocean. Most of the southern part of Oregon lies within the Great Basin hydrologic region. In this arid region, large through-flowing rivers have not developed, and each watershed drains into a sump, its

Lower Columbia Subregion

Lower Columbia Basin

COLUMBIA RIVER REGION

Middle Columbia Subregion

Youngs

Necanicum

Clatskanie

Nehalem

Lower Willamette

Lower Columbia Basin

Middle Columbia Basin

Lake Wallula

Lake Wallula

Mic

Hood

Hood

Willow

Wilson–Trask–Nestucca

Tualatin

Lower John Day

Yamhill

Middle Willamette

Molalla–Pudding

Sandy

Clackamas

Lower Deschutes

Trout

North

Siletz–

Willamette Subregion and Basin

North Santiam

John Day Ba

Yaquina

Upper Willamette

South Santiam

Deschutes Basin

Upper Jo

Alsea

McKenzie

Upper Deschutes

Lower Crooked

Upper Crooked

Beaver–South Fork Crooked

Siuslaw

Middle Fork Willamette

Siltcoos

Coast Fork Willamette

Little Deschutes

Silver

Umpqua

Coos

North Umpqua

Williamson

Summer Lake

Oregon Closed Bas

Coquille

Southern Oregon Coastal Basin

South Umpqua

Sixes

Lower Rogue

Middle Rogue

Upper Rogue

Upper Klamath Lake

Sprague

Lake Abert

Subregion

Warner Lakes

Gu

Illinois

Applegate

Lost

Goose Lake

Upper Sacramento Basin

Chetco

Upper Klamath

Lost sub-basin partially diverted into Klamath, and classified accordingly but colored here as Great Basin.

Sacramento Subregion

Goose Lake sub-basin drains into Sacramento only in very wet years.

Winchuck California/Oregon

Smith California/Oregon

Lower Klamath California/Oregon

Butte

Klamath River Basin

Klamath N California Coastal Subregion

CALIFORNIA REGION

GRE

lowest point, where the water is lost to evaporation and to groundwater recharge. Large watersheds are subdivided into smaller watersheds, which are further subdivided at several levels. The smallest watersheds shown here are called "cataloging units," each identified by a code number. The large map shows major watershed boundaries as dark brown and light brown lines; the boundaries of smaller watersheds within them are shown as black or light gray lines.

Each watershed is a unique area in which hillsides, soils, vegetation, runoff, river flow, water quality, fish and the aquatic ecosystem are connected. Any activity that affects the water quality, quantity or rate of movement at one location can influence water downstream. Watersheds therefore are important natural units for water quality, water supply, flood control and ecological planning. In most cases political units which have traditionally defined boundaries for planning (for example, counties) do not match watershed boundaries. Increasingly, however, watersheds are being used as management and planning units. Watershed councils have been established across the state as part of the Oregon Plan for Salmon and Watersheds, supported by the Oregon Watershed Enhancement Board. Watershed councils provide a structure for local residents and land owners to identify environmental problems in their watershed and undertake river and watershed restoration projects. Most watershed councils correspond to one cataloging unit as shown on this map.

Water Availability

These three maps show how water availability varies across Oregon during the dry season. The lowest stream flows typically occur in August or September. August natural streamflow (right) shows the quantity of water that would be in the river without human intervention. The streamflows shown are technically known as August 80 percent exceedance levels (the level of natural streamflow that is equaled or exceeded 80 percent of the time in August). Natural streamflow is important as an indicator of the conditions to which the local aquatic ecosystem is adapted.

August expected streamflow (middle) is natural streamflow (the 80 percent exceedance flow) minus consumptive use by humans. Consumptive use includes agricultural, domestic and industrial uses that actually reduce streamflow. Most consumptive use in Oregon is for irrigated agriculture. The Williamson River, upper Deschutes and Crooked Rivers, Umatilla, Owyhee and parts of other Eastern Oregon rivers are strongly affected by consumptive use, as are some watersheds in Western Oregon, particularly those in agricultural areas.

August water availability (bottom) is the quantity of water that could be appropriated for new out-of-stream consumptive water use. Natural streamflow minus existing use (in-stream water rights plus out-of-stream consumptive uses) determines the amount available. Oregon's water is essentially fully appropriated—there is no available water except in a few very limited areas. Newly identified ecological needs could further reduce the limited water availability shown on this map. Future human population growth will have to be accommodated by wiser use of existing water resources.

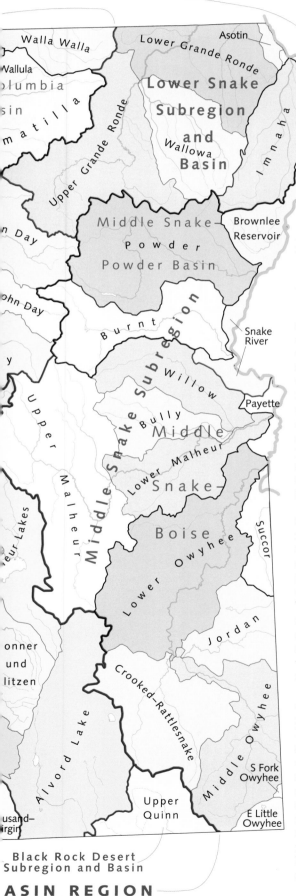

Black Rock Desert
Subregion and Basin

ASIN REGION

Major Drainage Basins of the Far West

Water Availability
August Natural Streamflow

August Expected Streamflow

August Water Availability

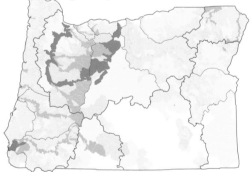

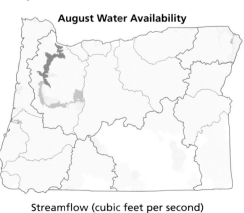

Streamflow (cubic feet per second)

0   1   10   100   1,000   No Data

Water Quality and Dams

Water Quality

The health of a river or stream depends on many chemical, physical and biological characteristics. The Oregon Department of Environmental Quality has established water quality standards for these characteristics to assess the health of Oregon's rivers, lakes and estuaries. Not all standards are applied to every body of water; each body of water is evaluated using standards related to how it is used (for example, water contact recreation, drinking water or resident fish and aquatic life).

The map at right shows two indicators of water quality in Oregon's rivers. The Oregon Water Quality Index (OWQI), shown as blue to red circles, is a numerical index that combines eight major water quality measures: water temperature, dissolved oxygen, biochemical oxygen demand, pH, nitrogen, total phosphates, total solids and fecal coliform bacteria. The OWQI is measured at about 150 water quality monitoring sites around the state. Based on the OWQI, the Cascades, the Blue Mountains and parts of the Coast Range have the best water quality in the state. The greater Portland area, the Ontario–Vale area in Eastern Oregon and the Klamath Basin tend to have the poorest water quality.

The second indicator, "303(d) listed streams and lakes," is shown on the map as rivers in orange. This list, required under section 303(d) of the federal Clean Water Act, includes bodies of water in which one or more applicable water quality standards is violated. The rivers shown in blue on the map meet all applicable standards or fall into one of two other categories: insufficient data to make a determination or not assessed. About half of Oregon's river miles have been assessed, and of these 30 percent meet all applicable standards, 26 percent are on the 303(d) list, and the remaining river miles meet standards but are threatened. For lakes (many of which were, like river miles, not assessed due to cost) 55 percent meet all applicable standards, 24 percent are on the 303(d) list, and 33 percent meet standards but are threatened. The 303(d) listed rivers and streams are found all across the state, in urban and rural areas. Water temperature is the standard most extensively violated; habitat modification, fecal coliform bacteria or sedimentation standards are also violated in at least 100 Oregon water bodies.

Water Quality

Water Quality Index

- ● Excellent (90–100)
- ● Good (85–89)
- ○ Fair (80–84)
- ● Poor (60–79)
- ● Very Poor (0–59)
- ─ 303(d) Listed Streams and Lakes

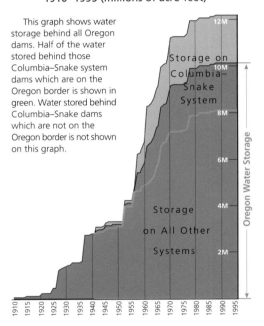

Dams

While dams and reservoirs serve many useful functions, they also have changed the character of Oregon's rivers. Dams are built for water storage, flood control, generation of electric power and recreation. Most dams and reservoirs serve more than one of these uses. Dams and reservoirs also impede fish migration, change river water temperature, interrupt sediment movement and convert river habitat to lake habitat. The major era of dam building occurred after World War II. Three times as many dams were constructed in 1941–1960 as in 1921–1940, but dam building slowed after the 1980s. Recently a few small dams that are obsolete or unsafe have been removed. At many of the larger dams, the timing and amount of water released has been modified to improve ecological conditions downstream. Today in Oregon there are about 1,100 dams that are at least 25 feet high or with at least 50 acre-feet of storage. This map shows 813 dams for which data are available. Most of Oregon's largest dams and reservoirs are operated by the U.S. Army Corps of Engineers, the U.S. Bureau of Reclamation or public utility companies.

Water Storage Behind Dams
1910–1995 (millions of acre-feet)

This graph shows water storage behind all Oregon dams. Half of the water stored behind those Columbia–Snake system dams which are on the Oregon border is shown in green. Water stored behind Columbia–Snake dams which are not on the Oregon border is not shown on this graph.

Dam Construction 1880–1998

● Dams constructed during time period   ● Dams constructed before time period

1880–1900   **1901–1920**   **1921–1940**

Dam Storage and Ownership

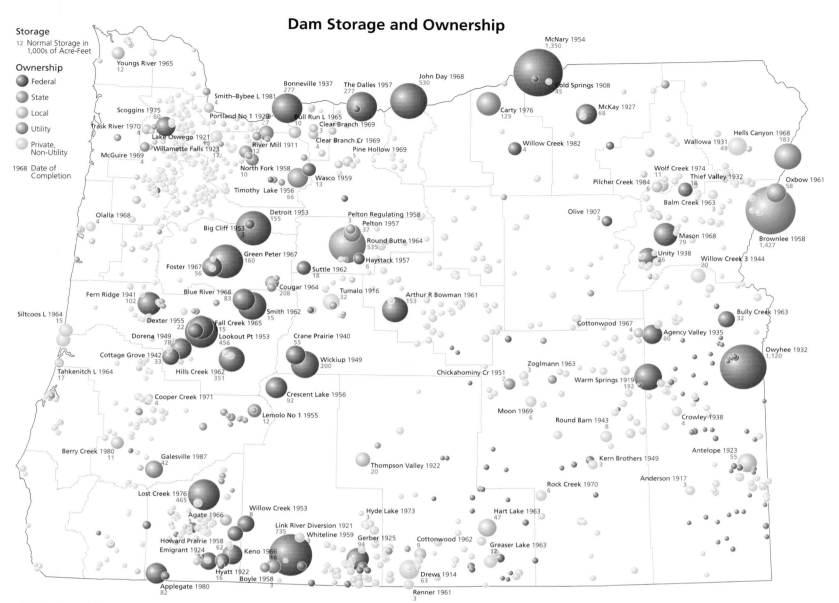

Storage
12 Normal Storage in 1,000s of Acre-Feet

Ownership
- Federal
- State
- Local
- Utility
- Private, Non-Utility

1968 Date of Completion

100 Largest Dams
(ranked by normal storage of reservoir in acre-feet)

#	Name	Storage	#	Name	Storage	#	Name	Storage	#	Name	Storage	#	Name	Storage
1	Brownlee	1,426,700	21	Fern Ridge	102,200	41	Galesville	42,225	61	Lemolo No 1	12,350	81	Smith–Bybee Lakes	4,100
2	McNary	1,350,000	22	Gerber	94,270	42	Emigrant	40,530	62	River Mill	12,200	82	Trask River	4,000
3	Owyhee	1,120,000	23	Crescent Lake	91,740	43	Pelton	37,300	63	Greaser Lake	12,000	83	Cooper Creek	3,900
4	Link River Diversion	735,000	24	Blue River	83,000	44	Cottage Grove	33,000	64	Youngs River	12,000	84	Cottonwood (Drewsey)	3,700
5	Round Butte	535,000	25	Applegate	82,200	45	Tumalo	32,300	65	Berry Creek	11,250	85	Crowley	3,700
6	John Day	530,000	26	Mason	78,500	46	Bully Creek	31,600	66	Wolf Creek	10,800	86	Olalla	3,650
7	Lost Creek	465,000	27	Dorena	77,500	47	Portland No. 1	26,640	67	Bull Run Lake	10,000	87	Clear Branch Cr	3,550
8	Lookout Point	455,840	28	McKay	67,800	48	Unity	25,800	68	North Fork	10,000	88	McGuire	3,550
9	Hills Creek	350,600	29	Timothy Lake	66,000	49	Dexter	22,200	69	Lake Oswego	9,800	89	John C Boyle	3,380
10	Bonneville	277,000	30	Drews	62,500	50	Willow Creek 3	20,400	70	Cottonwood (Lake Co)	8,740	90	Olive Lake	3,300
11	The Dalles	277,000	31	Howard Prairie	62,100	51	Thompson Valley	19,660	71	Round Barn	7,500	91	Pelton Regulating	3,270
12	Cougar	208,000	32	Scoggins	59,910	52	Keno	18,500	72	Willow Cr (Jackson Co)	7,500	92	Renner	3,270
13	Wickiup	200,000	33	Agency Valley	59,900	53	Suttle	17,700	73	Chickahominy Creek	7,228	93	Clear Branch	3,200
14	Warm Springs	192,400	34	Oxbow	58,000	54	Thief Valley	17,600	74	Pilcher Creek	5,910	94	Anderson (Malheur)	2,990
15	Hells Canyon	183,000	35	Foster	56,000	55	Willamette Falls	17,000	75	Rock Creek	5,818	95	Balm Creek	2,926
16	Green Peter	160,000	36	Crane Prairie	55,330	56	Tahkenitch Lake	16,580	76	Haystack	5,650	96	Hyde Lake	2,870
17	Detroit	155,000	37	Antelope (Malheur)	55,000	57	Hyatt	16,200	77	Moon	5,650	97	Kern Brothers	2,700
18	Arthur R Bowman	152,800	38	Wallowa Lake	49,257	58	Siltcoos Lake	15,070	78	Agate	4,780	98	Whiteline	2,692
19	Carty	129,000	39	Hart Lake	47,400	59	Smith	15,000	79	Pine Hollow	4,750	99	Big Cliff	2,630
20	Fall Creek	115,000	40	Cold Springs	44,668	60	Wasco	13,100	80	Willow Cr	4,326	100	Zoglmann	2,533

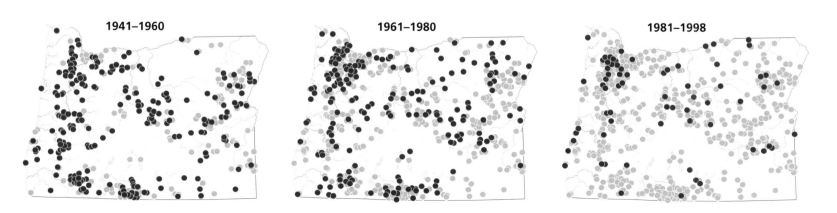

1941–1960 **1961–1980** **1981–1998**

Ecoregions

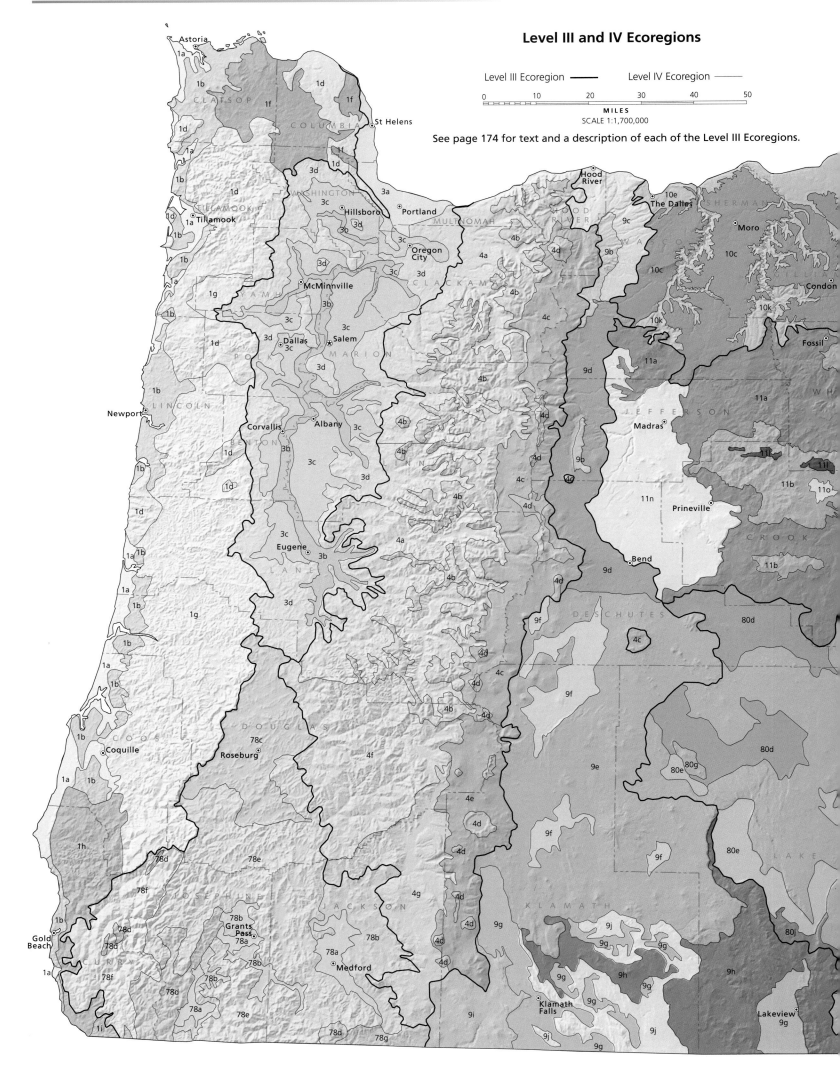

Level III and IV Ecoregions

Level III Ecoregion ——— Level IV Ecoregion ———

MILES
SCALE 1:1,700,000

See page 174 for text and a description of each of the Level III Ecoregions.

1. Coast Range
Coastal Lowlands   `1a`
Coastal Uplands   `1b`
Volcanics   `1d`
Willapa Hills   `1f`
Mid-Coastal Sedimentary   `1g`
Southern Oregon Coastal Mountains   `1h`
Redwood Zone   `1i`

3. Willamette Valley
Portland/Vancouver Basin   `3a`
Willamette River Gallery Forest   `3b`
Prairie Terraces   `3c`
Valley Foothills   `3d`

4. Cascades
Western Cascades Lowlands and Valleys   `4a`
Western Cascades Montane Highlands   `4b`
Cascade Crest Montane Forest   `4c`
Cascades Subalpine/Alpine   `4d`
High Southern Cascades Montane Forest   `4e`
Umpqua Cascades   `4f`
Southern Cascades   `4g`

9. Eastern Cascades Slopes and Foothills
Grand Fir Mixed Forest   `9b`
Oak/Conifer Eastern Cascades–Columbia Foothills   `9c`
Ponderosa Pine/Bitterbrush Woodland   `9d`
Pumice Plateau Forest   `9e`
Cold Wet Pumice Plateau Basins   `9f`
Klamath/Goose Lake Warm Wet Basins   `9g`
Fremont Pine/Fir Forest   `9h`
Southern Cascades Slope   `9i`
Klamath Juniper/Ponderosa Pine Woodland   `9j`

10. Columbia Plateau
Umatilla Plateau   `10c`
Pleistocene Lake Basin   `10e`
Yakima Folds   `10g`
Deep Loess Foothills   `10i`
Deschutes/John Day Canyon   `10k`

11. Blue Mountains
John Day/Clarno Uplands   `11a`
John Day/Clarno Highlands   `11b`
Maritime-Influenced Zone   `11c`
Melange   `11d`
Wallowas/Seven Devils Mountains   `11e`
Canyons and Dissected Highlands   `11f`
Canyons and Dissected Uplands   `11g`
Continental Zone Highlands   `11h`
Continental Zone Foothills   `11i`
Blue Mountains Basins   `11k`
Mesic Forest Zone   `11l`
Subalpine Zone   `11m`
Deschutes River Valley   `11n`
Cold Basins   `11o`

12. Snake River Plain
Treasure Valley   `12a`
Unwooded Alkaline Foothills   `12j`

13. Central Basin and Range
Salt Desert Shrub Valleys   `13h`

78. Klamath Mountains
Rogue/Illinois Valleys   `78a`
Siskiyou Foothills   `78b`
Umpqua Interior Foothills   `78c`
Serpentine Siskiyous   `78d`
Inland Siskiyous   `78e`
Coastal Siskiyous   `78f`
Klamath River Ridges   `78g`

80. Northern Basin and Range
Dissected High Lava Plateau   `80a`
Pluvial Lake Basins   `80d`
High Desert Wetlands   `80e`
Owyhee Uplands and Canyons   `80f`
High Lava Plains   `80g`
Semiarid Uplands   `80j`
Partly Forested Mountains   `80k`

173

Ecoregions Legend; Biotic Systems

Ecoregions (*Map on previous pages*)

Ecoregions, or ecological regions, denote areas of general similarity in ecosystems and in the type, quality and quantity of environmental resources. They serve as a useful spatial framework for individuals who research, assess, manage and monitor ecosystems and ecosystem components. A four-level scale is used to describe ecoregions at varying degrees of detail. The most general classification, level I, divides North America into 15 ecological regions, with level II splitting the continent into 51 regions. At level III, the continental U.S. contains 98 regions. The 10 that appear in Oregon are listed below. Level IV ecoregions are a further refinement of level III. Sixty-three level IV regions are shown on the ecoregions map.

Specialists delineate ecological regions after carefully analyzing the patterns and interplay of geography and other natural phenomena. They then define areas that share similar combinations of elements. The subjects of such an analysis include an area's geology, landforms, soils, land use, vegetation, climate, wildlife and hydrology. Ecoregions reflect an ecosystem's capacities and potentials as well as its range of likely responses to human disturbance. State agencies use the ecoregion framework as a tool in efforts to establish water quality standards and goals for managing non-point source pollution. These regions provide a kind of biological lingua franca that is critical for developing coordinated management strategies for federal and state agencies that have different responsibilities for the same geographic areas.

Oregon's ecosystems are shaped to a large degree by the position of major landforms. Ecoregions mapped in Oregon generally reflect moisture availability at various elevation levels. The Coast Range (1) and the Cascades (4) greatly reduce the effects of marine weather systems to create dry conditions in Eastern Oregon. Due to this rain shadow effect, the western Blue Mountains (11) are relatively dry; however, the northeast part of this ecoregion contains higher elevation areas of moist forest where the mountains lie in the path of the marine weather coming through the Columbia River Gorge. Southeastern Oregon contains a portion of the Northern Basin and Range (80) which is characterized by rolling sagebrush plains, fault block mountains and internally drained rain-holding basins. Geology is especially important to ecoregion character in some areas of the state. For example, Coast Range streams in volcanic areas are less prone to and recover more easily from disruption compared to stream in sedimentary areas, where bank erosion and sedimentation are long-term management concerns. Familiarity with ecoregion character, both past and present, and knowledge of ecoregion response to management activities are key factors in mounting major environmental initiatives such as salmon and watershed restoration efforts.

Legend

1. Coast Range

The low mountains of the Coast Range are covered by highly productive, rain-drenched coniferous forests. Sitka spruce forests originally dominated the fog-shrouded Coast, while a mosaic of western red cedar, western hemlock and Douglas-fir blanketed inland areas. Today Douglas-fir plantations are prevalent on the intensively logged and managed landscape.

3. Willamette Valley

Rolling prairies, deciduous–coniferous forests and extensive wetlands characterized the pre-settlement landscape of this broad lowland valley. The Willamette Valley is distinguished from the adjacent Coast Range and Cascades by lower precipitation, less relief and a different mosaic of vegetation. Landforms consist of terraces and floodplains that are interlaced with and surrounded by rolling hills. Productive soils and a temperate climate make it one of the most important agricultural areas in Oregon.

4. Cascades

This mountainous ecoregion is underlain by Cenozoic volcanics, and has been affected by alpine glaciations. It is characterized by steep ridges and river valleys in the west, a high plateau in the east and both active and dormant volcanoes. Its moist, temperate climate supports an extensive and highly productive coniferous forest. Subalpine meadows occur at high elevations.

9. Eastern Cascades Slopes and Foothills

In the rain shadow of the Cascade Mountains, this ecoregion's climate exhibits greater temperature extremes and less precipitation than ecoregions to the west. Open forests of ponderosa pine and some lodgepole pine distinguish this region from the higher ecoregions to the west where hemlock and fir forests are common, and the lower, drier ecoregions to the east where shrubs and grasslands are predominant. The vegetation is adapted to the prevailing dry, continental climate and is highly susceptible to wildfire. Volcanic cones and buttes are common in much of the region.

10. Columbia Plateau

This is an arid sagebrush steppe and grassland, surrounded on all sides by moister, predominantly forested, mountainous ecological regions. This region is underlain by lava rock up to two miles thick. Particularly in the region's eastern portion, where precipitation is greater, deep wind-deposited loess soils have been extensively cultivated for wheat.

11. Blue Mountains

This ecoregion is a complex of mountain ranges that are lower and much more open than the neighboring Cascades and northern Rocky Mountains. Like the Cascades but unlike the northern Rockies, the Blue Mountains ecoregion is mostly volcanic in origin. Only its highest ranges, particularly the Wallowa and Elkhorn Mountains, consist of intrusive rocks that rise above the dissected lava surface of the region. Much of this ecoregion is grazed by cattle, unlike the Cascades and northern Rockies.

12. Snake River Plain

This portion of the Basin and Range area is considerably lower and less rugged than surrounding ecoregions. Mostly because of water that is available for irrigation a large percentage of the alluvial valleys bordering the Snake River is used for agriculture. Cattle feedlots and dairy operations are also common in the river plain. Except for the scattered barren lava fields, the remainder of the plains and low hills in the ecoregion have sagebrush steppe natural vegetation and are used for cattle grazing.

13. Central Basin and Range

The Central Basin and Range is composed of north–south-trending fault block ranges and intervening, drier basins. In the higher mountains, woodland, mountain brush and scattered open forest are found. Lower elevation basins, slopes and alluvial fans are either shrub- and grass-covered, shrub-covered, or barren. The potential natural vegetation is, in order of decreasing elevation and ruggedness: scattered western spruce–fir forest, juniper woodland, Great Basin sagebrush and saltbush–greasewood. The region is internally drained by ephemeral streams and once contained ancient Lake Lahontan. In general, the Central Basin and Range is warmer and drier than the Northern Basin and Range and has more shrubland and less grassland than the Snake River Plain. Soils in this region grade upslope from mesic Aridisols to frigid Mollisols (see Soil Suborders, pages 150–151). The land is primarily used for grazing.

78. Klamath Mountains

The Klamath Mountain ecoregion is physically and biologically diverse. Highly dissected, folded mountains, foothills, terraces and floodplains occur and are underlain by igneous, sedimentary and some metamorphic rock. The mild, sub-humid climate of the Klamath Mountains is characterized by a lengthy summer drought. It supports a mix of Northern Californian and Pacific Northwest conifers.

80. Northern Basin and Range

This ecoregion consists of dissected lava plains, rolling hills, alluvial fans, valleys and scattered mountains. Mountains are less common in the west than in the east. Overall, it is higher and cooler than the Snake River Plain, it is drier and more suited to agriculture than the Columbia Plateau and it has fewer ranges than the Central Basin and Range. Sagebrush steppe is extensive. Juniper-dominated woodland occurs on rugged, stony uplands. Much of this region is used as rangeland. Generally all but the eastern third of the Oregon part of this ecoregion is internally drained.

Biotic Systems

Oregon's biotic systems reflect complex interactions of evolutionary factors with climate, geology, landforms, soils and living organisms. Both past and present human activities that affect the environment also significantly affect these systems. The closely related presentations of information in this portion of the *Atlas* illustrate Oregon's biotic systems in a number of ways.

Ecoregions, discussed on the facing page, are ecologically distinctive and homogeneous areas defined by climate, vegetation, landforms, soils and land use. The Ecoregions Legend on the facing page identifies important factors controlling biotic systems.

Vegetation, the total plant cover of an area, provides the basic framework for many kinds of biologically related mapping. The Vegetation map covers Oregon in four overlapping quadrants (see locator map below and pages 178–185). Information sources for this map include satellite imagery, aerial photography and field surveys. Oregon's plant cover is presented in 70 classes that describe vegetation cover types, often defined by dominant species. The number of classes shown on such a map depends in part on the scale at which information is being displayed. The classes shown here are a practical compromise, grouping similar but not identical types in order to show map units large enough to be legible, with a legend simple enough to be useful to non-specialists. Vegetation mapping issues are discussed below.

Wildlife habitat closely reflects vegetation distribution, since wildlife relies on vegetation for cover, food and reproductive needs. The Wildlife Habitat map was derived by analysis of 541 wildlife species and 119 types of habitat. The results are grouped in a single map showing 25 natural habitat types, representing about 85 percent of the state, and two "cultural habitat types," urban and agricultural. This small number of habitat types makes it possible to display small units legibly. The Wildlife Habitat map features requirements of wildlife species mostly defined by vegetation characteristics, while the Ecoregions map divides Oregon in an entirely different manner based on landforms and climate.

All three maps are closely related to vegetation mapping, which itself may be approached in various ways. Vegetation is an aggregation of diverse species with different growth forms, densities, compositional uniformity, spatial patterns, seasonal expressions and human uses. Any combination of these characteristics may be reflected in a given classification scheme. At a world scale, vegetation is usually classed on the basis of "physiognomy" or appearance, as forest, savanna, desert and so on. At the more detailed state scale, vegetation units may be defined by a combination of physiognomy and location—riparian forest, for example, or rimrock shrubland. Vegetation may also be classified by species composition, defined by various criteria. Among these are "dominance," the proportional area covered by a species. Dominance is frequently combined with physiognomic criteria—a ponderosa pine forest, an Oregon white oak savanna. Vegetation composition may also be keyed to "indicator species," a species that may be relatively minor but distinguishes one plant community from another—a Douglas-fir/oceanspray forest, a ponderosa pine/bitterbrush woodland.

Vegetation patterns are not fixed, but change over time. Vegetation mapping must take this into account. A mix of species mapped on the ground may be clearly in the process of changing: a cut-over area of alder and vine maple being overtopped by young Douglas-fir will probably become a Douglas-fir forest. But Douglas-fir will not regenerate in deep shade, though western hemlock will. Therefore in much of Western Oregon a mature Douglas-fir forest will tend eventually to be replaced by a western hemlock forest, unless forest fire, logging or blow-down intervene. Forest fires are a natural component of the environment, but human activity increases their frequency and also alters their intensity, with consequences for species composition and physiognomy. The Vegetation map portrays vegetation as it existed in the 1990s. For example, cut-over and burned areas are shown in their present state. Oregon white oak/Douglas-fir communities are classed according to present configurations, though in many cases the Douglas-fir will overtop and eventually shade out the oak. Grazed wetlands are shown as agricultural lands, because that is their present use. It is important to recognize that other species will be present (and perhaps locally dominant in some areas) and that the distinct boundaries mapped will probably be indistinct on the ground.

Vegetation Map Index

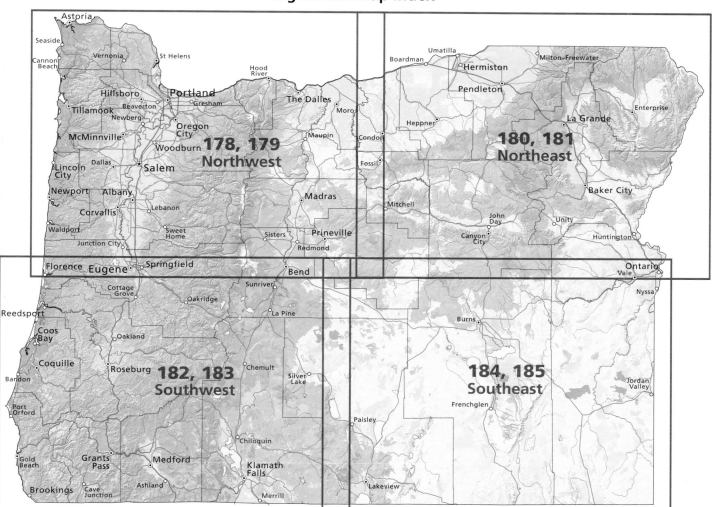

Scale 1:3,500,000

Vegetation Legend

Oregon's vegetation is organized here into 70 vegetation and land cover types. Many vegetation types are identified by dominant species; relative dominance within each community is indicated by the order of the names. For example, Douglas-fir is the predominant species in the map areas labeled Douglas-fir/Ponderosa/True Fir (dpf); Ponderosa Pine is predominant in areas labeled Ponderosa/Douglas-fir/True Fir (pdf). Botanical names are included for tree and important shrub species when first listed.

a **Alpine Barren Fell Fields**

Oregon's highest peaks and ridges, snow-covered most of the year, support low-growing alpine associations of herbaceous, dwarf shrub, cushion plant communities.

ag **Agriculture**

A land-use category; includes cultivated cropland and improved pasture. Livestock grazing is common in grassland communities and very widespread in many other vegetation types.

bb **Bitterbrush Scrub**

Bitterbrush (*Purshia tridentata*), a low shrub common in Ponderosa and Juniper types, is dominant at the Boardman Bombing Range and the Umatilla Army Depot in Morrow and northwest Umatilla Counties and in isolated small areas of northwestern Lake, northwestern Jefferson, southern Wheeler and northern Malheur Counties.

bp **Barren Playa**

Basin bottoms subject to intermittent flooding and mineral concentration from evaporation are characteristic of the Great Basin portions of southeastern Oregon.

bs **Big Sagebrush**

Big Sagebrush (*Artemisia tridentata*) covers more of the state than any other type. It is very widespread throughout the Great Basin portions of the state, as well as in the Snake River tributary drainages from the Powder River south. Western Juniper (*Juniperus occidentalis*), a great many grass species and other sage species are associated in the many communities grouped together here.

Built-up Area

A land-use category rather than a vegetation type.

Cutover/Burned

Areas of heavy recent logging or fires, or both. (Well-established second- and third-growth areas are not shown on the map; a satellite image of many stages of regrowth appears on page 93.) The rate and species composition of regrowth varies widely by community and site.

cg **Cleared Grasslands**

About 40 percent of the land in this type is dominated by Cheatgrass with Big Sagebrush, especially in Harney and Malheur Counties. Bluebunch Wheatgrass represents about 12 percent, mostly in central Malheur County. Annual grasses represent about 9 percent.

dd **Douglas-fir/Broadleaf Deciduous**

The Douglas-fir (*Pseudotsuga menziesii*)/Broadleaf Deciduous type occurs in drier and interior areas of the larger Douglas-fir/Western Hemlock region, and areas in the earlier successional stages of development toward "climax" Western Hemlock (*Tsuga heterophylla*) dominance. Significant broadleaf species include Red Alder (*Alnus rubra*) and Bigleaf Maple (*Acer macrophyllum*) in wetter sites, and Oregon White Oak (*Quercus garryana*), Madrone (*Arbutus menziesii*) and Tanoak (*Lithocarpus densiflorus*) on drier sites.

dh **Douglas-fir/Western Hemlock**

The Douglas-fir/Western Hemlock type is the most widespread in Western Oregon, and the most heavily logged. Douglas-fir dominates after clearing (disturbance by logging, fire or blowdown); shade-tolerant Western Hemlock eventually (over centuries) takes over in undisturbed moist sites. Communities generally include Grand Fir (*Abies grandis*) as an occasional component. Red Alder and Bigleaf Maple are important along watercourses. Coast Redwood (*Sequoia sempervirens*) is found very locally within this type, only in the extreme southwest corner of the state.

do **Douglas-fir/Oregon White Oak**

A combination of Douglas-fir and Oregon White Oak is typical of Western Oregon valley margins. Both are relatively fire tolerant; their dominance in part reflects the historic frequency of fire clearing in the valleys. Douglas-fir will eventually shade out and replace the oaks in most settings in the northern parts of Western Oregon.

dpf **Douglas-fir/Ponderosa/True Fir**

Douglas-fir, Ponderosa Pine (*Pinus ponderosa*) and true fir are widespread and occur in scattered mid-elevation mountain settings of the Cascade crest, from Mt. Hood to the southern Cascades and the southern Warner Range. It is widely scattered in the northeast quarter of the state. Western Larch (*Larix occidentalis*) makes an occasional appearance in Eastern Oregon.

dpi **Douglas-fir/Ponderosa/Incense Cedar**

Incense Cedar (*Calocedrus decurrens*) is widely scattered through the Cascades and Siskiyous on drier sites, but occurs as a co-dominant species (with Douglas-fir and Ponderosa Pine) only on the lower slopes of the Warner Mountains.

fd **True Fir/Douglas-fir**

Two large blocks of this association dominate Yamsey Mountain and Gearhart Mountain (both on the Klamath–Lake County line). These are relatively cool, wet islands rising from drier low country dominated by Ponderosa Pine.

fl **True Fir/Lodgepole**

Lodgepole Pine (*Pinus contorta*), a fire-successional species, is typically succeeded by shade-tolerant true firs, which eventually overtop Lodgepole. The dominant species is an indicator of time passed since the last major disturbance.

flw **True Fir/Lodgepole/Western Larch/Douglas-fir**

Large areas of this association are found southeast of Mt. Hood and in the Blue Mountains; smaller pockets occur on the east side of the central Cascade peaks. Western Larch is an indicator of past fire and disappears after about 100 years.

fsp **Subalpine Fir/Engelmann Spruce Parklands**

The highest forest zone in the Wallowas, the Elkhorns and the Strawberry Mountains. The Subalpine Fir (*Abies lasciocarpa*) and Engelmann Spruce (*Picea engelmannii*) type is the western outlier of a formation widespread in the Rockies.

g/gb **Grasslands/Bunchgrass**

Nearly 40 percent is a combination of Bluebunch Wheatgrass/Idaho Fescue/Sandberg's Bluegrass, in eastern Morrow and western Umatilla Counties and along the Snake River; a quarter in Idaho Fescue/Junegrass, typically upslope from the former community.

h **Mountain Hemlock**

Mountain Hemlock (*Tsuga mertensiana*) is the dominant species of the higher Cascade Range from the slopes of Mt. Hood to the California border. North of Willamette Pass it often is found in nearly pure stands, and with Whitebark Pine (*Pinus albicaulis*). Variants at timberline, and south and east of Willamette Pass, are defined below.

hf **Mountain Hemlock/Red Fir**

A Mountain Hemlock/Red Fir (*Abies magnifica* var. *shastensis*) community predominates along the Cascade crest south of Three Sisters to Aspen Butte west of Klamath Lake. This is a northern extension of a California complex. Douglas-fir, Western White Pine (*Pinus monticola*) and White Fir (*Abies concolor*) may be present.

hfl **Mountain Hemlock/Red Fir/Lodgepole**

Lodgepole Pine joins the Western Hemlock/Red Fir association south of Three Sisters, predominantly, though not exclusively, on the eastern side of the Cascade crest, with an eastern outlier on Newberry Crater south of Bend.

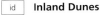 **Mountain Hemlock/Parklands**

The highest-elevation tree group in the Cascades. Subalpine Fir, Whitebark Pine and Mountain Hemlock are present in characteristic open parklands. At the highest elevations all three species appear as dwarf scrub. Whitebark Pine is almost always found not in association with Mountain Hemlock, but on ridges above parkland.

id **Inland Dunes**

Unvegetated active dunes.

jb **Juniper/Bitterbrush**

Bitterbrush is an important feature of the Ponderosa forests on the east side of the Cascades; it is co-dominant with Western Juniper at slightly lower elevations in Wasco, Jefferson and Deschutes Counties.

jg **Juniper/Grasslands**

Juniper/Grassland communities are found along with the various Juniper/Sage types throughout Central and Eastern Oregon. The varying influences of fire and of livestock grazing versus deer browsing and antelope grazing may determine which community becomes dominant in any given period.

jl **Juniper/Low Sage**

Low Sagebrush (*Artemisia arbuscula*) is widespread in Central and southeastern Oregon, both as a dominant species and in association with Western Juniper.

jm **Juniper/Mountain Big Sage**

This variant of the Juniper/Sage association, in which Mountain Big Sage (*Artemisia tilesii*) replaces Big Sagebrush, is typically intermediate in elevation between Juniper/Big Sage and Ponderosa.

jp **Juniper/Ponderosa**

Both trees are common at the margins of grasslands and sage communities. They occur as dominants in the "Lost Forest" north of Christmas Lake Valley.

js **Juniper/Big Sage**

Western Juniper has the lowest moisture requirement of any Oregon tree species. It dominates the forest/open country margins of Central Oregon, in association with grasses or with various sage species. Juniper/Big Sagebrush is especially dominant in Deschutes, Jefferson and Crook Counties.

l **Lodgepole**

Lodgepole Pine is widespread in its "genetically differentiated contorted" Shore Pine form along the coast, but is never dominant. It displays a very different form in the Cascades and to the east, where it is widespread in many communities and dominant in several. Lodgepole comes in after fire, commonly in dense, even-aged stands, with the characteristic straight, slender form that gives the tree its common name. The interior type comes in after fire.

lf **Lodgepole/True Fir**

This type is found west of the Elkhorns near the headwaters of the North Fork of the John Day River. The general successional sequence suggests that the fir (in this case, Grand or White Fir) will slowly replace Lodgepole.

ls **Low Sagebrush**

Low Sagebrush is second only to Big Sagebrush in the extent of its dominance in southeast Oregon.

lv sl **Open Lava, Sage on Lava**

The short snow-free growing season of the Cascades leaves recent Cascade lava flows virtually bare except for lichen and widely dispersed trees. Lower elevation flows, appearing in a diagonal strip across Central and Eastern Oregon, are typically colonized by sagebrush. In the Cascades, isolated Mountain Hemlock and Douglas-fir and, interestingly, Vine Maple (*Acer circinatum*), are scattered among the lava blocks. Ponderosa Pine is scattered farther to the east.

lw   **Lodgepole / Western Larch**

This type appears in small areas of the Wallowas and in the Blue Mountains north and west of the Elkhorns. It is a variant of wdp and wdf, typically but not always at higher elevations than either. Both species are seral, for a time dominating in areas which may be expected to be taken over by Grand Fir.

m   **Marsh / Wet Meadow**

The most widespread communities are alkaline grasslands and seasonal wetlands of Lake and Harney Counties, followed by Bullrush / Cattail / Burreed marshes in Klamath, Lake and Harney County depressions. Widely scattered mountain meadows dominated by Sedge and Tufted Hairgrass are also prominent in this category.

mb   **Manzanita / Buckbrush Chaparral**

Manzanita (*Arctostaphylos viscida*) and Buckbrush (*Ceanothus cuneatus*) are widely distributed as a shrub layer under open conifer overstories. As a dominant type, they are found in a few small pockets on the upper Illinois River in Josephine County.

mbs   **Mountain Big Sage**

The dominant species at mid-elevations in northwestern Malheur County, and in scattered locations around southeast Oregon.

ms   **Montane Shrublands**

Widely scattered in Central and Eastern Oregon, these communities reach their greatest extent in Hells Canyon on the Snake River, on the southern margins of the Grande Ronde Valley and on Steens Mountain. The principal dominants are Mountain Mahogany (*Cerocarpus betuloides* and *C. ledifolius*), Snowberry (*Symphoricarpos alba*) and Serviceberry (*Amelanchier alnifolia*).

od   **Oregon White Oak / Douglas-fir**

Oak dominates on drier sites in the central and southern Willamette, Umpqua and Rogue Valleys. Ponderosa Pine and Incense Cedar are often present.

om   **Oregon White Oak / Pacific Madrone**

Madrone is an important component of this White Oak / Douglas-fir variant. This type is commonly found at lower elevations in the Rogue and Umpqua Valleys, but also occurs locally north to the Columbia River and beyond.

op   **Oregon White Oak / Ponderosa**

This variant of the White Oak / Douglas-fir and White Oak / Madrone types is found in drier settings in the Rogue and Chetco River drainages in southwest Oregon, and also between Mt. Hood and the Deschutes River in Wasco County. Incense Cedar may be present; all are adapted to frequent low-intensity fires.

os   **Other Sagebrush**

Oregon is home to nine sagebrush species, in addition to the three widespread dominants noted above. Of these, Three-Tipped (*Artemisia tripartita*), Stiff (*A. rigida*) and Silver (*A. cana*) Sages are locally dominant in small areas throughout southeast Oregon. The largest area is in southern Crook County.

p   **Ponderosa**

Large areas of forests composed almost entirely of Ponderosa Pine extend the length of the state along the eastern slopes of the Cascades and are very widespread at lower and mid-elevations in the mountains of Central and northeast Oregon. The typical open "parkland" forest seen in historical photographs was largely the result of frequent fires set by Indians; fire suppression has promoted the present shift to much denser stands.

pdf   **Ponderosa / Douglas-fir / True Fir**

Found from Willamette Pass north to the Columbia River and throughout the mountains of northeast Oregon, typically higher in elevation than the neighboring pdw type.

pdw   **Ponderosa / Douglas-fir / Western Larch / Lodgepole**

This is a very widespread type at lower to mid-elevations on the eastern slopes of the northern Cascades, in the Ochocos, Blue Mountains and Wallowas, as far south as the Baker–Malheur County line. Western Larch is a minor and scattered component.

pg   **Ponderosa / Grasslands**

A mosaic, comparable to the Ponderosa / Shrub type ps found alongside that type in the Blue Mountains, and especially in the Grande Ronde and Imnaha River drainages in the northeast corner of the state.

pl   **Ponderosa / Lodgepole**

A combination of Ponderosa and Lodgepole Pine, often alternating in a sharply differentiated mosaic, covers much of the high country from Chemult to Bend. Ponderosa will overtop and eventually shade out Lodgepole in most settings. It apparently is kept in check here by the latter's advantages in pumice and in low areas where both water and very cold air pool.

po   **Ponderosa / White Oak**

Both species are widespread, as dominants and in association with many others. This combination is highly localized southwest of The Dalles.

pp   **Ponderosa on Pumice**

Ponderosa stands on immature pumice soils are characterized by low plant cover. The associated low shrub layer is dominated by Bitterbrush, Green Manzanita (*Arctostaphylos patula*), Snowbush (*Ceanothus velutinus*) and Buckbrush.

ps   **Ponderosa / Shrub**

Shrubs (Bitterbrush, Manzanita, Sage) are commonly present in the Ponderosa forests described above. The Ponderosa / Shrub type as mapped, along the lower northwest slopes of the Blue Mountains, is a mosaic of alternating forest and shrub communities.

qa   **Quaking Aspen**

This distinctive tree is widely scattered on the eastern slope of the Cascades, although it occurs rarely west of the crest. Quaking Aspen (*Populus tremuloides*) occurs as a dominant species only on Steens Mountain and southwest of Silver Lake.

rb   **Pasture / Riparian Bottomlands**

Oregon Ash (*Fraxinus latifolia*) and Black Cottonwood (*Populus trichocarpa*) dominate. Big Leaf Maple and Oregon White Oak are often present, with Ponderosa Pine on drier sites. River and stream bottomlands have been heavily farmed and grazed since the earliest White settlement. There is some pasturage, but not much. Oregon White Oak is a rare component (on drier sites), while some Oregon Ash is common.

rc/rw   **Cottonwood / Willow Riparian**

Black Cottonwood dominates most river bottomlands of Western Oregon valleys in association with Black Hawthorne (*Crataegus douglasii*) and Oregon Ash. (Oregon Ash is often locally dominant along the Columbia River.) Willow communities are found mostly in floodplains in Central and Eastern Oregon.

rs   **Rimrock Shrublands**

Sage species are prominent but combine with a number of other shrubs. Rimrock and the steep talus slopes below have extremely localized microclimates and moisture availability, supporting unusually diverse communities.

s   **Sitka Spruce**

Sitka Spruce (*Picea sitchensis*) is dominant within the range shown, especially near the ocean in sites exposed to intense wind and fog. It occurs generally on lower ocean-facing slopes, on north-facing slopes and in valley bottoms. Western Hemlock and Douglas-fir are intermixed throughout the inland portions of this type, and are often locally dominant.

sc   **Scrub**

Black Greasewood (*Sarcobatus vermiculatus*) and Shadscale (*Atriplex confertifolia*) tolerate both high salinity and alkali conditions, which will support few other species. Scrub communities dominated by these species cover large areas at the margins of fluctuating lakes and other basins throughout southeast Oregon.

sch   **Siskiyou Mixed Conifer (High Elevation)**

The higher-elevation variant of the Siskiyou Mixed Conifer type is dominated by White Fir, with lower percentages of Douglas-fir, Sugar (*Pinus lambertiana*), Ponderosa and Western White Pine. Lodgepole Pine appears in the Cascade Range areas of this type. Shasta Red Fir (*Abies magnifica shastensis*) appears at the highest elevations.

sf   **Silver Fir / Western Hemlock / Noble Fir**

The Silver Fir (*Abies amabilis*) / Western Hemlock / Noble Fir (*A. procera*) type occurs as far south as the Rogue–Umpqua Divide but is more common north of Willamette Pass and most extensive in the headwaters of the Clackamas and Warm Springs Rivers, south of Mt. Hood. It is intermediate between the Douglas-fir / Western Hemlock forests (at lower elevations in the Cascades) and the Mountain Hemlock which dominates the crest of the range.

sh   **Shorelands**

Includes coastal sand dunes, spits and beaches. Inland assemblages include dense shrub communities and Shore Pine (*Pinus contorta contorta*).

sm   **Saltmarsh**

Tidal areas dominated by Pickleweed, Sedge, Tufted Hairgrass, Rush and other herbaceous species often abruptly change to moist conifer forest above tidal influences.

smc   **Siskiyou Mixed Conifer**

The dominant type in eastern Curry, Josephine and Jackson Counties, where it occurs as the northernmost extension of California Coast Range and Sierra Nevada / Cascades vegetation formations. Douglas-fir, Sugar Pine, Ponderosa Pine, Incense Cedar and White Fir are abundant. Bigleaf Maple, Madrone and Western White Pine are common; Western Hemlock and Western Red Cedar (*Thuja plicata*) are found in wetter sites.

sme   **Siskiyou Mixed Evergreen**

A lower-elevation variant of the Siskiyou Mixed Conifer type, with a larger proportion of broadleaf trees. Madrone and Tanoak are common.

sp   **Siskiyou Jeffrey Pine**

Jeffrey Pine (*Pinus jeffreyi*) resembles Ponderosa but grows on serpentine soils with high magnesium, nickel and chromium content, which few species tolerate. On drier sites this type is distinctively open, with sparse grass cover. Higher sites include Douglas-fir, Incense Cedar and Knobcone (*Pinus attenuata*), Sugar and Western White Pine. This type appears widely within the area shown on the map, interspersed with Siskiyou Mixed Conifer (smc).

sl   **Subalpine Lodgepole**

Lodgepole forests are scattered along the crest of the Cascades. Lodgepole is a pioneer species after disturbance, but also thrives in poorly drained and very coarse soils (especially pumice), which discourage competing species.

ss   **Big Sage / Scrub**

An association of Big Sagebrush with Bitterbrush, or, less frequently, Squawapple (*Peraphyllum ramosissimum*), is dominant over significant areas on the Powder and Burnt River drainages.

wdf   **Western Larch / Douglas-fir / True Fir**

This type occurs in the Blue Mountains and Wallowas, northwest and southeast of Elgin, north of La Grande. The Western Larch is a relatively minor and rare component.

wdp   **Western Larch / Douglas-fir / Ponderosa / Lodgepole**

The deciduous conifer Western Larch appears along the eastern slope of the Cascades as a minor species in association with Douglas-fir, true fir, Ponderosa and Lodgepole Pine. The Larch-dominated association of all four species is found in large blocks in the Blue Mountains and also dominates the lower slopes of the Wallowas.

177

Vegetation: Northwest

Expanded legend is on pages 176–177

a	Alpine Barren Fell Fields
ag	Agriculture
bb	Bitterbrush Scrub
bp	Barren Playa
bs	Big Sagebrush
	Built-up Area
	Cutover/Burned
cg	Cleared Grasslands
dd	Douglas-fir/Broadleaf Deciduous
dh	Douglas-fir/Western Hemlock
do	Douglas-fir/Oregon White Oak
dpf	Douglas-fir/Ponderosa/True Fir
dpi	Douglas-fir/Ponderosa/Incense Cedar
fd	True Fir/Douglas-fir
fl	True Fir/Lodgepole
flw	True Fir/Lodgepole/Western Larch/Douglas-fir
fsp	Subalpine Fir/Englemann Spruce Parklands
g/gb	Grasslands/Bunchgrass
h	Mountain Hemlock
hf	Mountain Hemlock/Red Fir
hfl	Mountain Hemlock/Red Fir/Lodgepole
hp	Mountain Hemlock/Parklands
id	Inland Dunes
jb	Juniper/Bitterbrush
jg	Juniper/Grasslands
jl	Juniper/Low Sage
jm	Juniper/Mountain Big Sage
jp	Juniper/Ponderosa
js	Juniper/Big Sage
l	Lodgepole
lf	Lodgepole/True Fir
ls	Low Sagebrush
lv sl	Open Lava, Sage on Lava
lw	Lodgepole/Western Larch
m	Marsh/Wet Meadow
mb	Manzanita/Buckbrush Chaparral
ms	Montane Shrublands
od	Oregon White Oak/Douglas-fir
mbs	Mountain Big Sage
om	Oak/Pacific Madrone Forest and Woodland
op	Oak/Ponderosa
os	Other Sagebrush
p	Ponderosa
pdf	Ponderosa/Douglas-fir/True Fir
pdw	Ponderosa/Douglas-fir/Western Larch/Lodgepole
pg	Ponderosa/Grasslands
pl	Ponderosa/Lodgepole
po	Ponderosa/White Oak
pp	Ponderosa on Pumice
ps	Ponderosa/Shrub
qa	Quaking Aspen
rb	Pasture/Riparian Bottomlands
rc/rw	Cottonwood/Willow Riparian
rs	Rimrock Shrublands
s	Sitka Spruce
sc	Scrub
sch	Siskiyou Mixed Conifer (High Elevation)
sf	Silver Fir/Western Hemlock/Noble Fir
sh	Shorelands
sm	Saltmarsh
sme	Siskiyou Mixed Conifer
smc	Siskiyou Mixed Evergreen
sp	Siskiyou Jeffrey Pine
sl	Subalpine Lodgepole
ss	Big Sage/Shrub
wdf	Western Larch/Douglas-fir/True Fir
wdp	Western Larch/Doug-fir/Ponderosa/Lodgepole

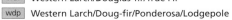

SCALE 1:850,000

MILES

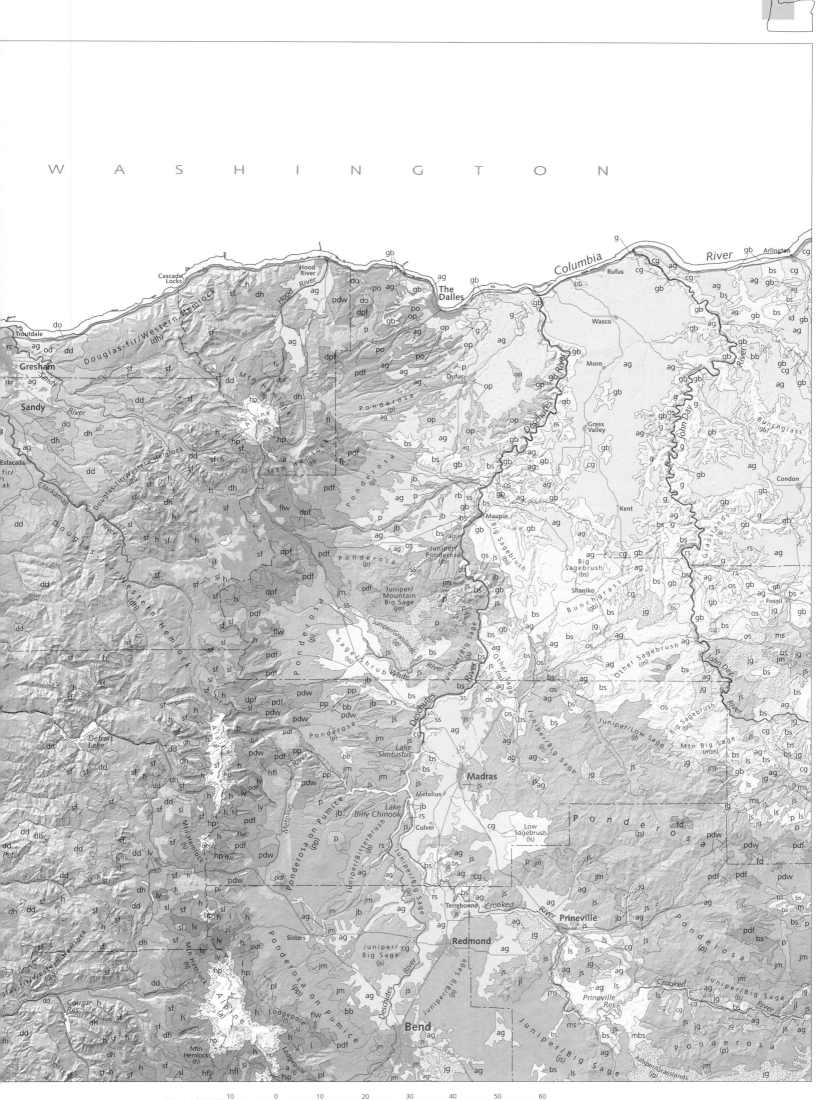

SCALE 1:850,000

10 0 10 20 30 40

MILES

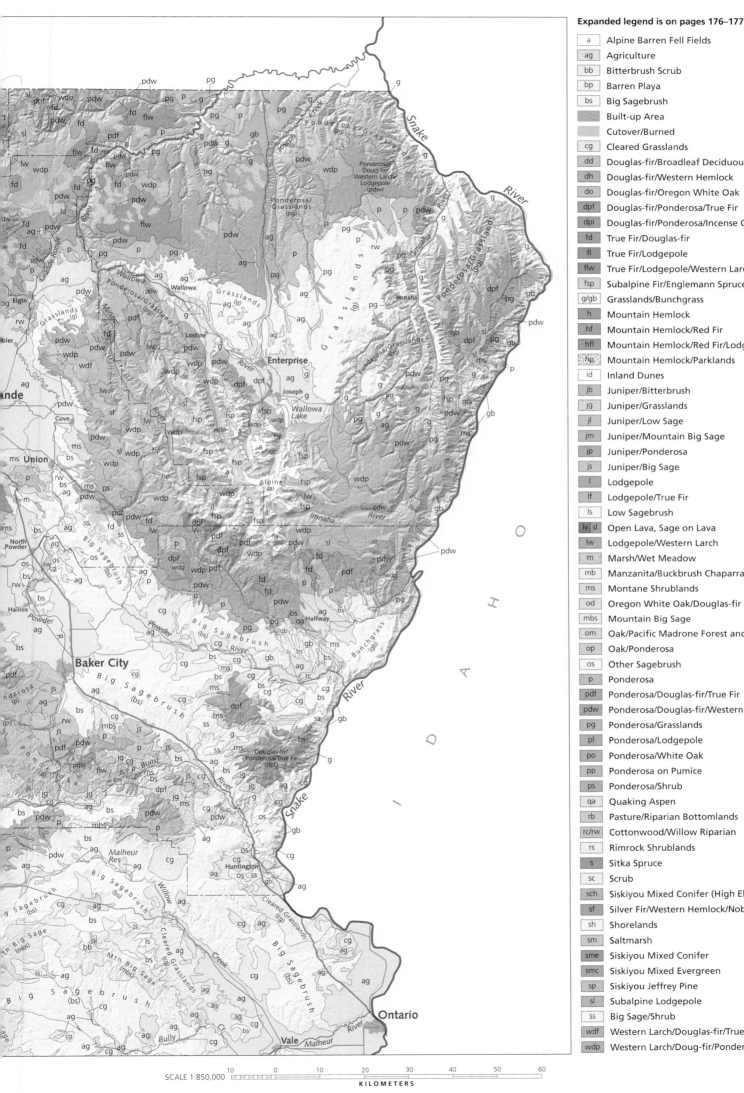

Expanded legend is on pages 176–177

a	Alpine Barren Fell Fields
ag	Agriculture
bb	Bitterbrush Scrub
bp	Barren Playa
bs	Big Sagebrush
	Built-up Area
	Cutover/Burned
cg	Cleared Grasslands
dd	Douglas-fir/Broadleaf Deciduous
dh	Douglas-fir/Western Hemlock
do	Douglas-fir/Oregon White Oak
dpf	Douglas-fir/Ponderosa/True Fir
dpi	Douglas-fir/Ponderosa/Incense Cedar
fd	True Fir/Douglas-fir
fl	True Fir/Lodgepole
flw	True Fir/Lodgepole/Western Larch/Douglas-fir
fsp	Subalpine Fir/Englemann Spruce Parklands
g/gb	Grasslands/Bunchgrass
h	Mountain Hemlock
hf	Mountain Hemlock/Red Fir
hfl	Mountain Hemlock/Red Fir/Lodgepole
hp	Mountain Hemlock/Parklands
id	Inland Dunes
jb	Juniper/Bitterbrush
jg	Juniper/Grasslands
jl	Juniper/Low Sage
jm	Juniper/Mountain Big Sage
jp	Juniper/Ponderosa
js	Juniper/Big Sage
l	Lodgepole
lf	Lodgepole/True Fir
ls	Low Sagebrush
lv sl	Open Lava, Sage on Lava
lw	Lodgepole/Western Larch
m	Marsh/Wet Meadow
mb	Manzanita/Buckbrush Chaparral
ms	Montane Shrublands
od	Oregon White Oak/Douglas-fir
mbs	Mountain Big Sage
om	Oak/Pacific Madrone Forest and Woodland
op	Oak/Ponderosa
os	Other Sagebrush
p	Ponderosa
pdf	Ponderosa/Douglas-fir/True Fir
pdw	Ponderosa/Douglas-fir/Western Larch/Lodgepole
pg	Ponderosa/Grasslands
pl	Ponderosa/Lodgepole
po	Ponderosa/White Oak
pp	Ponderosa on Pumice
ps	Ponderosa/Shrub
qa	Quaking Aspen
rb	Pasture/Riparian Bottomlands
rc/rw	Cottonwood/Willow Riparian
rs	Rimrock Shrublands
s	Sitka Spruce
sc	Scrub
sch	Siskiyou Mixed Conifer (High Elevation)
sf	Silver Fir/Western Hemlock/Noble Fir
sh	Shorelands
sm	Saltmarsh
sme	Siskiyou Mixed Conifer
smc	Siskiyou Mixed Evergreen
sp	Siskiyou Jeffrey Pine
sl	Subalpine Lodgepole
ss	Big Sage/Shrub
wdf	Western Larch/Douglas-fir/True Fir
wdp	Western Larch/Doug-fir/Ponderosa/Lodgepole

SCALE 1:850,000

10 0 10 20 30 40 50 60

KILOMETERS

Vegetation: Southwest

Expanded legend is on pages 176–177

a	Alpine Barren Fell Fields
ag	Agriculture
bb	Bitterbrush Scrub
bp	Barren Playa
bs	Big Sagebrush
	Built-up Area
	Cutover/Burned
cg	Cleared Grasslands
dd	Douglas-fir/Broadleaf Deciduous
dh	Douglas-fir/Western Hemlock
do	Douglas-fir/Oregon White Oak
dpf	Douglas-fir/Ponderosa/True Fir
dpi	Douglas-fir/Ponderosa/Incense Cedar
fd	True Fir/Douglas-fir
fl	True Fir/Lodgepole
flw	True Fir/Lodgepole/Western Larch/Douglas-fir
fsp	Subalpine Fir/Englemann Spruce Parklands
g/gb	Grasslands/Bunchgrass
h	Mountain Hemlock
hf	Mountain Hemlock/Red Fir
hfl	Mountain Hemlock/Red Fir/Lodgepole
hp	Mountain Hemlock/Parklands
id	Inland Dunes
jb	Juniper/Bitterbrush
jg	Juniper/Grasslands
jl	Juniper/Low Sage
jm	Juniper/Mountain Big Sage
jp	Juniper/Ponderosa
js	Juniper/Big Sage
l	Lodgepole
lf	Lodgepole/True Fir
ls	Low Sagebrush
lv sl	Open Lava, Sage on Lava
lw	Lodgepole/Western Larch
m	Marsh/Wet Meadow
mb	Manzanita/Buckbrush Chaparral
ms	Montane Shrublands
od	Oregon White Oak/Douglas-fir
mbs	Mountain Big Sage
om	Oak/Pacific Madrone Forest and Woodland
op	Oak/Ponderosa
os	Other Sagebrush
p	Ponderosa
pdf	Ponderosa/Douglas-fir/True Fir
pdw	Ponderosa/Douglas-fir/Western Larch/Lodgepole
pg	Ponderosa/Grasslands
pl	Ponderosa/Lodgepole
po	Ponderosa/White Oak
pp	Ponderosa on Pumice
ps	Ponderosa/Shrub
qa	Quaking Aspen
rb	Pasture/Riparian Bottomlands
rc/rw	Cottonwood/Willow Riparian
rs	Rimrock Shrublands
s	Sitka Spruce
sc	Scrub
sch	Siskiyou Mixed Conifer (High Elevation)
sf	Silver Fir/Western Hemlock/Noble Fir
sh	Shorelands
sm	Saltmarsh
sme	Siskiyou Mixed Conifer
smc	Siskiyou Mixed Evergreen
sp	Siskiyou Jeffrey Pine
sl	Subalpine Lodgepole
ss	Big Sage/Shrub
wdf	Western Larch/Douglas-fir/True Fir
wdp	Western Larch/Doug-fir/Ponderosa/Lodgepole

SCALE 1:850,000

MILES

SCALE 1:850,000

10   0   10   20   30   40   50   60

KILOMETERS

183

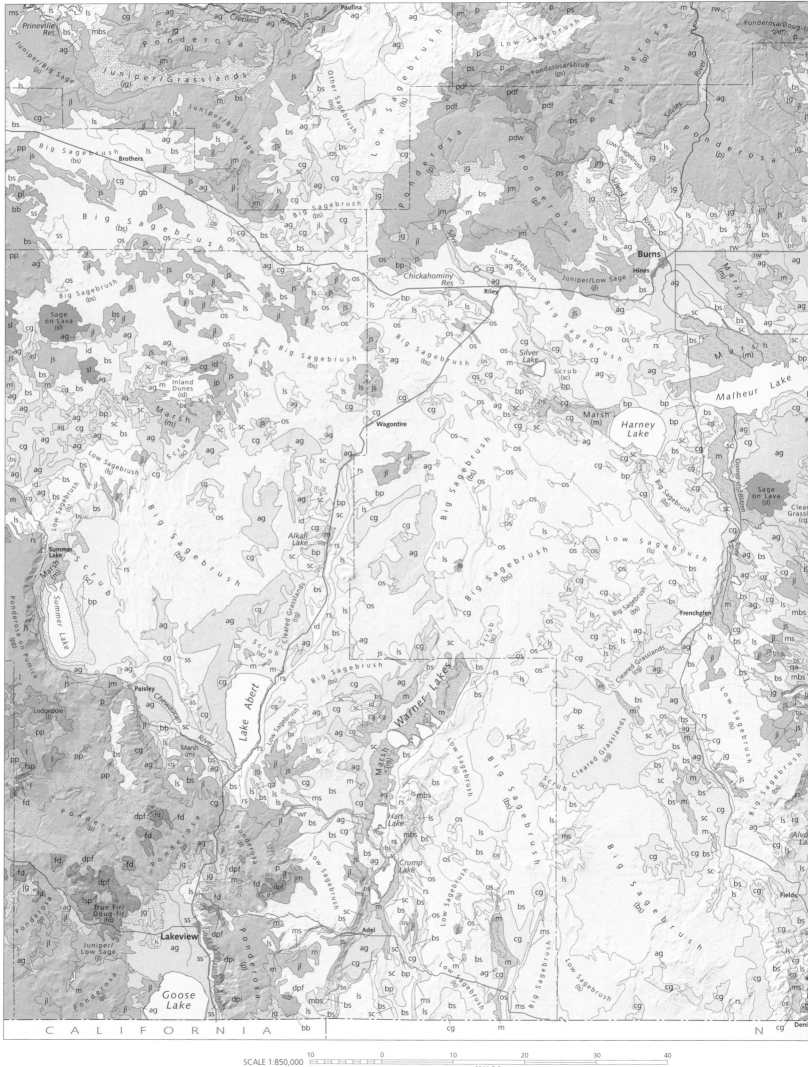

SCALE 1:850,000

10   0   10   20   30   40

MILES

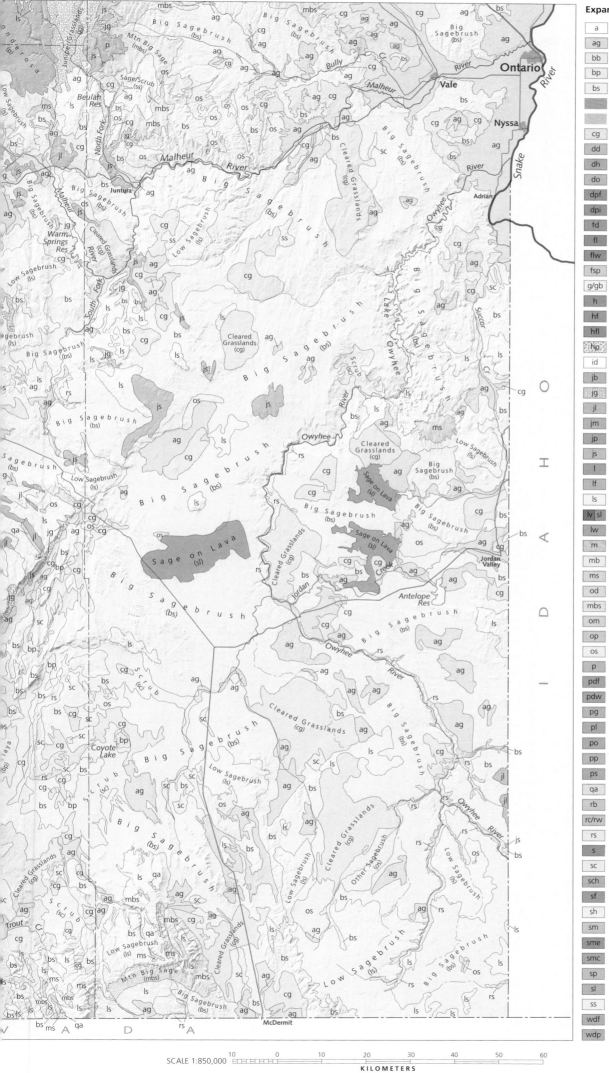
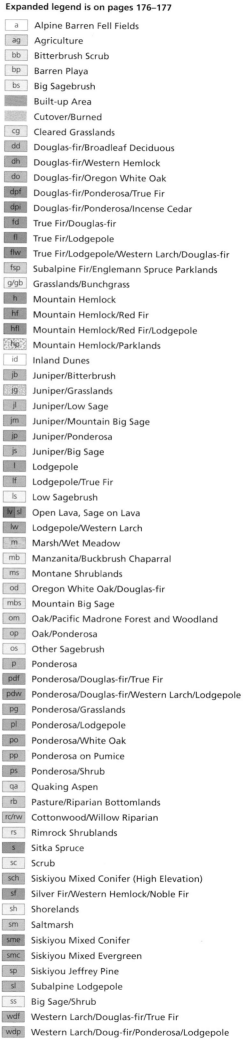

a	Alpine Barren Fell Fields
ag	Agriculture
bb	Bitterbrush Scrub
bp	Barren Playa
bs	Big Sagebrush
	Built-up Area
	Cutover/Burned
cg	Cleared Grasslands
dd	Douglas-fir/Broadleaf Deciduous
dh	Douglas-fir/Western Hemlock
do	Douglas-fir/Oregon White Oak
dpf	Douglas-fir/Ponderosa/True Fir
dpi	Douglas-fir/Ponderosa/Incense Cedar
fd	True Fir/Douglas-fir
fl	True Fir/Lodgepole
flw	True Fir/Lodgepole/Western Larch/Douglas-fir
fsp	Subalpine Fir/Englemann Spruce Parklands
g/gb	Grasslands/Bunchgrass
h	Mountain Hemlock
hf	Mountain Hemlock/Red Fir
hfl	Mountain Hemlock/Red Fir/Lodgepole
hp	Mountain Hemlock/Parklands
id	Inland Dunes
jb	Juniper/Bitterbrush
jg	Juniper/Grasslands
jl	Juniper/Low Sage
jm	Juniper/Mountain Big Sage
jp	Juniper/Ponderosa
js	Juniper/Big Sage
l	Lodgepole
lf	Lodgepole/True Fir
ls	Low Sagebrush
lv sl	Open Lava, Sage on Lava
lw	Lodgepole/Western Larch
m	Marsh/Wet Meadow
mb	Manzanita/Buckbrush Chaparral
ms	Montane Shrublands
od	Oregon White Oak/Douglas-fir
mbs	Mountain Big Sage
om	Oak/Pacific Madrone Forest and Woodland
op	Oak/Ponderosa
os	Other Sagebrush
p	Ponderosa
pdf	Ponderosa/Douglas-fir/True Fir
pdw	Ponderosa/Douglas-fir/Western Larch/Lodgepole
pg	Ponderosa/Grasslands
pl	Ponderosa/Lodgepole
po	Ponderosa/White Oak
pp	Ponderosa on Pumice
ps	Ponderosa/Shrub
qa	Quaking Aspen
rb	Pasture/Riparian Bottomlands
rc/rw	Cottonwood/Willow Riparian
rs	Rimrock Shrublands
s	Sitka Spruce
sc	Scrub
sch	Siskiyou Mixed Conifer (High Elevation)
sf	Silver Fir/Western Hemlock/Noble Fir
sh	Shorelands
sm	Saltmarsh
sme	Siskiyou Mixed Conifer
smc	Siskiyou Mixed Evergreen
sp	Siskiyou Jeffrey Pine
sl	Subalpine Lodgepole
ss	Big Sage/Shrub
wdf	Western Larch/Douglas-fir/True Fir
wdp	Western Larch/Doug-fir/Ponderosa/Lodgepole

SCALE 1:850,000

10   0   10   20   30   40   50   60
KILOMETERS

Wildlife Habitat

Westside Lowland Conifer–Hardwood Forest

Westside Oak/Douglas-fir Forest–Woodlands

SW Oregon Mixed Conifer–Hardwood Forest

Montane Mixed Conifer Forest

Eastside (Interior) Mixed Conifer Forest

Lodgepole Pine Forest and Woodlands

Ponderosa Pine/Eastside Oak Forest–Woodlands

Upland Aspen Forest

Subalpine Parklands

Alpine Grasslands and Shrublands

Ceanothus-Manzanita Shrublands

Western Juniper/Mountain Mahogany Woodlands

Eastside (Interior) Canyon Shrublands

Eastside (Interior) Grasslands

Shrub–Steppe

Dwarf Shrub-Steppe

Desert Playa and Salt Scrub

Agriculture, Pasture and Mixed Environs

Urban and Mixed Environs

Lakes, Rivers, Ponds and Reservoirs

Herbaceous Wetlands

Westside Riparian Wetlands

Montane Coniferous Wetlands

Eastside (Interior) Riparian Wetlands

Coastal Dunes and Beaches

Coastal Headlands and Islets

Bays and Estuaries

- - - - Indistinct Boundaries

A few habitat boundaries which are not clearly
defined on satellite imagery are shown here on
the basis of elevation (Montane Mixed Conifer
Forest) or are compiled from other sources and
drawn in as dotted lines.

Wildlife habitats are areas with the combination of necessary resources—water, food and shelter—and environmental conditions that allow a given species to survive and reproduce. Vegetation plays the key role in providing these basic biological needs. Major vegetation types, such as forests, shrublands, grasslands and wetlands, typically attract wildlife species uniquely adapted to survive in each of those particular environments. Other resident species may thrive in a range of habitat types. The plant and animal species that each of these major vegetation types support are the measure of its biological diversity; biological diversity is a critical element in maintaining viable ecosystems. This map defines 27 general habitat types, with local conditions within each providing a range of environments. The vegetation maps on pages 178–185 show more specifically defined vegetation groupings; this map illustrates the degree of interpenetration of different habitat types.

Wildlife Habitat Detail

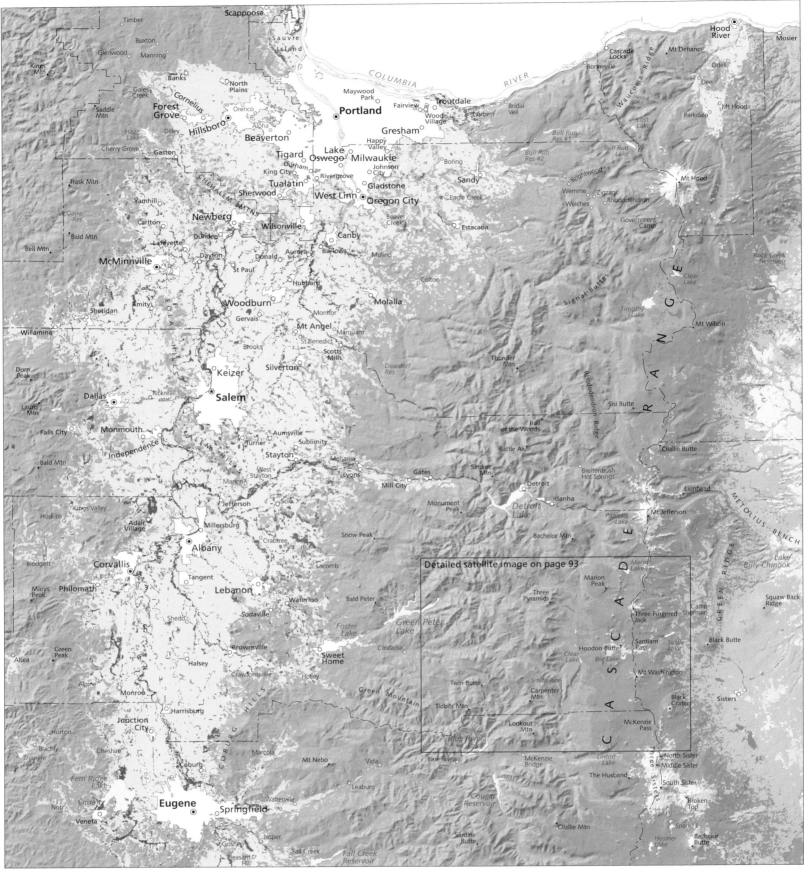

Westside Lowland Conifer–Hardwood Forest

Westside Oak/Douglas-fir Forest–Woodlands

SW Oregon Mixed Conifer–Hardwood Forest

Montane Mixed Conifer Forest

Eastside (Interior) Mixed Conifer Forest

Lodgepole Pine Forest and Woodlands

Ponderosa Pine/Eastside Oak Forest–Woodlands

Subalpine Parklands

Alpine Grasslands and Shrublands

Ceanothus–Manzanita Shrublands

Western Juniper/Mountain Mahogany Woodlands

Eastside (Interior) Grasslands

Shrub–Steppe

Dwarf Shrub–Steppe

Desert Playa and Salt Scrub

Agriculture, Pasture and Mixed Environs

Urban and Mixed Environs

Lakes, Rivers, Ponds and Reservoirs

Herbaceous Wetlands

Westside Riparian Wetlands

Montane Coniferous Wetlands

Eastside (Interior) Riparian Wetlands

MILES

KILOMETERS

SCALE 1:850,000

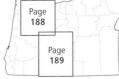

Page 188

Page 189

McKenzie
Bridge
Blue River
Cougar
Reservoir
Sardine Butte
Chucksney
Mtn
Moolack
Mtn
Irish Mtn
Koch Mtn
Waldo
Lake
Bunchgrass Ridge
The Twins
Juniper Ridge
Willamette
Pass
Diamond Peak
McGowan
Mtn
Sawtooth
Mtn
Lemolo
Lake
Diamond
Lake
Diamond
Lake
Mt Bailey
Mt Thielsen

The Husband
Three Sisters
North Sister
Middle Sister
South Sister
Broken Top
Hosmer
Lake
Sparks
Bachelor
Butte
Lava
Lake
Cultus
Lake
Sheridan
Mtn
Cultus
Mtn
Crane Prairie
Reservoir
Wickiup
Reservoir
Davis
Lake
Davis Mtn
Hamner
Butte
Odell
Lake
Crescent
Lake
Odell Butte
Crescent
Gilchrist
Crescent
Walker Rim
Miller
Lake
Chemult

Upper Tumalo
Res
Bend
Sunriver
Paulina
Mountains
Newberry Crater
La Pine

Badlands
Lava Beds
Pine Mtn
Brothers

MAURY MOUNTAINS
Antelope Flat
Reservoir
Hampton

Benjamin
Lake

FORT ROCK VALLEY
Fort Rock
Connley Hills
Christmas
Valley
CHRISTMAS LAKE
VALLEY

Paulina
Marsh
Silver Lake
Silver
Lake

CASCADE RANGE

Crater
Lake
Mt Scott
Devils Peak
Fourmile
Lake
Mt
McLoughlin
Fish
Lake
Lake of the
Woods
Aspen
Butte
Aspen
Lake

Klamath Marsh
Yamsay
Mtn
Thompson
Reservoir
Sycan
Marsh
SYCAN
FLAT
Summer
Lake
Summer
Lake
DIABLO RIM
WINTER RIDGE
COGLAN BUTTES
Lake Abert

Agency
Lake
Marsh
Fort
Klamath
Klamath
Agency
Agency Lake
Chiloquin
Pelican
Butte
Upper Klamath Lake
Medoc Rim
Klamath
Falls
Round
Lake
Altamont
Keno
Midland
Merrill

Sprague River Valley
Sprague
River
Muckney
Lake
Beatty
Swan Lake
Point
Swan
Lake
Whiteline
Res
Yainax
Butte
Bly
Campbell
Res
Gearhart
Mtn
Paisley
Upper
Chewaucam
Marsh
Lower
Chewaucam
Marsh

Dairy
Alkali
Lake
Bonanza
Mallory
Reservoir
Gerber
Reservoir
Cougar
Peak
Grizzly
Peak
Cottonwood
Reservoir
Lakeview
WARNER MOUNTAINS

Olene
Spring
Lake
Long Lake
Malin
LANGELL VALLEY
Willow Valley
Reservoir
Drews
Reservoir
Junipers
Reservoir
Strawberry
Reservoir
Dog
Lake
Renner
Lake
Goose
Lake
New Pine
Creek

189

Protected Areas

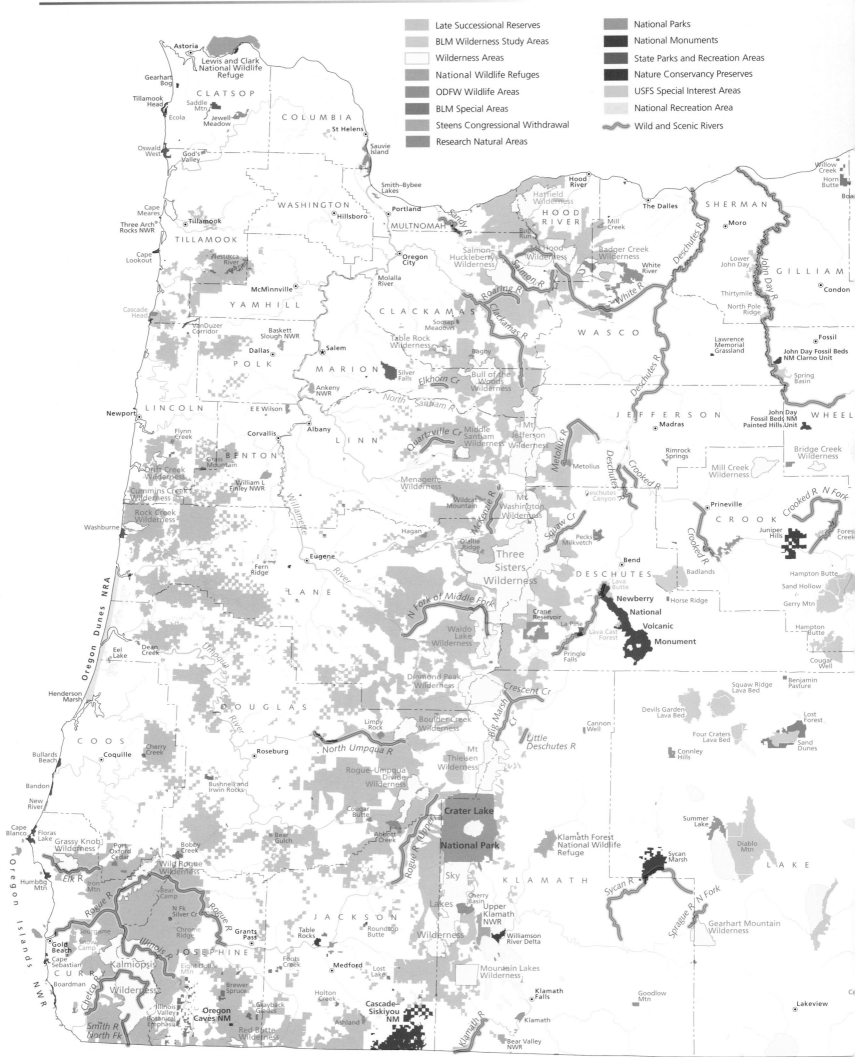

Legend:
- Late Successional Reserves
- BLM Wilderness Study Areas
- Wilderness Areas
- National Wildlife Refuges
- ODFW Wildlife Areas
- BLM Special Areas
- Steens Congressional Withdrawal
- Research Natural Areas
- National Parks
- National Monuments
- State Parks and Recreation Areas
- Nature Conservancy Preserves
- USFS Special Interest Areas
- National Recreation Area
- Wild and Scenic Rivers

This map shows lands managed primarily, or in large measure, for the protection of habitat. It does not include lands designated as parks or refuges but managed for other or multiple uses. Some small but significant municipal and county parks and most private preserves and watershed projects are not included, but the Nature Conservancy's preserves are shown.

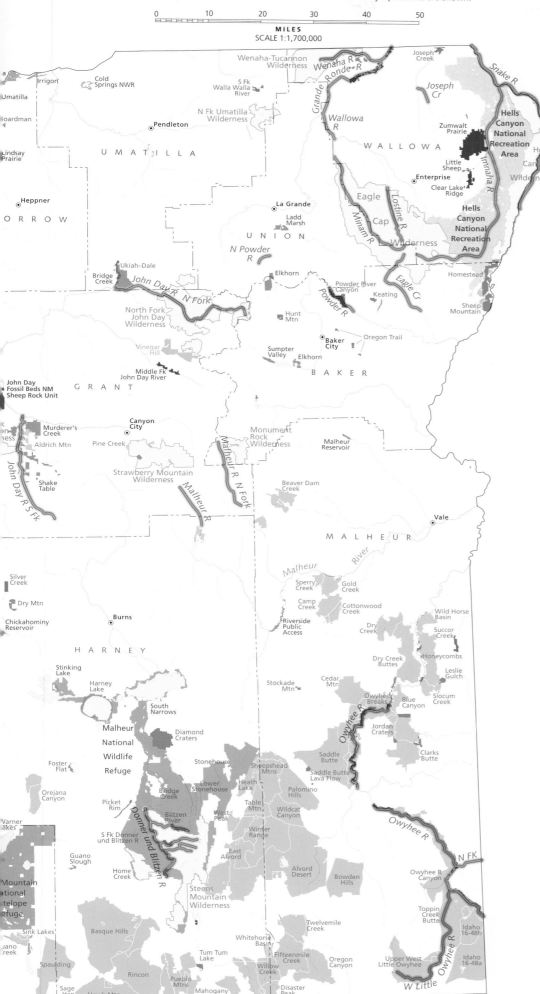

MILES
SCALE 1:1,700,000

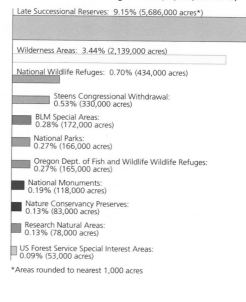

Protected Lands
15.18% of Total Oregon Area (62,132,185 acres)

Late Successional Reserves: 9.15% (5,686,000 acres*)

Wilderness Areas: 3.44% (2,139,000 acres)

National Wildlife Refuges: 0.70% (434,000 acres)

Steens Congressional Withdrawal: 0.53% (330,000 acres)

BLM Special Areas: 0.28% (172,000 acres)

National Parks: 0.27% (166,000 acres)

Oregon Dept. of Fish and Wildlife Wildlife Refuges: 0.27% (165,000 acres)

National Monuments: 0.19% (118,000 acres)

Nature Conservancy Preserves: 0.13% (83,000 acres)

Research Natural Areas: 0.13% (78,000 acres)

US Forest Service Special Interest Areas: 0.09% (53,000 acres)

*Areas rounded to nearest 1,000 acres

The protected areas mapped here afford varying levels of protection to the ecological systems and species found within them. Economic exploitation and human use of resources within these areas are limited to varying degrees. Designations on this map reflect the evolution of national sentiment and laws regarding the protection of natural systems. National Parks resulted from an early interest in reserving "scenic wonders" for public enjoyment. In 1902 President Theodore Roosevelt segregated Crater Lake National Park from the Cascade Forest Reserves, which were about to be opened to commercial logging, creating Oregon's first protected landscape. National Monuments, proclaimed by the President under the Antiquities Act of 1906 or legislated by Congress, historically protected geologic oddities and wonders as well as, most recently, ecological diversity. National Wildlife Refuges developed from early efforts to protect wildlife, preserve significant breeding grounds and maintain game stocks. Three Arch Rocks and Malheur National Wildlife Refuges, dating back to 1907 and 1908, are among the earliest in the country. State Parks acquired since the 1930s provided roadside scenery and recreation —the larger tracts shown here also include significant natural areas. Wilderness Areas, first designated in 1964, established a backcountry system of "cathedral" peaks and forests open to non-mechanized uses compatible with a "wilderness ethic"—an ideological bone of contention in Oregon, as elsewhere. Wilderness Study Areas provide interim protection for nearly three million acres that qualify for wilderness designation, mostly large roadless areas of shrub–steppe on the Oregon high desert. Late Successional Reserves (LSRs) are the state's largest protected designation. Beginning in 1994, the LSR system was comprehensively designed to protect large-scale ecosystems. The LSRs link Wilderness Areas, and extend toward lowland forests which would otherwise be isolated from higher-elevation natural systems. Other designations on the map constitute an array of representative natural ecosystems set aside for research and education, or unique habitats required to maintain special status species.

Reference Maps

Detailed Maps of the Entire State

Population Centers

Historic Growth

Sectional Maps

Population Centers Legend and Introduction

Legend

Maps are at a scale of 1:150,000.
1 inch equals approximately 2.4 miles on the ground.

Settlements

SALEM — Over 100,000 Population
Medford — 10,000 to 100,000
Philomath — 1,000 to 10,000
Monroe — Less Than 1,000
Buchanan — Locale, Site or Historic Place

✪ ◉ — State Capital, County Seats
○ — Incorporated
● — Unincorporated, Locale or Sites

Pop 52,215
1980 40,960
1960 20,669
1940 8,392

Populations for incorporated places are shown for 2000, 1980, 1960 and 1940. The figures for 2000 are estimates by the Center for Population Research. The U.S. Census figures for 2000, not available when these pages were prepared, are given for all cities on page 31.

Water Features

Rivers
Streams
Intermittent Streams
Canals
Cranberry Bogs
Lakes, Reservoirs
Intermittent Lakes
Marsh
Falls
Mill Ponds

Roads

Interstate
U.S. Highways
State Highways
Other Paved, Gravel or Dirt Roads
Railroads, Railroad Names

Boundaries

State Boundaries
POLK CO — County Boundaries, County Names
National Parks or Monuments
City Limits (black)
Urban Growth Boundaries (red)

Land Cover

Built-up Areas: Commercial/Industrial
Built-up Areas: Residential
Scattered Rural Settlement
Farmland
Forestlands
Wetlands
Cleared or Recently Cut
Barren

Other Symbols

Railroad Tunnel
Airports with Scheduled Service
Other Airports
246 — Airport Elevations in Feet
Dams, Peak Symbol, Pass
State Park Site
Courthouse, Hospital or Point of Interest
High School, College or University

Land Cover Explanation

The landcover categories shown in the Population Centers pages are similar, but not identical, to those described in the State Sectional Maps legend on the facing page. The differences in presentation are designed to make built-up areas, the focus of these pages, show up more clearly and legibly. **Commercial/Industrial** areas are large blocks of highly reflective surfaces, such as very large roofs, parking lots, freeway interchanges and roads with wide smooth shoulders. **Residential areas** are dense concentrations of smaller roofs; these may be masked by tall trees where urban and forested areas meet. **Farmland** is shown in lighter colors but is otherwise identical to the category on the Reference Maps. All **Forestlands** are shown in a single color. **Grassland** and **Shrubland** are not included at all, but grouped with **Barren** in a neutral background shading color. **Scattered Rural Settlement** is not derived from satellite imagery, which does not detect single buildings or small clusters of buildings. This category was compiled by hand from USGS 7.5' maps, most of them from 5 to 15 years old, a few as much as 25 years old. The pattern defines the areas where there are buildings within a few hundred yards, or less, of one another; the dots do not represent individual buildings.

Historic Growth Maps

Maps are at a scale of 1:333,333.
1 inch equals approximately 5 miles on the ground.

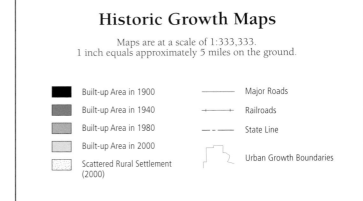

Built-up Area in 1900
Built-up Area in 1940
Built-up Area in 1980
Built-up Area in 2000
Scattered Rural Settlement (2000)

Major Roads
Railroads
State Line
Urban Growth Boundaries

The following 52 pages provide a close look at every one of Oregon's larger communities. All county seats and most other towns of significant size are mapped, including at least 95 percent of Oregon's population. These Population Centers maps are at a scale of 1:150,000—one inch equals nearly two and half miles on the ground. They combine satellite imagery (from 1993) of land cover with digital elevation models showing landforms; additional detail is taken from recent transportation and drainage data. These maps represent many decades of data collection by the U.S. Geological Survey (USGS).

The same sources are also used for the 24 pages of less-detailed Reference maps (see page 250), which immediately follow the Population Centers maps. The Reference maps cover the entire state in 12 overlapping two-page sections at a scale of 1:500,000—one inch equals about eight miles on the ground. The two map series are different both in scale and in emphasis, and are designed to complement one another. Population Centers maps include the corresponding Reference map page numbers.

The land-cover information presented is limited to what the satellite can detect—reflectance patterns, which must then be interpreted (see note on the facing page). A good way to learn to interpret these maps is by studying the map of an area you know well. The Population Centers maps also include a scattered rural settlement pattern. This is derived not from satellite data but from examination of USGS 1:24,000 quadrangle maps.

Finally, each of the Population Centers maps is accompanied by a smaller Historic Growth map (some of these maps cover more than one area and may be found on a separate page). Historic Growth maps show both the present extent of scattered settlement and the historic development of the built-up area in 1900, 1940, 1980 and 2000. These categories are based on historic maps, aerial photographs, street grid patterns, architectural styles and landscape plantings. All these sources record the expansion of dense settlement over time. The year 1980 marks the point when Oregon's land use controls began to limit expansion into outlying farmlands and forestlands. The continuous built-up area shown for 2000 generally corresponds to a density of about 5,000 people per square mile. This density may differ slightly from the satellite-derived "Built-up Area" on the corresponding Population Centers map, since the Historic Growth maps are based on information which is both more current and different in character. "Scattered Rural Settlement" covers a great range of densities, but includes all areas in which houses are typically within a few hundred yards of one another.

The Population Centers maps make it possible to visualize these places in their physical settings—to picture the farmlands, forests, rangelands or estuaries which border them, to grasp the extent and character of the places in a way which conventional road maps do not allow. The Historic Growth maps show the progress of development during the past century. Taken together they form a portrait of Oregon and provide a context for the social and economic topics which fill this atlas.

Population Centers Index

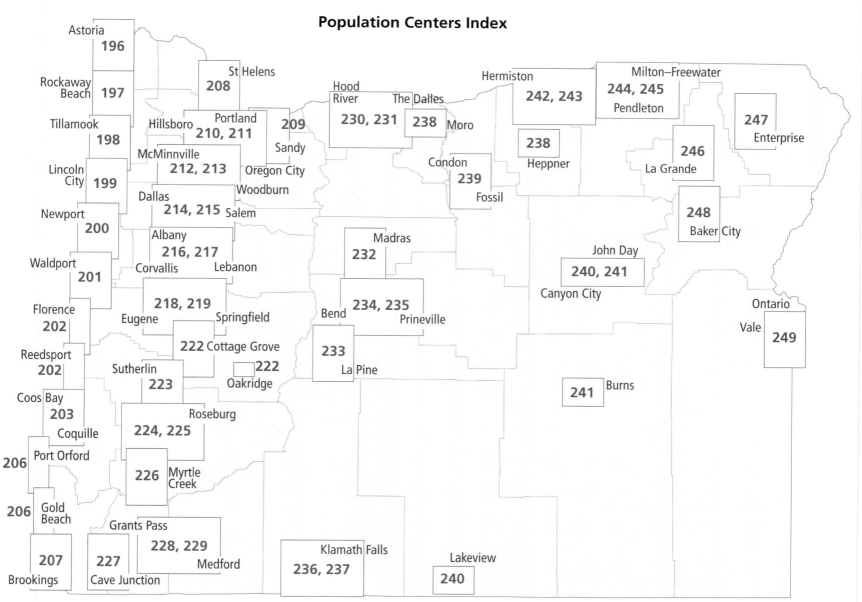

Scale 1:3,000,000

Astoria; Rockaway Beach

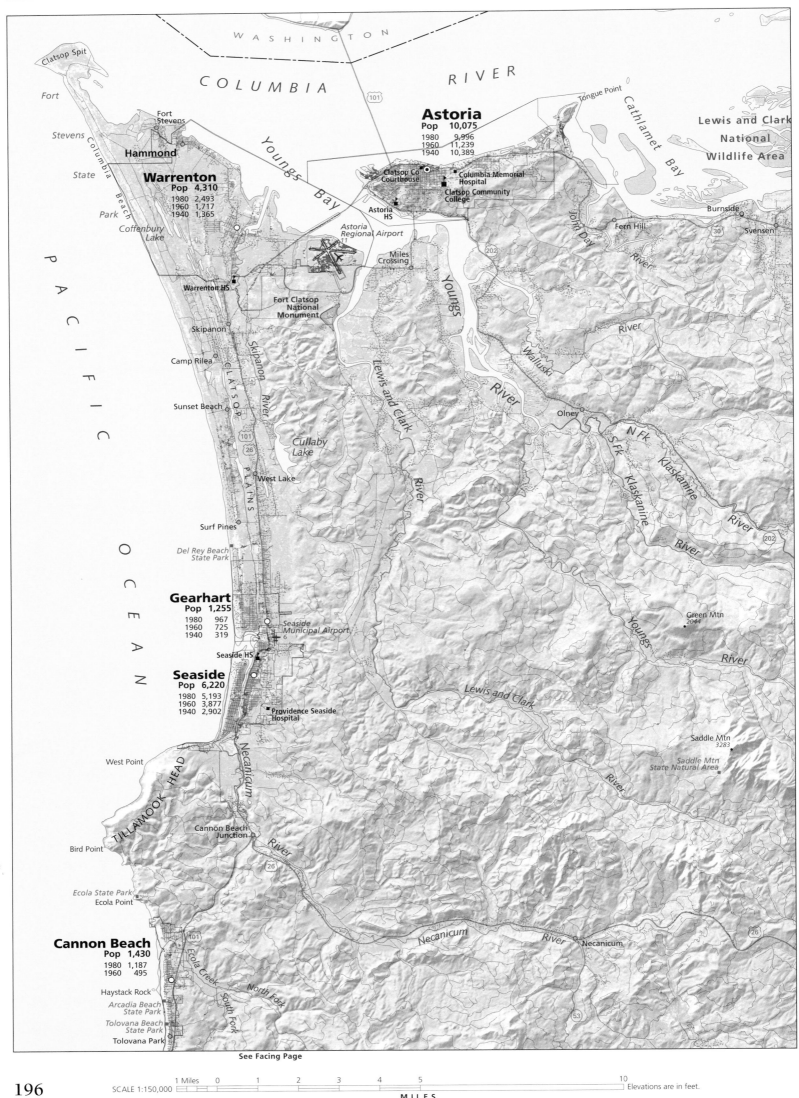

WASHINGTON

COLUMBIA RIVER

Clatsop Spit

Fort

Stevens

State

Fort
Stevens

Hammond

Warrenton
Pop 4,310

1980 2,493
1960 1,717
1940 1,365

Columbia Beach

Park

Coffenbury Lake

Youngs Bay

Astoria
Pop 10,075

1980 9,996
1960 11,239
1940 10,389

Clatsop Co
Courthouse

Columbia Memorial
Hospital

Clatsop Community
College

Astoria
HS

*Astoria
Regional Airport*
11

Tongue Point

Cathlamet Bay

Lewis and Clark
National
Wildlife Area

Burnside

Fern Hill

Svensen

30

John Day River

Warrenton HS

Skipanon

Camp Rilea

Sunset Beach

*Fort Clatsop
National
Monument*

Miles
Crossing

Youngs

Lewis and Clark

River

Youngs River

Waluski

202

Skipanon River

CLATSOP

PLAINS

*Cullaby
Lake*

West Lake

Surf Pines

*Del Rey Beach
State Park*

Olney

N Fk

S Fk

Klaskanine

Klaskanine River

River

202

Gearhart
Pop 1,255

1980 967
1960 725
1940 319

*Seaside
Municipal Airport*
6

Seaside HS

Seaside
Pop 6,220

1980 5,193
1960 3,877
1940 2,902

Providence Seaside
Hospital

Green Mtn
2044

Youngs

River

Lewis and Clark

River

P A C I F I C

O C E A N

West Point

TILLAMOOK HEAD

Necanicum River

Saddle Mtn
3283

*Saddle Mtn
State Natural Area*

Bird Point

Cannon Beach
Junction

River

Ecola State Park
Ecola Point

Necanicum

River

Necanicum

26

Cannon Beach
Pop 1,430

1980 1,187
1960 495

Haystack Rock

*Arcadia Beach
State Park*

*Tolovana Beach
State Park*

Tolovana Park

101

Ecola Creek

North Fork

South Fork

53

See Facing Page

1 Mile 0   1   2   3   4   5   10

SCALE 1:150,000   Elevations are in feet.

M I L E S

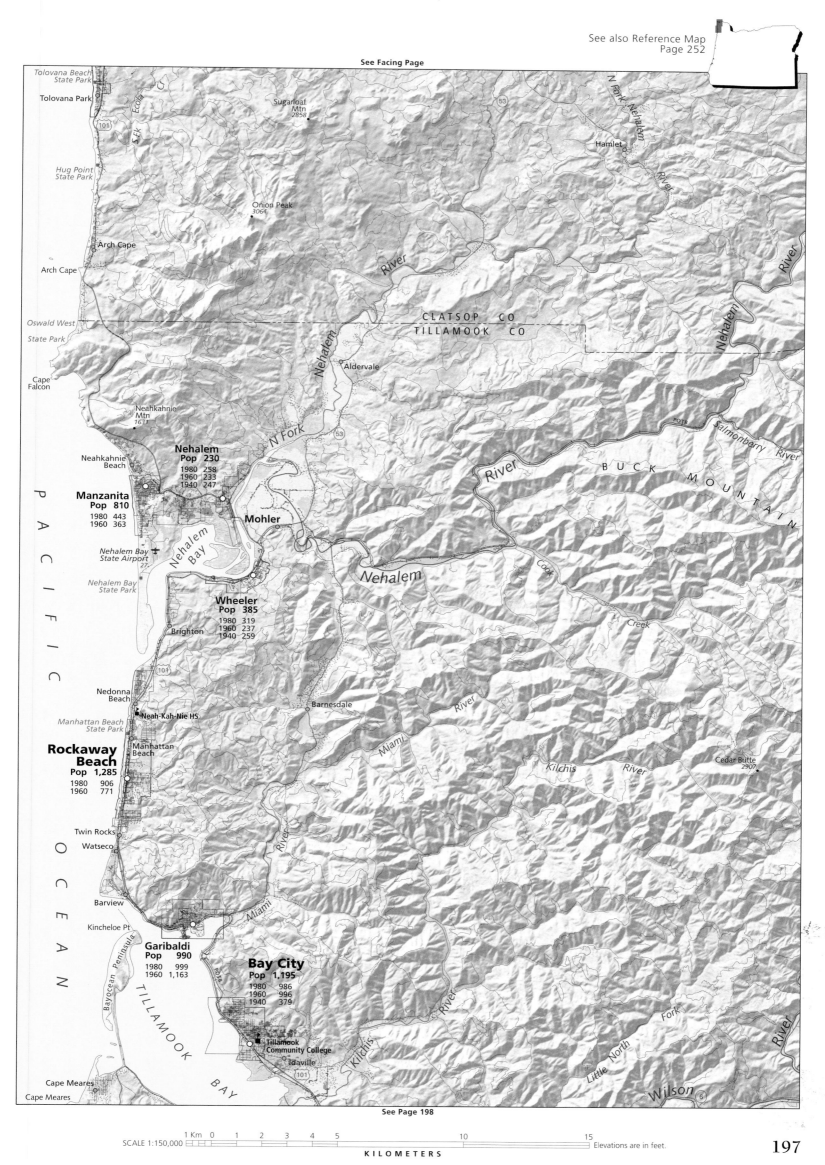

See Facing Page

Tolovana Beach
State Park

Tolovana Park

S Fk Ecola

Sugarloaf
Mtn
2858

Hug Point
State Park

101

Onion Peak
3064

Arch Cape

Arch Cape

Hamlet

N Fork Nehalem River

River

CLATSOP CO
TILLAMOOK CO

Oswald West
State Park

Aldervale

Nehalem River

53

Cape
Falcon

Neahkahnie
Mtn
1631

Nehalem River

POTB

Salmonberry River

N Fork

N Fork

Neahkahnie
Beach

Nehalem
Pop 230
1980 258
1960 233
1940 247

River

BUCK MOUNTAIN

Manzanita
Pop 810
1980 443
1960 363

Mohler

Nehalem Bay
State Airport
27

Nehalem Bay

Nehalem

Cook

Wheeler
Pop 385
1980 319
1960 237
1940 259

Creek

Nehalem Bay
State Park

Brighton

Nedonna
Beach

Barnesdale

River

Neah-Kah-Nie HS

Manhattan Beach
State Park

Manhattan
Beach

Miami

Kilchis River

Cedar Butte
2907

Rockaway
Beach
Pop 1,285
1980 906
1960 771

River

Twin Rocks

Watseco

Barview

Kincheloe Pt

Miami

Garibaldi
Pop 990
1980 999
1960 1,163

Bayocean Peninsula

Bay City
Pop 1,195
1980 986
1960 996
1940 379

Little North Fork

PACIFIC

OCEAN

TILLAMOOK

Tillamook
Community College

Idaville

Kilchis River

Wilson River

6

Cape Meares

Cape Meares

TILLAMOOK
BAY

101

See Page 198

SCALE 1:150,000   1 Km 0   1   2   3   4   5   10   15   Elevations are in feet.

KILOMETERS

197

Tillamook; Lincoln City

See Page 197

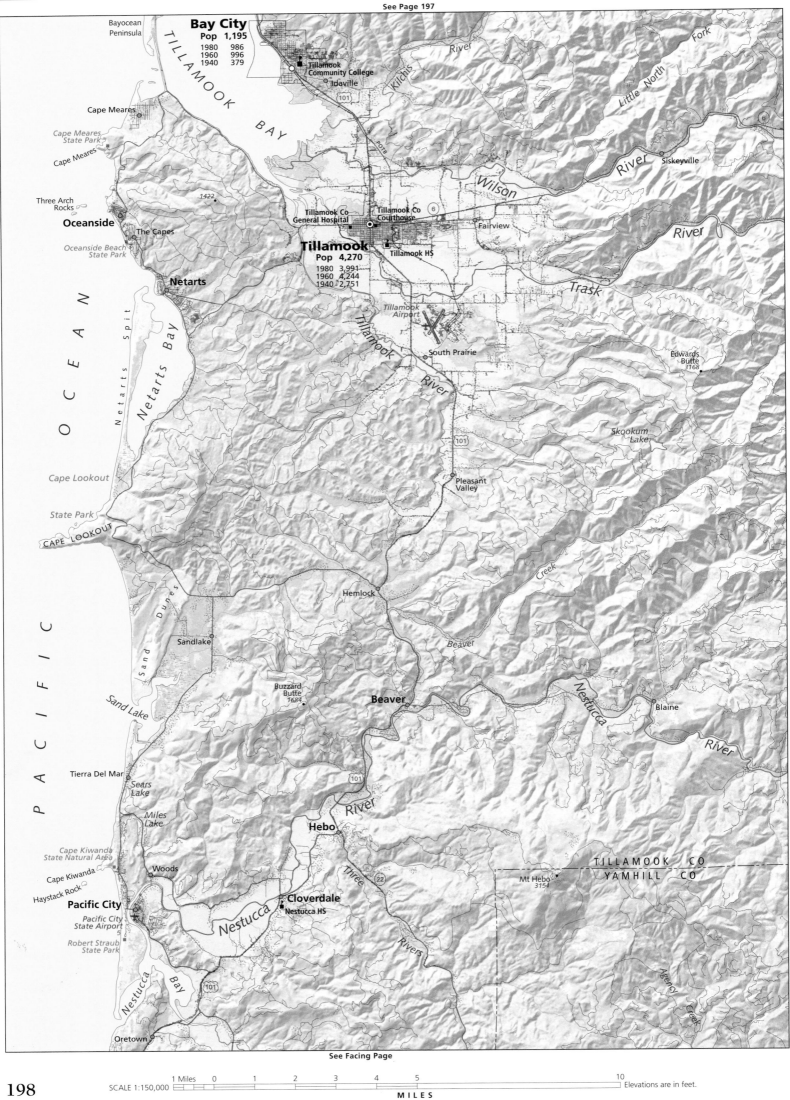

Bayocean
Peninsula

Bay City
Pop 1,195
1980   986
1960   996
1940   379

Tillamook
Community College

Idaville

Cape Meares

*Cape Meares
State Park*

Cape Meares

TILLAMOOK BAY

Kilchis River

Little North Fork

Siskeyville

*Three Arch
Rocks*

1422

Wilson River

River

Oceanside

The Capes

Tillamook Co
General Hospital

Tillamook Co
Courthouse

6

Fairview

River

*Oceanside Beach
State Park*

Tillamook
Pop 4,270
1980 3,991
1960 4,244
1940 2,751

Tillamook HS

Trask

Netarts

O
C
E
A
N

Netarts Spit

Netarts Bay

*Tillamook
Airport*
35

Tillamook River

South Prairie

*Edwards
Butte
3168*

Cape Lookout

*Skookum
Lake*

101

State Park

Pleasant
Valley

CAPE LOOKOUT

Creek

P
A
C
I
F
I
C

Sand Dunes

Hemlock

Beaver

Nestucca

Blaine

Sand Lake

Sandlake

*Buzzard
Butte
1684*

Beaver

River

Tierra Del Mar

*Sears
Lake*

River

*Miles
Lake*

River

Hebo

TILLAMOOK CO
YAMHILL CO

*Cape Kiwanda
State Natural Area*

Woods

Three

22

*Mt Hebo
3154*

Cape Kiwanda

Cloverdale
Nestucca HS

Haystack Rock

Pacific City

*Pacific City
State Airport*
5

Nestucca River

Rivers

Agency Creek

*Robert Straub
State Park*

Nestucca Bay

101

Oretown

See Facing Page

1 Miles   0   1   2   3   4   5   10

SCALE 1:150,000   Elevations are in feet.

MILES

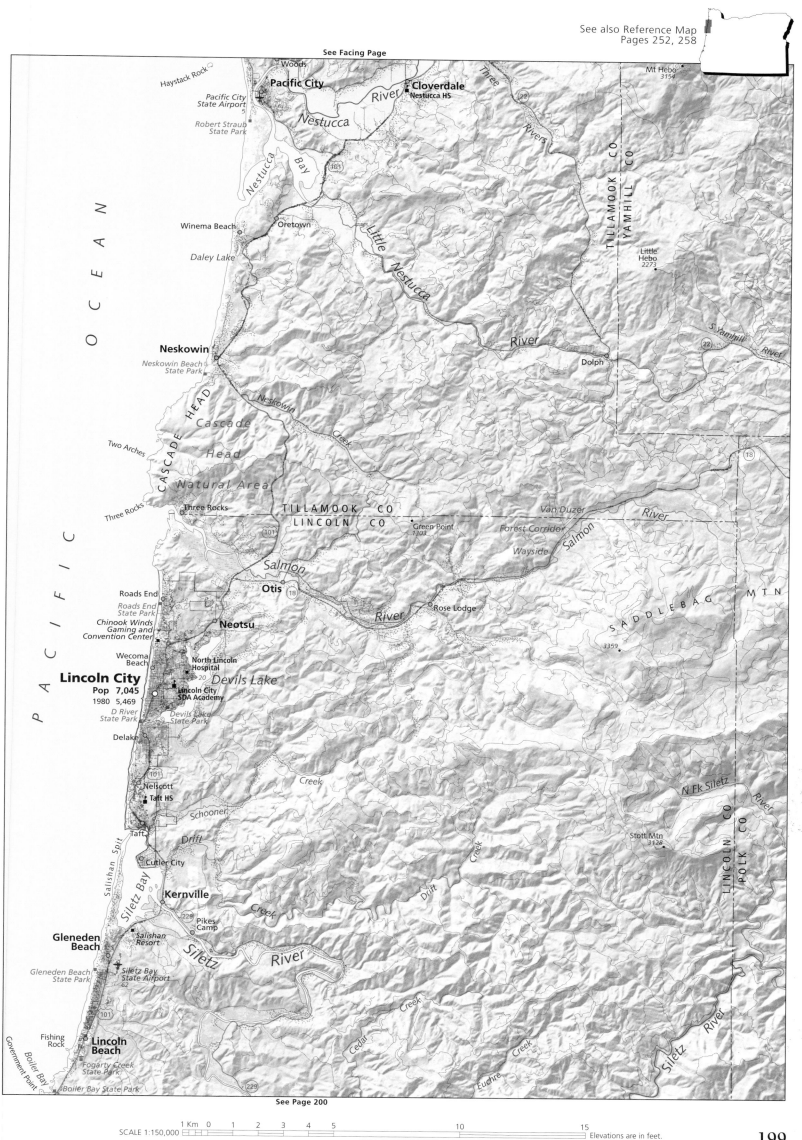

See Facing Page

Woods

Pacific City

Haystack Rock

Pacific City
State Airport
5

Three

River

Cloverdale
Nestucca HS

Mt Hebo
3154

TILLAMOOK CO
YAMHILL CO

Robert Straub
State Park

Nestucca

Bay

Rivers

O C E A N

P A C I F I C

Nestucca

101

Little

Winema Beach

Oretown

Nestucca

Little
Hebo
2273

Daley Lake

River

S Yamhill

River

Neskowin

Dolph

22

Neskowin Beach
State Park

Neskowin

18

Two Arches

CASCADE HEAD

Cascade

Creek

Head

Van Duzer

River

Natural Area

Three Rocks

TILLAMOOK CO

Forest Corridor

Salmon

Three Rocks

LINCOLN CO

Green Point
1303

Salmon

101

Wayside

SADDLEBAG MTN

Salmon

Otis

18

Roads End

River

Rose Lodge

3359

Roads End
State Park

Chinook Winds
Gaming and
Convention Center

Neotsu

Wecoma
Beach

North Lincoln
Hospital

20

Lincoln City
Pop 7,045
1980 5,469

Devils Lake

Lincoln City
SDA Academy

N Fk Siletz

D River
State Park

Devils Lake
State Park

Delake

Creek

101

Nelscott

Taft HS

Stott Mtn
3128

Schooner

Salishan Spit

Taft

Drift

Creek

Duft

LINCOLN CO
POLK CO

Cutler City

Siletz Bay

Kernville

Creek

229

Pikes
Camp

**Gleneden
Beach**

Salishan
Resort

Siletz

River

Gleneden Beach
State Park

Siletz Bay
State Airport
62

Creek

Fishing
Rock

Boiler Bay

Siletz

**Lincoln
Beach**

Cedar

Euchre

Creek

River

Government Point

Fogarty Creek
State Park

101

229

Boiler Bay State Park

See Page 200

SCALE 1:150,000   1 Km 0   1   2   3   4   5   10   15

KILOMETERS

Elevations are in feet.

199

Newport; Waldport

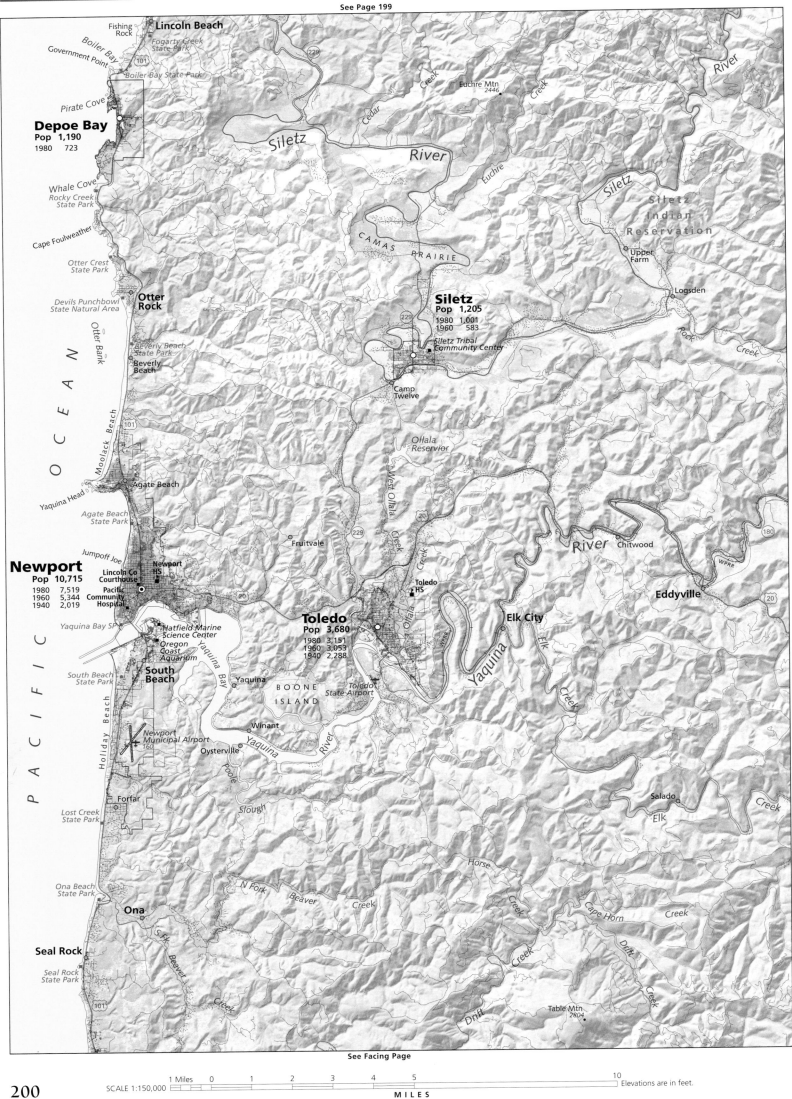

Lincoln Beach
Fishing Rock
Fogarty Creek State Park

Boiler Bay
Government Point
Boiler Bay State Park

Pirate Cove

Depoe Bay
Pop 1,190
1980   723

Whale Cove
Rocky Creek State Park

Cape Foulweather

Otter Crest State Park

Devils Punchbowl State Natural Area

Otter Rock

Beverly Beach State Park

Beverly Beach

Euchre Mtn 2446

Siletz River

River

CAMAS PRAIRIE

Siletz Indian Reservation

Upper Farm

Logsden

Siletz
Pop 1,205
1980   1,001
1960   583

Siletz Tribal Community Center

Camp Twelve

Ollala Reservior

Rock Creek

Euchre Creek

Cedar Creek

P A C I F I C   O C E A N

Otter Bank

Moolack Beach

Agate Beach

Yaquina Head

Agate Beach State Park

Jumpoff Joe

Newport
Pop 10,715
1980   7,519
1960   5,344
1940   2,019

Lincoln Co Courthouse
Pacific Community Hospital

Newport HS

Fruitvale

West Ollala Creek

Ollala Creek

Toledo
Pop 3,680
1980   3,151
1960   3,053
1940   2,288

Toledo HS

River

Chitwood

WPRR

Eddyville

Yaquina Bay SP

Hatfield Marine Science Center
Oregon Coast Aquarium

South Beach

South Beach State Park

Yaquina Bay

Yaquina

B O O N E   I S L A N D

Toledo State Airport

Elk City

Yaquina River

Elk Creek

Holiday Beach

Newport Municipal Airport 160

Winant

Oysterville

Poole Slough

Yaquina

Salado

Elk Creek

Forfar

Lost Creek State Park

N Fork Beaver Creek

Horse Creek

Cape Horn Creek

Ona

Ona Beach State Park

Seal Rock

Seal Rock State Park

S. Fk. Beaver

Creek

Drift Creek

Creek

Table Mtn 2804

SCALE 1:150,000   1 Miles   0   1   2   3   4   5   10
M I L E S   Elevations are in feet.

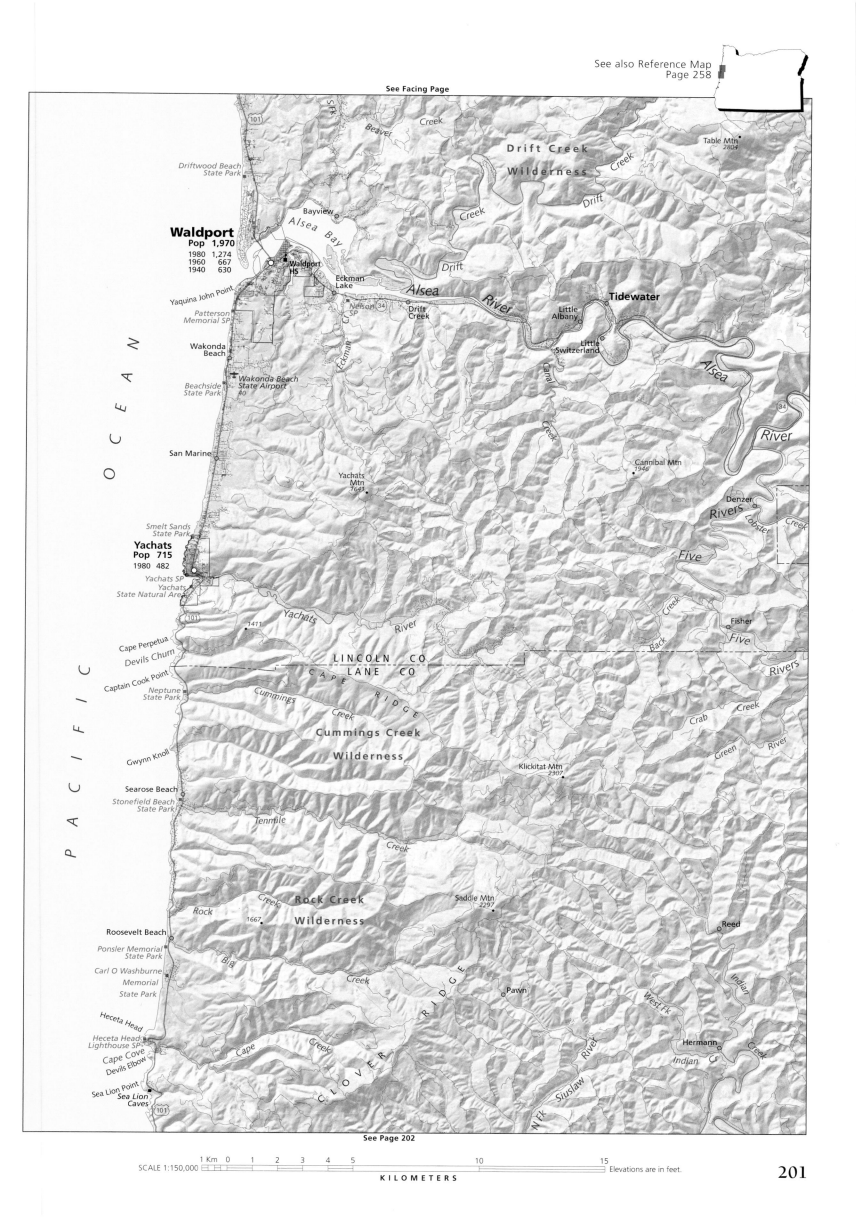

See also Reference Map
Page 258

See Facing Page

SFK

Beaver

Creek

Creek

Drift Creek

Wilderness

Table Mtn
2804

Driftwood Beach
State Park

Creek

Bayview

Drift

Creek

Waldport
Pop 1,970
1980 1,274
1960   667
1940   630

Alsea Bay

Waldport
HS

Eckman
Lake

Drift

Alsea

River

Tidewater

Yaquina John Point

Nelson
SP

Drift
Creek

Little
Albany

Patterson
Memorial SP

Eckman

Little
Switzerland

Wakonda
Beach

Canal

Alsea

Beachside
State Park

Wakonda Beach
State Airport
40

River

34

San Marine

Creek

Cannibal Mtn
1946

Yachats
Mtn
1641

Denzer

Rivers

Lobster

Creek

Smelt Sands
State Park

Yachats
Pop 715
1980 482

Five

Yachats SP
Yachats
State Natural Area

Fisher

Yachats

River

Back

Five

1411

Cape Perpetua

LINCOLN CO
LANE CO

Rivers

Devils Churn

Captain Cook Point

CAPE RIDGE

Creek

Neptune
State Park

Cummings

Crab

Creek

Creek

Gwynn Knoll

Cummings Creek

Wilderness

Green

River

Klickitat Mtn
2307

Searose Beach

Stonefield Beach
State Park

Tenmile

Rock Creek

Reed

Creek

Rock Creek

Saddle Mtn
2297

Rock

Wilderness

1667

Roosevelt Beach

CLOVER RIDGE

Ponsler Memorial
State Park

Big

Pawn

Carl O Washburne
Memorial
State Park

Creek

West Fk

Indian

Heceta Head

Heceta Head
Lighthouse SP

Cape

Creek

Hermann

Cape Cove
Devils Elbow

Siuslaw

Indian Cr

Sea Lion Point

Sea Lion
Caves

N Fk

River

See Page 202

1 Km 0   1   2   3   4   5   10   15
SCALE 1:150,000   Elevations are in feet.

KILOMETERS

201

Florence; Reedsport; Coos Bay, Coquille

See Page 201
See Map at Left

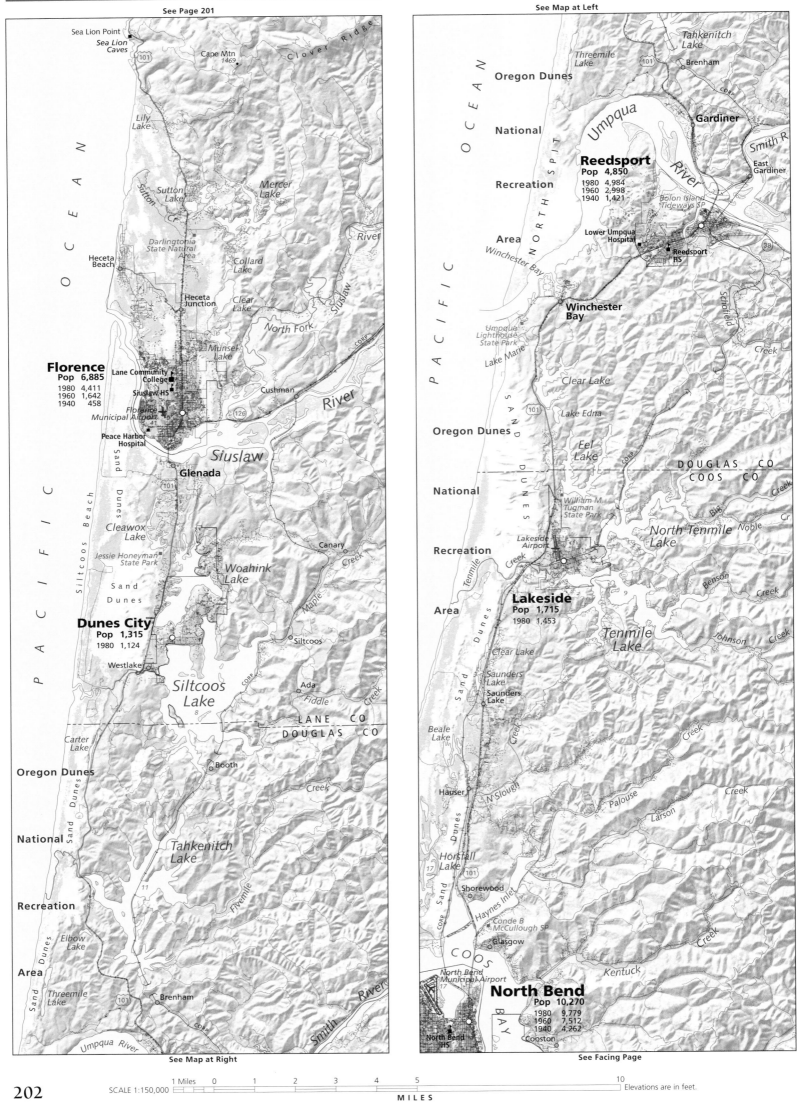

Sea Lion Point
Sea Lion Caves
Cape Mtn 1469

Clover Ridge

Lily Lake

Sutton Cr.

Sutton Lake

Mercer Lake

32

River

Darlingtonia State Natural Area

Heceta Beach

Collard Lake

Clear Lake

Heceta Junction

North Fork

Siuslaw

River

Munsel Lake

Cushman

Florence
Pop 6,885
1980 4,411
1960 1,642
1940 458

Lane Community College
Siuslaw HS
Florence Municipal Airport
101

River

126

Peace Harbor Hospital

Siuslaw

Glenada

101

Sand Dunes

Cleawox Lake

Jessie Honeyman State Park

Canary

Creek

Woahink Lake

Sand Dunes

Maple

Dunes City
Pop 1,315
1980 1,124

Siltcoos

Westlake

Ada

Fiddle

Creek

Siltcoos Lake

8

LANE CO
DOUGLAS CO

Carter Lake

Booth

Creek

Oregon Dunes

Sand Dunes

National

Tahkenitch Lake

Recreation

11

Fivemile

Elbow Lake

Area

Sand Dunes

Threemile Lake

101

Brenham

Smith River

CORP

Umpqua River

PACIFIC OCEAN

Siltcoos Beach

PACIFIC

Tahkenitch Lake

Threemile Lake

101

CORP

Brenham

Oregon Dunes

Umpqua

River

Smith R.

East Gardiner

National

Gardiner

Reedsport
Pop 4,850
1980 4,984
1960 2,998
1940 1,421

Bolon Island Tideways SP

Recreation

Lower Umpqua Hospital

38

Reedsport HS

NORTH SPIT

Area

Winchester Bay

Winchester Bay

Umpqua Lighthouse State Park

Lake Marie

Schofield

Creek

SAND

Clear Lake

101

Lake Edna

Oregon Dunes

Eel Lake

DOUGLAS CO
COOS CO

DUNES

National

William M. Tugman State Park

Big

North Tenmile Lake

Noble Cr

Lakeside Airport

Tenmile

Recreation

Lakeside
Pop 1,715
1980 1,453

Benson

Creek

Area

Sand Dunes

Clear Lake

Saunders Lake

Saunders Lake

Tenmile Lake

Johnson

Creek

Beale Lake

Hauser

N Slough

Palouse

Larson

Creek

Creek

Horsfall Lake

17

101

Shorewood

Haynes Inlet

Conde B McCullough SP

Glasgow

Kentuck

Creek

COOS BAY

North Bend Municipal Airport

17

North Bend
Pop 10,270
1980 9,779
1960 7,512
1940 4,262

North Bend HS

Coaston

See Map at Right
See Facing Page

1 Miles 0   1   2   3   4   5   10

SCALE 1:150,000   Elevations are in feet.

MILES

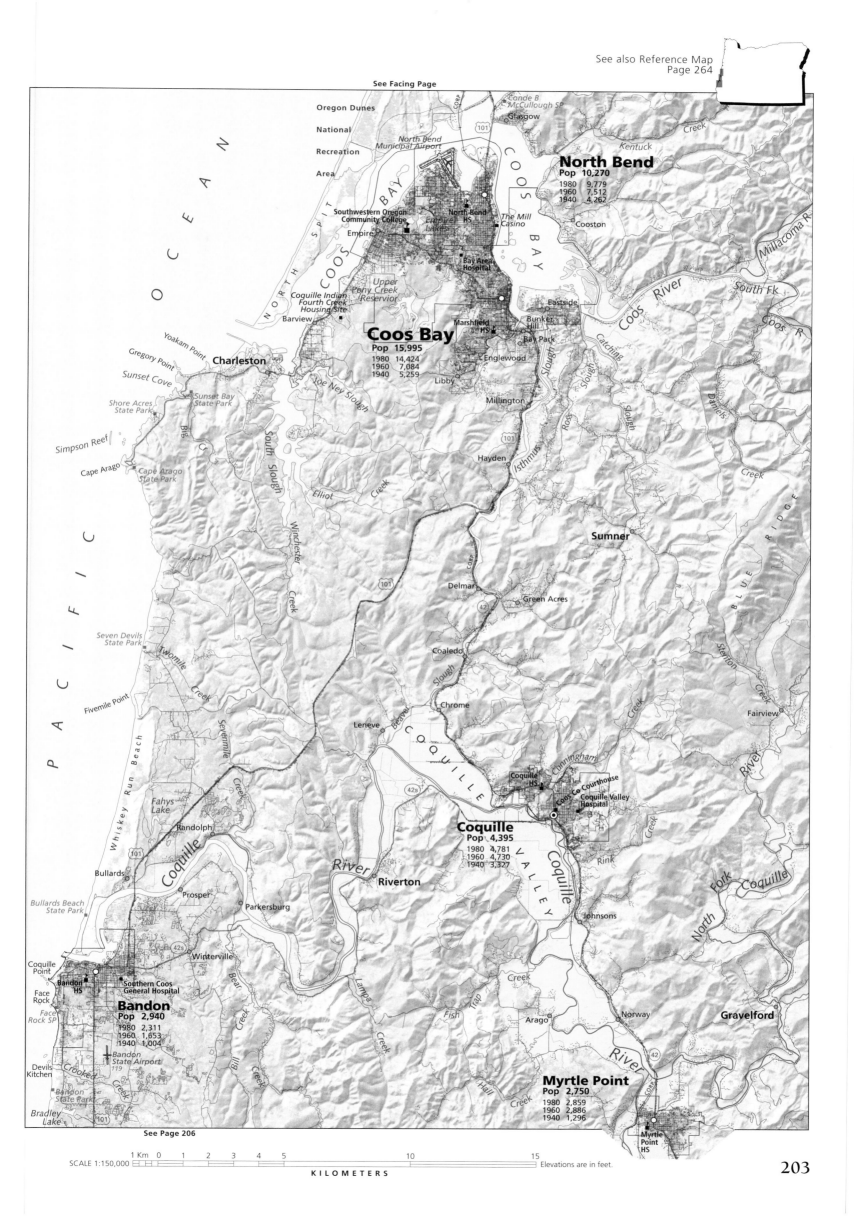

See Facing Page

Oregon Dunes

National

Recreation

Area

Conde B
McCullough SP

Glasgow

Kentuck
Creek

Creek

North Bend
Municipal Airport

North Bend
Pop 10,270

1980	9,779
1960	7,512
1940	4,262

Cooston

Southwestern Oregon
Community College

North Bend
HS

The Mill
Casino

COOS BAY

Empire
Lakes

Empire

NORTH SPIT

Bay Area
Hospital

Eastside

South Fk

Coos River

Millicoma R

Upper
Pony Creek
Reservoir

Coquille Indian
Fourth Creek
Housing Site

Barview

Marshfield
HS

Bunker
Hill

Bay Park

Catching Slough

Coos R

Coos Bay
Pop 15,995

1980	14,424
1960	7,084
1940	5,259

Englewood

Libby

Ross Slough

Slough

Yoakam Point

Gregory Point

Charleston

Sunset Cove

Shore Acres
State Park

Sunset Bay
State Park

Joe Ney Slough

Millington

Daniels Creek

Simpson Reef

Cape Arago

Cape Arago
State Park

Big Creek

South Slough

Elliot Creek

Creek

Hayden

Isthmus

101

Sumner

BLUE RIDGE

Seven Devils
State Park

Winchester Creek

Delmar

Green Acres

101

42

Fairview

Twomile Creek

Fivemile Point

Coaledo

Slough

Sterton Creek

River

Coquille

Chrome

Leneve

Beaver

Cunningham

Coquille
HS

Coos Co Courthouse

Coquille Valley
Hospital

Sevenmile Creek

Whiskey Run Beach

Fahys
Lake

Randolph

42s

River

Riverton

COQUILLE VALLEY

Coquille
Pop 4,395

1980	4,781
1960	4,730
1940	3,327

Rink

Creek

North Fork Coquille

Bullards

101

Coquille

Prosper

Parkersburg

Johnsons

Bullards Beach
State Park

Coquille
Point

42s

Winterville

Bear Creek

Bill Creek

Lampa Creek

Trap Creek

Arago

Norway

Gravelford

Bandon
HS

Southern Coos
General Hospital

Face
Rock

Face
Rock SP

Bandon
Pop 2,940

1980	2,311
1960	1,653
1940	1,004

Fish Creek

Hall Creek

42

River

Devils
Kitchen

Bandon
State Airport
119

Crooked Creek

Myrtle Point
Pop 2,750

1980	2,859
1960	2,886
1940	1,296

Bradley
Lake

Bandon
State Park

101

Myrtle
Point
HS

See Page 206

SCALE 1:150,000

| 1 Km | 0 | 1 | 2 | 3 | 4 | 5 | 10 | 15 |

Elevations are in feet.

KILOMETERS

203

Astoria to Coos Bay Historic Growth

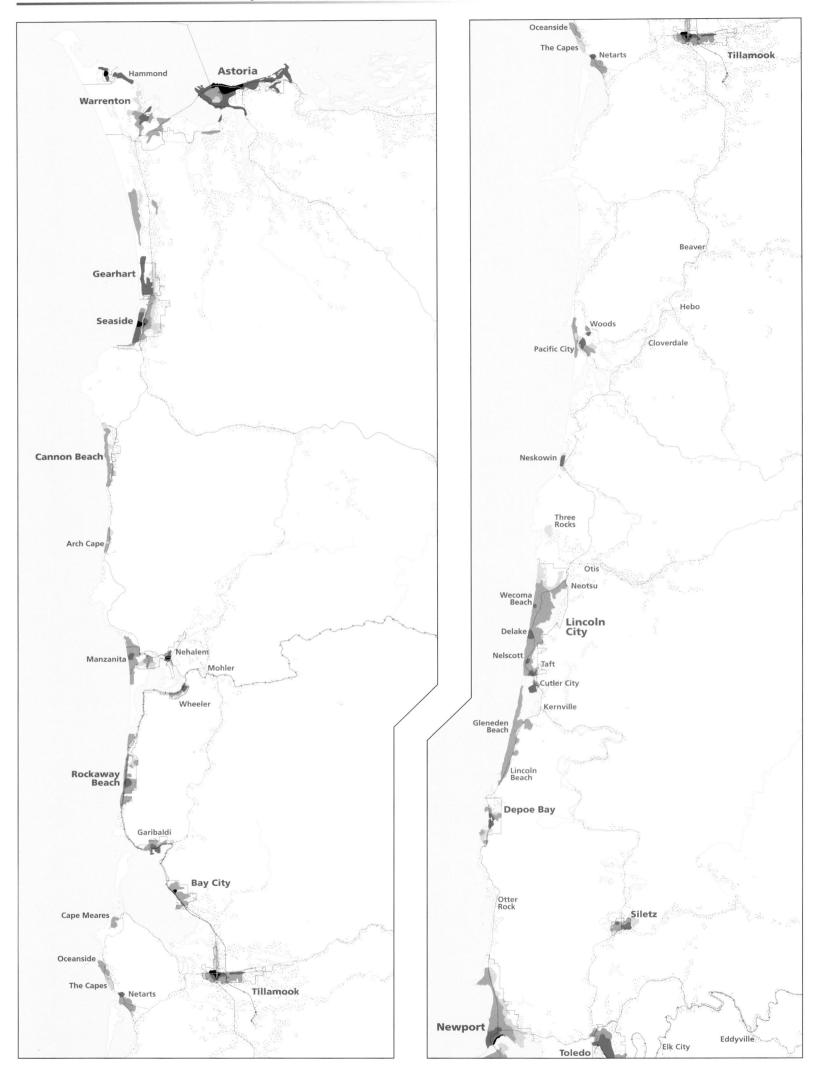

Hammond

Astoria

Warrenton

Gearhart

Seaside

Cannon Beach

Arch Cape

Manzanita
Nehalem
Mohler

Wheeler

Rockaway Beach

Garibaldi

Bay City

Cape Meares

Oceanside

The Capes
Netarts
Tillamook

Oceanside
The Capes
Netarts

Tillamook

Beaver

Hebo

Woods
Cloverdale

Pacific City

Neskowin

Three
Rocks

Otis
Wecoma
Beach
Neotsu
**Lincoln
City**
Delake
Nelscott
Taft
Cutler City
Kernville
Gleneden
Beach

Lincoln
Beach

Depoe Bay

Otter
Rock

Siletz

Newport

Elk City
Eddyville

Toledo

SCALE 1:333,333

0   5   10   15   20

MILES

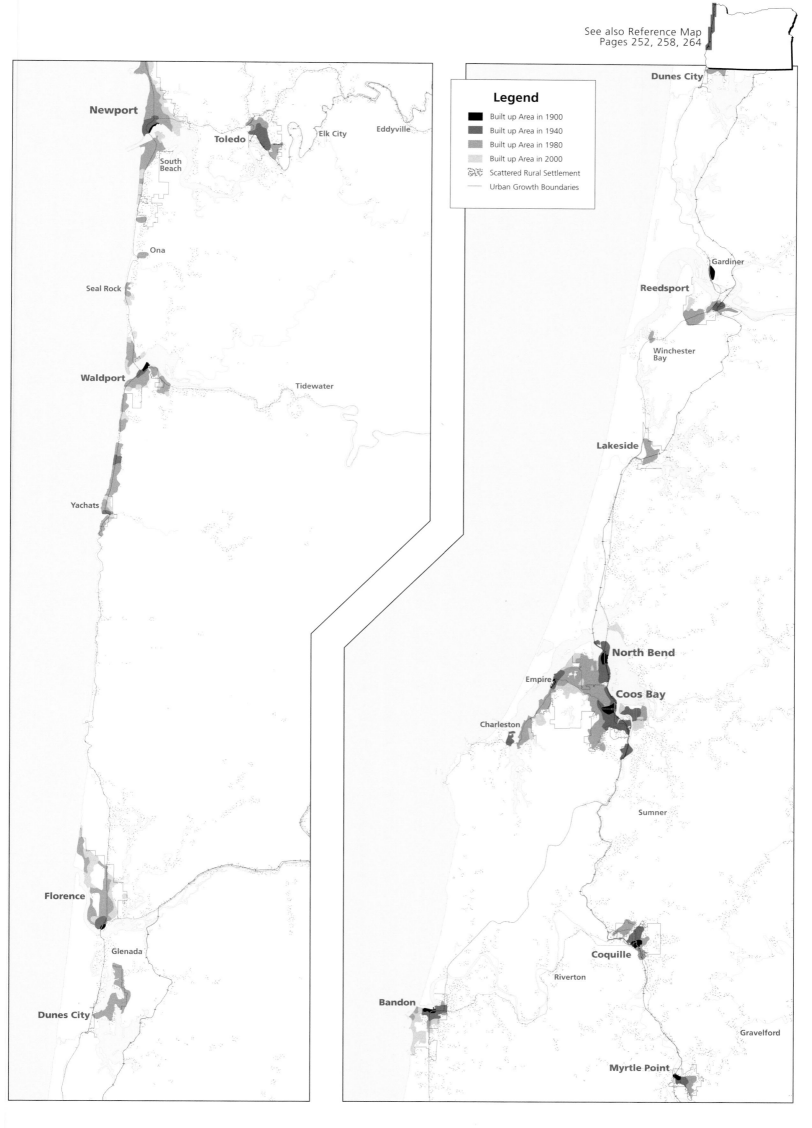

See also Reference Map
Pages 252, 258, 264

Legend

- Built up Area in 1900
- Built up Area in 1940
- Built up Area in 1980
- Built up Area in 2000
- Scattered Rural Settlement
- Urban Growth Boundaries

Dunes City

Newport

Toledo

Elk City

Eddyville

South
Beach

Ona

Seal Rock

Gardiner

Reedsport

Winchester
Bay

Waldport

Tidewater

Lakeside

Yachats

North Bend

Empire

Coos Bay

Charleston

Sumner

Florence

Glenada

Coquille

Riverton

Dunes City

Bandon

Gravelford

Myrtle Point

0   5   10   15   20   25   30   SCALE 1:333,333

KILOMETERS

Port Orford; Gold Beach; Brookings

See Page 203
See Map at Left

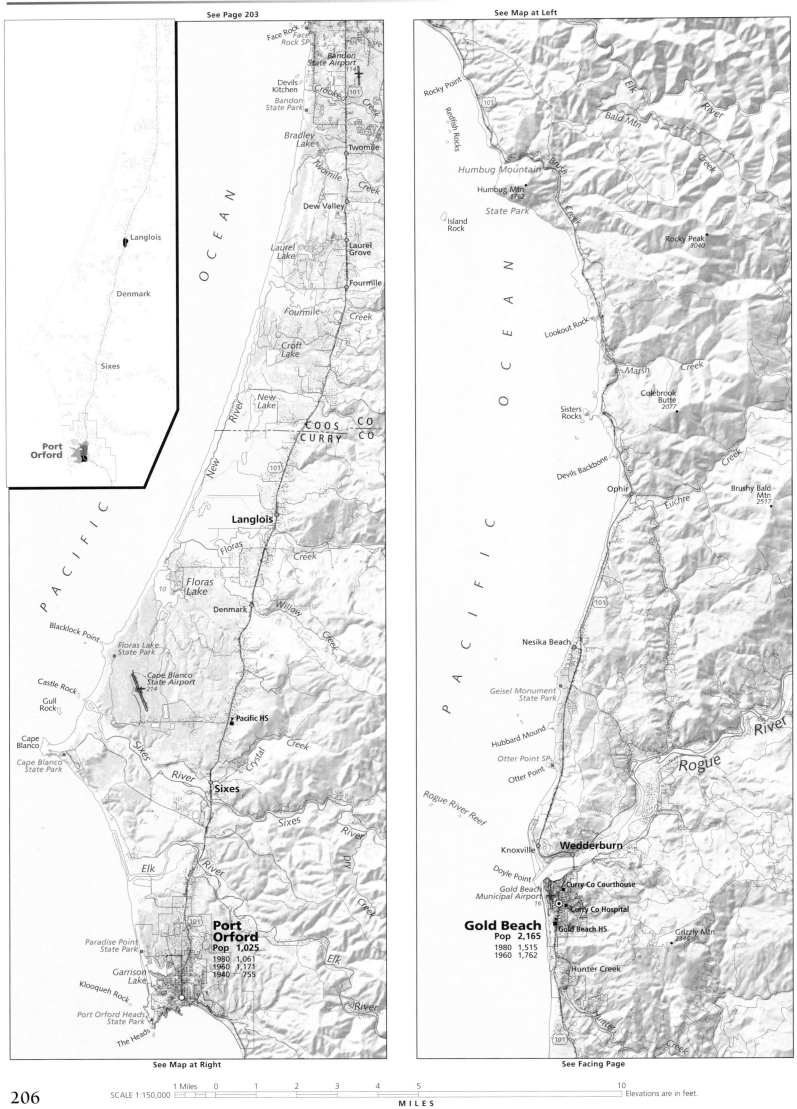

Face Rock
Face Rock SP
Bandon State Airport
Devils Kitchen
Bandon State Park
Crooked Creek
101
Bradley Lake
Twomile
Twomile Creek
Dew Valley
Laurel Lake
Laurel Grove
Fourmile
Fourmile
Croft Lake
Creek
New River
New Lake
COOS CO
CURRY CO
101
Langlois
Floras
Floras Creek
Floras Lake
10
Denmark
Willow Creek
Blacklock Point
Floras Lake State Park
Cape Blanco State Airport
214
Castle Rock
Gull Rock
Pacific HS
Crystal Creek
Cape Blanco
Cape Blanco State Park
Sixes River
Sixes
Sixes River
Dry Creek
Elk River
River
Paradise Point State Park
Port Orford
Pop **1,025**
1980 1,061
1960 1,171
1940 755
Garrison Lake
Klooqueh Rock
Elk River
Port Orford Heads State Park
The Heads

O C E A N
P A C I F I C

(inset, upper left)
Langlois
Denmark
Sixes
Port Orford

(right map)
Rocky Point
Redfish Rocks
101
Bald Mtn
Elk River
Humbug Mountain
Humbug Mtn 1762
Island Rock
State Park
Brush Creek
Rocky Peak 3040
Lookout Rock
Marsh Creek
Colebrook Butte 2077
Sisters Rocks
Devils Backbone
Euchre Creek
Ophir
Brushy Bald Mtn 2517
101
Nesika Beach
Geisel Monument State Park
Hubbard Mound
Otter Point SP
Otter Point
Rogue River Reef
Rogue River
Knoxville
Wedderburn
Doyle Point
Gold Beach Municipal Airport 76
Curry Co Courthouse
Curry Co Hospital
Gold Beach
Pop **2,165**
1980 1,515
1960 1,762
Gold Beach HS
Grizzly Mtn 2346
Hunter Creek
Hunter Creek

P A C I F I C   O C E A N

See Map at Right
See Facing Page

206

SCALE 1:150,000   1 Miles 0 1 2 3 4 5   10   Elevations are in feet.
MILES

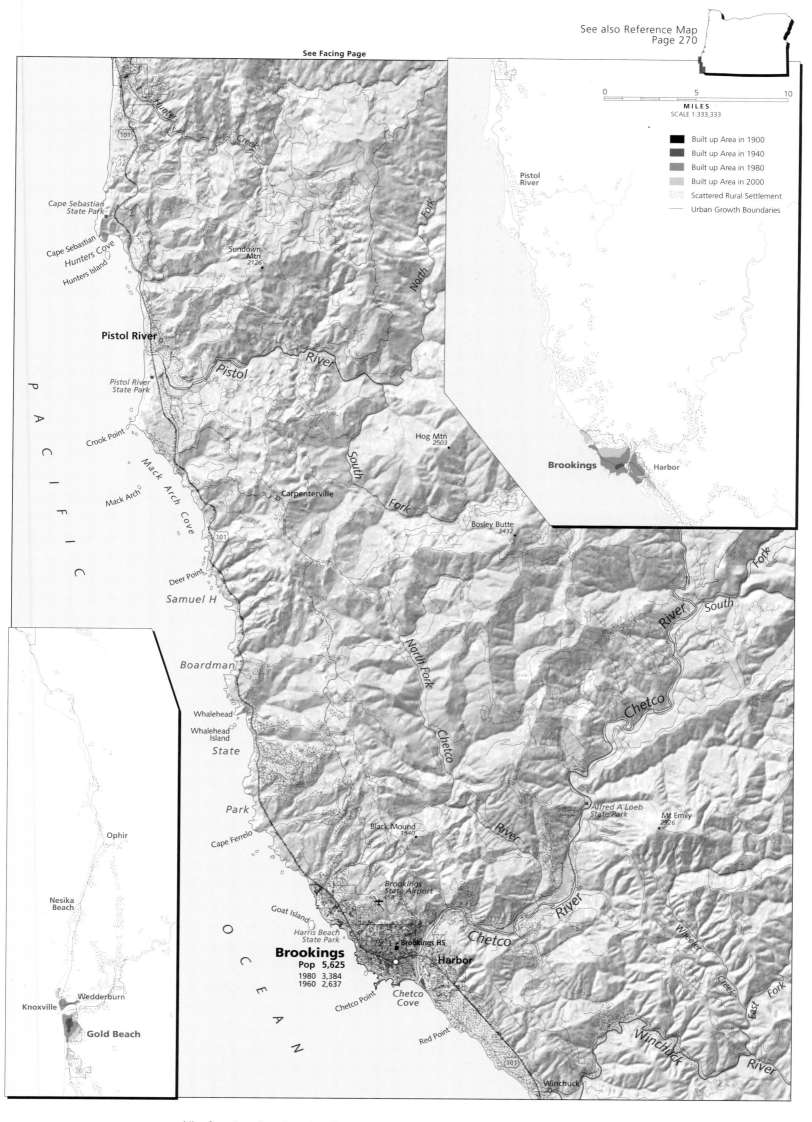

See Facing Page

MILES
SCALE 1:333,333

Built up Area in 1900
Built up Area in 1940
Built up Area in 1980
Built up Area in 2000
Scattered Rural Settlement
Urban Growth Boundaries

Pistol
River

Brookings   Harbor

Hunters Creek

Cape Sebastian
State Park

Cape Sebastian
Hunters Cove
Hunters Island

Sundown
Mtn
2126

North Fork

Pistol River

Pistol River
State Park

Pistol   River

Crook Point

Mack Arch

Mack Arch Cove

Carpenterville

Hog Mtn
2503

South
Fork

Bosley Butte
3432

Deer Point

Samuel H

P A C I F I C

Boardman

Whalehead

Whalehead
Island

State

North Fork

Chetco

Chetco   River   South   Fork

Alfred A Loeb
State Park

Mt Emily
2926

Ophir

Nesika
Beach

Park

Cape Ferrelo

Black Mound
1540

River

Brookings
State Airport
158

Goat Island

Harris Beach
State Park

Brookings HS

Brookings
Pop 5,625
1980 3,384
1960 2,637

Harbor

Chetco   River

Chetco

Wheeler   Creek

Knoxville

Wedderburn

Gold Beach

O C E A N

Chetco Point

Chetco
Cove

Red Point

Winchuck   River

East   Fork

Winchuck

1 Km 0   1   2   3   4   5   10   15
SCALE 1:150,000   Elevations are in feet.
K I L O M E T E R S

St Helens; Sandy

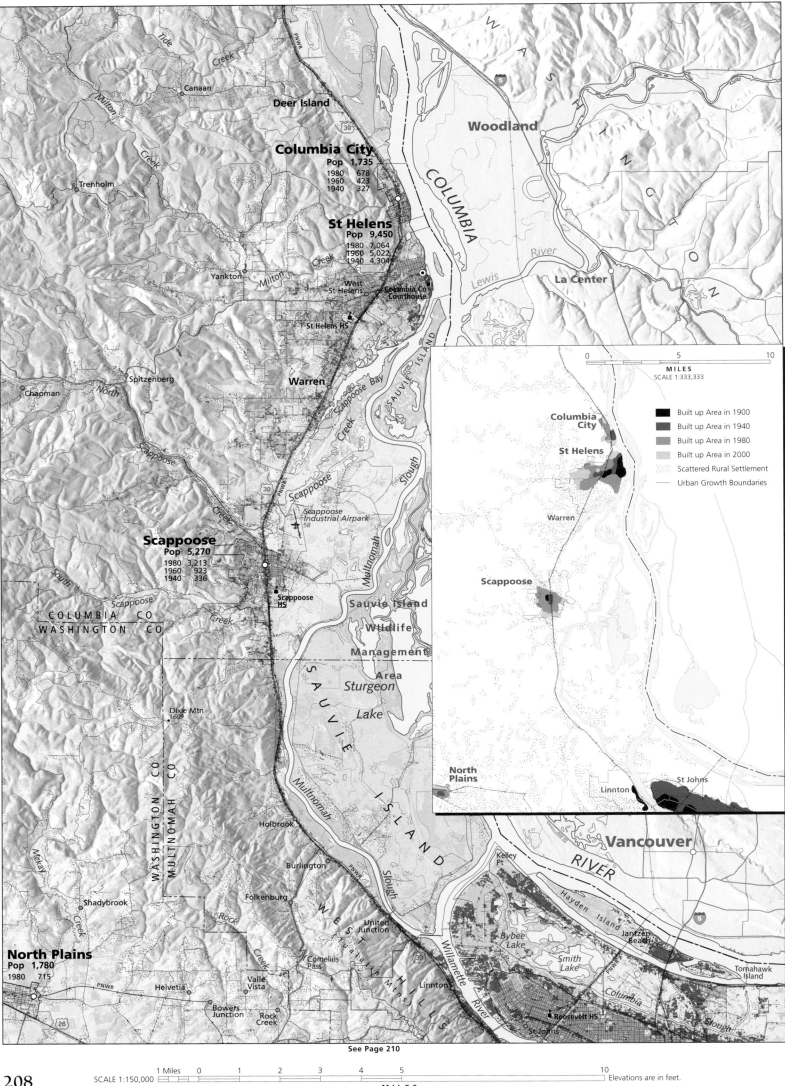

Deer Island

Columbia City
Pop 1,735
1980	678
1960	423
1940	327

St Helens
Pop 9,450
1980	7,064
1960	5,022
1940	4,304

West
St Helens

Columbia Co
Courthouse

St Helens HS

Warren

Spitzenberg

Chapman

Yankton

Trenholm

Canaan

Woodland

La Center

COLUMBIA RIVER

Lewis River

WASHINGTON

Scappoose Bay

SAUVIE ISLAND

Scappoose
Industrial Airpark
58

Scappoose
Pop 5,270
1980	3,213
1960	923
1940	336

Scappoose
HS

COLUMBIA CO
WASHINGTON CO

WASHINGTON CO
MULTNOMAH CO

Dixie Mtn
1609

Multnomah Slough

**Sauvie Island
Wildlife
Management
Area**
Sturgeon
Lake

SAUVIE ISLAND

Holbrook

Burlington

Folkenburg

Shadybrook

North Plains
Pop 1,780
1980	715

Helvetia

Bowers
Junction

Rock
Creek

Valle
Vista

Comelius
Pass

United
Junction

WEST TUALATIN MTNS

Linnton

Roosevelt HS

St Johns

Willamette River

Vancouver

COLUMBIA RIVER

Hayden Island

Kelley
Pt

Bybee
Lake

Smith
Lake

Jantzen
Beach

Tomahawk
Island

Columbia
Slough

Inset map legend

0   5   10
MILES
SCALE 1:333,333

**Columbia
City**

St Helens

Warren

Scappoose

**North
Plains**

Linnton

St Johns

■	Built up Area in 1900
■	Built up Area in 1940
■	Built up Area in 1980
■	Built up Area in 2000
·	Scattered Rural Settlement
—	Urban Growth Boundaries

See Page 210

1 Miles 0   1   2   3   4   5   10
SCALE 1:150,000   Elevations are in feet.
MILES

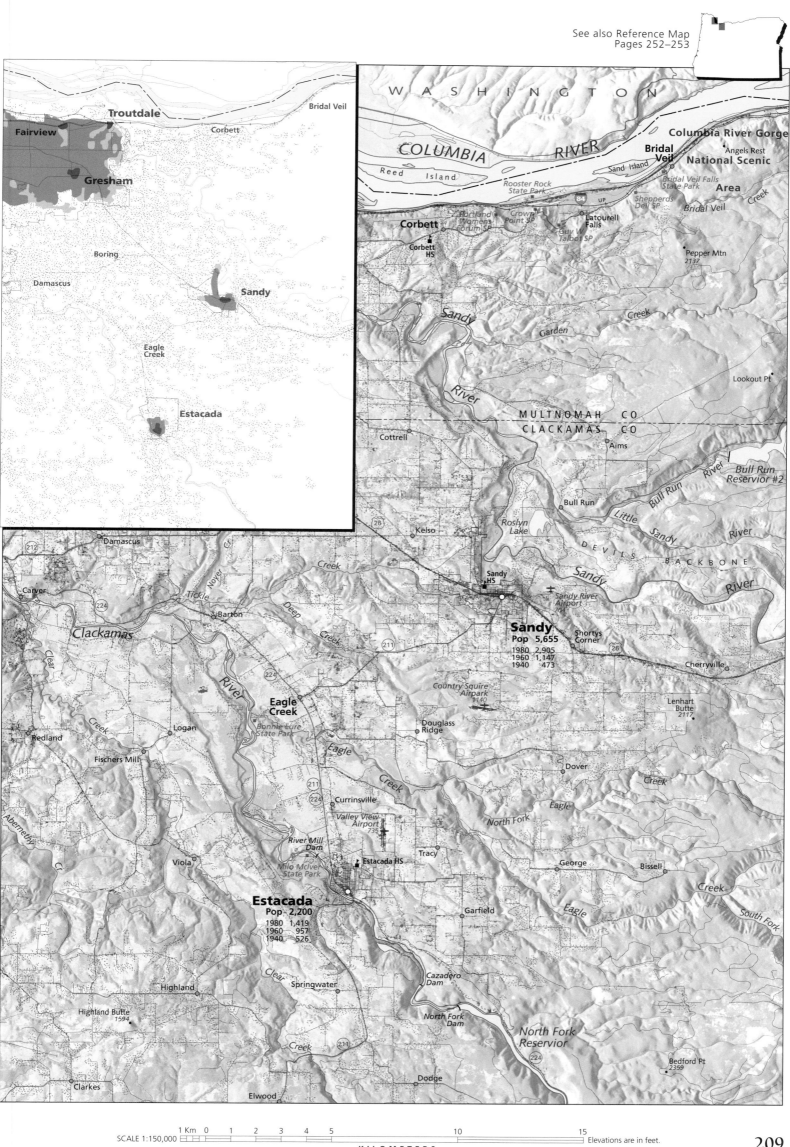

See also Reference Map
Pages 252–253

SCALE 1:150,000

1 Km 0 1 2 3 4 5 10 15

KILOMETERS

Elevations are in feet.

See Page 211

Portland, Hillsboro, Oregon City

See Page 208

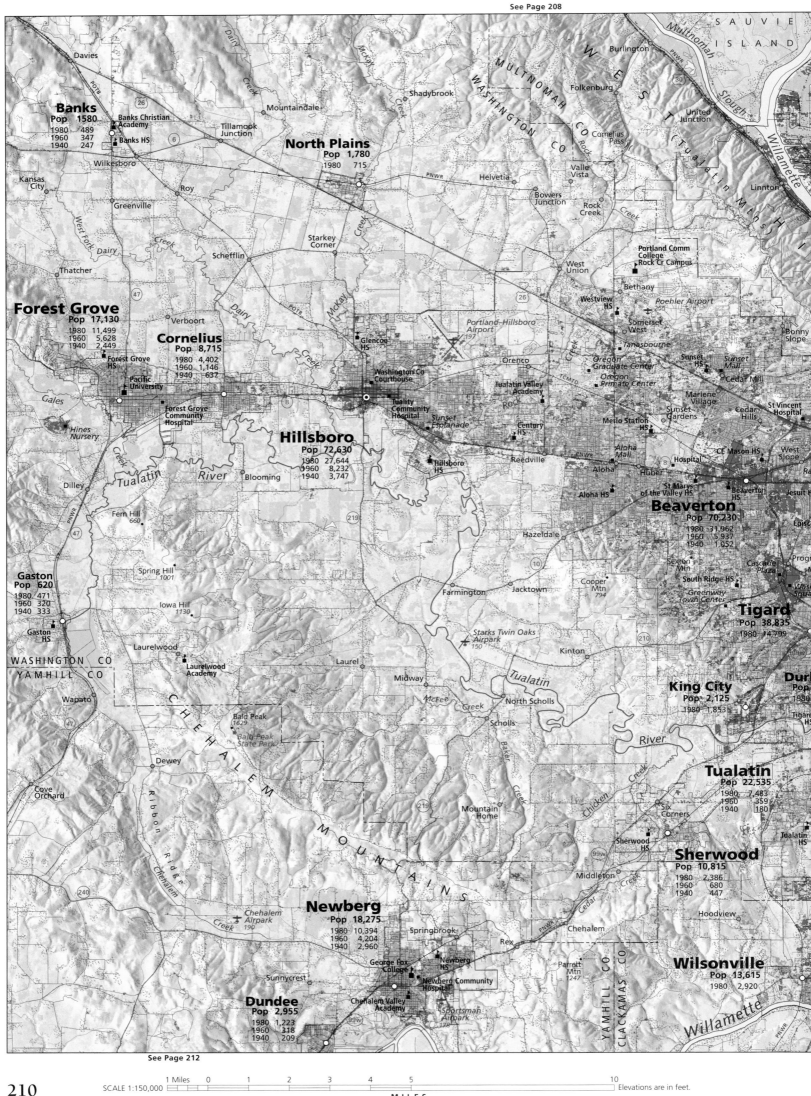

Banks
Pop 1580
1980 489
1960 347
1940 247

North Plains
Pop 1,780
1980 715

Forest Grove
Pop 17,130
1980 11,499
1960 5,628
1940 2,449

Cornelius
Pop 8,715
1980 4,402
1960 1,146
1940 637

Hillsboro
Pop 72,630
1980 27,644
1960 8,232
1940 3,747

Beaverton
Pop 70,230
1980 31,962
1960 5,937
1940 1,052

Gaston
Pop 620
1980 471
1960 320
1940 333

Tigard
Pop 38,835
1980 14,799

King City
Pop 2,125
1980 1,853

Tualatin
Pop 22,535
1980 7,483
1960 359
1940 180

Sherwood
Pop 10,815
1980 2,386
1960 680
1940 447

Newberg
Pop 18,275
1980 10,394
1960 4,204
1940 2,960

Wilsonville
Pop 13,615
1980 2,920

Dundee
Pop 2,955
1980 1,223
1960 318
1940 209

See Page 212

1 Miles 0 1 2 3 4 5 10
SCALE 1:150,000
MILES
Elevations are in feet.

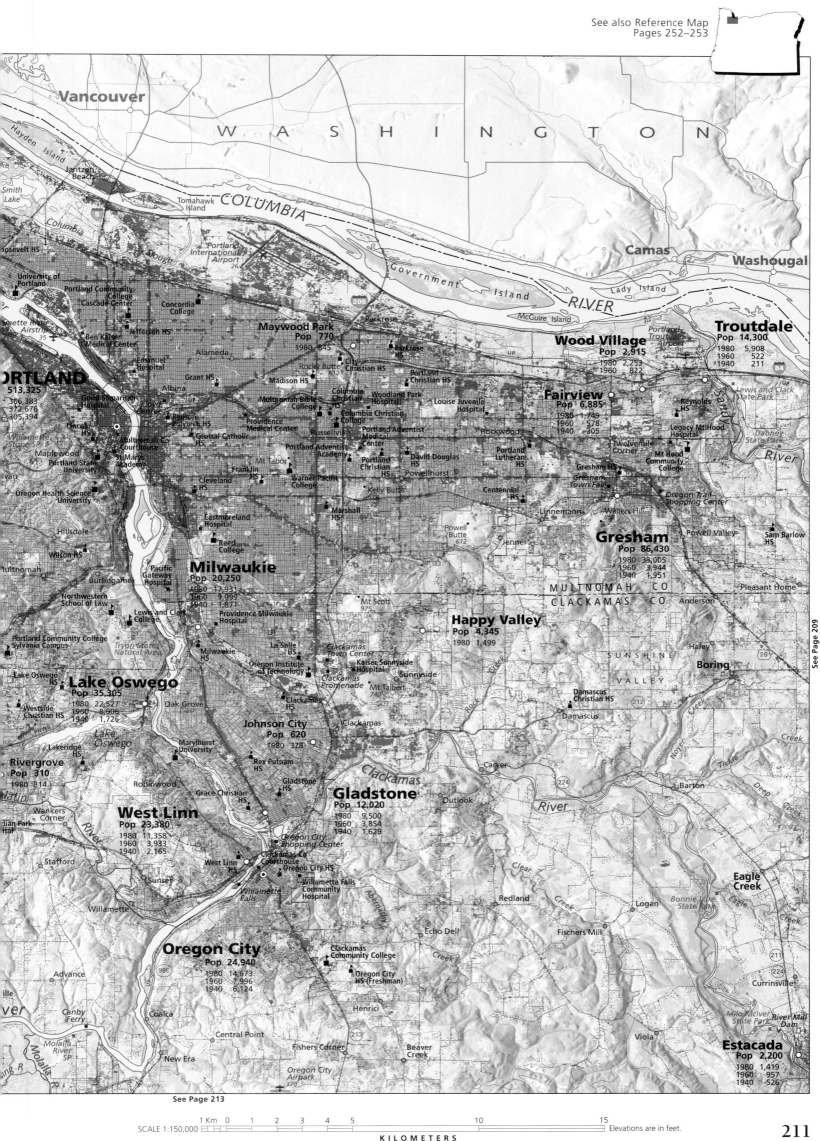

See also Reference Map
Pages 252–253

Vancouver

W A S H I N G T O N

Smith
Lake

Hayden
Island

Jantzen
Beach

COLUMBIA

Roosevelt HS

Tomahawk
Island

Columbia

University of
Portland

Willamette River
Airstrip 35

Portland Community
College
Cascade Center

Concordia
College

Ben Kaiser
Medical Center

Jefferson HS

Emanuel
Hospital

Portland
International
Airport 26

Maywood Park
Pop 770
1980 845

Parkrose

Camas

Washougal

Government   Island   RIVER

McGuire Island

Lady Island

Portland-
Troutdale
Airport

Troutdale
Pop 14,300
1980 5,908
1960 522
1940 211

Lewis and Clark
State Park

ORTLAND
513,325
366,383
372,676
305,394

Good Samaritan
Hospital

Lincoln
HS

Multnomah Co
Courthouse

St Mary's
Academy

Oregon Health Science
University

Maplewood

Portland State
University

Hillsdale

Wilson HS

ivan

Willamette
Stone St

Alameda

Grant HS

Albina

Benson
Polytech HS

Central Catholic
HS

Madison HS

Multnomah Bible
College

Providence
Medical Center

Franklin
HS

Mt Tabor

Cleveland
HS

Reed
College

Eastmoreland
Hospital

Rocky Butte
522

Columbia
Christian HS

Columbia
Christian
College

Russellville

Portland Adventist
Academy

Warner Pacific
College

Kelly Butte

Marshall
HS

Parkrose
HS

Christian HS

Portland
Christian HS

Woodland Park
Hospital

Portland Adventist
Medical
Center

Portland
Christian

David Douglas
HS

Powellhurst

Louise Juvenile
Hospital

Rockwood

Portland
Lutheran
HS

Fairview
Pop 6,885
1980 1,749
1960 578
1940 305

Reynolds
HS

Legacy Mt Hood
Hospital

Twelvemile
Corner

Mt Hood
Community
College

Dabney
State Park

River

Powell
Butte
612

Jenner

Centennial
HS

Gresham HS

Gresham
Town Fair

Linnemann

Walters Hill
858

Gresham
Pop 86,430
1980 33,005
1960 3,944
1940 1,951

Oregon Trail
Shopping Center

Powell Valley

Sam Barlow
HS

Pleasant Home

Multnomah

Pacific
Gateway
Hospital

Burlingame

Northwestern
School of Law

Portland Community College
Sylvania Campus

Lake Oswego
HS

Lewis and
Clark College

Tryon State
Natural Area

Milwaukie
Pop 20,250
1980 17,931
1960 9,099
1940 1,871

Mt Scott
975

Providence Milwaukie
Hospital

Milwaukie
HS

La Salle
HS

Oregon Institute
of Technology

Clackamas
Town Center

Clackamas
Promenade

Mt Talbert
740

Kaiser Sunnyside
Hospital

Sunnyside

MULTNOMAH CO

CLACKAMAS CO

Anderson

Happy Valley
Pop 4,345
1980 1,499

S U N S H I N E

V A L L E Y

Haley

Boring

Damascus
Christian HS

Damascus

Lake Oswego
Pop 35,305
1980 22,527
1960 8,906
1940 1,726

Westside
Christian HS

PNWR

Lake
Oswego

Lakeridge
HS

Oak Grove

Clackamas
HS

Marylhurst
University

Johnson City
Pop 620
1980 378

Rex Putnam
HS

Clackamas

Carver

Barton

Rivergrove
Pop 310
1980 314

Wankers
Corner

Robinwood

Grace Christian
HS

Gladstone
HS

Gladstone
Pop 12,020
1980 9,500
1960 3,854
1940 1,629

Clackamas

River

Outlook

Noyer

Creek

Deep

Creek

Eagle

Creek

West Linn
Pop 23,380
1980 11,358
1960 3,933
1940 2,165

Stafford

Sunset

West Linn
HS

Oregon City
Shopping Center

Clackamas Co
Courthouse

Oregon City HS

Willamette
Falls
Community
Hospital

Willamette
Falls

Redland

Clear

Logan

Creek

Bonnie Lure
State Park

**Eagle
Creek**

Willamette

Echo Dell

Fischers Mill

Milo McIver
State Park

River Mill
Dam

Advance

Canby
Ferry

Coalca

New Era

Oregon City
Pop 24,940
1980 14,673
1960 7,996
1940 6,124

Clackamas
Community College

Oregon City
HS (Freshman)

Henrici

Central Point

Fishers Corner

Beaver
Creek

Oregon City
Airpark
370

Viola

Currinsville

Estacada
Pop 2,200
1980 1,419
1960 957
1940 526

Molalla River SP

See Page 213

See Page 209

See Page 209

SCALE 1:150,000

1 Km 0   1   2   3   4   5   10   15

K I L O M E T E R S

Elevations are in feet.

211

McMinnville, Woodburn

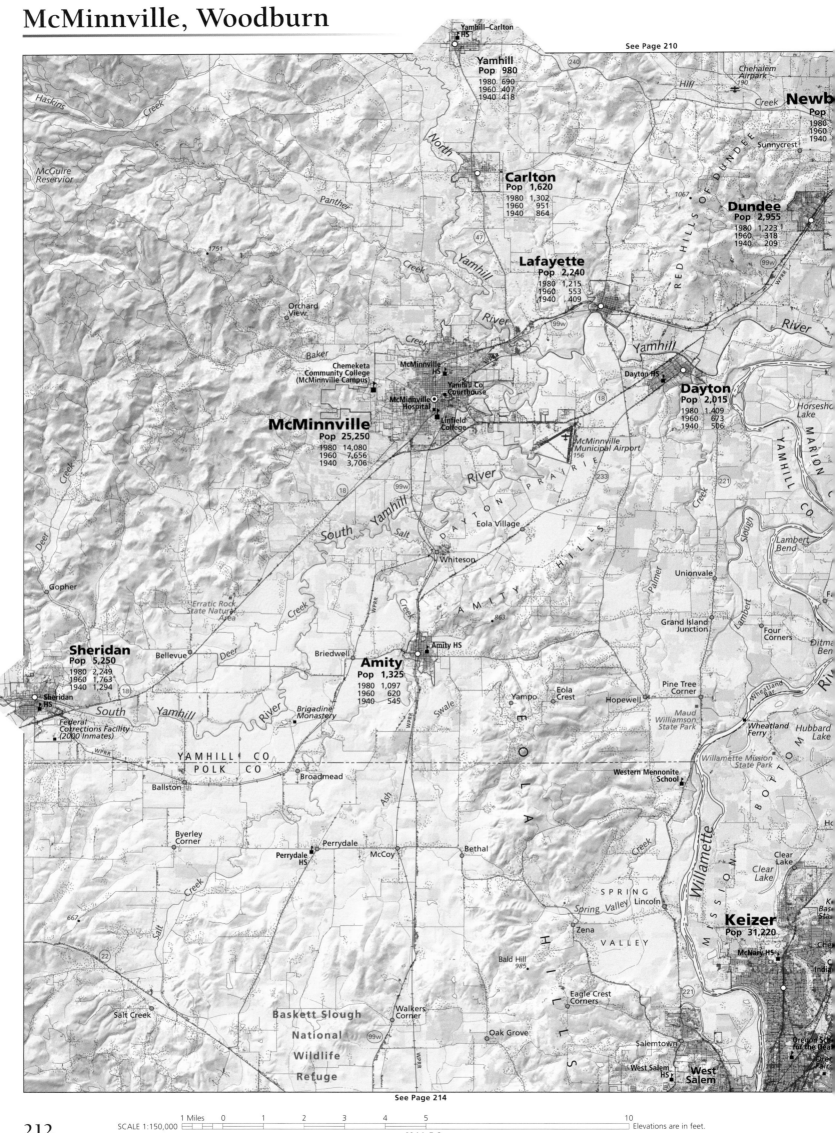

See Page 210

Yamhill
Pop 980
1980	690
1960	407
1940	418

Yamhill–Carlton HS

Newb
Pop
1980
1960
1940

Chehalem
Airpark

Sunnycrest

Carlton
Pop 1,620
1980	1,302
1960	951
1940	864

Dundee Pop 2,955
1980	1,223
1960	318
1940	209

RED HILLS OF DUNDEE

1067.

Lafayette
Pop 2,240
1980	1,215
1960	553
1940	409

99w

Yamhill River

Orchard View

Baker Creek

Chemeketa Community College (McMinnville Campus)

McMinnville HS

Yamhill Co Courthouse

McMinnville Hospital

Dayton HS

Dayton Pop 2,015
1980	1,409
1960	673
1940	506

Horsesho Lake

McMinnville
Pop 25,250
1980	14,080
1960	7,656
1940	3,706

Linfield College

McMinnville Municipal Airport
156

YAMHILL CO

MARION CO

Lambert Bend

DAYTON PRAIRIE

Eola Village

River

South Yamhill

Salt

Whiteson

AMITY HILLS

863.

Unionvale

Palmer Creek

Slough

Grand Island Junction

Four Corners

Ditma Ben

Gopher

Erratic Rock State Nature Area

Deer Creek

Creek

WPRR

Creek

Pine Tree Corner

Hopewell

Maud Williamson State Park

Wheatland Ferry

Hubbard Lake

Sheridan
Pop 5,250
1980	2,249
1960	1,763
1940	1,294

Bellevue

Briedwell

Amity HS

Yampo

Eola Crest

Wheatland Bar

Wheatland

Sheridan HS

Deer

18

Amity
Pop 1,325
1980	1,097
1960	620
1940	545

Willamette Mission State Park

Federal Corrections Facility (2000 Inmates)

South Yamhill River

Brigadine Monastery

Swale Creek

WPRR

O L A

Western Mennonite School

WPRR

YAMHILL CO
POLK CO

Broadmead

Ballston

Byerley Corner

Perrydale

Perrydale HS

McCoy

Bethal

Ash

Salt Creek

Spring Creek

SPRING VALLEY

Spring Valley

Lincoln

Clear Lake

Clear Lake

667.

Zena

VALLEY

H I L L S

B O T T O M

Willamette River

M I S S I O N

Keizer Pop 31,220

McNary HS

22

Bald Hill
985.

Eagle Crest Corners

Salemtown

Oregon Sch for the Dea

Salt Creek

Baskett Slough

National

Walkers Corner

Oak Grove

West Salem HS

West Salem

Wildlife

99w

Refuge

WPRR

221

SCALE 1:150,000

1 Miles 0 1 2 3 4 5 10

MILES

Elevations are in feet.

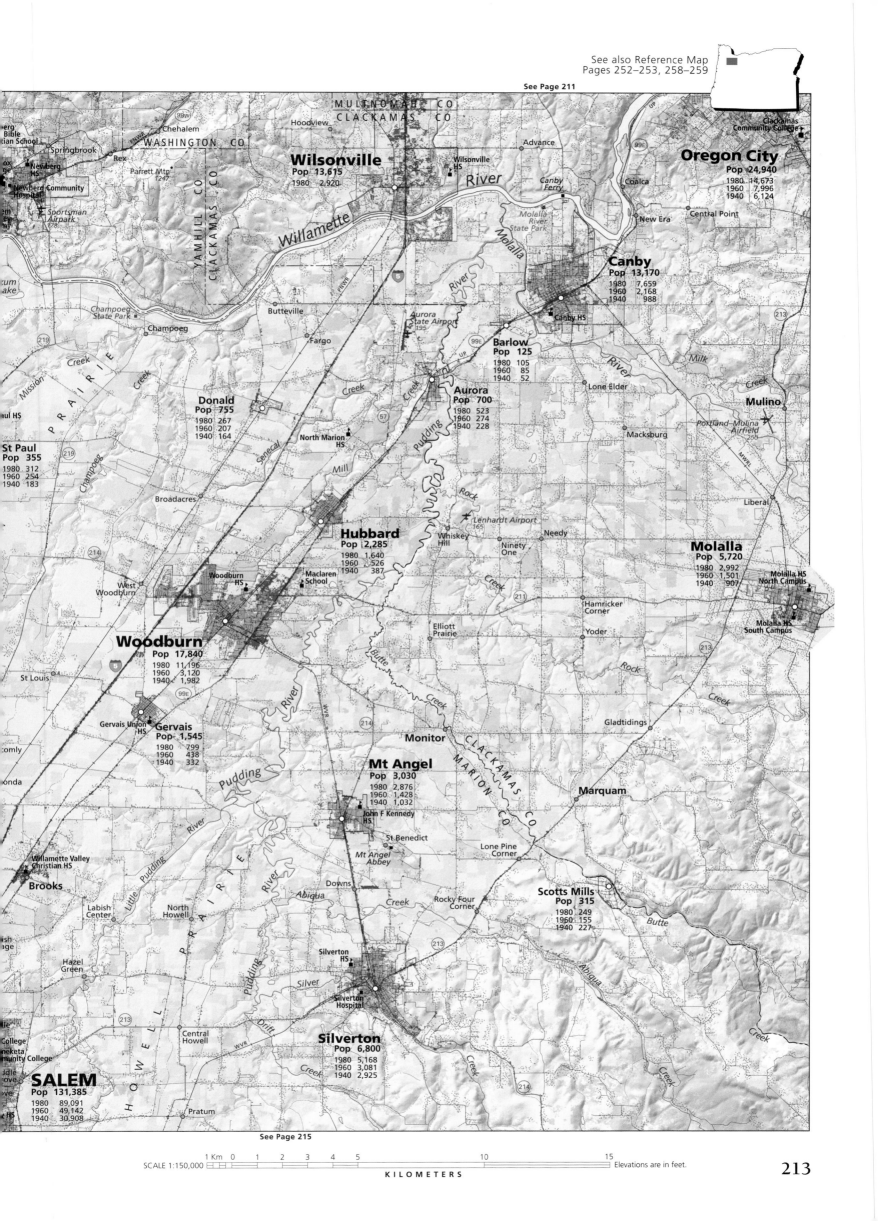

MULTNOMAH CO
CLACKAMAS CO

Hoodview

Advance

Oregon City
Pop 24,940
1980 14,673
1960 7,996
1940 6,124

Clackamas
Community College

Chehalem

WASHINGTON CO

Springbrook

Rex

Parrett Mtn
1247

Wilsonville
Pop 13,615
1980 2,920

Wilsonville
HS

River

Canby Ferry

Coalca

Central Point

Newberg Community
Hospital

Sportsman
Airpark
178

Willamette

Molalla
River
State Park

New Era

Champoeg
State Park

Butteville

Canby
Pop 13,170
1980 7,659
1960 2,168
1940 988

Milk

Champoeg

Fargo

Aurora
State Airport
195

Canby HS

Creek

Barlow
Pop 125
1980 105
1960 85
1940 52

Lone Elder

Donald
Pop 755
1980 267
1960 207
1940 164

99E

Aurora
Pop 700
1980 523
1960 274
1940 228

Macksburg

Mulino

Portland–Mulino
Airfield
250

St Paul
Pop 355
1980 312
1960 254
1940 183

North Marion
HS

Pudding

Rock

Lenhardt Airport
165

Needy

Liberal

Broadacres

Whiskey
Hill

Ninety
One

Molalla
Pop 5,720
1980 2,992
1960 1,501
1940 907

Hubbard
Pop 2,285
1980 1,640
1960 526
1940 387

Molalla HS
North Campus

West
Woodburn

Woodburn
HS

Maclaren
School

Creek

Hamricker
Corner

Molalla HS
South Campus

St Louis

Woodburn
Pop 17,840
1980 11,196
1960 3,120
1940 1,982

Elliott
Prairie

Yoder

213

5

99E

Gladtidings

comly

Gervais Union
HS

Gervais
Pop 1,545
1980 799
1960 438
1940 332

River

WVR

214

Rock

Marquam

onda

Monitor

CLACKAMAS CO

Pudding

Mt Angel
Pop 3,030
1980 2,876
1960 1,428
1940 1,032

MARION CO

Willamette Valley
Christian HS

River

John F Kennedy
HS

Lone Pine
Corner

Brooks

Labish
Center

North
Howell

St Benedict

Mt Angel
Abbey

Downs

Rocky Four
Corner

Scotts Mills
Pop 315
1980 249
1960 155
1940 227

Hazel
Green

Abiqua

Creek

Butte

Silverton
HS

213

College

Central
Howell

Silver

Silverton
Hospital

Abiqua

neketa
munity College

Pudding

WVR

Drift

Silverton
Pop 6,800
1980 5,168
1960 3,081
1940 2,925

214

Creek

SALEM
Pop 131,385
1980 89,091
1960 49,142
1940 30,908

HOWELL
PRAIRIE

Pratum

Creek

1 Km 0   1   2   3   4   5   10   15
SCALE 1:150,000   Elevations are in feet.
KILOMETERS

213

Salem, Dallas

Perrydale
Perrydale HS

McCoy

Bethal

EOLA

Spring Valley

Lincoln

SPRING

MISSI

BOTTO

Kei
Pop 3

Buell

667

Salt Creek

Zena

VALLEY

MARION CO.

POLK CO.

Bald Hill
985

Baskett Slough

National

Wildlife

Refuge

Walkers Corner

Oak Grove

Eagle Crest Corners

Salemtown

West Salem HS

West Salem

22

Salt Creek

Ellendale

Dallas
Pop 12,960
1980   8,530
1960   5,072
1940   3,579

Fir Villa

Rickreall

Rickreall

223

22

22

Brunks Corner

Eola

Holman Wayside SP

Winona

Marion Courthou
Will

Oakdale

Valley Community Hospital

Polk Co. Courthouse

Dallas HS

WPRR

Orrs Corner

51

Hayden Slough

Hayden Lake

Illahe Hill

Roberts

South Sal

Rickreall

Creek

Clow Corner

WPRR

Humbug Lake

Sprague HS

Liberty

Falls City
Pop 1,045
1980   804
1960   653
1940   715

Falls City HS

223

99w

Independence State Airport
175

Willamette River

CROISAN RIDGE

Prospect Hill
1119

Rosedale

Little Luckiamute

Bridgeport

Fern Corner

Western Oregon State University

Central HS

Orville

Independence
Pop 6,375
1980   4,024
1960   1,930
1940   1,372

Mt Pisgah
827

Monmouth
Pop 8,310
1980   5,594
1960   2,229
1940   965

SALEM

Burns Corner

1390

River

AMERICAN BOTTOM

Twin

Maple Grove

River

Luckiamute

Sarah Helmick State Park

Modeville

Sydney

Ankeny

National

Wildlife Refuge

Pedee

223

Luckiamute

Airlie

Parker

Buena Vista

Buena Vista Ferry

Talbot

MARION CO

River

Cole Island

Santiam

LINN CO.

Suver Junction

Suver

Soap

BENTON CO.

LINN CO.

Willamette River

BNSF

POLK CO.
BENTON CO.

Coffin Butte

Hale Butte
436

Kings Valley

CARDWELL HILLS

Creek

99w

WPRR

Palestine

River

BNSF

5

Santiam Christian

Adair Village
Pop 570
1980   589

223

Soap

SCALE 1:150,000   1 Miles   0   1   2   3   4   5   10   Elevations are in feet.

MILES

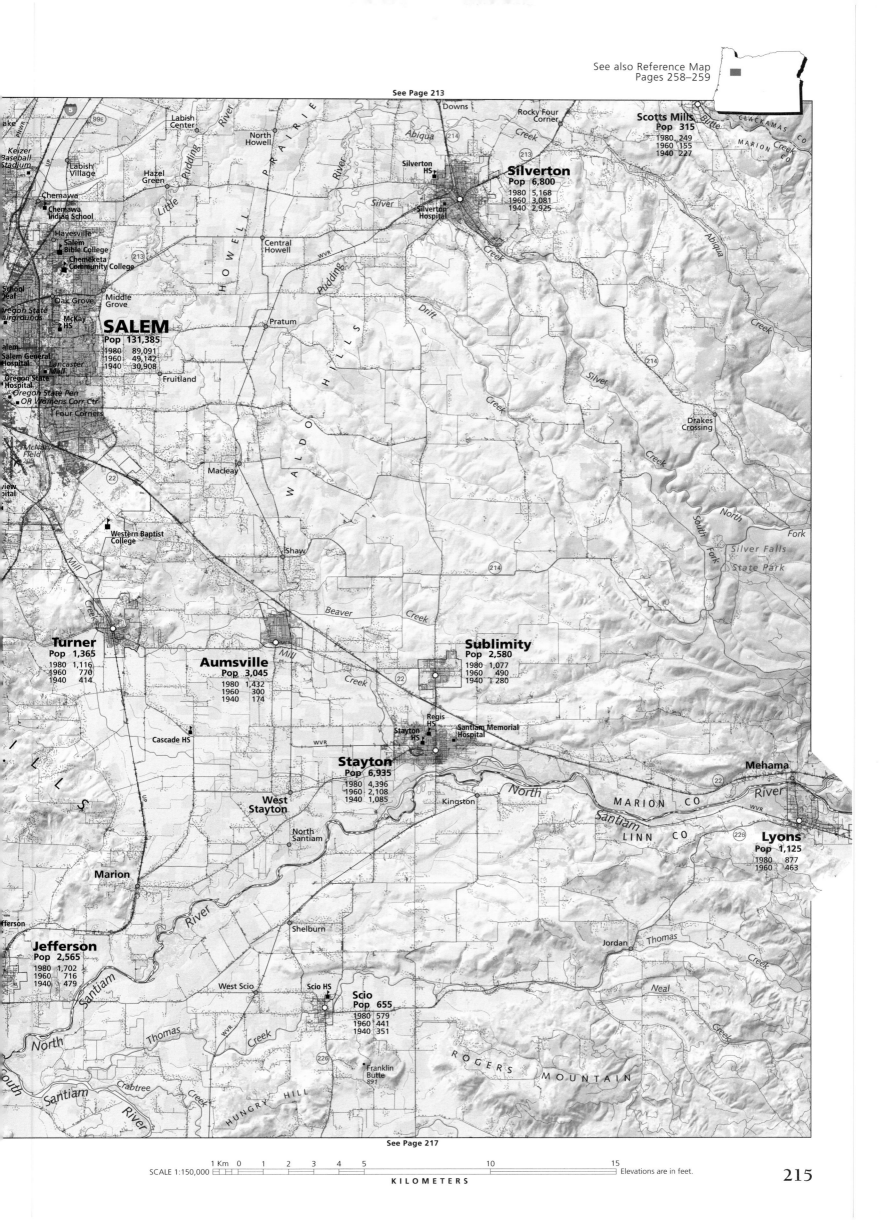

See Page 213

See also Reference Map
Pages 258–259

Scotts Mills
Pop 315
1980 249
1960 155
1940 227

Downs

Rocky Four Corner

CLACKAMAS CO

MARION CO

Abiqua

Creek

Silverton
HS

Silverton
Pop 6,800
1980 5,168
1960 3,081
1940 2,925

Silver

Creek

Silverton
Hospital

Labish
Center

North
Howell

Hazel
Green

Keizer
Baseball
Stadium

Labish
Village

Chemawa

Chemawa
Indian School

Hayesville

Salem
Bible College

Chemeketa
Community College

School
Deaf

Oak Grove

Middle
Grove

Pratum

Central
Howell

WVR

Pudding

River

Little Pudding River

HOWELL PRAIRIE

SALEM
Pop 131,385
1980 89,091
1960 49,142
1940 30,908

Oregon State
Fairgrounds

McKay
HS

Salem General
Hospital

Lancaster
Mall

Fruitland

Oregon State
Hospital

Oregon State Pen

OR Womens Corr Ctr

Four Corners

Macleay

WALDO HILLS

Drift

Silver

Creek

Drakes
Crossing

North Fork

South Fork

Silver Falls
State Park

McNary
Field

view
pital

Western Baptist
College

Shaw

Mill

Creek

Beaver

Creek

Turner
Pop 1,365
1980 1,116
1960 770
1940 414

Aumsville
Pop 3,045
1980 1,432
1960 300
1940 174

Mill

Creek

Sublimity
Pop 2,580
1980 1,077
1960 490
1940 280

Cascade HS

22

WVR

Regis
HS

Stayton
HS

Santiam Memorial
Hospital

Stayton
Pop 6,935
1980 4,396
1960 2,108
1940 1,085

West
Stayton

Kingston

North

Santiam

River

MARION CO

LINN CO

22

WVR

Mehama

Lyons
Pop 1,125
1980 877
1960 463

226

North
Santiam

Marion

Shelburn

Jordan

Thomas

Creek

Jefferson
Pop 2,565
1980 1,702
1960 716
1940 479

South
Santiam

North

River

West Scio

Scio HS

Scio
Pop 655
1980 579
1960 441
1940 351

Neal

Thomas

Creek

226

Franklin
Butte
891

ROGERS MOUNTAIN

HUNGRY HILL

Crabtree

Creek

WVR

Thomas

See Page 217

1 Km 0   1   2   3   4   5   10   15
SCALE 1:150,000   Elevations are in feet.

KILOMETERS

215

Corvallis, Albany, Lebanon

See Page 214

Palestine

Miller
Pop 7
1980 5

Santiam Christian
HS

Adair Village
Pop 570
1980   598

North
Albany

Dra
Albany
Municip
Airport
22

Country
Estate

Granger

Albany General
Hospital

Linn Co
Courthouse

Lewisburg

Crescent Valley
HS

Riverside

West Albany
HS

Heritage
Mall

Alba
Pop 41,
1980   26,5
1960   12,9
1940   5,6

Dimple Hill
1495

Good Samaritan
Hospital

Half Moon
Bend

South Albany
HS

Price Peak
1875

BENTON   CO

LINN   CO

Colorado
Lake

Linn–Benton
Community
College

Marys

Orleans

Wren   WPRR

Hewlett
Packard

34

River

Corvallis
Pop 52,215
1980   40,960
1960   20,669
1940   8,392

Corvallis HS

Benton Co
Courthouse

Oregon State
University

Avery

Marys

River

Muddy

Willamette

99E

Tangent
UP

Tangent
Pop 1,080
1980   478

Philomath
Philomath
HS

Pop 3,995
1980   2,673
1960   1,359
1940   856

BNSF

Calapooia

5

Muddy

K I G E R

I S L A N D

Corvallis
Municipal Airport
246

99w

Oakville

Creek

Fern

Shedd

Fayetteville

Saddle
Butte
669

Greenberry

Peoria

Island

Buchanan

Winkle
Butte

Hoacum

William L Finley

National

WPRR

Rickard

Island

Central Linn
HS

Wildlife

Bruce

Refuge

River

Paper
Mill

Barclay

Halsey
Pop 775
1980   693
1960   404
1940   305

Bellfountain

Bellfountain
Junction

Creek

Irish
Bend

Muddy

Dawson

WPRR

Little Muddy

228

BENTON   CO

LINN   CO

Long Tom

Little Muddy

Bond
503

Alpine

Alpine
Junction

Muddy

Monroe
Pop 550
1980   412
1960   374
1940   311

Glenbrook

Hammer   *Creek*

Monroe
HS

99w

Spoon

99E

Creek

Alford

See Page 218

1 Miles   0   1   2   3   4   5   10

SCALE 1:150,000   Elevations are in feet.

M I L E S

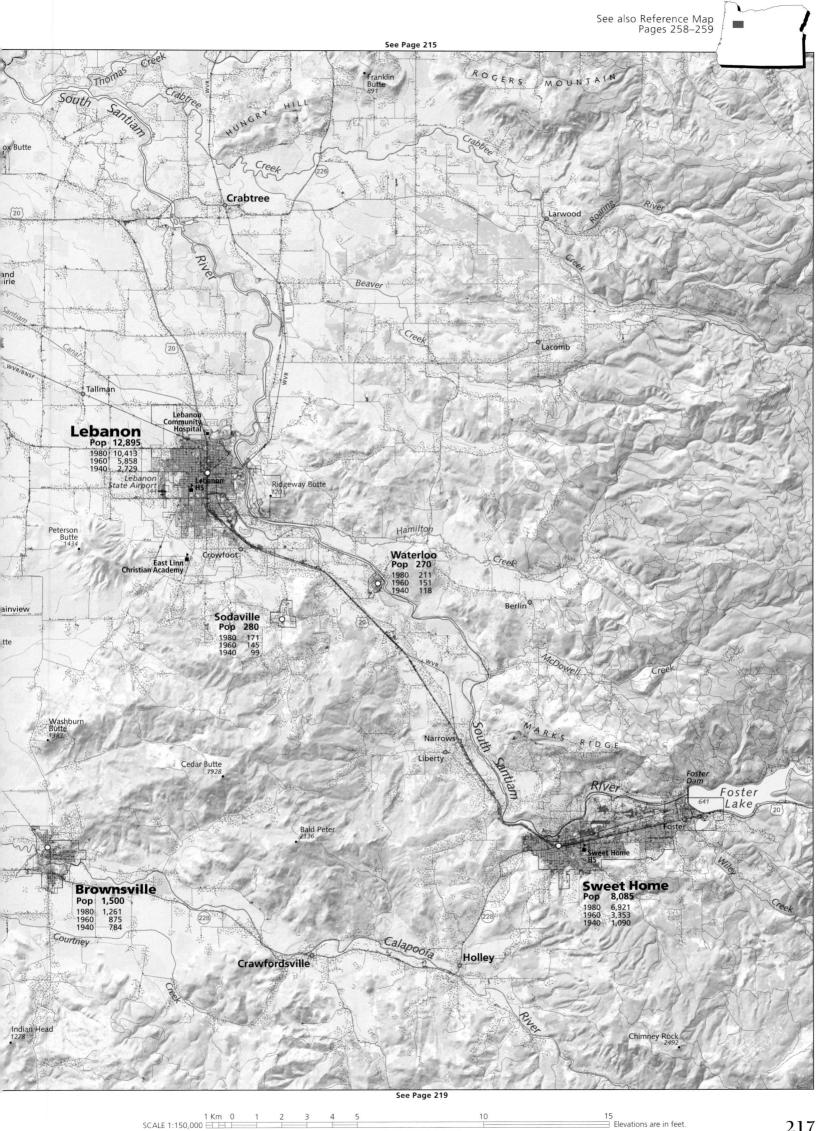

ROGERS MOUNTAIN

South Santiam

Thomas Creek

Crabtree Creek

HUNGRY HILL

Franklin
Butte
891

Crabtree

Larwood

Roaring River

226

Crabtree

Crabtree

20

Beaver Creek

Lacomb

WVR

Tallman

Lebanon
Pop 12,895
1980 10,413
1960   5,858
1940   2,729

Lebanon
Community
Hospital

Lebanon
State Airport

Lebanon
HS

Ridgeway Butte
1203

Hamilton Creek

Peterson
Butte
1434

Crowfoot

East Linn
Christian Academy

Waterloo
Pop 270
1980 211
1960 151
1940 118

Berlin

Sodaville
Pop 280
1980 171
1960 145
1940   99

20

WVR

McDowell Creek

Washburn
Butte
1383

Narrows

Liberty

South Santiam

MARKS RIDGE

Cedar Butte
1928

River

Foster
Dam

Foster
Lake

641

Foster

20

Bald Peter
2136

Sweet Home
HS

Brownsville
Pop 1,500
1980 1,261
1960   875
1940   784

Sweet Home
Pop 8,085
1980 6,921
1960 3,353
1940 1,090

Willey Creek

228

Courtney Creek

Indian Head
1228

Calapooia

Crawfordsville

Holley

228

River

Chimney Rock
2492

SCALE 1:150,000   1 Km 0   1   2   3   4   5   10   15   Elevations are in feet.
KILOMETERS

217

Eugene, Springfield

See Page 216

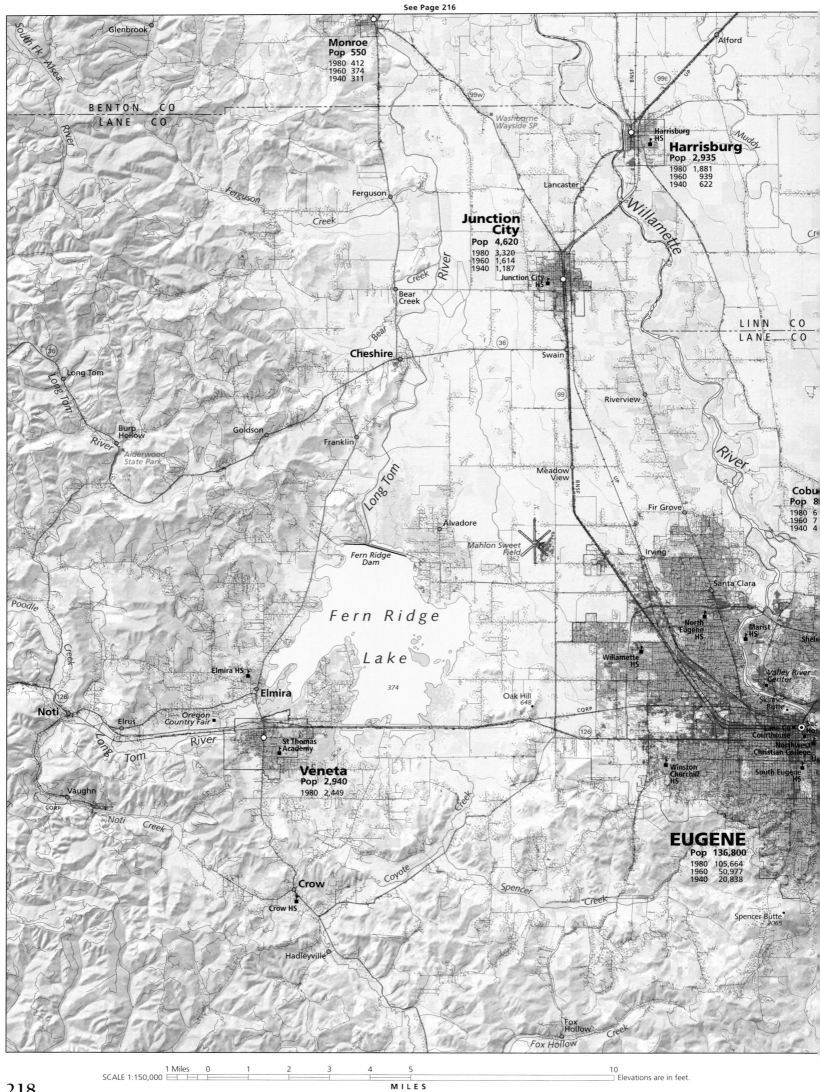

Glenbrook

Monroe
Pop 550

1980	412
1960	374
1940	311

South Fk Alsea River

BENTON CO
LANE CO

Ferguson Creek

Ferguson

Washburne Wayside SP

99w

Alford

BNSF

99E

UP

Harrisburg HS

Harrisburg
Pop 2,935

1980	1,881
1960	939
1940	622

Muddy

Lancaster

Willamette

Creek

River

Junction City
Pop 4,620

1980	3,320
1960	1,614
1940	1,187

Bear Creek

Junction City HS

LINN CO
LANE CO

36

Swain

Bear Creek

99

Riverview

River

Cheshire

36

Creek

Long Tom

36

Long Tom

Burp Hollow

River

Goldson

Alderwood State Park

Franklin

Meadow View

BNSF

UP

Fir Grove

Cobu
Pop 8

1980	6
1960	7
1940	4

Alvadore

Mahlon Sweet Field
362

Irving

Santa Clara

Poodle

Fern Ridge Dam

North Eugene HS

Marist HS

Shel

Fern Ridge

Creek

Lake

374

Willamette HS

Valley River Center

Ski River Butte

Elmira HS

Oak Hill
648

CORP

Sac Hos

Noti

Elrus

Oregon Country Fair

Elmira

River

126

Lane Co Courthouse

Northwest Christian College

Vaughn

CORP

St Thomas Academy

126

Winston Churchill HS

South Eugene HS

Noti

Creek

Veneta
Pop 2,940

1980	2,449

Creek

EUGENE
Pop 136,800

1980	105,664
1960	50,977
1940	20,838

Long Tom

Coyote

Spencer

Creek

Crow

Crow HS

Spencer Butte
2065

Hadleyville

Fox Hollow

Fox Hollow Creek

SCALE 1:150,000   1 Miles   0   1   2   3   4   5   10   Elevations are in feet.

MILES

218

See Page 217

See also Reference Map
Pages 258–259, 264–265

Calapooia
River

LINN CO
LANE CO

Pierce

Creek

Georges
Knob
2247

Mohawk

Creek

River

COBURG

Cash

Oshkosh
Mtn
2939

Mt Tom
3166

West Point
Hill
966

Parsons

Mabel

Creek

Wendling

Mill

Creek

Creek

Mt Nebo
3407

Marcola

Mohawk
HS

Cartwright

Creek

McGowan

River

Mohawk

Creek

Mohawk

CAMP CREEK RIDGE

Creek

Leaburg

126

Armitage
State Park

Mohawk

Camp

River

McKenzie

Deerhorn

McKenzie

River

Gateway
Mall

River

Walterville

5

McKenzie

River

Cedar Flat

Hendricks Bridge
State Park

Springfield
HS

McKenzie
Willamette
Hospital

Weyerhauser

Thurston
HS

126

Springfield
Pop 53,700
1980 41,621
1960 19,616
1940   3,805

Middle Fork

Natron

Mt Pisgah
1516

Willamette

Creek

Lane
Community
College

Jasper

Hills

Creek

Goshen

River

Little Fall

Short Mtn
1106

Fall

Creek

Coast Fork Willamette

**Pleasant
Hill**

38

River

Fall
Creek

Fall Creek
Dam

834

Fall Creek
Reservoir

CLACKAMAS CO

Pleasant Hill
HS

Pengra

Lost Cr

Elijah Bristow
State Park

Unity

5

Hobby Field
535

Trent

VALE

See Page 222

1 Km 0   1   2   3   4   5   10   15
SCALE 1:150,000 ⊨⊨⊨   ⊨ Elevations are in feet.
KILOMETERS

219

Portland to Eugene Historic Growth

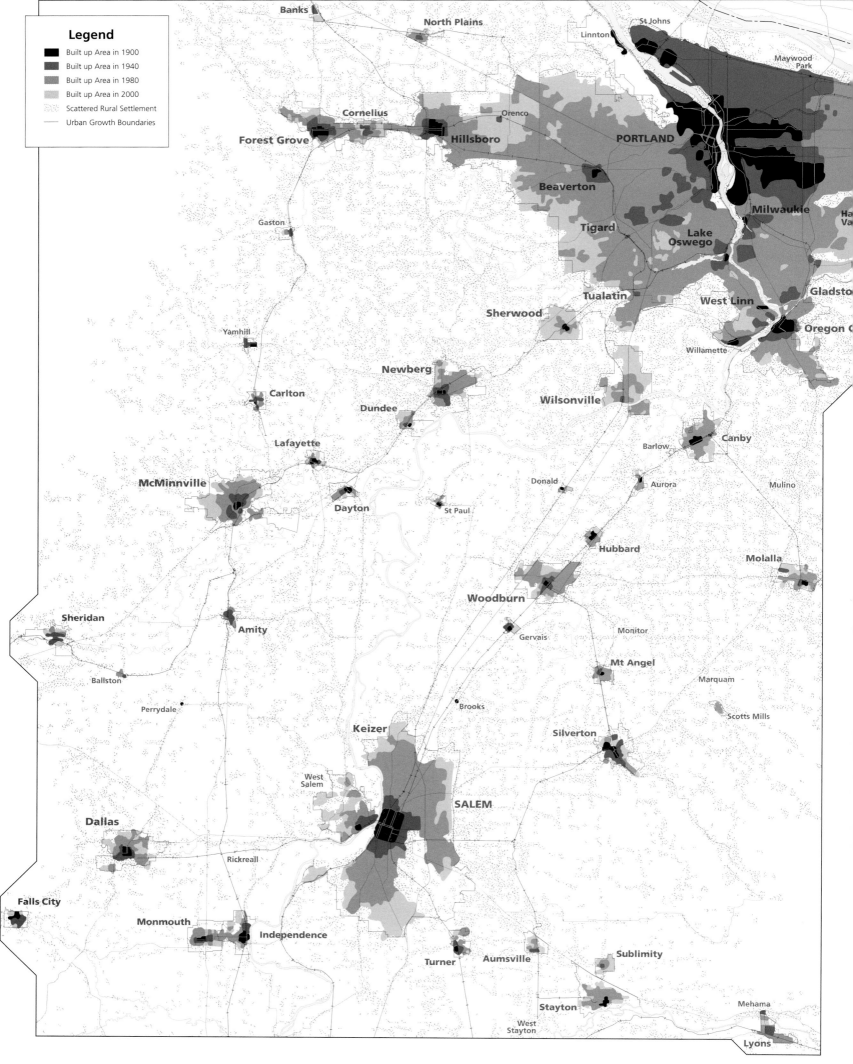

Legend

- Built up Area in 1900
- Built up Area in 1940
- Built up Area in 1980
- Built up Area in 2000
- Scattered Rural Settlement
- Urban Growth Boundaries

Banks
North Plains
St Johns
Linnton
Maywood Park
Cornelius
Orenco
Forest Grove
Hillsboro
PORTLAND
Gaston
Beaverton
Milwaukie
Ha
Va
Tigard
Lake Oswego
Yamhill
Tualatin
West Linn
Gladsto
Sherwood
Newberg
Oregon C
Carlton
Wilsonville
Willamette
Dundee
Lafayette
Barlow
Canby
McMinnville
Donald
Aurora
Mulino
Dayton
St Paul
Hubbard
Molalla
Woodburn
Sheridan
Amity
Monitor
Gervais
Ballston
Mt Angel
Marquam
Perrydale
Brooks
Scotts Mills
Keizer
Silverton
West Salem
SALEM
Dallas
Rickreall
Falls City
Monmouth
Independence
Turner
Aumsville
Sublimity
Stayton
Mehama
West Stayton
Lyons

220

SCALE 1:333,333

0   5   10   15   20

MILES

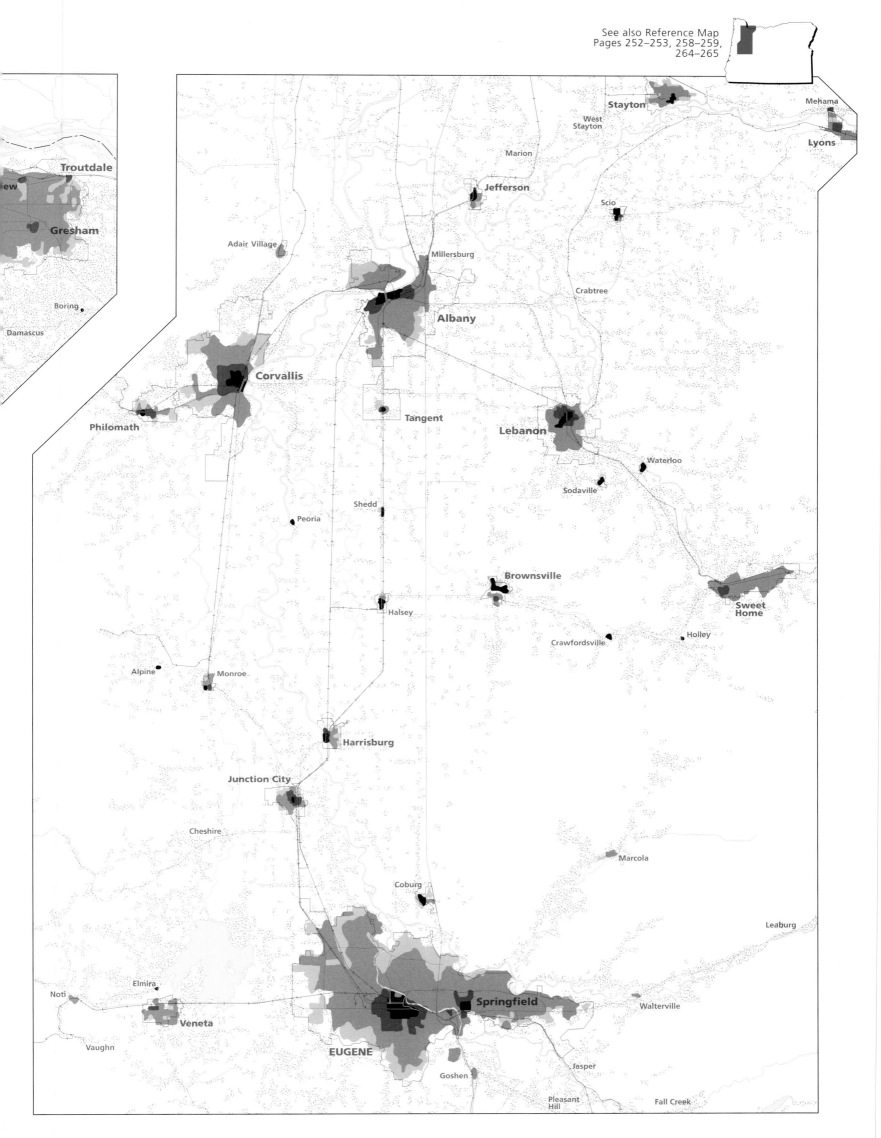

See also Reference Map
Pages 252–253, 258–259,
264–265

Troutdale

Gresham

Boring

Damascus

Stayton

West
Stayton

Mehama

Lyons

Marion

Jefferson

Scio

Adair Village

Millersburg

Crabtree

Albany

Corvallis

Tangent

Lebanon

Philomath

Waterloo

Sodaville

Shedd

Peoria

Brownsville

Halsey

Sweet
Home

Crawfordsville

Holley

Alpine

Monroe

Harrisburg

Junction City

Cheshire

Marcola

Coburg

Leaburg

Elmira

Noti

Veneta

Springfield

Walterville

Vaughn

EUGENE

Goshen

Jasper

Pleasant
Hill

Fall Creek

0   5   10   15   20   25   30   SCALE 1:333,333

KILOMETERS

Cottage Grove; Oakridge; Sutherlin

See Page 219

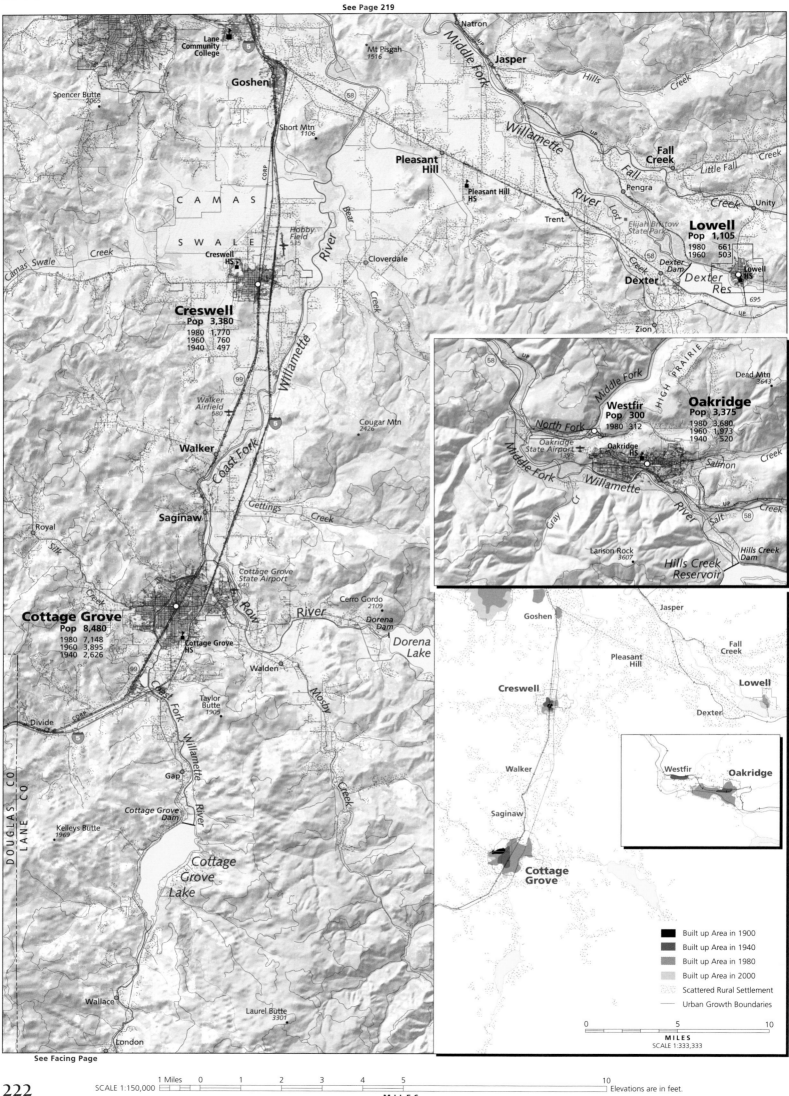

Natron

Jasper

Middle *Fork*

UP

Hills

Creek

Fall
Creek

Willamette

Fall

Pengra

River

Little Fall

Creek

Unity

UP

Lowell
Pop 1,105

1980	661
1960	503

Trent

Elijah Bristow
State Park

Creek

58

Dexter
Dam

Lowell
HS

Dexter

Dexter
Res

695

Zion

UP

Lane
Community
College

5

Goshen

Mt Pisgah
1516

Spencer Butte
2065

58

Short Mtn
1106

Pleasant
Hill

Pleasant Hill
HS

C A M A S

CORP

Bear

Cloverdale

S W A L E

Hobby
Field
535

Willamette

Creek

Creswell
HS

Creek

Creek

Camas Swale

Creswell
Pop 3,380

1980	1,770
1960	760
1940	497

River

99

Walker
Airfield
580

5

Walker

Cougar Mtn
2426

Saginaw

Coast Fork

Gettings

Creek

Royal

Silk

Cerro Gordo
2109

Dorena
Dam

Cottage Grove
State Airport
640

Raw

River

Dorena
Lake

Cottage Grove
Pop 8,480

1980	7,148
1960	3,895
1940	2,626

Cottage Grove
HS

Creek

Walden

Mosby

99

Coast Fork

CORP

Divide

5

Taylor
Butte
1905

Willamette

Gap

Creek

Cottage Grove
Dam

Kelleys Butte
1969

Cottage
Grove
Lake

DOUGLAS CO
LANE CO

Wallace

Laurel Butte
3301

London

See Facing Page

58

UP

Middle *Fork*

HIGH PRAIRIE

Dead Mtn
3643

North Fork

Westfir
Pop 300

1980 312

Oakridge
Pop 3,375

1980	3,680
1960	1,973
1940	520

Oakridge
State Airport
1335

Oakridge
HS

Salmon

Creek

Middle Fork

Willamette

Gray *Cr*

River

Salt

UP

Creek

58

Larison Rock
3607

Hills Creek
Reservoir

Hills Creek
Dam

Goshen

Jasper

Pleasant
Hill

Fall
Creek

Creswell

Lowell

Walker

Dexter

Saginaw

Westfir   **Oakridge**

Cottage
Grove

■	Built up Area in 1900
■	Built up Area in 1940
■	Built up Area in 1980
░	Built up Area in 2000
⋯	Scattered Rural Settlement
—	Urban Growth Boundaries

0   5   10
MILES
SCALE 1:333,333

---

1 Miles   0   1   2   3   4   5   10

SCALE 1:150,000   Elevations are in feet.

MILES

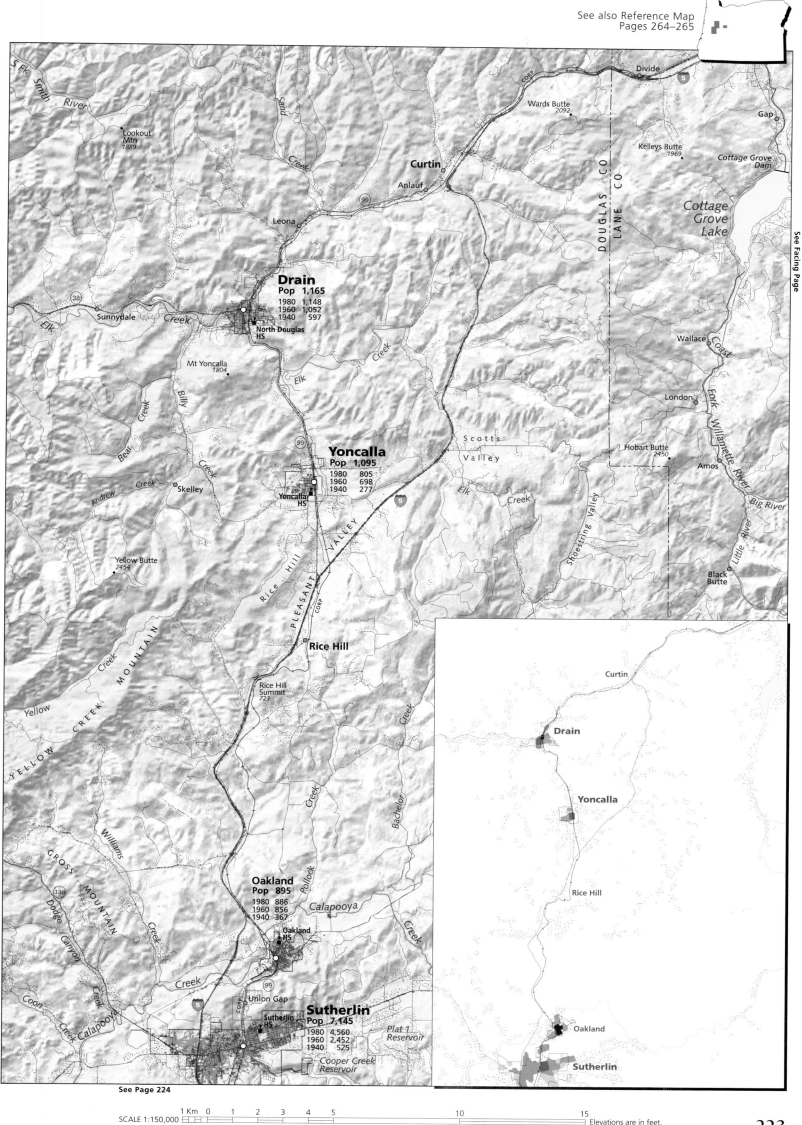

See also Reference Map
Pages 264–265

Divide

Wards Butte
2092

Gap

Kelleys Butte
1969

Cottage Grove
Dam

Lookout
Mtn
1889

Curtin

Anlauf

*Cottage
Grove
Lake*

Leona

DOUGLAS CO

LANE CO

Drain
Pop 1,165

1980	1,148
1960	1,052
1940	597

Sunnydale

North Douglas
HS

Wallace

Coast

Mt Yoncalla
1804

London

Yoncalla
Pop 1,095

1980	805
1960	698
1940	277

Scotts

Valley

Hobart Butte
2450

Skelley

Yoncalla
HS

Amos

Elk Creek

Shoestring Valley

Yellow Butte
2454

Black
Butte

CREEK MOUNTAIN

Rice Hill

Rice Hill
Summit
723

Yellow

GROSS MOUNTAIN

Oakland
Pop 895

1980	886
1960	856
1940	367

Calapooya

Oakland
HS

Union Gap

Sutherlin
Pop 7,145

1980	4,560
1960	2,452
1940	525

Sutherlin
HS

Plat 1
Reservoir

Cooper Creek
Reservoir

Curtin

Drain

Yoncalla

Rice Hill

Oakland

Sutherlin

See Page 224

See Facing Page

SCALE 1:150,000

1 Km 0   1   2   3   4   5   10   15

KILOMETERS

Elevations are in feet.

Roseburg

See Page 223

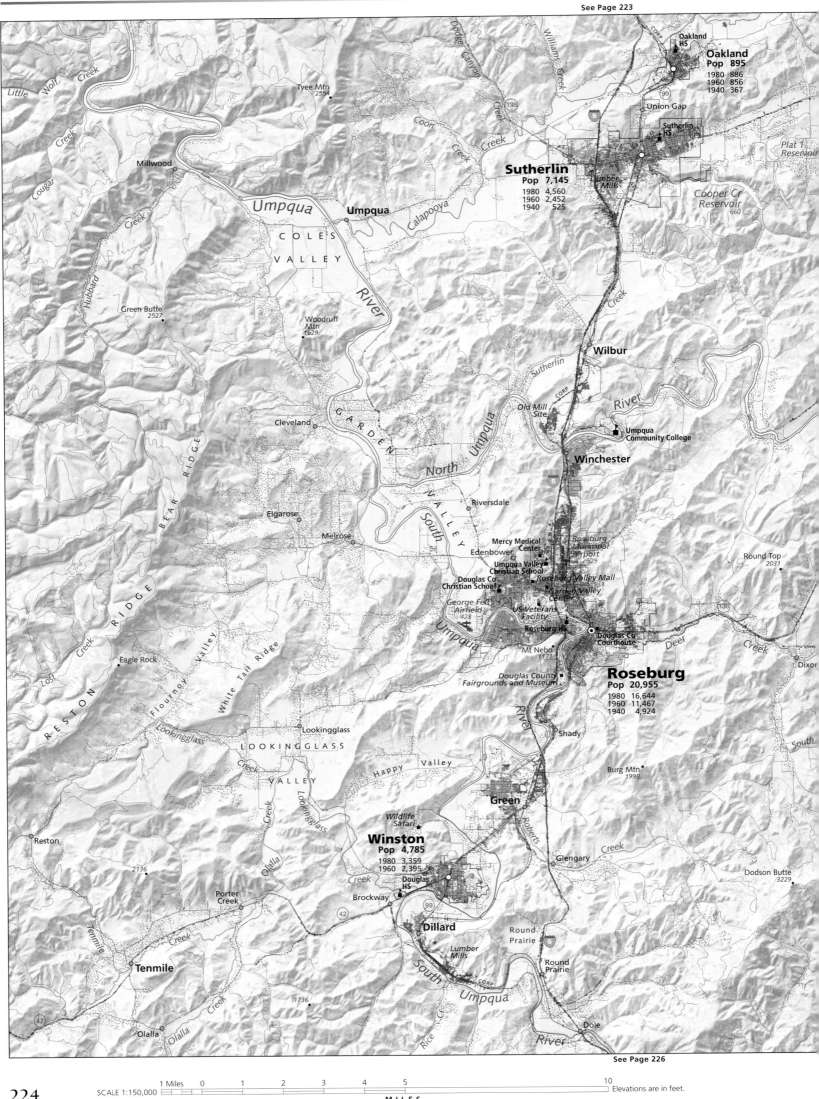

Oakland
Pop 895
1980 886
1960 856
1940 367

Union Gap

Sutherlin
Pop 7,145
1980 4,560
1960 2,452
1940 525

Sutherlin
HS

Lumber
Mills

Cooper Cr
Reservoir
660

Plat 1
Reservoir

Little
Wolf Creek

Cougar Creek

Dodge Canyon

Williams Creek

Tyee Mtn
2554

Coon Creek

Creek

Calapooya Creek

Millwood

Umpqua

Umpqua

COLES
VALLEY

River

Hubbard Creek

Green Butte
2527

Woodruff
Mtn
1629

Cleveland

GARDEN

VALLEY

North

Umpqua

South

River

Sutherlin
Creek

Old Mill
Site

Wilbur

Umpqua
Community College

Winchester

Riversdale

BEAR RIDGE

Elgarose

Melrose

Mercy Medical
Center

Edenbower

Umpqua Valley
Christian School

Douglas Co
Christian School

George Fell
Airfield
428

US Veterans
Facility

Roseburg
Municipal
Airport
529

Roseburg Valley Mall

Garden Valley
Center

Douglas Co
Courthouse

Round Top
2031

Roseburg HS

Mt Nebo
1171

Roseburg
Pop 20,955
1980 16,644
1960 11,467
1940 4,924

Deer Creek

Dixon

RESTON RIDGE

Lost Creek

Eagle Rock

FLOURNOY VALLEY

White Tait Ridge

Lookingglass

LOOKINGGLASS

VALLEY

Happy Valley

Douglas County
Fairgrounds and Museum

Umpqua River

Shady

Burg Mtn
1998

South Creek

Reston

2136

Olalla Creek

Lookingglass Creek

Green

Wildlife
Safari

Winston
Pop 4,785
1980 3,359
1960 2,395

Douglas
HS

Roberts Creek

Glengary Creek

Dodson Butte
3229

Porter
Creek

Brockway

Dillard

Lumber
Mills

Round
Prairie

Round
Prairie

Tenmile Creek

Tenmile

Olalla Olalla Creek

1736

Rice Creek

South Umpqua River

Dole

See Page 226

224

1 Miles 0   1   2   3   4   5   10
SCALE 1:150,000 ⊟⊟⊟⊟⊟   ⊟ Elevations are in feet.
                        MILES

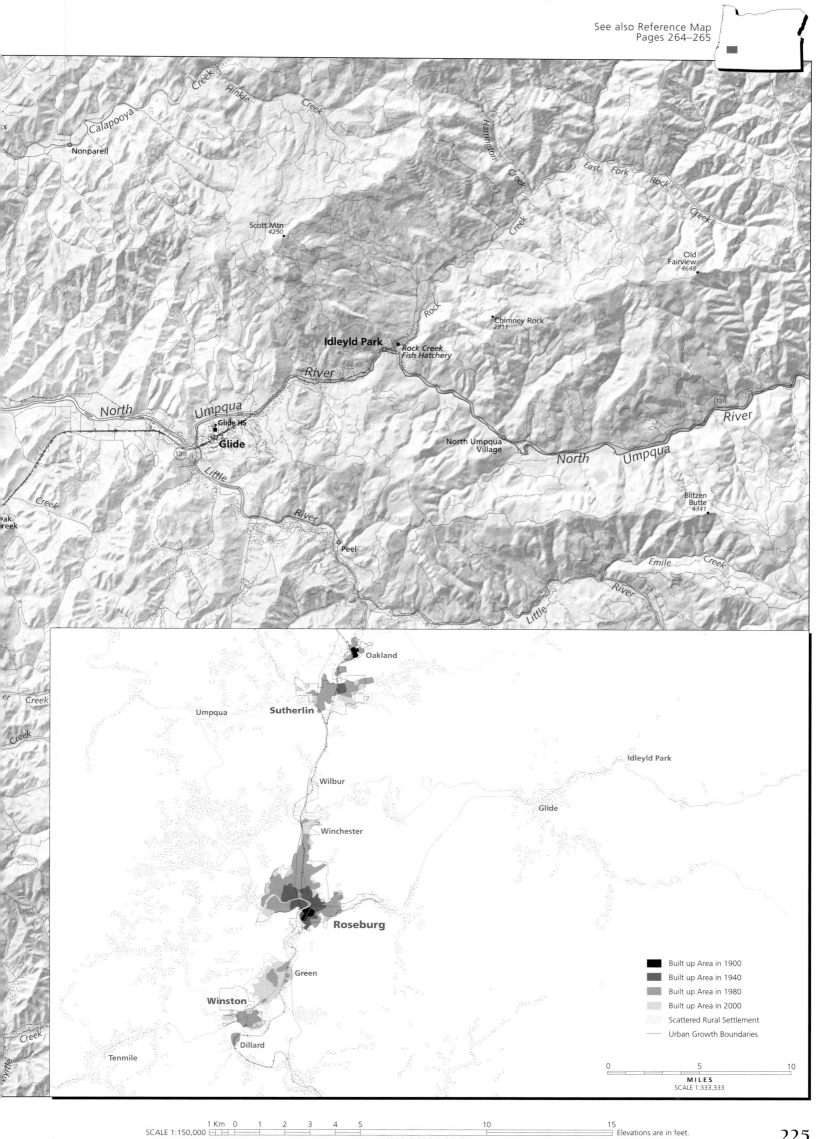

See also Reference Map
Pages 264–265

Nonpareil

Calapooya

Hinkle

Creek

Creek

Harrington

Creek

East

Fork

Rock

Creek

Creek

Scott Mtn
4250

Old
Fairview
4648

Rock

Chimney Rock
2811

Idleyld Park

Rock Creek
Fish Hatchery

North

Umpqua

River

138

River

Glide HS

Glide

North Umpqua
Village

North

Umpqua

138

Little

Creek

River

Blitzen
Butte
4341

ak
eek

Peel

Emile

Creek

Little

River

Oakland

Creek

Umpqua

Sutherlin

Idleyld Park

Creek

Wilbur

Glide

er
Creek

Winchester

Roseburg

Green

Built up Area in 1900

Built up Area in 1940

Built up Area in 1980

Built up Area in 2000

Scattered Rural Settlement

Urban Growth Boundaries

Winston

Dillard

Tenmile

0   5   10
MILES
SCALE 1:333,333

Creek

1 Km 0   1   2   3   4   5   10   15
SCALE 1:150,000 ⊞⊞⊞⊞⊞⊞   Elevations are in feet.
KILOMETERS

225

Myrtle Creek; Cave Junction

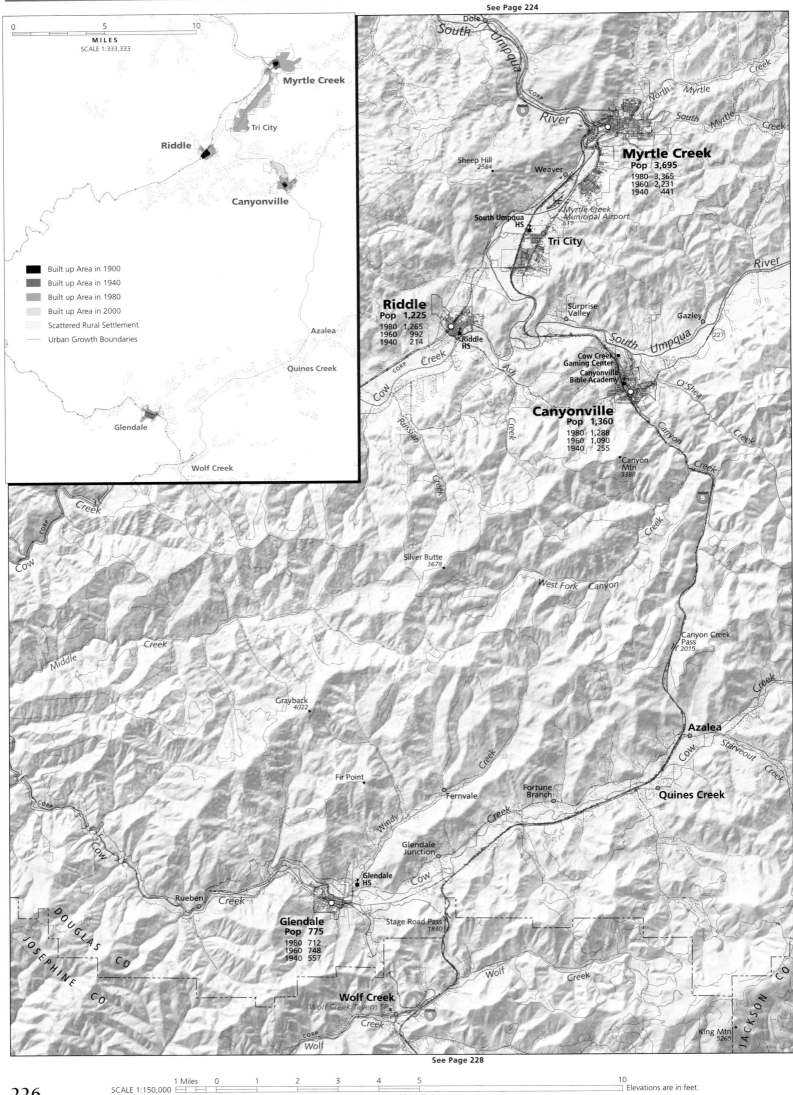

See Page 224

MILES
SCALE 1:333,333

Built up Area in 1900
Built up Area in 1940
Built up Area in 1980
Built up Area in 2000
Scattered Rural Settlement
Urban Growth Boundaries

Myrtle Creek

Tri City

Riddle

Canyonville

Azalea

Quines Creek

Glendale

Wolf Creek

South

Umpqua

River

Dole

North

Myrtle

South

Myrtle

Creek

Creek

Sheep Hill
2584

Weaver

Myrtle Creek
Pop 3,695
1980 3,365
1960 2,231
1940   441

Myrtle Creek
Municipal Airport
619

South Umpqua
HS

Tri City

River

Surprise
Valley

Gazley

227

Riddle
Pop 1,225
1980 1,265
1960   992
1940   214

Riddle
HS

South

Umpqua

Cow Creek
Gaming Center

Canyonville
Bible Academy

Canyonville
Pop 1,360
1980 1,288
1960 1,090
1940   255

O'Shea

Canyon

Creek

Cow

Creek

CORP

Ash

Creek

Russian

Creek

Creek

Canyon
Mtn
3388

Silver Butte
3678

West Fork   Canyon

5

Canyon Creek
Pass
2015

Middle

Creek

Creek

Grayback
4022

Azalea

Starveout

Creek

Fir Point

Fernvale

Fortune
Branch

Quines Creek

Windy

Cow

Creek

Glendale
Junction

Glendale
HS

Rueben

Creek

Creek

Glendale
Pop 775
1980 712
1960 748
1940 557

Stage Road Pass
1830

Cow

Creek

Wolf

Creek

DOUGLAS CO

JOSEPHINE CO

Cow

CORP

Wolf Creek
Wolf Creek Tavern SP

5

Creek

Wolf

King Mtn
5265

JACKSON CO

See Page 228

1 Miles   0   1   2   3   4   5   10
SCALE 1:150,000   Elevations are in feet.
MILES

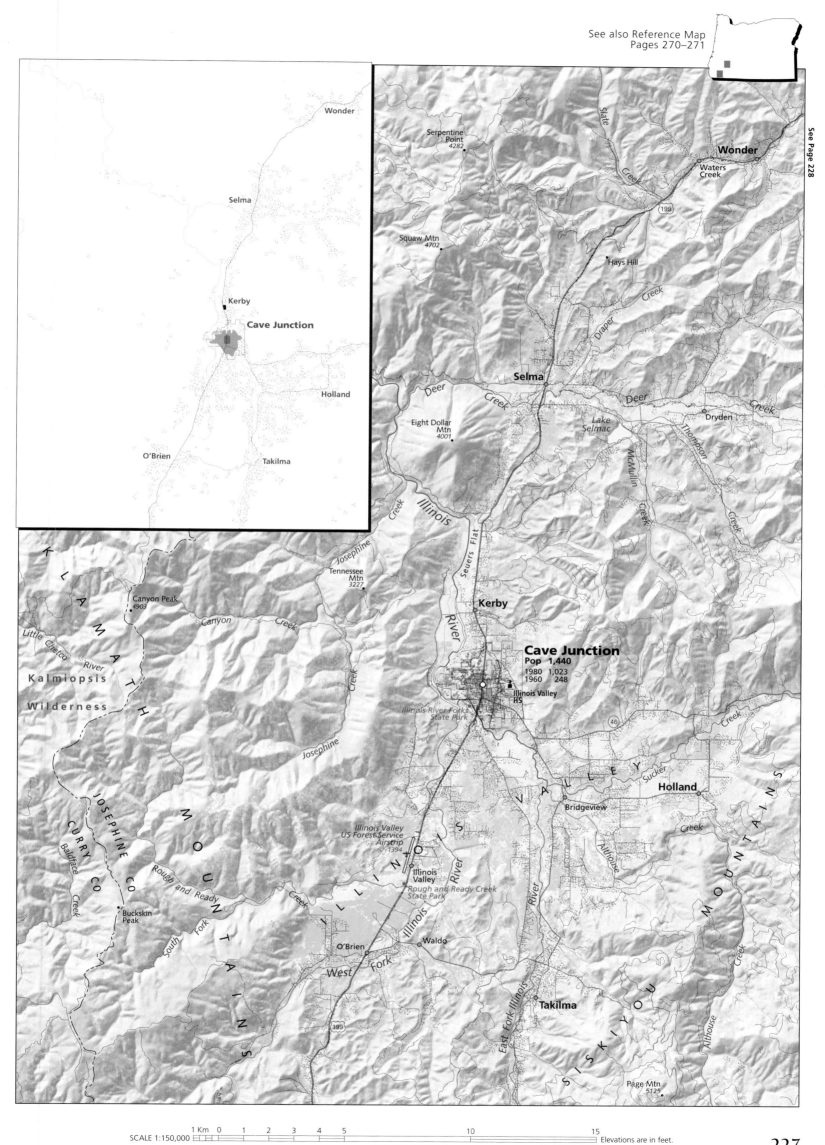

See also Reference Map
Pages 270–271

See Page 228

Wonder

Serpentine
Point
4282

Slate

Creek

Wonder

Waters
Creek

199

Squaw Mtn
4702

Hays Hill

Draper

Creek

Selma

Deer

Creek

Deer

Creek

Dryden

Lake
Selmac

McMullin

Thompson

Creek

Creek

Eight Dollar
Mtn
4001

Illinois

Deer

Creek

Severs Flat

K
L
A
M
A
T
H

Josephine

Tennessee
Mtn
3227

Canyon Peak
4903

Canyon

Creek

Kerby

Little Chetco

River

Kalmiopsis

Wilderness

Josephine

Creek

Cave Junction
Pop 1,440
1980 1,023
1960 248

Illinois Valley
HS

46

Creek

Sucker

Holland

J
O
S
E
P
H
I
N
E

C
O

Josephine

Illinois River Forks
State Park

Bridgeview

C
U
R
R
Y

C
O

Baldface

Rough and Ready

Creek

I
L
L
I
N
O
I
S

Creek

Illinois Valley
US Forest Service
Airstrip
1394

River

Illinois

V
A
L
L
E
Y

Althouse

S
I
S
K
I
Y
O
U

M
O
U
N
T
A
I
N
S

South Fork

Buckskin
Peak

M
O
U
N
T
A
I
N
S

Illinois

Illinois
Valley

Rough and Ready Creek
State Park

River

O'Brien

Waldo

West

Fork

East Fork Illinois

Takilma

Althouse

Creek

399

Page Mtn
5125

SCALE 1:150,000   1 Km 0   1   2   3   4   5   10   15
                                                        Elevations are in feet.

K I L O M E T E R S

Wonder

Selma

Kerby

Cave Junction

Holland

O'Brien

Takilma

Medford, Grants Pass

See Page 226

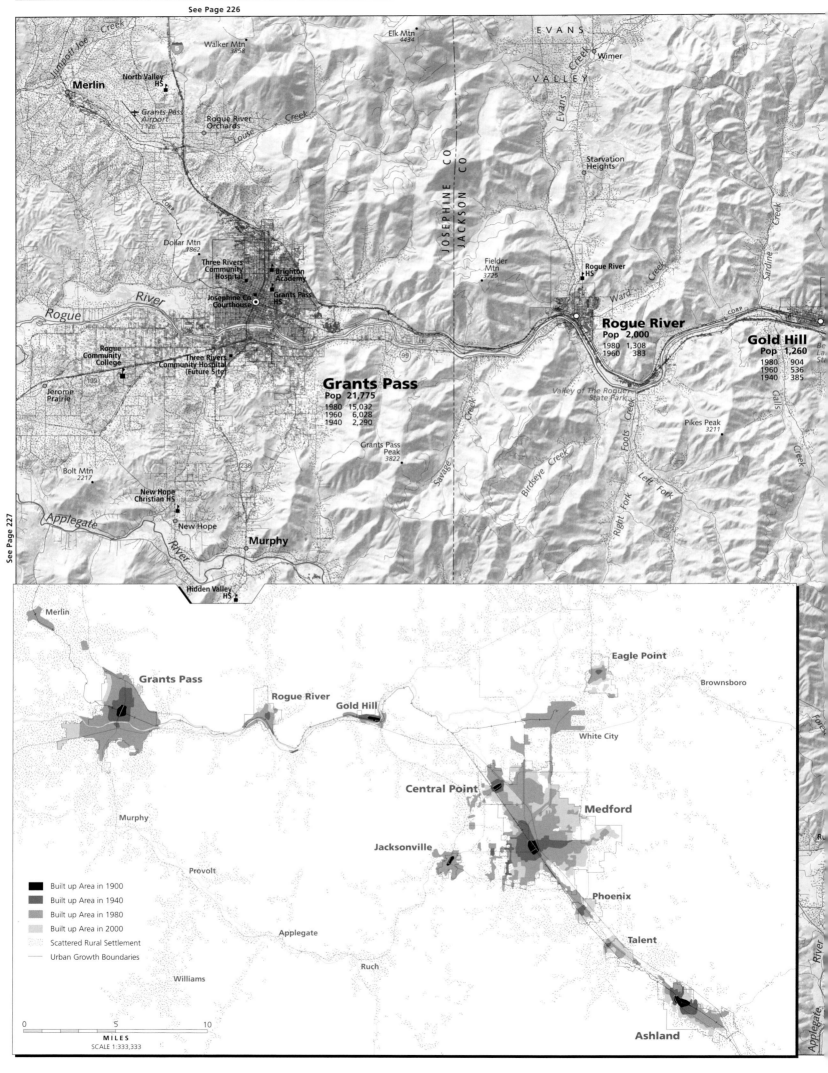

Merlin

Walker Mtn
3858

North Valley
HS

EVANS

Elk Mtn
4434

VALLEY

Wimer

Grants Pass
Airport
1126

Rogue River
Orchards

Starvation
Heights

Dollar Mtn
1862

Three Rivers
Community Hospital

Brighton
Academy

Fielder
Mtn
3725

Rogue River
HS

Josephine Co.
Courthouse

Grants Pass
HS

Rogue River
Pop **2,000**
1980   1,308
1960   383

Gold Hill
Pop **1,260**
1980   904
1960   536
1940   385

Rogue

River

Rogue Community
College

Three Rivers
Community Hospital
(Future Site)

Grants Pass
Pop **21,775**
1980   15,032
1960   6,028
1940   2,290

Valley of The Rogue
State Park

Jerome
Prairie

Grants Pass
Peak
3822

Pikes Peak
3211

Bolt Mtn
2217

New Hope
Christian HS

Applegate

New Hope

Murphy

River

See Page 227

Hidden Valley
HS

Merlin

Eagle Point

Grants Pass

Brownsboro

Rogue River

Gold Hill

White City

Central Point

Medford

Murphy

Jacksonville

Provolt

Phoenix

Applegate

Talent

Ruch

Williams

Ashland

- ■ Built up Area in 1900
- ■ Built up Area in 1940
- ■ Built up Area in 1980
- ▫ Built up Area in 2000
- ░ Scattered Rural Settlement
- — Urban Growth Boundaries

0   5   10

MILES

SCALE 1:333,333

1 Miles   0   1   2   3   4   5   10

SCALE 1:150,000   Elevations are in feet.

MILES

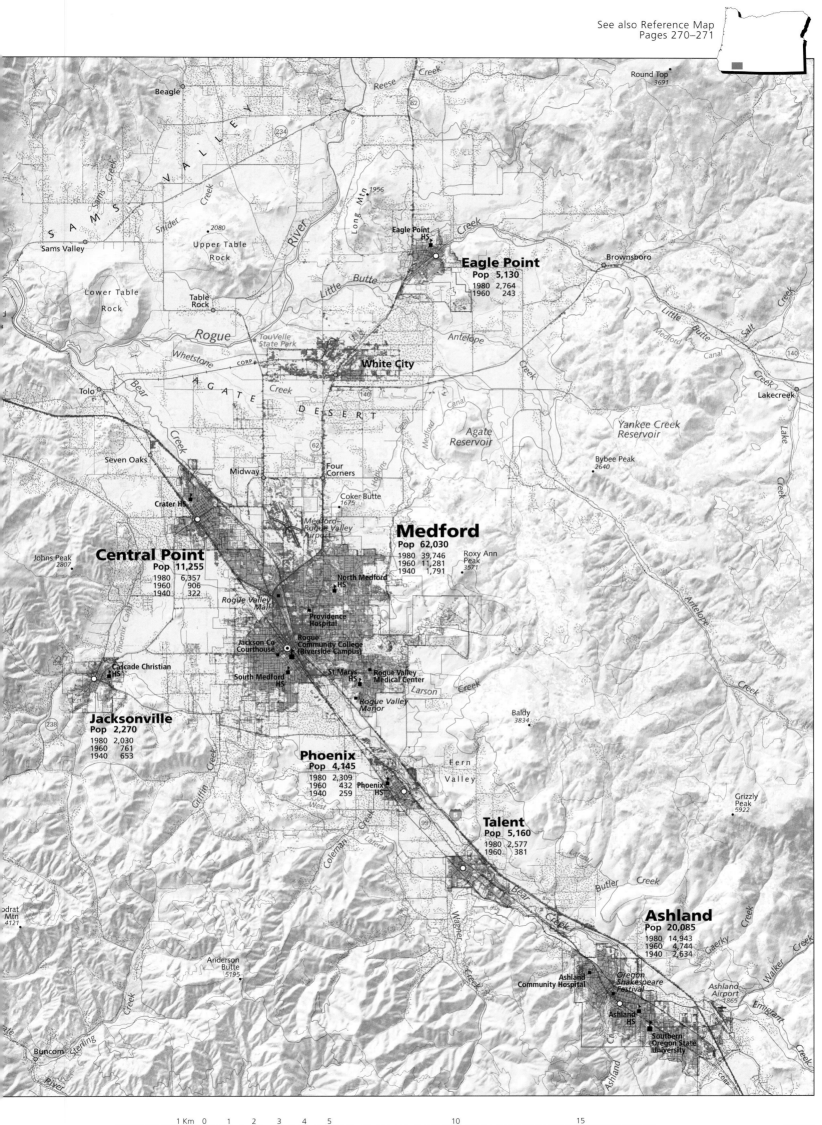

Round Top
3691

Beagle

Reese   Creek

62

234

S   A   M   S   V   A   L   L   E   Y

Snider   Creek

Sams   Creek

2080

Long Mtn *1956*

Eagle Point
HS

Eagle Point
Pop 5,130

1980	2,764
1960	243

Brownsboro

Sams Valley

Upper Table Rock

Little   Butte

Little   Butte   Creek

Antelope

Medford   Little   Butte   Canal

140

Salt   Creek

Lower Table Rock

Table Rock

Rogue

River

TouVelle State Park

Whetstone   Creek

CORP

White City

Lakecreek

Tolo

Bear   Creek

A   G   A   T   E   Creek

D   E   S   E   R   T

Canal

Medford   Canal

Agate Reservoir

Yankee Creek Reservoir

Bybee Peak *2640*

Seven Oaks

140

Midway

62

Four Corners

Hopkins   Canal

Crater HS

Coker Butte *1675*

Medford–Rogue Valley Airport *1335*

Medford
Pop 62,030

1980	39,746
1960	11,281
1940	1,791

Roxy Ann Peak *3571*

Johns Peak *2807*

Central Point
Pop 11,255

1980	6,357
1960	906
1940	322

North Medford HS

Rogue Valley Mall

Providence Hospital

Phoenix   Canal

Jackson Co Courthouse

Rogue Community College (Riverside Campus)

South Medford HS

St Marys HS

Rogue Valley Medical Center

Larson   Creek

Cascade Christian HS

Rogue Valley Manor

Baldy *3834*

Jacksonville
Pop 2,270

1980	2,030
1960	761
1940	653

238

Griffin   Creek

Phoenix
Pop 4,145

1980	2,309
1960	432
1940	259

Phoenix HS

Fern   Valley

Grizzly Peak *5922*

West   Creek

5

Coleman   Creek

Lateral

99

Talent
Pop 5,160

1980	2,577
1960	381

Bear   Creek

Lateral

Butler   Creek

...odrat Mtn *4121*

Anderson Butte *5195*

Wagner   Creek

Ashland
Pop 20,085

1980	14,943
1960	4,744
1940	2,634

Gaerky   Creek

Buncom

Sterling   Creek

Ashland Community Hospital

Oregon Shakespeare Festival

Ashland Airport *1865*

Walker   Creek

Ashland HS

Southern Oregon State University

Clay   Creek

Ashland   Creek

Emigrant   Creek

CORP

1 Km   0   1   2   3   4   5   10   15
SCALE 1:150,000 ⊟⊟⊟⊟   Elevations are in feet.
K I L O M E T E R S

229

The Dalles, Hood River

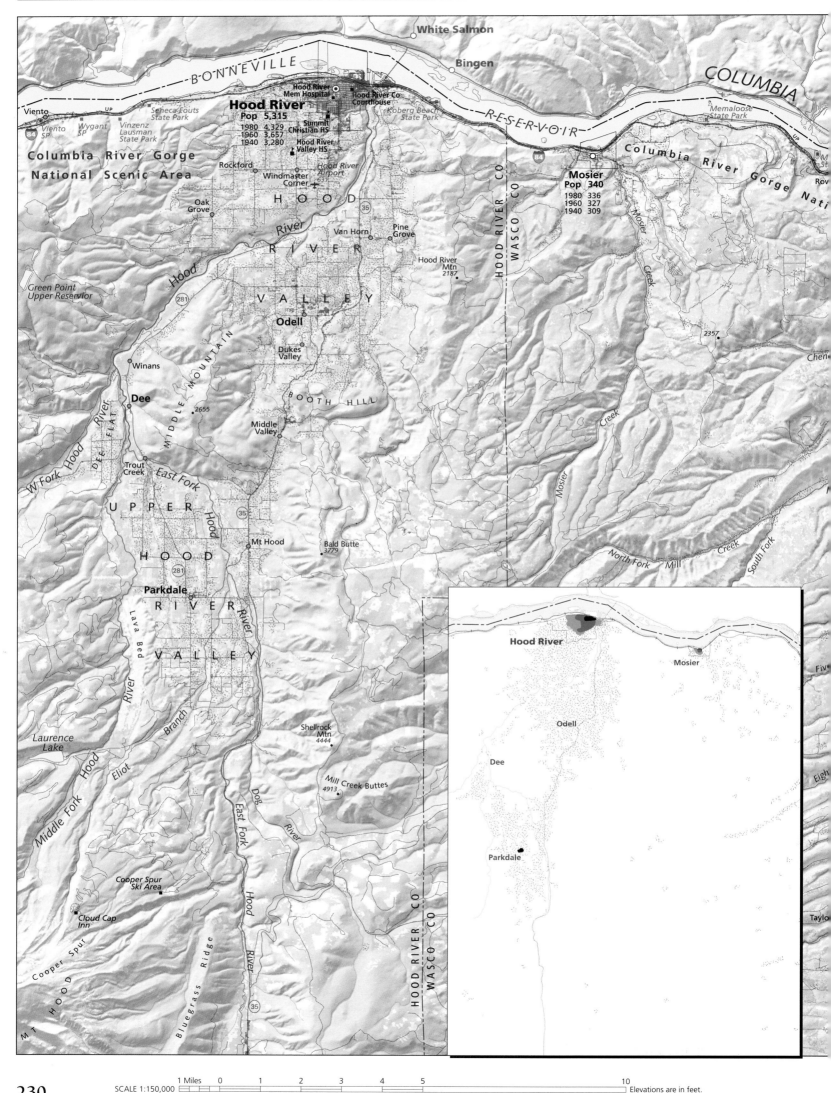

White Salmon

Bingen

BONNEVILLE

COLUMBIA

Viento

UP

Seneca Fouts
State Park

Wygant
SP

Viento
SP

Vinzenz
Lausman
State Park

Hood River
Mem Hospital

Hood River Co
Courthouse

Koberg Beach
State Park

RESERVOIR

UP

Memaloose
State Park

Columbia River Gorge Nati

Rov

Hood River
Pop 5,315
1980 4,329
1960 3,657
1940 3,280

Summit
Christian HS

Hood River
Valley HS

84

Mosier
Pop 340
1980 336
1960 327
1940 309

Columbia River Gorge

Columbia River Gorge
National Scenic Area

Rockford

Windmaster
Corner

Hood River
Airport
631

H   O   O   D

35

Van Horn

Pine
Grove

Oak
Grove

R   I   V   E   R

Hood River
Mtn
2187

Green Point
Upper Reservoir

Hood

River

281

V   A   L   L   E   Y

Odell

2357

Winans

Dukes
Valley

Chen

Dee

MIDDLE   MOUNTAIN

2655

B O O T H   H I L L

Middle
Valley

Creek

W. Fork Hood

River

DEE   FLAT

East Fork

Trout
Creek

Mosier

Mosier

Creek

U   P   P   E   R

35

Hood

Mt Hood

Bald Butte
3779

North Fork

Mill

Creek

South Fork

H   O   O   D

281

Parkdale

R   I   V   E   R

River

Lava   Bed

V   A   L   L   E   Y

Branch

Shellrock
Mtn
4444

Laurence
Lake

Hood

Eliot

Mill Creek Buttes
4913

Dog

Middle Fork

East Fork

River

Cooper Spur
Ski Area

Hood River

Mosier

Cloud Cap
Inn

Odell

Dee

Cooper   Spur

M   T   H   O   O   D

Bluegrass Ridge

Hood

River

35

Parkdale

HOOD RIVER CO

WASCO CO

Five

Eigh

Taylo

SCALE 1:150,000   1 Miles   0   1   2   3   4   5   10

M I L E S

Elevations are in feet.

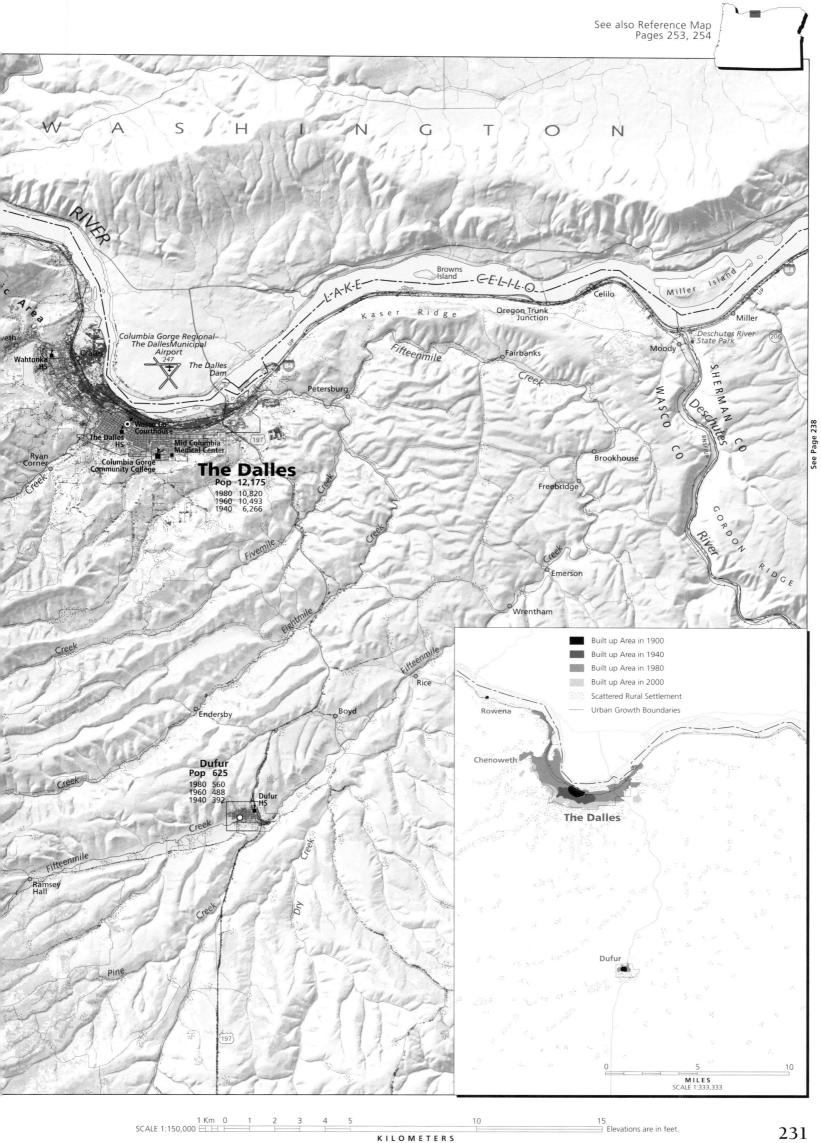

See Page 238

The Dalles
Pop 12,175

1980	10,820
1960	10,493
1940	6,266

Dufur
Pop 625

1980	560
1960	488
1940	392

Built up Area in 1900
Built up Area in 1940
Built up Area in 1980
Built up Area in 2000
Scattered Rural Settlement
Urban Growth Boundaries

The Dalles

MILES
SCALE 1:333,333

SCALE 1:150,000

1 Km 0 1 2 3 4 5 10 15

KILOMETERS

Elevations are in feet.

231

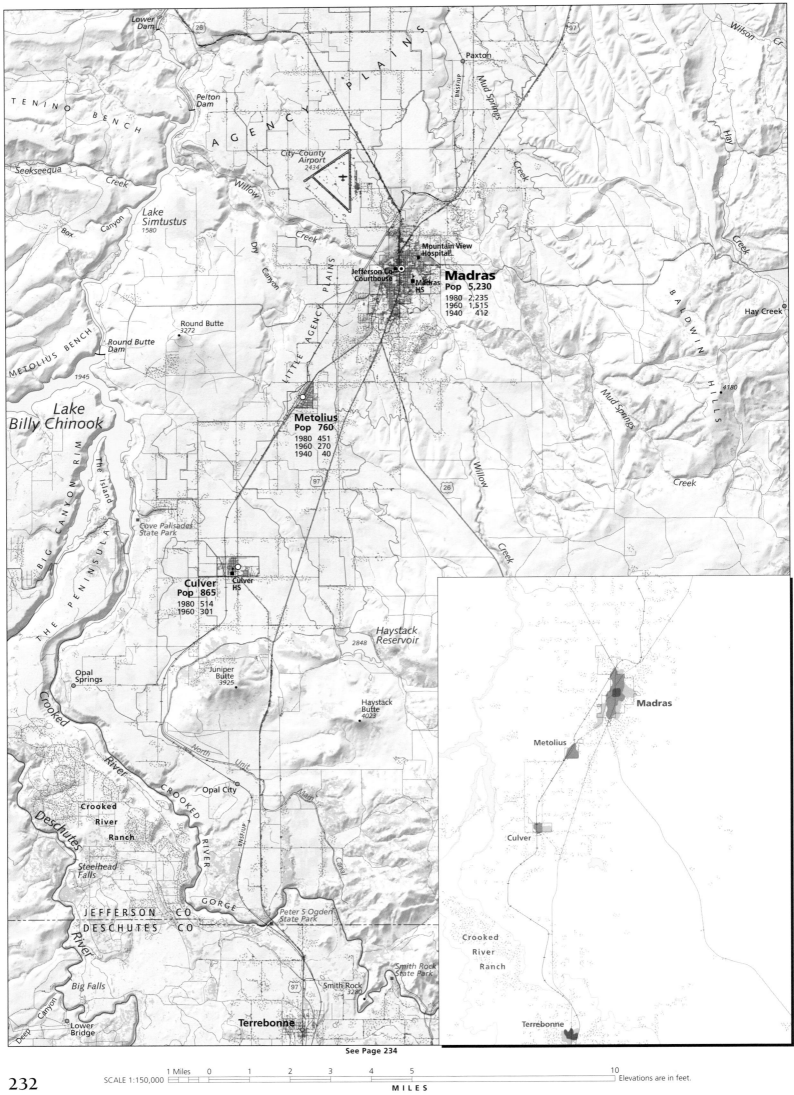

TENINO BENCH

Lower Dam

28

Pelton Dam

AGENCY PLAINS

Paxton

97

Wilson Cr

City-County Airport
2434

BNSF/up

Mud Springs

Hay Creek

Seekseequa Creek

Willow Creek

Lake Simtustus
1580

Box Canyon

Dry Canyon

LITTLE AGENCY PLAINS

Mountain View Hospital

Jefferson Co. Courthouse

Madras HS

Madras
Pop 5,230
1980 2,235
1960 1,515
1940   412

BALDWIN HILLS

4180

Hay Creek

METOLIUS BENCH

Round Butte Dam

Round Butte
3272

1945

Mud Springs

Lake
Billy Chinook

BIG CANYON RIM

The Island

Metolius
Pop 760
1980 451
1960 270
1940   40

97

26

Willow Creek

Cove Palisades State Park

THE PENINSULA

Culver
Pop 865
1980 514
1960 301

Culver HS

Haystack Reservoir
2848

Crooked River

Opal Springs

Juniper Butte
3925

Haystack Butte
4023

North Unit

Madras

Deschutes River

Crooked
River
Ranch

Steelhead Falls

CROOKED RIVER

Opal City

Main

BNSF/up

Canal

Metolius

GORGE

Peter S Ogden State Park

JEFFERSON CO
DESCHUTES CO

Culver

Deep Canyon

River

Big Falls

Lower Bridge

97

Smith Rock State Park

Smith Rock
3280

Crooked
River
Ranch

Terrebonne

Terrebonne

See Page 234

SCALE 1:150,000

1 Miles 0   1   2   3   4   5   10

MILES

Elevations are in feet.

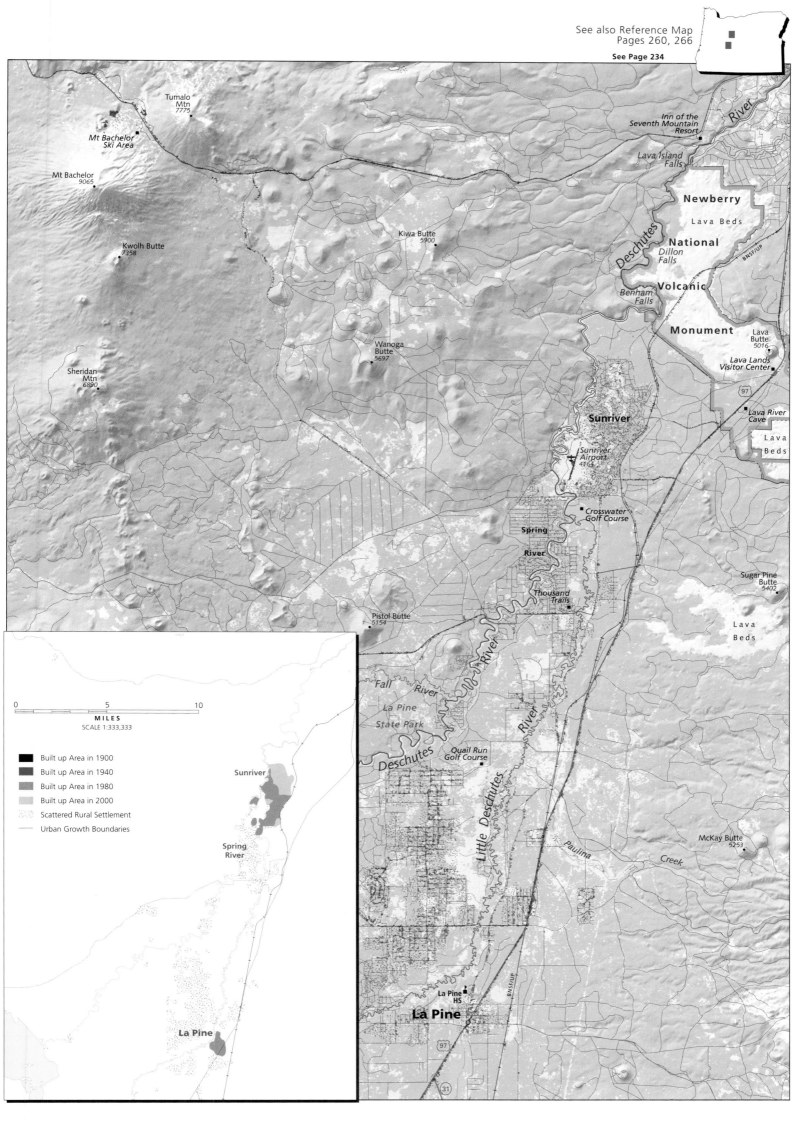

Tumalo
Mtn
7775

Mt Bachelor
Ski Area

Mt Bachelor
9065

Kwolh Butte
7358

Kiwa Butte
5900

Inn of the
Seventh Mountain
Resort

River

Lava Island
Falls

Newberry

Lava Beds

Deschutes

National

Dillon
Falls

Volcanic

Benham
Falls

Monument

Lava
Butte
5016

Lava Lands
Visitor Center

97

Lava River
Cave

Sheridan
Mtn
6890

Wanoga
Butte
5697

Sunriver

Sunriver
Airport
4164

Crosswater
Golf Course

Spring

River

Thousand
Trails

Lava

Beds

Sugar Pine
Butte
5402

Lava

Beds

Pistol Butte
5154

Fall

River

River

La Pine
State Park

Deschutes

Quail Run
Golf Course

Little Deschutes

River

Paulina

Creek

McKay Butte
5253

BNSF/UP

La Pine
HS

La Pine

97

31

MILES
SCALE 1:333,333

0   5   10

■ Built up Area in 1900
■ Built up Area in 1940
■ Built up Area in 1980
□ Built up Area in 2000
⬚ Scattered Rural Settlement
— Urban Growth Boundaries

Sunriver

Spring
River

La Pine

SCALE 1:150,000   1 Km 0   1   2   3   4   5   10   15   Elevations are in feet.

KILOMETERS

233

Bend, Prineville

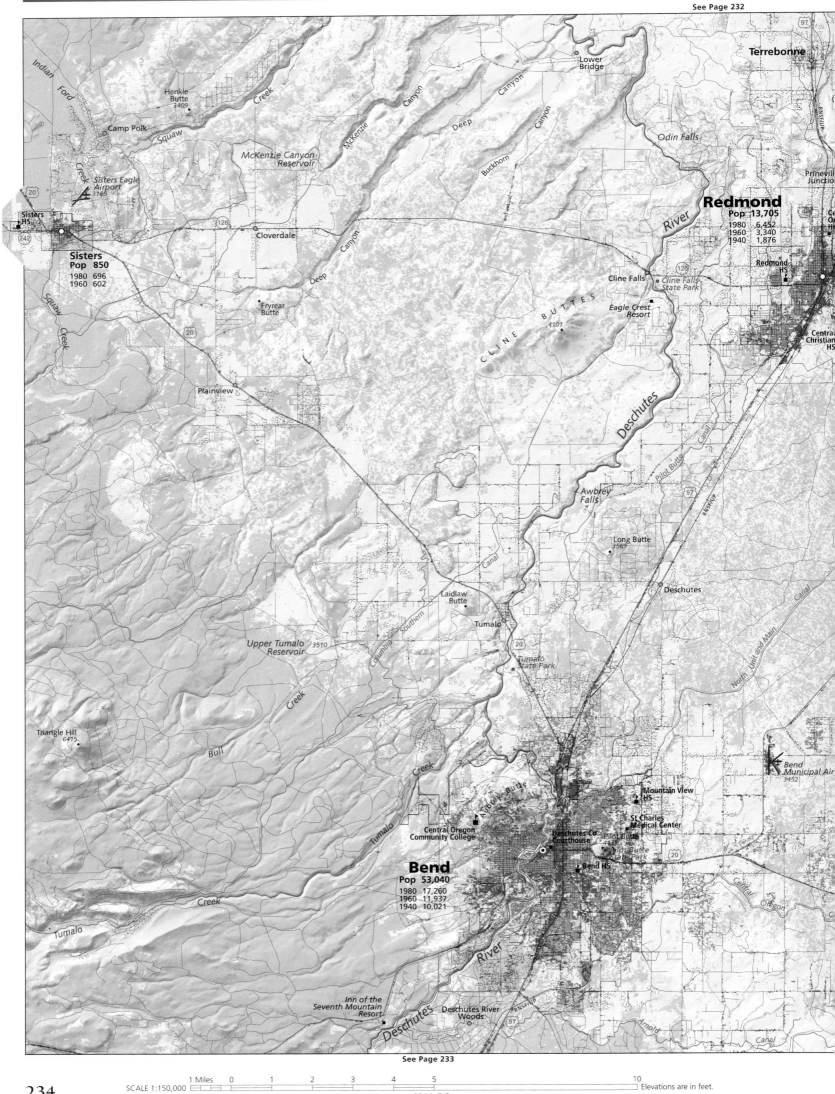

Terrebonne

Lower Bridge

Indian Ford

Creek

Squaw

Henkle Butte
3409

Camp Polk

McKenzie Canyon Reservoir

McKenzie

Canyon

Deep

Canyon

Buckhorn

Canyon

Canyon

Odin Falls

Prineville Junction

Sisters Eagle Airport
3165

Redmond
Pop 13,705
1980 6,452
1960 3,340
1940 1,876

River

Central Oregon HS

Sisters HS

126

Cloverdale

Sisters
Pop 850
1980 696
1960 602

Deep

Canyon

Cline Falls

Cline Falls State Park

Redmond HS

Central Christian HS

Fryrear Butte

20

C L I N E   B U T T E S
4101

Eagle Crest Resort

Squaw Creek

Plainview

Deschutes

Awbrey Falls

Pilot Butte

Canal

97

BNSF/UP

Long Butte
3569

Upper Tumalo Reservoir
3510

Columbia Southern

Canal

Laidlaw Butte

Deschutes

Triangle Hill
6415

Tumalo

Tumalo State Park

North Unit and Main

Canal

Creek

Bull

Creek

20

Creek

Tumalo

Inn of the Seventh Mountain Resort

Awbrey Butte

Central Oregon Community College

Deschutes Co Courthouse

Bend
Pop 53,040
1980 17,260
1960 11,937
1940 10,021

Mountain View HS

St Charles Medical Center

Pilot Butte
4138

Pilot Butte State Park

Bend HS

Bend Municipal Air
3452

20

Central Oregon

Creek

Deschutes River Woods

BNSF/UP

97

Deschutes

River

Arnold

Canal

1 Miles   0   1   2   3   4   5   10
SCALE 1:150,000   Elevations are in feet.
M I L E S

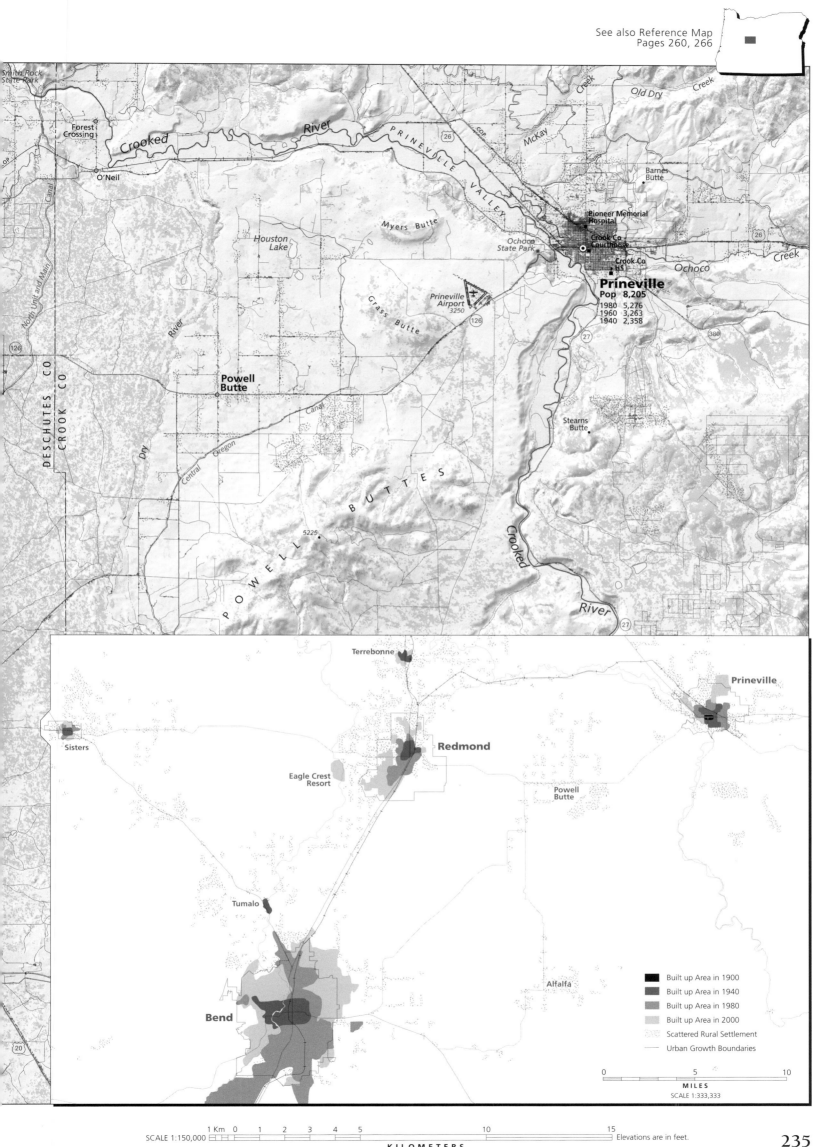

See also Reference Map
Pages 260, 266

Smith Rock
State Park

Forest
Crossing

Crooked   River   PRINEVILLE VALLEY

O'Neil

McKay

Old Dry   Creek

COP

26

Barnes
Butte

26

Myers Butte

Pioneer Memorial
Hospital

Houston
Lake

Ochoco
State Park

Crook Co
Courthouse

Crook Co
HS

Ochoco   Creek

Grass Butte

Prineville
Airport
3250

126

Prineville
Pop 8,205
1980 5,276
1960 3,263
1940 2,358

27

380

**Powell
Butte**

Stearns
Butte

DESCHUTES CO.

CROOK CO.

CROOK CO.

126

River

Dry

Central   Oregon   Canal

5225

P O W E L L   B U T T E S

Crooked

River

27

Terrebonne

Prineville

Sisters

Redmond

Eagle Crest
Resort

Powell
Butte

Tumalo

Alfalfa

Bend

20

	Built up Area in 1900
	Built up Area in 1940
	Built up Area in 1980
	Built up Area in 2000
	Scattered Rural Settlement
	Urban Growth Boundaries

0   5   10
MILES
SCALE 1:333,333

1 Km 0   1   2   3   4   5   10   15
SCALE 1:150,000   Elevations are in feet.
KILOMETERS

235

Klamath Falls

UPPER

KLAMATH

LAKE

Spence Mtn
5841

Naylor Mtn
5753

Whiteline
Reservoir

Grizzly Butte
4526

SWAN

MODOC

Howard Bay

Algoma

Swan
Lake

4139

Shady Pine

SWAN   LAKE

Upper Klamath   Hanks
National   Marsh
Wildlife Refuge

Caledonia
Marsh

Buck
Island

RIM

VALLEY

Running Y
Ranch Resort

Cove
Point

Wocus

PLUM   VALLEY

Hopp

Meadow
Lake

Round Lake
Hill
5043

Pelican City

Oregon Institute
of Technology

Klamath
Falls
Pop 19,365

Hogback Mtn
6198

Moyina Hill
5964

Lakeshore

Merle West
Medical Center

1980 16,661
1960 16,949
1940 16,497

Klamath Union
HS

Klamath Co
Courthouse

Hilltop Christian
Academy

Altamont

Triad
School

Round
Lake

Stewart-Lennox

Mazama
HS

Hager

MODOC

Lake Ewana

Hosanna
Christian School

Olene

The Gap

Henley
HS

River

RIDGE

Nuss
Lake

Klamath Falls–
Kingsley Field
4095

Henley

Keno

Midland

Miller Hill

Falcon
Heights

KLAMATH   VALLEY

Stukel
Mountain
6525

Stukel

Spring
Lake

4905

Hamaker
Mtn
6596

KLAMATH   HILLS

5188

Bear Valley
National
Wildlife Refuge

Worden

Lost

Lower Klamath
National
Wildlife Refuge

Merrill
Pop 870

1980 822
1960 804
1940 648

236

1 Miles   0   1   2   3   4   5   10
SCALE 1:150,000
MILES

Elevations are in feet.

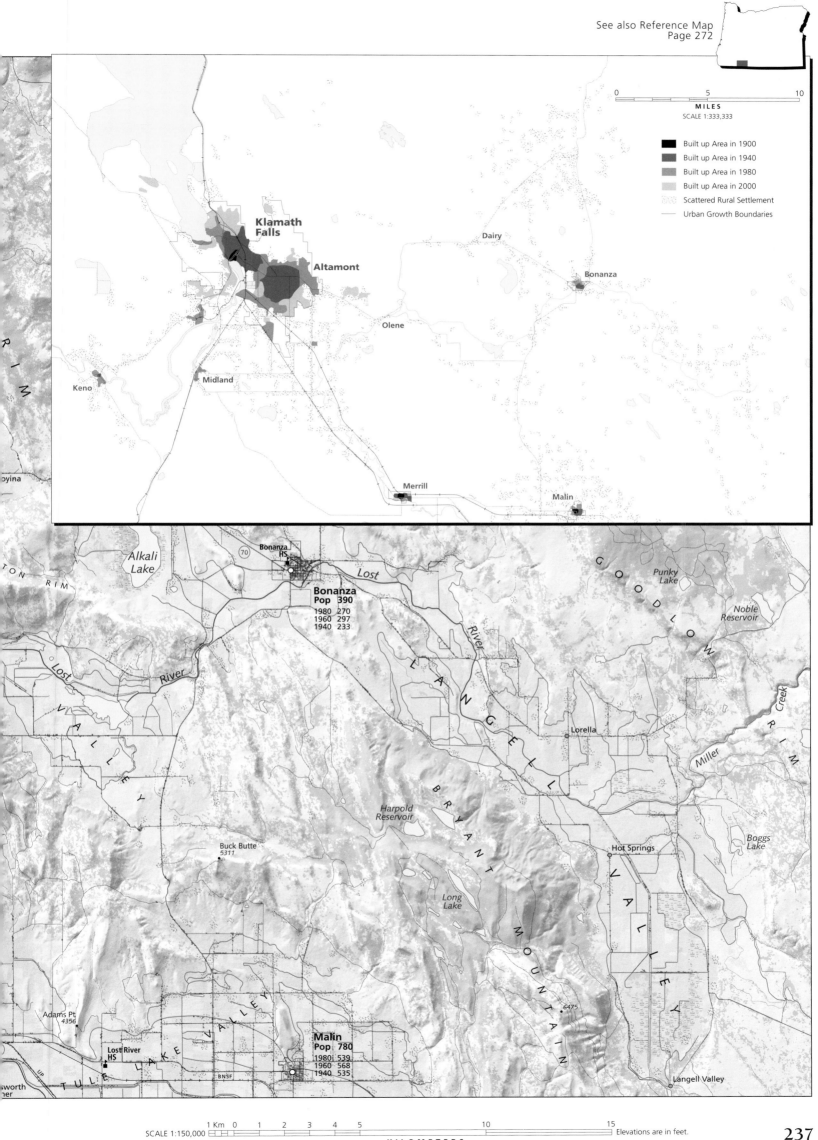

See also Reference Map
Page 272

0   5   10
MILES
SCALE 1:333,333

■ Built up Area in 1900
■ Built up Area in 1940
■ Built up Area in 1980
▨ Built up Area in 2000
▨ Scattered Rural Settlement
— Urban Growth Boundaries

Klamath
Falls

Dairy

Altamont

Bonanza

Olene

Keno

Midland

Merrill

Malin

Alkali
Lake

Bonanza
HS

70

Lost

River

Bonanza
Pop 390
1980 270
1960 297
1940 233

GOODLOW

Punky
Lake

Noble
Reservoir

RIM

Lost

River

L A N G E L L

Lorella

Miller

Creek

RIM

VALLEY

Harpold
Reservoir

B R Y A N T

Boggs
Lake

Buck Butte
5311

Hot Springs

V A L L E Y

Long
Lake

M O U N T A I N

Adams Pt
4356

6475

Lost River
HS

Malin
Pop 780
1980 539
1960 568
1940 535

Langell Valley

UP

sworth
er

TULE   LAKE   VALLEY

BNSF

1 Km 0   1   2   3   4   5   10   15
SCALE 1:150,000   Elevations are in feet.
KILOMETERS

237

Moro; Heppner; Condon, Fossil

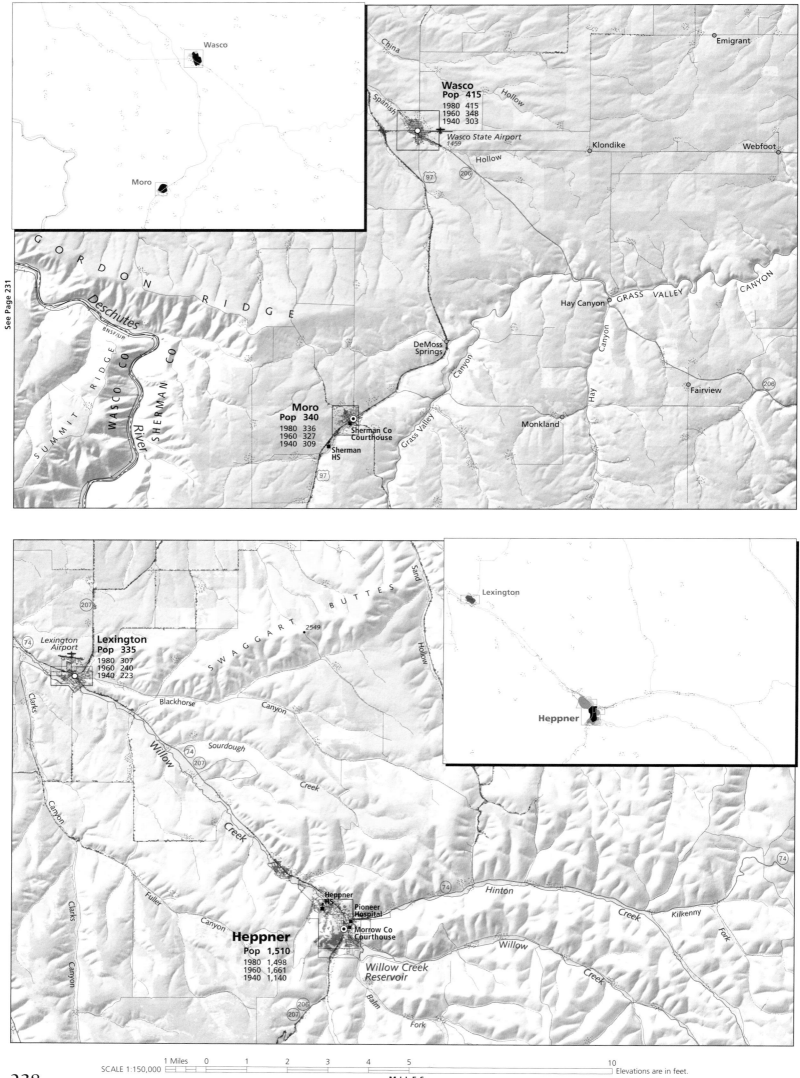

Wasco

Moro

See Page 231

China

Emigrant

Wasco
Pop 415
1980	415
1960	348
1940	303

Spanish

Hollow

Wasco State Airport
1459

Klondike

Webfoot

Hollow

GORDON RIDGE

Deschutes

BNSF/UP

SUMMIT RIDGE

WASCO CO

SHERMAN CO

Deschutes River

97

206

Hay Canyon

GRASS VALLEY

CANYON

DeMoss Springs

Canyon

Hay Canyon

Fairview

206

Moro
Pop 340
1980	336
1960	327
1940	309

Sherman Co Courthouse

Sherman HS

Grass Valley

Monkland

97

207

Lexington
Airport

74

Lexington
Pop 335
1980	307
1960	240
1940	223

SWAGGART BUTTES

2549

Sand

Hollow

Lexington

Heppner

Clarks

Blackhorse

Canyon

Willow

74

207

Sourdough

Creek

74

Hinton

Creek

Kilkenny

Canyon

Fuller Canyon

Clarks Canyon

Heppner HS

Pioneer Hospital

Morrow Co Courthouse

Willow

Fork

Heppner
Pop 1,510
1980	1,498
1960	1,661
1940	1,140

Willow Creek Reservoir

Creek

206

207

Balm

Fork

SCALE 1:150,000   1 Miles   0   1   2   3   4   5   10

MILES   Elevations are in feet.

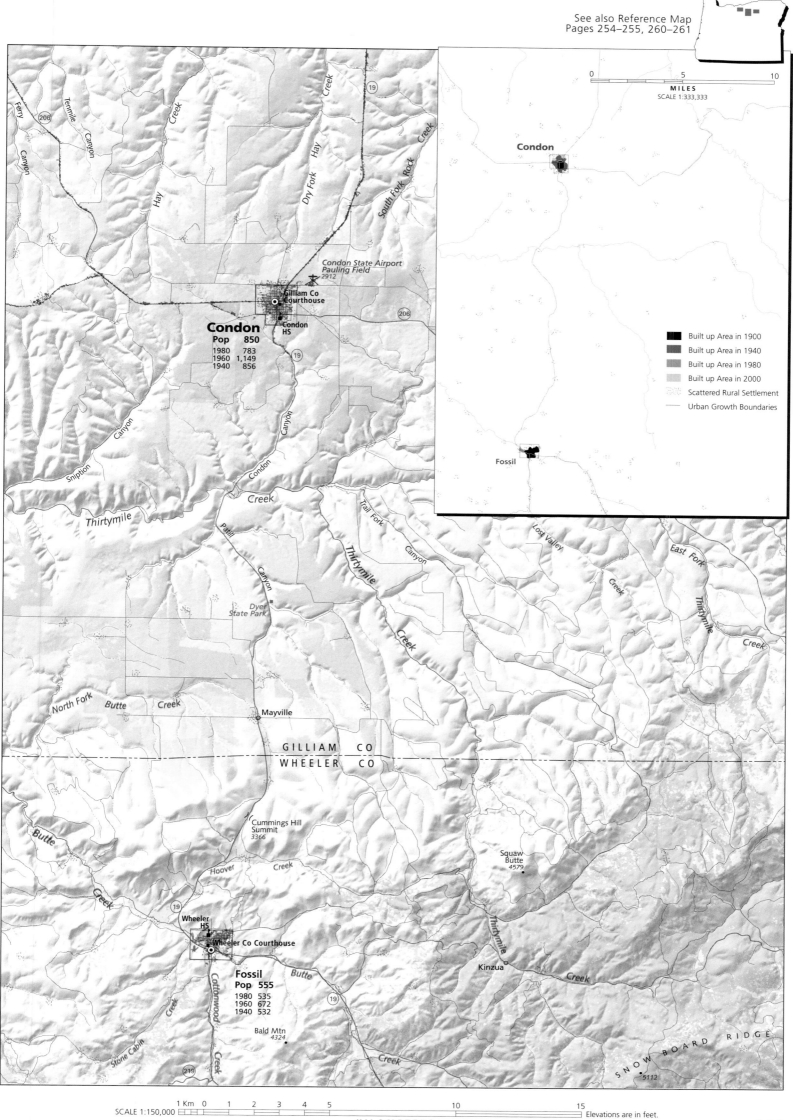

John Day, Canyon City; Lakeview; Burns

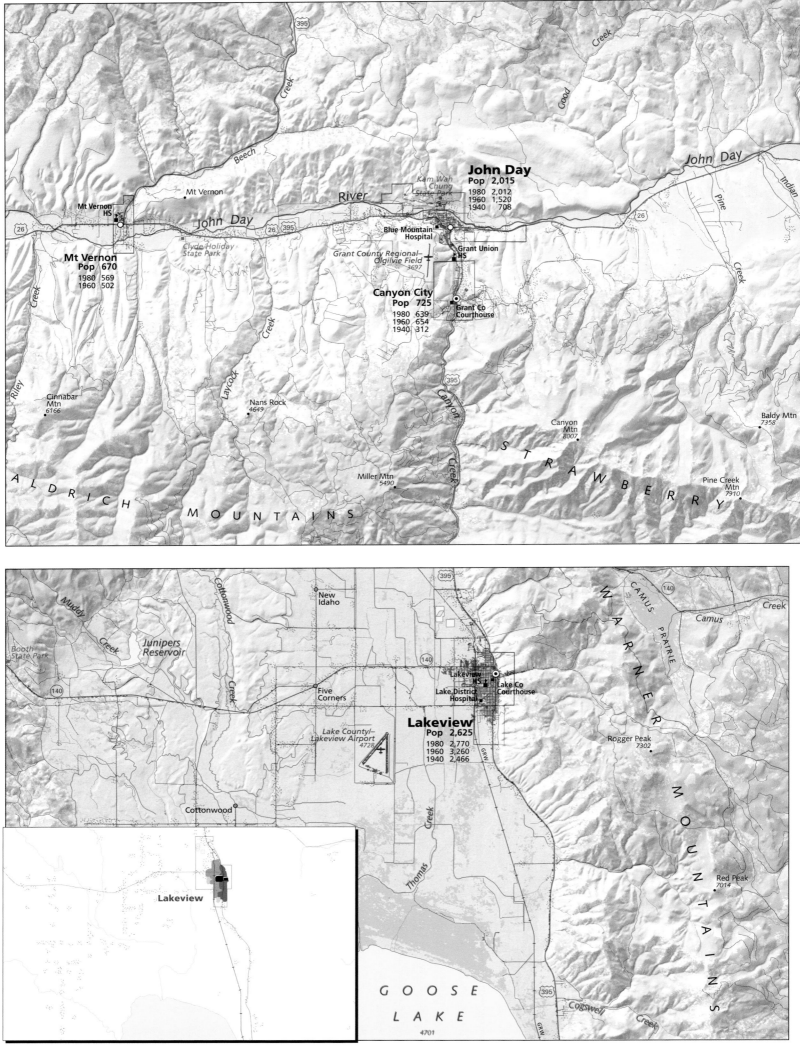

Mt Vernon

Mt Vernon HS

John Day
Pop **2,015**
1980 2,012
1960 1,520
1940   708

Kam Wah Chung State Park

River

Blue Mountain Hospital

Grant County Regional–Olgilvie Field
3697

Grant Union HS

Canyon City
Pop **725**
1980 639
1960 654
1940 312

Grant Co Courthouse

John Day

Mt Vernon
Pop **670**
1980 569
1960 502

Clyde Holiday State Park

John Day

Beech

Good

Creek

Pine

Indian

Creek

Creek

Riley

Creek

Laycock

Creek

Canyon

Creek

Cinnabar Mtn
6166

Nans Rock
4649

Miller Mtn
5490

Canyon Mtn
8007

Baldy Mtn
7358

Pine Creek Mtn
7910

A L D R I C H   M O U N T A I N S

S T R A W B E R R Y   R

New Idaho

Cottonwood

Muddy

Creek

Junipers Reservoir

Booth State Park

Creek

Five Corners

Lakeview HS
Lake District Hospital
Lake Co Courthouse

Lake County–Lakeview Airport
4728

Lakeview
Pop **2,625**
1980 2,770
1960 3,260
1940 2,466

Cottonwood

Thomas

Creek

W A R N E R

Camus

Creek

Camus

Creek

CAMUS PRAIRIE

Rogger Peak
7302

Red Peak
7014

M O U N T A I N S

GRW

Lakeview

G O O S E   L A K E
4701

Cogswell   Creek

GRW

SCALE 1:150,000

1 Miles 0   1   2   3   4   5   10

M I L E S

Elevations are in feet.

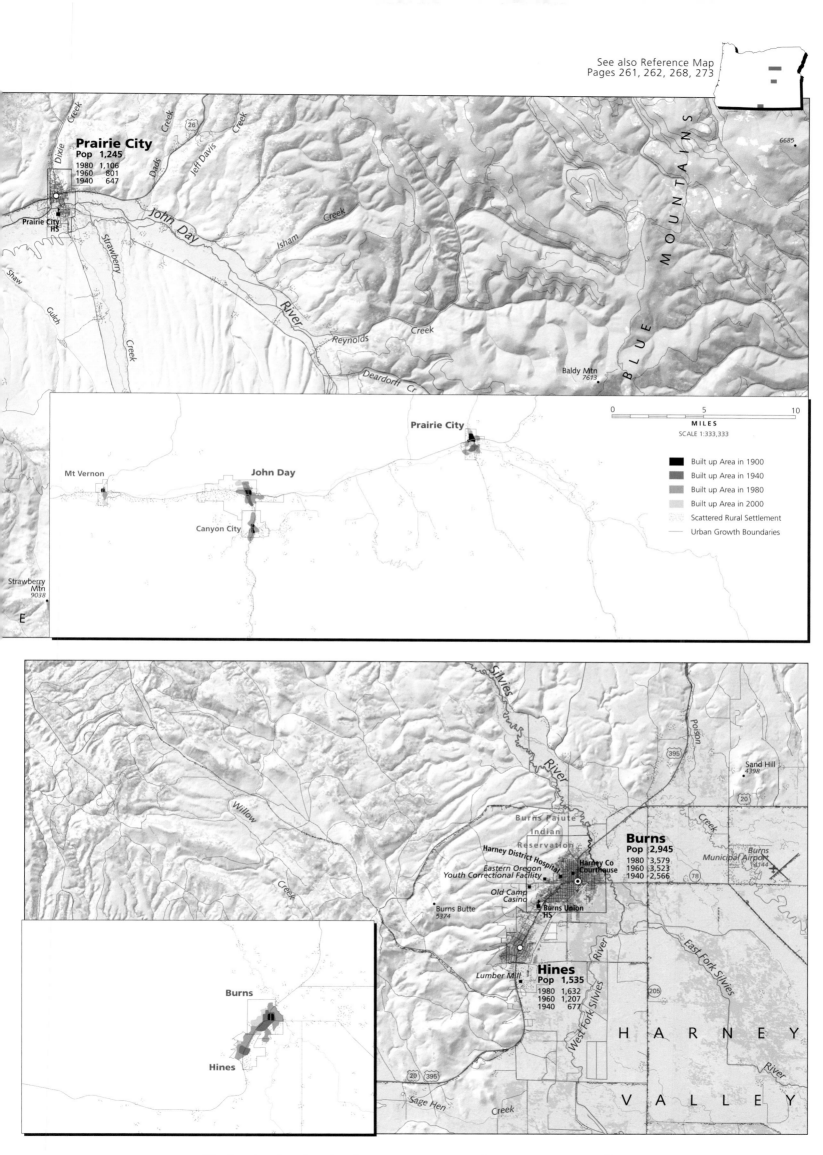

See also Reference Map
Pages 261, 262, 268, 273

Prairie City
Pop 1,245

1980	1,106
1960	801
1940	647

Prairie City HS

Dixie Creek

Dads Creek

Jeff Davis Creek

26

John Day River

Strawberry

Shaw

Gulch

Creek

Isham Creek

Creek

Reynolds Creek

Deardorff Cr

Creek

BLUE MOUNTAINS

6685

Baldy Mtn
7613

Mt Vernon

John Day

Prairie City

Canyon City

Strawberry
Mtn
9038

E

0   5   10

MILES
SCALE 1:333,333

■ Built up Area in 1900
■ Built up Area in 1940
■ Built up Area in 1980
□ Built up Area in 2000
⣿ Scattered Rural Settlement
— Urban Growth Boundaries

Silvies River

Poison Creek

Sand Hill
4398

395

20

Willow Creek

Burns Paiute
Indian
Reservation

Harney District Hospital

Eastern Oregon
Youth Correctional Facility

Harney Co
Courthouse

Burns
Pop 2,945

1980	3,579
1960	3,523
1940	2,566

Burns
Municipal Airport
4144

78

Burns Butte
5374

Old Camp
Casino

Burns Union
HS

Creek

East Fork Silvies

Lumber Mill

Hines
Pop 1,535

1980	1,632
1960	1,207
1940	677

205

West Fork Silvies

H A R N E Y

Burns

Hines

20 395

Sage Hen Creek

River

V A L L E Y

1 Km 0   1   2   3   4   5   10   15

SCALE 1:150,000   Elevations are in feet.

K I L O M E T E R S

241

Hermiston

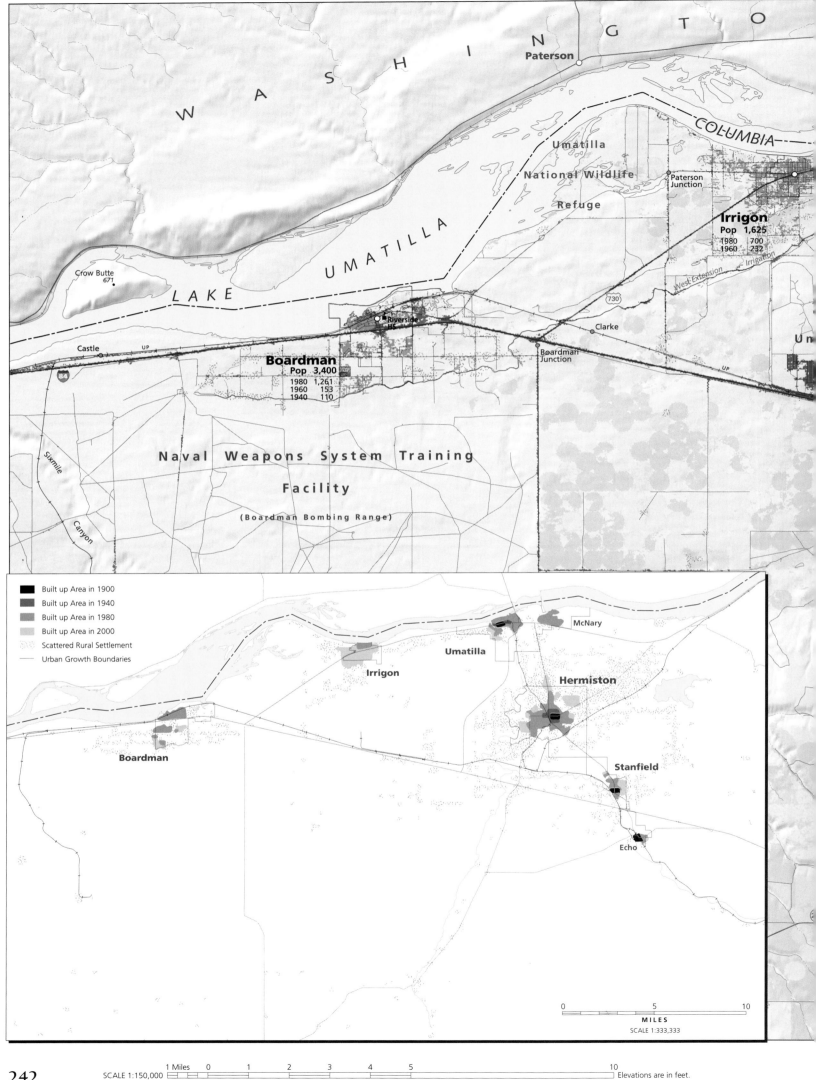

Paterson

W A S H I N G T O

Umatilla
National Wildlife
Refuge

COLUMBIA

Paterson
Junction

Irrigon
Pop 1,625
1980   700
1960   232

Crow Butte
671.

L A K E   U M A T I L L A

West Extension

Irrigation

730

Castle   UP

Riverside
HS

Clarke

Un

Boardman
Pop 3,400

1980   1,261
1960   153
1940   110

Boardman
Junction

UP

Naval Weapons System Training

Sixmile

Facility

(Boardman Bombing Range)

Canyon

84

- ■ Built up Area in 1900
- ■ Built up Area in 1940
- ■ Built up Area in 1980
- ■ Built up Area in 2000
- ░ Scattered Rural Settlement
- — Urban Growth Boundaries

McNary

Umatilla

Hermiston

Irrigon

Boardman

Stanfield

Echo

0   5   10

MILES

SCALE 1:333,333

SCALE 1:150,000

1 Miles   0   1   2   3   4   5   10

MILES

Elevations are in feet.

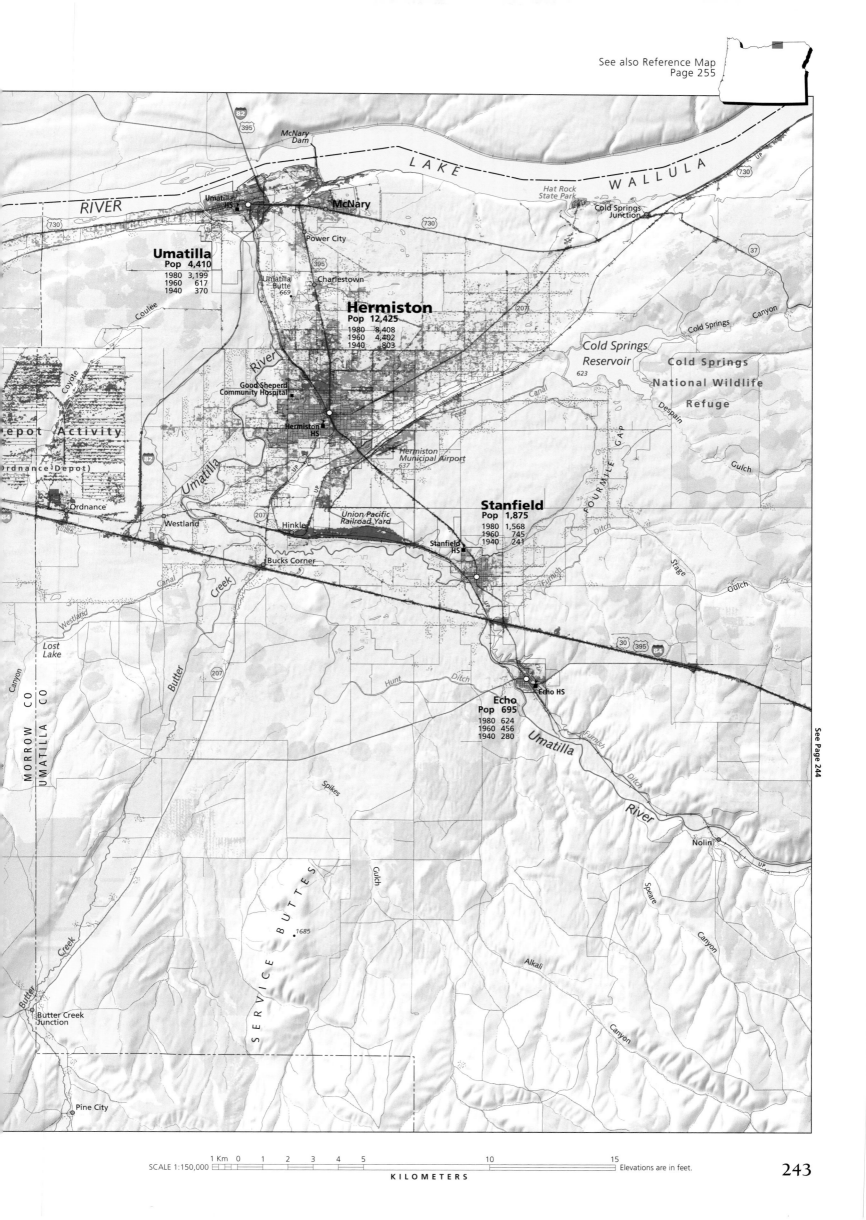

RIVER

McNary
Dam

LAKE   WALLULA

Umatilla
HS

McNary

Hat Rock
State Park

Cold Springs
Junction

730

730

Power City

Umatilla
Pop 4,410
1980 3,199
1960 617
1940 370

Umatilla
Butte
669

Charlestown

Hermiston
Pop 12,425
1980 8,408
1960 4,402
1940 803

Cold Springs

Cold Springs
Reservoir
623

Cold Springs

National Wildlife

Refuge

Despain

River

Good Sheperd
Community Hospital

Depot Activity

Ordnance Depot)

Ordnance

Westland

Umatilla

82

Hermiston
HS

Hinkle

Hermiston
Municipal Airport
637

UP

Union Pacific
Railroad Yard

Canal

FOURMILE GAP

Gulch

207

UP

Stanfield
Pop 1,875
1980 1,568
1960 745
1940 241

Stanfield
HS

Ditch

Furnish

Stage

Gulch

84

Bucks Corner

Canal

Westland

Lost
Lake

Creek

Butter

207

Hunt

Ditch

30   395   84

UP

Spikes

Echo HS

Echo
Pop 695
1980 624
1960 456
1940 280

Umatilla

Furnish

Ditch

River

Nolin

UP

MORROW CO
UMATILLA CO

Canyon

S E R V I C E   B U T T E S

Gulch

Speare

1685

Alkali

Canyon

Canyon

Butter
Creek

Butter Creek
Junction

Pine City

SCALE 1:150,000

1 Km 0   1   2   3   4   5   10   15
KILOMETERS   Elevations are in feet.

243

Pendleton, Milton–Freewater

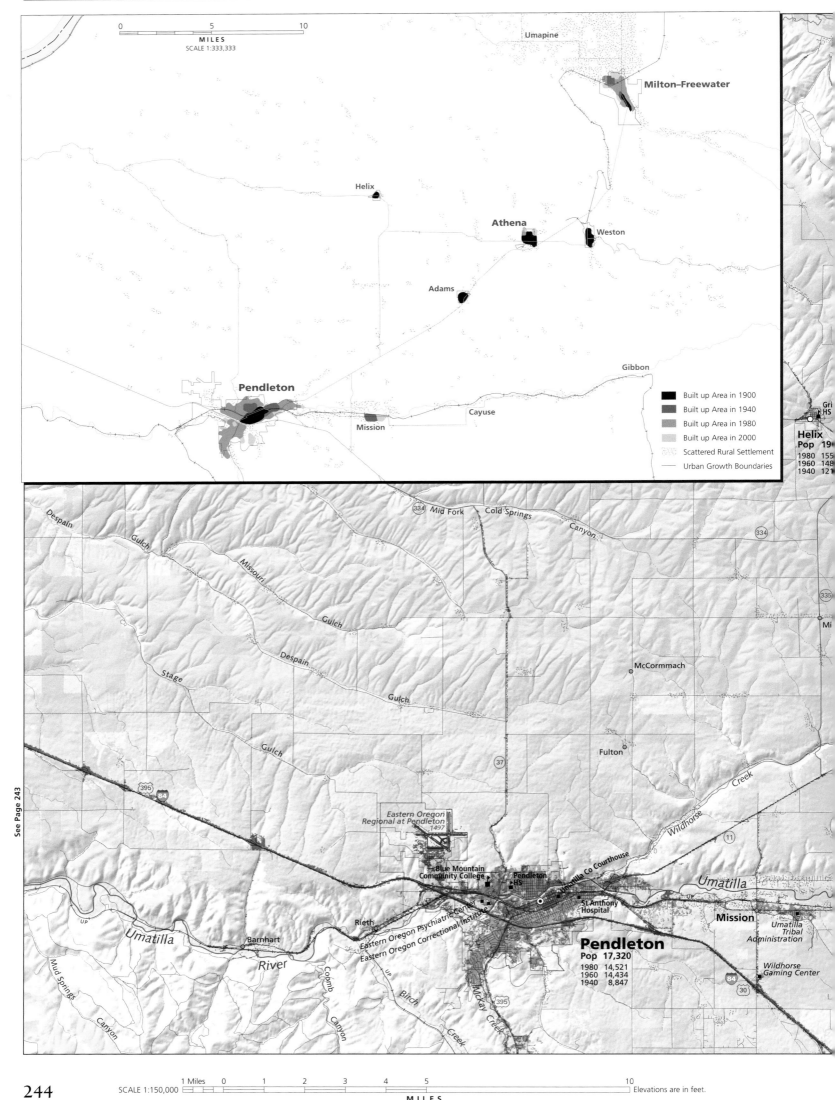

MILES
SCALE 1:333,333

0   5   10

Umapine

Milton–Freewater

Helix

Athena   Weston

Adams

Gibbon

Pendleton

Cayuse

Mission

- ■ Built up Area in 1900
- ■ Built up Area in 1940
- ■ Built up Area in 1980
- □ Built up Area in 2000
- Scattered Rural Settlement
- Urban Growth Boundaries

Gri
HS

Helix
Pop 19
1980 155
1960 148
1940 121

Despain

Gulch

334 Mid Fork   Cold Springs   Canyon   334

Missouri

Gulch   335

Despain   McCormmach   Mi

Stage

Gulch   37

Gulch   Fulton

395   84   Wildhorse   Creek   11

Eastern Oregon
Regional at Pendleton
1497

Blue Mountain
Community College   Pendleton   Umatilla Co Courthouse   Umatilla
HS

Rieth   St Anthony   **Mission**
Eastern Oregon Psychiatric Center   Hospital
Eastern Oregon Correctional Institute   Umatilla
Tribal
Administration

Barnhart   **Pendleton**
Pop 17,320
1980 14,521
1960 14,434
1940 8,847   Wildhorse
Gaming Center

Umatilla

River

Mud Springs   Coomb   Birch   McKay   395   84   30
Canyon   Canyon   Creek   Creek

1 Miles   0   1   2   3   4   5   10

SCALE 1:150,000   Elevations are in feet.

MILES

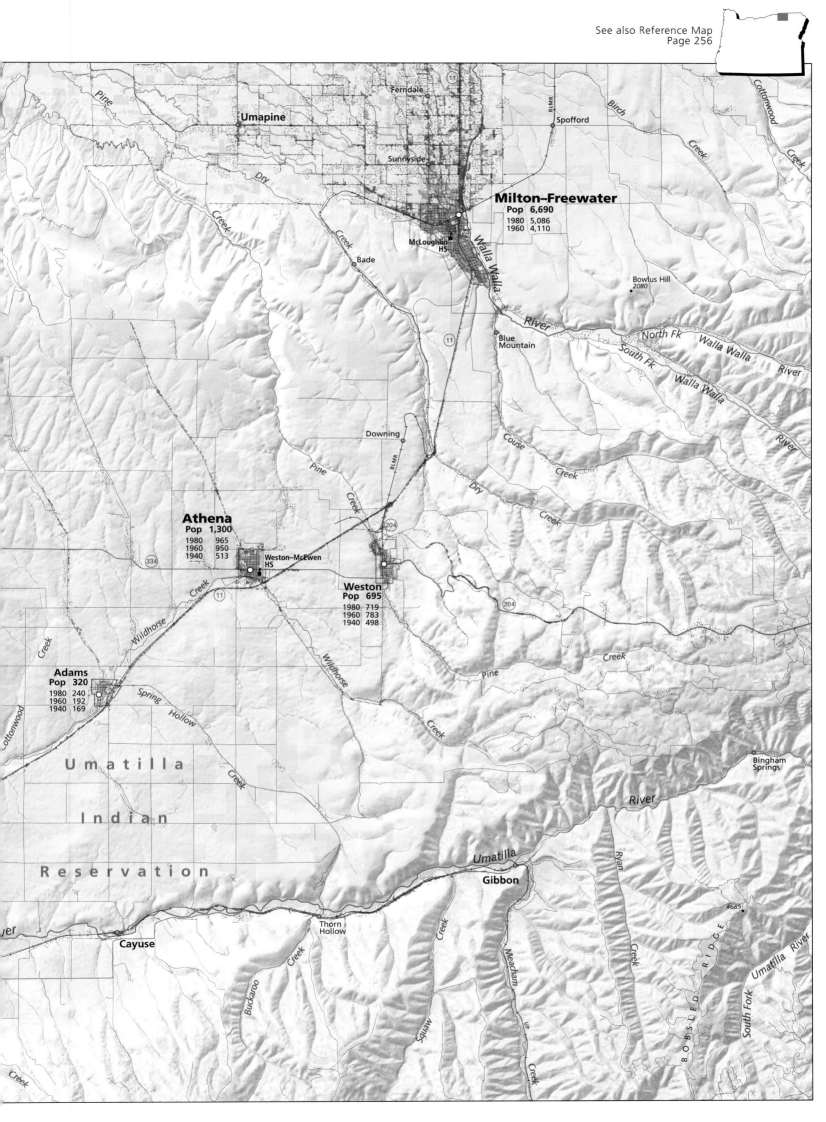

Umapine

Ferndale

Spofford

Sunnyside

Milton–Freewater
Pop 6,690
| 1980 | 5,086 |
| 1960 | 4,110 |

McLoughlin
HS

Bade

Bowlus Hill
2080

Blue
Mountain

North Fk

South Fk

Downing

Walla Walla River

Couse

Creek

Dry

Creek

Athena
Pop 1,300
1980	965
1960	950
1940	513

Weston–McEwen
HS

Weston
Pop 695
1980	719
1960	783
1940	498

Pine

Creek

Adams
Pop 320
1980	240
1960	192
1940	169

Spring

Hollow

Wildhorse

Creek

Umatilla

Bingham
Springs

Indian

River

Umatilla

Reservation

Gibbon

4685

Thorn
Hollow

Cayuse

Budaroo Creek

Squaw Creek

Meacham Creek

Ryan Creek

BOBSLED RIDGE

South Fork

Umatilla River

1 Km 0   1   2   3   4   5   10   15
SCALE 1:150,000   Elevations are in feet.
K I L O M E T E R S

245

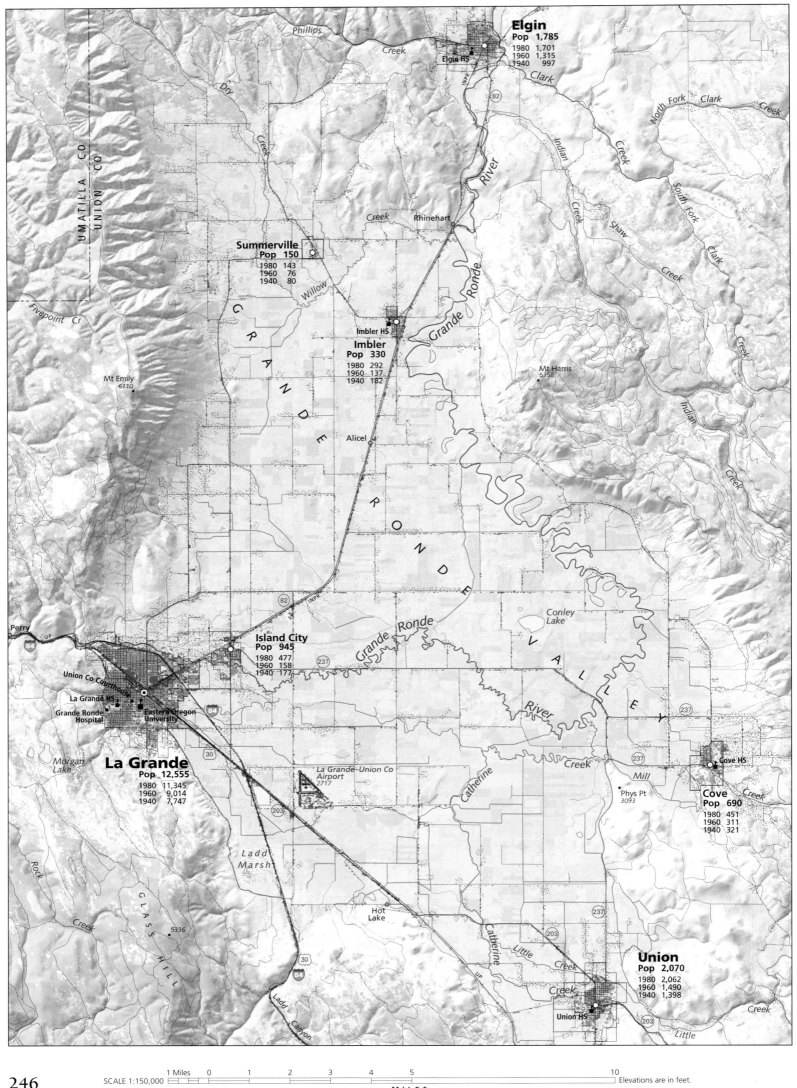

Elgin
Pop 1,785

1980	1,701
1960	1,315
1940	997

Phillips

Creek

Elgin HS

Clark

North Fork   Clark   Creek

Dry

Creek

UMATILLA CO
UNION CO

Creek

Rhinehart

River

Grande Ronde

Indian Creek

South Fork Clark

Shaw Creek

Fivepoint Cr

Summerville
Pop 150

1980	143
1960	76
1940	80

Willow

G R A N D E

Imbler HS

Imbler
Pop 330

1980	292
1960	137
1940	182

Mt Emily
6110

Mt Harris
5358

Indian Creek

R O N D E

Alicel

Grande Ronde

Conley Lake

Perry

UP

82   INPR

V A L L E Y

Island City
Pop 945

1980	477
1960	158
1940	177

237

Grande Ronde

237

Union Co Courthouse

84

La Grande HS

Grande Ronde
Hospital

Eastern Oregon
University

River

Cove HS

30

Morgan
Lake

La Grande
Pop 12,555

1980	11,345
1960	9,014
1940	7,747

La Grande–Union Co
Airport
2717

Catherine

Creek

Mill

237

Phys Pt
3093

Cove
Pop 690

1980	451
1960	311
1940	321

203

Ladd
Marsh

G L A S S   H I L L

Rock Creek

5336

Hot
Lake

30

84

Ladd Canyon

Catherine

Little   Creek

237

203

UP

Union
Pop 2,070

1980	2,062
1960	1,490
1940	1,398

Creek

Union HS

203

Little

Creek

SCALE 1:150,000   1 Miles   0   1   2   3   4   5   10   Elevations are in feet.

M I L E S

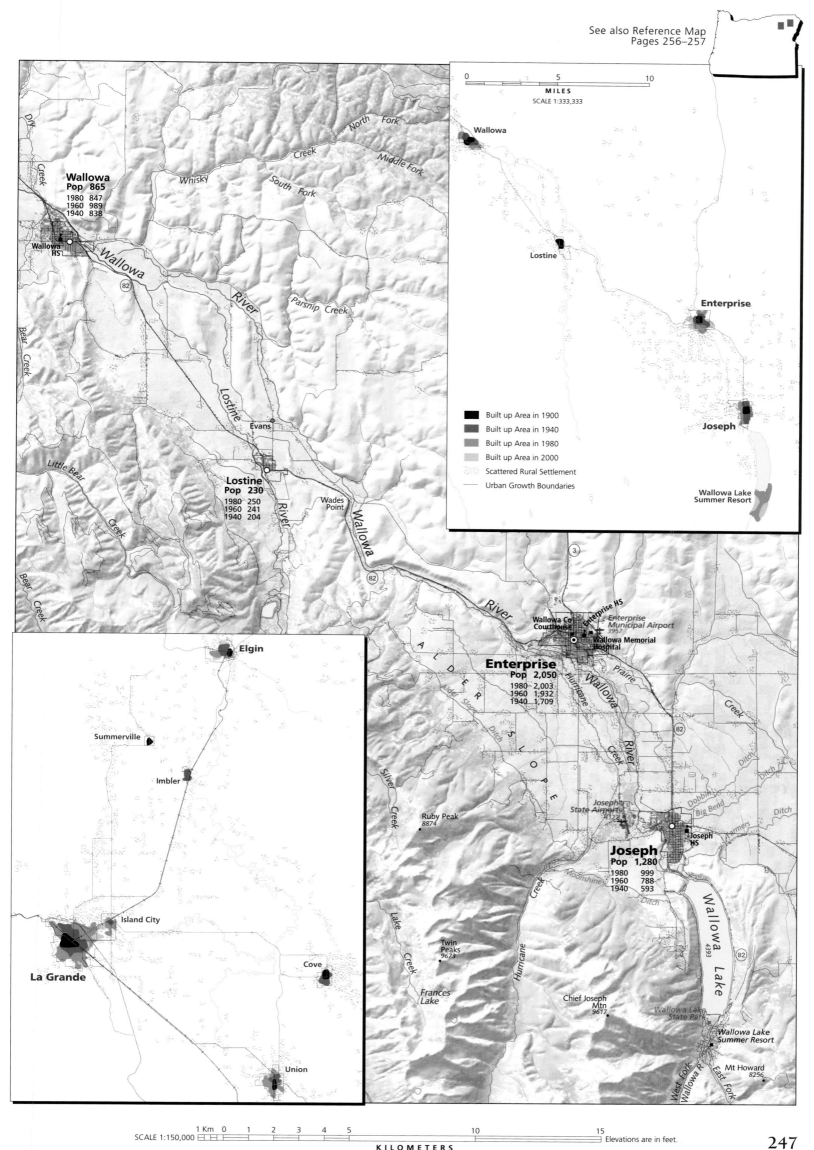

See also Reference Map
Pages 256–257

0   5   10
MILES
SCALE 1:333,333

Wallowa

Lostine

Enterprise

Joseph

Wallowa Lake
Summer Resort

■ Built up Area in 1900
■ Built up Area in 1940
■ Built up Area in 1980
□ Built up Area in 2000
⬚ Scattered Rural Settlement
— Urban Growth Boundaries

Dry Creek

North Fork

Creek

Middle Fork

Whisky

South Fork

Wallowa
Pop 865
1980 847
1960 989
1940 838

Wallowa HS

Wallowa River

82

Bear Creek

Parsnip Creek

Lostine

Evans

Little Bear

Creek

Lostine
Pop 230
1980 250
1960 241
1940 204

Wades Point

Wallowa

Bear Creek

82

River

3

Enterprise HS

Wallowa Co
Courthouse

*Enterprise
Municipal Airport*
3957

Wallowa Memorial
Hospital

Enterprise
Pop 2,050
1980 2,003
1960 1,932
1940 1,709

A L D E R   S L O P E

Alder Slope Ditch

Hurricane

Wallowa River

Prairie Creek

82

Silver Creek

Ruby Peak
8874

Joseph
State Airport
4122

Big Bend

Dobbin Ditch

Ditch

Farmers Ditch

Joseph HS

Joseph
Pop 1,280
1980 999
1960 788
1940 593

Moonshine

Ditch

Elgin

Summerville

Imbler

Lake Creek

Hurricane Creek

Twin Peaks
9673

Frances Lake

Chief Joseph
Mtn
9617

**Wallowa
Lake**
4393

Wallowa Lake
State Park

La Grande

Island City

Cove

Union

West Fork

East Fork

Wallowa R

Mt Howard
8256

*Wallowa Lake
Summer Resort*

1 Km 0   1   2   3   4   5
SCALE 1:150,000

10   15

KILOMETERS

Elevations are in feet.

Baker City; Ontario, Vale

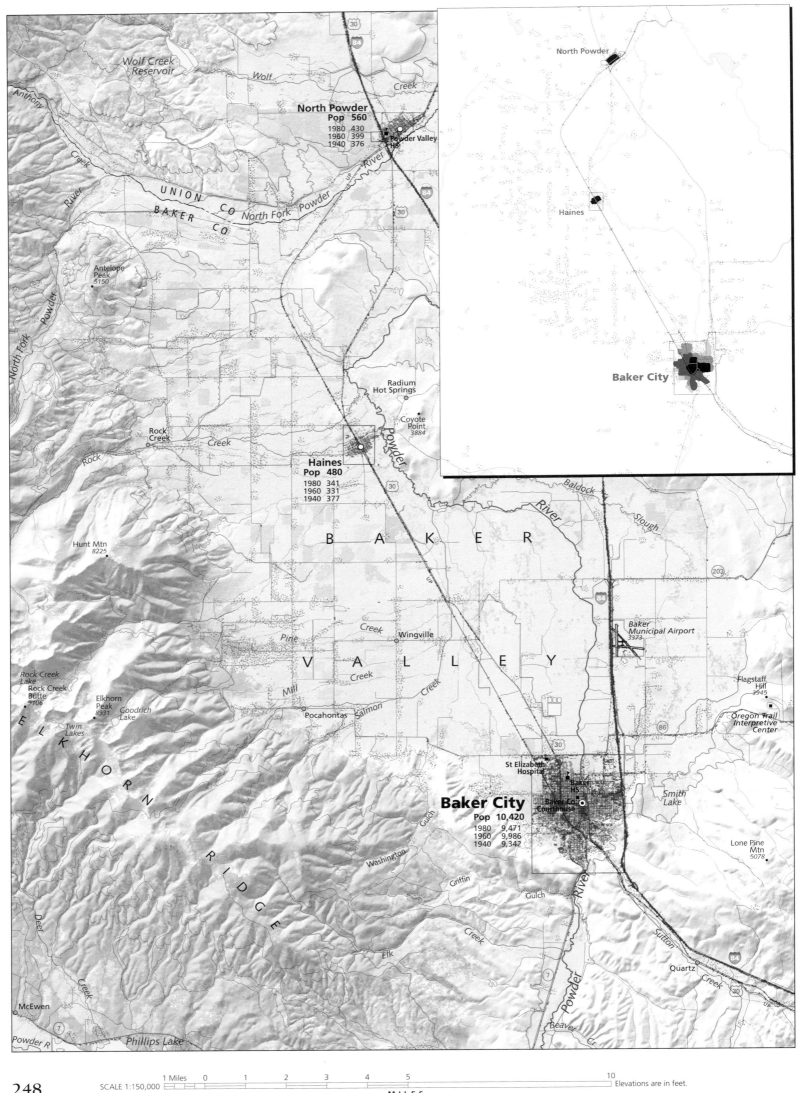

North Powder
Pop **560**

1980	430
1960	399
1940	376

Powder Valley HS

Wolf Creek Reservoir

Wolf Creek

Anthony Creek

River

UNION CO
BAKER CO

North Fork Powder

North Fork Powder River

Antelope Peak
5150

Radium Hot Springs

Coyote Point
3884

Rock Creek

Creek

Rock

Rock Creek

Haines
Pop **480**

1980	341
1960	331
1940	377

Powder

Hunt Mtn
8225

B A K E R

River

Baldock Slough

Rock Creek Lake
Rock Creek Butte
9106

Elkhorn Peak
8931

Goodrich Lake

Twin Lakes

E L K H O R N

R I D G E

V A L L E Y

Pine Creek

Creek

Wingville

Creek

Mill Creek

Salmon Creek

Pocahontas

Baker Municipal Airport
3373

Flagstaff Hill
3945

Oregon Trail Interpretive Center

St Elizabeth Hospital

Baker HS

Baker City
Pop **10,420**

1980	9,471
1960	9,986
1940	9,342

Baker Co. Courthouse

Gulch

Washington

Smith Lake

Lone Pine Mtn
5078

Griffin

Gulch

Creek

Elk

River

Powder

Deer

Creek

McEwen

Powder R

Phillips Lake

Beaver

Sutton

Creek

Quartz

Creek

North Powder

Haines

Baker City

SCALE 1:150,000

1 Miles 0 1 2 3 4 5   10   Elevations are in feet.

MILES

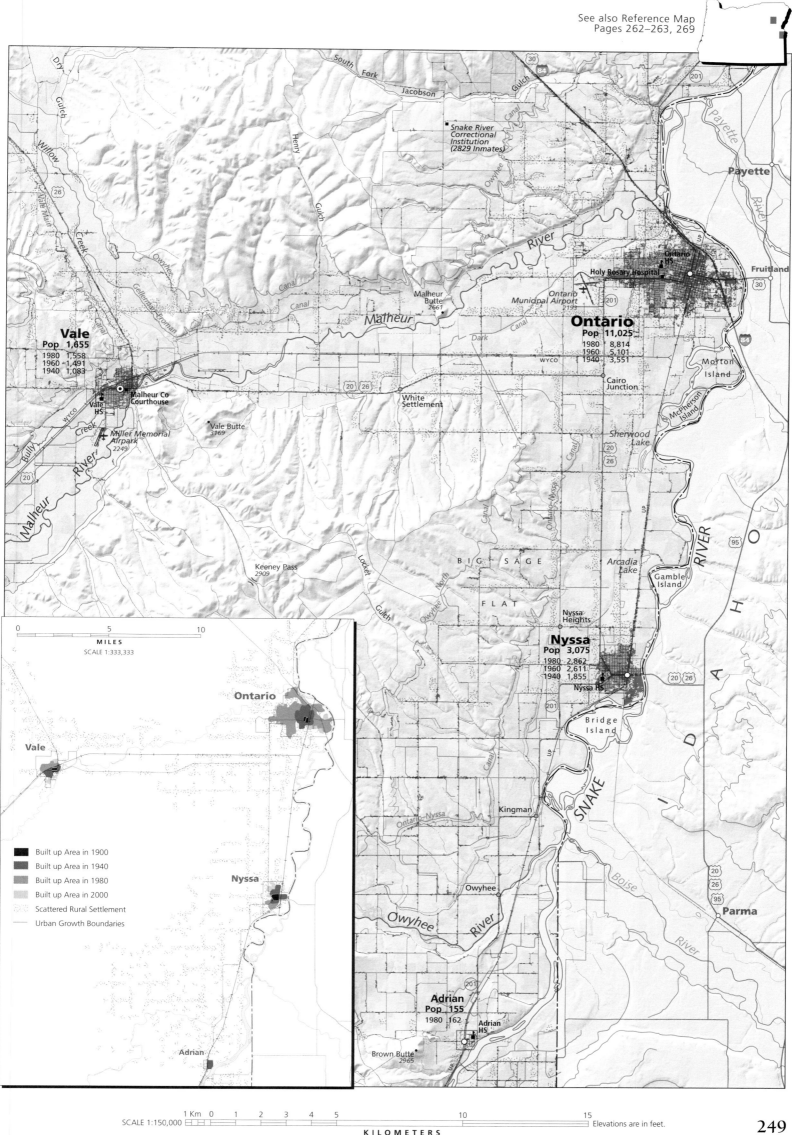

See also Reference Map
Pages 262–263, 269

Snake River
Correctional
Institution
(2829 Inmates)

Payette

Vale
Pop 1,655
1980 1,558
1960 1,491
1940 1,083

Malheur Co
Courthouse

Vale
HS

Miller Memorial
Airpark
2249

Vale Butte
3169

Malheur
Butte
2661

Ontario
Municipal Airport
2193

Holy Rosary Hospital

Ontario
HS

Ontario
Pop 11,025
1980 8,814
1960 5,101
1940 3,551

Fruitland

Morton
Island

McPherson
Island

Cairo
Junction

White
Settlement

Sherwood
Lake

Keeney Pass
2909

BIG SAGE

FLAT

Arcadia
Lake

Gamble
Island

Nyssa
Heights

Nyssa
Pop 3,075
1980 2,862
1960 2,611
1940 1,855

Nyssa HS

Bridge
Island

I D A H O

SNAKE RIVER

Kingman

Owyhee

Owyhee River

Boise River

Parma

Brown Butte
2965

Adrian
Pop 155
1980 162

Adrian
HS

0   5   10
MILES
SCALE 1:333,333

Ontario

Vale

Nyssa

Adrian

■ Built up Area in 1900
■ Built up Area in 1940
■ Built up Area in 1980
□ Built up Area in 2000
⋯ Scattered Rural Settlement
— Urban Growth Boundaries

Reference Maps Legend and Introduction

Legend

Maps are at a scale of 1:500,000.
1 inch equals approximately 8 miles on the ground.

Settlements

Portland	Over 100,000 Population	⊛ ◉	State Capital, County Seats
Tigard	10,000 to 100,000	○ ◦	Incorporated, Unincorporated
Seaside	2,500 to 10,000	□	Locale, Site, or Historical Place
Tangent	1,000 to 2,500	*el 176*	City Elevations in Feet
Paisley	Less Than 1,000		
Pengra	Locale or Site		

Roads and Boundaries

─(5)─	Interstate Highways	├─PNWR─┤	Railroads, Railroad Names
─(26)─	U.S. Highways	────────	Abandoned Railroads
─(140)─	State Highways		
────────	Other Paved Roads	─ ─ ─	State Boundaries
────────	Gravel or Dirt Roads	L I N N	County Boundaries, County Names
		▬▬▬▬	National Parks or Monuments

Township and Range

North

Meridian

	A		
2			
Initial Point (Willamette Stone)			
Base Line			

West — 3 2 1 | 1 2 3 — East

Principal Line

1			
2		**B**	

South

────────	Standard Baselines and Meridians
38	Township and Range Numbers
	Townships

Townships are identified by Township (T.) number north or south, and Range (R.) number east or west. In the example shown here, the shaded Townships are:
A) T. 2 N., R. 2 W.   **B)** T. 2 S., R. 2 E.

Water Features

∿∿	Rivers	⬭	Lakes, Reservoirs
～	Streams	⬯	Intermittent Lakes
～	Intermittent Streams	⬮	Marshes

Other Symbols

⊢→ ⊣ ⊢─	Railroad Tunnel	✈	Airports with Scheduled Service
≍	Pass	✛	Other Airports
◡ •¹⁹⁶³	Dams, Peak Symbol Elevations in Feet	─ ─ ─	Oregon Trail (Historical)

The alpha numeric grid on the reference pages is the 7.5-minute USGS Quadrangle grid. This can be used to locate a particular topographic quad for an area demanding further study. The quad names and locations can be found on pages 278–283.

Land Cover

▪	Built-up Areas	▪	Wetlands
▪	Farmland	▪	Shrub/Sage
▪	Evergreen Forests	▪	Cleared/Cut
▪	Mixed and Deciduous Forests	▪	Barren
▪	Grasslands	▪	Lava Fields

Landcover categories come from satellite images collected in 1990–1996. The images record reflection patterns, which are then compared to those of known features on the ground. **Built-up Areas** shown here include all urbanized areas. **Farmland** has a range of reflected characteristics, depending on crop type as well as growth and cultivation stage. It is shown here in four very similar colors in which large field patterns can be seen. **Evergreen Forests** are shown in dark green; **Mixed and Deciduous Forests** in lighter shades. **Grasslands** are uncultivated but relatively brush-free rangeland. **Wetlands** are of many types, some not corresponding to the "marsh" pattern on the base map. **Shrub/Sage** includes rangeland, and intergrades into Juniper Woodland classified here as **Evergreen Forests** (See Vegetation Maps, pages 182–189, for species composition). **Cleared/Cut** areas are recent burns or clearcuts. **Barren** includes sand dunes, alkali flats, high alpine barrens and similar areas. **Lava Fields** include recent flows with little plant cover.

The reference maps on the following pages are based on the same sets of data described at the beginning of the Populations Centers introduction on page 195. They portray the appearance and shape of the land at the more generalized level required by this map scale (about eight miles to the inch). The 12 page pairs are arranged in an overlapping

Reference Map Index

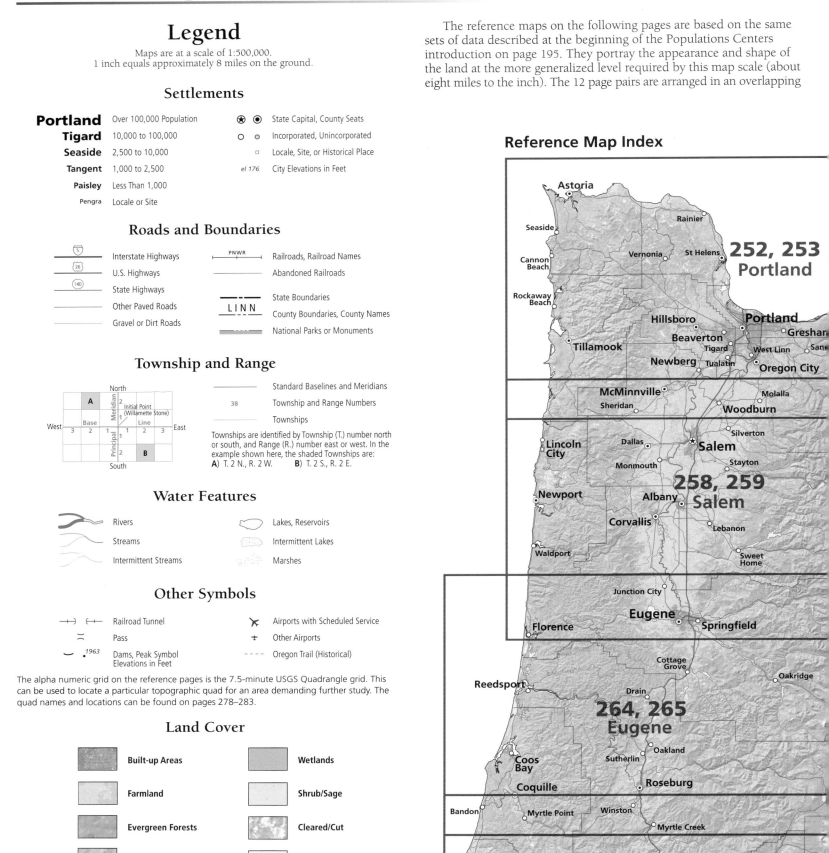

252, 253 Portland

258, 259 Salem

264, 265 Eugene

270, 271 Medford

grid. These are not discrete units, but pieces of a single picture. Oregon's regions typically fall on more than one page pair; readers can refer back and forth to the neighboring pages indicated on each map. A closer look at every major city and many smaller towns can be found by turning back to the Population Centers pages. Thus a reader interested in the Eugene area, for example, will turn in this section to pages 258–259 and 264–265, but also to pages 218–219 and 220–221 in the Population Centers section. In addition, the thematic maps that form the bulk of this atlas contain a great deal more information about how Eugene fits into statewide patterns of every sort. The reader is encouraged to browse.

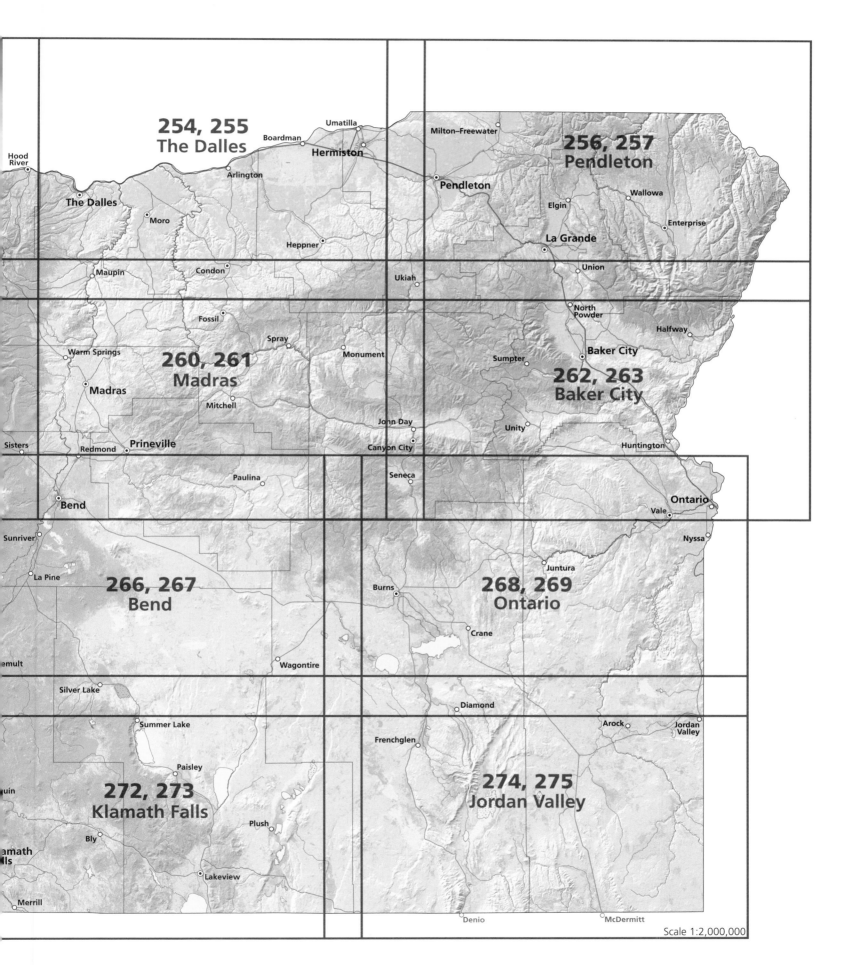

Scale 1:2,000,000

Portland

SCALE 1:500,000

10 Miles   0   10   20   30 Miles

MILES   Elevations are in feet

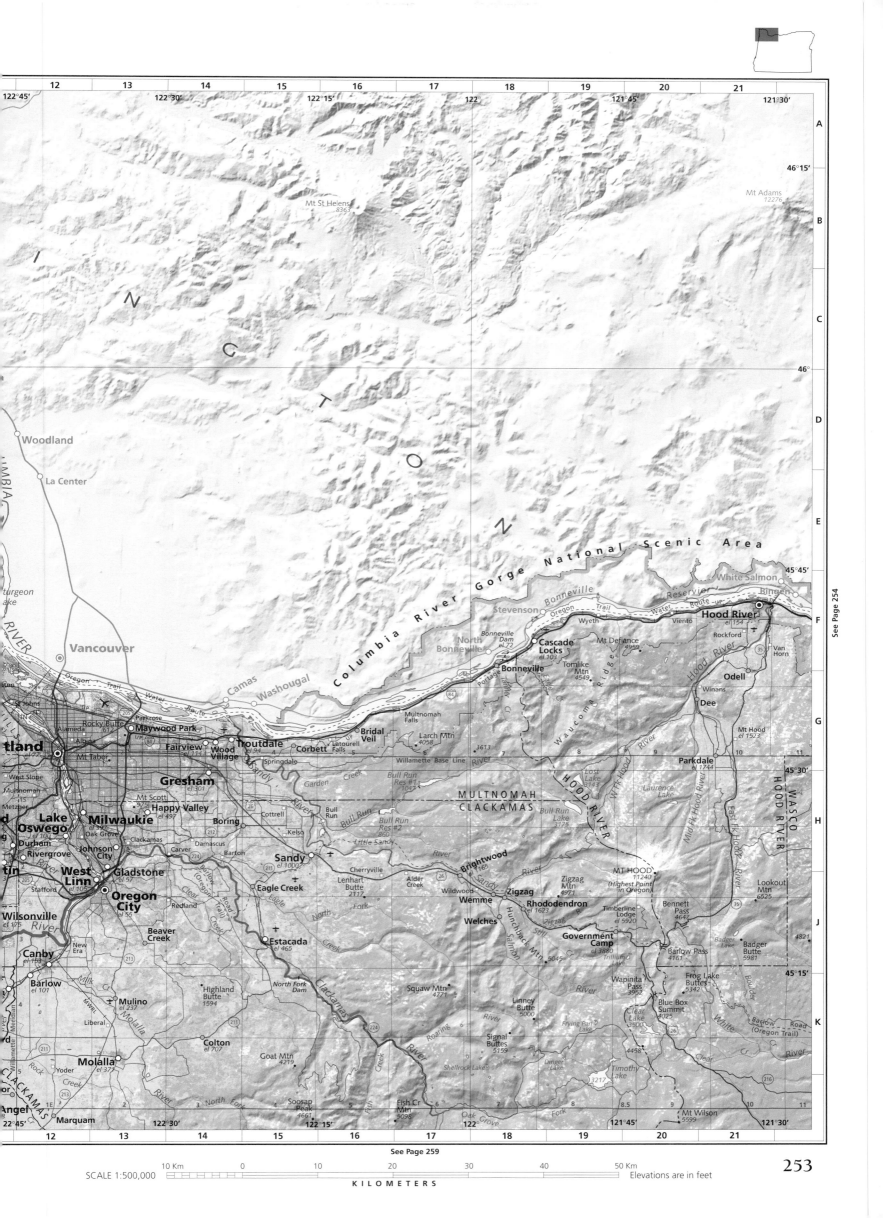

The Dalles

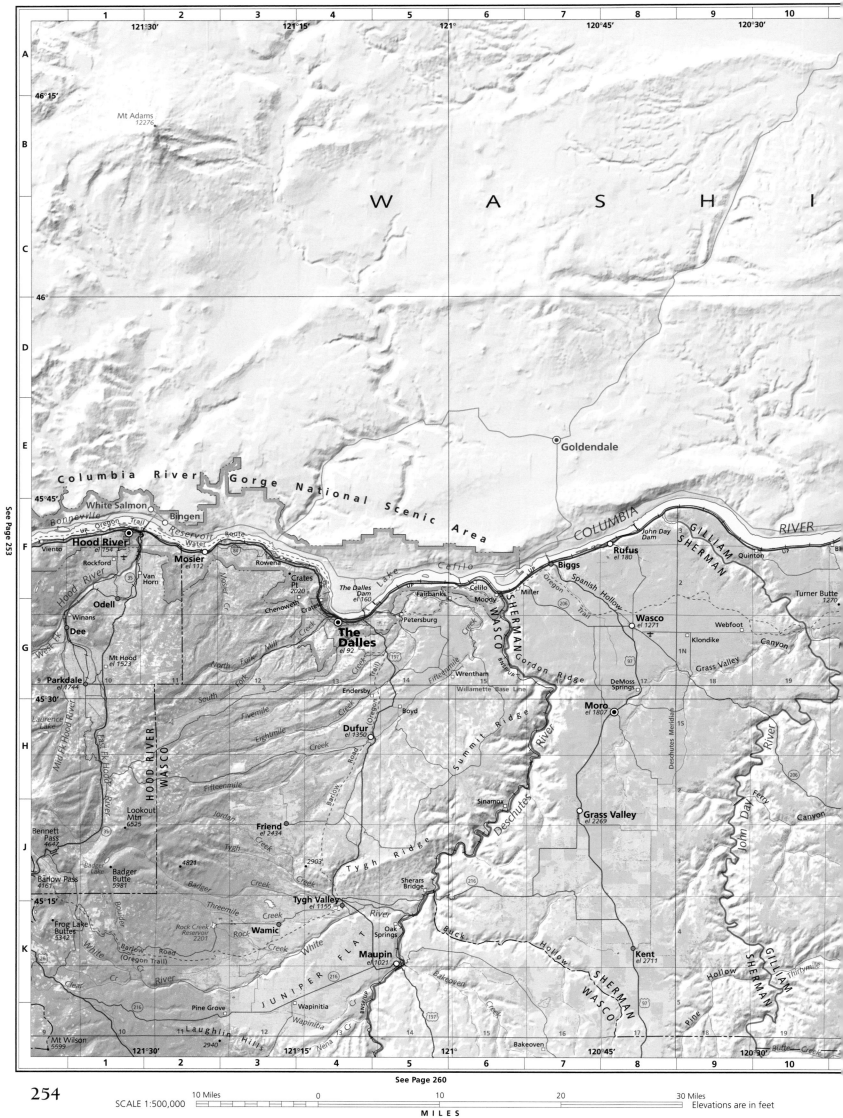

A

46°15'

B

C

46°

D

E

Goldendale

45°45'

W A S H I

Columbia River Gorge National Scenic Area

White Salmon
Bingen
Bonneville
Oregon Trail
Reservoir
Water
Route

Hood River
el 754
Viento
Rockford
Van Horn
Mosier
el 112
Rowena
Odell
Winans
Crates Pt
2020
Chenoweth
Crate
Dee
Mt Hood
el 1523

COLUMBIA SHERMAN
John Day Dam
Rufus
el 180
Biggs
Celilo
Fairbanks
Moody
Miller
The Dalles Dam
el 160
Petersburg
The Dalles
el 92

GILLIAM
SHERMAN
Quinton
Turner Butte
1270
Wasco
el 1271
Webfoot
Klondike
Canyon
Grass Valley

45°30'

Parkdale
el 1744
Laurence Lake
Mt Hood
West Fk
Mid Fk Hood River
East Fk Hood River
HOOD RIVER
WASCO

North Fork
South Fork
Fivemile
Eightmile
Fifteenmile

Endersby
Boyd
Dufur
el 1350
Wrentham
Willamette Base Line

Summit Ridge
Deschutes River
Bingham
Gordon Ridge
DeMoss Springs
Moro
el 1807

Deschutes Meridian

F

G

H

J

K

Bennett Pass
4647
Lookout Mtn
6525
Jordan
Fifteenmile
Barlow Road

Friend
el 2434
Tygh
2903

Sinamox

Grass Valley
el 2269

John Day River
Ferry Canyon

Barlow Pass
4161
Badger Lake
Badger Butte
5981
4821
Badger Creek
Tygh
Creek

Tygh Ridge
Sherars Bridge

Buck

206

45°15'

Frog Lake Buttes
5342
Boulder Creek
Barlow Road
(Oregon Trail)
White River
Threemile
Creek
Rock Creek Reservoir
2201
Rock Creek
Tygh Valley
el 1155
Wamic
White River
Oak Springs
Maupin
el 1021
Bakeoven

Hollow

SHERMAN
WASCO
Kent
el 2711

GILLIAM
SHERMAN

Mt Wilson
5599
Pine Grove
Laughlin Hills
2940
Wapinitia
Wapinitia Cr
Nena
JUNIPER FLAT
Bakeoven Creek
Pine Hollow
Thirtymile
Butte Creek

121°30'
121°15'
121°
120°45'
120°30'

1   2   3   4   5   6   7   8   9   10

SCALE 1:500,000
10 Miles   0   10   20   30 Miles
MILES
Elevations are in feet

Pendleton

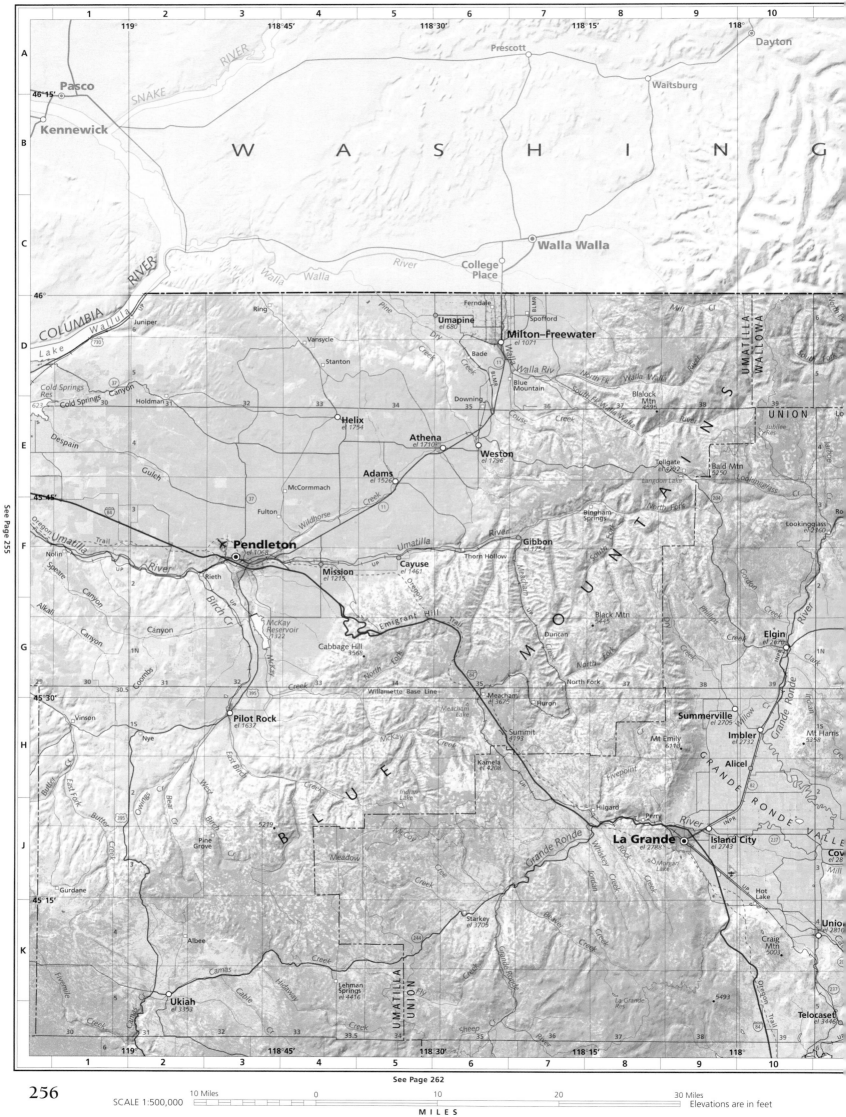

See Page 255

See Page 262

256

SCALE 1:500,000

10 Miles   0   10   20   30 Miles

MILES

Elevations are in feet

117°30' 117°15' 117° 116°45' 116°30'

Asotin

A

Winchester Craigmont 46°15'

B

Anatone

TON

Grande-Ronde River C

46°

Wenaha River Troy D
el 1615

Courtney SNAKE SALMON RIVER

Grande-Ronde Flora Joseph Horse Cr Cottonwood RIVER
el 4360 Cr

41 42 43 44 45 46 47 48 Chery Cr

Promise Table Mtn Brady E
4968

Maxville Red Hill 5333 5010 45°45'
5020

Powwatka Ridge Chico Chesnimnus Lightning Deep Creek H
Cr Creek

Top Cr Lewis Cr F

Minam River Whisky Creek Zumwalt Imnaha River Cow Creek Somers
el 2891 Deer Camp Point
5676

Wallowa Elk Mtn Grizzly Ridge Horse Suicide
el 2950 5122 Imnaha 5485 Creek Point G
Findley Buttes el 1965

41 42 82 43 44 45 46 47 48 49 50 45°30'

Evans Willamette Base Line SUMMIT RIDGE

Lostine Wallowa Creek Hat Point H
el 3200 River 6982

7552 Prairie Cr Little Sheep Dead Horse Ridge Creek Freezeout HELLS

Enterprise 8061 Creek Beeler Ridge Imnaha Bear Mtn
el 3757 Big Sheep 6895

8874 Joseph Hart Butte J
el 4190 6071

Mt Fanny Lookout Wallowa Lake Morgan Hells Canyon 45°15'
7153 Mtn 4393 Butte Dam
8831 Wallowa Mt Howard 6085 el 1514
Lake 8256

High Hat Frances Chief Joseph Aneroid 6708 K
Butte Lake Mtn Mtn
8160 9169 9617 Matterhorn 9702
9832 Aneroid
Lake Petes Pt
9675

Granite Butte Eagle Cap Minam Sugarloaf Mtn SNAKE
8679 9595 Lake S Fork 7938 WALLOWA
Eagle Imnaha River RIVER
Lake BAKER
UNION South Fork 41 42 43 44 45 46 47 48
BAKER

117°30' 117°15' 117° 116°45' 116°30'

See Page 263

SCALE 1:500,000 10 Km 0 10 20 30 40 50 Km Elevations are in feet
KILOMETERS

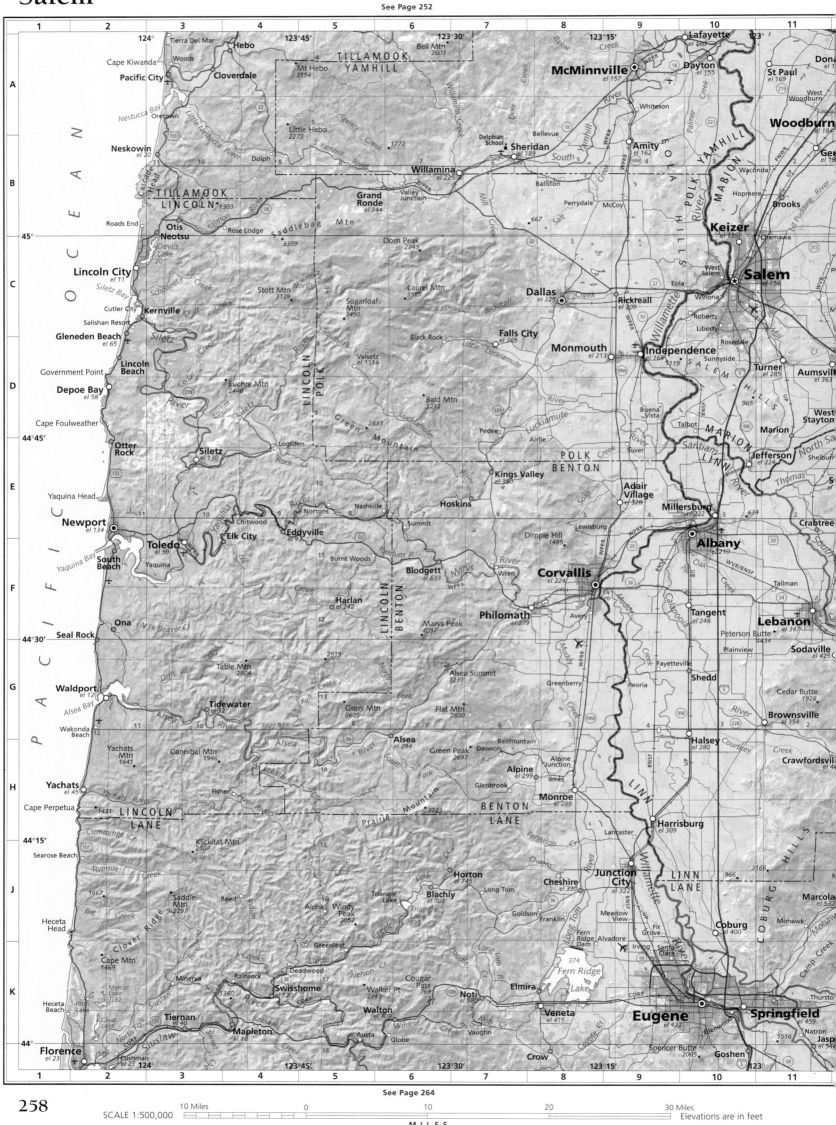

See Page 264

SCALE 1:500,000

10 Miles   0   10   20   30 Miles

MILES   Elevations are in feet

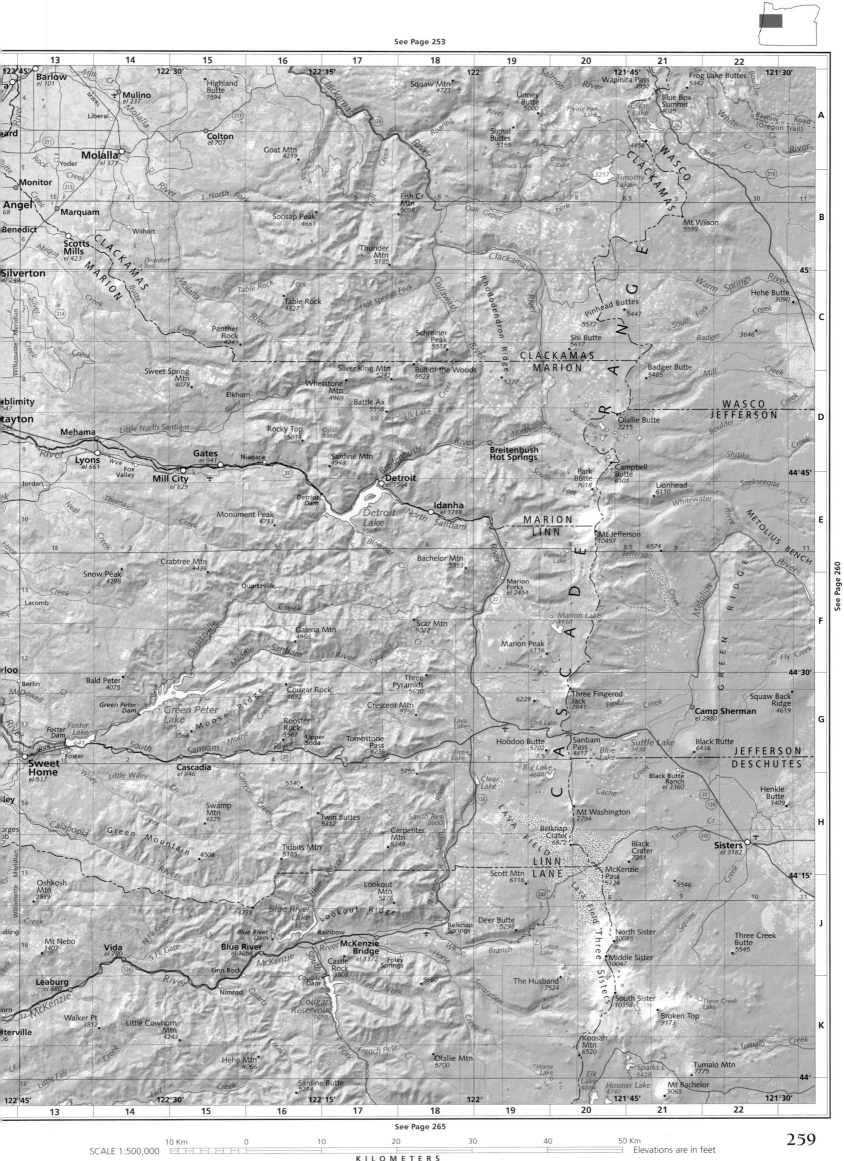

SCALE 1:500,000

KILOMETERS

10 Km   0   10   20   30   40   50 Km

Elevations are in feet

See Page 260

Madras

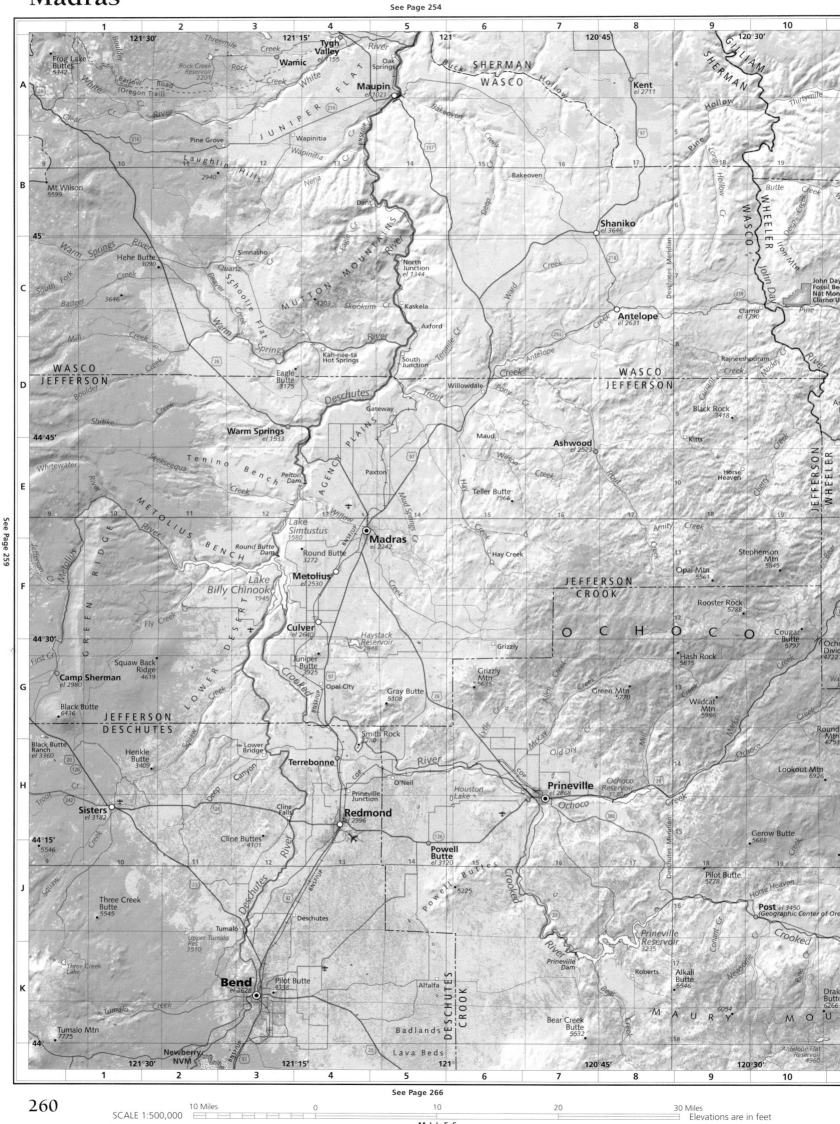

See Page 259

See Page 266

SCALE 1:500,000

10 Miles   0   10   20   30 Miles

MILES

Elevations are in feet

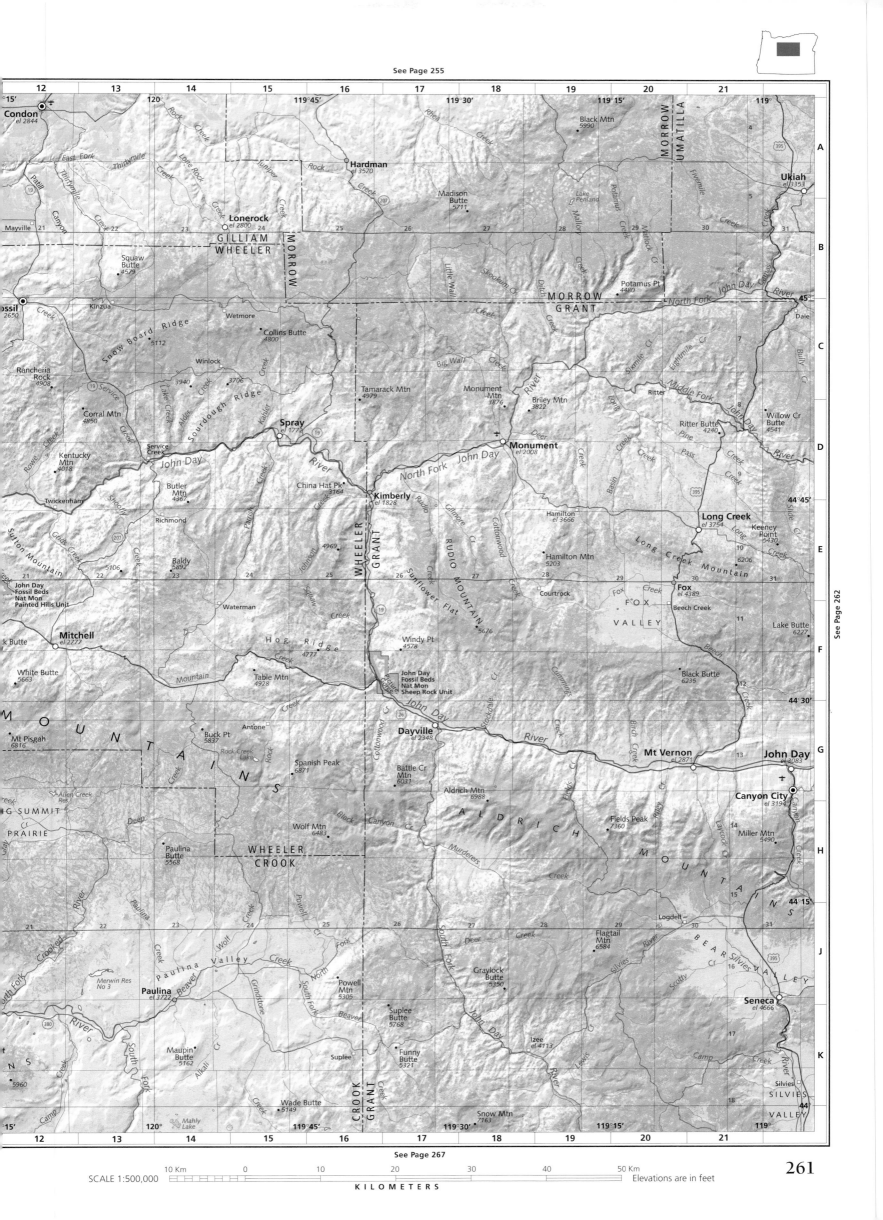

12 13 14 15 16 17 18 19 20 21

°15' 120° 119°45' 119°30' 119°15' 119°

Condon
el 2844

Mayville

East Fork
Thirtymile
Patili Canyon
Thirtymile

Rock Creek
Lone Rock
Juniper
Rock Creek

Hardman
el 3570

Black Mtn
5990

MORROW
UMATILLA

395

Ukiah
el 3353

A

Lonerock
el 2800

GILLIAM
WHEELER

Squaw
Butte
4579

MORROW

Madison
Butte
5711

Lake
Penland

Potamus Creek
Mallory

B

ossil
2650

Kinzua

Wetmore

Little Wall

Skookum Cr

MORROW
GRANT

Potamus Pt
4480

North Fork

John Day River

45'

Dale

Rancheria
Rock
4908

Snow Board Ridge

5112

Collins Butte
4800

Big Wall

Creek

Ditch

Creek

Eightmile Cr

Bully Cr

C

Corral Mtn
4850

Service

19

Winlock

3940

3706

Sourdough Ridge

Aider Creek
Kahler

Tamarack Mtn
4979

Monument
Mtn
3876

River

Briley Mtn
3822

Ritter

Middle Fork John Day

Willow Cr
Butte
4541

Kentucky
Mtn
4018

Lake Creek

Spray
el 1772

19

Ritter Butte
4240

Pine

Pass

D

Twickenham

John Day

Shoofly

Butler
Mtn
4367

China Hat Pk
3164

River

Kimberly
el 1828

North Fork John Day

Rudio

Gilmore Cr

Cottonwood

Deer Creek

Hamilton
el 3666

Basin

395

Long Creek
el 3754

44°45'

Keeney
Point
5430

Sutton Mountain

Richmond

207

Grubs Creek

Baldy
5892
23

Johnson

4969

Creek

WHEELER
GRANT

RUDIO MOUNTAIN

Hamilton Mtn
5203

Long Creek Mountain

6206

E

John Day
Fossil Beds
Nat Mon
Painted Hills Unit

21 22

5106

24

Waterman

25

Sellaw Creek

26

Sunflower Flat

27

Courtrock

28

29

Fox
Creek

Fox
el 4389

30

FOX
VALLEY

31

Lake Butte
6227

k Butte

Mitchell
el 2777

Hog Ridge

4777

Windy Pt
4578

5676

Beech Creek

11

Black Butte
6235

F

White Butte
5663

Mountain

Table Mtn
4928

Creek

John Day
Fossil Beds
Nat Mon
Sheep Rock Unit

Cr

Cummings

Beech

12

44°30'

M
O
U
N
T
A
I
N
S

Mt Pisgah
6816

Buck Pt
5837

Antone

Rock Creek Lake

Cottonwood

John Day

Dayville
el 2348

River

Stockdale

Creek

Mt Vernon
el 2871

13

John Day
el 3083

G

G SUMMIT

PRAIRIE

Allen Creek
Res

Spanish Peak
6871

Battle Cr
Mtn
6031

Aldrich Mtn
6988

ALDRICH

Fields Peak
7360

Riley

Canyon City
el 3194

Canyon

Miller Mtn
5490

Deep

Wolf Mtn
6483

Black Canyon Cr

Murderers

Creek

M
O
U
N
T
A
I
N
S

14

H

Paulina
Butte
5568

WHEELER
CROOK

Powell

Logdell

15

44°15'

River

21

22

Paulina

23

24

Powell
Mtn
5305

25

North Fork

26

South Fork

27

Deer Creek

28

Flagtail
Mtn
6584

29

River

30

BEAR

31

Silvies VALLEY

J

Crooked

Merwin Res
No 3

Paulina
el 3722

Beaver

Paulina Valley

Grindstone

Creek

Beaver

Graylock
Butte
5350

Silvies

Scotty

Seneca
el 4666

17

395

South Fork

River

Maupin
Butte
5162

Alkali Cr

Wolf Cr

Suplee

Suplee
Butte
5768

John Day

Lewis

Camp Creek

River

Silvies

SILVIES
VALLEY

K

5960

Mahly
Lake

Wade Butte
5149

CROOK
GRANT

Snow Mtn
7163

Funny
Butte
5321

Izee
el 4113

18

44'

°15' 120° 119°45' 119°30' 119°15' 119°

12 13 14 15 16 17 18 19 20 21

See Page 262

SCALE 1:500,000   10 Km   0   10   20   30   40   50 Km   Elevations are in feet

KILOMETERS

261

Baker City

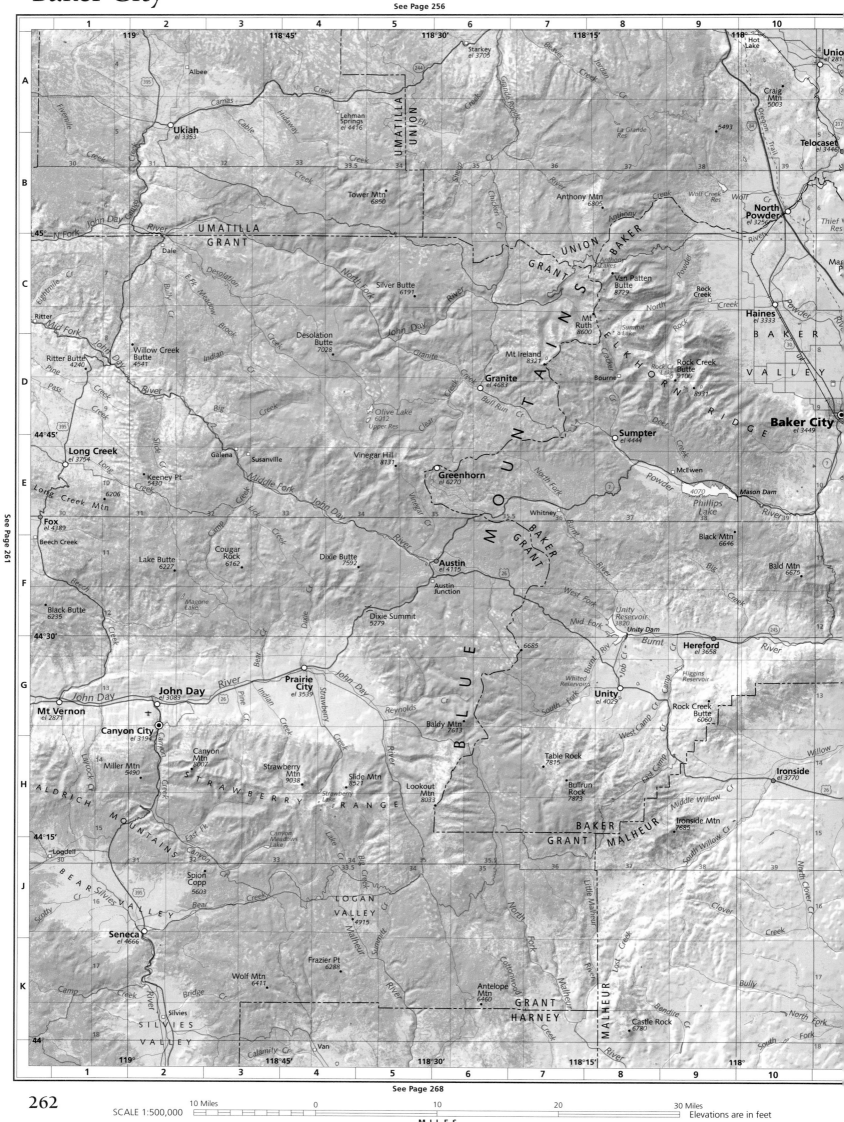

See Page 268

See Page 261

SCALE 1:500,000

10 Miles 0 10 20 30 Miles

MILES

Elevations are in feet

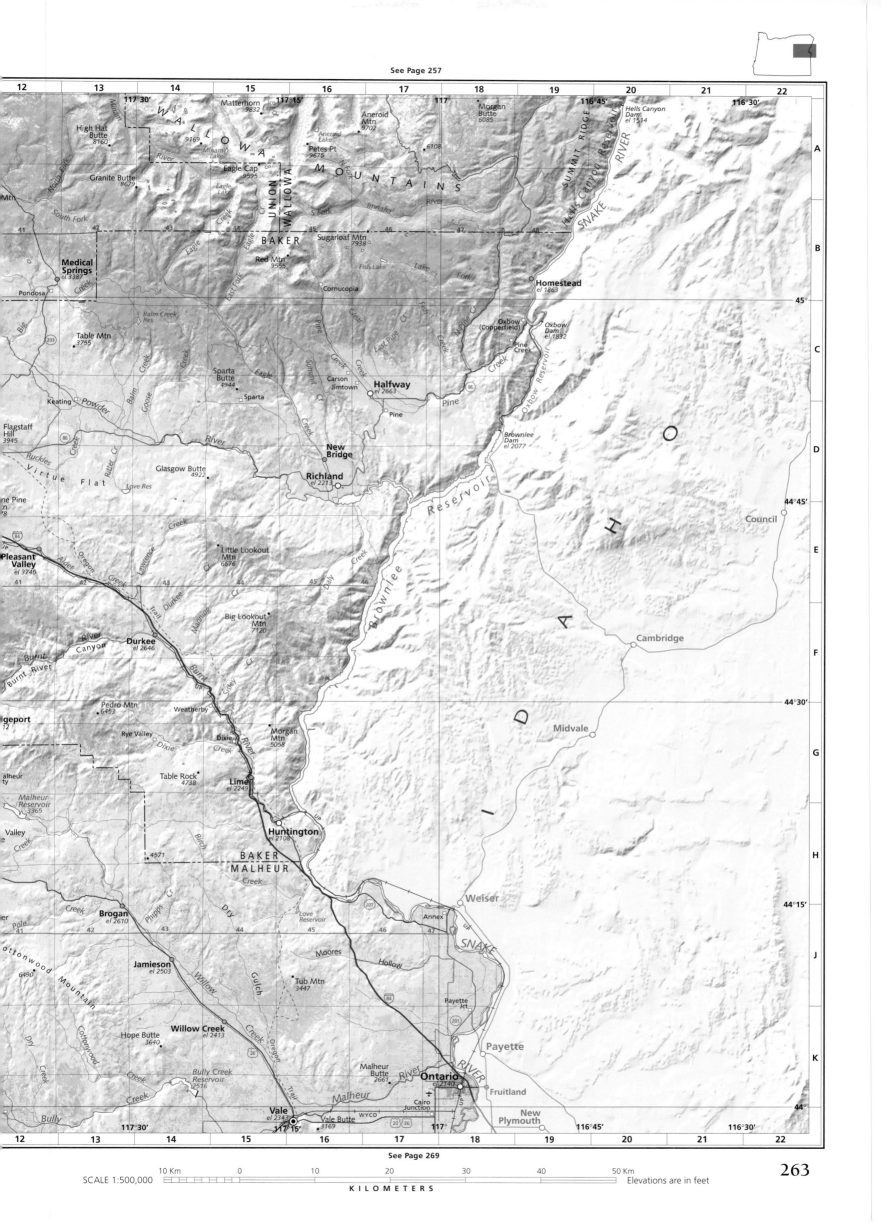

12 13 14 15 16 17 18 19 20 21 22

117°30' 117°15' 117° 116°45' 116°30'

W A L L O W A

Matterhorn
9832

High Hat
Butte
8160

9169

Minam Lake

Aneroid
Mtn
9702

Morgan
Butte
6085

Hells Canyon
Dam
el 1514

SUMMIT RIDGE

SNAKE RIVER

A

Granite Butte
8679

Eagle Cap
9595

Eagle Lake

Petes Pt
9675

Aneroid Lake

6108

U N I O N

W A L L O W A

M O U N T A I N S

North Fork

South Fork

41 42 43 44 45 46 47 48

B A K E R

Sugarloaf Mtn
7938

Imnaha River

Hells Canyon Reservoir

B

Medical
Springs
el 3387

Red Mtn
9555

Fish Lake

Homestead
el 1863

45°

Pondosa

Cornucopia

Lake Fork

Oxbow
(Copperfield)

Oxbow
Dam
el 1832

C

Big

Table Mtn
3755

Balm Creek
Res

Pine Creek

East Pine Cr

Fish Creek

Pine
Creek

Oxbow Reservoir

203

Sparta
Butte
4944

Eagle

Carson
Jimtown

Halfway
el 2663

Summit Creek

Clear Creek

86

Keating

Powder

Sparta

Pine

Brownlee
Dam
el 2077

Flagstaff
Hill
3945

Goose Cr

Balm Cr

Ritter Cr

86

New
Bridge

Pine

I
D
A

Council

44°45'

D

Ruckles Cr

Virtue Flat

Love Res

Glasgow Butte
4922

Richland
el 2213

Reservoir

ne Pine
n 8

84

UP

Pleasant
Valley
el 3745

Little Lookout
Mtn
6676

Lawrence Cr

Brownlee

E

41 42 43 44 45 46

Oregon

Durkee

Daly Cr

Cambridge

F

River

Canyon

Durkee
el 2646

Trail

Manning Cr

Big Lookout
Mtn
7120

Cr

Burnt

Burnt River

Burnt River

UP

Sisley Cr

44°30'

Pedro Mtn
6453

Weatherby

Midvale

G

geport
12

Rye Valley

Dixie

Dixie
Cr

Morgan
Mtn
5058

River

I
D

Table Rock
4738

Lime
el 2249

alheur
ty

Malheur
Reservoir
3365

4571

Huntington
el 2108

UP

H

Valley Creek

B A K E R
M A L H E U R

Creek

Birch Cr

Weiser

201

44°15'

Brogan
el 2610

Phipps Cr

Dry

Love
Reservoir

Annex

UP

SNAKE

pole
41

42 43 44 45 46 47

J

Cottonwood Mountain

Jamieson
el 2503

Willow

Gulch

Moores

Hollow

84

Payette
Jct

6490

Tub Mtn
3447

201

Payette

K

Hope Butte
3640

Willow Creek
el 2413

Creek

Oregon Trail

26

Malheur
Butte
2661

River

RIVER

Ontario
el 2140

Fruitland

Dry Creek

Cottonwood

Bully Creek
Reservoir
2516

Cairo
Junction

Bully

Vale
el 2343

Malheur

Vale Butte
3169

WYCO

20 26

New
Plymouth

44°

117°30' 117°15' 117° 116°45' 116°30'

12 13 14 15 16 17 18 19 20 21 22

SCALE 1:500,000   10 Km   0   10   20   30   40   50 Km   Elevations are in feet
K I L O M E T E R S

263

Eugene

See Page 258

See Page 270

SCALE 1:500,000

10 Miles   0   10   20   30 Miles

MILES

Elevations are in feet

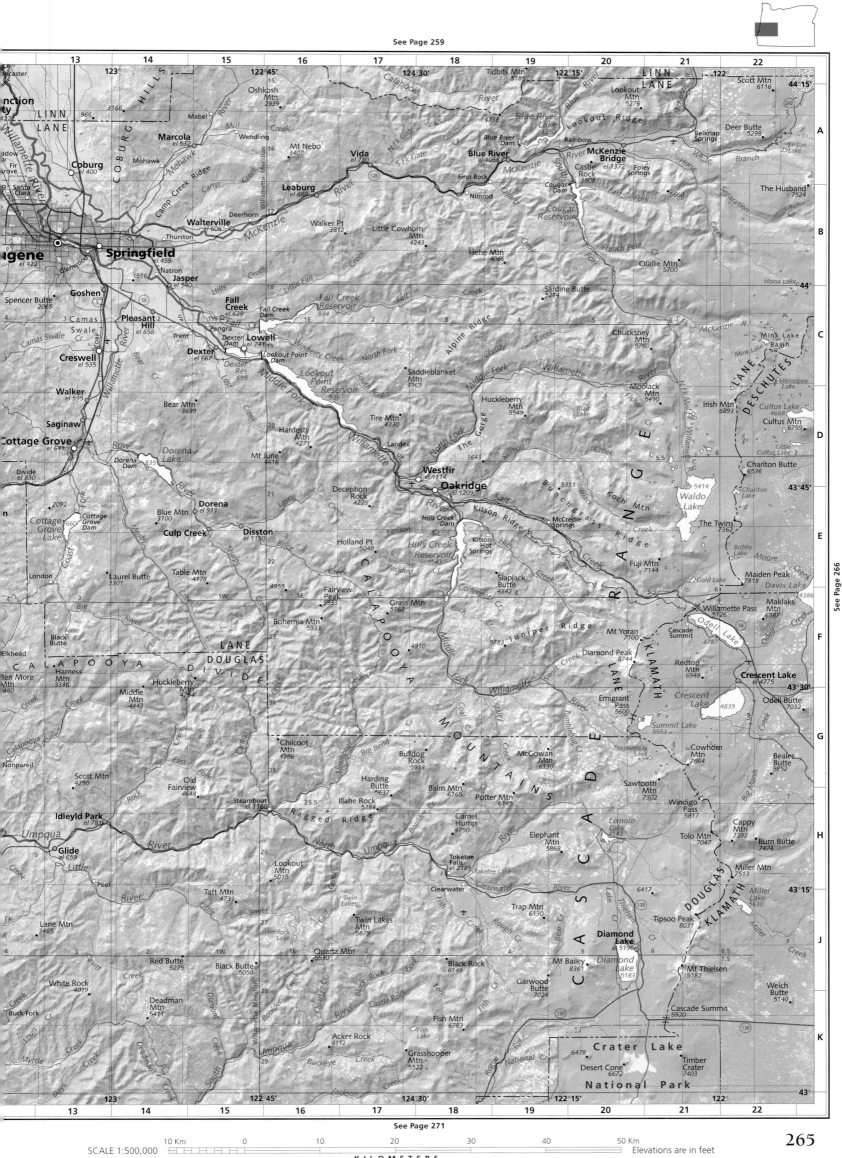

See Page 266

See Page 271

SCALE 1:500,000

KILOMETERS

Elevations are in feet

Bend

See Page 260

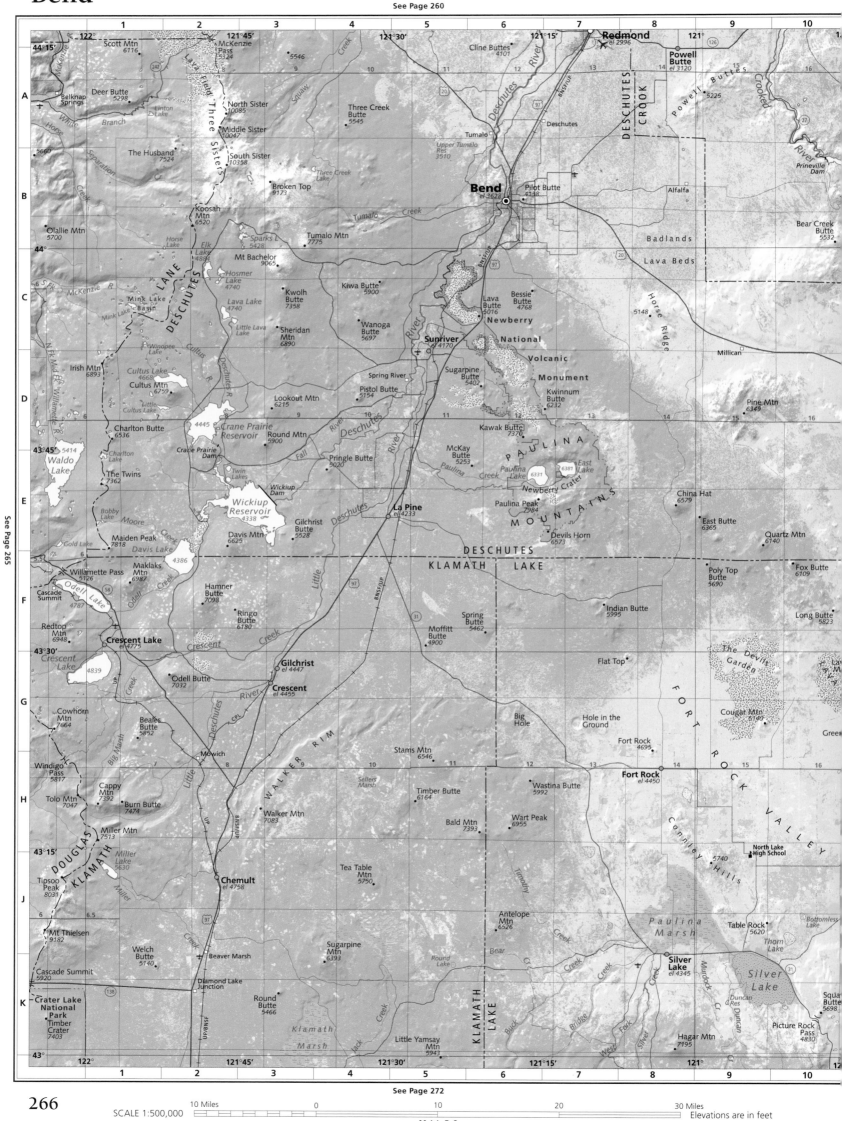

See Page 265

See Page 272

SCALE 1:500,000

10 Miles   0   10   20   30 Miles

MILES

Elevations are in feet

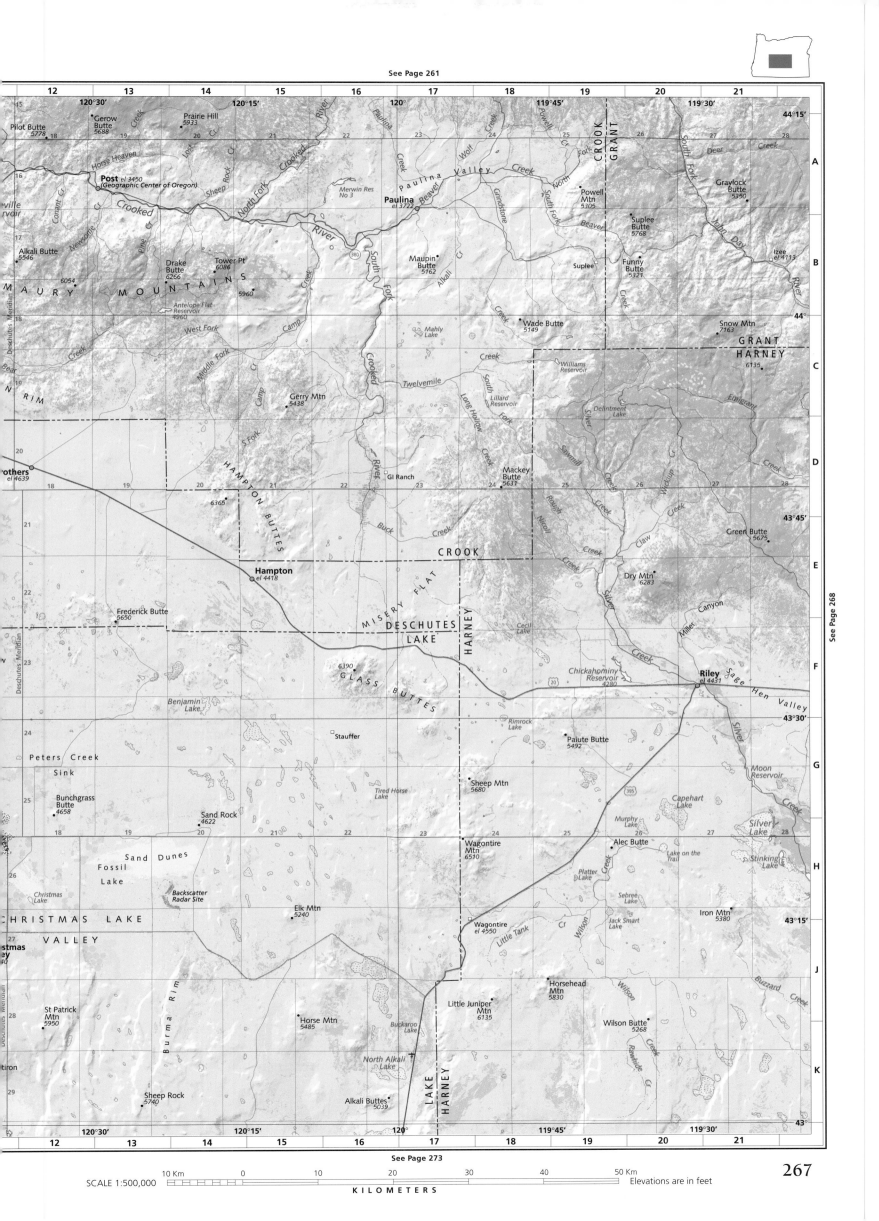

Ontario

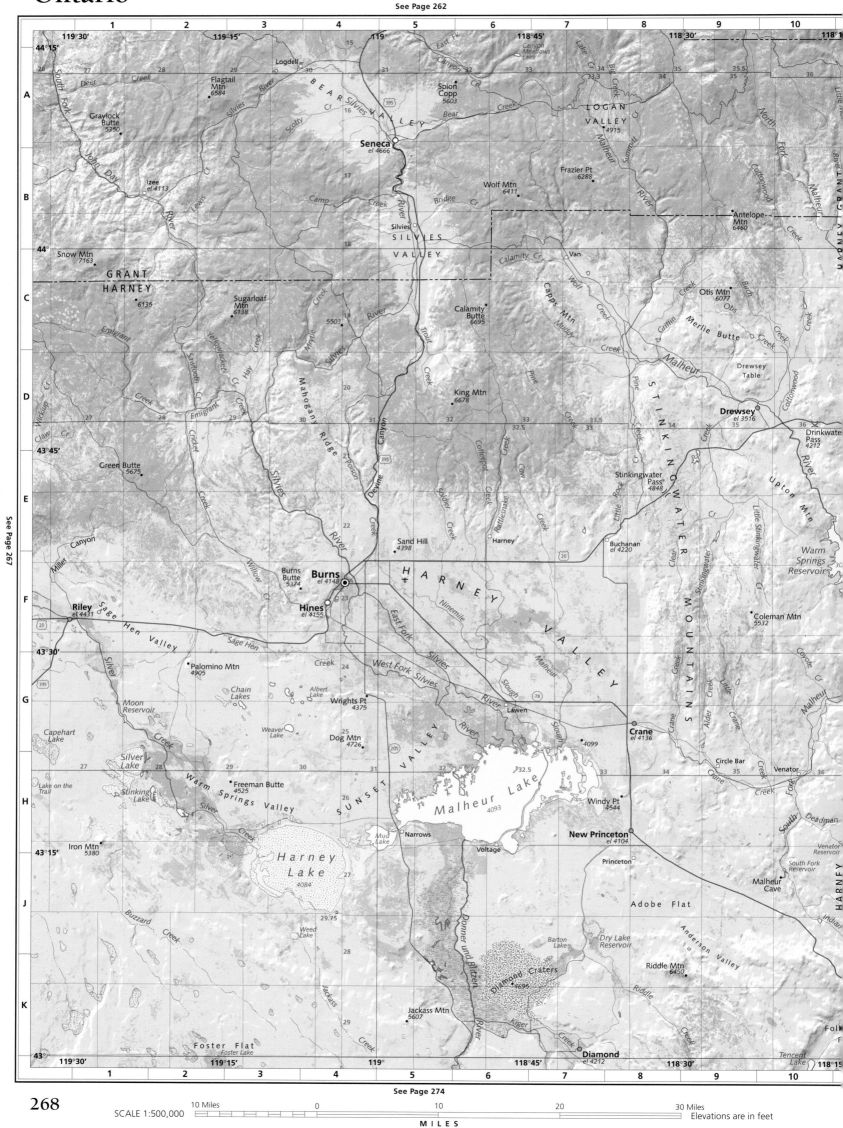

268

SCALE 1:500,000

10 Miles   0   10   20   30 Miles

MILES

Elevations are in feet

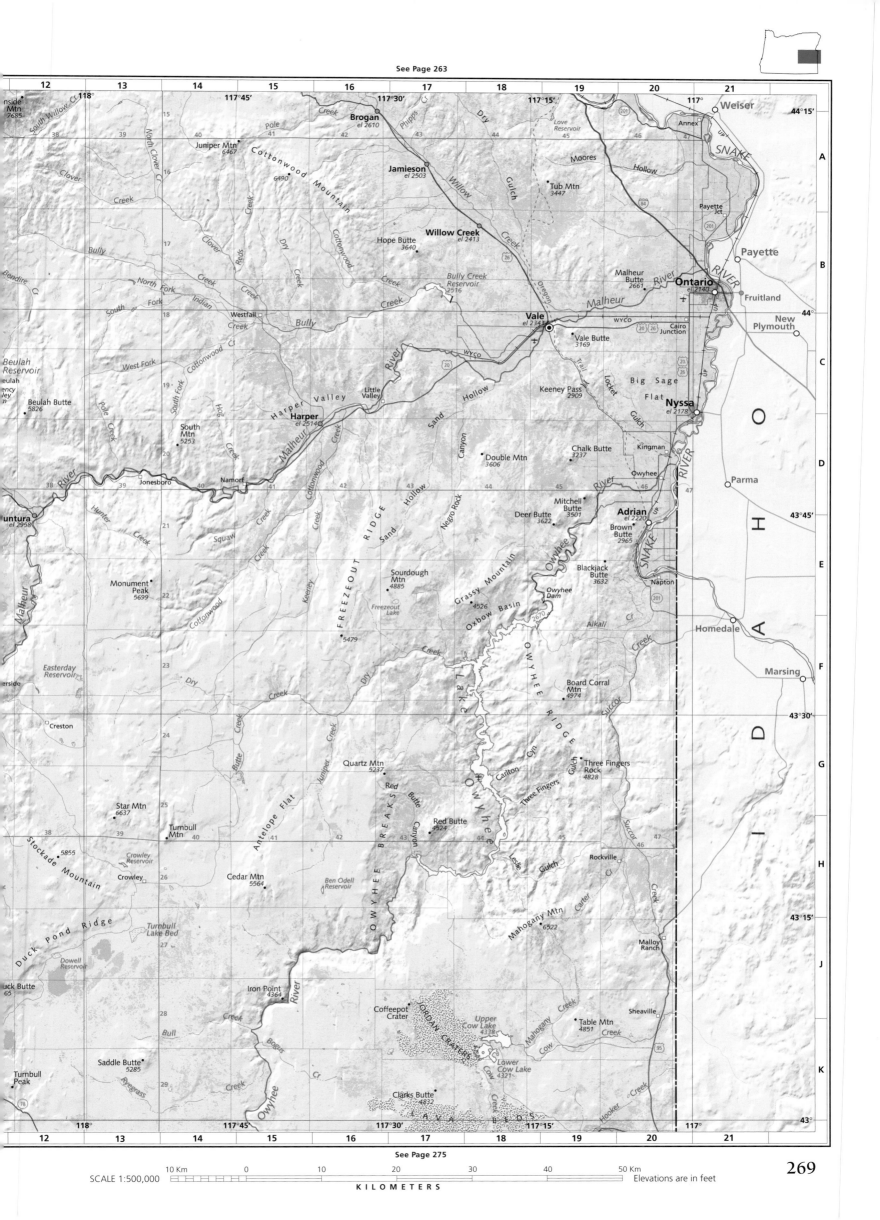

SCALE 1:500,000

10 Km   0   10   20   30   40   50 Km

KILOMETERS

Elevations are in feet

Medford

See Page 264

SCALE 1:500,000

MILES

Elevations are in feet

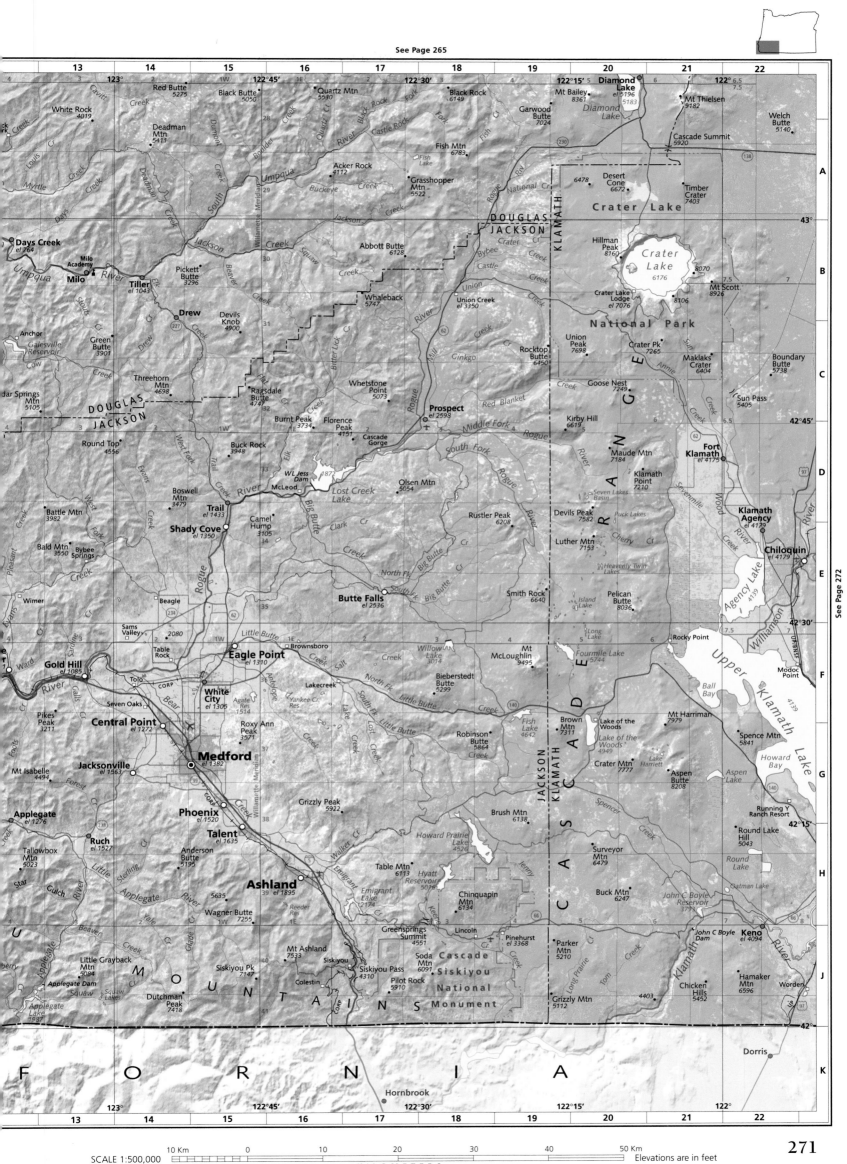

271

SCALE 1:500,000

10 Km   0   10   20   30   40   50 Km

KILOMETERS   Elevations are in feet

Klamath Falls

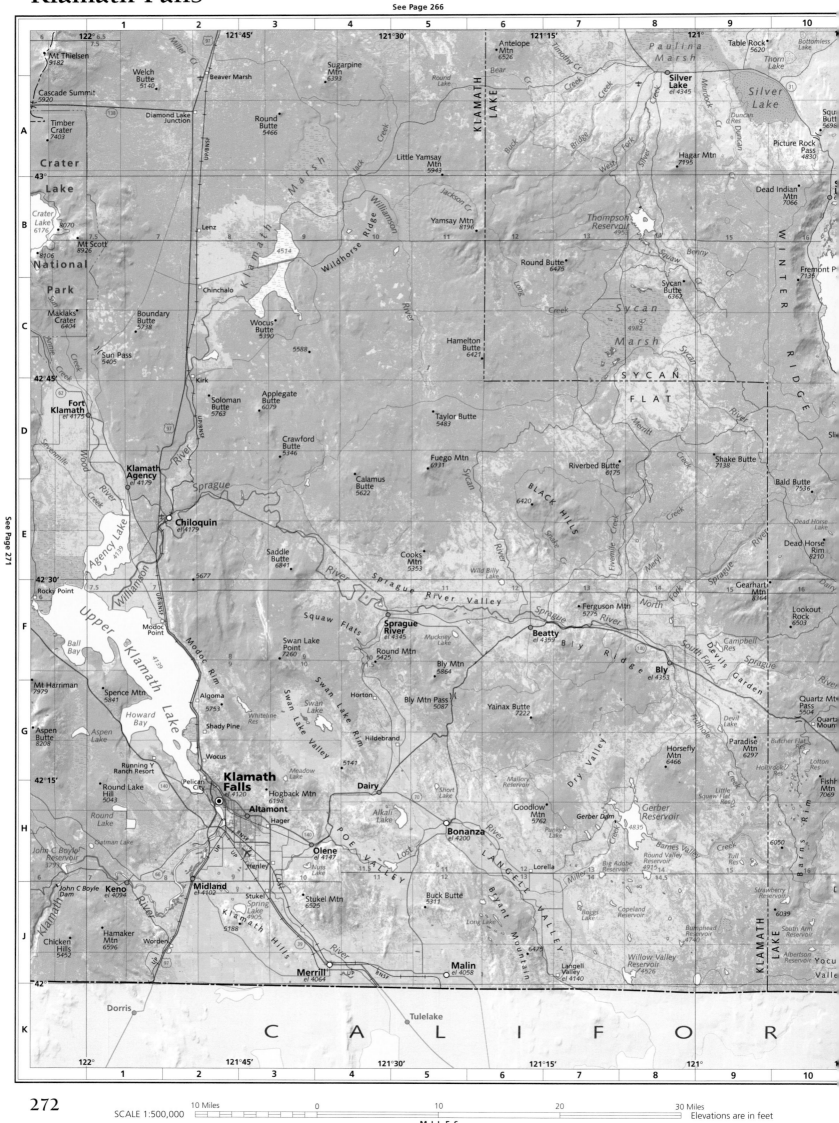

See Page 271

Mt Thielsen 9182

122° 6.5
7.5
6

Welch Butte 5140

121°45'

Beaver Marsh

Sugarpine Mtn 6393

Miller Cr

121°30'

Antelope Mtn 6526

Paulina Marsh

121°15'

Table Rock 5620

121°

Bottomless Lake

Thorn Lake

Cascade Summit 5920

Diamond Lake Junction

Round Butte 5466

Round Lake

Bear Cr

Silver Lake el 4345

Silver Lake

31

Timber Crater 7403

138

Little Yamsay Mtn 5943

West Fork

Bridge Cr

Buck

Hagar Mtn 7195

Duncan Res

Picture Rock Pass 4830

Squ Butte 5698

Crater

43°

Lake

Crater Lake 6176

8070

Lenz

Williamson Ridge

Wildhorse Ridge

Yamsay Mtn 8196

Jackson Cr

Thompson Reservoir 4953

12

13

Dead Indian Mtn 7066

15

16

Mt Scott 8926

8106

4514

Round Butte 6475

Sycan Butte 6362

Benny

Squaw

WINTER

Fremont P 7135

National

Chinchalo

Long

Sycan

Creek

4982

Marsh

RIDGE

Park

Maklaks Crater 6404

Boundary Butte 5738

Wocus Butte 5390

5588

Hamelton Butte 6421

SYCAN

FLAT

42°45'

Sun Pass 5405

Annie Creek

Kirk

Soloman Butte 5763

Applegate Butte 6079

Taylor Butte 5483

62

Merritt

Sycan

River

Shake Butte 7138

Fort Klamath el 4175

Sevenmile

Wood

97

UP/BNSF

Crawford Butte 5346

Fuego Mtn 6931

Riverbed Butte 6175

BLACK HILLS

Bald Butte 7536

Klamath Agency el 4179

River

Sprague

Calamus Butte 5622

6420

Shake Cr

Fivemile

Meryl

Dead Horse Lake

Dead Horse Rim 8210

Chiloquin el 4179

Agency Lake 4139

Saddle Butte 6841

5677

Cooks Mtn 5353

Sprague

River Valley

Wild Billy Lake

11

Sprague

12

13

14

Gearhart Mtn 8364

15

16

42°30'

Rocky Point

UP/BNSF

7

Williamson

River

Squaw Flats

Ferguson Mtn 5775

North Fork

Lookout Rock 6503

Upper

Ball Bay

Modoc Point

4139

Modoc Rim

Swan Lake Point 7260

Swan Lake

10

11.5

Round Mtn 5425

Sprague River el 4345

Muckney Cr

Beatty el 4359

Bly Ridge

Sprague River

Campbell Res

Devils Garden

Klamath

Mt Harriman 7979

Spence Mtn 5841

Algoma 5753

Whiteline Res

Bly Mtn 5864

Horton

Bly el 4353

140

South Fork

Quartz Mtn Pass 5504

Quartz Mtn

Lake

Howard Bay

Aspen Lake

Shady Pine

Swan Lake Valley

Swan Lake Rim

Hildebrand

Bly Mtn Pass 5087

Yainax Butte 7222

Pinehole

Devil Lake

Paradise Mtn 6297

Butcher Flat Res

Lofton Res

Aspen Butte 8208

5141

Horsefly Mtn 6466

Holbrook Res

Fishh Mtn 7069

42°15'

Round Lake Hill 5043

Running Y Ranch Resort

Wocus

Meadow Lake

Klamath Falls el 4120

Pelican City

140

Hogback Mtn 5198

Dairy

70

Short Lake

Goodlow Mtn 5762

Mallory Reservoir

Gerber Dam

Gerber Reservoir

Little Squaw Flat Res

6050

Round Lake

Altamont

Hager

Alkali Lake

Bonanza el 4200

4835

Barnes Valley

Creek

Barns

John C Boyle Reservoir 3793

Oatman Lake

Olene el 4147

Nuss Lake

140

POE VALLEY

Lost

Lorella

12

Punky Lake

Big Adobe Res

Round Valley 4915

13

14

Tull Res

Rim

6

66

8

Midland el 4102

Henley

10

11

River

LANGELL VALLEY

Miller

14.5

Strawberry Reservoir

Keno el 4094

John C Boyle Dam

US

Stukel 4905

Spring Lake

Stukel Mtn 6525

Buck Butte 5311

Bryant Mountain

Boggs Lake

Copeland Reservoir

6475

Bumphead Reservoir 4740

6039

Hamaker Mtn 6596

Chicken Hills 5452

Worden

Klamath Hills

5188

Langell Valley 4140

Willow Valley Reservoir 4526

Albertson Reservoir

KLAMATH LAKE

South Arm Reservoir

Yocu Valle

42°

39

Malin el 4058

Long Lake

Merrill el 4064

UP

BNSF

97

UP

River

Dorris

CALIFOR

Tulelake

K

122°

121°45'

121°30'

121°15'

121°

SCALE 1:500,000

10 Miles   0   10   20   30 Miles

MILES

Elevations are in feet

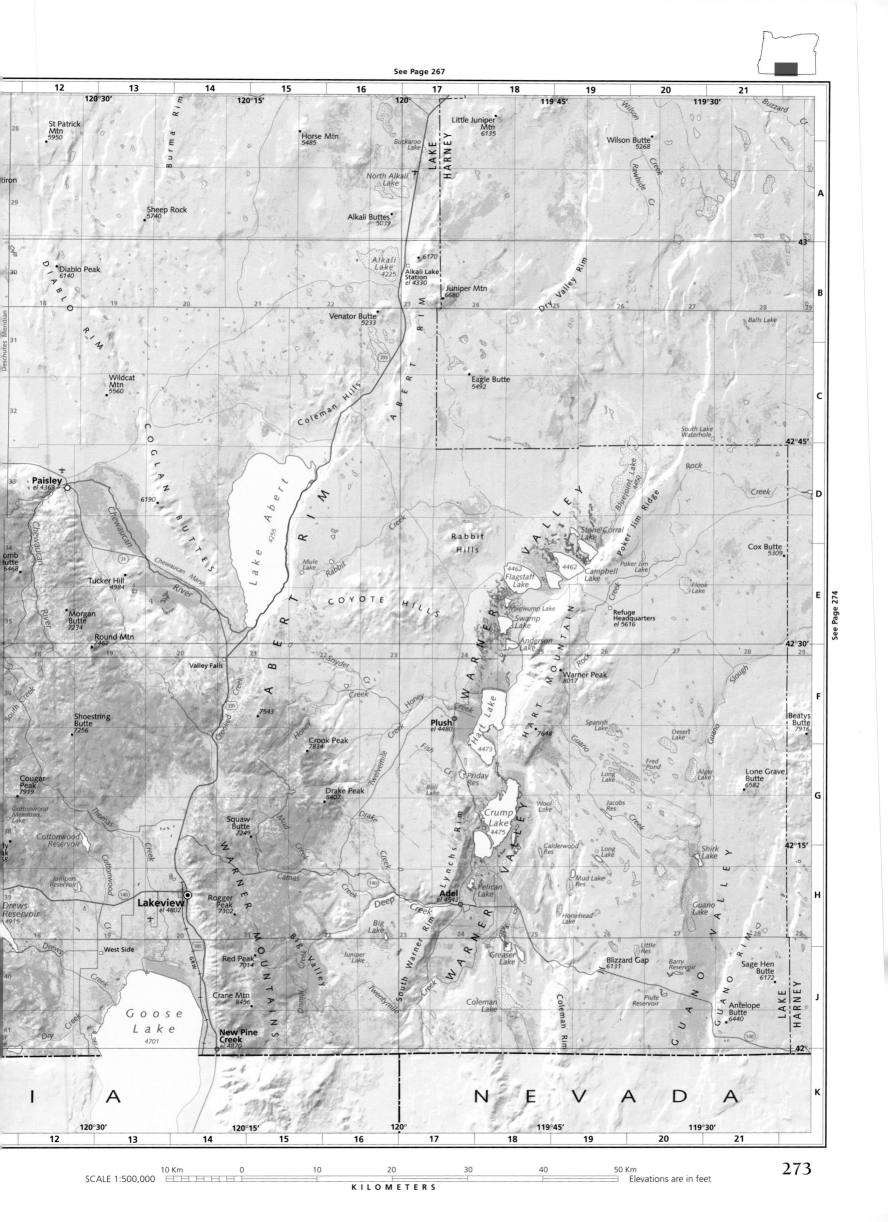

12 13 14 15 16 17 18 19 20 21

120°30′ 120°15′ 120° 119°45′ 119°30′

St Patrick
Mtn
5950

Horse Mtn
5485

Little Juniper
Mtn
6135

Wilson Butte
5268

Buzzard

Wilson

Rawhide Cr

Buckaroo
Lake

LAKE HARNEY

A

Sheep Rock
5740

North Alkali
Lake

Alkali Buttes
5039

43°

DIABLO RIM

Diablo Peak
6140

Alkali
Lake
4225

6170

Alkali Lake
Station
el 4330

Juniper Mtn
6680

Dry Valley Rim

Balls Lake

B

Deschutes Meridian

ABERT RIM

Venator Butte
5233

395

C

Wildcat
Mtn
5560

Coleman Hills

Eagle Butte
5492

South Lake
Waterhole

42°45′

COGLAN BUTTES

Paisley
el 4369

6190

Chewaucan

Lake Abert

4255

Rabbit
Hills

WARNER VALLEY

Bluejoint Lake

Stone Corral
Lake

Poker Jim Ridge

Rock

Creek

Cox Butte
5309

D

Comb
Butte
6468

31

Chewaucan Marsh

River

Tucker Hill
4984

ABERT RIM

Mule
Lake

Rabbit

Creek

4462
Flagstaff
Lake

4462

Campbell
Lake

Poker Jim
Lake

Flook
Lake

E

Chewaucan

River

Morgan
Butte
7234

Round Mtn
7462

COYOTE HILLS

Mingwump Lake

Swamp
Lake

Refuge
Headquarters
el 5616

42°30′

South Creek

Valley Falls

Snyder

Creek

395

7543

Crooked

Honey

Creek

Anderson
Lake

HART MOUNTAIN

Rock

Warner Peak
8017

Slough

Beatys
Butte
7916

F

Shoestring
Butte
7256

Creek

Crook Peak
7834

Honey

Twelvemile

Fish

Cr

Honey

Plush
el 4480

Hart Lake

4473

7648

Guano

Spanish
Lake

Desert
Lake

Guano

G

Cougar
Peak
7919

Cottonwood
Meadows
Lake

Thomas

Drake Peak
8407

Drake

Creek

Bull
Lake

Priday
Res

Guano

WARNER VALLEY

Long
Lake

Fred
Pond

Alger
Lake

Lone Grave
Butte
6582

Cottonwood
Reservoir

Squaw
Butte
7249

Mud

Creek

Crump
Lake
4475

Wool
Lake

Jacobs
Res

Shirk
Lake

42°15′

Junipers
Reservoir

Cottonwood

Camas

140

Lynchs Rim

Calderwood
Res

Long
Lake

H

Drews
Reservoir
4915

Lakeview
el 4802

Rogger
Peak
7302

Big Valley

Deep

Creek

Adel
el 4542

Pelican
Lake

Mud Lake
Res

Guano
Lake

Horsehead
Lake

Drews

395

GRW

West Side

Red Peak
7014

WARNER MOUNTAINS

Dismal

Juniper
Lake

South Warner Rim

Twentymile

Greaser
Lake

Blizzard Gap
6131

Barry
Reservoir

Little
Res

Sage Hen
Butte
6172

GUANO RIM

J

Goose
Lake
4701

Crane Mtn
8456

Big

New Pine
Creek
el 4870

Big
Lake

Coleman
Lake

Coleman Rim

Piute
Reservoir

Antelope
Butte
6440

GUANO VALLEY

LAKE HARNEY

140

42°

Dry

Creek

I A

N E V A D A

K

120°30′ 120°15′ 120° 119°45′ 119°30′

12 13 14 15 16 17 18 19 20 21

SCALE 1:500,000

10 Km 0 10 20 30 40 50 Km

KILOMETERS

Elevations are in feet

Jordan Valley

See Page 268

See Page 273

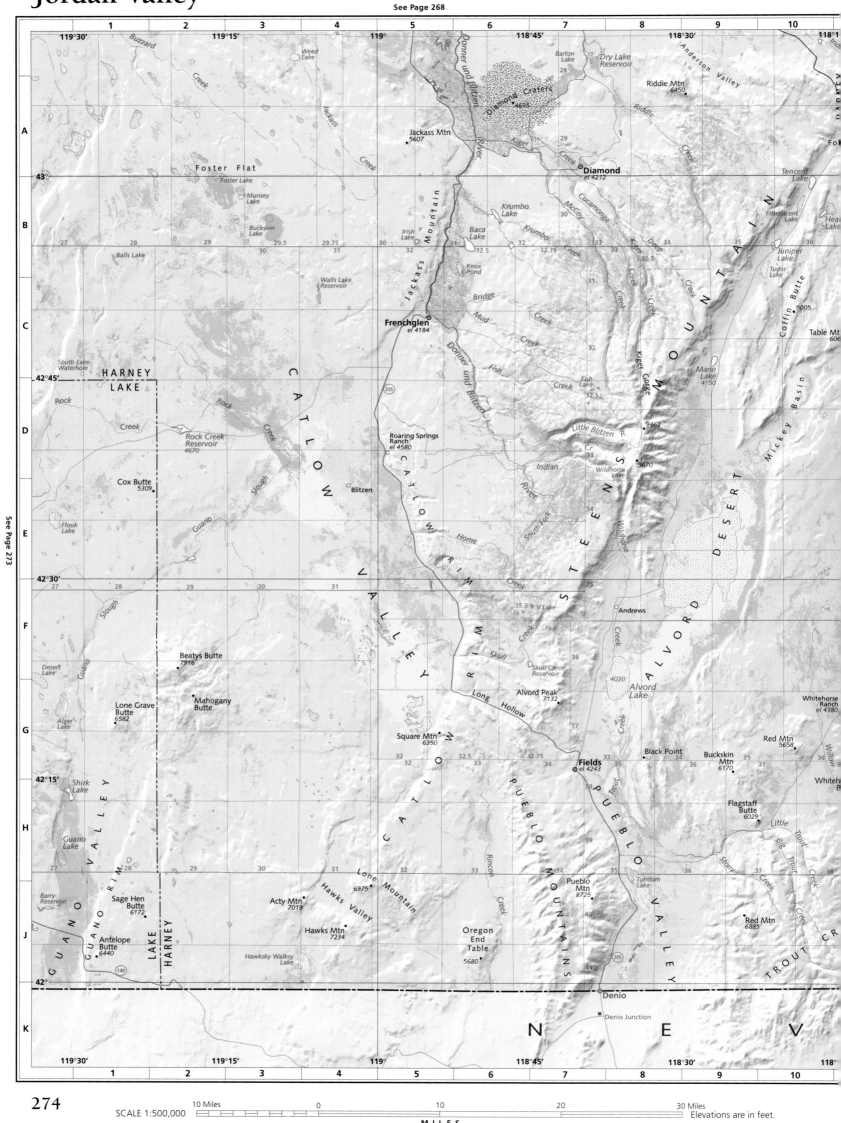

SCALE 1:500,000

10 Miles · 0 · 10 · 20 · 30 Miles

MILES

Elevations are in feet.

See Page 269

SCALE 1:500,000

KILOMETERS

Elevations are in feet.

Reference

USGS Map Index: Northwest

1:100,000 (30' x 60') Maps (see map at right)

1. ASTORIA	7. HERMISTON	13. MT HOOD	19. NEWPORT	25. BATES	47. ROSEBURG
2. MT ST HELENS	8. PENDLETON	14. CONDON	20. CORVALLIS	26. BAKER	48. DIAMOND LAKE
3. NEHALEM RIVER	9. WALLOWA	15. HEPPNER	21. N SANTIAM RIVER	27. McCALL	49. CRESCENT
4. VANCOUVER	10. GRANGEVILLE	16. LA GRANDE	22. MADRAS	28. WALDPORT	50. CHRISTMAS VALLEY
5. HOOD RIVER	11. YAMHILL RIVER	17. ENTERPRISE	23. STEPHENSON MTN	29. EUGENE	51. HARNEY LAKE
6. GOLDENDALE	12. OREGON CITY	18. RIGGINS	24. MONUMENT	30. MCKENZIE RIVER	52. MALHEUR LAKE
				31. BEND	53. MAHOGANY MTN
				32. PRINEVILLE	54. PORT ORFORD
				33. DAYVILLE	55. CANYONVILLE
				34. JOHN DAY	56. CRATER LAKE
				35. BROGAN	57. WILLIAMSON RIVER
				36. WEISER	58. LAKE ABERT
				37. REEDSPORT	59. BLUEJOINT LAKE
				38. COTTAGE GROVE	60. STEENS MTN
				39. OAKRIDGE	61. JORDAN VALLEY
				40. LA PINE	62. GOLD BEACH
				41. BROTHERS	63. GRANTS PASS
				42. BURNS	64. MEDFORD
				43. STINKING WATER MTNS	65. KLAMATH FALLS
				44. VALE	66. LAKEVIEW
				45. BOISE	67. ADEL
				46. COOS BAY	68. ALVORD LAKE
					69. LOUSE CANYON

1:24,000 (7.5' x 7.5') Quadrangles

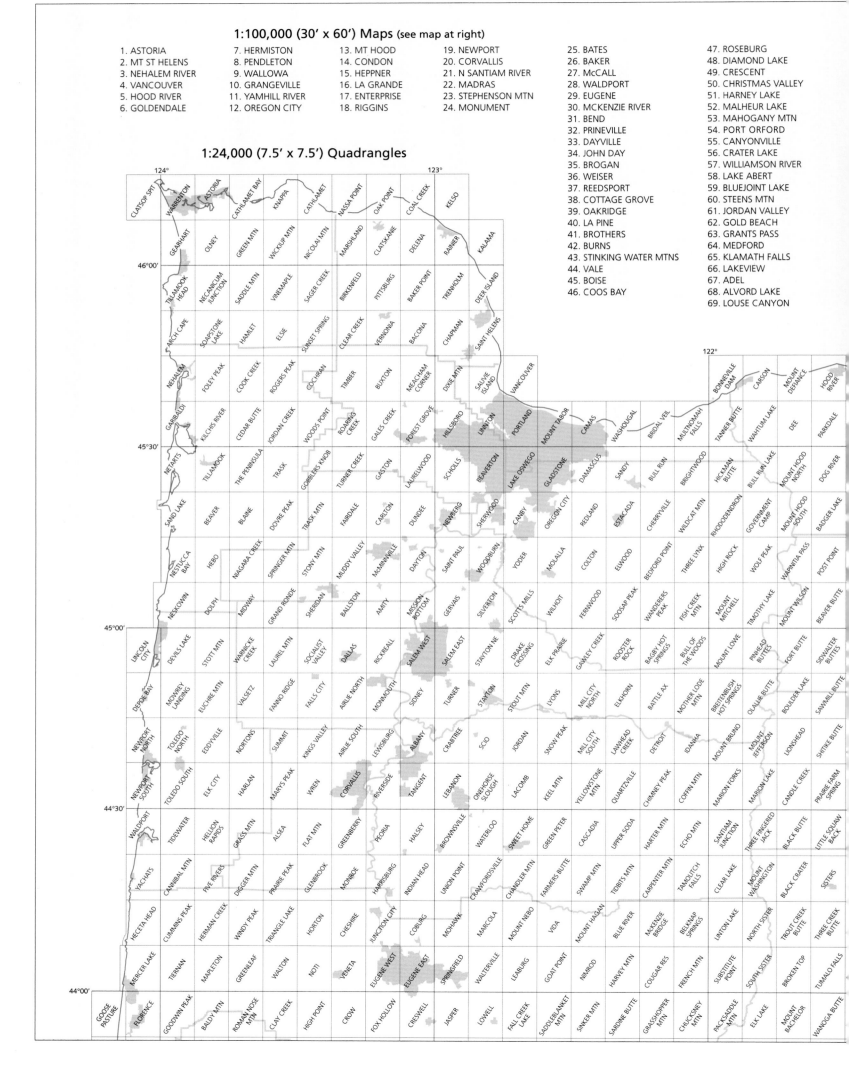

278

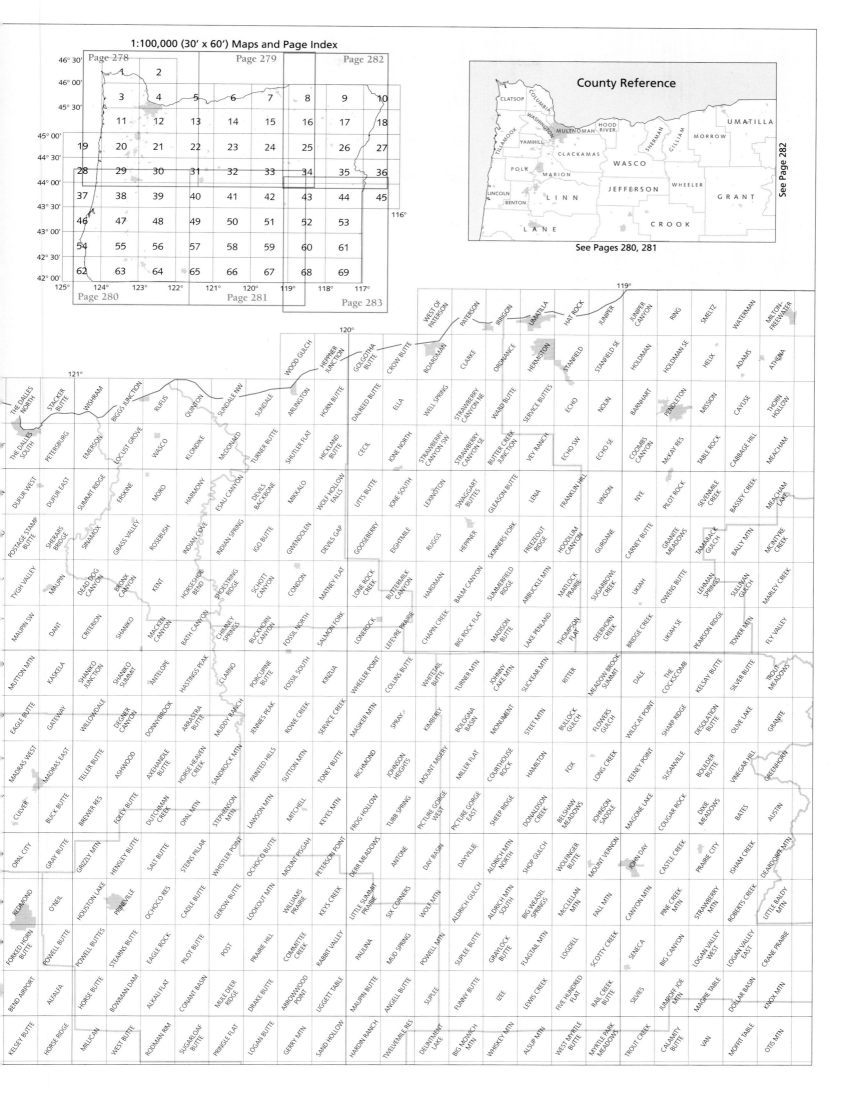

1:100,000 (30' x 60') Maps

	1	2	3	4	5	6	7
44° 00'	1	2	3	4	5	6	7
43° 30'	8	9	10	11	12	13	14
43° 00'	15	16	17	18	19	20	21
42° 30'	22	23	24	25	26	27	28
42° 00'	29	30	31	32	33	34	35
	124°	123°	122°	121°	120°	119°	

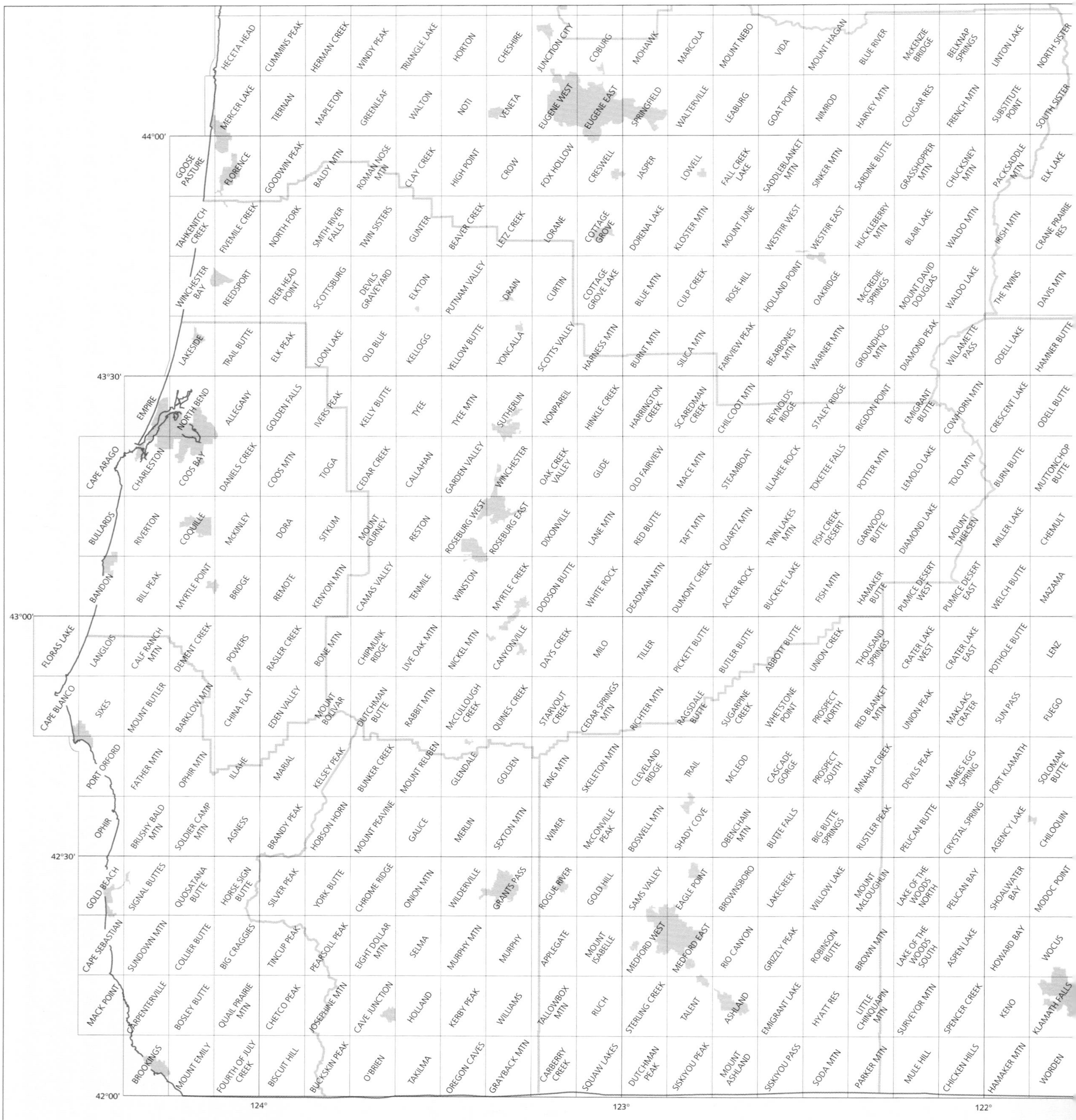

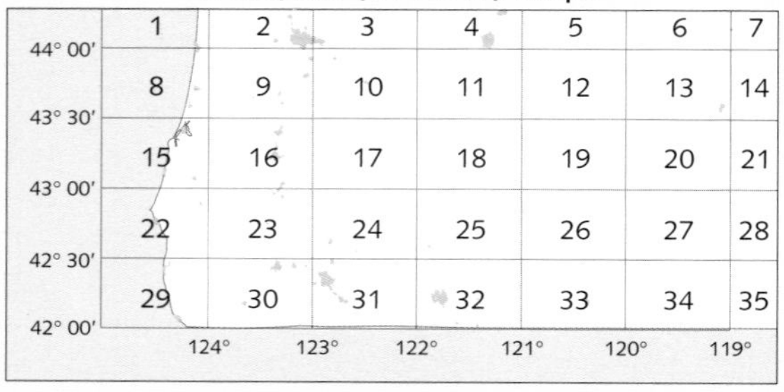

1. WALDPORT
2. EUGENE
3. McKENZIE RIVER
4. BEND
5. PRINEVILLE
6. DAYVILLE
7. JOHN DAY
8. REEDSPORT
9. COTTAGE GROVE
10. OAKRIDGE
11. LA PINE
12. BROTHERS
13. BURNS
14. STINKING WATER MTNS
15. COOS BAY
16. ROSEBURG
17. DIAMOND LAKE
18. CRESCENT
19. CHRISTMAS VALLEY
20. HARNEY LAKE
21. MALHEUR LAKE
22. PORT ORFORD
23. CANYONVILLE
24. CRATER LAKE
25. WILLIAMSON RIVER
26. LAKE ABERT
27. BLUEJOINT LAKE
28. STEENS MTN
29. GOLD BEACH
30. GRANTS PASS
31. MEDFORD
32. KLAMATH FALLS
33. LAKEVIEW
34. ADEL
35. ALVORD LAKE

121°   CALIFORNIA 120° NEVADA   119°

The southern Oregon boundary does not follow the 42nd parallel exactly. It wanders slightly due to survey errors, and crosses the parallel repeatedly. U.S. Geological Survey (USGS) 7.5′ quadrangles, however, end strictly at the parallel. Many very thin slices of Oregon therefore are mapped only on the neighboring California and Nevada quadrangles. These are not identified on this index, but adjacent quadrangles are listed on all USGS maps. The USGS 30′ x 60′ map series is not consistent in this respect. Some sheets extend their coverage beyond their nominal limits to the state boundary, others do not.

See Pages 278, 279

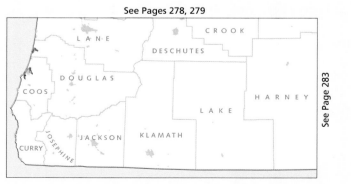

See Page 283

WASHINGTON | IDAHO

46°00'

JUNIPER	JUNIPER CANYON	RING	SMELTZ	WATERMAN	MILTON-FREEWATER	BOWLUS HILL	PETERSON RIDGE	BIG MEADOWS	BONE SPRING	WENAHA FORKS	ELBOW CREEK	EDEN	TROY	FLORA	PARADISE	TEEPEE BUTTE	JIM CREEK BUTTE	WAPSHILLA CREEK
STANFIELD SE	HOLDMAN	HOLDMAN SE	HELIX	ADAMS	ATHENA	WESTON MTN	BLALOCK MTN	TOLLGATE	JUBILEE LAKE	FRY MEADOW	DEEP CREEK	PROMISE	WOOD BUTTE	SHAMROCK CREEK	TABLE MTN	BILLY MEADOWS	POISON POINT	DEADHORSE RIDGE	CACTUS MTN	WOLF CREEK
NOLIN	BARNHART	PENDLETON	MISSION	CAYUSE	THORN HOLLOW	GIBBON	BINGHAM SPRINGS	ANDIES PRAIRIE	PARTRIDGE CREEK	RONDOWA	HOWARD BUTTE	AKERS BUTTE	SHEROD MEADOWS	SLED SPRINGS	ROBERTS BUTTE	GREENWOOD BUTTE	ZUMWALT	HAAS HOLLOW	FINGERBOARD SADDLE	LORD FLAT	GRAVE POINT
ECHO SE	COOMBS CANYON	MCKAY RES	TABLE ROCK	CABBAGE HILL	MEACHAM	DUNCAN	THIMBLEBERRY MTN	SANDERSON SPRING	ELGIN	CRICKET FLAT	MINAM	WALLOWA	EVANS	HICKS SPRING	ELK MTN	ELK MTN SE	FINDLEY BUTTES	IMNAHA	SLEEPY RIDGE	TEMPERANCE CREEK	KIRKWOOD CREEK

45°30'

VINSON	NYE	PILOT ROCK	SEVENMILE CREEK	BASSEY CREEK	MEACHAM LAKE	HURON	DRUMHILL RIDGE	SUMMERVILLE	IMBLER	GASSET BLUFF	MOUNT MORIAH	FOX POINT	LOSTINE	ENTERPRISE	JOSEPH NW	THREE LAKES COUNTRY	CLEAR LAKE RIDGE	SHEEP CREEK DIVIDE	HAT POINT	OLD TIMER MTN
GURDANE	CARNEY BUTTE	GRANITE MEADOWS	TAMARACK GULCH	BALLY MTN	MCINTYRE CREEK	KAMELA SE	HILGARD	LA GRANDE	CONLEY	COVE	MOUNT FANNY	JIM WHITE RIDGE	NORTH MINAM MEADOWS	CHIEF JOSEPH MTN	JOSEPH	KINNEY LAKE	HARL BUTTE	JAYNES RIDGE	SQUIRREL PRAIRIE
SUGARBOWL CREEK	UKIAH	OWENS BUTTE	LEHMAN SPRINGS	SULLIVAN GULCH	MARLEY CREEK	LITTLE BEAVER CREEK	LA GRANDE RES	GLASS HILL	CRAIG MTN	UNION	LITTLE CATHERINE CREEK	CHINA CAP	STEAMBOAT LAKE	EAGLE CAP	ANEROID MTN	LICK CREEK	GUMBOOT BUTTE	PUDERBAUGH RIDGE	WHITE MONUMENT
DEERHORN CREEK	BRIDGE CREEK	UKIAH SE	PEARSON RIDGE	TOWER MTN	FLY VALLEY	LIMBER JIM CREEK	ANTHONY BUTTE	TUCKER FLAT	NORTH POWDER	TELOCASET	MEDICAL SPRINGS	FLAGSTAFF BUTTE	BENNET PEAK	KRAG PEAK	CORNUCOPIA	DEADMAN POINT	DUCK CREEK	HOMESTEAD

45°00'

MEADOW BROOK SUMMIT	DALE	THE COCKSCOMB	KELSAY BUTTE	SILVER BUTTE	TROUT MEADOWS	CRAWFISH LAKE	ANTHONY LAKES	ROCK CREEK	HAINES	MAGPIE PEAK	KEATING NW	SAWTOOTH RIDGE	BALM CREEK RES	SPARTA BUTTE	JIMTOWN	HALFWAY	MCLAIN GULCH	OXBOW
FLOWERS GULCH	WILDCAT POINT	SHARP RIDGE	DESOLATION BUTTE	OLIVE LAKE	GRANITE	MOUNT IRELAND	BOURNE	ELKHORN PEAK	WINGVILLE	BAKER CITY	VIRTUE FLAT	KEATING	GLASGOW BUTTE	SPARTA	RICHLAND	POSY VALLEY	BROWNLEE DAM
LONG CREEK	KEENEY POINT	SUSANVILLE	BOULDER BUTTE	VINEGAR HILL	GREENHORN	WHITNEY	SUMPTER	PHILLIPS LAKE	BLUE CANYON	BOWEN VALLEY	ENCINA	OXMAN	LAWRENCE CREEK	LITTLE LOOKOUT MTN	DALY CREEK	STURGILL CREEK
JOHNSON SADDLE	MAGONE LAKE	COUGAR ROCK	DIXIE MEADOWS	BATES	AUSTIN	POGUE POINT	UNITY RES	BEAVERDAM CREEK	BRANNAN GULCH	DOOLEY MTN	FRENCH GULCH	LOST BASIN	DURKEE	BIG LOOKOUT MTN	CONNOR CREEK

44°30'

MOUNT VERNON	JOHN DAY	CASTLE CREEK	PRAIRIE CITY	ISHAM CREEK	DEARDORFF MTN	RAIL GULCH	UNITY	HEREFORD	DEVILS HEEL	WENDT BUTTE	BRIDGEPORT	MORMON BASIN	RYE VALLEY	LIME	HENLEY BASIN
FALL MTN	CANYON MTN	PINE CREEK MTN	STRAWBERRY MTN	ROBERTS CREEK	LITTLE BALDY MTN	BULRUN ROCK	RASTUS MTN	ELDORADO PASS	IRONSIDE	COW VALLEY WEST	COW VALLEY EAST	BECKER CREEK	BIRCH CREEK MEADOW	HUNTINGTON	OLDS FERRY	PORTERS FLAT
SCOTTY CREEK	SENECA	BIG CANYON	LOGAN VALLEY WEST	LOGAN VALLEY EAST	CRANE PRAIRIE	FLAG PRAIRIE	CLEVENGER BUTTE	DE BORD PEAKS	CLOVER CREEK RANCH	SCRATCH POST BUTTE	BRADY CREEK	BROGAN	JAMIESON	MCCARTHY RIDGE	TUB MTN	MOORES HOLLOW	WEISER SOUTH
RAIL CREEK BUTTE	SILVIES	JUMPOFF JOE MTN	MAGPIE TABLE	DOLLAR BASIN	KNOX MTN	BUCK TROUGH SPRING	CASTLE ROCK	HUNTER MTN	LITTLE JUNIPER SPRING	LOG CREEK	BUCKBRUSH CREEK	SWEDE FLAT	HOPE BUTTE	WILLOW CREEK	HENRY GULCH	MALHEUR BUTTE	PAYETTE

44°00'

| MYRTLE PARK MEADOWS | TROUT CREEK | CALAMITY BUTTE | VAN | MOFFIT TABLE | OTIS MTN | COTTONWOOD RES | BEULAH | DE ARMOND MTN | WESTFALL BUTTE | LITTLE BLACK CANYON | WESTFALL | LITTLE VALLEY | VINES HILL | VALE WEST | VALE EAST | CAIRO | NYSSA |

119° — 118° — 117°

1:100,000 (30' x 60') Maps

119°	118°	117°	116°	
1	2	3	4	46° 00'
5	6	7	8	45° 30'
9	10	11	12	45° 00'
13	14	15	16	44° 30'
17	18	19	20	44° 00'

1. HERMISTON
2. PENDLETON
3. WALLOWA
4. GRANGEVILLE
5. HEPPNER
6. LA GRANDE
7. ENTERPRISE
8. RIGGINS
9. MONUMENT
10. BATES
11. BAKER
12. McCALL
13. DAYVILLE
14. JOHN DAY
15. BROGAN
16. WEISER
17. BURNS
18. STINKING WATER MTNS
19. VALE
20. BOISE

UMATILLA | WALLOWA | UNION | GRANT | BAKER | MALHEUR | HARNEY

See Page 279

See Page 283

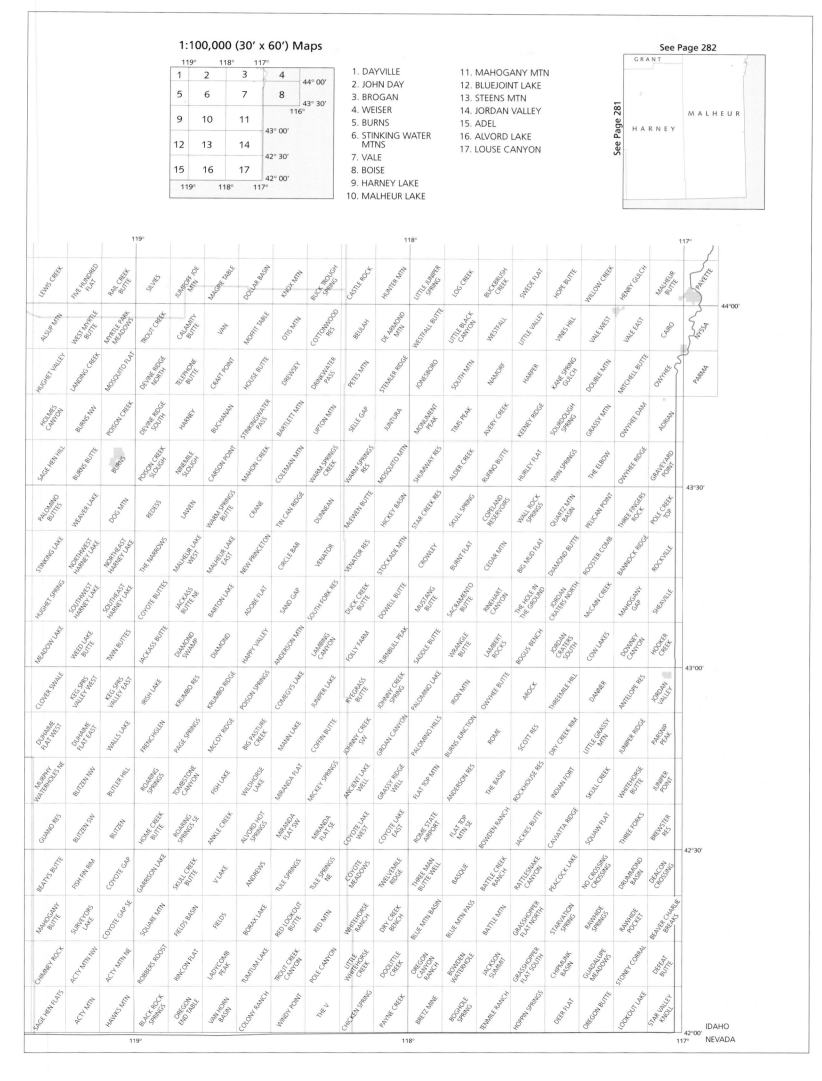

1:100,000 (30' × 60') Maps

1	2	3	4
5	6	7	8
9	10	11	
12	13	14	
15	16	17	

119° 118° 117°
44° 00'
43° 30'
116°
43° 00'
42° 30'
42° 00'

1. DAYVILLE
2. JOHN DAY
3. BROGAN
4. WEISER
5. BURNS
6. STINKING WATER MTNS
7. VALE
8. BOISE
9. HARNEY LAKE
10. MALHEUR LAKE
11. MAHOGANY MTN
12. BLUEJOINT LAKE
13. STEENS MTN
14. JORDAN VALLEY
15. ADEL
16. ALVORD LAKE
17. LOUSE CANYON

See Page 282

GRANT

See Page 281

HARNEY

MALHEUR

Reference Map Gazetteer

Names reflect the history of settlement. They are not merely the tags by which places are known, but rather the embodiment of an area's occupation by people. The definitive reference for Oregon place names is *Oregon Geographic Names* by Lewis A. and Lewis L. McArthur, now in its 6th edition, published by the Oregon Historical Society. *Oregon Geographic Names* explains in detail the origins of about 6,000 Oregon names. An essay on Oregon names immediately follows the gazetteer listings.

This gazetteer gives the page number and coordinates for the most important features named on the 1:500,000 scale reference maps. About a quarter of the physical features named on the maps are listed here. (Readers interested in a complete list may wish to consult the U.S. Geological Survey, or USGS, 7.5′ 1:24,000 scale maps (pages 252–275). The 7.5′ series is the foundation of most serious large-scale mapping in the U.S., and the best source for detailed geographic information.) The coordinates on the reference maps correspond to the 7.5′ quadrangle boundaries. The quadrangle names are given on the USGS quadrangle index maps (pages 278–283). A few very large features, such as the Cascade Range or the Columbia River, appear on many pages but are listed in the gazetteer only once, for the first page on which the name appears. Both currently populated and abandoned settlements are listed. Population estimates for 2000 are given in parentheses for all incorporated towns. All county seats and most other important communities are also shown at the larger scale of 1:150,000 on the Population Centers pages preceding these reference maps (pages 196–249). This gazetteer does not reference these pages; it locates names only on the reference maps. Population Centers maps are indexed on page 195.

Cities, Towns, Locales and Sites

Place Name	Inc. City Population	Page Number	Grid Location
Bend	(53,040)	204	K3

A
Ada 264 C5
Adair Village (570) 258 E9
Adams (320) 256 E5
Adel 273 H17
Adrian (155) 269 E20
Agness 270 E5
Airlie 258 D8
Alameda 253 G12
Albany (41,000) 258 F10
Albee 256 K2
Albina 253 G12
Alder Creek 253 J17
Aldervale 252 E3
Alfalfa 260 K5
Algoma 272 G2
Alicel 256 H9
Alkali Lake Station 273 B17
Allegany 264 G5
Almeda 270 E8
Aloha 252 H10
Alpha 258 J5
Alpine 258 H7
Alpine Junction 258 H8
Alsea 258 H6
Alston 252 C9
Altamont 272 H3
Alvadore 258 J8
Amity (1,325) 258 B9
Anchor 271 C12
Andrews 274 F8
Anlauf 264 E11
Annex 263 J17
Antelope (65) 260 C8
Antone 261 G15
Apiary 252 C9
Applegate 271 G12
Arago 270 A4
Arch Cape 252 E2
Arlington (535) 255 F11
Arock 275 B16
Ash 264 F7
Ashland (20,085) 271 H15
Ashwood 260 E7
Astoria (10,075) 252 B2
Athena (1,300) 256 E5

Aumsville (3,045) 258 D11
Aurora (700) 253 K11
Austa 258 K5
Austin 262 F6
Austin Junction 262 F6
Avery 258 F8
Axford 260 C5
Azalea 270 C11

B
Bacona 252 E8
Bade 256 D6
Bakeoven 260 B6
Baker City (10,420) 262 D10
Ballston 258 B8
Bandon (2,940) 270 A2
Banks (1,580) 252 G8
Barlow (125) 253 K12
Barnett 255 G11
Barton 253 H14
Barview [Tillamook] 252 G2
Barview [Coos] 264 H3
Basque Station 275 F13
Bay City (1,195) 252 G3
Beagle 271 E14
Beatty 272 F6
Beaver 252 J2
Beaver Creek 253 J13
Beaver Marsh 266 J2
Beaverton (70,230) 252 H10
Beech Creek 261 F20
Belknap Springs 259 J18
Bellevue 252 K7
Bellfountain 258 H7
Bend (53,040) 260 K3
Berlin 259 G13
Beulah 269 C11
Biggs 254 F7
Bingham Springs 256 F7
Birkenfeld 252 C6
Blachly 258 J6
Black Butte 265 F13
Black Butte Ranch 259 H21
Black Rock 258 C6
Blalock 254 F11
Blitzen 274 E4
Blodgett 258 F6
Blue Mountain 256 D7
Blue River 259 J15
Bly 272 F8
Boardman (3,400) 255 E16
Bonanza (390) 272 H5
Bonneville 253 G18
Booth 264 D5
Boring 253 H14
Bourne 262 D8
Bowers Junction 252 G10
Boyd 254 H5
Bradwood 252 B6
Breitenbush Hot Springs 259 D19
Bridal Veil 253 G16
Bridge 270 A5
Bridgeport 263 G12
Bridgeview 270 J9
Brightwood 253 H18
Broadbent 270 A4
Brogan 263 J13
Brookings (5,625) 270 J2
Brooks 258 B11
Brothers 267 D11
Brownsboro 271 F16
Brownsville (1,500) 258 G11
Buchanan 268 E8
Buck Fork 271 A12
Buena Vista 258 D9
Bull Run 253 H16
Bullards 264 J2
Burlington 252 F10
Burns (2,945) 268 F4
Burns Junction 275 C14
Burnt Woods 258 F5

Butte Falls (440) 271 E16
Butteville 253 J11
Buxton 252 F7
Bybee Springs 271 E13

C
Cairo Junction 269 C20
Camas Valley 270 A8
Camp Rilea 252 C2
Camp Sherman 259 G21
Canary 264 C5
Canby (13,170) 253 J12
Cannon Beach (1,430) 252 D1
Canyon City (725) 261 G21
Canyonville (1,360) 270 B11
Cape Meares 252 H2
Carlton (1,620) 252 J8
Carpenterville 270 H3
Carson 263 C16
Carver 253 H14
Cascade Gorge 271 D17
Cascade Locks (1,130) 253 F18
Cascade Summit 265 F21
Cascadia 259 G15
Castle 255 E15
Cave Junction (1,440) 270 H8
Cayuse 256 F5
Cecil 255 G14
Celilo 254 F6
Central Point (12,230) 271 G13
Charleston 264 H2
Chemawa 258 B11
Chemult 266 J2
Chenoweth 254 F3
Cherry Grove 252 H7
Cherryville 253 H16
Cheshire 258 J8
Chico 257 F16
Chiloquin (810) 272 E2
Chinchalo 272 C2
Chitwood 258 E4
Christmas Valley 267 J11
Circle Bar 268 H9
Clackamas 253 H13
Clarke 255 E17
Clarno 260 C9
Clatskanie (1,900) 252 C8
Clearwater 265 H18
Clem 255 H12
Cleveland 264 H9
Clifton 252 B5
Cline Falls 260 H3
Cloverdale 252 K2
Coaledo 264 J3
Coburg (805) 258 J10
Cochran 252 F6
Colestin 271 J16
Colton 253 K14
Columbia City (1,735) 252 D10
Condon (850) 255 K12
Coos Bay (15,995) 264 H3
Cooston 264 G4
Coquille (4,395) 264 J3
Corbett 253 G15
Cornelius (8,715) 252 G9
Cornucopia 263 B16
Corvallis (52,271) 258 F8
Cottage Grove (8,480) 265 D13
Cottrell 253 H15
Courtrock 261 E19
Cove (690) 256 J11
Cove Orchard 252 H8
Crabtree 258 E11
Crane 268 G8
Crater Lake Lodge 271 B20
Crates 254 G4
Crawfordsville 258 H11
Crescent 266 G3
Crescent Lake 266 F1
Creston 269 G12
Creswell (3,380) 265 C13

Crow 264 C11
Crowley 269 H13
Culp Creek 265 E15
Culver (865) 260 F3
Curtin 265 E12
Cushman 264 C5
Cutler City 258 C2

D
Dairy 272 H4
Dale 262 C2
Dallas (12,960) 258 C8
Damascus 253 H14
Danner 275 B17
Dant 260 B4
Dawson 258 H7
Days Creek 271 B12
Dayton (2,015) 252 K9
Dayville (185) 261 G17
Deadwood 258 K4
Dee 253 G21
Deer Island 252 D10
Deerhorn 259 K12
Dellwood 264 G5
Delmar 264 H4
DeMoss Springs 254 G8
Denmark 270 B2
Depoe Bay (1,190) 258 D1
Deschutes 260 J4
Detroit (380) 259 E17
Dexter 265 C14
Diamond 274 A7
Diamond Lake 265 J20
Diamond Lake Jct 272 A1
Dillard 270 A10
Dilley 252 H8
Disston 265 E15
Divide 265 D12
Dixie 263 G15
Dixonville 264 J11
Dolph 258 B4
Donald (755) 252 K10
Dora 264 J6
Dorena 265 E15
Downing 256 E6
Drain (1,165) 264 E11
Drew 271 B14
Drewsey 268 D9
Dryden 270 G9
Dufur (625) 254 H4
Duncan 256 G7
Dundee (2,955) 252 J9
Dunes City (1,315) 264 C4
Durham (1,570) 253 H12
Durkee 263 F13

E
Eagle Creek 253 J15
Eagle Point (5,130) 271 F15
East Gardiner 264 E5
Eastside 264 H4
Echo (695) 255 F20
Eddyville 258 E4
Eightmile 255 J15
Elgin (1,785) 256 G10
Elk City 258 F4
Elk Creek 270 J8
Elkhead 265 F12
Elkhorn 259 D15
Elkton (180) 264 F9
Elmira 258 K7
Elsie 252 E5
Empire 264 G3
Endersby 254 G4
Englewood 264 H3
Enright 252 F5
Enterprise (2,050) 257 H15
Eola 258 C9
Estacada (2,256) 253 J15
Eugene (136,800) 258 K9
Evans 257 G14

285

Reference Map Gazetteer

Plainview 258 G10
Pleasant Hill 265 C14
Pleasant Valley 263 E12
Plush 273 F17
Pondosa 263 B12
Port Orford (1,025) 270 C2
Portland (513,325) 253 G11
Post 260 J10
Powell Butte 260 J5
Powers (750) 270 B5
Prairie City (1,245) 262 G4
Pratum 258 C11
Prescott (60) 252 C10
Princeton 268 J7
Prineville (8,261) 260 H7
Prineville Junction 260 H4
Promise 257 E13
Prospect 271 C18
Prosper 264 J2
Provolt 270 G11

Q

Quartz Mountain 272 G10
Quartzville 259 F16
Quincy 252 B8
Quines Creek 270 C11
Quinton 254 F9

R

Rainbow 259 J16
Rainier (1,835) 252 C10
Rainrock 258 K4
Rajneeshpuram 260 D9
Rand 270 E8
Redland 253 J14
Redmond (13,705) 260 H4
Reed 258 J3
Reedsport (4,850) 264 E5
Reedville 252 G10
Refuge Headquarters 273 E19
Remote 270 B6
Reston 264 J9
Rhododendron 253 J18
Rice Hill 264 F11
Richland (175) 263 D16
Richmond 261 E14
Rickreall 258 C9
Riddle (1,225) 270 B10
Rieth 256 F3
Riley 267 F20
Ring 256 D3
Ritter 261 C20
Rivergrove (310) 253 H12
Riverside 269 F11
Riverton 264 J3
Roads End 258 B2
Roaring Springs Ranch 274 D5
Roberts [Marion] 258 C10
Roberts [Crook] 260 K8
Rock Creek [Gilliam] 254 G11
Rock Creek [Baker] 262 C9
Rockaway Beach (1,285) 252 G1
Rockford 253 F21
Rockville 269 H19
Rocky Point 271 F21
Rogue River (2,000) 271 F12
Rome 275 C15
Rondowa 256 F11
Rose Lodge 258 B4
Roseburg (20,955) 264 J11
Rosedale 258 D10
Rowena 254 F3
Roy 252 G9
Ruch 271 H13
Rufus (310) 254 F8
Running Y Ranch Resort 272 G1
Rye Valley 263 G13

S

Saginaw 265 D13
St Benedict 259 B12
St Helens (9,450) 252 E10
St Johns 253 G12
St Paul (355) 252 K10
Salem (131,385) 258 C10
Salishan Resort 258 C2
Sams Valley 271 F14
Sandlake 252 J2
Sandy (5,655) 253 H15
Santa Clara 258 K9
Scappoose (5,270) 252 F10
Scholls 252 H10
Scio (655) 258 E11
Scofield 252 F8
Scotts Mills (315) 259 B13
Scottsburg 264 E7
Seal Rock 258 F1
Searose Beach 258 J1
Seaside (6,276) 252 D2
Selma 270 G9
Seneca (225) 261 J21
Service Creek 261 D13
Seven Oaks 271 F13
Shady Cove (2,420) 271 E14
Shady Pine 272 G2
Shaniko (30) 260 B8
Shaw 258 C12
Sheaville 269 J20
Shedd 258 G10
Shelburn 258 E11
Sherars Bridge 254 J5
Sheridan (5,250) 258 B7
Sherwood (10,815) 252 J10
Shutler 255 F12
Siletz (1,261) 258 E3
Siltcoos 264 C5
Silver Lake 272 A8
Silverton (6,800) 259 C12
Silvies 262 K2
Simnasho 260 C3
Sinamox 254 H6
Siskiyou 271 J16
Sisters (850) 259 H22
Sitkum 264 J7
Sixes 270 C1
Skipanon 252 B2
Sodaville (280) 258 G11
South Beach 258 F1
South Junction 260 D5
Sparta 263 C15
Spofford 256 D7
Sprague River 272 F4
Spray (165) 261 D15
Springdale 253 G15
Springfield (53,700) 258 K10
Spring River 266 D5
Stafford 253 J12
Stanfield (1,875) 255 E20
Stanton 256 D4
Starkey 256 K6
Stauffer 267 G16
Stayton (6,935) 259 D12
Steamboat 265 H15
Stukel 272 J3
Sublimity (2,580) 259 D12
Sulphur Springs 264 D6
Summer Lake 272 B10
Summerville (150) 256 H9
Summit 258 E6
Sumner 264 H4
Sumpter (175) 262 E8
Sunny Valley 270 D10
Sunnyside 258 D10
Sunriver 266 C5
Suplee 261 K16
Susanville 262 E3
Sutherlin (7,145) 264 G11
Suver 258 E9
Svensen 252 B4

Sweet Home (8,085) 259 G13
Swisshome 258 K4

T

Table Rock 271 F14
Takilma 270 J9
Talbot 258 D9
Talent (5,160) 271 H15
Tallman 258 F11
Tangent (1,080) 258 F10
Telocaset 262 B11
Tenmile 270 A9
Terrebonne 260 H4
The Dalles (12,175) 254 G4
Thorn Hollow 256 F6
Three Forks 275 E19
Thurston 258 K11
Tidewater 258 G3
Tiernan 258 K3
Tierra del Mar 252 K1
Tigard (38,835) 253 H11
Tillamook (4,270) 252 H3
Tiller 271 B14
Timber 252 F7
Timberline Lodge 253 J19
Tioga 264 H7
Toketee Falls 265 H18
Toledo (3,680) 258 F3
Tollgate 256 E8
Tolo 271 F14
Tolvana Park 252 E2
Trail 271 D15
Trent 265 C14
Tri City 270 B11
Triangle Lake 258 J5
Trojan Nuclear Power Plant
  (decommissioned) 252 C10
Troutdale (14,300) 253 G15
Troy 257 D14
Tualatin (22,535) 253 J11
Tumalo 260 J2
Turner (1,365) 258 D11
Twickenham 261 D12
Twin Rocks 252 G1
Tyee 264 G9
Tygh Valley 254 K4

U

Ukiah (245) 256 K2
Umapine 256 D6
Umatilla (4,410) 255 D18
Umpqua 264 H10
Union (2,070) 256 K11
Union Creek 271 B18
Unity (165) 262 G8
Upper Soda 259 G16

V

Vale (1,655) 269 C18
Valley Falls 273 F14
Valley Junction 258 B6
Valsetz 258 D5
Van 268 C7
Van Horn 253 F21
Vansycle 256 D4
Vaughn 258 K7
Venator 268 H10
Veneta (2,940) 258 K8
Verboort 252 G8
Vernonia (2,460) 252 E8
Vida 259 J14
Viento 253 F20
Vincent 256 F11
Vinemaple 252 D5
Vinson 255 H21
Voltage 268 H6

W

Waconda 258 B10
Wagontire 267 J17
Wakonda Beach 258 G1

Waldo 270 J8
Waldport (1,970) 258 G1
Walker 265 D13
Wallowa (865) 257 G13
Wallowa Lake 257 J16
Walterville 259 K12
Walton 258 K5
Wamic 254 K3
Wapato 252 H8
Wapinitia 260 B4
Warm Springs 260 D3
Warner 270 B4
Warren 252 E11
Warrenton (4,310) 252 B2
Wasco (415) 254 G8
Waterloo (270) 259 F12
Waterman 261 F14
Wauna 252 B6
Weatherby 263 G14
Webfoot 254 G9
Wedderburn 270 F2
Welches 253 J18
Wemme 253 J18
Wendling 259 J12
West Fork 270 C9
West Linn (23,380) 253 J12
West Salem 258 C10
West Side 273 H13
West Slope 253 H11
West Stayton 258 D11
West Woodburn 252 K10
Westfall 269 C15
Westfir (300) 265 D18
Weston (695) 256 E6
Westport 252 C6
Wetmore 261 C14
Wheeler (385) 252 F2
White City 271 F15
Whitehorse Ranch 274 G10
Whiteson 252 K8
Whitney 262 E7
Wilbur 264 H10
Wilderville 270 F9
Wildwood 253 J17
Wilhoit 259 B14
Wilkesboro 252 G8
Willamina (1,875) 258 B6
Williams 270 H11
Willow Creek 263 K14
Willowdale 260 D6
Wilsonville (13,615) 253 J11
Wimer 271 E12
Winans 253 G21
Winchester 264 H11
Winchester Bay 264 E3
Winlock 261 C14
Winona 258 C10
Winston (4,785) 264 J10
Wocus 272 G2
Wolf Creek 270 D11
Wonder 270 G9
Wood Village (2,915) 253 G14
Woodburn (17,840) 252 K10
Woods 252 K2
Woodson 252 B7
Worden 272 J1
Wren 258 F7
Wrentham 254 G6
Wyeth 253 F19

Y

Yachats (715) 258 H1
Yamhill (980) 252 J8
Yaquina 258 F2
Yoder 253 K12
Yoncalla (1,095) 264 F11

Z

Zigzag 253 J18
Zumwalt 257 F18

Rivers, Lakes and Reservoirs

Feature Name	County Location	Page No.	Grid Location
Fish Lake [Baker]		207	B17

A

Agency Lake 272 E1
Alkali Lake [Klamath] 272 H4
Alkali Lake [Lake] 273 B16
Allen Creek Reservoir 261 G12
Alsea Bay 258 G2
Alsea River 258 G3
Alvord Lake 274 G8
Aneroid Lake 257 K16
Antelope Reservoir 275 B19
Anthony Lakes 262 C8
Applegate Lake 271 J12
Applegate River 270 F10
Aspen Lake 271 G21

B

Ben Irving Reservoir 270 A9
Beulah Reservoir 269 C11
Blue Lake 259 G20
Blue River Lake 265 A19
Bluejoint Lake 273 D19
Breitenbush River 259 D17
Brownlee Reservoir 263 E17
Bull Run Lake 253 J19
Bull Run Reservoir #1 253 H17
Bull Run Reservoir #2 253 H16
Bull Run River 253 H16
Bully Creek 269 C15
Bully Creek Reservoir 269 B17
Burnt River 263 G15

C

Calapooia River 258 F9
Calderwood Reservoir 273 H18
Campbell Lake 273 E19
Chetco River 270 J4
Chewaucan River 273 D13
Chickahominy Res 267 F19
Clackamas River 253 K16
Clatskanie River 252 C8
Clear Lake [Clack.] 253 K20
Clear Lake [Douglas] 264 E4
Clear Lake [Lane] 264 B5
Clearwater River 265 H18
Cleawox Lake 264 C5
Cold Springs Reservoir 255 E20
Collawash River 259 C18
Columbia River 252 B2
Coos Bay 264 G4
Coos River 264 H4
Coquille River 264 J3
Cottage Grove Lake 265 E13
Cottonwood Reservoir 273 G12
Cottonwood Mdw Lake 273 G11
Cougar Reservoir 265 B20
Cow Lakes 275 A18
Coyote Lake 275 E11
Crane Prairie Reservoir 266 D2
Crater Lake 271 B21
Crescent Lake 265 G22
Crooked River 260 G3
Crump Lake 273 G18
Cullaby Lake 252 C2
Cultus Lake 266 D2

D

Davis Lake 266 F2
Deschutes River 254 J6
Detroit Lake 259 E17
Devils Lake 258 C3
Diamond Lake 265 J20
Donner und Blitzen River 268 J6
Dorena Lake 265 D14
Drews Reservoir 273 H11

Physical Features

Feature Name	County Location	Page No.	Grid Location
Blue Mtn [Lane]	209	E14	

Hampton Buttes 267 D15
Hardesty Mountain 265 D16
Harl Butte 257 J18
Harness Mountain 265 F13
Hart Mountain 273 F18
Hash Rock 260 G9
Hat Point 257 H20
Heceta Head 258 J2
Hells Canyon 257 H20
High Point 264 C10
Highland Butte 253 K14
Hole in the Ground 266 G7
Horsefly Mountain 272 G8
Huckleberry Mtn [Doug.] 265 F15
Huckleberry Mtn [Lane] 265 D19
Humbug Mtn 270 D2

I

Iron Mtn 270 D4

J

Juniper Butte 260 G4
Juniper Mtn [Harney] 273 B17
Juniper Mtn [Malheur] 263 J12
Juniper Ridge 265 F19

K

Keeney Point 262 E2
Kenyon Mountain 270 A7
King Mountain 270 D11
Kitson Ridge 265 E19
Klamath Mountains 270 E4
Klamath Point 271 D21
Klickitat Mountain 258 J3
Koch Mountain 265 E20

L

Lane Mountain 265 J12
Lenhart Butte 253 J16
Little Grayback Mtn 271 J13
Little Juniper Mtn 273 A18
Long Creek Mtn 261 E21
Lookout Mtn [Crook] 260 H11
Lookout Mtn [Desch.] 266 D3
Lookout Mtn [Grant] 262 H5
Lookout Mtn [Hood R.] 254 J1
Lookout Mtn [Lane] 265 A20

M

Magpie Peak 262 C11
Mahogany Mountain 269 J19
Maiden Peak 265 E22
Marys Peak 258 F6
Matterhorn 257 K15
Maupin Butte 261 K14
Maury Mountains 267 B13
McKenzie Pass 259 H20
Middle Sister 259 J20
Mitchell Butte 269 D19
Monument Mtn 261 D18
Monument Peak 259 E16
Moolack Mountain 265 D21
Moose Ridge 259 G15
Mount Ashland 271 J16
Mount Bachelor 266 C3
Mount Bailey 265 J20
Mount Bolivar 270 C7
Mount Defiance 253 F20
Mount Emily [Curry] 270 J4
Mount Emily [Union] 256 H9
Mount Fanny 257 J12
Mount Hebo 252 K3
Mount Hood 253 J20
Mount Howard 257 J16
Mount Ireland 262 D7
Mount Isabelle 271 G13
Mount Jefferson 259 E20
Mount McLoughlin 271 F19
Mount Nebo 259 J13
Mount Peavine 270 E8
Mount Scott [Clack.] 253 H13
Mount Scott [Klam.] 271 B21

Mount Thielsen 265 J21
Mount Washington 259 H20
Mount Wilson 259 B21

N

Neahkahnie Mountain 252 F2
Newberry Crater 266 E7
Nickel Mountain 270 B10
Nicolai Mountain 252 C6
North Sister 259 J20

O

Ochoco Mountains 260 F10
Odell Butte 266 G2
Olallie Butte 259 D20
Old Fairview 265 H15
Olson Mountain 271 D17
Onion Mountain 270 F9
Onion Peak 252 E2
Owyhee Ridge 269 F18

P

Parker Mountain 271 J19
Parsnip Peak 275 C20
Paulina Butte 261 H14
Paulina Mountains 266 E7
Paulina Peak 266 E6
Pearsoll Peak 270 G7
Pedro Mountain 263 G13
Pelican Butte 271 E20
Picture Rock Pass 272 A10
Pilot Butte 266 B6
Pine Mountain 266 D9
Poker Jim Ridge 273 D19
Powell Buttes 260 J6
Powwatka Ridge 257 F14
Prairie Mountain 258 H6
Pueblo Mountains 274 H7

Q

Quartz Mtn [Douglas] 265 J16
Quartz Mtn [Malheur] 269 G16
Quartz Mtn Pass 272 G10

R

Red Butte 265 J14
Red Mountain 263 B15
Rhododendron Ridge 259 C19
Riddle Mountain 268 K9
Riverbed Butte 272 D8
Rocky Peak 270 D3
Roman Nose Mtn 264 C8
Round Butte 260 F4
Round Top 252 F7
Rudio Mountain 261 E18
Rustler Peak 271 D19

S

Saddle Butte [Mal.] 275 A13
Saddle Butte [Klam.] 272 E3
Saddle Mtn [Clatsop] 252 D4
Saddle Mtn [Curry] 270 F5
Saddle Bag Mtn [Linc.] 258 B4
Saddleblanket Mtn 265 C17
Santiam Pass 259 G20
Sardine Butte 265 C19
Sardine Mountain 259 D17
Sawtooth Rock 270 E4
Schreiner Peak 259 C18
Scott Mtn [Douglas] 265 G13
Scott Mtn [Lane] 259 J19
Service Buttes 255 F19
Sexton Mountain 270 E11
Sheepshead Mtns 275 B12
Sheridan Mountain 266 C3
Signal Buttes [Clack.] 253 K18
Signal Buttes [Curry] 270 F3
Silver King Mountain 259 D17
Silver Peak 270 F6
Sisi Butte 259 C20
Siskiyou Mountains 271 J14
Siskiyou Pass 271 J17

Slapjack Butte 265 E19
Slide Mountain 272 D11
Snow Mountain 267 C21
Snow Peak 259 F14
Soda Mountain 271 J18
Soosap Peak 259 B16
South Sister 259 K20
Spanish Peak 261 G15
Spencer Butte 265 C13
Spring Butte 266 F6
Squaw Back Ridge 260 G2
Squaw Butte 261 B13
Squaw Mtn [Clack.] 253 K17
Squaw Mtn [Joseph.] 270 G8
Steens Mountain 274 D8
Stephenson Mountain 260 F10
Stinkingwater Pass 268 E8
Stott Mountain 258 C4
Strawberry Mountain 262 H4
Strawberry Range 262 H4
Sugarloaf Mtn [Baker] 263 B17
Sugarloaf Mtn [Clatsop] 252 E3
Sugarloaf Mtn [Polk] 258 C5
Sugarpine Mountain 266 K4
Summit Ridge [Wall.] 257 G20
Summit Ridge [Wasco] 254 H6
Surveyor Mountain 271 H20
Sutton Mountain 261 E12
Swan Lake Point 272 F3
Sweet Spring Mtn 259 D15
Sycan Butte 272 C8

T

Table Mtn [Lane] 265 E15
Table Mtn [Lincoln] 258 G4
Table Mtn [Wallowa] 257 E16
Table Rock [Baker] 263 G14
Table Rock [Clack.] 259 C16
Tallowbox Mountain 271 H12
Three Fingered Jack 259 G20
Three Sisters 259 J20
Tidbits Mountain 259 H16
Tillamook Head 252 D2
Timber Crater 271 A21
Trap Mountain 265 J19
Trask Mountain 252 H6
Trout Creek Mtns 274 J10
Tub Mountain 263 J16
Turner Butte 254 F11
Twin Buttes 259 H17
Tyee Mountain 264 G10
Tygh Ridge 254 J5

U

Union Peak 271 C20

V

Vinegar Hill 262 E5

W

Wagontire Mountain 267 H17
Walker Mountain 266 H3
Walker Rim 266 H3
Wallowa Mountains 257 J14
White Butte 261 F12
White Rock 265 J13
Willamette Pass 265 F21
Willow Creek Butte 262 D2
Windigo Pass 265 H21
Windy Peak 258 J5
Winter Ridge 272 C10
Wolf Mountain 261 H16

Y

Yainax Butte 272 G6
Yamsay Mountain 272 B6
Yaquina Head 258 E2
Yellow Butte 264 F10

Z

Zigzag Mountains 253 J19

Oregon Place Names

Names on the Land

"Once, from eastern ocean to western ocean, the land stretched away without names. Nameless headlands split the surf; nameless lakes reflected nameless mountains; and nameless rivers flowed through nameless valleys into nameless bays.

"Men came at last, tribe following tribe, speaking different languages and thinking different thoughts. According to their ways of speech and thought, they gave names and in their generations laid their bones by the streams and hills they had named." These are the opening sentences of George R. Stewart's seminal work, *Names on the Land*. It would be difficult to improve upon these words.

Oregon is a new state. Only a handful of names are used by Whites prior to the beginning of the immigration and settlement period of the 1840s. Recording geographic name origins and histories for this area started well before the end of the nineteenth century and has continued without interruption. Consequently, basic information is available about a substantial percentage of Oregon place names. The origins of these names may be traced roughly to six periods in the state's history.

Native American Period

The period of Native American life is reflected in modern Oregon by the existence of a considerable number of Indian place names, some of which were applied by the Native Americans themselves, and some later by immigrants. Native Americans inhabited the Pacific Northwest at least 10,000 years ago and were well established in areas that provided sustenance. On the Coast the Clatsops, Tillamooks, Coos and other tribes ate shellfish, fish, berries and game while in the interior valleys the Kalapooians, Yamhills, Santiams and others relied on berries, camas, game and fish.

Most of the principal rivers west of the Cascade Range, other than the Columbia, bear names derived from the local Native American tribes or their descriptions. The names of the Willamette, Clackamas, Molalla, Santiam, Calapooya, Tualatin, Yamhill, Long Tom, Umpqua, Nehalem, Tillamook, Nestucca, Siuslaw, Alsea and Coos Rivers were all in use early and their forms standardized as mapping progressed. In Eastern Oregon the same pattern holds for rivers such as the Umatilla, Wallowa and Imnaha.

Native American names fall into three classes. The first category is of names actually used for geographic features by Native Americans in their languages. Though it seems likely that many such names were used, fewer than 100 survive. Native inhabitants had names for frequently visited places and routes of travel, but the record goes back only a few hundred years by stories and oral traditions. No tribe had a method of writing, and early explorers and immigrants found the Indian languages difficult to interpret. Nevertheless, settlers applied several hundred variations of these names to both natural and constructed features.

Names in a second class, almost entirely applied by non-natives, are taken from Chinook Jargon, a trade language originally developed to facilitate trade between Chinook nations along the Columbia and Nootka Indians who lived to the north.

A final class of names is made up of Eastern and Midwestern Native American names that settlers applied to Oregon features. Examples of this group include Missouri Flat, Iowa Bottom and Oswego.

Exploration Period

Exploration by sea resulted in Spanish and English names; overland exploration, spurred by the fur trade, brought English and French names. The 1542 Spanish expedition of Juan Rodriguez Cabrillo may have reached as far north as present-day Cape Mendocino in Northern California. After Cabrillo's death, the expedition's surviving pilot and now commander, Bartolome Ferrelo, sailed north of the Oregon border at 42° N latitude without sighting the Oregon coast. In the late 1860s, Cape Ferrelo, just north of the California border, was named in his honor.

In 1579, Sir Francis Drake explored the Pacific Coast. He was looking for a spot to careen his ship for repairs before continuing his voyage around the world. He reached at least 43° N and possibly farther. Drake's journal has never been found, but some historians believe he may have careened his ship in a bay north of Cape Arago in Oregon rather than, as others argue, in Drakes Bay north of San Francisco.

Sebastian Vizcaino commanded a Spanish expedition that sailed as far north as the Oregon border. On January 20, 1603, he sighted a prominent high bluff which he named Cabo Blanco de San Sebastian after his patron saint. Vizcaino's command included another ship captained by Martin de Aguilar, but the two vessels were separated in early January during a severe storm off Drakes Bay. After sailing farther north, Aguilar sighted a point or cape which he named Cabo Blanco. Cabo Blanco de San Sebastian and Cabo Blanco were the first features named by Europeans on the Oregon coast. It is not possible today to tell exactly which headlands were sighted, but both names persist on prominent features. In 1869, George Davidson, the well-known Pacific Coast head of the U.S. Coast Survey, shortened the former to Cape Sebastian, the name surviving today. Present-day Cape Blanco is the most westerly point in Oregon.

A 1775 expedition commanded by Bruno de Heceta in the frigate *Santiago* landed near the mouth of the Quinalt River in Washington. This was the first known landing on the Pacific Coast north of California (aside from Russian activity in Alaska). Continuing north, he reached the vicinity of Nootka Sound before the poor condition of both ship and crew forced a return south. Heceta's great discovery came on August 17, 1775, when he observed the mouth of the Columbia River, which he called the Bahía de la Asunción. He named the northern headland Cabo San Roque and the southern point Cabo Frondoso. These names have not persisted, but the name he gave Cape Falcon, a little south of Tillamook Head, survives. Heceta continued south to the vicinity of Port Orford, where he recorded Aguilar's Cabo Blanco as Cabo Diligencias. The discoveries and chartings of Heceta's command were of major importance; he is commemorated by Heceta Head, not far from Florence, and the offshore Heceta Bank. Both of these names were applied in 1862 by George Davidson.

In 1778 British explorer James Cook, then on his third voyage, sighted and named Cape Foulweather and Cape Perpetua on the Oregon Coast. The former was named for the rather typical March weather in Oregon, but the latter was named for Saint Perpetua, as it was sighted on the seventh day of March, her day. Cook made memorable discoveries on this voyage but missed both the Strait of Juan de Fuca and the Columbia River, apparently because of bad weather.

Ten years later—in May 1788—Englishman John Meares sailed to the West Coast to trade and explore. Heading south from Nootka Sound, he investigated Heceta's Bahía de la Asunción. After deciding there was no river feeding the bay, he gave Cabo San Roque a different name, Cape Disappointment, the name it carries today. Meares continued south and named Quicksand Bay, now Tillamook Bay. He then carefully described and named Cape Lookout just south of Tillamook Bay. Through an error on U.S. charts, the name Lookout was transferred 10 miles to the prominent headland south of Netarts Bay. In 1857, George Davidson decided to leave the name Cape Lookout on the new location and honor Meares by applying his name to the original discovery, Cape Meares.

On August 14, 1788, Robert Gray found and entered Tillamook Bay. This was the first landing of a U.S. citizen on the Pacific Coast (later on this same historic voyage, Gray's vessel became the first U.S. ship to circumnavigate the globe). During his second voyage, Gray found and entered the Columbia River on May 11, 1792. He christened the river Columbia after his ship, the *Columbia Rediviva*. His activity did much to establish the claim of the United States to what later was called the Oregon Country.

Gray sailed north, encountered George Vancouver and his British expedition and told them of his discovery. In October, Vancouver unsuccessfully attempted to enter the Columbia. He then ordered Lieutenant William Broughton in the armed tender *Chatham* to enter and explore. Broughton traveled up the Columbia in a longboat to the Sandy River east of present-day Portland. Tongue Point, named by Broughton for its shape, is believed to be the first inland geographic name in Oregon applied by an explorer. Broughton's most important contribution was naming Mount Hood for Lord Samuel Hood of the British Admiralty.

Journals from the Lewis and Clark Expedition of 1805–06 list many versions of Native American names for features in present-day Oregon, although only two of these and few of the English names they applied are in use today. Native American names survive for Fort Clatsop, the expedition's winter quarters in early 1806, and Ecola Creek near Cannon Beach, which was for many years called Elk Creek. Another significant Lewis and Clark name is Mount Jefferson, seen by Clark near the mouth of the Willamette River on a fortuitously clear day in early April. The famous explorers' Quicksand River has been only slightly abbreviated to what is today called the Sandy River.

By the 1830s, the land between the Mexican border at 42° N latitude and Alaska and between the Rocky Mountains and the Pacific Ocean came to be known as "the Oregon Country." The name Oregon was first used in a book, *Travels*, published in 1778, by Jonathon Carver, in which he applied it to the "River of the West." Carver apparently got the word from Major Robert Rogers, the British commander at Fort Mackinac (in present-day Michigan), who used the form Ouragon or Ourigan in a 1765 proposal to King George to explore the country west of the Great Lakes. While there has been much controversy over the origin of the name—various authorities have speculated that it came from a French, Spanish or Native American root—the most plausible present theory is that it was the result of an engraver's error on a map. George R. Stewart presented this plausible account after he discovered a French edition of Lahontan's early 1700s map. The map shows the Ouisconsink or Wisconsin River not only misspelled Ouariconsint but hyphenated Ouaricon- with the final syllable "sint" oddly offset above.

Early trade outposts, such as those of John Jacob Astor's Pacific Fur Company, the American Fur Company and the Hudson's Bay Company, are associated with a number of colorful place names in Oregon. Pudding River, south of Oregon City, was named by Joseph Gervais and Etienne Lucier in 1813 after a fortuitous midwinter elk hunt gave them the makings of blood pudding. The first use of the term "dalles" for the chutes of the Columbia, near present-day The Dalles, was applied by company clerk Gabriel Franchere in 1814. Donald McKenzie led a trapping party which named McKenzie River.

McKenzie is also believed to have named the Powder and Burnt Rivers about 1818. John Day, while in many ways inept and unfortunate, nevertheless left his name on the river east of The Dalles as well as a number of other features.

John McLoughlin, head of the Hudson's Bay Company, Columbia District, oversaw an operation that dominated the area until the middle 1840s. Mount McLoughlin in southern Oregon is named for him. The fur company's trapping expeditions led by such men as Peter Skene Ogden and John Work applied many names to the landscape. The Deschutes River was so called because it joined the Columbia near that river's falls, or chutes; the Deschutes itself is quite placid at its mouth. Ogden named the Malheur River for the misfortune of a fur cache being lost to theft (the word malheur means unfortunate in French). This was well to the east near the Idaho border, but the name migrated upriver to Malheur Lake and Valley. Ogden is remembered by the state park north of Bend. In December 2000 the name Ogden Hill was proposed for the high ground just northwest of Siskiyou Pass. Apparently the first use of the name Cascades for the rapids now inundated by Bonneville Dam was by John Work in 1825. Lewis and Clark used the term cascades, but not as a proper name. Silvies River bears the name of Antoine Sylvaille, an Ogden subordinate who led a trapping group into Harney Valley in 1826.

By the 1830s, the Oregon Country was provoking considerable interest in the Eastern United States. One early expedition that headed West included Nathaniel Wyeth, whose Fort Hall trading post tried unsuccessfully to compete with the Hudson's Bay Company. Trapper and explorer Benjamin Bonneville also traveled with this expedition. Bonneville recorded no names, but when the Oregon Railway & Navigation Company, now the Union Pacific, built tracks through the Columbia River Gorge in 1882, the railroad named a station west of Cascade Locks for him. Nationally known Bonneville Dam, built nearby, took its name from this long-abandoned railroad stop.

Pioneer Period

This period resulted in the application of a large number of eastern place names to Oregon communities and the use of many pioneer family names for features such as streams and mountains. A number of political subdivisions were named for well-known national figures, some of whom played a part in Oregon's development.

When Lieutenant Charles Wilkes and the U.S. Exploring Expedition visited the Oregon Country in 1841, the total non-Indian population was about 350. Retired Hudson's Bay Company employees, largely French Canadians, settled east of the Willamette River on what is now French Prairie. The next year the immigration of 1842, promoted by

Dr. Elijah White, is believed to have brought about 140 new residents. Methodist missionaries were already established on the Willamette River, and when they relocated to what is now Salem they gave it its biblical name.

By 1843, it was apparent to many settlers that some form of government was necessary. A meeting of those interested in addressing this need took place on May 2, 1843, at a site the settlers called Champooick and the French Canadians called Campment du Sable. By a vote of 52 to 50 the inhabitants voted to organize a provisional government. The spot is now Champoeg State Park.

The new Provisional Government met on July 5, 1843, at Oregon City. They elected an executive committee of David Hill, Joseph Gale and Alanson Beers. Hill, the chairman, was the founder of Hillsboro. Gale settled along Gales Creek west of Forest Grove. Beers' name was not geographically perpetuated.

Before the Champoeg meeting, settlers needed few place names other than those for major land features and rivers. This changed quickly as the part of the Oregon Country south of the Columbia River was divided into four districts. West of the Willamette River were Twality on the north and Yamhill on the south, both names of Native American tribes. East of the Willamette were Clackamas on the north and Champooick on the south. Clackamas was named for a Native American tribe, but Champooick is probably from a Kalapuyan word for a favorite edible root. Champoeg is now the common form.

The immigration of 1843 (also known as the Great Migration) brought over 800 new residents. These settlers spread across the fertile lands of the Willamette Valley. The number and arrangement of districts was adjusted as the population increased. Clatsop District was taken from Twality in 1844 and named for the Native American tribe at Astoria. Polk District, taken from Yamhill in 1845, was named for President James K. Polk. In 1847 Linn County—no longer a district—was taken from Champooick (later renamed Marion County) and named for Senator Lewis F. Linn of Missouri, a proponent of the donation land law. Benton County was taken from Polk District and named to honor Senator Thomas Hart Benton, also of Missouri. This arrangement was in place until August 14, 1848, when Oregon became a Territory of the United States.

In 1843 the region featured three sizeable communities: Astoria, Salem, then called Chemeketa or "The Mill," and Oregon City. Astoria had the first post office on the Pacific Coast, established March 3, 1847. Two years later it had the first U.S. Custom House in the West. As immigrants arrived, new communities formed. About 25 recognized settlements existed by 1848. The names of these communities largely fall into two classes, those named for individuals and those transferred from familiar places in the East. Dallas was named for George M. Dallas, Polk's

vice president. Albany was named for Albany, New York, the former home of its founders. Canemah, named for a Native American chief, was important as the south end of the portage at Willamette Falls. An exception to these classifications is Corvallis, descriptively named with the Latin for "heart of the valley."

Portland got its name by chance. The community started humbly as a local trading spot but began to flourish in 1845 when Captain John Couch determined seagoing vessels could not go farther upstream except during unusually high water. Francis W. Pettygrove and Asa Lovejoy tossed a coin to decide between the names Portland and Boston. Pettygrove, born in Calais, Maine, won.

Other towns were established, often with high hopes and some initial success. Linnton was named for Senator Lewis F. Linn. St. Helens—first called Plymouth—was renamed for its proximity to Mount St. Helens, itself named by Vancouver for Baron St. Helens, the British ambassador who negotiated the Nootka Treaty. Lafayette was named for Lafayette, Indiana, and Dayton was named for the city in Ohio. These four communities were in strategic locations on the Columbia and Yamhill Rivers, but as shipping patterns changed their growth lagged. Lebanon was a transfer from Lebanon, Tennessee. The names Milwaukie (with a slight spelling change) and Independence came from Wisconsin and Missouri.

There were also distinctive names. Buena Vista, south of Salem, was named by Reason B. Hall for the Mexican War battle of the same name. Government Camp, the popular outdoor recreation area on Mount Hood, was not named until the 1900s, but its origin was in the camp debris left by an 1849 Army contingent travelling along the Barlow Road. Amity owes its name to the peaceful settlement of a local dispute.

The foregoing were the main communities during the time of the Provisional Government, the period from 1843 to 1848. There is no count of the families in the Great Migration of 1843, but there were about 260 men 16 years of age and older. Some 25 of their names survive today on natural features, a few well known such as Applegate, Waldo, Howell and Nesmith, and others known locally such as John Hobson's Hobsonville north of Tillamook and Hess and Hawn Creeks near Newberg.

The 1843 migration increased the non-Native American population of the Oregon Country to around 1,500. Bernard DeVoto states that the population in 1846 was 6,000 to 7,000, while the 1850 census numbered residents at 12,000. The 1860 census figure was 52,000, a little more than four times the 1850 count.

All names on early maps are either those applied by the early explorers or the names of settlements established by early immigrants. There are no names of minor streams or features. The Augustus Mitchell map of 1846 has only 43 names. By the time of statehood, the geography of the western half of Oregon was well outlined, and the Military Map of 1859 has 122 names. The exact naming date of most minor features is unknown.

As the population rose, so did the need for ways to identify an ever greater number of specific locations. People had to move from place to place, and, since there was no road net, reference points were essential. Native American names were difficult for most English speakers to pronounce and did not easily fit the English alphabet. Consequently, myriad streams and hills were given descriptive names or the names of settlers. Including the 25 names directly traceable to the immigration of 1843, there were probably 250 to 300 minor feature names and 100 or more names for major features in use by 1849. By 1859, these numbers had probably quadrupled to a figure near 1,600, although the percentage of minor names increased as many descriptive Fish, Rock, Dry and Clear Creeks came to supplement those identified with settlers' names.

The names applied in the 1850s follow the patterns established earlier. There were 10 more counties: Tillamook, Coos, Multnomah and Wasco named for Native American tribes; Columbia for the river; Douglas and Jackson for national figures; Lane and Curry for territorial governors; and Josephine for an early resident, Josephine Rollins. Communities increased in number to almost 90, and named features of known date totaled almost 500. Important communities established in the 1850s with transferred names include McMinnville from Tennessee, Harrisburg from Pennsylvania and Ashland from Ashland County, Ohio. Brownsville, Eugene, Gardiner and Roseburg were all named for founding individuals. Camas Valley, Canyonville, Springfield and The Dalles owe their names to the physical surroundings. Most interesting are those named for some activity or arbitrary occurrence. Cedar Mill was where John Jones had his sawmill. Forest Grove was an arbitrary selection by founder J. Quinn Thorton. Sylvester Wait was agent for the Phoenix Insurance Company and so named Phoenix, while James Denny named Sublimity for "the sublime scenery." Not all the towns established in an aura of optimism grew to maturity. Jennyopolis, near Corvallis, is as forgotten as the reason for its name.

Indian Wars and Mining Period

The tumultuous period from the first pursuit of gold in the 1850s until the end of the Indian Wars by 1880 inspired some picturesque nomenclature. The military named myriad camps and forts for well-known officers or those killed in action. Most of these names did not last long, although Fort Stevens survives as a state park. Crook and Harney Counties are named for locally prominent officers. Major Enoch Steen gave

his name to Steens Mountain. Howluk Butte and the several Paulina features commemorate some of the military's Native American opponents.

Miners traditionally used names reeking with optimism such as Gold Bug, Luckyboy and Golconda ("mine of wealth"). Names derived from early mining activity are in use today on features other than mines. Arrastra Butte, for example, is named for an arrastra, a crude device to break up chunks of ore, while Placer in Josephine County is named for a method of mining used in the area.

Numerous military and mining names identify features in Western Oregon but far more of these names are found east of the Cascade Range. In this region both settlement and the use of settlers' names to designate places or features came later.

Homestead Period

During the 50 years between 1875 and 1925, nine million acres qualified for final entry (the passage of title for public lands to individuals), and thousands of family names were applied to creeks, buttes and other features. The names of geographic features and places are listed in the Geographic Names Information System (GNIS), a database maintained by the National Mapping Division of the U.S. Geological Survey. A study in 2001 indicates as many as 16,000 to 18,000 of the 48,000 names in the Oregon GNIS file may be attributed to those who occupied the land in this period. While a number of names were applied during the pioneer period and a few subsequent to the late 1920s, most came directly from the large influx of homesteaders.

This same influx created a need for more local government. Of Oregon's 36 present-day counties, eight were established before territorial status and 10 more before statehood in 1859. The last 18 counties came into being between 1862 and 1916, near the end of the homestead period. Communities flourished along with these larger political designations. The U.S. Topographical Engineers 1859 map shows 39 communities, while the State Highway Map of 1930 names more than 700.

The homestead era was also a time of extensive railroad construction. Railroads were the basic form of transportation, and main lines were augmented by numerous branches. Stations were needed not only for passengers and freight but also for railroad operation and were often only five or 10 miles apart. A rough count shows some 2,500 past and present railroad stations in Oregon. Many of them merely took the name of the community the railroad came to serve, but in many other cases, new communities were established as the railroad progressed. Glendale and Medford on the Southern Pacific Shasta Line are two communities that developed in this way. Many other stations existed primarily as railroad operating points; this group includes Bonneville and Wyeth on

the Union Pacific line up the Columbia River, and Cruzatte, Frazier and Fields on the Eugene to Klamath Falls line.

Modern Period

This period is dominated by made-up names, real estate phraseology and the current efforts to apply a suitable historic or Native American name to something that bears an unsatisfactory title. Vanport, Wood Village and Lincoln City represent the first two groups while Salishan is an example of the trend on the part of most public and private bodies currently applying new names. Both the Oregon Geographic Names Board and the U.S. Board on Geographic Names have rules and guidelines for any new or changed names that will appear on official maps. Both boards continue to receive proposals to name features for individuals, but such proposals must meet exacting standards to be approved. There is a movement to change names such as "squaw," believed by many to be demeaning, but, as with all geographic name changes, the process is deliberate to ensure a satisfactory replacement.

The Oregon GNIS file has approximately 51,500 names or records (of these, about 3,000 are North, South, Middle, Little or similar adjuncts of main features), a number that may represent between 85 and 90 percent of all the state's geographic names. What kinds of names does Oregon have? Of the names that have been carefully studied, 55 percent are or appear to be biographic, 25 percent are floral or faunal, 15 percent are descriptive and 5 percent are in the miscellaneous category.

Place names are integral to a full knowledge and understanding of history. All human activities, excepting those relying solely on intellect, involve spatial relationships, and these are, in turn, defined by place names. The disciplines of history, geography, linguistics and onomastics (the study of the origins and forms of proper names) each contribute valuable information to the understanding of these relationships.

Human Geography

Oregon in the World   2–3

U.S. Geological Survey, EROS Data Center. GTOPO 30 data, 1996.

Location   4–5

Cressman, L. S. *Prehistory of the Far West: Homes of Vanished Peoples*. Salt Lake City: University of Utah Press, 1977.

Goetzmann, William H. and Glyndwr Williams. *The Atlas of North American Exploration: From the Norse Voyages to the Race to the Pole*. New York: Prentice Hall General Reference, 1992.

Lavender, David. *Land of Giants: The Drive to the Pacific Northwest 1750–1950*. Garden City, New York: Doubleday & Company, Inc., 1958.

Oxford Atlas of Exploration. New York: Oxford University Press, 1997.

Peopling of the Americas Map. Washington, D.C.: National Geographic Society, 2000.

Maps: 1762–1814, 1838–1859   6–9

Cary, John. *A New Map of North America from the Latest Authorities*. London, 1806.

Diagram of a Portion of the Oregon Territory. Oregon City: General Land Office, 1852.

Greenhow, Robert. *Map of the Western and Middle Portions of North America*, 1844.

Hayes, Derek. *Historical Atlas of the Pacific Northwest: Maps of Exploration and Discovery*. Seattle: Sasquatch Books, 1999.

Janvier. *L'Amérique divisée par grands états*. Bordeaux. Paris, 1762.

Lewis, Samuel L. and William Clark. *A Map of Lewis and Clark's Track across the Western Portion of North America*. London: Longman, Hurst, Rees, Orme & Brown, 1814.

Parker, Samuel. *Map of Oregon Territory*. Ithaca, New York, 1838.

Preston, J. B. *A Diagram of a Portion of Oregon Territory*. Washington, D.C. General Land Office, 1852.

Sayer, Robert and Gerard Fridrikh Miller. *The Russian Discoveries: From the Map Published by the Imperial Academy of St. Petersburg*. London: Robert Sayer, Map & Printseller, 1775.

Indians   10–11

Driver, Harold E. and William C. Massey. "Comparative Studies of North American Indians." *Transactions of the American Philosophical Society* XLVII, 1957.

Goddard, Ives. "Native Languages and Language Families of North America." Map. In *Handbook of North American Indians*, vol. 17, *Languages*. William C. Sturtevant, ed. Washington, D.C.: Smithsonian Institution, 1996.

Graves, William, ed. *Indians of North America*. Washington, D.C.: National Geographic Society, 1990.

Kroeber, A. L. *Cultural and Natural Areas of Native North America*. Berkeley: University of California Press, 1963.

Loy, William G., Stuart Allan, Clyde P. Patton and Robert D. Plank. *Atlas of Oregon*. Eugene: University of Oregon Books, 1976.

Schwartz, E. A. *Rogue River Indian War and Its Aftermath 1850–1980*. Norman: University of Oklahoma Press, 1997.

Suttles, Wayne. *Native Languages of the Northwest Coast*. Map. Portland: Western Imprints, 1985.

Voegelin, C. F. and F. M. *Map of North American Indian Languages*. American Ethnological Society. Rand McNally, 1966.

Exploration   12–13

Dean, William G. et al., eds. *Concise Historical Atlas of Canada*. University of Toronto Press, 1998.

Farmer, Judith A. *A Historical Atlas of Early Oregon*. Portland: Historical Cartographic Publications, 1973.

Goetzmann, William H. and Glyndwr Williams. *The Atlas of North American Exploration: From the Norse Voyages to the Race to the Pole*. New York: Prentice Hall General Reference, 1992.

Hayes, Derek. *Historical Atlas of the Pacific Northwest: Maps of Exploration and Discovery*. Seattle: Sasquatch Books, 1999.

On to Oregon: Over the Oregon and Applegate Trails. Medford: Southern Oregon Historical Society, 1993.

The Oregon Trail   14–15

Franzwa, Gregory M. *Maps of the Oregon Trail*. St. Louis, Missouri: The Patrice Press, 1990.

Goetzmann, William H. and Glyndwr Williams. *The Atlas of North American Exploration: From the Norse Voyages to the Race to the Pole*. New York: Prentice Hall General Reference, 1992.

Epidemics, Wars and Reservations   16–17

Beckham, Stephen Dow. *Requiem for a People: The Rogue Indians and the Frontiersmen*. Norman: University of Oklahoma, 1971.

Boyd, Robert T. *The Coming of the Spirit of Pestilence: Introduced Infectious Diseases and Population Decline among the Northwest Coast Indians, 1774–1874*. Seattle: University of Washington Press, 1999.

Boyd, Robert T. "Demographic History, 1774–1874." In *Handbook of North American Indians*, vol. 7, Northwest Coast. Wayne Suttles, ed. Washington, D.C.: Smithsonian Institution, 1990.

Douthit, Nathan. *Uncertain Encounters: Indian–White Relations in Southern Oregon, 1820s to 1850s*.

Fuller, George W. *A History of the Pacific Northwest, with a Special Emphasis on the Inland Empire*. New York: Alfred A. Knopf, 1960.

Knuth, Priscilla. "Cavalry in Indian Country, 1864." *Oregon Historical Quarterly* 65 (1964): 5–118.

O'Donnell, Terence. *An Arrow in the Earth: General Joel Palmer and the Indians of Oregon*. Portland: Oregon Historical Society Press, 1991.

Oregon Geospatial Data Clearinghouse, originator. Ownership data updated since 1994 by the Bureau of Land Management.

Schwartz, E. A. *The Rogue River Indian War and Its Aftermath, 1850–1980*. Norman: University of Oklahoma, 1997.

Thompson, Erwin N. *The Modoc War: Its Military History and Topography*. Sacramento: Argus Books, 1997.

Waldman, Carl. *Atlas of the North American Indian*. New York: Checkmark Books, 2000.

Zucker, Jeff. *Oregon Indians*. Portland: Western Imprints, Oregon Historical Society, 1983.

Donation Land Claims, Public Land Survey   18–19

American Congress on Surveying and Mapping. "Surveying and Land Information Systems." *Journal of American Congress on Surveying and Mapping* 51, no. 4 (1991).

Loy, William G., Stuart Allan, Clyde P. Patton and Robert D. Plank. *Atlas of Oregon*. Eugene: University of Oregon Books, 1976.

U.S. Department of the Interior, U.S. Geological Survey. National Mapping Center: *1:100,000 Digital Line Graph Data, Public Land Survey*. Oregon Geospatial Data Clearinghouse [on-line].

Political Boundaries   20–21

Historical Atlas of the United States. Washington, D.C.: National Geographic Society, 1988.

Loy, William G., Stuart Allan, Clyde P. Patton and Robert D. Plank. *Atlas of Oregon*. Eugene: University of Oregon Books, 1976.

Land Grants   22–23

Loy, William G., Stuart Allan, Clyde P. Patton and Robert D. Plank. *Atlas of Oregon*. Eugene: University of Oregon Books, 1976.

O'Callaghan, Jerry A. *Disposition of the Public Domain in Oregon: Memorandum of the Chairman to the Committee on Interior and Insular Affairs*, 6 Nov. 1960.

Oregon Geospatial Data Clearinghouse, originator. Ownership data updated since 1994 by the Bureau of Land Management.

Richardson, Elmo. *BLM's Billion-Dollar Checkerboard: Managing the O & C Lands*. Santa Cruz, California, 1980.

Schools, Counties and Logs: Federal Lands Payment Programs in the Pacific Northwest. The Wilderness Society, Pacific Northwest Regional Office, 2000.

U.S. Department of the Interior, U.S. Geological Survey. National Mapping Center: "1:100,000 Digital Line Graph Data, Public Land Survey." Oregon Geospatial Data Clearinghouse [on-line].

Place Names   24–25

McArthur, Lewis A. *Oregon Geographic Names*, 6th ed. Portland: Oregon Historical Society Press, 1992.

County Populations   26–27
Cities: 1870–1960   28–29
Cities: 1970–2000   30–31

U.S. Department of Commerce, Bureau of the Census. *Census of the Population*. Decennially 1860–2000.

Historic Portland   32–33

Aerial photographs. Spencer B. Gross, Inc. Photogrammetric Engineering. Portland, Oregon, 1998.

Price, Larry W., ed. *Portland's Changing Landscape*. Department of Geography, Portland State University and the Association of American Geographers. Occasional Paper no. 4, 1987.

Sanborn Fire Insurance Maps. Portland, annotated ed. 1879, 1908, 1955.

Willamette Valley Population   34–35

Keisling, Phil. *1999–2000 Oregon Blue Book*. Tim Torgerson, ed. Office of the Secretary of State.

Population of Oregon Cities, Counties and Metropolitan Areas, 1850–1957: A Compilation of Census Counts and Estimates in Oregon. Bureau of Municipal Research and Service, University of Oregon, 1958.

Price, Larry W., ed. *Portland's Changing Landscape*. Department of Geography, Portland State University and the Association of American Geographers. Occasional Paper no. 4, 1987.

Vaughan, Thomas and Virginia Guest Ferriday, eds. *Space, Style and Structure: Building in Northwest America*. Portland: Oregon Historical Society Press, 1974.

Population Growth and Density   36–37

Metro Growth Management Services Data Resource Center. *1999 Population, Households, Dwelling Units. Census Tract Estimates, Portland–Vancouver Metropolitan Area*, 2000.

U.S. Department of Commerce. Bureau of the Census. *Census of the Population*, 1990.

U.S. Department of Commerce, Bureau of the Census. *Oregon's Census 2000 Population Totals for Legislative Redistricting*. Economics and Statistics Administration, 2001.

Age Structure   38–39

U.S. Department of Commerce, Bureau of the Census. *2000 Census of Population and Housing. Profiles of General Demographic Characteristics, Oregon*, 2001.

U.S. Department of Commerce, Bureau of the Census. *Census of Population and Housing*. Decennially 1950–1990.

Immigration   40–41

Martin, Philip and Elizabeth Midgley. "Immigration to the United States." *Population Bulletin* 54, no. 2 (1999). Washington D.C.: Population Reference Bureau.

Portes, Alejandro and Ruben G. Rumbaut. *Immigrant America: A Portrait*. Berkeley: University of California Press, 1996.

Smith, James and Barry Edmonston, eds. *The New Americans: Economic, Demographic and Fiscal Effects of Immigration*. Washington, D.C.: National Academy Press, 1997.

U.S. Department of Commerce, Bureau of the Census. *Census of the Population*. Decennially 1870–1990.

Race and Ethnicity   42–43

Bosco–Milligan Foundation. *Cornerstones of Community: Building of Portland's African American History*. Portland: Bosco–Milligan Foundation, Architectural Heritage Center, 1977.

Bunn, Stan. *Oregon School Directory 2000–2001*. Oregon Department of Education.

"Changes in Race, Ethnicity and Diversity." *The Oregonian*, article series: April–June, 2001.

Gamboa, Erasmo and Carolyn M. Buan, eds. *Nosotros: The Hispanic People of Oregon: Essays and Recollections*. Portland:

Sources

Oregon Council for the Humanities, 1990.

Gamboa, Erasmo. *Under the Thumb of Agriculture: Bracero and Mexican Workers in the Pacific Northwest, 1942–47.* Austin: University of Texas Press, 1990.

Latz, Gil. "Portland's East Asian Connection." In *Portland's Changing Landscape,* Larry W. Price, ed. Occasional Paper no. 4. Department of Geography, Portland State University, 1987.

Millner, Darrell. *On the Road to Equality: a 50 Year Retrospective, 1945–95.* The Urban League of Portland, 1995.

U.S. Department of Commerce, Bureau of the Census. *Compendium of the Tenth Census,* 1883.

U.S. Department of Commerce, Bureau of the Census. *1970 Census of the Population: Volume 1, Characteristics of the Population: Part 39, Oregon,* 1973.

U.S. Department of Commerce, Bureau of the Census. *Report on the Population of the United States,* 1973.

U.S. Department of Commerce, Bureau of the Census. "1990 Census of Population and Housing" [on-line].

U.S. Department of Commerce, Bureau of the Census. *The Statistics of the Population of the United States,* 1873.

Note: The U.S. Census Bureau has recorded the Hispanic population in different ways throughout the years. The census did not recognize this category until 1980. The population graphed for the earlier years are the foreign-born from Latin America and Caribbean countries. Census listings for 1960 and 1970 include "foreign stock" (people whose parents were foreign-born), and that group is included for those two time periods. Values from the 1980 and 1990 census are for Hispanics of all origins.

Income   44–45

Economic Policy Institute, Center on Budget and Policy Priorities, 2000 [on-line].

Government Information Sharing Project. U.S. Department of Commerce. Bureau of Economic Analysis [on-line].

Religion   46–47

Archdiocese of Portland and the Diocese of Baker. *2000 Oregon Catholic Directory.*

Assembly of God State Denominational Headquarters.

Berry, John W. *Profile of Oregon Churches, 1926–52, 1962–63.* Research and Planning Department, Oregon Council of Churches, 1963.

Bradley, Martin B., Norman M. Green, Jr., Dale E. Jones, Mac Lynn and Lou McNeil. *Churches and Church Membership in the United States 1990: An Enumeration by Region, State and County,* 1992.

Bunn, Stan. *Oregon School Directory 2000–2001.* Oregon Department of Education.

Central Lutheran Church. *2000 Yearbook, Roster of Congregations.*

Christian Churches and Churches of Christ. *1998 Directory of Churches.* Directory of the Ministry, 1997.

Church of Jesus Christ of Latter-day Saints. Eugene Mission, Portland Mission, Boise Mission, Church of Jesus Christ of Latter-day Saints Headquarters, Salt Lake City, Utah.

Conservative Baptist Association Northwest. *Directory of Churches.*

Episcopal Church Annual, 2000.

First United Methodist Church. *Report on the Oregon–Idaho Annual Conference,* 2000.

Glenmary Research Center. Atlanta, Georgia.

Jewish Federation of Portland. "Community Resources: Congregations" [on-line].

Johnson, Douglas W., Paul R. Picard and Bernard Quinn. *Churches and Church Membership in the United States: An Enumeration by Region, State and County.* Washington, D.C.: Glenmary Research Center, 1971. *Note: The 2000 Glenmary data was not available for this atlas.*

Kosmin, Barry A. and Seymour P. Lachman. *One Nation under God: Religion in Contemporary America.* New York: Crown Trade Paperbacks, 1993.

Loy, William G., Stuart Allan, Clyde P. Patton and Robert D. Plank. *Atlas of Oregon.* Eugene: University of Oregon Books, 1976.

National Muslim Student's Association.

Northwest Baptist Convention Headquarters.

Oregon School Activities Association.

Presbyterian General Assembly Reports, vol. 2, 1999.

Regional Seventh-day Adventist Headquarters.

Wardin, Albert W. Jr. Nashville, Tennessee. Conservative Baptist Association data, 2000.

Zelinsky, Wilbur. "An Approach to the Religious Geography of the United States: Patterns of Church Membership in 1952." *Annals of the Association of American Geographers,* 1961.

Politics   48–49

Abbott, Carl. *Portland: Planning, Politics and Growth in a Twentieth-Century City.* Lincoln: University of Nebraska Press, 1983.

Balmer, Don and Bill Lunch. *Oregon in an Era of Uncertainty: The Politics of the Property Tax Limit.* Corvallis: Program for Governmental Research and Education, 1995.

Cronin, Thomas E. *Direct Democracy: The Politics of Initiative, Referendum and Recall.* Cambridge: Harvard University Press, 1989.

Dodds, Gordon B. *Oregon: A History.* New York: W. W. Norton, 1977.

Edwards, G. Thomas and Carlos A. Schwantes. *Experiences in a Promised Land: Essays in Pacific Northwest History.* Seattle: University of Washington Press, 1986.

Keisling, Phil. *1999–2000 Oregon Blue Book.* Tim Torgerson, ed. Office of the Secretary of State.

Lee, Kai N. *Compass and Gyroscope: Integrating Science and Politics for the Environment.* Washington, D.C.: Island Press, 1993.

Lunch, William M. "Oregon Politics, Upstate and Down." *Oregon Humanities:* Winter, 1995.

Myers, Clay. *1973, 1974 Oregon Blue Book.* George Bell, Linda Koellmann, eds. Office of the Secretary of State.

Population of Oregon Cities, Counties and Metropolitan Areas, 1850–1957: A Compilation of Census Counts and Estimates in Oregon. Bureau of Municipal Research and Service, University of Oregon, 1958.

Robbins, William G. *Landscapes of Promise: The Oregon Story, 1800–1940.* Seattle: University of Washington Press, 1997.

Schwantes, Carlos A. *The Pacific Northwest: An Interpretive History.* Lincoln: University of Nebraska Press, 1989.

Swarthout, John M. "Oregon: Political Experiment Station." In *Western Politics.* Salt Lake City: University of Utah Press, 1961.

Walth, Brent. *The Fire at Eden's Gate: Tom McCall and the Oregon Story.* Portland: Oregon Historical Society Press, 1994.

Wilkinson, Charles F. *Crossing the Next Meridian.* Washington, D.C.: Island Press, 1992.

School Districts   50–51

Bunn, Stan. *Oregon School Directory 2000–2001.* Oregon Department of Education.

Oregon School Activities Association. Wilsonville.

Education   52–53

Oregon Department of Education. *Summary of Students, Staff and Organization, Certificated Personnel Report, Student Personnel Accounting Report,* annual school directories, various years.

Colleges and Universities   54–55

College Board, The. *College Handbook 2000.* New York: College Entrance Examination Board, 2000.

Kaplan–Newsweek. *College Catalog.* New York: Simon & Schuster, 2001.

Office of Community College Services. "Oregon Community College 1998–1999 Profile" [on-line].

Office of Degree Authorization, Oregon Student Assistance Commission.

Oregon Independent Colleges Association. Portland.

Oregon University System. *Fact Book 2000.* Institutional Research Services.

Crime and Prisons   56–57

Federal Bureau of Investigation. *Crime in the United States 1999: Uniform Crime Reports,* 2000.

Justice Research and Statistics Association. "Crime and Justice Atlas 2000" [on-line].

Oregon Department of Corrections, Research & Evaluation.

Oregon State Police. *Report of Criminal Offenses & Arrests.* Annual.

Oregon Youth Authority. *1995–1997 Biennial Report,* 1998.

Oregon Youth Authority. MacLaren Youth Correctional Facility [on-line].

Health Care   58–59

Center for Disease Control. *MMWR Surveillance Summaries,* vol. 49, SS-11. 8 Dec. 2000.

Department of Human Services, Oregon State Health Division. *Acute Care Provider List.* Health Care Licensure and Certification, 2000.

Information for VA Hospitals: Portland VA Medical Center and on-line.

National Center for Health Statistics. "Health, United States 1999, with Health and Aging Chartbook" [on-line].

Office for Oregon Health Plan Policy and Research. "The Uninsured in Oregon, 1998" [on-line].

Office for Oregon Health Plan Policy and Research. "An Overview of Nursing Homes, 1990–1996" [on-line].

Oregon Department of Human Services, Senior and Disabled Services Division, 2000.

Oregon Health Department. Collection of rates from county health departments. Average of 1996, 1997 and 1998 ITARS rates.

Oregon Vital Statistics County Data: 1995–1998. Table 1. Four-year average.

Oregon Vital Statistics Report. vols. 1 and 2, 1997; vol. 2, 1998 [on-line].

Newspapers and Broadcasting   60–61

Bittner, John R. *Broadcasting, an Introduction.* Englewood Cliffs, New Jersey: Prentice–Hall, Inc., 1980.

Editor and Publisher International Yearbook, 7th ed. 1999.

Gale Research. *Gale Directory of Publications and Broadcast Media,* 133rd ed., 1999.

Head, Sydney W., and Christopher H. Sterling. *Broadcasting in America,* 5th ed. Boston: Houghton Mifflin Co., 1987.

Mott, Frank Luther. *American Journalism, a History 1690–1960,* 3rd ed. New York: The Macmillan Co., 1962.

Nielsen Media Research.

Oregon Association of Broadcasters. *Official Directory 2000.*

Oregon Newspaper Publishers Association. *Annual Directory 2000–2001.*

Oregon Newspaper Publishers Association. "Newspapers Published in Oregon 1999–2000." Oregon Blue Book Media Directories [on-line].

Smith, F. Leslie. *Perspectives on Radio and Television, Telecommunication in the United States,* 3rd ed. New York: Harper and Row, 1990.

The Economy

Economic Sectors   64–65

Greenwood, M. J., G. L. Hunt, D. S. Rickman and G. I. Treyz. "Migration, Regional Equilibrium and the Estimation of Compensating Differentials." *The American Economic Review* 81, no. 5 (1991): 1382–1390.

State of Oregon, Employment Department. *1999 Oregon In-Migration Study.*

U.S. Department of Commerce, Bureau of the Census. *Statistical Abstract of the United States.* Various years.

U.S. Department of Commerce, Bureau of Economic Analysis [on-line].

U.S. Department of Commerce, Economics and Statistics Administration, Bureau of Economic Analysis. *Regional Economic Information System 1969–98* (on CD-ROM). RCN-0250, 2000.

Warren, D. D. *Production, Prices, Employment and Trade in Northwest Forest Industries.* U.S. Department of Agriculture, Forest Service, Pacific Northwest Research Station, various years.

Labor   66–67

Oregon Employment Department. *2000 Regional Economic Profile.*

U.S. Department of Commerce, Bureau of the Census [on-line].

U.S. Department of Labor, Bureau of Labor Statistics [on-line].

Public Employment   68–69

Oregon Employment Department.

U.S. Department of Commerce, Bureau of Economic Analysis.

Taxation and Revenue   70–71

Internal Revenue Service. "Internal Revenue Gross Collections, by State, Fiscal Year 1998." "1998 IRS Data Book, Publication 55B" [on-line].

Oregon Department of Revenue. "Oregon Property Tax Statistics, Fiscal Year 1997–98." Table A.2 [on-line], revised 1998.

Oregon Department of Revenue. "Personal Income Tax Annual Statistics, Tax Year 1997." Section 6, Table A [on-line], revised 1999.

Oregon Legislative Revenue Office. *Oregon Public Finance: Basic Facts.* Research Report #1-01, 2001.

Oregon Legislative Revenue Office. Research Report #1-99, Basic Tax Packet 1999.

Oregon Liquor Control Commission. *Liquor Sales by County and City*, 2000.

Oregon Lottery. *Oregon Lottery Dollars, Working for Oregon, 1997–99 Biennium*, 1999.

Oregon Lottery. *Oregon Lottery Revenue History*, 2000.

U.S. Department of Commerce, Bureau of the Census. "1997 Census of Governments" [on-line].

U.S. Department of Commerce, Bureau of the Census. "U.S. Census Bureau Statistical Abstract of the United States" [on-line], 1998.

Manufacturing   72–73

U.S. Department of Commerce, Bureau of the Census. *County Business Patterns 1980–98, 1982–2000.*

Lumber and Wood Products   74–75

Ehinger, Paul F. Eugene, Oregon: Paul F. Ehinger and Associates, 2001.

U.S. Department of Commerce, Bureau of the Census. *County Business Patterns 1977–97.*

High Technology   76–77

Hillsboro Chamber of Commerce. *Resource Guide, Oregon High Technology*, 2000.

U.S. Department of Commerce, Bureau of the Census. *County Business Patterns 1977–97.*

Business Activity   78–79

Bank & Thrift Branch Office Data Book, Table 7. Data Book 6, 1998.

D & B Regional Directory Oregon Area, 1999. Bethlehem, Pennsylvania: Dun and Bradsteet, Inc.

FDIC Division of Research and Statistics. *Statistics on Banking*, 1997, 1998.

Oregon Economic and Community Development Department.

U.S. Department of Commerce, Bureau of the Census. *Census of Retail Trade*, 1972, 1977, 1982, 1987, 1992, 1997.

U.S. Department of Commerce, Bureau of the Census. *Census of Wholesale Trade*, 1972, 1977, 1982, 1987, 1992, 1997.

International Investments   80–81

Foreign Direct Investment in the United States. Operations of U.S. Affiliates of Foreign Companies. Annual.

Oregon Economic & Community Development Department. *Oregon, Year 2000: International Companies Operating in Oregon*, 2000.

U.S. Department of Commerce, Bureau of the Census. *Statistical Abstract of the United States: 1998*, 118th ed. Table 1309.

U.S. Department of Commerce, Bureau of Economic Analysis. *Survey of Current Business*, June 1998.

Public Lands   82–83

O'Callaghan, Jerry A. *Disposition of the Public Domain in Oregon: Memorandum of the Chairman to the Committee on Interior and Insular Affairs.* United States Senate, 6 Nov. 1960

Oregon Geospatial Data Clearinghouse, originator. Ownership data updated since 1994 by the Bureau of Land Management.

Land Ownership   84–85

Atterbury Consultants, Inc., U.S. Forest Service, Oregon Wilderness Society and Oregon State Forestry Science Lab, 1994.

Disposition of the Public Domain in Oregon: Memorandum of the Chairman to the Committee on Interior and Insular Affairs. United States Senate. 6 Nov. 1960.

O'Callaghan, Jerry A. *Western Oregon Industrial Forestland Ownership.* Map, 1960.

Oregon Geospatial Data Clearinghouse, originator. Ownership data updated since 1994 by the Bureau of Land Management.

Zoning   86–87

Bill 100. Oregon Senate, 1973.

Benner, Dick. *Growth and Northwest Landscape.* Oregon Department of Land Conservation and Development. Spring 1998.

Oregon Department of Land Conservation and Development. *Biennial Report for 1999–2001.*

Oregon Department of Land Conservation and Development. "Fast Facts: Oregon's Statewide Land Use Planning Program 2000" [on-line].

Oregon Department of Land Conservation and Development. Generalized zoning data, 1983–86.

Oregon Department of Land Conservation and Development. *Inside the Boundaries* newsletter, Spring 2000.

Oregon Department of Land Conservation and Development. *Oregon's 19 Statewide Planning Goals and Guidelines*, 1970s.

Oregon Department of Land Conservation and Development. *The Oregon Livability Initiative*, September 1999.

Oregon Department of Land Conservation and Development. *Oregon's Verdant Willamette Valley: Growing Crops While Growing Cities*, May 1999.

Oregon Department of Land Conservation and Development. *Planning for Natural Hazards: Oregon Technical Resource Guide*, July 2000.

Oregon Department of Land Conservation and Development. "Rural Lands Planning" [on-line].

Oregon Department of Land Conservation and Development. *Secondary Lands Backgrounder*, 5 Feb. 1999.

Oregon Geospatial Data Clearinghouse, originator. Ownership data updated since 1994 by the Bureau of Land Management.

Minerals and Mining   88–89

Brooks, Howard C. and Len Ramp. *Gold and Silver in Oregon.* State Department of Geology and Mineral Industries, Bulletin 61, 1968.

Ferns, M. L. *Preliminary Report on Northeastern Oregon Lignite and Coal Resources, Union, Wallowa, and Wheeler Counties.* Oregon Department of Geology and Mineral Industries Open File Report O-85-02, 1985.

Ferns, M. L. and H. C. Brooks. *Geology and Coal Resources of the Arbuckle Mountain Coal Field, Morrow County.* Oregon Department of Geology and Mineral Industries Open File Report O-86-05, 1986.

Gray, Jerry J. *Mineral Information Layer for Oregon by County (MILOC).* Oregon Department of Geology and Mineral Industries Open File Report 93-08, 1993.

Gray, Jerry J. and Klaus K. E. Neuendorf. *Directory of Mineral Producers in Oregon.* Oregon Department of Geology and Mineral Industries Open File Report 0-93-9, 1993.

Mined Land Reclamation Database. Oregon Department of Geology and Mineral Industries (updated weekly).

Mineral industry surveys, 1971–94.

Oregon Department of Geology and Mineral Industries. Unpublished files.

Potter, Miles F. *Oregon's Golden Years: Bonanza of the West.* Caldwell, Idaho: The Caxton Printers, 1976.

U.S. Geological Survey. "Map of Principal Mineral Localities" [on-line], 1998.

U.S. Geological Survey, Bureau of Mines. *State Minerals Summaries*, 1991.

U.S. Geological Survey, Bureau of Mines. *Oregon Annual Report*, 1992.

Wheelan, Robert. *Oregon's Mineral Industry: An Assessment of the Size and Economic Importance of Mineral Extraction.* Oregon Department of Geology and Mineral Industries Open File Report 0-94-31, 1994.

Fisheries   90–91

Oregon Department of Fish and Wildlife. *1997 Pounds and Value of Commercially Caught Fish and Shellfish Landed in Oregon. Commercial Fish and Shellfish Landings (Pounds Round) by Port in Oregon*, 2000.

Beiningen, K. T. *Fish Runs, an Investigative Report of Columbia River Fisheries Project.* Vancouver, Washington: Pacific Northwest Regional Commission, 1976.

Oregon Department of Fish and Wildlife. *Ex-Vessel Value of Oregon Commercial Food Fish Landings by Fishery/Species Group and Oregon Commercial Food Fish Landings by Fishery/Species Group*, May 2001.

Pacific Fishery Management Council [on-line].

Pacific States Marine Fisheries Commission. PacFIN, Regional Fisheries Data Network [on-line].

U.S. Bureau of Economic Analysis. Regional accounts data, local area personal income. Detailed county annual tables. Table CA05: "Personal Income by Major Source and Earnings by Industry." Portland, Oregon.

U.S. Department of Commerce, National Oceanic and Atmospheric Administration and the National Marine Fisheries Service. *Fisheries of the United States 1998.*

Washington Department of Fish and Wildlife, Oregon Department of Fish and Wildlife. *Status Report: Columbia River Fish Runs and Fisheries, 1938–1998.* Table 3, 98–101.

Timber   92–93

Bourhill, Bob. *History of Oregon's Timber Harvests and Lumber Production.* Oregon Department of Forestry, 1994.

Elliot, T. S. and Theodore Rowland. *Oregon Department of Forestry*, 1914.

FEMAT. *Forest Ecosystem Management: An Ecological, Economic and Social Assessment.* Report of the Forest Ecosystem Management Assessment Team (FEMAT). 1993-793-071. Washington, D.C.: 1993.

Johnson, K. "Summary of Current Status and Health of Oregon's Forests." In: Risser, P. (chair). *Oregon State of the Environment Report 2000.* Prepared for the Oregon Progress Board, 2000.

Lettman, Gary. *Oregon Department of Forestry*, 2000.

Pacific Northwest Ecosystem Research Consortium. 19 Aug. 1995, 3 Aug. 1995, 13 Sept. 1995. Satellite image.

Risser, P. (chair). *Oregon State of the Environment Report 2000 Statewide Summary.* Prepared for the Oregon Progress Board.

Sessions, J. (coordinator). *Timber for Oregon's Tomorrow: The 1989 Update.* Oregon State University, Forest Research Laboratory, 1991.

Stere, David. *Oregon Department of Forestry and the Oregon State Service Center Geographical Information System*, 1993.

USDA Forest Service/USDI Bureau of Land Management. *Status of the Interior Columbia Basin: Summary of Scientific Findings.* General Technical Report PNW-GTR-381. Portland, Oregon: U.S. Department of Agriculture, Forest Service, Pacific Northwest Research Station, 1996.

Wimberley, M., T. Spies, C. Long and C. Whitlock. "Simulating Historical Variability in the Amount of Old Forests in the Oregon Coast Range." *Conservation Biology* 14, no. 1 (2000): 1–13.

Farmlands   94–95

Kiilsgaard, Chris. *Manual and Land Cover Type Descriptions, Oregon GAP Analysis 1998 Land Cover for Oregon.* OR-GAP Northwest Habitat Institute, 1999.

U.S. Department of Agriculture. *Census of Agriculture. Statistics for the State and Counties: Oregon*, 1925, 1954, 1964, 1974, 1982, 1992.

U.S. Department of Agriculture. *1997 Census of Agriculture*, vol. 1: part 37, ch. 2. Oregon County-Level Data.

Sources

U.S. Department of Agriculture and Oregon Department of Agriculture. Oregon Agricultural Statistics Service. *Oregon Agriculture & Fisheries Statistics*, 1998–1999.

Cattle and Crops   96–97
Crops and Wine   98–99

Grassel, Rhonda. Oregon Agricultural Information Network. *2000 Oregon County and State Agricultural Estimates. Special Report 790.* Corvallis: Oregon State University Extension Service, 2001.

Oregon Wine Advisory Board. "New Oregon Appellation Approved: Applegate Valley Becomes Sixth Nationally Recognized Oregon Wine Region." Press Release, 2001.

Rowley, Homer K. and Bruce Eklund, Oregon Agricultural Statistics Service. *1999–2000 Oregon Agriculture and Fisheries Statistics.* U.S. Department of Agriculture National Agricultural Statistics Service and Oregon Department of Agriculture, Salem, 2000.

U.S. Department of Agriculture, Oregon Agricultural Statistics Service. *1987 Oregon Vineyard and Winery Report.*

U.S. Department of Agriculture, Resource Economics Division, Economic Research Service. *Structural and Financial Characteristics of U.S. Farms: 2001 Family Farm Report.* Robert A. Hoppe, ed. Agriculture Information Bulletin No. 768, Washington, D.C.: 2001.

Energy Sources   100–101

Bonneville Power Administration [on-line].

Energy Information Administration. "Consumption Source Detailed Data 1960–97, State Rankings of Consumption" [on-line].

Loy, William G., Stuart Allan, Clyde P. Patton and Robert D. Plank. *Atlas of Oregon.* Eugene: University of Oregon Books, 1976.

Northwest Power Planning Council [on-line].

Northwest Natural Gas. *South Mist Pipeline Extension Project.* Portland, Oregon, 2000.

Oregon Department of Transportation. *Freight Moves the Oregon Economy,* 1999.

Oregon Department of Transportation. *Transportation Key Facts,* 2000.

"Oregon Pipeline Draws Attention." *The Oregonian,* 4 Aug. 1999, sec. B, p. 9.

Pennwell MapSearch. *Express Pipeline Map,* 1998.

PG&E Gas Transmission Company [on-line].

Quinn, Beth. "Pipe Dream Celebrates a Victory at the Polls." *The Oregonian,* 4 Nov. 1999.

Resource Data International. *Refined Products Systems Map,* 1998.

Resource Data International. *North American Natural Gas System Map,* 2000.

Energy Distribution   102–103

Bonneville Power Administration.

California Energy Commisssion. *California Power Plant—Statewide Map,* 2001.

Donley, Michael, Stuart Allan, Patricia Caro and Clyde Patton. *Atlas of California.* Culver City, California: Pacific Book Center, 1979.

Energy Information Administration. "Consumption by Sector Detailed Data 1960–97" [on-line].

Geo-Heat Center, "Oregon State Geothermal Projects" [on-line].

Kale, Steven and B. Alexander Sifford III. *Atlas of the Pacific Northwest,* Philip Jackson and A. Jon Kimerling, eds. Corvallis: Oregon State University Press, 1993.

Northwest Power Planning Council. *Draft Northwest Conservation and Electric Power Plan,* Appendix A. Portland, 1996.

Oregon Department of Geology and Mineral Industries.

Oregon Department of Transportation. *Freight Moves the Oregon Economy.*

Oregon Office of Energy. "Renewable Energy: Biomass, Geothermal and Windpower" [on-line].

Oregon Public Utilities Commission. *1999 Oregon Utility Statistics.*

Pacific Gas & Electric [on-line].

Pacific Northwest Laboratory. "Oregon Annual Wind Power, Wind Energy Resource Atlas of the United States" [on-line].

Resource Data International. *North American Natural Gas System Map,* 2000.

Sifford, B. Alexander III. "Energy Resources of the Pacific Northwest." In *The Pacific Northwest: Geographical Perspectives,* James Ashbaugh, ed. Dubuque, Iowa: Kendall/Hunt Publishing, 1997.

Development of the Road Network   104–105

Loy, William G., Stuart Allan, Clyde P. Patton and Robert D. Plank. *Atlas of Oregon.* Eugene: University of Oregon Books, 1976.

Oregon Department of Transportation, *Official State Map,* 1980, 1990, 2000–01.

Highway Traffic   106–107

Oregon Department of Transportation. "Oregon Vehicle Miles of Travel for State-Owned Highways" [on-line], 2000.

Oregon Department of Transportation. *Transportation Volume Tables,* various years.

U.S. Department of Transportation, Federal Highway Administration. *Highway Statistics,* 1999.

Railroads   108–109

American Association of Railroads. *Railroad Service in Oregon.* Washington, D.C.: 2000.

Loy, William G., Stuart Allan, Clyde P. Patton and Robert D. Plank. *Atlas of Oregon.* Eugene: University of Oregon Books, 1976.

Oregon Department of Transportation. *Transportation Key Facts,* 2000.

Oregon Department of Transportation. *Freight Moves the Oregon Economy,* July 1999.

Oregon Department of Transportation Rail Division.

Pacific Northwest Chapter of the National Railway Historical Society. Portland, Oregon.

Steam Powered Videos. *Railroad Atlas of North America,* 1998.

Surface Transportation Board. *Waybill Data.* Washington, D.C.: 2000.

Public Transportation and Airports   110–111

Amtrak. *Thruway Ridership Reports,* 2000.

Kaiser, I. C. F. et al. *Commodity Flow Analysis for the Portland Metropolitan Area.* Fairfax, Virginia: Metro and the Port of Portland, 1999.

Loy, William G., Stuart Allan, Clyde P. Patton and Robert D. Plank. *Atlas of Oregon.* Eugene: University of Oregon Books, 1976.

National Transit Resource Center. Washington, D.C.: 2000.

Oregon Department of Transportation. *Oregon Public Transportation Plan,* 1997.

Oregon Department of Transportation. *Freight Moves the Oregon Economy,* 1999.

Oregon Department of Transportation. *Transportation Key Facts,* 2000.

Oregon Department of Transportation. "Amtrak Routes and Depots" [on-line].

Oregon Department of Transportation, Aeronautics Division. *2000 Oregon Aviation Plan: An Element of the Oregon Transportation Plan,* 2000.

Oregon Department of Transportation. "Intercity Bus Routes and Depots" [on-line].

U.S. Department of Transportation, Federal Aviation Administration. *Airport Activity Statistics of Certificated Route Carriers,* various years.

U.S. Department of Transportation, Federal Transit Administration. *1998 National Transit Database,* 2000.

Ports and Trade   112–113

Cockle, Richard. "Tiny Town Sees Tons of Traffic," *The Oregonian,* 27 May 1999, sec. B, p. 1.

Oregon Department of Economic and Community Development, International Division [on-line].

Oregon Department of Transportation. *Freight Moves the Oregon Economy,* 1999.

Oregon Department of Transportation. *Transportation Key Facts,* 2000.

Oregon Economic Development Department. *Statewide Ports Study,* Technical Document, 1997.

Port of Portland. *Fast Facts,* 2000

U.S. Army Corps of Engineers. *Waterborne Commerce of the United States,* 2000.

U.S. Department of Commerce, International Trade Administration. *State Export Data,* 2000.

U.S. Department of Transportation. *Transborder Surface Freight Data,* 2000.

Wilbur Smith Associates, et al. *Western Transportation Trade Network. Phase 1 Report.* Columbia, South Carolina: Western Association of State Highway and Transportation Officials, 1997.

Tourism and Recreation   114–115

Dean Runyan Associates. *Oregon Travel Impacts 1991–99.*

Oregon Department of Fish and Wildlife. *Summary of 1999 Licenses by County of Residence,* 1999.

Oregon Department of Fish and Wildlife. "Vision 2006: A Six-Year Strategic Plan" [on-line].

Oregon Golf Commerce. "Directory 2000" [on-line].

Oregon Parks and Recreation Department. *Annual Attendance Data Set,* 1999.

Oregon State Marine Board [on-line].

Oregon Tourism Commission. "Travel Oregon" [on-line].

Pacific Northwest Ski Areas Association.

U.S. Department of Commerce, Bureau of the Census [on-line].

Physical Geography

Landforms   118–129
Cross Sections   130–131

U.S. Department of the Interior, U.S. Geological Survey. *National Elevation Data Set,* 1999.

U.S. Department of the Interior, U.S. Geological Survey. National Mapping Center: *1:100,000 Digital Line Graph Data, Hydrography and Transportation,* 1993.

U.S. Department of Transportation. *National Transportation Atlas Data.*

Ice Age Lakes and Floods   132–133
Ice Age Glaciers   134–135

Baker, Victor R. "Late-Pleistocene Fluvial Systems in Late-Quaternary Environments of the United States." H. E. Wright, Jr., ed. *Volume 1: The Late Pleistocene,* Stephen C. Porter, ed. Minneapolis: University of Minnesota Press, 1983.

Bentley, Elton B. *The Glacial Morphology of Eastern Oregon Uplands.* Ph.D. dissertation, University of Oregon, 1974.

Crandell, D. R. "The Glacial History of Western Washington and Oregon." In *The Quaternary of the United States: A Review Volume for the VII Congress of the International Association for Quaternary Research.* H. E. Wright and D. G. Frey, eds. Princeton, New Jersey: Princeton University Press, 1965.

Loy, William G., Stuart Allan, Clyde P. Patton and Robert D. Plank. *Atlas of Oregon.* Eugene: University of Oregon Books, 1976.

Orr, Elizabeth and William. *Geology of Oregon,* 2nd ed. Dubuque, Iowa: Kendall/Hunt, 1999.

Orr, Elizabeth and William. *Oregon Fossils.* Dubuque, Iowa: Kendall/Hunt, 1999.

Orr, Elizabeth and William. *Geology of the Pacific Northwest,* 5th ed. Dubuque, Iowa: McGraw–Hill, 2001.

Smith, George I. and F. Alayne Street–Perrott. "Pluvial Lakes of the Western United States." In *Late-Quaternary Environments of the United States.* H. E. Wright, Jr., ed. *Volume 1: The Late Pleistocene,* Stephen C. Porter, ed. Minneapolis: University of Minnesota Press, 1983.

U.S. Department of the Interior, U.S. Geological Survey. *Great Basin Geoscience Data Base,* digitally compiled by Gary L. Raines, Don L. Sawatzky and Katherine A. Connors, 1996.

Waitt, Richard B. and Robert M. Thorson. "The Cordilleran Ice Sheet in Washington, Idaho and Montana." In *Late-Quaternary Environments of the United States.* H. E. Wright, Jr., ed. *Volume 1: The Late Pleistocene,* Stephen C. Porter, ed. Minneapolis: University of Minnesota Press, 1983.

Note: Glacial Lake Modoc is defined here by the 4,300' elevation contour from the USGS GTOPO 30 data set.

Volcanoes   136–137

Global Volcanism Program. *Holocene Volcano Basic Data.* Smithsonian National Museum of Natural History, 2001.

Late-Quaternary Environments of the United States. H. E. Wright, Jr., ed. *Volume 1: The Late Pleistocene,* Stephen C. Porter, ed. Minneapolis: University of Minnesota Press, 1983

Mats, Stephen E. "The Mazama–Tephra Falls: Volcanic Hazards and Prehistoric Populations." *Anthropology Northwest* 5 (1991).

Orr, Elizabeth and William. *Geology of Oregon,* 2nd ed. Dubuque, Iowa: Kendall/Hunt, 1999.

Orr, Elizabeth and William. *Oregon Fossils.* Dubuque, Iowa: Kendall/Hunt, 1999.

Orr, Elizabeth and William. *Geology of the Pacific Northwest,* 5th ed. Dubuque, Iowa: McGraw–Hill, 2001.

U.S. Department of the Interior, U.S. Geological Survey. "Cascades Volcano Observatory" [on-line].

Earthquakes   138–139

Johnson, A. G., Portland State University; D. H. Scofield, Squier Associates and I. P. Medin, Oregon Department of Geology and Mineral Industries. *Earthquake Database for Oregon, 1833–1993.* Oregon Department of Geology and Mineral Industries, 1994.

Madin, Ian and Matthew Mabey. *Earthquake Hazard Maps for Oregon.* Oregon Department of Geology and Mineral Industries, Geologic Map Series 100, 1996.

Wang, Yumei. *Earthquake Damage and Loss Estimate for Oregon.* Oregon Department of Geology and Mineral Industries, 1998.

Wang, Yumei and J. L. Clark. *Earthquake Damage in Oregon: Preliminary Estimates of Future Earthquake Losses.* Oregon Department of Geology and Mineral Industries, Special Paper 29, 1999.

Wang, Yumei, Oregon Department of Geology and Mineral Industries and Ray J. Weldon and Dennis Fletcher, Department of Geological Sciences, University of Oregon. "Creating a Map of Oregon UBC Soils: A New Approach to Earthquake Hazard Identification in Oregon." *Oregon Geology* 60, no. 4 (1998): 75–80.

Landslides   140–141

Oregon Department of Geology and Mineral Industries. "Status Map: Inventory of Landslides in Oregon for the 1996 and 1997 Storm Events" [on-line].

Oregon State University, Forest Science Research Network. "H. J. Andrews Experimental Forest: Long-Term Ecological Research Site" [on-line].

Orr, E. and W. Orr. "The Other Face of Oregon: Geologic Processes That Shape Our State." *Oregon Geology* 61, no. 6 (1999).

U.S. Department of the Interior, U.S. Geological Survey. *National Elevation Data Set.*

Geology   142–143

Loy, William G., Stuart Allan, Clyde P. Patton and Robert D. Plank. *Atlas of Oregon.* Eugene: University of Oregon Books, 1976.

Oregon Department of Geology and Mineral Industries.

Orr, Elizabeth and William. *Geology of Oregon,* 2nd ed. Dubuque, Iowa: Kendall/Hunt, 1999.

Orr, Elizabeth and William. *Oregon Fossils.* Dubuque, Iowa: Kendall/Hunt, 1999.

Orr, Elizabeth and William. *Geology of the Pacific Northwest,* 5th ed. Dubuque, Iowa: McGraw–Hill, 2001.

University of Oregon, Department of Geological Sciences.

U.S. Deptartment of the Interior. U.S. Geological Survey *1:2,000,000 Geology Data,* Oregon Geospatial Data Clearinghouse [on-line].

Geologic Ages   144–145

U.S. Deptartment of the Interior. U.S. Geological Survey *1:500,000 Geology Data,* Oregon Geospatial Data Clearinghouse [on-line], 1991.

Geologic Evolution   146–147

Bayer, Kenneth C. *Generalized Structural Lithologic and Physiographic Provinces in the Fold and Thrust Belts of the United States.* U.S. Geological Survey Map, 1:2.5M, 1983.

Christiansen, R. L. *Post-Laramide Major Tectonic, Sedimentary and Igneous Features in the U.S. Cordillera.* Boulder, Colorado: Geological Society of America, Inc., 1992.

Christiansen, R. L. and R. S. Yeats "Post-Laramide Geology of the U.S. Cordilleran Region." In *Cordilleran Oregon: Conterminous U.S.* B. C Burchfiel, P. W. Lipman and M. L. Zoback, eds. *The Geology of North America, Volume G-3.* Boulder, Colorado: Geological Society of America. Used with permission No. 21669, The Geological Society of America, Inc., 1992.

Orr, E. L., W. N. Orr and E. M. Baldwin. *Geology of Oregon,* 4th ed.: Dubuque, Iowa: Kendall/Hunt, 1992.

Yeats, R. S., E. P. Graven, K. S. Werner, C. Goldfinger and T. A. Popowski. *Tectonics of the Willamette Valley, Oregon:* U.S. Geological Professional Paper 1560, 1996.

Soil Orders   148–149
Soil Suborders   150–151

U.S. Department of Agriculture, Soil Survey Staff. *Soil Taxonomy. A Basic System of Soil Classification for Making and Interpreting Soil Surveys.* USDA Agricultural Handbook 436, 2nd ed., 1999.

U.S. Department of Agriculture, *State Soil Geographic Data Base.* Miscellaneous Publication no. 1492, 1994.

Soil Interpretations   152–153

Hurt, G. W., P. M. Whited and R. F. Pringle, eds. *Field Indicators of Hydric Soils in the United States,* version 4.0. USDA Natural Resources Conservation Service, Fort Worth, Texas, 1998.

Klingebiel, A. A. and P. H. Montgomery. *Land Capability Classification.* USDA Agricultural Handbook 210, 1961.

Richardson, J. L., and M. J. Vepraskas, eds. *Wetland Soils: Genesis, Hydrology, Landscapes and Classification.* New York: Lewis, 1998.

U.S. Department of Agriculture. Pacific Northwest Soil Survey Region Office. *Potential Prime Farmland Oregon Map,* 1998.

U.S. Department of Agriculture, *State Soil Geographic Data Base.* Miscellaneous Publication no. 1492, 1994.

Annual Precipitation   154–155

Daly, C., R. P. Neilson and D. L. Phillips. "A Statistical–Topographic Model for Mapping Climatological Precipitation over Mountainous Terrain." *Journal of Applied Meteorology* 33 (1994): 140–158.

Liptsitz, B. B. *Climatic Estimates for Locations between Weather Stations in the Pacific Northwest: Comparison and Application of Two Linear Regression Analysis Methods.* M.A. thesis, University of Oregon, 1988.

Taylor, G. H., C. Daly, W. P. Gibson and J. Sibul-Weisberg. "Digital and Map Products Produced Using PRISM." In *Proceedings of the 10th AMS Conference on Applied Climatology.* Reno, Nevada: American Meteorological Society, 1997.

Thompson, R. S., K. H. Anderson and P. J. Bartlein. 1999. *Atlas of Relations between Climatic Parameters and Distributions of Important Trees and Shrubs in North America—Introduction and Conifers.* U.S. Geological Survey Professional Paper 1650-A, 1999.

Precipitation and Seasonality   156–157

Folland, C. K. and T. R. Karl. "Observed Climate Variability and Change." In *Intergovernmental Panel on Climate Change, Working Group I, Climate Change 2001: The Scientific Basis.* Cambridge University Press, 2001.

Liptsitz, B. B. *Climatic Estimates for Locations between Weather Stations in the Pacific Northwest: Comparison and Application of Two Linear Regression Analysis Methods.* M.A. thesis, University of Oregon, 1988.

Mock, C. J. *Modern Climate Analogues of Late-Quaternary Paleoclimates for the Western United States.* Ph.D. dissertation, University of Oregon, 1994.

Mock, C. J. "Climatic Controls and Spatial Variations of Precipitation in the Western United States." *Journal of Climate* 5 (1996): 1111–1125.

Oregon Climate Service [on-line].

Thompson, R. S., K. H. Anderson and P. J. Bartlein. *Atlas of Relations between Climatic Parameters and Distributions of*

Important Trees and Shrubs in North America—Introduction and Conifers. U.S. Geological Survey Professional Paper 1650-A, 1999.

WeatherDisc Associates, Inc. *World WeatherDisc Version 2.0.* Seattle, Washington, 1990.

Temperature   158–159

Folland, C. K. and T. R. Karl. "Observed Climate Variability and Change." In *Intergovernmental Panel on Climate Change, Working Group I. Climate Change 2001, The Scientific Basis.* Cambridge University Press, 2001.

Liptsitz, B. B. *Climatic Estimates for Locations between Weather Stations in the Pacific Northwest: Comparison and Application of Two Linear Regression Analysis Methods.* M.A. thesis, University of Oregon, 1988.

Mock, C. J. *Modern Climate Analogues of Late-Quaternary Paleoclimates for the Western United States.* Ph.D. dissertation, University of Oregon, 1994.

Oregon Climate Service [on-line].

Thompson, R. S., K. H. Anderson and P. J. Bartlein. *Atlas of Relations between Climatic Parameters and Distributions of Important Trees and Shrubs in North America—Introduction and Conifers.* U.S. Geological Survey Professional Paper 1650-A, 1999.

Climate Indicators and Change   160–161

Albritton, D. and G. Meira-Filho. "Technical Summary." In *Intergovernmental Panel on Climate Change, Working Group I. Climate Change 2001: The Scientific Basis.* Cambridge University Press, 2001.

Intergovernmental Panel on Climate Change Data Distribution Center [on-line].

Intergovernmental Panel on Climate Change, Summary for Policymakers. "A Report of Working Group I of the Intergovernmental Panel on Climate Change" [online]. Figure 5 used with permission, 2001.

Melillo, J. M., I. C. Prentice, G. D. Farquhar, E. D. Schulze and O. D. Sala. "Terrestrial Biotic Responses to Environmental Change and Feedbacks to Climate." In Houghton, J. T., L. G. Meira Hilho, B. A. Callander, N. Harris, A. Kattenburg and K. Maskell, eds. *Climate Change 1995: The Science of Climate Change.* Cambridge University Press, 1996.

Miller, D. A. and R. A. White. "A Conterminous United States Multilayer Soil Characteristics Dataset for Regional Climate and Hydrology Modeling." *Earth Interactions* 2: paper 2 (1998).

National Assessment Synthesis Team. *Climate Change Impacts on the United States: The Potential Consequences of Climate Variability and Change.* Cambridge University Press, 2000.

Prentice, I. C., et al. 1992. "A Global Biome Model Based on Plant Physiology and Dominance, Soil Properties and Climate." *Journal of Biogeography* 19 (1992): 117–134.

Shafer, S. L. *Potential Vegetation Response to Future Climate Change in Western North America and Its Implications for Biological Conservation and Geographical Conceptualizations of Place.* Ph.D. dissertation, University of Oregon, 2000.

U.S. Department of Commerce, National Oceanic and Atmospheric Administration cooperative sites, map produced using PRISM.

Rivers   162–163

National Imagery and Mapping Agency. *Digital Chart of the World, Edition 1,* 1994.

U.S. Environmental Protection Agency. *Basins Version 2.0,* January 1999.

Streamflow   164–165

Hubbard, L. E., T. A. Herrett, J. E. Poole, G. P. Ruppert and M. L. Courts. *Water Resources Data Oregon, Water Year 1999.* U.S. Geological Survey Water-Data Report OR-99-1, 2000.

Moffatt, Robert L., Roy E. Wellman and Janice M. Gordon. *Statistical Summaries of Streamflow Data in Oregon: Volume 1—Monthly and Annual Streamflow, and Flow-Duration Values.* U.S. Geological Survey Open File Report 90-118, 1990.

Wellman, Roy E., Janice M. Gordon and Robert L. Moffatt. *Statistical Summaries of Streamflow Data in Oregon: Volume 2—Annual Low and High Flow and Instantaeous Peak Flow.* U.S. Geological Survey Open File Report 93-63, 1993.

Sources

Lakes   166–167

Johnson, Daniel M., Richard R. Petersen, D. Richard Lycan, James W. Sweet and Mark E. Neuhaus, Portland State University, in cooperation with Andrew L. Schaedel, Oregon Department of Environmental Quality. *Atlas of Oregon Lakes*. Corvallis: Oregon State University Press, 1985.

Drainage Basins   168–169

Bastasch, R. *Waters of Oregon: A Source Book on Oregon's Water and Water Management*. Corvallis: Oregon State University Press, 1998.

Oregon Department of Water Resources. "Water Availability Report System" [on-line], 2001.

Oregon Department of Administrative Services, Geospatial Data Clearing House [on-line].

Oregon Watershed Enhancement Board.

Water Quality and Dams   170–171

Oregon Department of Environmental Quality. "Listing Criteria for Oregon's 1998 303(d) List of Water Quality Limited Water Bodies" [on-line], 1998.

Oregon Department of Environmental Quality. "Oregon Water Quality Index Summary Report, Water Years 1990–1999" [on-line], 2000.

Oregon Department of Environmental Quality. "Interpretation and Communication of Water Quality Data Using the Oregon Water Quality Index" [on-line].

U.S. Army Corps of Engineers. "National Inventory of Dams" [on-line].

U.S. Environmental Protection Agency. "Oregon 1998 303(d) Impaired/Threatened Waters." Map [on-line].

Water Control Infrastructure. *National Inventory of Dams*, 2001.

Ecoregions   172–174

Bryce, S. A., et al. *Ecoregions of Oregon*. Poster, in preparation. U.S. Geological Survey, 1:1.5M, 2002.

Clarke, S. E. and S. A. Bryce. *Hierarchical Subdivisions of the Columbia Plateau and Blue Mountain Ecoregions, Oregon and Washington*. General Technical Report PNW-GTR-395. Portland: U.S. Department of Agriculture, Forest Service, Pacific Northwest Research Station, 1997.

Gallant, A. L., T. R. Whittier, D. P. Larsen, J. M. Omernik and R. M. Hughes. *Regionalization As a Tool for Managing Environmental Resources*. EPA/600/3-89/060. Corvallis, Oregon: U.S. Environmental Protection Agency, Environmental Research Laboratory, 1989.

Omernik, J. M. "Ecoregions of the Conterminous United States." Map, 1:7.5M. *Annals of the Association of the American Geographers* 77, no. 1 (1982): 118–125.

Omernik, J. M. "Ecoregions: A Spatial Framework for Environmental Management." In *Biological Assessment and Criteria: Tools for Water Resource Planning and Decision Making*. Davis, W. S. and T. P. Simon, eds. Boca Raton, Florida: Lewis Publishers, 1995.

Omernik, J. M., S. S. Chapman, R. A. Lillie and R. T. Dumke. "Ecoregions of Wisconsin." *Transactions of the Wisconsin Academy of Science Arts and Letters* 88 (2000): 77–103.

Pater, D. E., S. A. Bryce, T. D. Thorson, J. Kagan, C. Chappell, J. M. Omernik, S. H. Azevedo and A. J. Woods.

Ecoregions of Western Washington and Oregon. Map. U.S. Geological Survey, 1998.

Wiken, E. *Terrestrial Ecozones of Canada*. Environment Canada. Ecological Classification Series No. 19. Ottawa, Ontario, 1998.

Vegetation   175-185

Kagan, Jimmy and Steve Caicco. *Manual of Oregon Actual Vegetation*. Oregon Natural Heritage Program, Idaho Cooperative Fish & Wildlife Research Unit. Oregon Geospatial Data Clearinghouse. GAP vegetation, 1:250,000, 1992.

Wildlife Habitat   186–189

Johnson, David H. and Thomas A. O'Neil, managing directors. *Wildlife–Habitat Relationships in Oregon and Washington*. Corvallis: Oregon State University Press. Map compilation by Chris Kiilsgaard and Charley Barret, Northwest Habitat Institute, Corvallis, Oregon, 2001.

Protected Areas   190–191

Bean, Michael J. "Strategies for Biodiversity Protection," Bruce A. Stein, Lynn S. Kutner, and Jonathan S. Adams, eds. *Precious Heritage: The Status of Biodiversity in the United States*. A joint project of The Nature Conservancy and the Association for Biodiversity Information. Oxford University Press, 2000.

Bureau of Land Management. "Northwest Forest Plan, Late Successional Reserves" [on-line].

Green, Sarah E., Robert E. Frenkel and Charles A. Wellner. "Pacific Northwest Natural Area Program: A Successful Partnership." *Natural Areas Journal* 5, no. 4 (1985): 14–23.

Meffe, Gary K., C. Ronald Carroll and contributors. *Principles of Conservation Biology*. Sunderland, Massachusetts: Sinaur Associates Inc., 1994.

The Nature Conservancy. Southwest Oregon Field Office.

Office of the Secretary of State. "State Parks" [on-line].

Oregon Natural Heritage Program. *Gap Analysis 2001 Data Set—Oregon Land Management*. 1:100,000.

U.S. Department of the Interior, National Park Service. "Crater Lake National Park History" [on-line].

U.S. Department of the Interior, National Park Service. "John Day Fossil Beds, Administrative History" [on-line].

U.S. Department of the Interior, National Park Service. "National Park System Timeline" [on-line].

U.S. Fish and Wildlife Service. "Refuges" [on-line].

White House. Proclamation. 9 June 2000. "Establishment of the Cascade–Siskiyou National Monument" [on-line].

The Wilderness Society. "America's Wilderness Facts" [on-line].

Reference

Population Centers   194–249

American Automobile Association. *Oregon County Road Maps Series, 1990s–2000*, various dates. AAA Oregon, Auto Travel Services, Portland, Oregon.

Loy, William G., Stuart Allan, Clyde P. Patton and Robert D. Plank. *Atlas of Oregon*. Eugene: University of Oregon Books, 1976.

Oregon Department of Transportation. *City Transportation Map* series, various dates.

Satellite imagery: *National Land Cover Data*, preliminary ed., 1999.

U.S. Department of Commerce, Bureau of the Census.

U.S. Department of the Interior, U.S. Geological Survey. *National Elevation Data Set*, 1999.

U.S. Department of the Interior, U.S. Geological Survey. National Mapping Center: *1:100,000 Digital Line Graph Data, Hydrography and Transportation*, 1993.

U.S. Department of Transportation. *National Transportation Atlas Data*.

Reference Maps   250–275

Satellite imagery: *National Land Cover Data*, preliminary ed., 1999.

U.S. Department of Commerce, Bureau of the Census.

U.S. Department of the Interior, U.S. Geological Survey. *National Elevation Data Set*, 1999.

U.S. Department of the Interior, U.S. Geological Survey. National Mapping Center: *1:100,000 Digital Line Graph Data, Hydrography and Transportation*, 1993.

U.S. Department of Transportation. *National Transportation Atlas Data*.

Note on Usage

The basic style guides for the *Atlas of Oregon* (2nd ed.) were *The Chicago Manual of Style* (14th ed.) and the *1993 Grammar and Style Guide for Publications of the University of Oregon*. Occasional variances in punctuation, abbreviation and capitalization were made to recognize the special needs of atlases and the house style of the University of Oregon Press. The choices made reflect our best attempt to fairly correlate historical and current usage. For instance, after consultation with historians, anthropologists and tribal members, the *Atlas* adopted the use of both "Indian" and "Native American." Readers may note the occasional use of unfamiliar spellings, such as "Douglas-fir." This spelling is common in current technical usage. Capitalization of a limited number of easily identifiable geographic areas (such as the Coast and Western, Central and Eastern Oregon) represents another editorial decision based on a mixture of common usage, historical data and the desire for clarity in the text.

Index

Place names are listed in the Gazetteer, pages 284–289, where their Reference Map page numbers and coordinates are given. The place names included in this index are those which appear on the Population Centers maps, pages 194–249; in the climate graphs on pages 156–159; or in relation to specific page topics.

Index